Oracle
High-Performance Tuning
with STATSPACK

Oracle
High-Performance Tuning
with STATSPACK

Donald Keith Burleson

Osborne/**McGraw-Hill**

New York Chicago San Francisco
Lisbon London Madrid Mexico City
Milan New Delhi San Juan
Seoul Singapore Sydney Toronto

Osborne/McGraw-Hill
2600 Tenth Street
Berkeley, California 94710
U.S.A.

To arrange bulk purchase discounts for sales promotions, premiums, or fund-raisers, please contact Osborne/**McGraw-Hill** at the above address. For information on translations or book distributors outside the U.S.A., please see the International Contact Information page immediately following the index of this book.

Oracle High-Performance Tuning with STATSPACK

1234567890 CUS CUS 01987654321
ISBN 0-07-213378-3

Publisher
Brandon A. Nordin

Vice President & Associate Publisher
Scott Rogers

Acquisitions Editor
Lisa McClain

Project Editor
Betsy Manini

Acquisitions Coordinator
Ross Doll

Technical Editor
Michael R. Ault

Copy Editor
Dennis Weaver

Proofreader
Stefany Otis

Indexer
Donald K. Burleson

Computer Designers
Carie Abrew
Michelle Galicia

Illustrators
Michael Mueller
Beth E. Young

Series Design
Jani Beckwith

Cover Design
Will Voss

This book was composed with Corel VENTURA™ Publisher.

This text is dedicated to my wife Janet, whose love and support made it possible for me to write this text.

About the Author

Donald Keith Burleson is one of the world's top Oracle Database experts with 20 years of full-time experience. He specializes in creating database architectures for very large online databases, and he has worked with some of the world's most powerful and complex systems. A leading database author, Don has written 10 books, published more than 60 articles in national magazines, and serves as editor-in-chief of Oracle Internals, a leading Oracle database journal. Don's professional Web sites include:

http://www.dba-oracle.com/images/don_burleson.jpg
http://www.dba-oracle.com/
http://www.remote-dba.net/

In addition to his services as a consultant, Don also is active in charitable programs to aid visually impaired individuals. Don pioneered a technique for delivering tiny pigmy horses as guide animals for the blind and manages a non-profit corporation called The Guide Horse Foundation dedicated to providing guide horses to blind people free-of-charge. The Web site for The Guide Horse Foundation is http://www.guidehorse.org/.

Don Burleson's books include:

Oracle High-Performance SQL Tuning (Osborne/**McGraw-Hill**, Oracle Press, 2001)
Oracle High-Performance Tuning with STATSPACK,
   (Osborne/**McGraw-Hill**, Oracle Press, 2001)
Unix for the Oracle DBA (O'Reilly & Associates, 2000)
Oracle SAP Administration (O'Reilly & Associates, 1999)
Inside the Database Object Model (CRC Press, 1998)
High Performance Oracle Data Warehousing (Coriolis Publishing, 1997)
High Performance Oracle 8 Tuning (Coriolis Publishing, 1997)
High Performance Oracle Database Applications (Coriolis Publishing, 1996)
Oracle Databases on the Web (Coriolis Publishing, 1996)
Managing Distributed Databases (John Wiley & Sons, 1994)
Practical Application of Object-Oriented Techniques to Relational
   Databases (John Wiley & Sons, 1993)

Contents at a Glance

Contents

PART I
Overview of the Method and the Tools

ix

PART II
Tuning the Oracle Database with STATSPACK

PART III
Tuning the Oracle Database with STATSPACK

Acknowledgments

There is always a team effort in the creation of any technical book, and this book was created as the direct result of the dedicated efforts of many individuals. I would like to thank Lisa McClain for her diligent efforts in helping with the concept and fruition of the idea for this book. Ross Doll was instrumental in the coordination of the technical editing and graphics efforts, and Betsy Manini did a great job project editing and correcting my atrocious grammar. I would also like to thank Mike Ault for doing a superb job as the technical review for this text, and Dennis Weaver for copyediting.

Introduction

ver since Oracle first released the STATSPACK utility, there has been a great deal of interest in how STATSPACK data can be used to assist with database tuning activities. Unlike most other Oracle products, STATSPACK was rolled-out without fanfare, and most Oracle professionals were not aware of this powerful new tool or how it could be used for database tuning.

STATSPACK is a simple tool that is used to capture Oracle statistical snapshots into Oracle tables. STATSPACK is the natural successor to the Oracle UTLBSTAT-UTLESTAT utility programs, which captured a beginning snapshot and ending snapshot, and then produced a report showing all database activity for the time period between the snapshots.

There has always been a need to capture Oracle performance statistics into tables. I wrote a utility that extended the UTLESTAT functionality to capture Oracle data into tables and published an article on the topic in 1996. Since that time, I created my own precursor to STATSPACK to remotely monitor Oracle databases and report on their performance. With the introduction of STATSPACK, everyone now has a standardized mechanism for capturing Oracle statistics into tables, and the historical archive of Oracle statistics provides an unparalleled opportunity to analyze Oracle performance for any desired period of time. Even more importantly, the historical collection of performance statistics allows the DBA to create trend analysis reports that can predict the future behavior of the database.

While the basic installation and configuration of STATSPACK are quite simple, Oracle has only provided a single report to display the information from the STATSPACK tables. Because I had the benefit of many years of experience with analyzing Oracle statistics from tables, I was able to quickly modify my existing scripts to read the data from the STATSPACK tables and create extremely useful reports.

While the value of these scripts alone will justify the costs of this book, I have included detailed techniques for interpreting the output from STATSPACK. In this book, I show the reader a step-by-step approach on how to use the STATSPACK reports to ensure that their database is properly tuned. I have deliberately reproduced only the most important STATSPACK scripts in the body of the text. However, I have provided you with an appendix of the full listings of all of the scripts, conveniently alphabetized, and I highly encourage you to refer to the Appendix so that you can understands the details about how each report was generated.

My goal for this text was to encapsulate my 20 years of experience in database tuning into a comprehensive treatise on database tuning. This is my third book on Oracle tuning, and I have gathered a great deal of insight into what you need to know in order to properly tune your database. It is very easy to get lost in a mind-boggling mass of statistics, but I am very careful to keep a tight focus and show the reader only the information that is pertinent to improving the performance of their database.

It's also important to note that this book uses an entirely different approach to Oracle tuning. Whereas virtually every one of the existing Oracle tuning books focuses on what do about a performance problem right now, this book focuses on how the use Oracle STATSPACK utility in order to proactively tune the database by looking at historical trends and performance patterns. This proactive approach to tuning ensures that the database is tuned for all Oracle processing requirements, not just those that the DBA happens to notice in real-time.

In the opinion of many Oracle DBAs, there's very little that can be done while your database is experiencing a performance problem. You can go to the Oracle Enterprise Manager performance pack, you can run customized scripts against the Oracle v$ views, and you may be able to determine the cause of the performance bottlenecks. However, you would not be able to actually make a change to the running database in real-time to correct the problem.

Instead, this book focuses on collecting relevant performance statistics using the Oracle STATSPACK utility, and providing a structured method for the DBA to take a look at all of the Oracle components and see how they interact. The goal of proactive Oracle tuning is to avoid future performance problems. In Oracle tuning, it is very true that "those who ignore the past are condemned to repeat it."

In my 20 years of tuning databases, I have found this proactive technique is the best approach for the long-term overall performance of the database. In my databases, I achieve success by constantly monitoring performance of the database with STATSPACK and by using automating scripts that will alert me to unusual situations. I have found that Oracle database performance can become a largely automated task.

Another distinct feature of this text is that I've deliberately organized the book so that all of the performance dependencies are addressed in their proper sequence. For example, Oracle tuning within the Oracle database will not alleviate a performance problem that relates to the database server. In other words, the performance of the server directly impacts the performance of the Oracle database that is running on the database server. These types of dependencies exist with regard to the database servers, the disk I/O subsystems, and the Oracle network. In order to properly tune any Oracle database, these external factors must be addressed before starting the tuning of the database.

It was also important to recognize the non-sequential nature of Oracle tuning. For example, the tuning of individual SQL statements can make a huge performance difference for those individual SQL statements. However, there is a direct trade-off in terms of RAM memory usage for individual SQL statements and the performance of the database as a whole. For example, SQL statements can be turbocharged by using more internal storage, but they will do so at the expense all other SQL statements that are executing within the database.

I also deliberately deferred addressing the issues of Oracle database design. This is because most Oracle DBAs do not have the ability to redesign the Oracle tables, and this is especially true for a third-party application or an in-house application that is already being used in a production environment. However, I firmly believe that a proper Oracle design is the singlemost important factor in Oracle performance.

In this book, I show the reader how to extend STATSPACK utility in order to capture relevant performance metrics of the database server, the disk I/O subsystem, and Oracle tables. By adding these factors to the STATSPACK database, the Oracle DBA can develop an overall picture of database performance.

This book is different from other Oracle tuning books for several reasons.

1. This is the first book to develop a comprehensive approach to Oracle tuning with the STATSPACK utility.

2. This book examines Oracle tuning from a *proactive method*, which is a new approach from other Oracle tuning books that use a reactive tuning methodology. Using a proactive approach, the Oracle professional can examine the detailed past performance of their database, and develop an overall tuning strategy that best suits the processing characteristics of their Oracle system.

3. This book is also different because it examines all of the factors that effect Oracle performance. While other books confine their discussion to the internals of the Oracle database, this book examines all relevant environmental issues, including the database server, the network, and the disk I/O.

This book will provide a complete methodology for tuning any Oracle database, and has dozens of ready-to-run STATSPACK scripts that encapsulate the important factors such that even a beginner can quickly identify performance bottlenecks.

This book's greatest strength is that it simplifies Oracle tuning and expands the scope of Oracle statistics. This book is more than the standard rehash of Oracle tuning techniques. The introduction of the STATSPACK utility changes the method of Oracle tuning, and this book will focus on using STATSPACK to collect, interpret, and correct Oracle performance problems.

In addition to the day-to-day Oracle tuning, the reader will learn to use STATSPACK to collect ongoing performance information for alert mechanisms, trend analysis and long-term resource planning. It is my hope that this book will become an indispensable weapon in your arsenal of Oracle tuning tools.

PART I

Overview of the Method and the Tools

CHAPTER
1

Overview
of Oracle Tuning

racle tuning has always been the most difficult area of Oracle database management. Because of the flexibility of Oracle, the internal software is phenomenally complex and there are many hundreds of causes of Oracle performance problems. The inherent complexity of the Oracle database leaves many shops unable to certify that their database is properly tuned.

In addition to the complex nature of the Oracle software, we also have the issue of the dynamic nature of Oracle applications. An Oracle database is constantly changing, and it is never exactly the same at any two times. Because of the dynamic nature of tuning an Oracle environment, it is very difficult for the Oracle database administrator to get a handle on what's going on inside their database. Many people who've attempted to tune an Oracle database say that it's analogous to attempting to work on a car while it is flying down the highway at 60 miles per hour!

While it may be true that the Oracle databases are in a constant state of flux, there is a general approach that most Oracle experts use when tuning the Oracle database. It's very important to take a top-down approach to tuning Oracle databases, such that you start at a very high level, taking a look at the overall Oracle environment and then successively drill down into more detail as you begin to tune the individual components within the database engine. For Oracle, the top-down approach means starting with the server, drilling down to the instance, drilling down to the objects, and finally examining the Oracle SQL.

The goal of this text is to give you the STATSPACK tools and diagnostic techniques that are required to ensure that your Oracle database is performing at an optimal level. While you may not become an Oracle tuning expert from reading this book, you will have a high-level understanding of the important Oracle tuning issues and know how to run STATSPACK queries to get performance metrics.

The Overall Tuning Approach

While there is no silver bullet for tuning Oracle databases, a comprehensive approach to Oracle tuning can help ensure that all of the bases are covered, and that no important tuning facts have been overlooked. In tuning an Oracle database, you have to start by taking a broad look at the external environment and successively drill down for more details (see Figure 1-1).

The concept of using a drill-down technique is very important to Oracle tuning. We must start at a very broad level, examining the overall environment and looking carefully at the database server for any problems that might exist within CPU, RAM, or disk configurations, as shown in Figure 1-2. No amount of tuning is going to help in an Oracle database when the Oracle database server is short on resources.

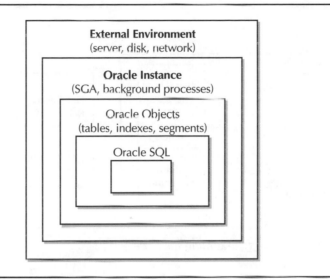

FIGURE 1-1.   *The Oracle database tuning hierarchy*

Once we've completed the tuning of the Oracle server environment, we can then begin to take a look at the global parameters that affect the Oracle database (the Oracle instance). When looking at the Oracle database, we take a look at the database as a whole, and we pay careful attention to the Oracle initialization parameters that govern the configuration of the SGA and the overall behavior of the database, as shown in Figure 1-3.

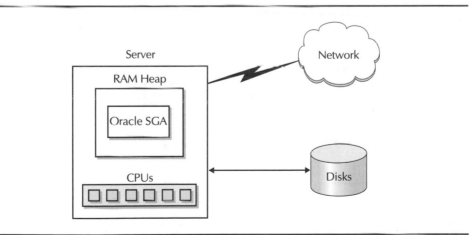

FIGURE 1-2.   *Tuning the Oracle environment*

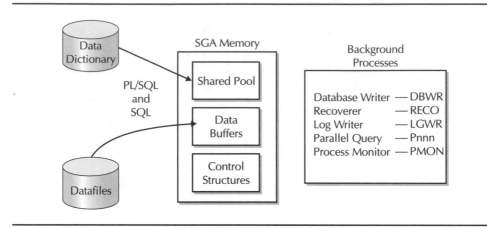

FIGURE 1-3. *Tuning the Oracle instance*

Once the database server in the Oracle instance has been tuned, we can then begin the work of taking a look at individual Oracle tables and indexes within the database. At this phase, we take a look at the storage settings that can govern the behavior of a table and take a look at how well the settings accommodate the processing needs of the individual objects (see Figure 1-4).

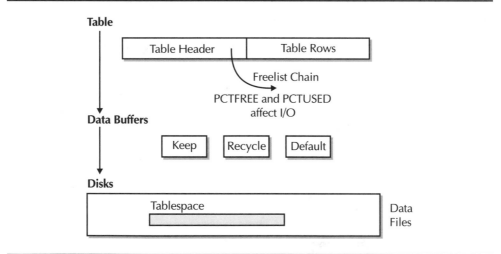

FIGURE 1-4. *Tuning Oracle objects*

Once the Oracle objects are tuned, we then move into tuning the individual SQL queries that are issued against the Oracle database. This is one of the most challenging of all of the areas of Oracle tuning because there can be many thousands of SQL statements issued against a highly active Oracle database. The task for the person tuning the Oracle SQL is to identify those SQL statements that are used most frequently and apply the tools necessary in order to tune each statement for the optimal execution plan (see Figure 1-5). We will also explore static binding and show how to improve execution by keeping bind plans for the SQL.

In summary, Oracle tuning involves the following steps, with each step being more general and broad than the step beneath it:

1. **Server, network, and disk tuning**   If there is a problem with the Oracle server, such as an overloaded CPU, excessive memory swapping, or disk I/O bottleneck, then no amount of tuning within the Oracle databases is going to improve your performance. Hence, the first thing the Oracle professional examines is the server, disk, and network environment.

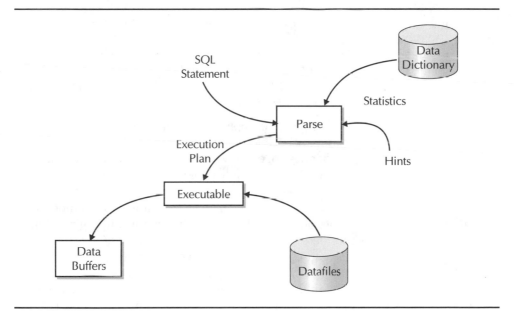

FIGURE 1-5.   *Tuning Oracle SQL*

2. **Instance tuning**   The Oracle SGA is tuned, and all of the Oracle initialization parameters are reviewed to ensure that the database has been properly configured. This phase of Oracle tuning is directed at looking for resource shortages in the *db_block_buffers*, *shared_pool_size*, and *sort_area_size*. We also investigate important default parameters for Oracle such as *optimizer_mode*.

3. **Object tuning**   This phase of tuning looks at the setting for Oracle tables and indexes. Settings such as *pctfree*, *pctused*, and *freelists* can have a dramatic impact on Oracle performance, and each object can benefit from proper storage settings.

4. **SQL tuning**   This is the most time-consuming tuning operation because there can be many thousands of individual SQL statements that access the Oracle database. At a high level, we identify the most common SQL statements and tune each statement by carefully reviewing the execution plan for the SQL and adjusting the execution plan using Oracle hints. For Oracle8i, we will also be investigating the new optimizer plan stability feature. Optimizer plan stability allows improved performance by storing a ready-to-go execution plan for SQL statements. We will also see how to implement optimizer plan stability with the OUTLINE package, so that we can modify execution plans for specific SQL statements. This is especially useful in cases where you are using vendor-supplied SQL and you cannot change the SQL source code. For example, in Oracle Applications and SAP, you are not allowed to change the SQL, but with optimizer plan stability you can tune the SQL by changing the stored execution plan for the SQL.

5. **Design tuning**   The design of the application is the single most important factor in Oracle performance. Unfortunately, most Oracle administrators are unable to change a poor design, either because they are using proprietary software or because the design is already implemented in production.

It is critical to the success of your Oracle tuning effort to follow the tuning steps in their proper order. Many neophyte Oracle DBAs will immediately begin to tune SQL statements without considering the environment in which the SQL is running. Mistakes like these can often cause problems with the overall tuning effort because the broader tuning issues have not yet been identified and corrected.

While later chapters will explore each of these areas in great detail, let's begin by covering the major areas so that we can understand their impact on Oracle performance.

Server Tuning

Many Oracle professionals discount the server environment because they have not been trained to understand how the Oracle database interacts with the server. As a practicing Oracle tuning consultant, I have learned that the external environment is the very first thing an Oracle DBA should take a look at when a performance problem has been reported. When checking the external server, the Oracle administrator must carefully check the settings for the operating system kernel parameters on the database server and carefully monitor the usage of RAM memory and CPU on the database server (see Figure 1-6). If the database server is experiencing disk or network bottlenecks or shortages of hardware resources, no amount of Oracle tuning can alleviate the problem.

Once we understand the basic nature of CPU and memory consumption on the server, we will turn our attention to extending the STATSPACK utility in order to capture server information. We will show how the UNIX *vmstat* utility can be extended in order to capture information regarding the usage on each CPU and memory within the computer, and to show how this information can be stored inside a STATSPACK table. We will also show how alert reports can then be generated from the STATSPACK table, such that the Oracle administrator becomes aware of all server-related problems that will impact the Oracle database performance.

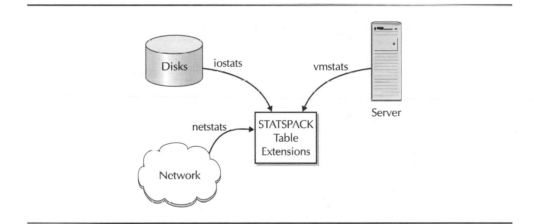

FIGURE 1-6. *Detailed Oracle server tuning*

We will also show how this extension of STATSPACK can be used in order to monitor other servers in an Oracle enterprise environment. We will show how this remote vmstat collection utility can be used to monitor the behaviors of Web servers and application servers in an Oracle database environment.

Network Tuning

With many Oracle databases shared across geographical areas, it is very important for the Oracle professional to recognize the importance of network communications on the performance of their databases. As you may know, Oracle provides for distributed communications between databases by using its Transparent Network Substrate (TNS). The TNS is a distributed protocol that allows for transparent database communications between remote systems. The TNS acts as an insulator between Oracle's logical request for data and the physical communications between the distributed servers. Because of this insulation between the Oracle logical data request and the internal workings of the network, much of the network performance tuning is in the hands of the network administrator. In other words, the Oracle administrator has very little direct control over the network configuration settings that can affect the overall performance of their database (see Figure 1-7).

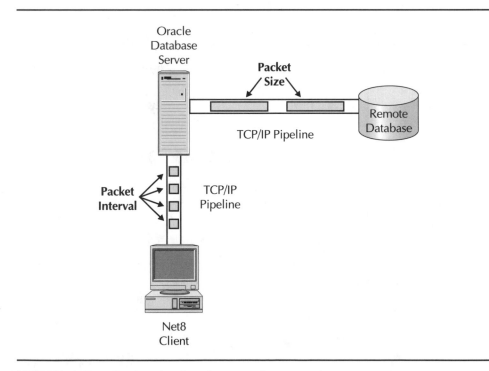

FIGURE 1-7. *Tuning the Oracle network*

However, there are some important settings that can be used in order to improve the performance of distributed transactions. This chapter will take a careful look at the *init.ora* parameters that relate to distributed communications, and also take a look at some of the TCP parameters such as *tcp.nodelay*, which can be used in order to change the basic packet-shipping mechanisms within the Oracle database.

We will also take a look at different parameters within the *sqlnet.ora, tnsnames.ora,* and *protocol.ora* files, which can be used to change the size and configuration of the TCP packets. These tools can often have a profound impact on the behavior of the underlying network transport layer and improve throughput of all Oracle transactions.

Disk Tuning

The largest single component of Oracle response time is disk I/O (input/output). Anything that the Oracle DBA can do to reduce disk I/O will have a positive benefit on the performance of the database. The reduction of disk I/O is a goal that will be mentioned in each of the chapters. For example, changing Oracle initialization parameters can reduce disk I/O and tuning SQL can also greatly reduce disk I/O.

Once we recognize that disk I/O is the single most important factor in tuning any Oracle database, it is understandable that the Oracle DBA needs to fully understand the internal operations of the disk I/O subsystem. In this day and age of using disk cache storage devises such as EMC, many Oracle DBAs are not always paying careful attention to the interaction between Oracle database and the disk I/O subsystem (see Figure 1-8). Another confounding issue is that the disk arrays often have a separate RAM cache, and an I/O request from Oracle does not always translate into a physical disk I/O.

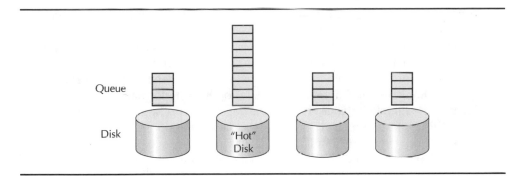

FIGURE I-8.   *Tuning Oracle disk I/O*

Because there are many dozens of ways to configure a disk I/O subsystem, Chapter 8 will focus on all of the common disk placement techniques, the use of RAID, and how the Oracle DBAs can "map" their disks, from the logical mount points to the physical disks. Once the mapping between the Oracle datafiles in the physical disks is clearly understood, the Oracle professional can then move on to create tools that will monitor the behavior of the disk I/O subsystem, and relocate files to overcome disk I/O bottlenecks.

In keeping with the theme of using STATSPACK, Chapter 8 will show how the Oracle DBA can extend the STATSPACK tables in order to capture I/O statistics using the generic UNIX iostat utility. Once the iostat utility is in place and constantly monitoring the behavior of the disk, the Oracle DBAs can create automated exception reports that will alert them to times when the disk I/O subsystem is undergoing contention.

Chapter 8 also goes into detail on what the Oracle DBA can do to remedy disk I/O bottlenecks and will include discussions on file striping and other RAID techniques that are used by the Oracle professional in order to ensure that the load is evenly balanced among all of the physical disk spindles.

Instance Tuning

The concept of instance tuning is one of the most misunderstood areas of Oracle tuning. In practice, an overstressed Oracle SGA can cause serious performance problems, but once tuned, the Oracle SGA really needs little attention from the Oracle professional. This section will show the Oracle DBA how to capture SGA information directly from the STATSPACK tables and provide an automated mechanism for alerting the DBA to shortages within Oracle's library cache, shared pool, and data block buffers, as shown in Figure 1-9.

The tuning of the Oracle instance involves checking all of the initialization parameters for the Oracle database. As most Oracle professionals know, the Oracle *init.ora* parameters are getting more complex as the Oracle database becomes more sophisticated. Chapter 9 will take a very close look at all of the Oracle *init.ora* parameters and provide techniques and guidelines for understanding how to change the Oracle initialization parameters for optimal performance.

Because the Oracle instance contains the data buffer cache, we'll also discuss how STATSPACK measures the behavior of the data buffer pools. These pools include the DEFAULT pool, the KEEP pool, and RECYCLE pool. We will show STATSPACK techniques that can be used to identify when the size of the data storage buffer pools need to be increased, and how to tune to the lowest common denominator setting for the size of the buffer pools.

We'll also take a look at tuning the shared pool and library cache within the Oracle SGA. We will show how STATSPACK information can be collected on the behavior of the SGA, and show techniques whereby we can adjust the relevant initialization parameters in order to maximize the behavior of objects within Oracle's shared pool.

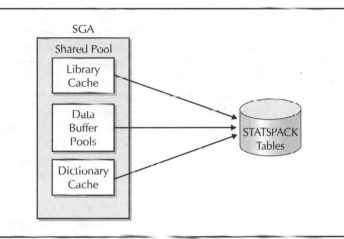

FIGURE 1-9.   *Tuning the Oracle SGA and background processes*

Object Tuning

Very few Oracle professionals recognize that the storage parameters for Oracle tables
and indexes can have a great impact on the performance of the database. This section
will explore each of the relevant storage parameters for Oracle objects and offer
guidelines for setting the storage parameters according to the behavior of the object.
This section will also explore object fragmentation, as shown in Figure 1-10, and offer
several techniques to ensure that expensive database reorganizations are minimized.

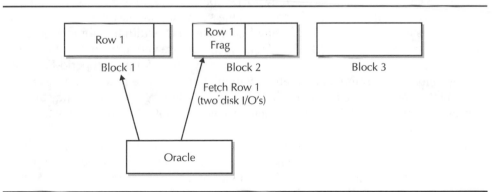

FIGURE 1-10.   *Oracle objects, freelists, and fragmentation*

Chapter 10 will also go into the internals of Oracle data blocks and show the internal mechanisms for linking and unlinking from Oracle's freelists. By understanding the detail in the internal operations of Oracle tables, the Oracle professional will gain insight into how to optimally set the storage parameters for maximum Oracle performance. Of course, this chapter will also focus on the STATSPACK utility, and show how you can derive useful information regarding the behavior of individual Oracle objects within your database. We will also look into the STATSPACK tables that measure block wait activities on objects and see scripts that can identify those objects that require adjustment to their storage parameters to improve performance. We will take a close look at the PCTFREE and PCTUSED Oracle object parameters, and understand how the settings for these parameters can dramatically improve the performance of SQL INSERT and UPDATE tasks. We'll also take a look at the use of freelists within Oracle tables to understand how to identify tables that are experiencing freelist contention, and how to set the freelists for Oracle objects in order to maximize the throughput of high-volume transactions against these tables.

SQL Tuning

The tuning of individual SQL statements is the most time-consuming of all of the processes in Oracle tuning. While Oracle SQL tuning is a very time-consuming job, the tuning of SQL also promises the most benefits in the overall performance of the Oracle system. It is not uncommon to increase performance by an order of magnitude by using the proper Oracle SQL tuning techniques. Chapter 11 will focus on identifying the high-use SQL statements within your database and will present a proven technique for tuning the SQL to ensure that it always runs in an optimal fashion.

This chapter will also show how to use the Oracle STATSPACK utility in order to monitor the behavior of SQL within your library cache and periodically alert the Oracle professional to SQL statements that may not be optimized for maximum performance. This is done by examining the SQL source in the stats$sql_summary table.

There is also a section on managing SQL statements within the library cache. As every Oracle professional knows, SQL statements are very transient within the Oracle instance, and may only reside in the library cache for a short period of time. At any given point in time, information with the library cache may change. SQL statements that enter the library cache remain in the library cache until they age-out and are no longer available to the Oracle instance. Chapter 11 will show you that you can capture SQL execution information from the library cache. This valuable technique will allow you to interrogate the library cache at any given point in time and prepare detailed reports showing the execution plans for all of the important SQL statements that are in the Oracle library cache.

The STATSPACK utility monitors the library cache information and can be used to create automated alert reports that will show whenever poorly tuned SQL statements are being executed within the Oracle instance.

We will also go into detail regarding the various optimizer modes for Oracle SQL. We will take a close look at the relative advantages and disadvantages of the cost-based optimizer (CBO), and also examine the rule-based optimizer and where it can be used to improve the throughput of Oracle SQL. We will also look at the differences between the first_rows and all_rows modes within the cost-based optimizer.

When tuning individual SQL statements, we will show how to change the execution plans with the use of SQL hints. We will examine actual examples for SQL tuning and show how the execution time of SQL statements can be reduced from hours down to only a few minutes. We'll also take a look at initialization parameters that affect the performance of Oracle SQL and take a close look at the Oracle8i feature of static SQL binding with the optimizer plan stability feature. For Oracle8i, we will also examine the query rewrite feature within SQL and see how it can be used to improve SQL performance.

Tuning with Oracle Parallel Query

Chapter 12 will focus on Oracle Parallel Query and show different methods that can be used to invoke parallelism in cases where full table scans are being performed against large tables. We begin by showing how to find large-table full table scans and then discuss the different methods that can be used for parallelizing these kinds of queries. We'll also show how to set the degree of parallelism in order to maximize the throughput and execution time of the individual query, based on the number of CPUs and the number of disks for the table's file.

We will also discuss parallel DML and how operations such as parallel index rebuilds can improve the speed of database maintenance activities. Chapter 12 also examines how submitting concurrent requests to Oracle can parallelize many large Oracle tasks.

Tuning the Oracle Parallel Server Environment

Chapter 13 will discuss the Oracle Parallel Server (OPS) product (known as Real Application Clusters in Oracle9i), and describe the characteristics of application systems that will benefit from using an Oracle Parallel Server environment. We will discuss the hardware configurations necessary for Oracle Parallel Server, and also take a look at application partitioning techniques that can be used maximize throughput in an Oracle Parallel Server environment. This chapter will also take a look at determining the optimal number of instances for Oracle Parallel Server, and will focus on the Integrated Distributed Lock Manager (IDLM). We will take a close look at the IDLM parameters, and show how STATSPACK can be extended in order to collect information on the behavior of the IDLM in a production environment. We'll also take a close look at pinging between instances, and understand how pinging can be minimized by partitioning application structures.

Now that we have covered the overall approach to tuning, we need to look at how STATSPACK is used to facilitate the tuning effort.

Oracle and STATSPACK

While the main focus of this text is on practical techniques for Oracle tuning, you'll find its STATSPACK is used as a common thread throughout the body of this text. Using STATSPACK as a vehicle for aiding performance tuning is a very important concept that will be the main focus of the chapters in this book. While you can back-port STATSPACK to Oracle 8.0 releases by using the statsrep80.sql report, there are some known problems with the utility. The report from STATSPACK on an Oracle release level prior to 8.1.6 has inaccuracies with the data and cannot always be trusted.

We will begin in Chapter 2 with an overview of the STATSPACK utility and show how Oracle STATSPACK is installed and configured in order to measure Oracle server metrics. We will show the installation procedure for the STATSPACK tables, the architecture of all of the STATSPACK tables, and a complete listing showing you where to find all of the salient server metrics that you need in order to pull useful information from the STATSPACK tables.

We will also take a look at the nature of STATSPACK snapshots, and show how to create reports that average metrics over time, as well as look at specific time intervals, spanned over long periods of time. This is an especially important technique because it shows the Oracle professional how to slice the STATSPACK information in order to get exactly what they are looking for.

We will take a look at sample queries that can be run against the STATSPACK tables and learn how we can get relevant metrics from STATSPACK to identify what was happening in our database at any given point in time.

While this text will utilize prewritten STATSPACK scripts, it's very important for the Oracle professional to understand the nature of STATSPACK queries and be able to formulate their own queries based upon the specific problem that they encounter within the Oracle environment. There are many dozens of scripts that come as a part of this text, but the Oracle professional will always be encouraged to extend upon these reports, and use them to see additional details about their system.

Because the STATSPACK utility is limited to the domain of the Oracle database, we will show some of the ways that Oracle STATSPACK can be extended to capture information from the external environment. We will begin by showing how STATSPACK can be extended to capture server metrics, and we will devote Chapter 5 to exploring how the UNIX vmstat utility can be used to capture server information and store them in STATSPACK extension tables. We will also show how the Oracle professional can interrogate these tables and see what's going on inside the database server when performance problems occur.

We will also extend the STATSPACK tables by capturing information on disk I/O. We will devote Chapter 8 to the tuning of the disk I/O subsystem so that the Oracle professional can understand the nature of disk I/O, the interaction between Oracle file placement and disk I/O, and how STATSPACK can be extended to monitor what's going on in the I/O subsystem over time.

Towards the end of this book we will also take a look at the extension of STATSPACK towards long-term statistical trend reporting. In Chapters 14 and 15, you'll find dozens of useful scripts that allow you to plot important Oracle metrics over time and use the existing statistics as a predictive model for developing a plan for additional database resources. While it is not necessary to have a background in statistics to fully understand the techniques in Chapter 15, it is important the Oracle administrator have a general knowledge of the Oracle performance metrics and how they may change over time.

When doing Oracle trend analysis with STATSPACK, it's important to understand that we will be aggregating information along many dimensions. For example, we will use Oracle scripts that will show you how to aggregate information by day of the week, so that you can see the relative stress on your system during specific days of the week, as shown in Figure 1-11.

We will also show how to break down Oracle STATSPACK information by hour of the day, so the Oracle professional can see on an hourly basis when end-user processes are causing stress on the Oracle database, as shown in Figure 1-12.

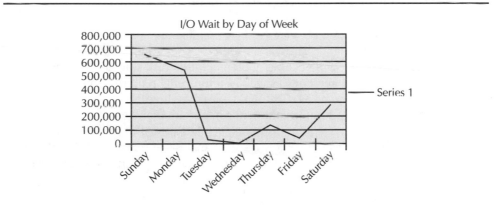

FIGURE 1-11.   *A day-of-the-week average report*

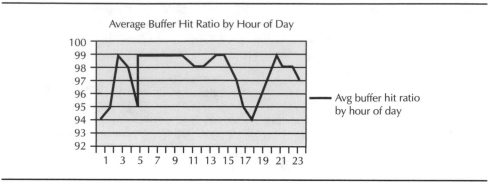

FIGURE 1-12. *An hour-of-the-day average activity summary*

We will use the same techniques for the measurement of daily and hourly information to extrapolate the overall performance of the database over periods of weeks and months. By taking summarized STATSPACK information and feeding it into statistical analysis routines, we can use predictive models to perform linear regression and predict the future performance of the Oracle database based upon the existing metrics.

We will also briefly cover the different methods for linear regression, including single, double, and triple exponential smoothing techniques as well as the more common sum-of-the-least-squares techniques for predicting overall Oracle performance.

These long-term trend reports are especially useful for the manager who is charged with predicting the amount of hardware resources required for the Oracle systems. We will show scripts that will accurately predict future disk storage requirements, future RAM memory requirements, as well as future CPU requirements—all based on statistics gathered from the STATSPACK tables over time.

For plotting STATSPACK information, it is important that we use a tool that is available to almost all Oracle administrators. While a powerful statistical package such as SAS or SPSS can give incredibly detailed analysis of statistics, we've chosen in this book to use the Microsoft Excel worksheet product. By confining our examples to MS Excel, we can provide easy to understand methods for extracting, plotting, and predicting the behavior of our database all using tools that are readily available on most desktops, as shown in Figure 1-13.

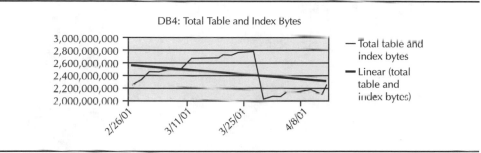

FIGURE I-13. *A sample of a predictive STATSPACK trend analysis using MS Excel*

Because STATSPACK has been configured to capture virtually everything that's going on in an Oracle database at any given point in time, you'll find that there are many hundreds of metrics that are useful when captured within the STATSPACK tables. While it is very tempting for this author to cover every single one of these metrics, it's more important to the practicing Oracle professional that we focus only on those server metrics of the most importance for the tuning of the Oracle system. Hence, we will confine our discussion to those metrics that will provide the Oracle professional with the information they need to very quickly make intelligent performance and tuning decisions for their system.

Conclusion

Throughout this book you will be directed to various STATSPACK tables that will allow you to investigate the values that relate to the concepts we are discussing. This combination of experienced Oracle tuning techniques and the use of STATSPACK makes this a truly unique text.

Now, let's get started and begin with an overview of the STATSPACK utility.

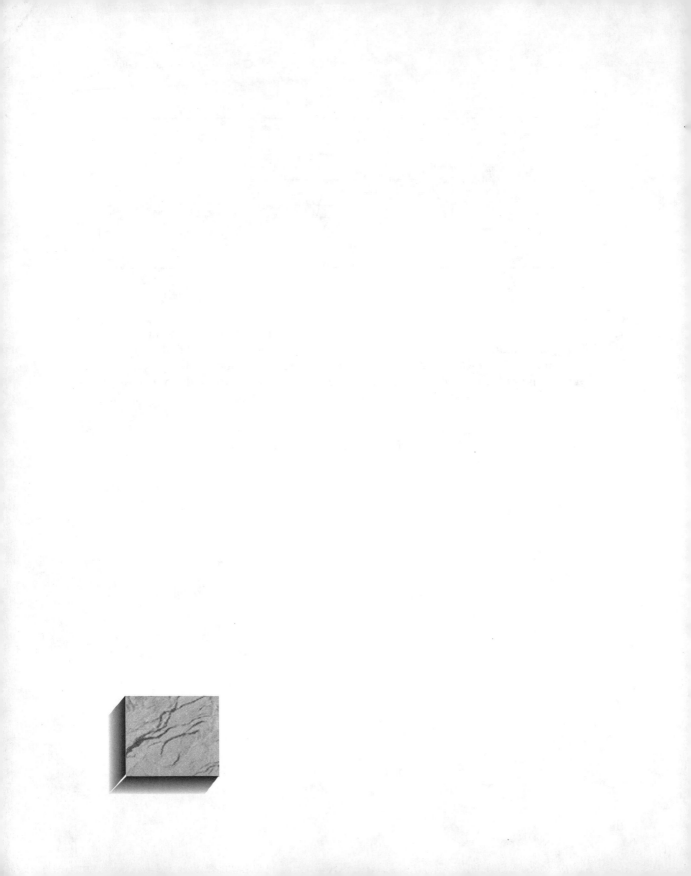

CHAPTER
2

Overview
of STATSPACK

he focus of this chapter will be on understanding the internal architecture of the STATSPACK utility, the basic information included in the STATSPACK tables, and appreciating how the information in the STATSPACK tables can be used to tune and monitor your Oracle database.

As you may know, Oracle offers several software tools for performance and tuning. Oracle has the Oracle Enterprise Manager (OEM) performance pack, which directly interrogates the memory of the v$ structures to show what is going on in your database at the time the performance problem is being experienced. Oracle Enterprise Manager also offers data collection mechanisms via the intelligent agents to capture information from remote databases and has a central repository where performance data can be analyzed at a later time.

However, the OEM tools have several shortcomings. First, up until Oracle9i, it rarely does the Oracle administrator any good to see what's happening the specific moment in time you encounter a performance problem by virtue of the fact that there's little that can be done immediately to correct the problem. However, with Oracle9i, the DBA can dynamically change the memory within the SGA. A later edition of this text will show how the DBA can automatically monitor Oracle and the database server, and adjust the size of the SGA depending on the current processing within Oracle9i. Oracle9i will create a foundation for a self-tuning database instance, and this is a very exciting new development in Oracle. In short, reactive tuning monitors are often less valuable than proactive monitors such as STATSPACK.

The second part of the problem with OEM addresses the inherent complexity of using Oracle Enterprise Manager with intelligent agents to capture long-term trend statistics. Many shops with hundreds of databases spend thousands of hours installing and configuring OEM and the intelligent agents.

In contrast with OEM, Oracle STATSPACK is very straightforward and easy to manage. The STATSPACK tables can be easily defined, and the data collection mechanisms can be easily started. Whereas Oracle Enterprise Manager can often take weeks to define the intelligent agents for a large enterprise, the Oracle STATSPACK utility can be very quickly installed, and useful information can be provided almost immediately.

While the benefits of STATSPACK will become very clear in coming chapters, suffice it to say for now that the Oracle STATSPACK utility can easily become the foundation for a comprehensive Oracle tuning environment. STATSPACK has open code, it is easy to understand, and it allows for a wealth of sophisticated reports.

Of course, STATSPACK is like any other vendor product because you cannot alter the existing code and tables. However, you can easily add new STATSPACK tables and write customized code. We will be looking at how we can extend STATSPACK in several chapters.

The STATSPACK Architecture

To fully understand the STATSPACK architecture, we have to look at the basic nature of the STATSPACK utility. As we discussed in the Preface, the STATSPACK utility is an outgrowth of the Oracle UTLBSTAT and UTLESTAT utilities, which have been around Oracle since the very earliest versions. As the experienced DBA may recall, the BSTAT-ESTAT utilities capture information directly from the Oracle's in-memory structures and then compare the information from two snapshots in order to produce an elapsed-time report showing the activity of the database.

Whenever an automated collection occurs, STATSPACK simply grabs the relevant information from the in-memory structures and stores the information inside the STATSPACK tables. This information now becomes available for any Oracle SQL queries, and it is quite easy to make time series reports from the information in the STATSPACK tables.

To understand the structure for STATSPACK, let's begin by taking a high-level overview of all of the different tables that comprise the STATSPACK collection mechanisms.

How STATSPACK Collects Data

The STATSPACK utility works by taking snapshots of the current state of the database. Most users of STATSPACK schedule a job to collect data on an hourly basis, and then request additional snapshots when required. While we will go into details on the various methods for obtaining STATSPACK snapshots in Chapter 3, the listing here shows two common methods for getting an immediate snapshot:

```
sql> execute dbms_job.run(x)   -- where x is the job number of the statspack job
sql> execute statspack.snap;
```

When a snapshot is executed, the STATSPACK software will sample from the RAM in-memory structures inside the SGA and transfer the values into the corresponding STATSPACK tables, as shown in Figure 2-1. These values are then available for comparing with other snapshots.

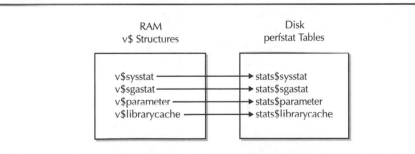

FIGURE 2-1. *Data collection mechanism for STATSPACK*

Note that in most cases, there is a direct correspondence between the v$ view in the SGA and the corresponding STATSPACK table. In the next example, we see that the stats$sysstat table is identical to the v$sysstat view:

```
SQL> desc v$sysstat;
 Name                                      Null?    Type
 ----------------------------------------- -------- --------------------
 STATISTIC#                                         NUMBER
 NAME                                               VARCHAR2(64)
 CLASS                                              NUMBER
 VALUE                                              NUMBER

SQL> desc stats$sysstat;
 Name                                      Null?    Type
 ----------------------------------------- -------- --------------------
 SNAP_ID                                   NOT NULL NUMBER(6)
 DBID                                      NOT NULL NUMBER
 INSTANCE_NUMBER                           NOT NULL NUMBER
 STATISTIC#                                NOT NULL NUMBER
 NAME                                      NOT NULL VARCHAR2(64)
 VALUE                                              NUMBER
```

The data collection mechanism for STATSPACK corresponds closely with the behavior of the utlbstat.sql and utlestat.sql (commonly called BSTAT-ESTAT) utilities that have been used for many years with Oracle. As we may recall from many years of using BSTAT-ESTAT, the utility samples data directly from the v$ views. If we look inside utlbstat.sql, we see the SQL that samples directly from the view:

utlbstat.sql   insert into stats$begin_stats select * from v$sysstat;

utlestat.sql   insert into stats$end_stats select * from v$sysstat;

It is critical to your understanding of the STATSPACK utility that you understand that the information captured by a STATSPACK snapshot are accumulated values. The information from the v$ views collect database information at startup time and continue to add to the values until the instance is shut down (see Figure 2-2).

In order to get a meaningful elapsed-time report, you must run a STATSPACK report that compares two snapshots, as shown in Figure 2-3. In later chapters we will examine methods for creating reports that stack elapsed-time reports, showing the changes in values over long periods of time.

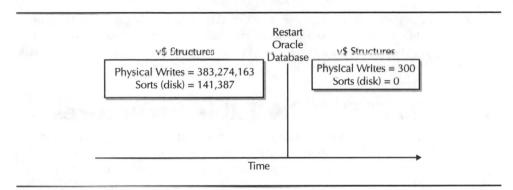

FIGURE 2-2. *Accumulated snapshot values*

CAUTION
It is critical that the user of the STATSPACK reports understand that a report will be invalid if the database is shut down between snapshots. This is because all of the accumulated values will be reset, causing the second snapshot to have smaller values than the original snapshot. When this happens, the STATSPACK report will display negative values.

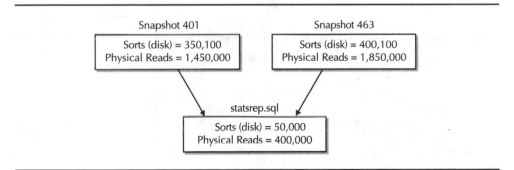

FIGURE 2-3. *A STATSPACK snapshot comparison report*

Now that we understand the basic functionality of STATSPACK, let's examine the tables that contain the STATSPACK information. Throughout the text you will be introduced to each of these tables, and you will eventually become intimate with the data contained within each table.

The STATSPACK Table Structures

The STATSPACK tables can be broken down into several areas. These areas measure all areas of the Oracle instance, including file I/O, system-wide statistics, data buffer statistics, SQL statistics, and a host of other information. We will become intimate with these tables in later chapters, but we should introduce the major STATSPACK tables at this time.

The STATSPACK utility is designed to measure Oracle information both from the perspective of a single database as well as a distributed enterprise consisting of many databases. In Figure 2-4, we see the basic hierarchical structure of the tables.

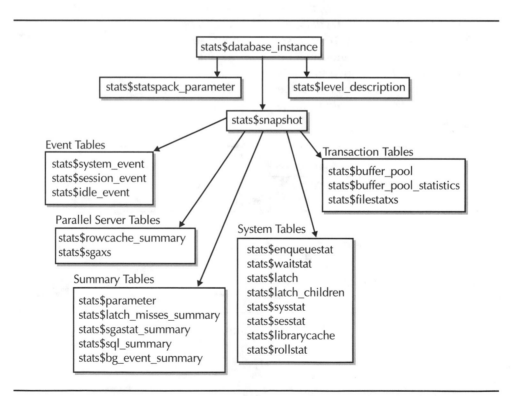

FIGURE 2-4.   *A high-level overview of the STATSPACK tables*

Let's begin our discussion by looking at the control tables for STATSPACK. We will then look at the parameter tables, and then describe the information collected in each of the subordinate data tables.

STATSPACK Control Tables

As we can see from this high-level entity relation model, the main anchor for the STATSPACK tables is a table called stats$database_instance. This table contains the database ID, the instance number, and the database server host name for the database that you are measuring. By associating the host name with this table, the DBA can populate database information from several database servers into a single collection mechanism. While the STATSPACK developers have not yet implemented a mechanism for collecting STATSPACK data from many databases in a distributed environment, they have laid the foundation for this functionality in this table:

```
SQL> desc STATS$DATABASE_INSTANCE;
 Name                                      Null?    Type
 ----------------------------------------- -------- --------------------
 DBID                                      NOT NULL NUMBER
 INSTANCE_NUMBER                           NOT NULL NUMBER
 DB_NAME                                   NOT NULL VARCHAR2(9)
 INSTANCE_NAME                             NOT NULL VARCHAR2(16)
 HOST_NAME                                          VARCHAR2(64)
```

For each database instance, we have many occurrences of the stats$snapshot table. This table contains the snapshot ID, the database ID, the instance number, and also the time the snapshot was taken. The stats$snapshot table is going to be very important in all of the scripts in our book because it contains the time that the snapshot was taken. Hence, all of the scripts that will be presented in this book must join into the stats$snapshot table so that you can correlate the time of the snapshot with the individual snapshot details.

```
SQL> desc STATS$SNAPSHOT;
 Name                                      Null?    Type
 ----------------------------------------- -------- --------------------
 SNAP_ID                                   NOT NULL NUMBER(6)
 DBID                                      NOT NULL NUMBER
 INSTANCE_NUMBER                           NOT NULL NUMBER
 SNAP_TIME                                 NOT NULL DATE
 STARTUP_TIME                              NOT NULL DATE
 SESSION_ID                                NOT NULL NUMBER
 SERIAL#                                             NUMBER
 SNAP_LEVEL                                          NUMBER
 UCOMMENT                                            VARCHAR2(160)
 EXECUTIONS_TH                                       NUMBER
```

```
PARSE_CALLS_TH                                       NUMBER
DISK_READS_TH                                        NUMBER
BUFFER_GETS_TH                                       NUMBER
```

In the stats$snapshot table, we see that there are three levels for STATSPACK data collection. In the next chapter we will see how these levels control what data is placed into the STATSPACK tables. We will also examine the four threshold columns (executions_th, parse_calls_th, disk_reads_th, buffer_gets_th) and see how these thresholds can be used to limit the number of stats$sql_summary rows that are added when a STATSPACK snapshot is executed.

STATSPACK Parameter Tables

The STATSPACK utility has numerous parameter tables that are used to record the thresholds and level of each snapshot in the STATSPACK collection process. There are two tables for parameters, the stats$snapshot_parameter table and the stat$level_description table.

stats$statspack_parameter

The stats$statspack_parameter table contains the default snapshot level for the database instance:

```
SQL> desc STATS$STATSPACK_PARAMETER;
 Name                                     Null?    Type
 --------------------------------------   -------- ------------------------
 DBID                                     NOT NULL NUMBER
 INSTANCE_NUMBER                          NOT NULL NUMBER
 SESSION_ID                               NOT NULL NUMBER
 SNAP_LEVEL                               NOT NULL NUMBER
 NUM_SQL                                  NOT NULL NUMBER
 EXECUTIONS_TH                            NOT NULL NUMBER
 PARSE_CALLS_TH                           NOT NULL NUMBER
 DISK_READS_TH                            NOT NULL NUMBER
 BUFFER_GETS_TH                           NOT NULL NUMBER
 PIN_STATSPACK                            NOT NULL VARCHAR2(10)
 LAST_MODIFIED                                     DATE
 UCOMMENT                                          VARCHAR2(160)
 JOB                                               NUMBER
```

The stats$level_description Table

This table is used to describe the data collection for each level of STATSPACK collection. There are only three levels of STATSPACK collection—0, 5, and 10—

and the rules are quite simple. A level 0 collection populates all tables except
stats$sql_summary and stats$latch_children. A level 5 collection adds collection
for stats$sql_summary, and a level 10 collection adds data for the stats$latch_children
table. A level 5 collection is the default.

```
SQL> desc STATS$LEVEL_DESCRIPTION;
 Name                                      Null?    Type
 ----------------------------------------- -------- ----------------------
 SNAP_LEVEL                                NOT NULL NUMBER
 DESCRIPTION                                        VARCHAR2(300)
```

Now that we understand the basic structure of STATSPACK, let's review some
of the uses for STATSPACK. These uses will be a central theme throughout the
body of this text, and we will be showing dozens of examples of each approach.

Uses for STATSPACK Information

Now that we have a high-level understanding of the STATSPACK tables and the
information captured in STATSPACK, we can begin to take a look at how this
information can help us in our Oracle tuning endeavors. There are many uses
for STATSPACK in addition to standard database tuning. The information in the
STATSPACK tables can be used for resource planning and predictive modeling,
as can also be used for reports that can tell the Oracle professional those times
in which the Oracle databases experienced stress.

While we will be going into a great amount of detail on the uses for the STATSPACK
tables in later chapters, suffice it to say for now that we will have scripts available
for virtually every type of event that affects Oracle performance.

For the first time in the history of Oracle, we have a tool provided by Oracle that
is capable of capturing complete database statistics over long periods of time. Because
of this ability to capture Oracle statistics over long periods of time, STATSPACK offers
the database administrator a huge opportunity to be able to go backwards and analyze
the behavior of their database during specific processing periods for the application.
Due to the time-oriented nature of the STATSPACK data, the Oracle administrator
can do far more than simply tune the database. The DBA now has the capability of
doing long-term trend analysis, post hoc analysis of performance problems, resource
planning, and predictive modeling that will help everyone in the IT organization
understand the growth demands of the Oracle database.

Let's begin by taking a brief look at how the STATSPACK tables will enable us to
do Oracle tuning far more efficiently than ever before.

Database Tuning with **STATSPACK**

Ever since the first releases of Oracle, the Oracle DBA has been charged with making sure that the Oracle database performs at the optimal levels. In order to do this, the DBA was forced to interrogate Oracle's internal structures in real time so that they might be able to see what's going on inside the Oracle database when the problem occurs. The DBA would then adjust Oracle parameters to maximize the throughput of information through the Oracle database.

This mode of tuning is generally referred to as *reactive* tuning. In reactive tuning mode, the Oracle database administrator captures information about a current performance problem, and then queries the Oracle database in order to ascertain its cause. In reactive tuning, the Oracle database administrator does not have any immediate options for fixing the database, and will make changes later on in order to remedy the problem that occurred in the previous point in time.

With the advent of STATSPACK, we see that the Oracle administrators now have a data repository at their disposal that will allow them to leisurely analyze Oracle performance statistics and trends over time. This allows the DBAs to come up with a general tuning strategy that addresses all of the different kinds of processing that can take place within the Oracle application.

This approach is commonly known as *proactive* tuning. In proactive tuning mode, the Oracle database administrator's goal is to tune the database by coming up with global parameters and settings that will maximize Oracle throughput at any given point in time. By using a proactive approach to Oracle tuning, the Oracle administrator can ensure that the database is always optimally tuned for the type of processing that is being done against the database.

As we discussed, the STATSPACK tables do nothing more than interrogate the in-memory v$ structures and place the information in the Oracle STATSPACK tables. While this may be a bit of an oversimplification, having STATSPACK information captured over periods of time gives the DBA the opportunity to use this data to model an optimal performance plan for the database. Over the course of the rest of this book we will be specifically addressing how the STATSPACK tables can be used in order to allow the Oracle database to perform this type of proactive tuning, and we will come up with an overall plan that is best suited for the database.

Resource Planning

As we just mentioned, the STATSPACK utility captures performance and tuning statistics over long periods of time. Hence, the STATSPACK utility is very useful for doing resource planning for an entire IT organization. Within an IT organization, managers are often charged with predicting the amount of resources that are going to be needed by Oracle and ensuring that those resources are delivered in time so that the Oracle database does not experience any kind of resource related outages. A typical sample resource plan is shown in Figure 2-5.

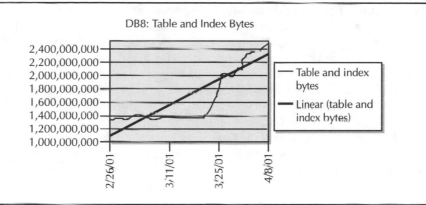

FIGURE 2-5.   *A sample resource plan for an Oracle database*

By using the STATSPACK tables, resource managers can plot the growth patterns of objects (tables and indexes) within the Oracle database, and come up with linear regression models that will accurately predict the disk storage needs of the Oracle database at future points in time. This resource modeling capability can also be used for predicting hardware resources, such as pending needs within the central processing units and the RAM memory structures. In Chapters 5 through 8 we will be taking a close look at how we can extend the STATSPACK tables in order to capture these types of server statistics and how we can plot the statistics in order to do predictive resource modeling for all areas within the Oracle enterprise.

Predictive Modeling

Predictive modeling is one of the most important new areas of Oracle tuning, and one that lends itself very well to the use of the STATSPACK tables. In a predictive model, the Oracle DBA is charged with taking existing statistics and predicting future needs for all areas within the Oracle database. For example, the Oracle DBA could analyze the STATSPACK data buffer hit ratio and compare it to the memory usage within the Oracle *db_block_buffers*. The DBA can then extrapolate the information from the studies, and predict the times at which the Oracle data buffers would need to be increased in order to maintain the current levels of performance.

Likewise, the Oracle DBA can also make a detailed analysis of Oracle's data buffer caches (the KEEP pool, DEFAULT pool, and the RECYCLE pool), and accurately measure the performance of each one of these pools over long periods of time. Based upon existing usage, the Oracle DBA can accurately predict at what time additional RAM memory is needed for each of these data buffers in order to keep the current performance levels for the system.

When discussing predictive modeling, the STATSPACK tables also offer the Oracle DBA an opportunity to slice off the information according to previously unavailable parameters. In the real world, Oracle applications commonly follow cyclical patterns. For example, an Oracle Financials application may be very active on the last Friday of every month when all of the books are being closed and financial reports are being prepared. Using the STATSPACK data, the Oracle DBA can extract information from the last Friday of every month for the past year, and take a look at the specific performance needs of the end-of-month Oracle Financials applications.

In Oracle8i, and on into Oracle9i, we see new features that allow the database administrator to dynamically change the database depending upon the performance needs of the applications. In Oracle9i, the Oracle DBA has the ability to dynamically alter the memory configuration of the Oracle instance. With these new features, Oracle is moving towards a dynamic database configuration, whereby the configuration of the system can be adjusted according to the needs of the Oracle application.

Once the Oracle administrators recognize cyclic performance patterns in the Oracle database, they are now in a position to reconfigure the database in order to meet the specific processing needs of the system. For example, it is not uncommon in the real world to find several versions of Oracle's init.ora files, each one customized to the processing needs of the application that is running at the time. For example, it is not uncommon to see a special version of the Oracle instance (with a different initialization file) that is dedicated towards batch processing tasks that might occur, say, on every Friday, while another version of the init.ora file is customized for OLTP transactions. Some Oracle shops also create additional init.ora files that are suited to data warehouse processing that might occur on the weekend. In each of these cases, the Oracle database is stopped and restarted with the appropriate init.ora configuration file.

Conclusion

Now that we understand the basic structure and uses for STATSPACK, we are ready to install and configure the STATSPACK software. The next chapter will review all of the installation steps, and Chapter 4 will show you all of the performance information that is contained within a STATSPACK snapshot.

CHAPTER
3

Installing
and Configuring
STATSPACK

he installation steps for STATSPACK are relatively simple and straightforward. This chapter will walk you, step by step, through the installation and configuration of STATSPACK. We will be including a complete description of the following steps:

- Creating the perfstat tablespace

- Creating the perfstat user

- Creating the tables

- Installing the packages

- Collecting data

- Scheduling data collection snapshots with dbms_job

- Testing your installation

In addition to just describing each step, we will describe some considerations that will make your use of STATSPACK more beneficial.

Back-Porting STATSPACK for Oracle 8.0 through 8.1.5

STATSPACK was officially introduced with Oracle 8.1.6, but it can be back-ported to run on Oracle 8.0–Oracle 8.1.5. If you are planning to use STATSPACK with pre-8.1.6 versions of Oracle, you will need the following modifications:

- **statscbps.sql**   This script adds a v$buffer_pool_statistics view that is required for pre-8.1.6 versions of Oracle. This script should be run after **connect internal** and before running the statscre.sql script.

- **statsrep80.sql**   This is the only STATSPACK supplied report for Oracle 8.0–8.1.5.

These SQL scripts to back-port STATSPACK can be downloaded from http://www.oracle.com/oramag/oracle/00-Mar/statspack-other.html.

CAUTION
*While you can back-port STATSPACK to Oracle 8.0
releases by using the statsrep80.sql report, there are
some known problems with the utility. The report
from STATSPACK on an Oracle release level prior
to 8.1.6 has known problems with the data and
cannot always be trusted. Check Oracle MetaLink
for details about the reporting problems.*

Overview of the STATSPACK Scripts

All of the STATSPACK scripts are located in the $ORACLE_HOME/rdbms/admin
directory, and you can see all of the scripts by going to this directory and listing
all files that begin with "stat":

```
>cd $ORACLE_HOME/rdbms/admin
server1*db01-/u01/app/oracle/product/8.1.6_64/rdbms/admin
>ls -al stat*
-rw-r--r--  1 oracle   oinstall    1739 Dec   6  1999 statsauto.sql
-rw-r--r--  1 oracle   oinstall     843 Dec   6  1999 statscre.sql
-rw-r--r--  1 oracle   oinstall   27183 Nov  10  1999 statsctab.sql
-rw-r--r--  1 oracle   oinstall    4686 Nov  10  1999 statscusr.sql
-rw-r--r--  1 oracle   oinstall     792 Aug  27  1999 statsdrp.sql
-rw-r--r--  1 oracle   oinstall    3236 Nov  10  1999 statsdtab.sql
-rw-r--r--  1 oracle   oinstall    1081 Nov  10  1999 statsdusr.sql
-rw-r--r--  1 oracle   oinstall   26667 Dec   6  1999 statspack.doc
-rw-r--r--  1 oracle   oinstall   49821 Nov  10  1999 statspack.sql
 rw-r--r--  1 oracle   oinstall   46873 Nov  10  1999 statsrep.sql
-rw-r--r--  1 oracle   oinstall     559 Aug  27  1999 statsuexp.par
```

Let's begin by reviewing the functions of each of these files. Several of the files
call subfiles, so it helps if we organize the files as a hierarchy:

- **statscre.sql** This is the first install script run after you create the
  tablespace. It calls several subscripts:

  - **statscusr.sql** This script creates a user called PERFSTAT with
    the required permissions.

- **statsctab.sql** This creates the STATSPACK tables and indexes, owned by the PERFSTAT user.

- **statspack.sql** This creates the PL/SQL package called STATSPACK with the STATSPACK procedures.

- **statsauto.sql** This script contains the dbms_job.submit commands that will execute a STATSPACK snapshot every hour.

- **statsdrp.sql** This script is used to drop all STATSPACK entities. This script calls these subscripts:

  - **statsdtab.sql** This drops all STATSPACK tables and indexes.

  - **statsdusr.sql** This script drops the PERFSTAT user.

- **statsuexp.par** This is an export parameter file for exporting the STATSPACK objects. This can be useful if you want to consolidate STATSPACK reports for several databases into a single STATSPACK structure.

- **statspack.doc** This is a generic read-me file explaining the installation and operation of the STATSPACK utility.

- **statsrep.sql** This is the only report provided in STATSPACK. It prompts you for the start and end snapshots, and then produces an elapsed-time report.

- **statsrep80.sql** This is a version of the STATSPACK report for Oracle 8.0.

Now that we understand the functions of each of the files, we are ready to install STATSPACK. Our first step is to create a tablespace for the STATSPACK data.

Step 1: Create the perfstat Tablespace

The STATSPACK utility requires an isolated tablespace to contain all of the objects and data. For uniformity, it is suggested that the tablespace be called perfstat, the same name as the schema owner for the STATSPACK tables. Note that I have deliberately not used the AUTOEXTEND option. It is important for the Oracle DBA to closely watch the STATSPACK data to ensure that the stats$sql_summary table is not taking an inordinate amount of space. We will talk about adjusting the STATSPACK thresholds later in this chapter.

Next, we create a tablespace called perfstat with 500 megabytes of space in the datafile:

```
>sqlplus /

SQL*Plus: Release 8.1.6.0.0 - Production on Tue Dec 12 14:08:11 2000

(c) Copyright 1999 Oracle Corporation. All rights reserved.


Connected to:
Oracle8i Enterprise Edition Release 8.1.6.1.0 - 64bit Production
With the Partitioning option
JServer Release 8.1.6.1.0 - 64bit Production

SQL> create tablespace perfstat
  2  datafile '/u03/oradata/prodb1/perfstat.dbf'
size 500m;
```

Step 2: Run the create Script

Now that the tablespace exists we can begin the installation process of the STATSPACK software. This script creates a user called PERFSTAT, executes the script to create all of the STATSPACK tables and installs the STATSPACK PL/SQL package. When you run this script, you will be prompted for the following information:

- Specify PERFSTAT user's default tablespace: perfstat
- Specify PERFSTAT user's temporary tablespace: temp
- Enter tablespace where STATSPACK objects will be created: perfstat

Install Prerequisites

Note that this script assumes that you have run the catalog synonym script, so make sure you have run catdbsyn.sql when connected as INTERNAL. You will also be using the dbms_shared_pool package, so you must also run dbmspool.sql as INTERNAL.

NOTE
This script is designed to stop whenever an error is encountered. The statsctab.sql script contains the SQL*Plus directive `whenever sqlerror exit;`. *This means that the script will cease execution if any error is encountered. If you encounter an error and you need to restart the script, just comment out the* `whenever sqlerror exit` *line and run the script again. Also, note that the STATSPACK install script contains SQL*Plus commands. Hence, be sure you run it from SQL*Plus and do not try to run it in SVRMGRL or SQL*Worksheet.*

Once you have completed running the statscre.sql script, you will need to ensure that you do not have errors. The STATSPACK utility creates a series of files with the .lis extensions as shown here:

```
prodb2-/u01/app/oracle/product/8.1.6_64/rdbms/admin
>ls -al *.lis
-rw-r--r--   1 oracle    oinstall    4170 Dec 12 14:28 statsctab.lis
-rw-r--r--   1 oracle    oinstall    3417 Dec 12 14:27 statscusr.lis
-rw-r--r--   1 oracle    oinstall     201 Dec 12 14:28 statspack.lis
```

To check for errors, you need to look for any lines that contain "ORA-" or the word "error", since the presence of these strings indicates an error. If you are using Windows NT, you can check for errors by searching the output file in MS Word. However, most Oracle administrators on NT get a freeware grep for DOS, which is readily available on the Internet.

The code here shows the UNIX **grep** commands that are used to check for creation errors.

```
prodb2-/u01/app/oracle/product/8.1.6_64/rdbms/admin> grep ORA- *.lis

prodb2-/u01/app/oracle/product/8.1.6_64/rdbms/admin> grep -i error *.lis
statsctab.lis:STATSCTAB complete. Please check statsctab.lis for any errors.
statscusr.lis:STATSCUSR complete. Please check statscusr.lis for any errors.
statspack.lis:No errors.
statspack.lis:No errors.
statspack.lis:STATSPACK complete. Please check statspack.lis for any errors.
```

Now that we have installed the user, tables, indexes, and the package, we are ready to start collecting STATSPACK data. We will begin by testing the STATSPACK functionality and then schedule a regular STATSPACK collection job.

Step 3: Test the STATSPACK Install

To ensure that everything is installed correctly, we can demand two snapshots and then request an elapsed-time report. To execute a STATSPACK snapshot, we enter the statspack.snap procedure. If we do this twice, we will have two snapshots, and we can run the statsrep.sql report to ensure that everything is working properly. Here is the test to ensure that the install works properly. If you get a meaningful report after entering **statsrep**, then the install was successful. Also, note that the *statsrep.sql* script has an EXIT statement, so it will return you to the UNIX prompt when it has completed:

```
SQL> execute statspack.snap
PL/SQL procedure successfully completed.
SQL> execute statspack.snap
PL/SQL procedure successfully completed.
SQL> @statsrep
. . .
```

Step 4: Schedule Automatic STATSPACK Data Collections

Now that we have verified that STATSPACK is installed and working, we can schedule automatic data collection. By using the statsauto.sql script we can automatically schedule an hourly data collection for STATSPACK. The *statsauto.sql* script contains the following directive:

```
SQL> execute dbms_job.submit(:jobno, 'statspack.snap;',
trunc(sysdate+1/24,'HH'), 'trunc(SYSDATE+1/24,''HH'')', TRUE, :instno);
```

The important thing to note in this call to dbms_job.submit is the execution interval. The SYSDATE+1/24 is the interval that is stored in the dba_jobs view to produce hourly snapshots. You can change this as follows for different sample times. There are 1,440 minutes in a day, and you can use this figure to adjust the execution times.

Table 3-1 gives you the divisors for the snapshot intervals.

Hence, if we want a snapshot every ten minutes we would issue the following command:

```
SQL> execute dbms_job.submit(:jobno, 'statspack.snap;',
trunc(sysdate+1/144,'MI'), 'trunc(SYSDATE+1/144,''MI'')', TRUE, :instno);
```

Minutes per Day	Minutes between Snapshots	Required Divisor
1,440	60	24
1,440	30	48
1,440	10	144
1,440	5	288

TABLE 3-1. *Determining the Snapshot Interval*

In the real world, you may have times where you want to sample the database over short time intervals. For example, if you have noticed that a performance problem happens every day between 4:00 P.M. and 5:00 P.M., you can request more frequent snapshots during this period.

For normal use, you probably want to accept the hourly default and execute a snapshot every hour. Below is the standard output from running the *statsauto.sql* script:

```
SQL> connect perfstat/perfstat;
Connected.
SQL> @statsauto
PL/SQL procedure successfully completed.

Job number for automated statistics collection for this instance
~~~~~~~~~~~~~~~~~~~~~~~~~~~~~~~~~~~~~~~~~~~~~~~~~~~~~~~~~~~~~~~~~~~
Note that this job number is needed when modifying or removing
the job:

     JOBNO
----------
         1


Job queue process
~~~~~~~~~~~~~~~~~~
Below is the current setting of the job_queue_processes init.ora
parameter - the value for this parameter must be greater
than 0 to use automatic statistics gathering:

NAME                                 TYPE    VALUE
------------------------------------ ------- ----------------------------
job_queue_processes                  integer 1
```

```
Next scheduled run
~~~~~~~~~~~~~~~~~~
The next scheduled run for this job is:

       JOB NEXT_DATE NEXT_SEC
---------- --------- --------
         1 12-DEC-00 16:00:00
```

We can now see that a STATSPACK snapshot will automatically be executed every hour. We see that this is scheduled as job number 1, and we can use this job number to cancel this collection at any time using the dbms_job.remove procedure:

```
SQL> execute dbms_job.remove(1);

PL/SQL procedure successfully completed.
```

Now that we have installed and tested STATSPACK, we are ready to look at the configuration and maintenance issues.

STATSPACK Configuration and Maintenance

This section will investigate the procedures for viewing and modifying your STATSPACK jobs. In this section we will examine a quick script for viewing your STATSPACK snapshots, adjusting the STATSPACK levels, and adjusting the STATSPACK thresholds for capturing SQL into the stats$sql_summary table.

Viewing STATSPACK Snapshots

Because STATSPACK reports are generally made by comparing a starting snapshot with an ending snapshot, it is useful to have a tool to quickly display all of the available snapshots. To see the snapshots, you can enter a query directly from SQL*Plus:

```
SQL> select * from stats$snapshot;

    SNAP_ID      DBID INSTANCE_NUMBER SNAP_TIME STARTUP_T SESSION_ID
ERIAL#
---------- ---------- ---------- ---------- ---------- ---------- ---------
SNAP_LEVEL
----------
UCOMMENT
```

```
--------------------------------------------------------------------------
EXECUTIONS_TH PARSE_CALLS_TH DISK_READS_TH BUFFER_GETS_TH
------------- -------------- -------------- --------------
            1 2289877879                 1 12-DEC-00 12-DEC-00          0             0
            5

              100           1000           1000         10000
```

An easier method to see your snapshots is to invoke a UNIX shell script that you can call directly from the UNIX prompt. The script next quickly lists all of the snapshots in a single command. Let's look at this script, *list_snaps.ksh*.

list_snaps.ksh

```ksh
#!/bin/ksh

# First, we must set the environment . . . .
ORACLE_SID=$ORACLE_SID
export ORACLE_SID
ORACLE_HOME=`cat /etc/oratab|grep ^$ORACLE_SID:|cut -f2 -d':'`
#ORACLE_HOME=`cat /var/opt/oracle/oratab|grep ^$ORACLE_SID:|cut -f2 -d':'`
export ORACLE_HOME
PATH=$ORACLE_HOME/bin:$PATH
export PATH

$ORACLE_HOME/bin/sqlplus -s perfstat/perfstat<<!
select
   name,
   snap_id,
   to_char(snap_time,' dd Mon YYYY HH24:mi:ss')
from
   stats\$snapshot,
   v\$database
order by
   snap_id
;
exit
!
```

When executed from the UNIX prompt, this script gives you a fast and complete description of all available snapshots. Let's now execute this script and see the results:

```
UNIX> list_snaps.ksh
NAME          SNAP_ID TO_CHAR(SNAP_TIME,'DD
--------- ----- -- -------------------
PRODB1            1  12 Dec 2000 15:30:03
PRODB1            2  12 Dec 2000 15:51:09
PRODB1            3  12 Dec 2000 15:51:14
PRODB1            4  12 Dec 2000 15:51:57
PRODB1            5  12 Dec 2000 15:52:02
PRODB1            6  12 Dec 2000 15:54:26
PRODB1            7  12 Dec 2000 15:54:31
```

Here we see each snapshot, the snapshot number, and the date of the snapshot. This script is useful because we must be careful never to run queries that span times where the database instance has been shut down and restarted. As we know, this resets the v$ accumulators, and causes invalid STATSPACK reports.

Now let's look at how we can restrict the amount of SQL that is collected in a snapshot by setting the collection thresholds.

Adjusting the STATSPACK Collection Thresholds

As we have already mentioned, STATSPACK has two types of collection options, *level* and *threshold*. The *level* parameter controls the type of data collected from Oracle, while the *threshold* parameter acts as a filter for the collection of SQL statements into the stats$sql_summary table.

Snapshot Levels

There are three snapshot levels used in STATSPACK, and level 5 is the default:

- **Level 0: General Performance Statistics**   This level collects general performance statistics, such as wait statistics, system events, system statistics, rollback segment data, row cache, SGA, background events, session events, lock statistics, buffer pool statistics, and parent latch statistics.

- **Level 5: Add SQL Statements**   This level includes all level 0 statistics plus SQL statements into the stats$sql_summary table.

■ **Level 10: Add Child Latch Statistics**   The level 10 snapshot includes everything in the level 5 statistics plus the addition of child latches into the stats$latch_children table. You rarely, if ever, need this level of detail, and you should only do a level 10 snapshot when directed by Oracle technical support.

The default for a snapshot is always level 5, but you can use the statspack package to change the default or request a special snapshot at a different level. You can change the default level of a snapshot with the statspack.snap function. In the example here, we remove all SQL collection from all future snapshots by specifying a default level 1 snapshot:

```
SQL>  execute statspack.snap -
      (i_snap_level=>0, i_modify_parameter=>'true');
```

Once set, all future snapshots will be level 0. If you want a single snapshot at a different level without changing the default, you just omit the i_modify_parameter argument. In the next example, we take a single snapshot at level 10, while leaving the default at level 5 for all subsequent snapshots:

```
SQL>  execute statspack.snap -
      (i_snap_level=>10);
```

Snapshot Thresholds

The snapshot thresholds only apply to the SQL statements that are captured in the stats$sql_summary table. The stats$sql_summary table can easily become the largest tables in the STATSPACK schema because each snapshot might collect several hundred rows, one for each SQL statement that was in the library cache at the time of the snapshot.

The thresholds are stored in the stats$statspack_parameter table. Let's take a look at each threshold:

■ **executions_th**   This is the number of executions of the SQL statement (default is 100).

■ **disk_reads_th**   This is the number of disk reads performed by the SQL statement (default is 1,000).

■ **parse_calls_th**   This is the number of parse calls performed by the SQL statement (default is 1,000).

■ **buffer_gets_th**   This is the number of buffer gets performed by the SQL statement (default is 10,000).

It is important to understand that each SQL statement will be evaluated against all of these thresholds, and the SQL statement will be included in the stats$sql_summary table if *any one* of the thresholds is exceeded. In other words, these thresholds are not AND'ed together as we might expect, but they are OR'ed together such that any value exceeding any of the thresholds will cause a row to be populated.

The main purpose of these thresholds is to control the rapid growth of the stats$sql_summary table that will occur when a highly active database has hundreds of SQL statements in the library cache. In the next chapter we will be discussing clean-up strategies for removing unwanted snapshots from the database.

You can change the threshold defaults by calling the statspack.modify_statspack_ parameter function. In the example here, we change the default threshold for buffer_gets and disk_reads to 100,000. In all subsequent snapshots, we will only see SQL that exceeds 100,000 buffer gets or disk reads.

```
SQL> execute statspack.modify_statspack_parameter -
     (i_buffer_gets_th=>100000, i_disk_reads_th=>100000);
```

Removing Old STATSPACK Snapshots

At some point, your collection of STATSPACK data will be too old to be useful. Some shops choose to roll up old STATSPACK data into average values and store these summaries in extensions to the STATSPACK tables, and we will be presenting scripts in later chapters for that purpose.

Fortunately, STATSPACK uses foreign-key referential integrity constraints with the ON CASCADE DELETE option. This means that all information for a given snapshot can be deleted by deleting the corresponding stats$snapshot record. For example, suppose that you wanted to delete all snapshots for 1999, and these were snapshots that have a snap_id of less than 10,000. The following DELETE would remove all of these snapshots, and all subordinate detail rows:

```
SQL > delete from stats$snapshot where snap_id < 10000;
28923563 rows deleted.
```

Of course, you can selectively delete rows from STATSPACK. For example, you might want to keep all of the system statistics and delete all of the SQL statements that were more than six months old. In this case, you could selectively remove the rows from stats$sql_summary:

```
SQL > delete from stats$sql_summary where snap_time < sysdate - 180;
2888363 rows deleted.
```

Now let's take a look at some handy shell scripts that will make your use of STATSPACK easier.

Handy STATSPACK Shell Scripts

Once you have become comfortable with the STATSPACK data collection, you may need some easy scripts that you can use to quickly get reports from STATSPACK. While the Web site mentioned in the Preface contains dozens of STATSPACK scripts, let's look at one that is frequently used by the DBA.

A Quick Elapsed-Time STATSPACK Script

This is a great Korn shell script that shows the Oracle database behavior change between snapshots. This report is very handy if you get an end-user report of a performance problem and you want to capture details about what is happening right now. The script is called quick.ksh, and it will become one of the most frequently used of all the STATSPACK scripts.

The *quick.ksh* script will take an immediate snapshot, sleep for the period you specify, and then take another snapshot and produce an elapsed-time report. This is a very similar procedure to the old utlbstat/utlestat utilities, but it is much easier to execute and interpret the results.

quick.ksh

```
#!/bin/ksh

# First, we must set the environment . . . .
ORACLE_SID=$ORACLE_SID
export ORACLE_SID
ORACLE_HOME=`cat /etc/oratab|grep ^$ORACLE_SID:|cut -f2 -d':'`
export ORACLE_HOME
PATH=$ORACLE_HOME/bin:$PATH
export PATH

echo "Please enter the number of seconds between snapshots."
read elapsed


$ORACLE_HOME/bin/sqlplus -s perfstat/perfstat<<!
execute statspack.snap;
exit
!

sleep $elapsed
```

```
$ORACLE_HOME/bin/sqlplus -s perfstat/perfstat<<!
execute statspack.snap;

select
   name,
   snap_id,
   to_char(snap_time,' dd Mon YYYY HH24:mi:ss')
from
   stats\$snapshot,
   v\$database
where
   snap_id > (select max(snap_id)-2 from stats\$snapshot)
;

@rpt_last
```

Now that we have captured two quick snapshots, we execute the *rpt_last.sql*
script to give us a report on the important metrics. Let's take a close look at this
SQL*Plus report. After completing the two snapshots, this script invokes *rpt_last.sql*,
which is a STATSPACK script that always compares the last two snapshots in the
database. The rpt_last.sql script is very valuable, and is included in the Oracle Press
Web site for these scripts. Here is a sample of the output from the *rpt_last.sql* script.
This script will identify almost every possible cause of the performance problem.

rpt_last.sql

```
*************************************************************
This will identify any single file who's read I/O
is more than 10% of the total read I/O of the database.

The "hot" file should be examined, and the hot table/index
should be identified using STATSPACK.

- The busy file should be placed on a disk device with
"less busy" files to minimize read delay and channel
contention.

- If small file has a hot small table, place the table
in the KEEP pool

- If the file has a large-table full-table scan, place
the table in the RECYCLE pool and turn on parallel query
for the table.
*************************************************************
```

```
MYDATE              FILE_NAME                                    READS
---------------     -----------------------------------------   ------------
2000-12-20 11       /u03/oradata/PROD/pod01.dbf                  1,766


*************************************************************
This will identify any single file who's write I/O
is more than 10% of the total write I/O of the database.

The "hot" file should be examined, and the hot table/index
should be identified using STATSPACK.

- The busy file should be placed on a disk device with
"less busy" files to minimize write delay and channel
contention.

- If small file has a hot small table, place the table
in the KEEP pool

*************************************************************


no rows selected

*************************************************************
When the data buffer hit ratio falls below 90%, you
should consider adding to the db_block_buffer init.ora parameter

*************************************************************




MYDATE              phys_writes BUFFER HIT RATIO
---------------     ----------- ----------------
20 Dec 11:23:47         101,888               91

1 row selected.

*************************************************************
When there are high disk sorts, you should investigate
increasing sort_area_size, or adding indexes to force index_full scans


*************************************************************
```

```
MYDATE              SORTS_MEMORY    SORTS_DISK             RATIO
----------------    ------------    ------------    --------------
20 Dec 11:23:47             109               1    .0001743119266

1 row selected.



************************************************************
When there is high I/O waits, disk bottlenecks may exist
Run iostats to find the hot disk and shuffle files to
remove the contention



************************************************************



no rows selected



************************************************************
Buffer Busy Waits may signal a high update table with too
few freelists. Find the offending table and add more freelists.



************************************************************



MYDATE              BUFFER_BUSY_WAIT
----------------    ----------------
20 Dec 11:23:47                   20

1 row selected.



************************************************************
High redo log space requests indicate a need to increase
the log_buffer parameter



************************************************************
```

```
no rows selected


*************************************************************
Table fetch continued row indicates chained rows, or fetches of
long datatypes (long raw, blob)

Investigate increasing db_block_size or reorganizing tables
with chained rows.


*************************************************************



MYDATE          TABLE_FETCH_CONTINUED_ROW
---------------- -------------------------
20 Dec 11:23:47                      1,551

1 row selected.



*************************************************************
Enqueue Deadlocks indicate contention within the Oracle
shared pool.

Investigate increasing shared_pool_size


*************************************************************



MYDATE          ENQUEUE_DEADLOCKS
---------------- -----------------
20 Dec 11:23:47                  0

1 row selected.



*************************************************************
Long-table full table scans can indicate a need to:

- Make the offending tables parallel query
(alter table xxx parallel degree yyy;)
```

```
- Place the table in the RECYCLE pool
- Build an index on the table to remove the FTS

To locate the table, run access.sql

See Oracle Magazine September 2000 issue for details
************************************************************


MYDATE                   FTS
----------------    ------------
20 Dec 11:23:47          148

1 row selected.
```

Note that quick.ksh requires that you specify the ORACLE_SID, so that you can run it on a server that contains many Oracle instances. Also, you may need to change the location of the oratab file from /etc/ to /var/opt/oracle if you are running Solaris.

Conclusion

This chapter should cover all of the areas that are required for the installation and maintenance of STATSPACK. We are now ready to start tuning the Oracle database, and we will begin with examining the data inside the STATSPACK tables. The next chapter will serve as an excellent quick reference for all of the STATSPACK values.

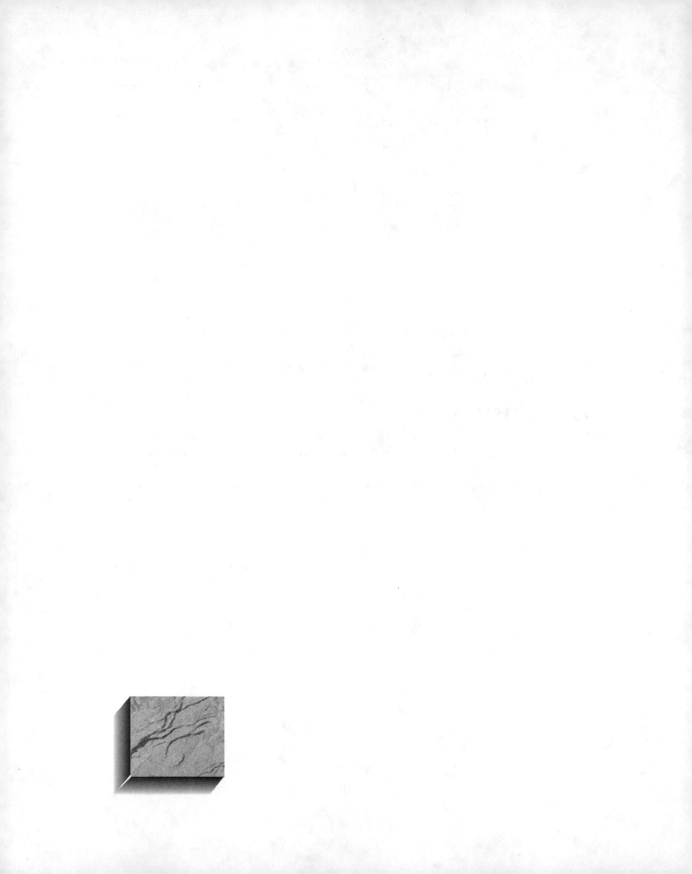

CHAPTER
4

Data Inside
the STATSPACK Tables

his chapter will review all of the subordinate data tables within STATSPACK and describe all of the Oracle database information that is contained within each table. While this chapter provides a basic overview, we will be returning to these tables many times during the tuning sections of this text, so do not be concerned if there is not enough detail in this chapter. This chapter will make a great reference section after you have completed the book.

In the last chapter we discussed the control tables stats$database_instance and stats$snapshot, and the parameter table stats$statspack_parameter. Now let's look at the detail tables and see how the data from these tables can provide information for Oracle tuning.

What Is Missing from STATSPACK?

It is important to note that STATSPACK fails to capture all of the information that you require to fully analyze performance problems. As we discussed in Chapter 1, Oracle performance problems are sometimes related to external issues such as disk I/O bottlenecks, RAM swapping, CPU enqueues, and network bottlenecks. To make up for these shortcoming and extend STATSPACK to measure environmental performance, we can add new STATSPACK tables for the following areas:

- **Server statistics** We will look at extending STATSPACK to capture server statistics in Chapter 5.

- **Disk statistics** We will show how to extend STATSPACK for disk I/O statistics in Chapter 8.

- **Object statistics** We will see how to extend STATSPACK to capture and report on tables and indexes in Chapter 10.

We will look at extending the STATSPACK structure to capture these external statistics in later chapters, but for now let's focus on the details of the existing STATSPACK tables.

STATSPACK Subordinate Table Structures

Starting from the stats$snapshot table, we see a wealth of other tables that capture information from the in-memory v$ structures. It's important to note that some of these will only have single snapshot rows, whereas other tables will have many rows. For example, the stats$sesstat table will contain many rows, one row for each statistic measured at the time that the snapshot was taken. Hence, it is important to distinguish in the overall structure of the STATSPACK tables those tables that have individual rows per snapshot and those that have multiple rows.

While at first glance the structure and complexity of the STATSPACK tables may seem overwhelming, remember that this book will provide dozens of prewritten scripts that you will be able to run to get the relevant information for your purposes. Also bear in mind that the script templates provided in this book can lay the foundation for additional queries.

The next sections will describe the layout and data within the subordinate STATSPACK tables. The STATSPACK tables are divided into four areas: the summary tables that report on system-wide summaries, the system tables that contain system-wide information relating to the Oracle instance, the transaction tables that contain information relating to Oracle transaction processing, and the event tables that record Oracle system events.

STATSPACK Summary Tables

There are several system-wide summary tables that can be used from within STATSPACK, as shown in Figure 4-1.

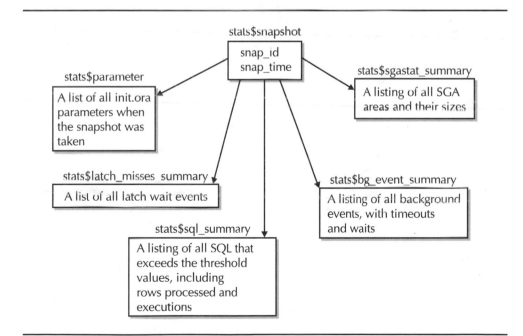

FIGURE 4-1. *The STATSPACK summary tables*

These summary tables are useful for several reporting areas that we will discuss in detail in Chapter 14. For example, the stats$parameter table shows all of the *init.ora* parameters at the time of the snapshot, and this table is very useful when comparing the performance of the database before and after a change to an initialization parameter. Let's examine the data inside each of these tables.

The stats$latch_misses_summary Table

This table records latch misses for the Oracle database. When we observe latches, we must remember that there are two types of latches:

- **Willing-to-wait latch** A willing-to-wait latch will repeatedly try to reacquire the latch. The redo allocation latch is a good example.

- **Immediate latch** These latches must acquire a latch immediately or the task will abort. The redo copy latch is a good example of an immediate latch.

Latch sleeps are very important because they indicate the number of times we had to sleep because we could not get a latch. The latches with the highest sleep values are the ones to concentrate on. Latch misses are recorded in the nwfail_count column of this table, and misses are important because they indicate system resource shortages:

```
SQL> desc stats$latch_misses_summary;
Name                                     Null?      Type
---------------------------------------- --------   -------------------
SNAP_ID                                  NOT NULL   NUMBER(6)
DBID                                     NOT NULL   NUMBER
INSTANCE_NUMBER                          NOT NULL   NUMBER
PARENT_NAME                              NOT NULL   VARCHAR2(50)
WHERE_IN_CODE                            NOT NULL   VARCHAR2(64)
NWFAIL_COUNT                                        NUMBER
SLEEP_COUNT                                         NUMBER
```

There are more than a dozen types of latches, but there are only a few that impact Oracle performance. Here is a brief listing of some important latches and the remedy to shortages.

Latch Name	Willing-to-Wait?	Action
Redo copy	Yes	Increase redo log size
Redo allocation	No	Increase log_small_entry_max_size

Latch Name	Willing-to-Wait?	Action
Library cache	Yes	Increase shared_pool_size
Shared pool	Yes	Increase shared_pool_size

We will be discussing Oracle latches in detail in Chapter 9.
Here is a sample STATSPACK report from the information in this table.

rpt_latch_misses.sql

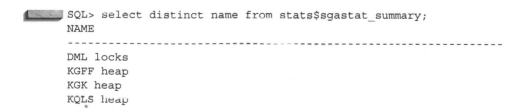

```
SNAP_DAT PARENT_NAME                    WHERE_IN_C SUM_NWFAIL SUM_SLEEP
-------- ------------------------------ ---------- ---------- ----------
12-12-00 cache buffers chains           kcbbxsv             0          3
         cache buffers chains           kcbget: pi          0          3
                                        n buffer
12-13-00 cache buffers chains           kcbbxsv             0         24
         channel operations
            parent latch                ksrwait()           0         96
         library cache                  kglhdgn: c          0         48
                                        hild:
         library cache                  kglic               0        384
         row cache objects              kqrpre: fi          0         24
                                        nd obj
```

The stats$sgastat_summary Table

The stats$sgastat_summary table sums up some of the important system-wide values for the Oracle database:

```
SQL> desc stats$sgastat_summary;
 Name                                      Null?    Type
 ----------------------------------------- -------- -------------------
 SNAP_ID                                   NOT NULL NUMBER
 DBID                                      NOT NULL NUMBER
 INSTANCE NUMBER                           NOT NULL NUMBER
 NAME                                      NOT NULL VARCHAR2(64)
 BYTES                                              NUMBER
```

In the *name* column for this table we see that 22 rows are added for each STATSPACK snapshot:

```
SQL> select distinct name from stats$sgastat_summary;
NAME
-------------------------------------------------------------------
DML locks
KGFF heap
KGK heap
KQLS heap
```

```
PL/SQL DIANA
PL/SQL MPCODE
PL/SQL SOURCE
PLS non-lib hp
SEQ S.O.
SYSTEM PARAMETERS
State objects
branches
character set object
db_block_buffers
db_block_hash_buckets
dictionary cache
distributed_transactions-
enqueue_resources
event statistics per sess
fixed allocation callback
fixed_sga
free memory
ktlbk state objects
library cache
log_buffer
long op statistics array
message pool freequeue
miscellaneous
sessions
sql area
state objects
table columns
table definiti
temporary tabl
transaction_branches
transactions
trigger defini
trigger inform
trigger source
type object de
view columns d
```

The stats$sgastat_summary table is most beneficial for long-term trending reports in STATSPACK. Here is a sample from the data in this table showing the change in size of SGA areas.

rpt_sga_summary.sql

NAME	MIN_BYTES	MAX_BYTES	CHG_BYTES
KQLS heap	1,827,000	8,520,208	6,693,208
PL/SQL DIANA	6,601,096	13,886,264	7,285,168
PL/SQL MPCODE	1,430,384	3,216,128	1,785,744

PL/SQL SOURCE	1,008	8,672	7,664
dictionary cache	1,910,280	5,253,304	3,343,024
free memory	139,558,232	194,640,008	55,001,776
library cache	7,395,640	24,541,760	17,146,120
miscellaneous	665,112	916,864	251,752
sql area	3,368,200	23,797,248	20,429,040
state objects	126,600	270,448	151,848
table columns	35,064	387,104	352,040
table definition	5,496	29,416	23,920
temporary table	608	8,576	7,968
trigger definition	7,016	97,072	90,056
trigger source	7,000	49,760	42,760
view columns	1,112	92,032	90,920

The stats$sql_summary Table

The SQL statistics summary is one of the most important tables within the STATSPACK facility. As we discussed in Chapter 1, tuning of SQL can often have a profound impact on the performance of your Oracle system, and the stats$sql_summary table provides the text of each SQL statement and a detailed description of the resources used by each and every SQL statement that met the necessary thresholds conditions to be captured in a snapshot.

We will be returning to this table many times in this text, and especially in Chapter 11. For now, all we need to know is that this table tracks the number of executions, the number of parse calls, and the number of data blocks read and written for each SQL statement. This information can be an invaluable tool when it comes time to tune the SQL within your Oracle database.

It also bears mentioning that the stats$sql_summary table is the most highly populated of all of the STATSPACK tables. If your threshold values are set very low and you have a busy database, it's not uncommon to get 300 to 500 rows added to the stats$sql_summary table each and every time STATSPACK requests a snapshot. Hence, it is very important that the DBA remove unwanted rows from the stats$sql_summary table once they are no longer used for SQL tuning.

```
SQL> desc STATS$SQL_SUMMARY;
 Name                                      Null?    Type
 ----------------------------------------- -------- -------------------
 SNAP_ID                                   NOT NULL NUMBER(6)
 DBID                                      NOT NULL NUMBER
 INSTANCE_NUMBER                           NOT NULL NUMBER
 SQL_TEXT                                           VARCHAR2(1000)
 SHARABLE_MEM                                       NUMBER
 SORTS                                              NUMBER
 MODULE                                             VARCHAR2(64)
 LOADED_VERSIONS                                    NUMBER
```

```
EXECUTIONS                                          NUMBER
LOADS                                               NUMBER
INVALIDATIONS                                       NUMBER
PARSE_CALLS                                         NUMBER
DISK_READS                                          NUMBER
BUFFER_GETS                                         NUMBER
ROWS_PROCESSED                                      NUMBER
ADDRESS                                  NOT NULL RAW(8)
HASH_VALUE                               NOT NULL NUMBER
VERSION_COUNT                                       NUMBER
```

For details on the use of the stats$sql_summary table for Oracle tuning, please refer to Chapter 11.

The stats$parameter Table

The stats$parameter table contains the initialization parameters that were in effect when the snapshot was taken. This is taken directly from the v$parameter view, and the values correspond directly to the initialization parameters when the instance started. This table is sometimes useful when you want to compare the before and after performance after changing an initialization parameter. For example, after changing optimizer_mode, we might want to see changes in the physical I/O for the database.

Uses for stats$parameter

The stats$parameter table is most commonly used when performing comparisons of the database performance with different *init.ora* parameter settings. The most common uses include:

- Comparing the buffer hit ratio after increasing db_block_buffers

- Comparing I/O after changing optimizer_mode

- Comparing shared pool misses after increasing shared_pool_size

- Comparing disk sorts after increasing sort_area_size

```
SQL> desc STATS$PARAMETER;
 Name                                     Null?    Type
 ---------------------------------------- -------- -------------------
 SNAP_ID                                  NOT NULL NUMBER(6)
 DBID                                     NOT NULL NUMBER
 INSTANCE_NUMBER                          NOT NULL NUMBER
 NAME                                     NOT NULL VARCHAR2(64)
 VALUE                                             VARCHAR2(512)
 ISDEFAULT                                         VARCHAR2(9)
 ISMODIFIED                                        VARCHAR2(10)
```

In addition to the values from v$parameter, the stats$parameter table also contains 285 hidden initialization parameters. A *hidden* parameter is an internal initialization parameter that is seldom modified by the DBA, and they always begin with an underscore character. For example, to see the hidden parallel parameters for parallel processing, you can enter the query here:

```
  1  select name, value from stats$parameter
  2* where snap_id = 2000 and name like '_parallel%'
SQL> /


NAME                                   VALUE
------------------------------ --------- ----------------------------
_parallel_adaptive_max_users           1
_parallel_default_max_instances        1
_parallel_execution_message_align      FALSE
_parallel_fake_class_pct               0
_parallel_load_bal_unit                0
_parallel_load_balancing               TRUE
_parallel_min_message_pool             64560
_parallel_recovery_stopat              32767
_parallel_server_idle_time             5
_parallel_server_sleep_time            10
_parallel_txn_global                   FALSE
_parallelism_cost_fudge_factor         350
```

It is sometimes useful to compare the performance of the database after a change to an initialization parameter, and you can use the stats$parameter table for this purpose. For example, we might want to compare the average data buffer hit ratio before and after a change to the db_block_buffers parameter. In this case we would create a SQL query on stats$buffer_pool_statistics with a JOIN into the stats$parameter table both before and after our change to db_block_buffers. We will show this type of script in Chapter 9.

STATSPACK System Tables

The STATSPACK system tables keep track of system-wide statistics, the library cache, data on rollback segments, latches, sessions and a wealth of other data, as shown in Figure 4-2.

Let's take a close look at each of these tables and examine the type of data contained in each.

The stats$rollstat Table

The stats$rollstat table keeps information on the activity of the Oracle rollback segments. The data from this table is useful for the initial tuning of the rollback

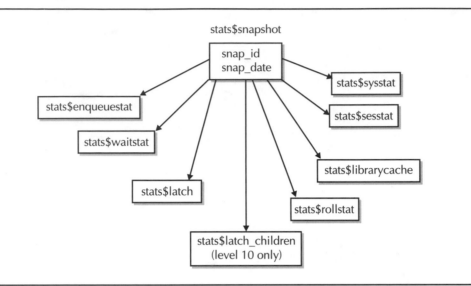

FIGURE 4-2. *The STATSPACK system tables*

segment sizes and initialization parameters, but once tuned, the data in this table is seldom required:

```
SQL> desc STATS$ROLLSTAT;
 Name                                      Null?    Type
 ----------------------------------------- -------- --------------------
 SNAP_ID                                   NOT NULL NUMBER(6)
 DBID                                      NOT NULL NUMBER
 INSTANCE_NUMBER                           NOT NULL NUMBER
 USN                                       NOT NULL NUMBER
 EXTENTS                                            NUMBER
 RSSIZE                                             NUMBER
 WRITES                                             NUMBER
 XACTS                                              NUMBER
 GETS                                               NUMBER
 WAITS                                              NUMBER
 OPTSIZE                                            NUMBER
 HWMSIZE                                            NUMBER
 SHRINKS                                            NUMBER
 WRAPS                                              NUMBER
 EXTENDS                                            NUMBER
 AVESHRINK                                          NUMBER
 AVEACTIVE                                          NUMBER
```

The stats$latch Table

Internal to Oracle, latches are used to serialize transactions and are closely tied to the OS semaphores. If the user is planning to perform operations such as accessing data, this user must first obtain all latch data from the table and then become the owner of the latch. If the user's process is forced to wait for a latch because there isn't enough space available, a slowdown will occur and we would experience internal contention for latches.

As we can see from the listing of the v$latch view next, there are many different kinds of latches that are used internally within Oracle. Regardless of the types of latches the important thing is the hit ratio.

The key latches are:

- Cache buffers lru chain latch
- Enqueues latch
- Redo allocation latch
- Redo copy latch
- Library cache latch

If the hit ratio for any of these key latches is lower than 99 percent, there is substantial latch contention within the database. The contention for these key latches can be reduced in a variety of ways, including tuning the database writer, tuning the redo log files, and reducing buffer cache latch contention. We will be going into detail on these techniques in Chapter 9.

The latch hit ratio is the ratio of the total number of latch misses to the number of latch gets for all latches. A low value for this ratio indicates a latching problem, whereas a high value is generally good. However, as the data is rolled up over all latches, a high latch hit ratio can artificially mask a low get rate on a specific latch. Oracle tuning professionals will cross-check this value with the top 5 wait events to see if latch free is in the list, and refer to the Latch sections of the report.

```
SQL> desc STATS$LATCH;
 Name                                      Null?    Type
 ----------------------------------------- -------- --------------------
 SNAP_ID                                   NOT NULL NUMBER(6)
 DBID                                      NOT NULL NUMBER
 INSTANCE_NUMBER                           NOT NULL NUMBER
 NAME                                      NOT NULL VARCHAR2(64)
 LATCH#                                    NOT NULL NUMBER
 LEVEL#                                             NUMBER
 GETS                                               NUMBER
```

```
MISSES                                          NUMBER
SLEEPS                                          NUMBER
IMMEDIATE_GETS                                  NUMBER
IMMEDIATE_MISSES                                NUMBER
SPIN_GETS                                       NUMBER
SLEEP1                                          NUMBER
SLEEP2                                          NUMBER
SLEEP3                                          NUMBER
SLEEP4                                          NUMBER
```

The stats$latch_children Table

The stats$latch_children table is only populated when a level 10 collection is requested. The STATSPACK documentation suggests that a level 10 only be collected at the request of Oracle technical support.

```
SQL> desc STATS$LATCH_CHILDREN;
 Name                                    Null?    Type
 --------------------------------------- -------- -------------------
 SNAP_ID                                 NOT NULL NUMBER(6)
 DBID                                    NOT NULL NUMBER
 INSTANCE_NUMBER                         NOT NULL NUMBER
 LATCH#                                  NOT NULL NUMBER
 CHILD#                                  NOT NULL NUMBER
 GETS                                             NUMBER
 MISSES                                           NUMBER
 SLEEPS                                           NUMBER
 IMMEDIATE_GETS                                   NUMBER
 IMMEDIATE_MISSES                                 NUMBER
 SPIN_GETS                                        NUMBER
 SLEEP1                                           NUMBER
 SLEEP2                                           NUMBER
 SLEEP3                                           NUMBER
 SLEEP4                                           NUMBER
```

The stats$librarycache Table

As you may know from our introduction to Oracle, the library cache is the memory space where SQL statements are parsed and executed. Each one of the values in the stats$librarycache table is for a specific event.

Following is a list of all of the possible values for the library cache. As we will discuss in detail in Chapter 9, the important thing is that the hit ratio for each one of these library cache entries remains above 90 percent for online transaction databases. If not, some tuning of the Oracle shared pool within the SGA will be necessary. Data warehouses and decision support systems may have much lower data buffer hit ratios because of the high amount of full-table scans.

Also note that the DLM parameters in the stats$librarycache table only apply to systems running Oracle Parallel Server. If you're not running OPS, you don't need to be concerned with any of the DLM values in this table.

```
SQL> desc STATS$LIBRARYCACHE;
 Name                                      Null?    Type
 ----------------------------------------- -------- --------------------
 SNAP_ID                                   NOT NULL NUMBER(6)
 DBID                                      NOT NULL NUMBER
 INSTANCE_NUMBER                           NOT NULL NUMBER
 NAMESPACE                                 NOT NULL VARCHAR2(15)
 GETS                                               NUMBER
 GETHITS                                            NUMBER
 PINS                                               NUMBER
 PINHITS                                            NUMBER
 RELOADS                                            NUMBER
 INVALIDATIONS                                      NUMBER
 DLM_LOCK_REQUESTS                                  NUMBER
 DLM_PIN_REQUESTS                                   NUMBER
 DLM_PIN_RELEASES                                   NUMBER
 DLM_INVALIDATION_REQUESTS                          NUMBER
 DLM_INVALIDATIONS                                  NUMBER
```

The stats$waitstat Table

The system wait statistics described in the stats$waitstat table can be useful if you suspect that your database is undergoing resource bottlenecks.

By looking at the total time, you can often determine which one of the wait statistics is causing a bottleneck within your Oracle database. We will return to the use of the wait statistics table later on in the chapter where we investigate SGA tuning.

The most common wait event we will be taking a look at in our chapter on object tuning is waits on the *freelists*. One of the best ways to find out if you've got an object that has improper storage parameter settings is to take a look at *freelist* waits. If your *freelist* waits are very high, there is a good chance you have tables that have competing INSERT or UPDATE tasks and these tables do not have enough *freelists* defined. This is arguably the most important section in the report because it shows how long Oracle is waiting for resources. This will be the starting point for looking at tuning Oracle. Again, we will go into detail on tuning waits in Chapter 9.

```
SQL> desc STATS$WAITSTAT;
 Name                                      Null?    Type
 ----------------------------------------- -------- --------------------
 SNAP_ID                                   NOT NULL NUMBER(6)
 DBID                                      NOT NULL NUMBER
 INSTANCE_NUMBER                           NOT NULL NUMBER
```

```
CLASS                                    NOT NULL VARCHAR2(18)
WAIT_COUNT                                        NUMBER
TIME                                              NUMBER
```

Here is a sample report on the data from stats$waitstat, showing various classes and the wait counts and times for each class.

rpt_waitstat.sql

```
Yr.  Mo Dy Hr CLASS                    WAIT_COUNT        TIME
------------ --------------------     ----------  ------------
2001-09-21 15 data block                       3           0
2001-10-02 15 data block                       3           0
2001-10-02 15 undo block                       8           0
2001-12-11 18 undo header                     19           4
```

The stats$enqueuestat Table

It's important when you take a look at the stats$enqueuestat table to remember that enqueue waits are a normal part of Oracle processing. It is only when you see an excessive amount of enqueue waits for specific processes that you need to be concerned in the tuning process.

Oracle locks protect shared resources and allow access to those resources via a queuing mechanism. A large amount of time spent waiting for enqueue events can be caused by various problems, such as waiting for individual row locks or waiting for exclusive locks on a table. Look at the highly contended enqueues in the enqueue activity section of the STATSPACK report to determine which enqueues are waited for. At snapshot time, this table is populated by querying the x$ksqst view:

```
SELECT  ksqsttyp "Lock",
        ksqstget "Gets",
        ksqstwat "Waits"
   FROM X$KSQST where KSQSTWAT>0;
```

Here is a description for this table:

```
SQL> desc STATS$ENQUEUESTAT;
 Name                                      Null?    Type
 ---------------------------------------- -------- -------------------
 SNAP_ID                                   NOT NULL NUMBER(6)
 DBID                                      NOT NULL NUMBER
 INSTANCE_NUMBER                           NOT NULL NUMBER
 NAME                                      NOT NULL VARCHAR2(2)
 GETS                                               NUMBER
 WAITS                                              NUMBER
```

There are 26 lock types that could be captured in the stats$enqueuestat table, but only a handful of these are meaningful for Oracle tuning:

- **CI (Cross-instance lock)**   The CI lock is called the cross-instance lock, but it is not an Oracle Parallel Server lock. The name of this lock is misleading because it doesn't have to do with distributed transactions. Rather, the CI lock is used to invoke specific actions in background processes on a specific instance or all instances. Examples would include checkpoints, log switches, or when the instance is shut down.

- **CU (Cursor bind lock)**   This is a cursor bind lock that is set whenever a cursor is used in a SQL statement.

- **JQ (Job queue lock)**   When a job is submitted using dbms_job.submit, the running job is protected by a JQ enqueue lock.

- **ST (Space management enqueue lock)**   This lock is usually associated with too much space management activity due to too-small extent sizes. The ST enqueue needs to be held every time the session is allocating or deallocating extents.

- **TM (DML enqueue lock)**   This is a general table lock. Every time a session wants to lock a table (for an UPDATE, INSERT, or DELETE), a TM enqueue is requested. These locks are normally of very short duration, but they can be held for long periods when updating a table when foreign-key constraint have not been properly indexed.

- **TX (Transaction lock)**   A transaction is set when a change begins and is held until the transaction issues a COMMIT or ROLLBACK. When simultaneous tasks want to update the same rows, the TX locks allow the tasks to enqueue, waiting until the row is freed.

- **US (User lock)**   This lock is set when a session has taken a lock with the dbms_lock.request function. Application developers sometimes use this function to set serialization locks on parallelized tasks.

You can use the standard statsrep.sql script, or the custom rpt_enqueue.sql script to identify possible lock contention issues over time. Here is a sample report against the stats$enqueuestat table:

rpt_enqueue.sql

```
Yr.  Mo Dy Hr NAME                    GETS        WAITS
------------- -------------------- -------- ------------
2000-12-11 16 TX                      1,784            2
2000-12-11 18 TM                      1,789           20
```

The stats$sysstat Table

You should note that the structure of this STATSPACK table is identical to the v$sysstat structure, with 226 distinct statistic names in Oracle8i. Every snapshot that you take with STATSPACK will add these 226 rows to the stats$sysstat table:

```
SQL> desc STATS$SYSSTAT;
 Name                                      Null?    Type
 ----------------------------------------- -------- -------------------
 SNAP_ID                                   NOT NULL NUMBER(6)
 DBID                                      NOT NULL NUMBER
 INSTANCE_NUMBER                           NOT NULL NUMBER
 STATISTIC#                                NOT NULL NUMBER
 NAME                                      NOT NULL VARCHAR2(64)
 VALUE                                              NUMBER
```

While many of these statistics are seldom used in tuning Oracle, there are some statistics that you will find quite useful. In Chapter 14 you will see STATSPACK scripts that will report on specific statistic names within stats$sysstat. Here are the most important system statistics for Oracle tuning. Again, we will return to this table in detail in Chapter 9 on instance tuning.

```
STATISTIC# NAME
---------- ------------------------------------------------------------
         3 opened cursors current
         9 session logical reads
        12 CPU used by this session
        13 session connect time
        15 session uga memory
        20 session pga memory
        23 enqueue waits
        24 enqueue deadlocks
        39 consistent gets
        40 physical reads
        41 db block changes
        44 physical writes
        46 summed dirty queue length
        67 hot buffers moved to head of LRU
        84 prefetched blocks
        85 prefetched blocks aged out before use
        86 physical reads direct
        87 physical writes direct
       106 redo log space requests
       107 redo log space wait time
       151 table scans (long tables)
       158 table fetch continued row
```

```
169 parse time cpu
174 bytes sent via SQL*Net to client
175 bytes received via SQL*Net from client
176 SQL*Net roundtrips to/from client
177 bytes sent via SQL*Net to dblink
178 bytes received via SQL*Net from dblink
179 SQL*Net roundtrips to/from dblink
181 sorts (disk)
203 OS User level CPU time
204 OS System call CPU time
211 OS Wait-cpu (latency) time
213 OS Major page faults
214 OS Swaps
222 OS System calls
223 OS Chars read and written
```

Uses for the stats$sysstat Table

This table is most commonly used when analyzing overall database load under certain conditions. The common uses of this table include:

- Comparing *OS major page faults* to vmstat page-in values

- Comparing *OS swaps* to vmstat page-in values

- Using *OS chars read and written* to measure overall I/O load on the database

- Reviewing redo log space behavior to measure configuration of the online redo logs

- Determining the overall data buffer hit ratio using *consistent gets*

- Monitoring *enqueue deadlocks* to locate sources of contention

- Monitoring *sorts (disk)* to identify contention in the TEMP tablespace

- Monitoring *table fetch continued row* to seek chained rows

- Monitoring SQL*Net metrics to identify times of peak network usage

The stats$sesstat Table

Session statistics are captured from the v$sesstat view. As you may remember from basic DBA class, this table only contains the statistic number and the value. To see the corresponding name for the value, you need to JOIN into the v$statname view. The statistics numbers for stats$sesstat are the same as the stats$sysstat table.

CAUTION
The stats$sesstat table only takes a snapshot of the sessions that were active at the exact moment that the snapshot was executed. If your database has hundreds of small transactions each minute, you will only see a small number of the total transactions in this table. Also, elapsed-time comparisons are meaningless with this table because of the transient nature of Oracle sessions.

```
SQL> desc STATS$SESSTAT;
 Name                                      Null?    Type
 ----------------------------------------- -------- -------------------
 SNAP_ID                                   NOT NULL NUMBER(6)
 DBID                                      NOT NULL NUMBER
 INSTANCE_NUMBER                           NOT NULL NUMBER
 STATISTIC#                                NOT NULL NUMBER
 VALUE                                              NUMBER
```

If you want to see the actual values for all 226 session statistics, you must join from the stats$sesstat into the v$statname view. The statistic names are the same as for the v$sysstat view.

Uses for stats$sesstat

Because of the incomplete information in this table (it only snaps sessions that are active at the time of the snapshot), this table has limited use for Oracle tuning. However, the information can be used in long-term trend reports to display common session information.

The stats$sgastat Table

This is a simple table that provides the total size of the SGA in bytes at the time that the snapshot was taken. This table has limited use within Oracle tuning, and the same values can be computed from summing the memory structures within the stats$parameter table.

```
SQL> desc STATS$SGASTAT_SUMMARY;
 Name                                      Null?    Type
 ----------------------------------------- -------- -------------------
 SNAP_ID                                   NOT NULL NUMBER
 DBID                                      NOT NULL NUMBER
 INSTANCE_NUMBER                           NOT NULL NUMBER
 NAME                                      NOT NULL VARCHAR2(64)
 BYTES                                              NUMBER
```

STATSPACK Transaction Tables

The STATSPACK transaction tables capture information related to the processing of transactions within Oracle. This data includes data buffer pool usage and Oracle file I/O (see Figure 4-3).

Let's take a close look at these tables and see how they can be used to assist with Oracle tuning.

The stats$buffer_pool Table

The stats$buffer_pool table is used to hold basic information about the number of buffers in each data buffer pool. The three pools are the DEFAULT pool (db_block_buffers), the KEEP pool (buffer_pool_keep) and the RECYCLE pool (buffer_pool_recycle).

There are normally only four rows in this table for each snap_id. The following query shows the data for a specific snapshot:

```
SQL> select snap_id, instance_number, name, buffers
  2  from stats$buffer_pool where snap_id = 1;
   SNAP_ID INSTANCE_NUMBER NAME                              BUFFERS
---------- --------------- ----------------------------- ----------
         1               1 -                                       0
         1               1 KEEP                                    0
         1               1 RECYCLE                                 0
         1               1 DEFAULT                             20000
```

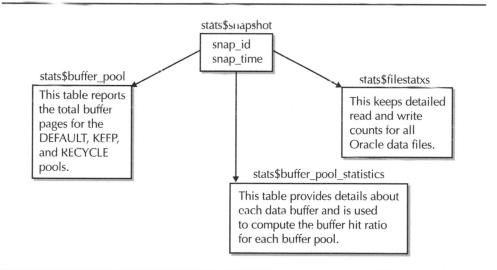

FIGURE 4-3.   *The STATSPACK transaction tables*

The stats$buffer_pool_statistics Table

There are two tables that report on the activity within the Oracle data buffer pools. The stats$buffer_pool table gives the summary information for the data buffer pools, and will generally have three rows per snapshot—one showing the data buffer activity in each pool. The three rows per snapshot are for the DEFAULT pool, the RECYCLE pool, and the KEEP pool.

NOTE
The stats$buffer_pool table is only supported in Oracle 8.1.6 and above. If you are back-porting STATSPACK to Oracle 8.0–Oracle 8.1.5, you must run the statscbps.sql script to create the v$buffer_pool_statistics view:

```
SQL> desc STATS$BUFFER_POOL_STATISTICS;
 Name                                      Null?    Type
 ----------------------------------------- -------- -------------------
 SNAP_ID                                   NOT NULL NUMBER(6)
 DBID                                      NOT NULL NUMBER
 INSTANCE_NUMBER                           NOT NULL NUMBER
 ID                                        NOT NULL NUMBER
 NAME                                               VARCHAR2(20)
 SET_MSIZE                                          NUMBER
 CNUM_REPL                                          NUMBER
 CNUM_WRITE                                         NUMBER
 CNUM_SET                                           NUMBER
 BUF_GOT                                            NUMBER
 SUM_WRITE                                          NUMBER
 SUM_SCAN                                           NUMBER
 FREE_BUFFER_WAIT                                   NUMBER
 WRITE_COMPLETE_WAIT                                NUMBER
 BUFFER_BUSY_WAIT                                   NUMBER
 FREE_BUFFER_INSPECTED                              NUMBER
 DIRTY_BUFFERS_INSPECTED                            NUMBER
 DB_BLOCK_CHANGE                                    NUMBER
 DB_BLOCK_GETS                                      NUMBER
 CONSISTENT_GETS                                    NUMBER
 PHYSICAL_READS                                     NUMBER
 PHYSICAL_WRITES                                    NUMBER
```

As you can see from the columns in the stats$buffer_pool_statistics table, we get a wealth of information about the behavior of each data buffer pool. This information can be used to calculate the data buffer hit ratio, a generalized measure of the efficiency of the buffer pool.

Some Oracle tuning professionals have conducted studies into the relative efficiency of the buffer pools using the details from this table, but we are only concerned with the standard measures of the data buffer hit ratio.

Note that there are two ways to compute the data buffer hit ratio. For a system-wide metric, you can query the stats$sysstat table. If you want detail on each data buffer, you use the stats$buffer_pool_statistics table. Here is a sample from statspack_alert.sql that identifies periods when the data buffer hit ratio is too low:

```
SNAP-TIME            BUFFER HIT RATIO
-- ----------        ----------------
2001-12-21 19        84
2001-12-21 20        83
2001-12-21 21        85
2001 12-21 22        82
2001-12-21 23        83
2001-12-22 00        86
2001-12-22 02        85
2001-12-22 03        82
2001-12-22 04        86
```

The stats$filestatxs Table

The stats$filestatxs table is one of the most important tables with respect to Oracle tuning. As we discussed in Chapter 1, I/O is the single most expensive operation in any Oracle database. The stats$filestatxs table will give us detailed information on each data file within Oracle database, including the amount of read I/O, the amount of write I/O, and any wait contention that may have been experienced during the processing.

We will return in detail to this table in Chapter 8 at which time we'll discuss tuning disk I/O within an Oracle. The most important column in this table is the *wait_count* and *time* columns. The *time* column is a very easy way to indicate if there were key resources waiting on disk I/O.

However, it is critical to note that an Oracle I/O does not always equal a disk I/O. If you are using a storage management system such as EMC, Oracle reads and writes may be cached for asynchronous I/O at a later time. Hence, the READTIM and WRITETIM may not be accurate because the physical I/O subsystem will acknowledge (ACK) a successful I/O, even though the I/O is not actually written to disk.

Uses for stats$filestatxs

This table gives a great picture of the distribution of I/O for your Oracle database. This table is most commonly referenced for:

- Load balancing of the I/O subsystem
- Finding "hot" files and "hot" tables
- Finding times of peak read and write activity for the database

```
SQL> desc STATS$FILESTATXS;
 Name                                       Null?    Type
 ------------------------------------------ -------- --------------------
 SNAP_ID                                    NOT NULL NUMBER(6)
 DBID                                       NOT NULL NUMBER
 INSTANCE_NUMBER                            NOT NULL NUMBER
 TSNAME                                     NOT NULL VARCHAR2(30)
 FILENAME                                   NOT NULL VARCHAR2(257)
 PHYRDS                                              NUMBER
 PHYWRTS                                             NUMBER
 READTIM                                             NUMBER
 WRITETIM                                            NUMBER
 PHYBLKRD                                            NUMBER
 PHYBLKWRT                                           NUMBER
 WAIT_COUNT                                          NUMBER
 TIME                                                NUMBER
```

STATSPACK Event Tables

The STATSPACK event tables record all system events, as shown in Figure 4-4.
These events include standard system events, background events, session events,
and idle events.

Let's take a look at each of the event tables and see how they can help with
Oracle tuning.

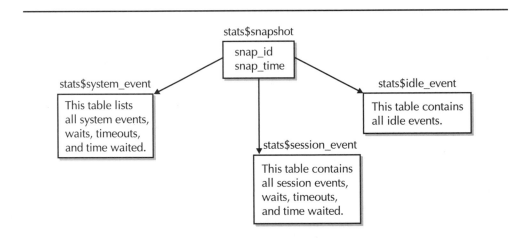

FIGURE 4-4. *The STATSPACK event tables*

The stats$system_event Table

The stats$system_event table is one of the tables that will be populated with many rows for each snapshot. The Oracle database captures information on many system events, and most of these events are of little interest when tuning the database.

```
SQL> desc STATS$SYSTEM_EVENT;
 Name                                     Null?    Type
 ---------------------------------------- -------- -------------------
 SNAP_ID                                  NOT NULL NUMBER(6)
 DBID                                     NOT NULL NUMBER
 INSTANCE_NUMBER                          NOT NULL NUMBER
 EVENT                                    NOT NULL VARCHAR2(64)
 TOTAL_WAITS                                       NUMBER
 TOTAL_TIMEOUTS                                    NUMBER
 TIME_WAITED                                       NUMBER
```

The important metric here is the event column. In Oracle8i, there are 55 events that are captured in this table. Let's look at a list of these events:

```
SQL> select distinct event from stats$system_event;

EVENT
-----------------------------------------------------------------
BFILE closure
BFILE get length
BFILE internal seek
BFILE open
BFILE read
LGWR wait for redo copy
Null event
PX Deq: Join ACK
PX Deq: Signal ACK
PX Deq: Txn Recovery Start
PX Idle Wait
SQL*Net break/reset to client
SQL*Net message from client
SQL*Net message from dblink
SQL*Net message to client
SQL*Net message to dblink
SQL*Net more data from client
```

```
SQL*Net more data to client
Wait for stopper event to be increased
buffer busy waits
checkpoint completed
control file parallel write
control file sequential read
db file parallel read
db file parallel write
db file scattered read
db file sequential read
db file single write
direct path read
direct path write
dispatcher timer
enqueue
file identify
file open
instance state change
latch free
library cache load lock
library cache pin
local write wait
log file parallel write
log file sequential read
log file single write
log file switch (checkpoint incomplete)
log file switch completion
log file sync
pmon timer
process startup
rdbms ipc message
rdbms ipc reply
refresh controlfile command
reliable message
single-task message
smon timer
undo segment extension
virtual circuit status
```

Uses for stats$system_event

Many of these events are of little interest when tuning Oracle. The most commonly used events for tuning Oracle include:

- **buffer busy waits**   This can indicate object contention in a segment header block.

- **db file scattered read**   This is for a multiblock read that is most often associated with a full table scan or index fast full scans. Oracle reads up to *db_file_multiblock_read_count* consecutive blocks at a time and scatters them into buffers in the buffer cache.

■ **db file sequential read**   This is a table access using an index or a rowid probe.

■ **enqueue**   An enqueue is sometimes associated with a held lock.

■ **latch free**   A latch free event is sometimes associated with waiting for a lock to be released.

■ **LGWR wait for redo copy**   This can indicate problems with the size and configuration of the online redo log files.

■ **SQL*Net message to/from client**   This gives information regarding the amount of network traffic between the database and Net8 clients.

■ **SQL*Net message to/from dblink**   This gives information on the amount of network traffic between distributed Oracle servers.

The stats$session_event Table

The session event table is unpredictable because it will only capture information from those sessions that are active at the time that the snapshot was taken. Hence, just like the stats$sesstat table, you will only get a sample of what was happening at the time of the snapshot.

```
SQL> desc STATS$SESSION_EVENT;
 Name                                      Null?    Type
 ----------------------------------------- -------- ------------------
 SNAP_ID                                   NOT NULL NUMBER(6)
 DBID                                      NOT NULL NUMBER
 INSTANCE_NUMBER                           NOT NULL NUMBER
 EVENT                                     NOT NULL VARCHAR2(64)
 TOTAL_WAITS                                        NUMBER
 TOTAL_TIMEOUTS                                     NUMBER
 TIME_WAITED                                        NUMBER
```

Note that this table will have very few rows because it will only capture statistics when a session_wait is active.

The stats$bg_event_summary Table

This table summarizes the background events for the overall database instance. This table is very similar to the stats$system_event table in content and uses the same events. This table is used to display background process wait events.

```
SQL> desc STATS$BG_EVENT_SUMMARY;
 Name                                    Null?    Type
 --------------------------------------- -------- -------------------
 SNAP_ID                                 NOT NULL NUMBER(6)
 DBID                                    NOT NULL NUMBER
 INSTANCE_NUMBER                         NOT NULL NUMBER
 EVENT                                   NOT NULL VARCHAR2(64)
 TOTAL_WAITS                                      NUMBER
 TOTAL_TIMEOUTS                                   NUMBER
 TIME_WAITED                                      NUMBER
```

This table is used to display general information on background wait events. Here is a sample of the data from this table in the statsrep.sql STATSPACK script. Our custom script rpt_bg_event_waits.sql will report on exceptional conditions within this table.

rpt_bg_event_waits.sql

```
Yr.  Mo Dy Hr EVENT                      tot waits time wait timeouts
------------ ---------------------------- --------- --------- --------
2001-12-11 18 LGWR wait for redo copy        2,387       515       50
2001-12-11 18 enqueue                          422    52,785       20
2001-12-12 10 enqueue                           33     1,035        0
```

As we can see, our primary concern for sampling this table is to find circumstances where the time waits (expressed in microseconds) are out of the ordinary.

The stats$idle_event Table

This table is not particularly interesting for Oracle tuning purposes.

```
SQL> desc STATS$IDLE_EVENT;
 Name                                    Null?    Type
 --------------------------------------- -------- -------------------
 EVENT                                   NOT NULL VARCHAR2(64)
```

Oracle Parallel Server Tables (Real Application Clusters)

This section covers the tables that relate to the use of Oracle Parallel Server (OPS), which has been renamed to Real Application Clusters (RAC) in Oracle9i. The first table, stats$rowcache_summary, contains information relating to each of the many instances in the OPS environment. For the benefit of those who have never used

Oracle Parallel Server, an OPS environment allows you to define multiple instances that share the same database. Because there are multiple instances for each database, the Oracle Integrated Distributed Lock Manager (IDLM), is used to manage the transportation of data blocks between the buffers in many instances. This process of transferring data blocks between instances is called *pinging*.

The stats$rowcache_summary Table

The activity within the IDLM is the purpose of the stats$rowcache_summary table. The stats$rowcache_summary table tracks block usage within each one of the instances in the OPS environment.

When using STATSPACK with OPS, you must connect to the instance you wish to collect data for and for running the report. If you are using statsauto.sql in an OPS environment, the statsauto.sql script must be run once on each instance in the cluster. Similarly, the job_queue_processes parameter must also be set for each OPS instance.

```
SQL> desc STATS$ROWCACHE_SUMMARY;
 Name                                      Null?    Type
 ----------------------------------------- -------- ------------------
 SNAP_ID                                   NOT NULL NUMBER(6)
 DBID                                      NOT NULL NUMBER
 INSTANCE_NUMBER                           NOT NULL NUMBER
 PARAMETER                                 NOT NULL VARCHAR2(32)
 TOTAL_USAGE                                        NUMBER
 USAGE                                              NUMBER
 GETS                                               NUMBER
 GETMISSES                                          NUMBER
 SCANS                                              NUMBER
 SCANMISSES                                         NUMBER
 SCANCOMPLETES                                      NUMBER
 MODIFICATIONS                                      NUMBER
 FLUSHES                                            NUMBER
 DLM_REQUESTS                                       NUMBER
 DLM_CONFLICTS                                      NUMBER
 DLM_RELEASES                                       NUMBER
```

The stats$sgaxs Table

The stats$sgaxs table is used to cross-reference the multiple SGAs that are used in a single OPS environment. In many OPS environments, the database administrator can dynamically change the number of instances that are referencing an individual database, such that the number of databases in an OPS set of instances at any given time may be different.

```
SQL> desc STATS$SGAXS;
 Name                                      Null?    Type
 ----------------------------------------- -------- --------------------
 SNAP_ID                                   NOT NULL NUMBER(6)
 DBID                                      NOT NULL NUMBER
 INSTANCE_NUMBER                           NOT NULL NUMBER
 STARTUP_TIME                              NOT NULL DATE
 PARALLEL                                  NOT NULL VARCHAR2(3)
 NAME                                      NOT NULL VARCHAR2(64)
 VERSION                                            VARCHAR2(17)
 VALUE                                              NUMBER
```

Conclusion

Now that we understand the location of the statistics, we are ready to begin tuning the Oracle database with this valuable tool. We will begin by looking at external environments and see how STATSPACK can be extended to capture server and disk statistics. We will then delve into the details of tuning Oracle.

PART
II

Tuning
the Oracle Database
with STATSPACK

CHAPTER
5

Extending STATSPACK
to Collect
Server Statistics

s we discussed in our overview of Oracle tuning, the database server is the first place we look when tuning an Oracle database. Oracle runs within the domain of the server, and no amount of Oracle tuning will help if the server is experiencing CPU or memory shortages. The Oracle database does not run in a vacuum. Rather, the Oracle database is very dependent upon the server, and no amount of Oracle tuning can remedy a server resource problem.

With the rapid acceptance of STATSPACK for monitoring databases, it is important for you to extend STATSPACK to capture server statistics. This chapter will describe a technique to show how to extend the STATSPACK tables to capture everything that may cause a slowdown, including RAM memory, CPU, and server waits.

One of the challenges in tuning a Web-based Oracle system is to identify and correct bottlenecks in CPU, I/O, and memory on the servers. If a UNIX server is experiencing a bottleneck, you will commonly see system tasks that are waiting for CPU resources. This chapter will be in three sections:

- **Overview of server tuning**   Because the vast majority of an Oracle database runs under the UNIX operating system, we will show how to use the UNIX vmstat utility to identify CPU and memory problems.

- **Capturing vmstat data inside STATSPACK**   This section will show you how to use my prewritten method to extend STATSPACK to capture database server information.

- **Capturing vmstat data for other Oracle servers**   If your installation uses separate application servers or Web servers, it is important to capture information on their memory and CPU behavior. This section will show you how to capture vmstat information on any remote UNIX server that is running a Net8 client. It will also explain how you can use this data for predictive load balancing between application servers and Web servers.

To be as generic as possible, we have chosen the vmstat utility for capturing server performance information. While each UNIX vendor offers their own proprietary monitor software, almost all dialects of UNIX offer the vmstat utility. Hence, we will show how to collect vmstat information and store the results inside an Oracle table.

Overview of the vmstat Utility

The vmstat utility is the most common UNIX monitoring utility, and it is found in the majority of UNIX dialects (vmstat is called osview on IRIX). The vmstat utility displays various server values over a given time interval. The vmstat utility is invoked from the UNIX prompt, and it has several numeric parameters. The first numeric argument to vmstat represents the time interval (expressed in seconds) between server samples.

The second argument specifies the number of samples to be reported. In the example that follows, vmstat is executed to take 5 samples at 2-second intervals:

```
Root> vmstat 2 5
```

Almost all UNIX servers have some version of vmstat. Before we look at the details for this powerful utility, let's explore the differences that you are likely to see.

Dialect Differences in vmstat

Because each hardware vendor writes their own vmstat utility, there are significant differences in vmstat output. The vmstat output is different depending on the dialect of UNIX, but each dialect contains the important server metrics.

Because vendors have written their own versions of the vmstat utility, it can be useful to consult the online UNIX documentation to see the display differences. In UNIX, you can see your documentation by invoking the man pages. The term *man* is short for manual, and you can see the documentation for your particular implementation of vmstat by entering **man vmstat** from your UNIX prompt.

Following is a sample of vmstat output for the four most popular dialects of UNIX. In each example, the important metrics appear in bold.

vmstat for Solaris

In the Sun Solaris operating environment, the output from vmstat will appear like this:

```
>vmstat 2 5
```

procs			memory				page			disk				faults			cpu		
r	h	w	swap	free	re	mf	**pi**	po	…	s6	--	--	in	sy	cs	**us**	**sy**	id
0	0	0	2949744	988800	0	4	**0**	0	…	0	0	0	148	200	41	**0**	**0**	99
0	0	0	2874808	938960	27	247	**0**	1	…	0	0	0	196	434	64	**1**	**2**	98
0	0	0	2874808	938960	0	0	**0**	0	…	0	0	0	134	55	32	**0**	**0**	100
0	0	0	2874808	938960	0	0	**0**	0	…	0	0	0	143	114	39	**0**	**0**	100
0	0	0	2874808	938960	0	0	**0**	0	…	0	0	0	151	86	38	**0**	**0**	100

vmstat for Linux

In the Linux operating environment, the output from vmstat will appear like this:

```
>vmstat 2 5
```

procs						memory	swap		io		system			cpu		
r	b	w	swpd	free	buff	cache	**si**	…	bi	bo	in	cs	**us**	**sy**	id
1	0	0	140	90372	726988	26228	**0**	…	0	0	14	7	**0**	**0**	4
0	0	0	140	90372	726988	26228	**0**	…	0	2	103	11	**0**	**0**	100
0	0	0	140	90372	726988	26228	**0**	…	0	5	106	10	**0**	**0**	100
0	0	0	140	90372	726988	26228	**0**	…	0	0	101	11	**0**	**0**	100
0	0	0	140	90372	726988	26228	**0**	…	0	0	102	11	**0**	**0**	100

vmstat for AIX

In the IBM AIX operating environment, the output from vmstat will appear like this:

```
>vmstat 2 5

kthr      memory              page                    faults         cpu
-----  -----------  ------------------------  ------------  -----------
 r  b    avm    fre   re  pi  po   fr   sr  cy   in      sy   cs  us  sy id wa
 7  5  220214    141   0   0   0   42   53   0  1724  12381 2206  19  46 28  7
 9  5  220933    195   0   0   1  216  290   0  1952  46118 2712  27  55 13  5
13  5  220646    452   0   0   1   33   54   0  2130  86185 3014  30  59  8  3
 6  5  220228    672   0   0   0    0    0   0  1929  25068 2485  25  49 16 10
```

vmstat for HP/UX

In the Hewlett Packard HP/UX operating environment, the output from vmstat will appear like this:

```
>vmstat 2 5
 r  b  w    avm     free re at  pi  po  ...    in   sy    cs  us sy  id
 1  0  0  70635  472855 10  5   2   0  ...  2024 2859   398   4  1  96
 1  0  0  74985  472819  9  0   1   0  ...  1864 1820   322   0  0 100
 0  0  0  83056  472819  2  0   0   0  ...  1846 1684   302   0  0 100
 0  0  0  81390  472819  0  0   0   0  ...  1847 1571   288   0  0 100
 0  0  0  78788  472819  0  0   0   0  ...  1852 1608   291   0  0 100
```

Now that we have seen the different display options for each dialect of vmstat, let's take a look at the data items in vmstat and understand the common values that we can capture in STATSPACK tables.

What to Look for in vmstat

As you can see, each dialect of vmstat reports different information about the current status of the server. Despite these dialect differences, there are only a small number of metrics that are important for server monitoring. These metrics include:

- **r (runqueue)**   The runqueue value shows the number of tasks executing and waiting for CPU resources. When this number exceeds the number of CPUs on the server, a CPU bottleneck exists, and some tasks are waiting for execution.

- **pi (page in)**   A page-in operation occurs when the server is experiencing a shortage of RAM memory. While all virtual memory servers will page out to the swap disk, page-in operations show that the servers has exceeded the available RAM storage. Any nonzero value for pi indicates excessive activity as RAM memory contents are read in from the swap disk.

- **us (user CPU)**   This is the amount of CPU that is servicing user tasks.

- **sy (system CPU)**   This is the percentage of CPU being used to service system tasks.

- **id (idle)**   This is the percentage of CPU that is idle.

- **wa (wait—IBM-AIX only)**   This shows the percentage of CPU that is waiting on external operations such as disk I/O.

Note that all of the CPU metrics are expressed as percentages. Hence, all of the CPU values (us + sy + id + wa) will always sum to 100. Now that we have a high-level understanding of the important vmstat data, let's look into some methods for using vmstat to identify server problems.

Identifying CPU Bottlenecks with vmstat

Waiting CPU resources can be shown in UNIX **vmstat** command output as the second column under the kthr (kernel thread state change) heading. Tasks may be placed in the wait queue ("b") if they are waiting on a resource, while other tasks appear in the run queue ("r") column. As we see in Figure 5-1, server tasks are queued for execution by the server.

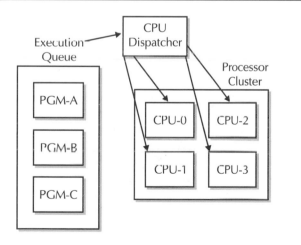

FIGURE 5-1.   *Tasks queuing for service by the CPUs*

In short, the server is experiencing a CPU bottleneck when "r" is greater than the number of CPUs on the server. To see the number of CPUs on the server, you can use one of the following UNIX commands.

Display the Number of CPUs in IBM AIX and HP/UX

In AIX and HP/UX the **lsdev** command can be used to see the number of CPUs on a server. This is very important, because it shows the number of Parallel Query processes that can be used on that server. That, in turn, limits the value that you can use following the DEGREE keyword in a Parallel Query or DML statement. The following example is taken from an AIX server, and shows that the server has four CPUs:

```
>lsdev -C|grep Process|wc -l
4
```

Display Number of CPUs in Solaris

In Solaris, the **prsinfo** command can be used to count the number of CPUs on the processor. Here we see that we have two CPUs on this server:

```
>psrinfo -v|grep "Status of processor"|wc -l
2
```

Display Number of CPUs in Linux

To see the number of CPUs on a Linux server, you can **cat** the */proc/cpuinfo* file. In the example here we see that our Linux server has four CPUs:

```
>cat /proc/cpuinfo|grep processor|wc -l
4
```

Remember that we need to know the number of CPUs on our server because the vmstat runqueue value must never exceed the number of CPUs. A runqueue value of 32 is perfectly acceptable for a 36-CPU server, while a value of 32 would be a serious problem for a 24-CPU server.

In the following example, we run the vmstat utility. For our purposes, we are interested in the first two columns: the run queue "r," and the kthr wait "b" column. In the next listing we see that there are an average of about eight new tasks entering the run queue every five seconds (the "r" column), while there are five other tasks that are waiting on resources (the "b" column). Also, a nonzero value in the ("b") column may indicate a bottleneck.

```
vmstat 5 5

kthr     memory            page                    faults        cpu
----- ----------- ------------------------- ------------ -----------
 r  b   avm    fre  re  pi  po  fr   sr  cy   in    sy   cs us sy id wa
 7  5 220214   141   0   0   0  42   53   0 1724 12381 2206 19 46 28  7
```

9	5	220933	195	0	0	1	216	290	0	1952	46118	2712	27	55	13	5
13	5	220646	452	0	0	1	33	54	0	2130	86185	3014	30	59	8	3
6	5	220338	673	0	0	0	0	0	0	1939	35068	3485	35	49	16	10

The rule for identifying a server with CPU resource problems is quite simple. Whenever the value of the runqueue "r" column exceeds the number of CPUs on the server, tasks are forced to wait for execution. There are several solutions to managing CPU overload, and these alternatives are presented in their order of desirability:

1. Add more processors (CPUs) to the server.

2. Load balance the system tasks by rescheduling large batch tasks to execute during off-peak hours.

3. Adjust the dispatching priorities (nice values) of existing tasks.

To understand how dispatching priorities work, we must remember that incoming tasks are placed in the execution queue according to their nice value (see Figure 5-2). Here we see that tasks with a low nice value are scheduled for execution above those tasks with a higher nice value.

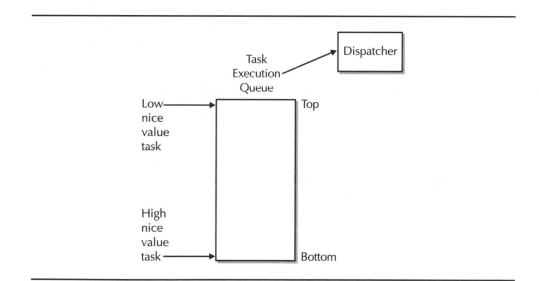

FIGURE 5-2. *Tasks queued for execution according to their nice value*

We will go into detail about these resolutions later in this chapter. Now that we can see when the CPUs are overloaded, let's look into vmstat further and see how we can tell when the CPUs are running at full capacity.

Identifying High CPU Usage with vmstat

We can also easily detect when we are experiencing a busy CPU on the Oracle database server. Whenever the "us" (user) plus "sy" (system) times approach 100, the CPUs are operating at full capacity as shown in the next listing.

Please note that it is not uncommon to see the CPU approach 100 percent even when the server is not overwhelmed with work. This is because the UNIX internal dispatchers will always attempt to keep the CPUs as busy as possible. This maximizes task throughput, but it can be misleading for a neophyte.

Remember, it is not a cause for concern when the user + system CPU values approach 100 percent. This just means that the CPUs are working to their full potential. The only metric that identifies a CPU bottleneck is when the run queue ("r" value) exceeds the number of CPUs on the server.

```
vmstat 5 1

kthr      memory              page                    faults          cpu
-----  -----------   ------------------------   ------------   -----------
 r  b   avm    fre   re  pi  po  fr   sr  cy   in   sy   cs  us  sy id wa
 0  0 217485   386    0   0   0   4   14    0  202  300  210  20  75  3  2
```

Now let's take a look at measuring the memory utilization on the server.

Identifying RAM Memory Bottlenecks

Contention for random access memory (RAM) has always been a problem for Oracle. All database servers have a limited amount of available RAM, and this RAM must be shared between the Oracle database and all external sessions that connect to the server and consume RAM in their Program Global Area (PGA).

However, before we go into detecting if your server memory is exceeded, we must first give you a tool for determining how much memory you have available on your server. Next is a command that you can issue to see how much RAM exists on your server.

Display RAM Size on DEC-UNIX

In DEC-UNIX, you can use the **uerf** command in conjunction with grep to display memory size. For example:

```
uerf -r 300 | grep -i mem
```

Here, the output of the **uerf** command is piped to grep to filter out and display the segments relating to memory. The –i option causes grep to find both uppercase and lowercase strings. With respect to the example shown here, grep –i mem looks for both "MEM" and "mem."

Display RAM Size on HP/UX
In HP/UX, the **dmesg** command can display memory information:

```
dmesg
Memory Information:
physical page size = 4096 bytes, logical page size = 4096 bytes
Physical: 5242880 Kbytes,lockable: 4051216 Kbytes,available: 4651796 Kbytes
```

Display RAM Size on AIX
In IBM's AIX dialect of UNIX, you must issue two separate commands. You start with the **lsdev** command followed by the **lsattr** command to display the amount of memory on a server. First, execute **lsdev** to list all devices. Then pipe that output through grep to filter out everything not related to memory. That will get you the name of the memory devices that are installed. For example:

```
>lsdev -C|grep mem

mem0        Available 00-00            Memory
```

Here you can see that mem0 is the name of the memory device. Now that you have the name, you can issue the **lsattr –El** command to see the amount of memory on the server. In the following example, the server has 3GB of RAM installed:

```
>lsattr -El mem0

size    3064 Total amount of physical memory ...
```

You must issue the **lsattr –El** command separately for each memory device.

Display RAM Size on Solaris
The **prtconf** command can also be used on all Solaris servers to quickly see the amount of available memory:

```
>prtconf|grep -i mem

Memory size: 2048 Megabytes
    memory (driver not attached)
    virtual-memory (driver not attached)
```

Display RAM Size in Linux

In Linux, the **free** command can be used to quickly display the amount of RAM memory on the server:

```
>free
              total      used      free    shared   buffers    cached
Mem:        3728668    504688   3223980     41316    430072     29440
-/+ buffers/cache:      45176   3683492
Swap:        265032       608    264424
```

Using the Top Utility for Displaying RAM

While each dialect has unique mechanisms and commands to display RAM, most UNIX servers support the *top* utility. The top utility is invoked by issuing the **top** command from the UNIX prompt. This will display the total amount of RAM available, and will also show the usage of both RAM and virtual memory:

```
root> top

  9:43am  up 16 days, 22:33, 24 users,  load average: 0.00, 0.00, 0.00
123 processes: 122 sleeping, 1 running, 0 zombie, 0 stopped
CPU states:  0.0% user,  0.9% system,  0.0% nice, 99.0% idle
Mem:    257568K av, 244988K used, 12580K free,  88732K shrd,  179772K buff
Swap:  530104K av,    9972K used, 520132K free                15452K cached

  PID USER     PRI  NI  SIZE  RSS SHARE STAT  LIB %CPU %MEM   TIME COMMAND
22417 oracle    14   0   904  904   668 R       0  0.9  0.3   0:00 top
    1 root       1   0   160  120    88 S       0  0.0  0.0   0:11 init
    2 root       0   0     0    0     0 SW      0  0.0  0.0   0:00 kflushd
    3 root       0   0     0    0     0 SW      0  0.0  0.0   0:08 kupdate
    4 root       0   0     0    0     0 SW      0  0.0  0.0   0:00 kpiod
```

In this example, we see from the top utility that we have 257,568 kilobytes of RAM on the server. The top utility is also great for seeing the top CPU consumer tasks on your server.

Using Glance to See Memory

In HP/UX and Solaris, you can enter the glance utility in order to see the amount of RAM available. The glance utility displays a screen showing CPU and memory utilization for the system as a whole, and for individual processes (see Figure 5-3). For more information on glance, look to the man pages on your UNIX server. Glance is started by entering **glance** from the UNIX prompt, and exited by entering CTRL-C.

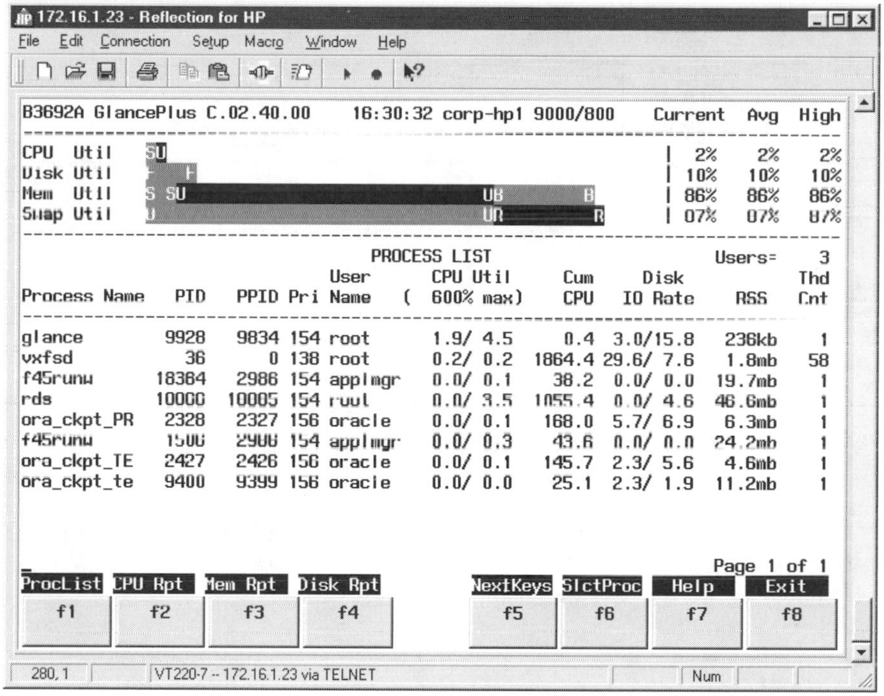

FIGURE 5-3. *A sample glance screen*

Glance is a great tool for reactive tuning because it shows the current status of your Oracle server, along with consumption details for the CPU and RAM.

RAM Memory and the Swap Disk

Now that we know the amount of RAM on our server, we are ready to investigate the RAM and swap disk usage for the Oracle server. Whenever the memory demands of the server exceed that amount of RAM, the virtual memory facility is invoked. With virtual memory, segments of RAM are moved onto a special disk segment called the *swap* disk. The swap disk is a special segment of disk defined by the systems administrator to hold excess RAM memory contents. The virtual memory system commonly pages-out memory segments, and this is not an indicator of a memory problem. However, a page-in operation indicates that the server has exceeded the amount of available RAM, and is recalling memory segments from the swap disk (see Figure 5-4).

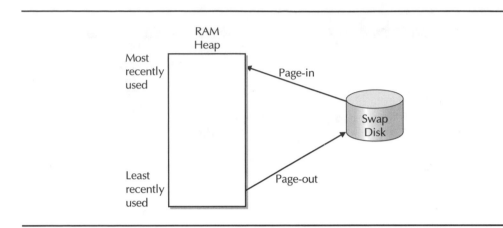

FIGURE 5-4. *RAM memory paging from the swap disk*

Swapping (pi) slows down a server because it takes a large amount of time to copy memory segments from the swap disk back into RAM. On an Oracle database server, the solution to a page-in problem involves:

- **Smaller SGA**   Reduce the demand for RAM by making the SGA smaller. The SGA can be made smaller by reducing the *db_block_buffers* or *shared_pool_size* init.ora parameters.

- **More RAM memory**   Add additional RAM memory to the server. (Remember that some 32-bit versions of Oracle cannot use more than 1.7 gigabytes of RAM.)

- **Reduce RAM demand**   Reduce RAM consumption of a database server by reducing the demands on Program Global Area (PGA) memory. Oracle parameters such as *sort_area_size* can greatly increase the amount of RAM allocated to each connected user's PGA.

A memory-bound database server always experiences paging from the swap disk. This is displayed in the vmstat utility as the po (page-out) and pi (page-in) columns of vmstat. Here we see that the database server is experiencing five page-in and nine page-out operations. You can tell that a server is having excessive memory requests by looking at page-in operations.

```
Root> vmstat 1 2

kthr     memory            page              faults        cpu
-----  -----------  -----------------------  -----------  -----------
r  b   avm   fre  re  pi  po   fr   sr   cy   in   sy  cs  us sy id wa
```

```
0  0 218094   166   0  4    0   4   16   0 202   301 211 14 19 45 22
0  0 218094   166   0  5    9   4   14   0 202   301 211 14 19 45 22
```

In sum, page-out operations are a normal part of virtual memory operation, but page-in (pi) operations indicate that the server has excessive RAM demands. Now let's take a look at a vmstat metric that is sometimes associated with a disk I/O bottleneck.

Detecting Potential I/O Bottlenecks in AIX

Using IBM's AIX dialect of UNIX, an I/O bound database server is usually evidenced by a high value in the wa (wait) column of vmstat. In the next listing , we see that 22 percent of the CPU time is being used waiting for database I/O:

```
root> vmstat
kthr        memory              page              faults        cpu
-----  -----------  ------------------------  -----------  ------------
r  b   avm   fre re pi po fr   sr  cy  in   sy  cs us sy id wa
0  0 217485   386  0  0  0  4   14   0 202  300 210 14 19 45 22
```

It is important to note that a high wait value does not always signal an I/O bottleneck. The CPU wait could be due to other factors, and this metric simply means that the CPU is waiting for external OS services.

Now that we understand the basics of the vmstat utility, let's explore an easy method for capturing vmstat data, storing it inside an Oracle table, and producing server performance reports.

Capturing Server Performance Data Inside STATSPACK

Now that we have seen that vmstat can provide useful information about the status of the Oracle database server, how can we create a mechanism for monitoring these vmstat statistics? As we noted from our discussion of vmstat, system-level resource contention is transient and fleeting, and it is often very easy to miss a bottleneck unless we are constantly vigilant. For this reason, we need to create an extension to the STATSPACK tables that will constantly poll the hardware and collect any data relating to resource contention.

The concept behind this extension is to execute the vmstat utility and capture the performance information within an Oracle table called stats$vmstat.

While this technique works very well for monitoring the Oracle database server, these operating system statistics can also be used to monitor the other computers in your system. These include the application servers (Web servers) and the Oracle database server. We will show you how to collect vmstats on a remote server later in this chapter.

A Script to Capture vmstat Information

It is a simple matter to create an Oracle table to store this information and use a script to populate the table. Creating the automated vmstat monitor begins by creating an Oracle table to contain the vmstat output:

```
connect perfstat/perfstat;

drop table stats$vmstat;
create table stats$vmstat
(
      start_date          date,
      duration            number,
      server_name         varchar2(20),
      runque_waits        number,
      page_in             number,
      page_out            number,
      user_cpu            number,
      system_cpu          number,
      idle_cpu            number,
      wait_cpu            number
)
tablespace perfstat
storage (initial   10m
         next        1m
         pctincrease 0)
;
```

Now that we have defined an Oracle table to capture the vmstat information, we need to write a UNIX script that will execute vmstat, capture the vmstat output, and place it into the Oracle table.

The main script to collect the vmstat information is a Korn shell script called *get_vmstat.ksh*. As we noted earlier, each dialect of UNIX displays vmstat information in different columns, so we need slightly different scripts for each type of UNIX.

The idea is to write a script that continually runs the vmstat utility and then directs the results into our Oracle table, as shown in Figure 5-5.

The script shows the vmstat capture utility script for the Linux operating system. Note that you must change this script in several places to make it work for you:

■ You must set the ORACLE_HOME to your directory:

```
ORACLE_HOME=/usr/app/oracle/admin/product/8/1/6
```

■ You must set your ORACLE_SID in the sqlplus command:

```
$ORACLE_HOME/bin/sqlplus -s perfstat/perfstat@testsys1<<EOF
```

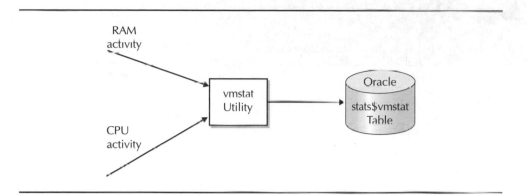

FIGURE 5-5.   *Capturing vmstat output into a STATSPACK extension table*

■ You can change the duration of samples by setting SAMPLE_TIME:

```
SAMPLE_TIME=300
```

get_vmstat.ksh (Linux version)

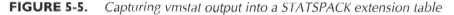

```
#!/bin/ksh

# This is the Linux version

ORACLE_HOME=/usr/app/oracle/admin/product/8/1/6
export ORACLE_HOME

PATH=$ORACLE_HOME/bin:$PATH
export PATH
SERVER_NAME=`uname -a|awk '{print $2}'`
typeset -u SERVER_NAME
export SERVER_NAME

# sample every five minutes (300 seconds) . . . .
SAMPLE_TIME=300

while true
do
   vmstat ${SAMPLE_TIME} 2 > /tmp/msg$$


# run vmstat and direct the output into the Oracle table . . .
cat /tmp/msg$$|sed 1,3d | awk  '{ printf("%s %s %s %s %s %s\n", $1, $8, $9,
14, $15, $16) }' | while read RUNQUE PAGE_IN PAGE_OUT USER_CPU SYSTEM_CPU
```

```
IDLE_CPU
  do

    $ORACLE_HOME/bin/sqlplus -s perfstat/perfstat@testsys1<<EOF
    insert into perfstat.stats\$vmstat
                         values (
                           sysdate,
                           $SAMPLE_TIME,
                           '$SERVER_NAME',
                           $RUNQUE,
                           $PAGE_IN,
                           $PAGE_OUT,
                           $USER_CPU,
                           $SYSTEM_CPU,
                           $IDLE_CPU,
                           0
                                  );
      EXIT
EOF
  done
done

rm /tmp/msg$$
```

Because of the differences in implementations of vmstat, the first task is to identify the columns of the vmstat output that contain the information that we want to capture. Once we know the columns that we want to capture, we can add these columns to the vmstat script to put the output into our Table 5-1.

Dialect	Run Queue column	Page-In column	Page-Out column	User column	System column	Idle column	Wait column
HP/UX	1	8	9	16	17	18	NA
AIX	1	6	7	14	15	16	17
Solaris	1	8	9	20	21	22	NA
Linux	1	8	9	14	15	16	NA

TABLE 5-1.   *Column locations for vmstat dialects*

Using this table, you can adjust the capture script according to your operating system. You customize the script by changing the line in the script that reads the vmstat output and places it into the stats$vmstat table. Here is a summary of the UNIX dialect changes to this line.

HP/UX vmstat Columns

```
cat /tmp/msg$$|sed 1,3d |\
   awk '{ printf("%s %s %s %s %s %s\n", $1, $8, $9, $16, $17, $18) }' |\
   while read RUNQUE PAGE_IN PAGE_OUT USER_CPU SYSTEM_CPU IDLE_CPU
```

IBM AIX vmstat Columns

```
cat /tmp/msg$$|sed 1,3d |\
   awk '{ printf("%s %s %s %s %s %s\n", $1, $6, $7, $14, $15, $16, $17) }' |\
   while read RUNQUE PAGE_IN PAGE_OUT USER_CPU SYSTEM_CPU IDLE_CPU WAIT_CPU
```

Sun Solaris vmstat Columns

```
cat /tmp/msg$$|sed 1,3d |\
   awk '{ printf("%s %s %s %s %s %s\n", $1, $8, $9, $20, $21, $22) }' |\
   while read RUNQUE PAGE_IN PAGE_OUT USER_CPU SYSTEM_CPU IDLE_CPU
```

Linux vmstat Columns

```
cat /tmp/msg$$|sed 1,3d |\
   awk '{ printf("%s %s %s %s %s %o\n", $1, $8, $9, $14, $15, $16) }' |\
   while read RUNQUE PAGE_IN PAGE_OUT USER_CPU SYSTEM_CPU IDLE_CPU
```

Internals of the vmstat Capture Script

It is important to understand how the *get_vmstat.ksh* script functions, so let's examine the steps in this script:

1. It executes the vmstat utility for the specified elapsed-time interval (SAMPLE_TIMF=300).

2. The output of the vmstat is directed into the /tmp directory.

3. The output is then parsed using the awk utility, and the values are inserted into the mon_vmstats table.

Once started, the *get_vmstat.ksh* script will run continually and capture the vmstats into your stats$vmstat table. This script is an example of a UNIX daemon process, and it will run continually to sample the server status. However, the script may be terminated if your server is rebooted, so it is a good idea to place a crontab entry to make sure that the *get_vmstat* script is always running. Next is a script called *run_vmstat.ksh* that will ensure that the vmstat utility is always running on your server.

Note that you must make the following changes to this script:

■ Set the file location variable vmstat to the directory that contains your *get_vmstat.ksh* script:

```
vmstat=`echo ~oracle/vmstat`
```

■ Create a small file in your UNIX file directory ($vmstat) called *mysid*. This file will contain one line and specify the name of your ORACLE_SID.

```
ORACLE_SID=`cat ${vmstat}/mysid`
```

run_vmstat.ksh

```
#!/bin/ksh

# First, we must set the environment . . . .
vmstat=`echo ~oracle/vmstat`
export vmstat
ORACLE_SID=`cat ${vmstat}/mysid`
export ORACLE_SID

ORACLE_HOME=`cat /etc/oratab|grep $ORACLE_SID:|cut -f2 -d':'`
export ORACLE_HOME
PATH=$ORACLE_HOME/bin:$PATH
export PATH

#----------------------------------------
# If it is not running, then start it . . .
#----------------------------------------
check_stat=`ps -ef|grep get_vmstat|grep -v grep|wc -l`;
oracle_num=`expr $check_stat`
if [ $oracle_num -le 0 ]
 then nohup $vmstat/get_vmstat_linux.ksh > /dev/null 2>&1 &
fi
```

The *run_vmstat.ksh* script can be scheduled to run hourly on the server. As we can see by examining the code, this script checks to see if the *get_vmstat.ksh* script is executing. If it is not executing, the script resubmits it for execution. In practice, the *get_vmstat.ksh* script will not abort, but if the server is shut down and restarted, the script will need to be restarted.

Here is an example of the UNIX crontab file. For those not familiar with cron, the cron facility is a UNIX scheduling facility that allows tasks to be submitted at specific times. Note that it schedules the *run_vmstat.ksh* script every hour, and runs a vmstat exception report every day at 7:00 A.M.

```
00 * * * * /home/vmstat/run_vmstat.ksh > /home/vmstat/r.lst

00 7 * * * /home/vmstat/run_vmstat_alert.ksh prodb1 > /home/vmstat/v.lst
```

Now that we see how to monitor the Oracle database server, let's examine how we can use this technique to report on other Oracle-related servers. This technique is very handy for reporting on Oracle Web servers and application servers.

Reporting vmstat Information on Other Oracle Servers

To get a complete picture of the performance of your total Oracle system, you must also monitor the behavior of all of the servers that communicate with Oracle. For example, many Oracle environments have other servers:

- **Oracle Applications**   In Oracle Applications products, you generally have separate application servers communicating with the database server.

- **SAP with Oracle**   In SAP, you have separate application servers that communicate with Oracle.

- **Real Application Clusters (Oracle Parallel Server)**   With RAC, you have multiple Oracle database servers, all sharing the same database.

- **Oracle Web Applications**   When using Oracle databases on the Web, you have separate Web servers that direct the communications into the database.

This technique in *get_vmstat.ksh* can easily be extended to measure the performance of other servers in your Oracle environment. Note that the stats$vmstat table has a column to store the server name. Since we can separate vmstat metrics by server, we simply need to create a remote vmstat script that will capture the performance of the other servers and send the data to a central database. Because only the database server contains an Oracle database, the vmstat data will be sent to the database from the remote server using database links. Any server that has a Net8 client can be used to capture vmstat information.

If we take a close look at the *get_vmstat* script from before, we see that this script can be executed on a remote server. The script will send the vmstat data to the server that contains our Oracle database using a database link. Note where the script enters sqlplus using sqlplus perfstat/perfstat@prod.

By collecting the data remotely, we can capture a complete picture of the performance of all of the components of the Oracle environment, not just the database server. This is important in cases where you need to track slow performance of e-commerce systems. Using this vmstat information, you can go back to the time of the slowdown and see which Web servers may have been overloaded and also examine the load on the database server.

Conclusion

Now that we see how to capture server statistics into Oracle tables, we are ready to see how we can use this valuable information to ensure that our server is not the cause of Oracle performance problems. In the next chapter we will look at some of the specific causes of server resource shortages and see techniques that can be used to reduce demands on the CPU and RAM. We will also explore some prewritten scripts that will automatically alert us to exceptional server conditions.

CHAPTER

6

Tuning
the Server Environment

t should now be clear that the tuning of the server environment is a prerequisite to tuning the Oracle database. As we repeatedly demonstrated in earlier chapters and in our discussion in Chapter 5, no amount of Oracle tuning is going to help a performance problem if the CPU or memory on the server is experiencing an overload or a bottleneck.

When tuning an Oracle database server, we must always remember the goal of fully loading the CPUs and RAM on the server. Unused processing and RAM power can never be reclaimed, and with the significant depreciation of the value of most servers, maximizing the utilization is a noble goal. On any server that is dedicated to an Oracle database, we want to dedicate as much hardware resources to Oracle as possible without causing a server-related slowdown. This chapter will look at the details of Oracle database server tuning and will be divided into several sections:

- **Online server monitor tools**   This will look at ancillaries to vmstat and will show the top and sar utilities to see details about CPU and memory activity.

- **Tuning CPU consumption**   This will describe the basic causes of CPU overload and explore remedies for excessive CPU consumption. When you experience a shortage of CPU, you will need to add more processors or reduce the amount of work on the database server.

- **Tuning memory consumption**   This section will explore basic memory management and show some tricks for partitioning memory on the server. When an Oracle server runs short of real memory, segments of RAM are swapped out to a swap disk. Such page-out operations happen frequently, but a page-in indicates that the Oracle server is exceeding the amount of RAM memory. The usual remedies for swapping are to reduce the size of the SGA and/or to buy more RAM for the database server.

- **Reporting on server statistics**   This section will look at some handy scripts that will alert you to server exceptions and show you how to create trend and usage reports for your server.

Let's begin with a review of some online tools for server monitoring. We already covered vmstat in the last chapter, but we also need to understand the glance, top, and sar utilities.

The Relationship Between the Database Administrator and the Systems Administrator

In many Oracle shops, computer professionals called systems administrators are responsible for the setup, configuration, and tuning of the Oracle database server. The abilities of system administrators vary widely, from excellent support and cooperation to neophyte support and complete noncooperation.

Because of the tight coupling between database performance and server performance, it is imperative that the Oracle DBA have access to the tools that we describe here. By themselves, the systems administrators will not have enough information about what is happening inside the database to properly tune the server. Conversely, the DBAs cannot get the information they need to properly configure Oracle if they cannot get access to the server monitor utilities.

Many Oracle shops give *root* access to the DBA so they will have full control over their database server. The system administrator continues to be responsible for the configuration and system software on the server, but the DBA accepts responsibility for setting the kernel parameters and managing the interface layer between Oracle and the operating system environment.

A small minority of shops will restrict access to the root account, but these shops will provide the Oracle DBA with access to all of the server monitor tools and system utilities. In either case, it is imperative that the Oracle DBA have access to the system monitor tools.

Online Server Monitor Tools

Before we address the specific tuning techniques for your database server, let's begin with a brief tour of several online tools that can help us tune the server. There are many companies that provide third-party server performance monitors, but there are several "freeware" server monitors that can help you see what is happening on the server.

Using glance

The glance utility is provided on HP/UX systems to provide a graphical display of server performance. Glance displays current CPU, memory, and disk and swap consumption, and also reports on the top processes. The glance utility is invoked by entering **glance** from the UNIX prompt. The name for glance is quite appropriate because it gives you a complete glance at the whole server. Figure 6-1 shows an example glance screen.

The histograms at the top of the glance screen show the amount of consumption on CPU, disk, memory, and swap. The output within each histogram shows the high-water mark, and the amount of the resource in system and user mode. For example, from Figure 6-1 we see that this server is only using 4 percent of the CPU capacity, but the RAM memory is at 90-percent capacity.

The second part of the glance utility shows the most intensive tasks on the database server. The glance screen in Figure 6-1 was for an Oracle server running Oracle Applications, and we see that the Oracle Forms 4.5 runtime task (f45runw) is the most intensive task on the server. For each task displayed, we also can see the amount of disk I/O currently being consumed by the task. The glance screen will refresh every few seconds, so we get a continual picture of the load on the Oracle server. To exit glance, you enter CTRL-C. Now let's look at another server monitor tool that is quite similar to glance.

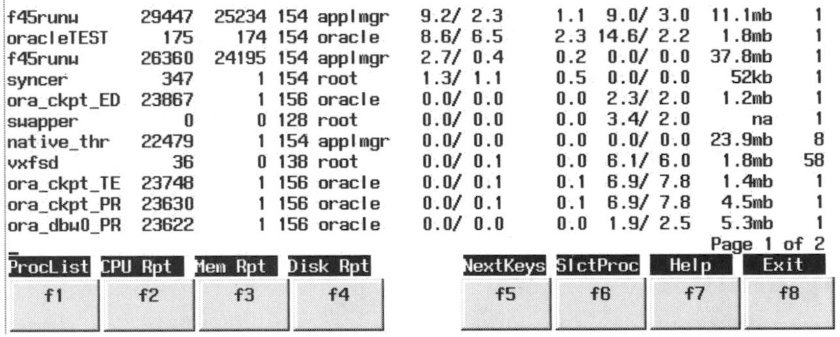

```
B3692A GlancePlus C.02.40.00     08:57:46 corp-hp1 9000/800    Current  Avg  High
-----------------------------------------------------------------------------------
CPU  Util  SUU                                           |   4%    3%    8%
Disk Util  F       F                                     |  13%    6%   14%
Mem  Util  S SU              UB                        B |  90%   90%   90%
Swap Util  U                              UR          R |  92%   92%   92%
-----------------------------------------------------------------------------------
                                PROCESS LIST               Users=     2
                              User    CPU Util   Cum    Disk          Thd
Process Name   PID   PPID Pri Name  ( 600% max)  CPU  IO Rate   RSS   Cnt
-----------------------------------------------------------------------------------
f45runw       29447 25234 154 applmgr   9.2/ 2.3  1.1   9.0/ 3.0  11.1mb   1
oracleTEST      175   174 154 oracle    8.6/ 6.5  2.3  14.6/ 2.2   1.8mb   1
f45runw       26360 24195 154 applmgr   2.7/ 0.4  0.2   0.0/ 0.0  37.8mb   1
syncer          347     1 154 root      1.3/ 1.1  0.5   0.0/ 0.0    52kb   1
ora_ckpt_ED   23867     1 156 oracle    0.0/ 0.0  0.0   2.3/ 2.0   1.2mb   1
swapper           0     0 128 root      0.0/ 0.0  0.0   3.4/ 2.0      na   1
native_thr    22479     1 154 applmgr   0.0/ 0.0  0.0   0.0/ 0.0  23.9mb   8
vxfsd            36     0 138 root      0.0/ 0.1  0.0   6.1/ 6.0   1.8mb  58
ora_ckpt_TE   23748     1 156 oracle    0.0/ 0.1  0.1   6.9/ 7.8   1.4mb   1
ora_ckpt_PR   23630     1 156 oracle    0.0/ 0.1  0.1   6.9/ 7.8   4.5mb   1
ora_dbw0_PR   23622     1 156 oracle    0.0/ 0.0  0.0   1.9/ 2.5   5.3mb   1
                                                                Page 1 of 2
-----------------------------------------------------------------------------------
ProcList CPU Rpt Mem Rpt Disk Rpt        NextKeys SlctProc  Help    Exit
   f1      f2      f3      f4               f5      f6       f7       f8
```

FIGURE 6-1.   *A sample screen from glance*

Using top to Monitor the Server

The top utility is used to show CPU consumption, RAM memory consumption, and the top sessions on a UNIX server. The top utility is invoked by entering **top** from the UNIX prompt. The output from top is displayed in three sections.

The top Load Averages

At the very beginning of the following top output we see a series of three numbers. These are the called load average metrics. The *load average* is an arbitrary number that describes the load on the system. The first load average value is the immediate load for the past minute. The next value represents the load average from 5 minutes in the past. The third value is the load average from 15 minutes ago. Whenever the load average rises above 1, you can assume that the processors are fully burdened and you should immediately run vmstat to check the run queue values.

```
System: corp-hp9 Thu Jul  6 09:14:23 2000
Load averages: 0.04, 0.03, 0.03
340 processes: 336 sleeping, 4 running
```

The top CPU Summary

The first output from top shows the load on each processor and the current top sessions in terms of CPU utilization. Top gives details on each CPU on the server, and we can immediately see from the listing here that this server has six CPUs, numbered 0–5:

```
root> top

Cpu states:
CPU   LOAD   USER   NICE    SYS    IDLE BLOCK   SWAIT    INTR   SSYS
 0    0.06   5.0%   0.0%    0.6%   94.4%  0.0%    0.0%    0.0%   0.0%
 1    0.06   0.0%   0.0%    0.8%   99.2%  0.0%    0.0%    0.0%   0.0%
 2    0.06   0.8%   0.0%    0.0%   99.2%  0.0%    0.0%    0.0%   0.0%
 3    0.06   0.0%   0.0%    0.2%   99.8%  0.0%    0.0%    0.0%   0.0%
 4    0.00   0.0%   0.0%    0.0%  100.0%  0.0%    0.0%    0.0%   0.0%
 5    0.00   0.2%   0.0%    0.0%   99.8%  0.0%    0.0%    0.0%   0.0%
---   ----  -----  -----  -----  -----  -----   -----   -----  -----
avg   0.04   1.0%   0.0%    0.2%   98.8%  0.0%    0.0%    0.0%   0.0%
```

Top Sessions

Now let's look at the second section from the **top** command. The second section of top output details the current top sessions in terms of CPU utilization, and appears as follows:

```
System: core-hp1                              Mon Dec 25 07:17:56 2000
Load averages: 0.03, 0.04, 0.05
372 processes: 368 sleeping, 4 running
Cpu states:
CPU   LOAD   USER   NICE    SYS    IDLE  BLOCK  SWAIT   INTR   SSYS
 0    0.11   0.0%   0.0%   0.0% 100.0%   0.0%   0.0%   0.0%   0.0%
 1    0.02   0.0%   0.0%   0.0% 100.0%   0.0%   0.0%   0.0%   0.0%
 2    0.02   0.0%   0.0%   0.0% 100.0%   0.0%   0.0%   0.0%   0.0%
 3    0.03   0.0%   0.0%   0.0% 100.0%   0.0%   0.0%   0.0%   0.0%
 4    0.00   0.0%   0.0%   0.0% 100.0%   0.0%   0.0%   0.0%   0.0%
 5    0.01   0.0%   0.0%   0.0% 100.0%   0.0%   0.0%   0.0%   0.0%
---   ----  -----  -----  -----  -----  -----  -----  -----  -----
avg   0.03   0.0%   0.0%   0.0% 100.0%   0.0%   0.0%   0.0%   0.0%

Memory: 736056K (417860K) real, 733560K (422192K) virtual, 1101512K free  Page#
1/54

CPU TTY      PID USERNAME PRI NI   SIZE    RES STATE    TIME  %WCPU  %CPU COMMAND
 3   ?     16664 oracle   154 20 20304K 1892K sleep   15:32   2.21  2.21 oracleTE
 5   ?        36 root     152 20    0K     0K run     57:52   1.65  1.65 vxfsd
 2   ?       477 root     154 20   32K    80K sleep  160:55   0.71  0.71 syncer
 3   ?     14963 oracle   154 20 4448K  2780K sleep    4:39   0.32  0.32 oraweb
 0   ?     15980 oracle   154 20 4704K  3020K sleep    4:41   0.31  0.31 oraweb
 0 pts/tb 21355 root     158 20  536K   184K sleep    0:00   0.77  0.30 sh
```

In this section of the top output, we see the process ID (PID), username, the dispatching priority (PRI), the nice value (NI), the size of each task's memory (SIZE), the state, the execution time, and the percentage of CPU being used by each process.

While top has many columns of information, there are only a few columns that are of interest to you as the Oracle DBA:

- **Load averages**   These are the load averages for the entire server. Values greater than 1 may indicate an overload problem on the server.

- **CPU**   The first section of the top output shows a load summary for each CPU. The CPU column in the detailed listing shows which CPU is servicing each individual task.

- **LOAD**   The LOAD column shows the load on each of the CPUs.

- **NI**   The NI (nice) value is the dispatching priority of the task, and refers to the rate that the task receives services from the CPUs.

- **IDLE**   This shows the percentage of time that each CPU has been idle.

In sum, the top and glance utilities are reliable reactive utilities that allow the DBA to see what is happening on the database server. Now let's take a look at a more detailed online monitor, the System Activity Reporter, or sar for short.

Using sar to Monitor Server Statistics

The sar utility (System Activity Reporter) is a system activity reporter that is quite popular with HP/UX and Solaris, and sar is also available for AIX. Just like top, sar gives detailed information about Oracle tasks from the UNIX level. You will be able to see the overall consumption of CPU, disk, memory, and Journal File System (JFS) buffer usage. There are three major flags that you can use with sar:

- **sar –u**   Shows CPU activity

- **sar –w**   Shows swapping activity

- **sar –b**   Shows buffer activity

NOTE
Each flavor of UNIX has a different implementation of sar. For example, some of the key flags used in the Sun version of sar are not available on HP/UX. The examples in this book show the HP/UX version of sar.

The output from sar reports usually shows a time-based snapshot of activity. This is true for all reports that you'll see in this section. When you issue the **sar** command, you pass two numeric arguments. The first represents the time interval between samples, and the second represents the number of samples to take. For example:

```
sar -u 10 5
```

The **sar** command in this example is requesting five samples taken at 10-second intervals.

sar –u: The CPU Report

The **sar –u** command is very useful for seeing the overall CPU consumption over time. In the example that follows, I execute **sar –u** to see the state of the CPU. CPU time can be allocated into the following four sections: user mode, system mode, waiting on I/O, and idle.

```
>sar -u 2 5

HP-UX corp-hp1 B.11.00 U 9000/800    12/25/00

07:18:44    %usr    %sys    %wio    %idle
07:18:46       0       0       1      99
07:18:48       0       0       1      99
07:18:50       4       0      13      83
07:18:52       2       1       7      90
07:18:54       0       0       3      98

Average        1       0       5      93
```

sar –w: The Memory Switching and Swapping Activity Report

The **sar –w** command is especially useful if you suspect that your database server is experiencing a memory shortage. The following example shows the swapping activity report that you get from sar:

```
>sar -w 5 5

HP-UX corp-hp1 B.11.00 U 9000/800    12/25/00

07:19:33 swpin/s bswin/s swpot/s bswot/s pswch/s
07:19:38    0.00     0.0    0.00     0.0     261
07:19:43    0.00     0.0    0.00     0.0     231
07:19:48    0.00     0.0    0.00     0.0     326
07:19:53    0.00     0.0    0.00     0.0     403
07:19:58    0.00     0.0    0.00     0.0     264

Average     0.00     0.0    0.00     0.0     297
```

The column descriptions are as follows:

- **swpin/s**   Number of process swap-ins per second.
- **swpot/s**   Number of process swap-outs per second.
- **bswin/s**   Number of 512-byte swap-ins per second.
- **bswot/s**   Number of 512-byte swap-outs per second.
- **pswch/s**   Number of process context switches per second.

sar –b: The Buffer Activity Report

The **sar -b** command causes sar to report buffer activity, which equates to disk
I/O activity and is especially useful if you suspect that your database is I/O bound.
The report shows real disk I/O, and the interaction with the UNIX Journal File
System (JFS) buffer. For example, here we see a sample of sar output over a
5-second interval:

```
>sar -b 1 5

HP-UX corp-hp1 B.11.00 U 9000/800     12/25/00

07:20:40 bread/s lread/s %rcache bwrit/s lwrit/s %wcache pread/s pwrit/s
07:20:41       0      72     100       6       7      14       0       0
07:20:42       0       3     100       3       3       0       0       0
07:20:43       0       3     100       0       9     100       0       0
07:20:44       0      26     100       6      12      50       0       0
07:20:45       0      19     100       3      15      80       0       0

Average        0      25     100       4       9      61       0       0
```

In the output shown here, you see the following data columns:

- **Bread/s**   Number of physical reads from disk per second.

- **lread/s**   Number of reads per second from the UNIX JFS buffer cache.

- **%rcache**   Buffer cache hit ratio (for the UNIX JFS buffer cache) for
  read requests.

- **bwrit/s**   Number of physical writes to disk per second. This gives the DBA
  an indication of the overall write activity on the server.

- **lwrit/s**   Number of writes per second to the UNIX JFS buffer cache.

- **%wcache**   Buffer cache hit ratio (for the UNIX JFS buffer cache) for
  write requests.

- **pread/s**   Number of reads per second from disk. This is an excellent
  measure of the load on the I/O subsystem.

- **pwrit/s**   Number of writes per second to disk.

The **sar –b** command is often used in reactive tuning when you want to correlate
what is happening inside Oracle with what is happening on the database server.
Now let's turn our attention to the detection of server problems. We will begin by
examining CPU consumption of the database server.

Monitoring Server CPU Consumption

CPU consumption on an Oracle server is a simple matter because the server manages all CPU transactions automatically. All servers are configured to use CPU cycles on an as-needed basis, and the Oracle database will use CPU resources freely. The internal machine code will manage the assignment of processors to active tasks and ensure that the maximum amount of processing power is applied to each task.

CPU shortages are evidenced in cases where the CPU run queue is greater than the number of CPUs, as shown in Figure 6-2. In these cases, the only solutions are to increase the number of CPUs on the processor or reduce the CPU demands on Oracle. You can decrease CPU demands on Oracle by turning off Oracle Parallel Query, replacing the standard Oracle listener with the multithreaded server (MTS), and other actions that would reduce the processing demands on the hardware.

Tasks are serviced in UNIX according to their internal dispatching priority. Important tasks such as the UNIX operating system tasks will always have a more favorable dispatching priority because the UNIX system tasks drive the operating system

CPU overload is usually evidenced by high values in the vmstat run queue column. Whenever the run queue value exceeds the number of CPUs of the server, some task may be waiting for service. When we see a CPU overload, we have several alternatives:

1. **Add additional processors** This is usually the best solution, because an Oracle server that is overloading the CPU will always run faster with additional processors.

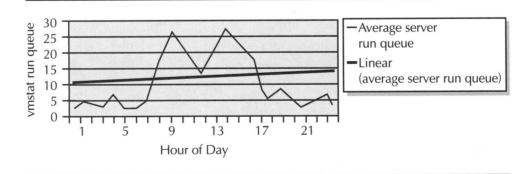

FIGURE 6-2. *CPU overload on an Oracle server with 12 CPUs*

2. **Reduce server load** If the CPU overload is not constant, task load balancing may be the solution. For example, It is not uncommon to see a server overloaded during peak work hours, and then return to 80-percent idle in the evenings. In these cases, batch tasks can be rescheduled to execute when there are more idle CPU resources available.

3. **Alter task dispatching priorities** Most all operating systems allow the root user to change the dispatching priority for tasks. As a general rule, the online database background tasks are given more priority (a smaller priority value), while less critical batch processes are placed with less priority (a higher priority value). However, altering the default dispatching priorities is not a good long-term solution, and it should only be undertaken in emergency situations.

Upgrading an Entire Server

On mission-critical databases where speed is a primary concern, adding additional processors may not be the best solution. Oracle tuning professionals will sometimes recommend upgrading to a faster server architecture. For example, many of the new 64-bit CPU processors will handle Oracle transactions an order of magnitude faster than their 32-bit predecessors. For example, in the IBM AIX environment, the IBM SP2 processors run on 32 bits. IBM's next generation of processors utilize a 64-bit technology, and these systems can process information far faster than their 32-bit ancestors. The new IBM Blackbird servers will often double the overall processing speed of an Oracle database.

When making recommendations for upgrades of entire servers, many Oracle tuning professionals use the analogy of the performance of a 16-bit PC compared to the performance of 32-bit PC. In general, moving to faster CPU architecture can greatly improve the speed of Oracle applications, and many vendors such as IBM will allow you to actually load your production system onto one of the new processors for speed benchmarks prior to purchasing the new servers.

Adding Additional CPU Processors

Most symmetric multiprocessor (SMP) architectures for Oracle databases servers are expandable, and additional processors can be added at any time. Once added, the processor architecture will immediately make the new CPUs available to the Oracle database.

The problem with adding additional processors is the high cost that can often outweigh the cost of a whole new server. Adding additional processors to an existing server can commonly cost over $100,000, and most managers require a detailed cost-benefit analysis when making the decision to buy more CPUs.

Essentially, the cost-benefit analysis compares the lost productivity of the end users (due to the response time latency) with the additional costs of the processors.

Another problem with justifying additional processors is the sporadic nature of CPU overloads. Oracle database servers often experience "transient" overloads, and there will be times when the processors are heavily burdened and other times when the processors are not at full utilization. Before recommending a processor upgrade, most Oracle tuning professionals will perform a load-balancing analysis to ensure that any batch-oriented tasks are presented to the server at nonpeak hours.

Load Balancing of Server Tasks

When CPU overload is experienced, the DBA will generally see periods during the days when the run queue gets quite long and other periods at night when the processors are mostly idle (Figure 6-3). A common question asked by a systems administrator is "The CPU is 40-percent idle for 16 hours a day, so why should we add more processors?"

However, there are times when it makes sense to add more processors, even if the processors are idle during off-peak times. For example, if you are working in an online environment, the only response time that matters is the time between 7:00 A.M. and 8:00 P.M. when your online users are active. The fact that the server is largely idle during the middle of the night has no bearing on the decision to upgrade with additional CPUs.

Once we identify the times when the CPU activity is excessive, we need to go to STATSPACK and examine the activity at the times of the overload. Once we have identified the times when the processors are overloaded, we must then see if it is

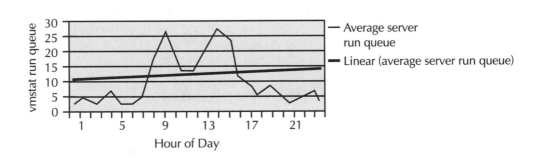

FIGURE 6-3.   *Average Oracle server run queue values before task load balancing*

possible to reschedule batch tasks to run at off-peak hours. On an Oracle database server, tasks may be scheduled in many ways:

- The dbms_job utility
- The UNIX cron utility
- A TP monitor such as Tuxedo
- Oracle Concurrent Manager (for Oracle Applications)
- SAPGUI if we are running SAP

Regardless of the method of scheduling Oracle tasks, the idea is to find large batch tasks that may be scheduled during peak processing times. From the graph in Figure 6-2, we see that the CPU overloads peak at 10:00 A.M. and again at 3:00 P.M. Our task is to find a large regularly scheduled SQL task that runs during these times.

STATSPACK Solutions for Finding High-Impact Tasks

Within STATSPACK, we can examine the stats$sql_summary table, looking for SQL statements that are executed during the peak hours. The high-impact tasks will generally be associated with SQL statements that have a high value for *rows processed*. Here is an easy STATSPACK table query to find the SQL:

rpt_top_sql.sql

```
set lines 80;
set pages 999;
set heading off;

select
   to_char(snap_time,'yyyy-mm-dd hh24'),
   substr(sql_text,1,50)
from
   stats$sql_summary a,
   stats$snapshot    sn
where
   a.snap_id = sn.snap_id
and
   to_char(snap_time,'hh24') = 10
or
   to_char(snap_time,'hh24') = 15
order by
   rows processed desc;
```

Here is a sample of the output from this report, showing the beginning of all SQL statements, ordered in descending order of rows_processed. This tells the DBA which SQL statements are causing the most I/O resources.

```
Yr.  Mo dy Hr SQL_TEXT
------------- ---------------------------------------------------
2000-09-20 10 begin :retCode := toc_maint . toc_insert_entry ( :
2000-09-20 10 begin :retCode := toc_maint . toc_insert_entry ( :
2000-09-20 15 INSERT INTO TOC_ENTRY ( ISBN,TOC_SEQ_NBR,VISUAL_PA
2000-09-20 15 INSERT INTO TOC_ENTRY ( ISBN,TOC_SEQ_NBR,VISUAL_PA
2000-09-20 15 SELECT PAGE_SEQ_NBR   FROM PAGE  WHERE (ISBN = :b1
2000-09-20 15 SELECT PAGE_SEQ_NBR   FROM PAGE  WHERE (ISBN = :b1
2000-09-21 10 select 'ALTER ' || substr(object_type,1,20) || ' '
2000-09-21 10 DECLARE job BINARY_INTEGER := :job; next_date DATE
2000-09-21 10 DECLARE job BINARY_INTEGER := :job; next_date DATE
2000-09-21 10 DECLARE job BINARY_INTEGER := :job; next_date DATE
2000-09-20 15 SELECT IMAGE_BLOB   FROM PAGE_IMAGE  WHERE (ISBN =
2000-09-20 15 SELECT IMAGE_BLOB   FROM PAGE_IMAGE  WHERE (ISBN =
2000-09-20 15 begin pageimages_curs . page_get_image ( :myisbn:i
2000-09-20 15 SELECT IMAGE_BLOB   FROM PAGE_IMAGE  WHERE (ISBN =
2000-09-20 15 BEGIN sys.dbms_ijob.remove(:job); END;
2000-09-20 15 begin pageimages_curs . page_get_image ( :myisbn:i
2000-09-20 15 BEGIN sys.dbms_ijob.remove(:job); END;
```

If we are diligent, we can locate the online or batch SQL tasks that are overwhelming the server. Once we reschedule the offending tasks to run during off-peak hours, our average run queue for the server falls below the number of CPUs, as shown in Figure 6-4.

Of course, load balancing Oracle tasks is often not as trivial as it might appear. The Oracle DBA generally has no control over when members of the end-user

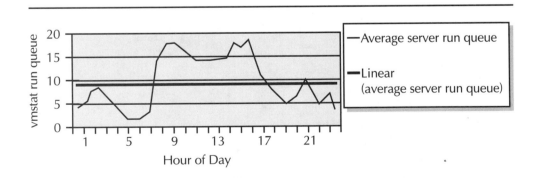

FIGURE 6-4. *Average Oracle server run queue values after task load balancing*

community submit batch-oriented work against the Oracle database. Unless you are using scheduling tools such as Oracle's Concurrent Manager, the end users are free to submit large resource-intensive reports against Oracle anytime they feel like it. In shops where end users generate ad hoc SQL statements, there are three Oracle features that can govern end-user query resources:

- The dbms_resource_manager PL/SQL package can be used to govern end-user resources. In the following example, dbms_resource_manager is called to assign CPU, SQL plan, and Parallel Query options for the ADHOC_Group of end users:

```
SQL> execute dbms_resource_manager.update_plan_directive(
           plan -> 'SINGLE_LEVEL_PLAN',
           group_or_subplan => 'ADHOC_Group',
           new_comment => 'ADHOC day users sessions at level 1',
           new_cpu_p1 => 10,
           new_parallel_degree_limit_p1 => 0);
```

- Oracle Applications systems have a profile feature to restrict ad hoc queries. For ad hoc users, their Oracle user ID is associated with a group, and the group is linked to a profile that governs the amount of server resources the end users are allowed to use.

- SQL*Plus profiles are for end users who execute queries from SQL*Plus. The product_user_profile table can be used to restrict access.

Hence, it is up to the Oracle professional to become a detective, and hunt through the library cache in order to see when high-resource statements are being added to the Oracle system. We will discuss the techniques for hunting for SQL in the library cache in Chapter 11.

The stats$sql_summary table is one STATSPACK table that has a great deal of information to help you find offending SQL statements. SQL statements within the stats$sql_summary table can be sorted according to a number of resource utilization metrics, including rows processed, buffer gets, disk reads, and executions.

In Chapter 11, we will also introduce a revolutionary script called *access.sql* that will allow you to automatically fish SQL from the library cache and produce meaningful reports showing the activity of all of the SQL statements in your system.

Even though Oracle developers write most SQL, it is still the duty of the Oracle DBA to monitor the behavior of the SQL within the system in order to determine those SQL statements that are creating excessive load upon the server processor. The Oracle DBA must also load balance those intensive SQL statements by requiring the end users to submit them during less active times.

This next section will discuss a very short-term technique that can be used in order to remedy sporadic CPU overload at times when an upgrade to the CPUs or load balancing is not possible. Using nice to change the dispatching priorities of Oracle tasks is a last-resort measure, and should only be undertaken in extreme circumstances when it is critical to keep the system running until more resources are available.

Using nice and priocntl to Change Execution Priority

While CPU shortages generally require the addition of more processors on the server, there are some short-term things that you can do to keep running until the new processors arrive. Within the server, all tasks are queued to the CPUs according to their dispatching priority, and the dispatching priority is commonly referred to as the nice value for the task. Those tasks with a low nice value are scheduled ahead of other tasks in the CPU queue, while those tasks with a high nice value are serviced later (see Figure 6-5).

In emergency situations where you cannot immediately get more CPUs, you can assign a very low dispatching priority to the Oracle background process, causing them to get CPU cycles ahead of other tasks on the server. This will ensure that Oracle gets all of the CPU that it requires, but it will slow down any external tasks that are accessing the Oracle database. To do this, the systems administrator

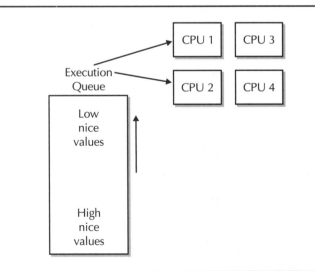

FIGURE 6-5. *Task list and dispatching priorities*

can alter the CPU dispatching priority of tasks with the UNIX **nice** or **priocntl** commands. The UNIX **nice** command is used to change dispatching priorities, but these numeric ranges vary by operating system. In general, the lower the nice value, the higher the priority.

Displaying the nice Values

In UNIX, you can use the **ps –elf** command to see each task and its dispatching priority. In the following example, the NI column shows the existing dispatching priority for the task. Note that there are special nice values—SY (system) and RT (real time)—and these have the highest dispatching priority.

```
>ps -elf|more
 F S     UID  PID  PPID  C  PRI  NI  ...  SZ  ...  STIME TTY   TIME CMD
19 T    root    0     0  0    0  SY  ...   0  ...  Dec 21 ?   0:00 sched
 8 S     oot    1     0  0   41  20  ...  98  ...  Dec 21 ?   0:00 /etc/init -
19 S    root    2     0  0    0  SY  ...   0  ...  Dec 21 ?   0:00 pageout
19 S    root    3     0  1    0  SY  ...   0  ...  Dec 21 ?  22:13 fsflush
 8 S    root  182     1  0   41  20  ... 217  ...  Dec 21 ?   0:00 /usr/lib/saf/sac -t 3
 8 S  qmaill  173   161  0   41  20  ... 207  ...  Dec 21 ?   0:00 splogger qmail
 8 S    root   45     1  0   48  20  ... 159  ...  Dec 21 ?   0:00 /usr/lib/devfseventd
 8 S    root   47     1  0   49  20  ... 284  ...  Dec 21 ?   0:00 /usr/lib/devfsadmd
 0 C    root  139     1  0   46  20  ... 425  ...  Dec 21 ?   0:00 /usr/sbin/syslogd
 8 S    root  126     1  0   77  20  ... 247  ...  Dec 21 ?   0:00 /usr/sbin/inetd -s
 8 S    root 1600     1  0    0  RT  ... 268  ...  Dec 22 ?   0:00 /usr/lib/inet/xntpd
```

Changing nice Values

Again, we need to note that there are huge dialect differences when using the **nice** command. In Linux, you can use **nice** to change the dispatching priority, but in Solaris you must use the **priocntl** command. You must have root authority to change the dispatching priority, and you will need to consult with your systems administrator before changing CPU dispatching priorities.

Now that we have an understanding of the processors on an Oracle database server, let's turn our attention to monitoring the RAM memory consumption on our Oracle server.

Monitoring Server Memory Consumption

In the UNIX environment, RAM memory is automatically managed by the operating system. In systems with "virtual" memory, a special disk called *swap* is used to hold chunks of RAM that cannot fit within the available RAM on the server. In this fashion, a virtual memory server can allow tasks to allocate memory above the RAM capacity on the server. As the server is used, the operating system will move some memory pages out to the swap disk in case the server exceeds its physical capacity. This is called a page-out operation. Page-out operations occur even when the database server has not exceeded the RAM capacity.

RAM memory shortages are evidenced by page-in operations. Page-in operations cause Oracle slowdowns because tasks must wait until their memory region is moved back into RAM from the swap disk (see Figure 6-6). The remedy for memory overload is to add more memory or to reduce the demands on memory by reducing *sort_area_size*, implementing the multithreaded server, or reducing the values for *shared_pool* or *db_block_buffers*.

Let's begin by looking at how memory is configured for a database server and explore how to manage memory on a large server.

Server Memory Settings

The first step when tuning server memory is to review the kernel settings that relate to available memory. The kernel settings for memory usage (i.e., *SHMMAX, SHMMNI, db_max_pct*) are critical to effective Oracle performance, and you should double-check all of your kernel parameters to ensure that the server memory is properly configured.

We also must verify the configuration of the swap disk. As you may know, the swap disk is a special system disk that is reserved to accept memory frames that are paged-out from physical RAM. Most servers recommend that the size of the swap disk be set to double the amount of physical RAM.

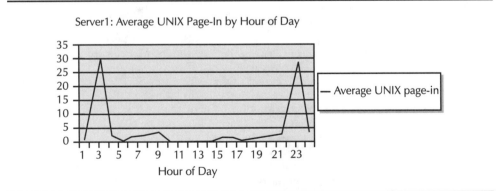

FIGURE 6-6. *Periodic RAM memory overload on a database server*

Very Large Memory and Oracle

It is important to note that some servers are not capable of addressing "high memory." The high-memory boundary is a physical constraint that is determined by the bit-size of the application, and the only way to utilize above-the-line memory is to use special OS techniques. For example, in all 32-bit versions of Oracle, all memory over 1.7 gigabytes cannot be addressed regardless of the amount of RAM on the server. This can cause a very perplexing problem, since the database server will experience page-in operations, while top and glance utilities report that there is excess memory on the server. In short, the sum of all SGA memory for all of the Oracle instances on the server cannot exceed 1.7 gigabytes. For some UNIX environments such as Solaris, there are special patches that can be applied on a 32-bit server to allow the DBA to create SGA regions in excess of 2 gigabytes.

If you cannot upgrade to 64-bit Oracle and you want to address memory above the line, operating system techniques can be used. For example, in HP/UX, special patches can be applied to allow Oracle regions to run above 1.7 gigabytes. HP calls this technique "memory windows," and it uses a SHARED_MAGIC executable to route application to above-the-line memory regions.

Bear in mind that all 32-bit applications are required to run in low memory. For example, Oracle applications are currently 32-bit and will not be able to address high memory, above the 1.7 gigabyte limit. Fortunately, all versions of 64-bit Oracle are capable of addressing high memory. However, you must ensure that your Oracle Database and any other applications are capable of addressing all of the available memory. For example, next we see a clear case of RAM overload, even though the CPU appears to be 99-percent idle:

TO_CHAR(START_DA	RUNQUE_WAITS	PAGE_IN	SYSTEM_CPU	USER_CPU	IDLE_CPU
06/02/2000 05:01	2	85	1	0	99
06/02/2000 13:47	2	193	0	0	99
06/03/2000 05:04	0	114	2	3	95
06/03/2000 22:31	1	216	0	1	99
06/04/2000 05:02	0	146	1	1	99
06/04/2000 22:34	1	71	1	8	90
06/05/2000 06:57	1	213	0	0	99
06/05/2000 07:25	1	113	0	0	99
06/05/2000 07:35	1	72	0	0	99
06/05/2000 11:06	1	238	0	1	99

Making Oracle Memory Nonswappable

Just like with CPU shortages, the best remedy to a RAM problem is to add additional RAM to the server. However, there are some short-term techniques that can be used to prevent the Oracle SGA memory from paging. On some operating systems, it is possible to use a memory-fencing technique to ensure that the Oracle SGA is never paged-out to the swap disk.

Memory fencing with the *lock_sga* Initialization Parameter

The *lock_sga init.ora* parameter will lock the entire SGA into physical RAM memory, making it ineligible for swapping. The *lock_sga* parameter does not work for Windows NT or AIX, and the setting for *lock_sga* will be ignored. For AIX 4.3.3 and above, you can set the SHM_PIN parameter to keep the SGA in RAM, and you can get details about this from your AIX documentation.

Solaris Memory Fencing

In Sun Solaris, you can set the *use_ism* parameter to invoke intimate shared memory for the Oracle SGA. In releases of Oracle prior to Oracle8i you can set the *init.ora* parameter *use_ism=true*. The *use_ism init.ora* parameter was obsoleted in 8.1.3, and in Oracle8i *use_ism* becomes a hidden parameter that defaults to True. Memory page locking is implemented in Solaris by setting some bits in the memory page's page structure. The page-out, which runs if free memory gets low, checks the status of the page's lock fields. If the field is nonzero, the page is considered locked in memory and thus not marked as a candidate for freeing.

CAUTION
There is a bug associated with use_ism *on some versions of Solaris. For details, see MetaLink for Note:1057644.6, Note:69863.1, Note:1055268.6, Doc ID 77604.1, Note:48764.1, and Note:1054590.6. You can access MetaLink at: http://metalink.oracle.com/home.html.*

Reporting on Server Statistics

Once the data is captured in the stats$vmstat table, there is a wealth of reports that can be generated. Because all of the server statistics exist inside a single Oracle table, it is quite easy to write SQL*Plus queries to extract the data.

The vmstat data can be used to generate all types of interesting reports. There are four classes of vmstat reports:

- **Exception reports**   These reports show the time period where predefined thresholds are exceeded.

- **Daily trend reports**   These reports are often run and used with Excel spreadsheets to produce trending graphs.

- **Hourly trend reports**   These reports show the average utilization, averaged by the hour of the day. These reports are very useful for showing peak usage periods in a production environment.

- **Long-term predictive reports**   These reports generate a long-term trend line for performance. The data from these reports is often used with a linear regression to predict when additional RAM memory or CPU power is required for the server. We will cover this report in Chapter 16.

Let's now examine the script that can be used to generate these server reports and see how this information can help us tune our Oracle database.

Server Exception Reports

The SQL script *vmstat_alert.sql* can quickly give a complete exception report on all of the servers in our Oracle environment. This report will display times when the CPU and RAM memory exceed your predefined thresholds:

```
set lines 80;
set pages 999;
set feedback off;
set verify off;

column my_date heading 'date       hour' format a20
column c2       heading runq   format 999
column c3       heading pg_in   format 999
column c4       heading pg_ot   format 999
column c5       heading usr     format 999
column c6       heading sys     format 999
column c7       heading idl     format 999
column c8       heading wt      format 999


ttitle 'run queue > 2|May indicate an overloaded CPU|When runqueue exceeds
the number of CPUs| on the server, tasks are waiting for service.';


select
 server_name,
 to_char(start_date,'YY/MM/DD    HH24') my_date,
 avg(runque_waits)       c2,
 avg(page_in)            c3,
 avg(page_out)           c4,
 avg(user_cpu)           c5,
 avg(system_cpu)         c6,
 avg(idle_cpu)           c7
from
perfstat.stats$vmstat
WHERE
```

```
runque_waits > 2
and start_date > sysdate-&&1
group by
 server_name,
 to_char(start_date,'YY/MM/DD    HH24')
ORDER BY
 server_name,
 to_char(start_date,'YY/MM/DD    HH24')
;

ttitle 'page_in > 1|May indicate overloaded memory|Whenever Unix performs
a page-in, the RAM memory | on the server has been exhausted and swap pages
are being used.';


select
 server_name,
 to_char(start_date,'YY/MM/DD    HH24') my_date,
 avg(runque_waits)      c2,
 avg(page_in)           c3,
 avg(page_out)          c4,
 avg(user_cpu)          c5,
 avg(system_cpu)        c6,
 avg(idle_cpu)          c7
from
perfstat.stats$vmstat
WHERE
page_in > 1
and start_date > sysdate-&&1
group by
 server_name,
 to_char(start_date,'YY/MM/DD    HH24')
ORDER BY
 server_name,
 to_char(start_date,'YY/MM/DD    HH24')
;

ttitle 'user+system CPU > 70%|Indicates periods with a fully-loaded CPU
subsssystem.|Periods of 100% utilization are only a | concern when runqueue
values exceeds the number of CPs on the server.';


select
 server_name,
 to_char(start_date,'YY/MM/DD    HH24') my_date,
 avg(runque_waits)      c2,
 avg(page_in)           c3,
 avg(page_out)          c4,
 avg(user_cpu)          c5,
 avg(system_cpu)        c6,
 avg(idle_cpu)          c7
```

```
from
perfstat.stats$vmstat
WHERE
(user_cpu + system_cpu) > 70
and start_date > sysdate-&&1
group by
 server_name,
 to_char(start_date,'YY/MM/DD    HH24')
ORDER BY
 server_name,
 to_char(start_date,'YY/MM/DD    HH24')
;
```

The standard vmstat alert report is used to alert the Oracle DBA and systems administrator to out-of-bounds conditions on each Oracle server. These conditions include:

- **CPU waits > 40% (AIX version only)** This may indicate I/O-based contention. The solution is to spread files across more disks or add buffer memory.

- **Run queue > xxx – (where xxx is the number of CPUs on the server, 2 in this example)** This indicates an overloaded CPU. The solution is to add additional processors to the server.

- **Page_in > 2** Page-in operations indicate overloaded memory. The solution is to reduce the size of the Oracle SGA, PGA, or add additional RAM memory to the server.

- **User CPU + System CPU > 90%** This indicates periods where the CPU is highly utilized.

While the SQL here is self-explanatory, let's look at a sample report and see how it will help our systems administrator monitor the server's behavior:

```
SQL> @vmstat_alert 7

Wed Dec 20                                                    page    1
                          run queue > 2
                   May indicate an overloaded CPU.
             When runqueue exceeds the number of CPUs
             on the server, tasks are waiting for service.


SERVER_NAME     date        hour      runq pg_in pg_ot  usr  sys  idl
--------------  ----------  --------- ---- ----- ----- ---- ---- ----
AD-01           00/12/13    17           3     0     0   87    5    8
```

```
Wed Dec 20                                                    page    1
                            page_in > 1
                   May indicate overloaded memory.
             Whenever Unix performs a page-in, the RAM memory
       on the server has been exhausted and swap pages are being used.


SERVER_NAME            date        hour      runq pg_in pg_ot  usr  sys  idl
-------------------    ----------  --------  ---- ----- ----- ---- ---- ----
AD-01                  00/12/13    16           0     5     0    1    1   98
AD-01                  00/12/14    09           0     5     0   10    2   88
AD-01                  00/12/15    16           0     6     0    0    0  100
AD-01                  00/12/19    20           0    29     2    1    2   98
PROD1DB                00/12/13    14           0     3    43    4    4   93
PROD1DB                00/12/19    07           0     2     0    1    3   96
PROD1DB                00/12/19    11           0     3     0    1    3   96
PROD1DB                00/12/19    12           0     6     0    1    3   96
PROD1DB                00/12/19    16           0     3     0    1    3   96
PROD1DB                00/12/19    17           0    47    68    5    5   91


Wed Dec 20                                                    page    1
                         user+system > 70%
            Indicates periods with a fully-loaded CPU sub-system.
                 Periods of 100% utilization are only a
        concern when runqueue values exceeds the number of CPUs on the server.


SERVER_NAME            date        hour      runq pg_in pg_ot  usr  sys  idl
-------------------    ----------  --------  ---- ----- ----- ---- ---- ----
AD-01                  00/12/13    14           0     0     2   75    2   22
AD-01                  00/12/13    17           3     0     0   87    5    8
AD-01                  00/12/15    15           0     0     0   50   29   22
AD-01                  00/12/15    16           0     0     0   48   33   20
AD-01                  00/12/19    07           0     0     0   77    4   19
AD-01                  00/12/19    10           0     0     0   70    5   24
AD-01                  00/12/19    11           1     0     0   60   17   24
PROD1                  00/12/19    12           0     0     1   52   30   18
PROD1                  00/12/19    13           0     0     0   39   59    2
PROD1                  00/12/19    14           0     0     0   39   55    6
PROD1                  00/12/19    15           1     0     0   57   23   20
```

You may notice that this exception report gives the hourly average for the vmstat information. If you look at the *get_vmstat.ksh* script, you will see that the data is captured in intervals of every 300 elapsed seconds (5-minute intervals). Hence, if you see an hour where your server is undergoing stress, you can modify your script to show the vmstat changes every five minutes. You can also run this report in conjunction with other STATSPACK reports to identify what tasks may have precipitated the server problem. The stats$sql_summary table is especially useful for this purpose.

Daily vmstat Trend Reports

One of the jobs of the Oracle tuning expert is to monitor the database and the server for regular trends. This is not just an exercise in searching for trends because every database will exhibit regular patterns of CPU and memory consumption.

Using the stats$vmstat table, it is very easy to write a query that will aggregate the CPU and memory. Here is a sample SQL script that aggregates server values:

```
connect perfstat/perfstat;
set pages 9999;

set feedback off;
set verify off;

column my_date heading 'date' format a20
column c2        heading runq   format 999
column c3        heading pg_in   format 999
column c4        heading pg_ot   format 999
column c5        heading usr     format 999
column c6        heading sys     format 999
column c7        heading idl     format 999
column c8        heading wt      format 999


select
 to_char(start_date,'day')  my_date,
--  avg(runque_waits)         c2
--  avg(page_in)              c3,
--  avg(page_out)             c4,
avg(user_cpu + system_cpu)                c5,
--  avg(system_cpu)           c6,
--  avg(idle_cpu)             c7,
avg(wait_cpu)              c8
from
   stats$vmstat
```

```
group  BY
 to_char(start_date,'day')
order by
 to_char(start_date,'day')
;
```

Here we can see that we can easily get any of the vmstat values aggregated by day. In the output here we see the average user and wait CPU times for each day of the week:

```
SQL> @rpt_vmstat_dy
Connected.

date                    usr   wt
------------------- ---- ----
friday                    8    0
monday                   10    0
saturday                  1    0
sunday                    1    0
thursday                  6    0
tuesday                  15    0
wednesday                11    0
```

This data can be extracted into MS-Excel and quickly plotted for graphical reference, as shown in Figure 6-7. We will cover the method of plotting STATSPACK data in MS-Excel in Chapter 15.

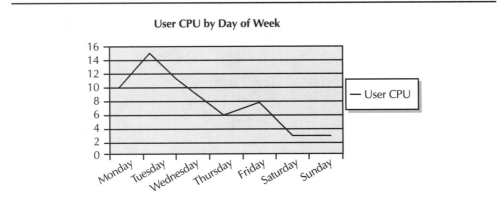

FIGURE 6-7. *A daily report of vmstat metrics*

Hourly vmstat Trend Reports

We can use the same techniques to average vmstat information by the hour of the day. An average by hour of the day can provide very valuable information regarding times when the server is experiencing stress:

```
connect perfstat/perfstat;
set pages 9999;

set feedback off;
set verify off;

column my_date heading 'date'  format a20
column c2        heading runq   format 999
column c3        heading pg_in  format 999
column c4        heading pg_ot  format 999
column c5        heading cpu    format 999
column c6        heading sys    format 999
column c7        heading idl    format 999
column c8        heading wt     format 999


select
  to_char(start_date,'day') my_date,
-- avg(runque_waits)         c2
-- avg(page_in)              c3,
-- avg(page_out)             c4,
avg(user_cpu + system_cpu)            c5,
-- avg(system_cpu)           c6,
-- avg(idle_cpu)             c7,
avg(wait_cpu)          c8
from
   stats$vmstat
group  BY
 to_char(start_date,'day')
order by
 to_char(start_date,'day')
;
```

Here we see the output from this script and we get the average run queue and user + system CPU values and wait CPU values, aggregated by hour of the day:

```
SQL> @rpt_vmstat_hr
Connected.
```

```
date                   runq  cpu   wt
------------------     ----  ----  ----
00                       0    4     0
01                       0    5     0
02                       0    3     0
03                       0    1     0
04                       0    1     0
05                       0    1     0
06                       0    1     0
07                       0    1     0
08                       0    1     0
09                       0    1     0
10                       0    1     0
11                       0    1     0
12                       0    11    0
13                       0    21    0
14                       0    23    0
15                       0    20    0
16                       0    15    0
17                       0    20    0
18                       0    12    0
19                       0    10    0
20                       0    5     0
21                       0    1     0
22                       0    1     0
23                       0    1     0
```

This hourly information can also be extracted into MS-Excel for graphical plotting charts that show trends that may not be evident from a raw observation.

Long-Term Server Analysis and Trending

You can also use the data from stats$vmstat to gather information for long-term trend analysis, as shown in Figure 6-8. The nature of the vmstat tables allows the DBA to extract an ongoing average and then chart the data in MS-Excel. This Excel chart can also be enhanced to add a linear regression that can be used to predict future usage.

This long-term trend analysis is very useful for IT managers who must plan for additional server resources. For these managers, knowing the rate at which CPU and memory are being consumed on the server is critical, since there is often a lag time of several weeks between ordering and installing new hardware resources. We will go into more detail on using STATSPACK information for management planning in Chapter 15.

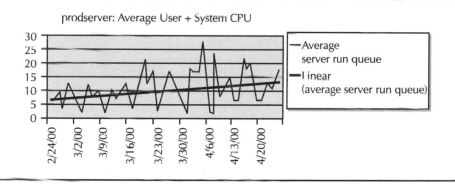

FIGURE 6-8. *A long-term hardware resource predictive report*

Conclusion

Now that we have an understanding of the methods for extending STATSPACK to monitor our database server, we are ready to look at the Oracle network environment. Distributed Oracle databases have become commonplace, and the time required to transfer information over the network can have a huge impact on the overall performance of the Oracle database application.

CHAPTER
7

Tuning the
Network Environment

common misconception about Net8 is that you can tune Oracle network parameters to realize performance gains across a network. With a few minor exceptions, all network traffic is outside the scope of Oracle and cannot be tuned from within the Oracle environment. Net8 is simply a layer in the OSI model and it resides above the network-specific protocol stack. In other words, virtually all network tuning is external to the Oracle environment. When a remote data request is initialed, Net8 will get the data for the packet and hand it over to the protocol stack for transmission. The protocol stack will then create a packet with this data and send it over the network. Because Net8 simply passes data to the protocol stack, there is very little Net8 can do to improve performance.

However, the DBA can control the size and frequency of the network packets. The Oracle DBA has a wealth of tools that can change the packet size and frequency that packets are sent over the network. For a simple example, the refresh interval for a snapshot can be changed to ship larger amounts over the network at a less frequent interval.

To understand how the Oracle DBA can configure Oracle for better network performance, we must first start with a brief overview of a distributed Oracle database. We will then explore the internals of Oracle transparent network substrate (TNS), and then look at the tools that network administrators use to tune network traffic.

This chapter has the following sections that address network tuning issues:

- Optimizing Oracle Net8 configuration

- Other Oracle features that affect network performance

- Monitoring network performance using STATSPACK

- Tuning the distributed network

In each of these sections we will discuss the tuning options that are available to help the DBA manage and tune distributed Oracle communications. Let's begin by looking at the configuration parameters that affect network performance.

Optimizing Oracle Net8 Configuration

There are several tuning parameters that will affect the performance of Net8 connections between servers. However, we must always remember that the tuning of the network is outside the scope of Oracle, and the services of a qualified network administrator should be used for tuning the network. The following parameter files contain settings that affect the size and frequency of packet shipping across the network:

- *sqlnet.ora* server file
  - *automatic_ipc*
- *sqlnet.ora* client file
  - *break_poll_skip*
- *tnsnames.ora* file
  - *SDU, TDU*
- *listener.ora* file
  - *SDU, TDU*
- *protocol.ora* file
  - *tcp.nodelay*

Remember, these are the only tuning parameters that will affect the performance of the Oracle Net8 layer. Let's discuss those parameters and see how they can be adjusted to improve Net8 throughput.

The tcp.nodelay Parameter in protocol.ora

By default, Net8 waits before transmitting a request until the buffer is filled up. This can mean on some occasions that a request is not sent immediately to its destination. Most often, this behavior occurs when large amounts of data are streamed from one end to another, and Net8 waits until the buffer is full before transmitting the packet. To remedy this problem, you can add a *protocol.ora* file and specify *tcp.nodelay* to stop delays in the buffer flushing process.

For all TCP/IP implementations, the *protocol.ora* file can be specified to indicate no data buffering. This parameter can be used on both the client and the server. The statement in *protocol.ora* is:

```
tcp.nodelay = yes
```

By specifying this parameter, TCP buffering is skipped and every request is sent immediately. In some cases, setting this parameter can cause network slowdowns. The network traffic can increase due to the smaller (and more frequent) network packets being transmitted between the client and the server.

Oracle recommends that *tcp.nodelay* should only be used if TCP timeouts are encountered. However, in conditions of high-volume traffic between database servers, setting *tcp.nodelay* can have a huge improvement in performance.

The automatic_ipc Parameter of sqlnet.ora

The *automatic_ipc* parameter speeds local connections to a database because it bypasses the network layer. If *automatic_ipc*=on, Net8 will first check to see if a local database with the same alias definition exists. If so, the connection will be translated to a local IPC connection and will therefore bypass the network layers. This is, of course, only useful on database servers, and is a completely useless feature on Net8 clients.

On the database server, the *automatic_ipc* parameter should only be used in cases where a Net8 connection must be made to the local database. If no local database connections are needed or required, put this parameter to off, and all Net8 clients should have this setting to improve performance.

SDU and TDU Parameters in tnsnames.ora

The *SDU* and *TDU* parameters are placed in the *tnsnames.ora* and *listener.ora* files. *SDU* is the session data unit, and specifies the size of the packets to send over the network. Ideally, this size should not surpass the size of the *MTU* (maximum transmission unit). This *MTU* value is fixed and depends on the actual network implementation used. Oracle recommends that *SDU* should be set to *MTU*.

NOTE
Prior to release 7.3.3, both SDU *and* TDU *were fixed at 2K and couldn't be changed.*

The *TDU* (transport data unit) is the default packet size used within Net8 to group data together. Ideally, the *TDU* parameter should be a multiple of the *SDU* parameter. The default values for *SDU* and *TDU* are 2,048, and the maximum value is 32,767 bytes.

The following guidelines apply for *SDU* and *TDU:*

- On fast network connections (T1 or T3 lines), you should set *SDU* and *TDU* equal to the *MTU* for your network. On standard Ethernet networks, the default *MTU* size is set to 1,514 bytes. On standard token ring networks, the default *MTU* size is 4,202.

- The *SDU* should never be set greater than *TDU* because you will waste network resources by shipping wasted space in each packet.

- If your users are connecting via modem lines, you may want to set *SDU* and *TDU* to smaller values because of the frequent resends that occur over modem lines.

- If the Multi-Threaded Server (MTS) is used, you must also set the *mts_dispatchers* with the proper *MTU TDU* configuration.

Here is an example of these parameters on a token ring network with an *MTU* of 4,202:

listener.ora

```
SID_LIST_LISTENER =
  (SID_LIST =
    (SID_DESC =
      (SDU = 4202)
      (TDU = 4202)
      (SID_NAME = ORCL)
      (GLOBAL_DBNAME = ORCL.WORLD)
    )
  )
```

tnsnames.ora

```
ORCL.WORLD =
  (DESCRIPTION =
    (SDU=4202)
    (TDU=4202)
    (ADDRESS =
      (PROTOCOL = TCP)
      (HOST = fu.bar)
      (PORT = 1521)
    )
    (CONNECT_DATA = (SID = ORCL))
  )
```

Again, we must remember that the *SDU* and *TDU* settings are a direct function of the connection speed between the hosts. If you have a fast T1 line, set *SDU=TDU=MTU*. For slower modem lines, you need to experiment with smaller values of *SDU* and *TDU*.

If you are using Oracle8i, the database will automatically register instances in the *listener.ora* file unless you take one of the following actions:

- Implement the Multi-Threaded Server (MTS) and define the *mts_dispatchers* in your *init.ora* file:

```
MTS_DISPATCHERS="(DESCRIPTION=(SDU=8192)(TDU=8192)\
ADDRESS=(PARTIAL=TRUE)(PROTOCOL=TCP)(HOST=supsund3)))\

                  (DISPATCHERS=1)"
```

- Use *service_name=global_dbname* in the Connect_Data section of the *tnsnames.ora* file, where *global_dbname* is configured in *listener.ora*. Note that this setting will disable the use of Transparent Application Failover (TAF), which is not supported using *global_dbname*. For details, see "Configuring Transparent Application Failover" in the Net8 Administrator's Guide.

- Do not use automatic service registration. To do this, you must set the *init.ora* parameter *local_listener* to use a different TCP port than the one defined in your *listener.ora* file.

Next, let's look at the *queuesize* parameter and see how it affects network performance.

The queuesize Parameter in listener.ora

The undocumented *queuesize* parameter determines the number of requests the listener can store while Oracle is working to establish a connection. This parameter is only used for very high-volume databases, where the listener is spawning thousands of connections per hour. The size of the *queuesize* parameter should be equal to the number of expected simultaneous connections. Here is an example of this parameter in the *listener.ora* file:

```
LISTENER =
  (ADDRESS_LIST =
       (ADDRESS =
          (PROTOCOL = TCP)
          (HOST = marvin)
          (PORT = 1521)
          (QUEUESIZE = 32)
        )
    )
```

The disadvantage of this parameter is that it uses more memory and resources because it is preallocating resources for anticipated connect requests. If you have high-volume connections into a dedicated listener, you may want to implement the Multi-Threaded Server (MTS), and use prespawned Oracle connections. Also, note that there are some restrictions of the MTS queue size, and some versions of UNIX do not allow queues greater than five.

The break_poll_skip Parameter of sqlnet.ora

This value specifies the number of packets to skip before checking for a user break. This is a client-only *sqlnet.ora* parameter and affects the amount of CPU consumed on the Net8 client.

The general rules for *break_poll_skip* are as follows:

- The higher the *break_poll_skip* value, the less frequent CTRL-C checking, and the less CPU overhead used.

- The lower the *break_poll_skip* value, the more frequent CTRL-C checking, and the more CPU overhead used.

The default value for *break_poll_skip* is 4. Remember, this parameter is only useful on a Net8 client *sqlnet.ora* file, and only functions on servers that support in-band breaks.

The disable_oob Parameter of sqlnet.ora

Out-of-band break checks can be disabled by adding this parameter to the *sqlnet.ora* file. If for some specific reason the checks should not be performed, set this parameter to ON. By default, Net8 assumes OFF for this parameter and will perform out-of-band checks.

When *disable_oob*=on, Oracle's use of urgent data messages is disabled. The negative impact of using this parameter is the usage of the interrupt key. When you use *disable_oob*, you lose the break functionality of the interrupt key such as CTRL-C. A break is a function in Net8 that allows a user of an application to interrupt or stop a transaction before it is complete, returning both the client and the server to a state from which they can continue.

The epc_disabled Environment Variable

Starting in Oracle 7.3.2, the Oracle Server Tracing (otrace) is enabled by default. A practical implication of this is that every connection and every request sent over Net8 is logged in the Oracle trace files *process.dat* and *regid.dat*. After long-term use of the database, these trace files can become enormous, slowing down the connection time dramatically.

The solution is to implement a crontab job to periodically remove the trace files, or to disable the otrace facility. It is highly recommended that the DBA disable the otrace facility unless they require it for session tracing. Here are the steps:

1. Shut down the databases and listeners.

2. Remove the **.dat* files from your $ORACLE_HOME/otrace/admin directory.

3. Re-create the *dat* files with the UNIX **touch** command.

4. Specify '*epc_disabled*=TRUE' in the runtime environment of the UNIX Oracle *.profile, .login*, or *.cshrc* login file. This will disable the otrace facility.

5. Modify the *listener.ora* file to specify *epc_disabled*=TRUE in the *sid_desc* for each database.

6. Restart the database and listeners.

7. Run the **otrccref** command from $ORACLE_HOME/bin.

Other Oracle Features that Affect Network Behavior

Now that we have covered the basic Oracle parameters that govern network traffic, let's look at some techniques that are used within the Oracle environment that can be used to manage network activity. In general, there are several options:

■ Using array fetches

■ Using the Multi-Threaded Server (MTS)

■ Using connection pooling

■ Using ODBC

■ Using Oracle replication

Using Array Fetches to Improve Network Throughput

In databases that are using PL/SQL stored procedures and functions or a language such as C that supports array fetches, you can reduce Oracle network calls by using bulk array fetches. For example, instead of fetching one row at a time from a cursor, it is more efficient to fetch 10 rows with a single network round trip.

Many Oracle tools such as SQL*Plus, SQL*Forms and the language precompilers allow for the use of the *arraysize* parameter. The *arraysize* parameter allows multiple rows to be returned in a single databases access. This has the effect on the network of making fewer TCP/IP packets, each with more data inside each packet. This technique can often greatly aid the performance of long-running client/server tasks.

Oracle8i also offers enhanced bulk fetching through the Oracle Call Interface (OCI). The programming aspects of array fetching are beyond the scope of this text, but you can get more information on array fetch techniques in the Oracle-supplied documentation and on Oracle's MetaLink Web site.

Using the Multi-Threaded Server

When your database server experiences a large volume of incoming connections, the overhead of spawning a dedicated process to service each request can cause measurable overhead on the server. This is because the default listener process "bequeaths" the incoming connection, creating a process (PID) on the Oracle server and directing this process to establish the connection to Oracle.

To reduce this overhead, the MTS can be implemented to allow new connections to attach to prespawned shadow processes. Note that Oracle does not recommend using the MTS unless you average more than 300 connections on the server.

The basic premise of the MTS is that Oracle creates dispatcher processes, each with a set of preestablished connections into the Oracle database. Each dispatcher owns a set of prespawned connections into the database. By preestablishing the connections to Oracle, server resources are minimized, and RAM storage is also minimized because each session will not allocate a personal *sort_area_size* in the Program Global Area (PGA). Instead, all dispatchers share the same User Global Area (UGA), thereby reducing memory demands on the database server.

One of the problems with the dedicated listener is that each incoming transaction is spawned by the listener as a separate operating system task. With the MTS, all communications to a database are handled through a single dispatcher instead of separate UNIX process IDs (PIDs) on each database. If you have constant connection loads of 300 users or more, using the MTS translates into faster performance for most online tasks. The only real downside to using the MTS is that the DBA cannot directly observe Oracle connections using the UNIX **ps-cf | grep oracle** command.

However, be aware that the MTS is not a panacea, especially at times when you want to invoke a dedicated process for your program. For Pro*C programs and I/O-intensive SQL*Forms applications, or any batch processes that have little idle time, you may derive better performance using a dedicated listener process. For shops that segregate tasks into online and batch modes, the DBA sometimes creates separate listeners—one with the MTS and another for dedicated connections.

In general, the MTS offers benefits such as reduced memory use, fewer processes per user, and automatic load balancing. However, the DBA must be careful to set the proper number of dispatcher processes, and the proper number of servers within each dispatcher. Also, because the MTS uses the *shared_pool* for process sorting, the DBA will also see increased demands on the *shared_pool*.

Connections using the MTS will place the UGA inside the Oracle SGA. To hold the UGA storage for MTS connections, Oracle has provided the *large_pool init.ora* parameter. The LARGE pool is an area of the SGA similar to the SHARED pool, but with restrictions on its usage such that only certain types and sizes of memory can be allocated in this pool. When using the MTS, Oracle recommends that the *large_pool* be set to a value greater than the default of 614,000 bytes.

Inside Oracle, the v$queue and v$dispatcher system views will indicate if the number of MTS dispatchers is too low. Even though the number of dispatchers is specified in the *init.ora* file, you can change it online in SQL*DBA with the **ALTER SYSTEM** command:

```
SVRMGRL> ALTER SYSTEM SET MTS_DISPATCHERS = 'TCPIP,4';
```

If you encounter problems with the MTS, you can quickly regress to dedicated servers by issuing an **ALTER SYSTEM** command. The following command turns off the MTS by setting the number of MTS servers to zero:

```
SVRMGRL> ALTER SYSTEM SET MTS_SERVERS=0;
```

The DBA must be careful when bouncing the database and listener. In some cases, the instance must be bounced if the listener is stopped, or it will restart in dedicated mode. Whenever an instance is to be bounced, stop the listener, shut down the instance, restart the listener, and start up the instance. The listener reads the MTS parameters only if it is running before startup of the instance. Therefore, bouncing the listener can disable the MTS. To implement the MTS, you need to add the following *init.ora* parameters:

```
# ---------------------
# Multi-threaded Server parameters
# ---------------------
local_listener="(address_list=

    (address=(protocol=tcp)(host=sting.janet.com)(port=1521))

    )"
MTS_MAX_DISPATCHERS=5
MTS_MAX_SERVERS=20
MTS_DISPATCHERS="(ADDRESS=

    (PROTOCOL=tcp)(HOST=sting.janet.com))(DISPATCHERS=3)

    "
service_names=testb1
```

Now that we see how the MTS can relieve stress on the server, let's look at the connection pooling features of Oracle8i.

Connection Pooling and Network Performance

Connection pooling is a resource utilization feature that enables you to reduce the number of physical network connections to an MTS dispatcher. This reduction is achieved by sharing or pooling a set of connections among the client processes. Connection pooling effectively allows Oracle to maximize the number of physical network connections to the Multi-Threaded Server. Connection pooling is achieved by sharing or pooling a dispatcher's set of connections among multiple client processes (Figure 7-1).

Connection pooling reuses physical connections and makes them available for incoming clients, while still maintaining a logical session with the previous idle connection. By using a timeout mechanism to temporarily release transport connections that have been idle for a specified period, connection pooling will *suspend* a previous connection and reuse the physical connection. When the idle client has more work to do, the physical connection is reestablished with the dispatcher. When the idle client has more work to do, the physical connection is reestablished with the dispatcher.

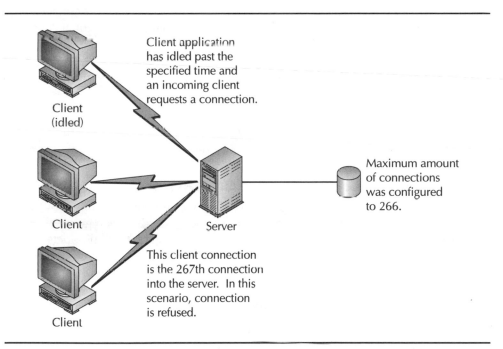

FIGURE 7-1. *Multi-Threaded Server connections*

By default, connection pooling is disabled on both incoming and outgoing network connections. To enable connection pooling, you must alter the *mts_dispatchers* parameter in the *init.ora* file. Next, we can enable the Net8 connection pooling feature by adding the POOL argument to the *mts_dispatchers* parameter:

```
MTS_DISPATCHERS = "(PROTOCOL=TCP)(DISPATCHERS=3)(POOL=3)"
```

If a number is specified, then connection pooling is enabled for both incoming and outgoing network connections and the number specified is the timeout in ticks for both incoming and outgoing network connections.

```
MTS_DISPATCHERS = "(PROTOCOL=TCP)(DISPATCHERS=3)(POOL=ON)"
```

If ON, YES, TRUE, or BOTH is specified, connection pooling is enabled for both incoming and outgoing network connections and the default timeout (set by Net8) will be used for both incoming and outgoing network connections.

```
MTS_DISPATCHERS = "(PROTOCOL=TCP)(DISPATCHERS=3)(POOL=IN)"
```

If IN is specified, connection pooling is enabled for incoming network connections and the default timeout (set by Net8) will be used for incoming network connections.

```
MTS_DISPATCHERS = "(PROTOCOL=TCP)(DISPATCHERS=3)(POOL=OUT)"
```

If OUT is specified, connection pooling is enabled for outgoing network connections and the default timeout (set by Net8) will be used for outgoing network connections.

In practice, connection pooling is rarely used except in cases where the database server is overwhelmed with incoming Net8 requests.

ODBC and Network Performance

The Open Database Connectivity (ODBC) product was initially developed by Microsoft as a generic database driver. Its architecture has now been generalized and many different vendors are offering open database connectivity products that are based on ODBC. ODBC consists of more than 50 functions that are invoked from an application using a call-level API. The ODBC API does not communicate with a database directly. Instead, it serves as a link between the application and a generic interface routine. The interface routine, in turn, communicates with the database drivers via a Service Provider Interface (SPI).

ODBC has become popular with database vendors such as Oracle, and Oracle is creating new ODBC drivers that will allow ODBC to be used as a gateway into their database products. Essentially, ODBC serves as the traffic cop for all data within the client/server system. When a client requests a service from a database,

ODBC receives the request and manages the connection to the target database. ODBC manages all of the database drivers, checking all of the status information as it arrives from the database drivers.

It is noteworthy that the database drivers should be able to handle more than just SQL. Many databases have a native API that requires ODBC to map the request into a library of functions. An example would be a SQL Server driver that maps ODBC functions to database library function calls. Databases without a native API (i.e., non-SQL databases) can also be used with ODBC, but they go through a much greater transformation than the native API calls.

Database connectivity using ODBC has a high amount of overhead in many Oracle applications. The inherent flexibility of ODBC means that the connection process to Oracle is not as efficient as a native API call to the database. Most companies that experience ODBC-related performance problems will abandon ODBC and replace it with a native communications tool such as the Oracle Call Interface (OCI). In sum, ODBC is great for ad hoc database queries from MS Windows, but it is too slow for most production applications. Now let's turn our attention to Oracle replication and see how the replication parameters can affect Oracle performance.

Tuning with Oracle Replication

Oracle replication was first introduced as a method to allow Oracle tables to reside on widely separated servers. Replication was a godsend for companies that needed to have synchronized databases across the globe. Of course, it is still far faster to process a table on a local host than it is to process a remote table across the Net8 distributed communication lines.

Several factors influence the decision about replicating Oracle tables. The foremost considerations are the size of the replicated table and the volatility of the tables, as shown in Figure 7-2. Large, highly active tables with many updates, deletes, and inserts will require a lot of system resources to replicate and keep synchronized with the master table. Smaller, less active tables would be ideal candidates for replication, since the creation and maintenance of the replicated table would not consume a high amount of system resources.

Oracle's advanced replication facility is relatively mature, and Oracle now supports multimaster replication whereby many sites can accept new rows and propagate them to the other snapshots.

From a performance perspective, we need to be concerned about how often the snapshots are refreshed. We can refresh the replicated table in full, we can re-create the snapshot at will, we can choose periodic refreshes of the snapshot, and we can use database triggers to propagate changes from a master table to the snapshot table. Although the choice of technique depends upon the individual application, some general rules apply.

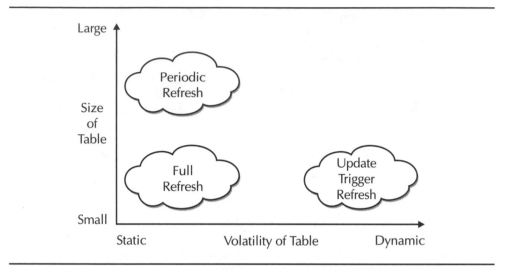

FIGURE 7-2. *The replication alternatives based on size and volatility*

Tiny Static Tables

If a replicated table is small and relatively static, it is usually easier to drop and re-create the snapshot than to use Oracle's REFRESH COMPLETE option. A crontab file can be set up to invoke the drop and re-creation at a predetermined time each day, completely refreshing the entire table.

Another popular alternative to the snapshot is using Oracle's distributed SQL to create a replicated table directly on the slave database. In the following example, the New York database creates a local table called emp_nc, which contains New York employee information from the master employee table at corporate headquarters:

```
CREATE TABLE emp_nc
AS SELECT
    emp_nbr,
    emp_name,
    emp_phone,
    emp_hire_date
FROM
    emp@hq
WHERE
    department = 'NC';
```

For highly static tables that seldom change, we can also specify refreshes to run quarterly. The example here refreshes a table completely on the first Tuesday of each quarter:

```
CREATE SNAPSHOT
    cust_snap1
REFRESH COMPLETE
    START WITH SYSDATE
    NEXT NEXT_DAY(ADD_MONTHS(trunc(sysdate,'Q'),3),'TUESDAY')
AS
SELECT
    cust_nbr, cust_name
FROM
    customer@hq
WHERE
    department = 'NC';
```

Large Dynamic Tables

Very large replicated tables will consume too much time if you drop and re-create the snapshot, or if you use the REFRESH COMPLETE option. For static tables, a snapshot log would not contain very many changes—we could direct Oracle to propagate the changes to the replicated table at frequent intervals. Let's take a look at the different refresh intervals that can be specified for a snapshot:

```
CREATE SNAPSHOT
    cust_snap1
REFRESH FAST
    START WITH SYSDATE
    NEXT SYSDATE+7
AS
SELECT
    cust_nbr, cust_name
FROM
    customer@hq
WHERE
    department = 'NC';
```

Now that we have covered the parameters and techniques that affect network performance, let's look at how we can use STATSPACK to see the network activity.

Monitoring Network Performance from Oracle STATSPACK

From STATSPACK, you can query the stats$system_event table to see the amount of time Oracle has waited for network packets. As you recall, there are several system events that can show us network activity:

```
SQL> select distinct event from stats$system_event
  2  where event like 'SQL%';

EVENT
---------------------------------------------------------------
SQL*Net break/reset to client
SQL*Net message from client
SQL*Net message from dblink
SQL*Net message to client
SQL*Net message to dblink
SQL*Net more data from client
SQL*Net more data to client
```

From this STATSPACK table, we can select all of the significant events, the number of waits, and the average wait time in seconds. Remember, most networks such as TCP/IP send an acknowledgment when a packet has been received, as shown in Figure 7-3.

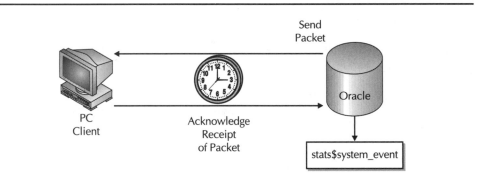

FIGURE 7-3.   *Tracking network latency by timing between send and acknowledgment*

The *rpt_event.sql* script here can be run to see all Oracle system events that
were captured in the STATSPACK stats$system_event table.

rpt_event.sql

```
set pages 999;

column mydate heading 'Yr. Mo Dy Hr'      format a13;
column event                              format a30;
column waits                              format 999,999;
column secs_waited                        format 999,999,999;
column avg_wait_secs                      format 99,999;

select
   to_char(snap_time,'yyyy-mm dd HH24')            mydate,
   e.event,
   e.total_waits - nvl(b.total_waits,0)            waits,
   ((e.time_waited - nvl(b.time_waited,0))/100) /
   nvl((e.total_waits - nvl(b.total_waits,0)),.01)  avg_wait_secs
from
   stats$system_event b,
   stats$system_event e,
   stats$snapshot      sn
where
   e.snap_id = sn.snap_id
and
   b.snap_id = e.snap_id-1
and
   b.event = e.event
and
   e.event like 'SQL*Net%'
and
   e.total_waits - b.total_waits  > 100
and
   e.time_waited - b.time_waited > 100
;
```

Here is a sample of the output from this report, showing the events and the wait
times for each event. This is a great report for showing specific times when the
network is overloaded with packet traffic.

```
Yr.   Mo Dy Hr EVENT                            WAITS AVG_WAIT_SECS
------------- ------------------------------ -------- -------------
2001-09-20 15 SQL*Net message from client       1,277             1
2001-09-20 16 SQL*Net message from client         133            64
2001-09-20 18 SQL*Net message from client         325             1
2001-09-20 19 SQL*Net message from client         410             0
2001-09-20 20 SQL*Net message from client         438            22
```

```
2001-09-20 22 SQL*Net message from client          306              8
2001-09-21 10 SQL*Net message from client          253              4
2001-09-21 12 SQL*Net message from client          208              0
2001-09-21 13 SQL*Net message from client          230              6
2001-09-21 14 SQL*Net message from client          311              6
2001-09-21 17 SQL*Net message from client          269             21
2001-09-21 18 SQL*Net message from client          222             29
2001-09-21 19 SQL*Net message from client          362             22
2001-09-22 11 SQL*Net message from client          111             32
2001-09-22 15 SQL*Net message from client          353             10
2001-09-22 20 SQL*Net message from client          184             18
2001-09-22 22 SQL*Net message from client          642            104
2001-09-23 11 SQL*Net message from client          125             22
2001-09-23 12 SQL*Net message from client          329             11
2001-09-23 13 SQL*Net message from client          329            172
2001-09-23 14 SQL*Net message from client          310              4
2001-09-23 15 SQL*Net message from client          501             17
2001-09-23 16 SQL*Net message from client          197             49
2001-09-23 19 SQL*Net message from client          214             20
2001-09-24 16 SQL*Net message from client          343            251
```

These STATSPACK reports can often give the DBA an idea about potential network problems because Oracle captures the number of seconds that have been waited for each distributed event. Of course, Oracle can identify a latency problem, but we need to go out to the network to find the exact cause of the network problem.

While network tuning is very complex, let's take a brief overview of the standard tools that are used in a UNIX environment to monitor network transmissions.

Tuning the Distributed Network

Tuning a network is a very long painstaking process of gathering statistics and analyzing them. Unfortunately, there are no quick or simple answers that will solve all network performance issues. Basically, you will have to generate a sniffer trace and check for utilization statistics, retransmissions, and delta times.

Note that while it is easy to extend STATSPACK to monitor disk I/O information, it is extremely difficult to extend STATSPACK to capture network traffic information. Network information varies widely between systems, and it is almost impossible to capture meaningful disk I/O information into STATSPACK extension tables.

The most basic tool used by network administrators is the UNIX netstat utility. Unfortunately, netstat is implemented differently by all of the UNIX vendors, and the output from netstat looks very different depending on the operating system that you are using. Let's take a brief tour of netstat and see how it can be used by the Oracle DBA to monitor network activity.

Using netstat to Monitor Network Activity

Netstat is a generic UNIX utility that displays the contents of various network-related structures in various formats. These formats are determined by the options passed to the **netstat** command.

Netstat is very good at telling the DBA what is happening on the network at the current time, but netstat does not give a good trending capability or periodic snapshot functionality. Most network administrators purchase a specialized third-party tool for long-term network monitoring. Let's look at some of the differences in netstat and see some of the network information that netstat provides about the current state of the network.

Netstat on Solaris

On a Sun Solaris server, the netstat utility provides information about all network traffic touching the server:

```
>netstat

TCP: IPv4
Local Address    Remote Address        Swind Send-Q Rwind Recv-Q  State
-------------    --------------        ----- ------ ----- ------  ---------
sting.32773      ting.1521             32768      0 32768      0  ESTABLISHED
sting.1521       ting.32773            32768      0 32768      0  ESTABLISHED
sting.32774      ting.1521             32768      0 32768      0  ESTABLISHED
sting.1521       ting.32774            32768      0 32768      0  ESTABLISHED
sting.32775      ting.1521             32768      0 32768      0  ESTABLISHED
sting.1521       ting.32775            32768      0 32768      0  ESTABLISHED
sting.1521       az.janet.com.32777    24820      0 24820      0  ESTABLISHED
sting.1521       rumpy.jan.com.34601   24820      0 24820      0  ESTABLISHED
sting.22         onsrv1.jan.com.1120   31856      0 24616      0  ESTABLISHED
sting.1521       rumpy.jan.com.35460   24820      0 24820      0  ESTABLISHED

Active UNIX domain sockets
Address      Type        Vnode        Conn      Local Addr Remote Addr
300021bda88  stream-ord  30002225e70  00000000  /var/tmp/  .oracle/s#255.1
300021bdc30  stream-ord  300021f02c0  00000000  /var/tmp/  .oracle/sextproc_key
300021bddd8  stream-ord  300021f0848  00000000  /var/tmp/  .oracle/s#252.1
```

netstat for Linux

In Linux, we see that the output from netstat is quite different from Solaris:

```
Proto Recv-Q Send-Q Local Address            Foreign Address              State
tcp   0      0      donsrv1.rov:netbios-ssn  intranet.janet.com:1351      ESTABLISHED
tcp   0      0      donsrv1.janet.com:1120   sting.janet.com:ssh          TIME_WAIT
tcp   0      40     donsrv1.janet.com:ssh    hpop3-146.gloryroa:1096      ESTABLISHED
```

```
tcp   0      0      donsrv1.rov:netbios-ssn 192.168.1.105:1025      ESTABLISHED
tcp   0      0      donsrv1.janet.com:6010  donsrv1.janet.com:1104  CLOSE_WAIT
tcp   0      0      donsrv1.janet.com:6010  donsrv1.janet.com:1103  CLOSE_WAIT
tcp   0      0      donsrv1.janet.com:1023  grumpy.janet.com:ssh    ESTABLISHED
tcp   0      0      donsrv1.janet.com:ssh   exodus-rtr-2.arsdi:2195 ESTABLISHED
tcp   0      0      donsrv1.rov:netbios-ssn 192.168.1.107:1025      ESTABLISHED
tcp   0      0      donsrv1.rov:netbios-ssn 192.168.1.126:1030      ESTABLISHED
Active UNIX domain sockets (w/o servers)
Proto RefCnt Flags       Type     State        I-Node Path
unix  1      [ ]         STREAM   CONNECTED    741    @0000002a
unix  1      [ ]         STREAM   CONNECTED    745    @0000002b
unix  0      [ ]         STREAM   CONNECTED    182    @0000001a
unix  1      [ ]         STREAM   CONNECTED    763    @00000030
unix  8      [ ]         DGRAM                 397    /dev/log
unix  0      [ ]         DGRAM                 234471
unix  0      [ ]         DGRAM                 234252
unix  0      [ ]         DGRAM                 843
unix  1      [ ]         STREAM   CONNECTED    764    /tmp/.X11-unix/X0
unix  1      [ ]         STREAM   CONNECTED    746    /tmp/.font-unix/fs-1
unix  1      [ ]         STREAM   CONNECTED    748    /tmp/.X11-unix/X0
unix  0      [ ]         DGRAM                 654
unix  0      [ ]         DGRAM                 589
unix  0      [ ]         DGRAM                 560
unix  0      [ ]         DGRAM                 419
[oracle@donsrv1 oracle]$ netstat -sp tcp
Ip:
    15753092 total packets received
    1 with invalid headers
    0 forwarded
    0 incoming packets discarded
    99397 incoming packets delivered
    20325485 requests sent out
Icmp:
    1041 ICMP messages received
    37 input ICMP message failed.
    ICMP input histogram:
        destination unreachable: 972
        timeout in transit: 31
        echo requests: 27
        echo replies: 11
    490 ICMP messages sent
    0 ICMP messages failed
    ICMP output histogram:
        destination unreachable: 463
        echo replies: 27
Tcp:
    131 active connections openings
    0 passive connection openings
    14 failed connection attempts
    0 connection resets received
    6 connections established
```

```
     15652680 segments received
     20276668 segments send out
     6933 segments retransmited
     2 bad segments received.
     25 resets sent
Udp:
     97289 packets received
     11 packets to unknown port received.
     3 packet receive errors
     48279 packets sent
TcpExt:
     9 packets pruned from receive queue because of socket buffer overrun

     unix    0      [ ]        DGRAM                 407
```

Hopefully, this brief description of the netstat utility will give you an appreciation for the scope and complexity of network tuning.

Conclusion

Now that we understand the tools we have to change Oracle packet characteristics and how to use STATSPACK to identify potential network problems, let's move on and take a look at tuning and monitoring the most important external areas of all: the disk I/O subsystem. Remember, disk I/O is the cause of almost all Oracle slow-downs, and almost all Oracle tuning efforts are directed at reducing disk I/O.

CHAPTER
8

Tuning
the Disk I/O Subsystem
with STATSPACK

his chapter deals with the single most important component of Oracle tuning: the time required to fetch data blocks from disk. Because I/O bottlenecks are the greatest source of response time problems in any Oracle database, the Oracle DBA must constantly be alert for I/O-related slowdowns. Every time that Oracle has to visit the disk to retrieve a database block, time is wasted and Oracle must wait for the I/O to complete.

The purpose of this chapter is to show how to minimize the amount of I/O in Oracle. This chapter will be divided into several sections.

- **Oracle tuning factors that affect disk I/O** This section will discuss the Oracle configurations and parameters that affect the amount of disk I/O.

- **Oracle internals and disk I/O** This section will show the transient nature of disk hot spots and show how hot spots are related to table parameters such as *pctused*.

- **Mapping Oracle disk architectures** This section will demonstrate the benefits of segregating large tables into separate tablespaces and mapping the tablespaces to specific datafiles. We will also examine the various file organization techniques and show their relative merits.

- **STATSPACK reports for Oracle datafiles** This section will show how STATSPACK reports can be used to identify "hot" datafiles in your environment and provide the DBA with an alert mechanism for hot files.

- **Extending STATSPACK for disk I/O data** This section will show how to extend STATSPACK to capture data from the UNIX iostat utility. We will also show how the data from stats$filestatxs and stats$iostat can be compared.

- **Viewing I/O signatures with STATSPACK** This important section shows how to develop I/O signatures for a database and how to compare the I/O of datafiles to the entire database.

This chapter deals exclusively with I/O at the Oracle level, and how the Oracle DBA can identify patterns within the I/O subsystem and load balance their database for optimal performance.

NOTE
You are encouraged to run these prepared STATSPACK scripts against your database. It is only after you get insight into the I/O patterns within your database that you will be able to properly load balance your I/O subsystem.

This chapter emphasizes that there are many techniques that can be performed within Oracle to reduce the amount of I/O, and stresses that the primary motive for all Oracle tuning is to reduce I/O on the disks. These techniques will be discussed in detail in Chapters 9–11, but we need to briefly mention them here because they directly relate to the reduction of disk I/O.

Oracle Tuning Factors that Influence Disk I/O

As you know, one of the primary goals of all Oracle tuning activities is to reduce disk I/O. We will be discussing these techniques in Chapter 9, but we need to mention them here so you will understand how the instance parameters can affect disk I/O. There are three areas where the settings for Oracle have a direct impact on the amount of disk I/O. The settings for the Oracle instance (*init.ora*) impact disk I/O, the settings for Oracle objects (tables and indexes) affect disk I/O, and the execution plans for Oracle SQL also have a direct impact on disk I/O.

1. **Oracle instance** There are several database instance parameters that have a direct impact on lowering physical disk I/O:

   - **Large *db_block_size*** The block size of the database has a dramatic effect on the amount of disk I/O. As a general rule, the larger the block size, the less the disk I/O.

   - **Large *db_block_buffers*** The greater the number of data buffers, the smaller the chance that Oracle will need to perform disk I/O.

   - **Multiple database writers (DBWR) processes** Multiple database writer background processes allow for more efficient writing to the datafiles.

   - **Large *sort_area_size*** The greater the *sort_area_size* in RAM, the less disk sorting will take place in the TEMP tablespace.

   - **Large online redo logs** The larger the online redo logs, the less frequent the log switches.

2. **Oracle objects** Inside the database, settings for tables and indexes can reduce physical disk I/O

   - **Low *pctused*** The smaller the value of *pctused*, the less I/O will occur on subsequent SQL inserts.

   - **Low *pctfree*** If *pctfree* is set to allow all rows to expand without fragmenting, the less disk I/O will occur on subsequent SQL selects.

- **Reorganizing tables to cluster rows with indexes** If tables are placed in the same physical order as the most frequently used index, disk I/O will drop dramatically.

3. **Oracle SQL** Within SQL statements, there are many techniques to reduce physical disk I/O:

   - **Preventing unnecessary full table scans using indexes or hints** This is the most important way to reduce disk I/O because many SQL queries can use indexes to reduce disk I/O.

   - **Using bitmapped indexes** The use of bitmapped indexes will reduce full table scans on tables with low-cardinality columns, thereby reducing disk I/O.

   - **Applying SQL hints** Many hints make SQL run faster and with less disk I/O. For example, the USE_HASH hint will reduce disk I/O by performing joins within SGA memory, reducing calls for database blocks.

Now that we have reviewed some of the things that we can do within Oracle to reduce disk I/O, let's take a close look at the nature of disk I/O and examine the internal workings of the disk I/O subsystem.

Oracle Internals and Disk I/O

From an Oracle perspective, most databases can be characterized as either online transaction processing (OLTP) systems or decision support (DSS) systems. The patterns of I/O vary greatly between a data warehouse and decision support type of application and one that processes online transactions. While OLTP may appear random, upon closer inspection, we will see clear areas of impact to the Oracle database, and understand methods to alleviate I/O contention.

Oracle File Organization Techniques

Regardless of whether or not you use RAID, it is very important for the Oracle DBA to identify all high-volume and high-activity tables and move them into isolated tablespaces. By keeping the high-volume tables in a separate tablespace, the Oracle administrator can manipulate the datafiles in the tablespace to minimize I/O contention on the disk, as shown in Figure 8-1.

Without segregation, some tablespaces may have hundreds of tables and indexes, and it is impossible to tell which objects are experiencing the high I/O. The stats$filestatxs table will provide details about read and write I/O at the file level, but it is often difficult to tell the tables that are causing the high I/O because a file may contain many objects.

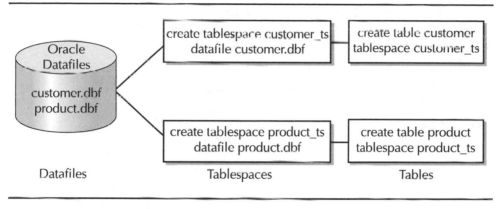

FIGURE 8-1. *Segregating Oracle tables into separate tablespaces*

With segregation, the DBA can generate STATSPACK file I/O reports from the stats$filestatxs table that show all read and write I/O for the datafile. If the Oracle datafile maps to only one table, we can easily see the total I/O for the table. Later in this chapter we will see a STATSPACK script called *rpt_io_pct.sql* that serves this purpose.

Because of the high-speed transaction oriented nature of most Oracle applications, we generally see high activity in specific areas within each tablespace. While this chapter describes the basics of I/O load balancing for Oracle datafiles and tablespaces, the settings for the individual tables will also have a profound influence on the performance of the entire database. We will look at disk I/O within Oracle and examine several areas:

- Transient disk hot spots

- Disk I/O patterns within highly active tables

Transient Disk Hot Spots

In any Oracle database it is not uncommon to see sporadic hot spots appear on disks as the I/O signature changes. As you know, Oracle offers a wealth of data buffering tools that are designed to keep Oracle data blocks within RAM and prevent disk I/O. These techniques include table caching and separate data buffers. However, unless you have your database fully cached in the data buffers, you will always experience I/O activity.

I/O Patterns Within High-Update Tables

There is a special case of disk I/O that occurs when a transaction table experiences high-volume **insert** and **update** operations. For example, consider an order processing system with 3,000 data entry operators constantly slamming orders into a large order table. Let's further assume that at any given time, there are 200 transactions inserting into this table. As we will see, a close inspection of the datafiles will reveal several important characteristics within tables that have high-volume inserts:

- Roving hot spots on disk
- The sparse table phenomenon

Roving Hot Spots on Disk

To understand roving hot spots on disk we will give a simple example. Let's assume that our database has a table named transaction that has 200 data entry operators constantly adding rows. The transaction table is defined with 200 freelists, and the table is gathering free blocks by raising the high-water mark for the Oracle table. This example assumes that there are not any free blocks on the freelists for the table, such as the case where the APPEND hint is used with the **insert** statements. Since we know that Oracle bumps the high-water mark for a table in increments of five blocks, our 200 concurrent inserts would generate intensive SQL **insert** activity that is isolated to a set of 1,000 blocks within the table.

Because each of the **insert** transactions must request a separate free block from the transaction table to insert their new transactions, Oracle will grab free blocks (five at a time) from sequential free space in the tablespace. These free blocks are likely to be contiguous blocks on the disk. Since these contiguous blocks are likely to reside on the same disk cylinder, it is likely that this disk would experience I/O contention at the end of the table.

As our data entry operators continue to hand key entries into the transaction table, we see the hot spot moving along the disk as new cylinders are accessed by the table (see Figure 8-2).

As we can see, the hot spot will travel through the tablespaces as Oracle blocks become full and the Oracle tables expand. So long as all of the SQL **insert** statements add blocks into a new data block, the hot spot will travel cleanly across the disks.

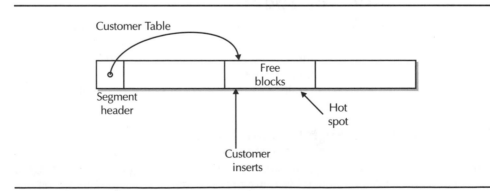

FIGURE 8-2. *The roving hot spot within a transaction table*

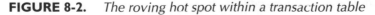

However, what happens after a transaction purge job is run? When older transactions are deleted from the table, blocks become free and are added to one of the 200 freelists for the table. As the freelists are loaded with newly empty blocks from the purge job, the hot spot will travel backward in the table, returning to the area of the table where the purge job removed the rows, as shown in Figure 8-3.

Oracle tablespaces that contain high-volume tables often experience the "roving hot spot" phenomenon. This is especially true for tables where rows are inserted and deleted on a date-time basis, such as a *fact* table within an Oracle data warehouse.

We see this type of time-based entry into many Oracle tables. For example, orders for goods are inserted in a time-based sequence, data warehouses load their data in a time sequence, and most every online system adds and purges rows based on a time sequence.

So, given that these roving hot spots will appear, what can you do to manage the activity? The trick to managing roving hot spots is to ensure that the free blocks always reside on adjacent cylinders. When Oracle data blocks are re-added to the freelists, we cannot guarantee that they will be close together on the disk, and this condition can create a "disk thrashing" situation. Disk thrashing occurs when free blocks are located on widely distant cylinders on the disk (see Figure 8-4). As our 200 tasks compete for free blocks, the read-write heads thrash back and forth attempting to meet the needs of each transaction. The time required for a disk's read-write head to move between cylinders is called "seek" delay, and seek delay is the single most time-consuming factor in disk access.

There are several techniques that can be done to remedy this problem:

■ **Segregate objects**   Identify all tables with high insert activity and segregate them into a separate tablespace.

■ **Use fresh data blocks**   Ensure that all new inserts go onto new data blocks at the end of the table by using the APPEND hint in all **insert** statements.

■ **Reorganize tables**   Reorganize the table after purge jobs are run to reclaim the freed blocks onto the end of the table.

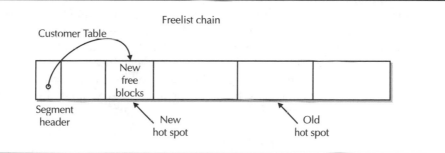

FIGURE 8-3.   *The hot spot travels back in the table*

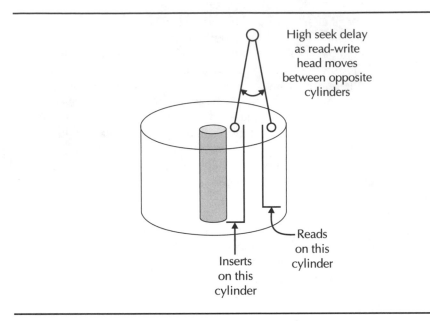

High seek delay
as read-write
head moves
between opposite
cylinders

Reads
on this
cylinder

Inserts
on this
cylinder

FIGURE 8-4. *High seek delay on a disk*

In addition to roving hot spots, these highly active Oracle tables will also manifest themselves as sparse tables.

The Sparse Table Phenomenon

Sparse tables generally occur when a highly active table is defined with many freelists, and the table has heavy **insert** and **delete** activity. In a sparse table, the table will appear to have thousands of free blocks, yet the table will continue to extend, and the table will behave as if Oracle does not have any free data blocks. A sparse table in a data warehouse can consume a huge amount of unnecessary storage, consuming many gigabytes of new storage while the table appears to have lots of free space. Remember, when you have multiple freelists, the freelists are independent and Oracle cannot share freelist blocks. An **insert** task will only attach to one freelist, and it is only able to use free blocks that are attached to that freelist.

The cause of a sparse table is a lack of balance between **insert** and **delete** activity. In our example, we have three freelists defined for the table, and each freelist gets new blocks in five-block chunks as the table expands. Next, a single job is run to remove the blocks, as shown in Figure 8-5.

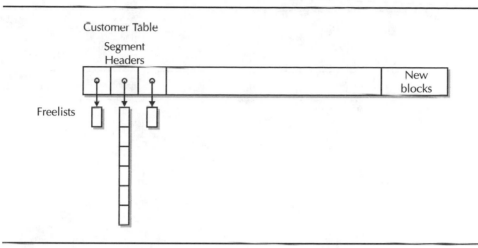

FIGURE 8-5. *Unbalanced freelists*

As we can see, only one of the three freelists is populated with the free blocks! The other two freelists remain empty, and must request blocks by increasing the high-water mark for the table. This causes the table to extend, even though it may be largely empty. Extension occurs because each freelist is unaware of the contents of other freelists inside the segment header.

The remedy, of course, is to parallelize the purge job into three simultaneous **delete** tasks. By parallelizing the purge, all three freelists are evenly populated with newly empty blocks, as shown in Figure 8-6.

Of course, we must set the number of freelists to the number of simultaneous **insert** or **update** operations, so we cannot reduce the number of freelists without introducing segment header contention.

So, what can we do to identify sparse tables? The following query selects tables that contain multiple freelists, with more than one extent, where there is excessive free space.

To find tables with excessive free blocks on a freelist, we must compute the amount of data used within the table. First, we calculate the average row length (*avg_row_len*) in the data dictionary view and the number of rows (*num_rows*) by performing a table **analyze** (that is, **analyze table xxx estimate statistics**). When we multiply the number of rows in the table by the average row length, we approximate the actual consumed size of the data within the table. We then compare this value with the actual number of allocated bytes in the table.

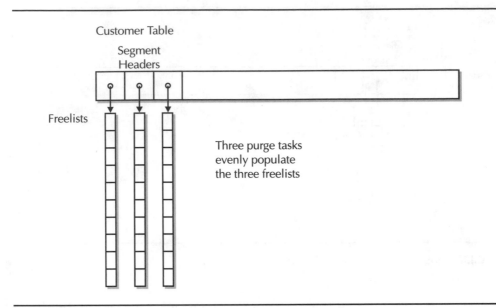

FIGURE 8-6. *Parallelizing a purge for a table with multiple freelists*

The idea is that a sparse table will have far more allocated space than consumed space because a single freelist contains a disproportional number of free blocks. Here is a script called *sparse.sql* that generates this report.

sparse.sql

```
column c1   heading "Tablespace";
column c2   heading "Owner";
column c3   heading "Table";
column c4   heading "Bytes M" format 9,999;
column c5   heading "Extents" format 999;
column c7   heading "Empty M" format 9,999;
column c6   heading "Blocks M" format 9,999;
column c8   heading "NEXT M" format 999;
column c9   heading "Row space M" format 9,999;
column c10  heading "Pct Full" format .99;

select
        substr(dt.table_name,1,10) c3,
        ds.extents c5,
```

```
        ds.bytes/1048576 c4,
        dt.next_extent/1048576 c8,
        (dt.empty_blocks*4096)/1048576 c7,
        (avg_row_len*num_rows)/1048576 c9,
        (ds.blocks*4096)/1048576 c6,
        (avg_row_len*num_rows)/(ds.blocks*4096) c10
from     sys.dba_segments ds,
         sys.dba_tables   dt
where    ds.tablespace_name = dt.tablespace_name
  and    ds.owner = dt.owner
  and    ds.segment_name = dt.table_name
and dt.freelists > 1
and ds.extents > 1
and dt.owner not in ('SYS','SYSTEM')
and (avg_row_len*num_rows)/1048576 > 50
and ds.bytes/1048576 > 20
order by c10;
```

Next is the output from *sparse.sql*. This will identify tables that have lots of free
space within their existing extents. If any of these tables extend before using up
their free blocks, we can assume that the table has a freelist imbalance. The remedy
for this imbalance is to reorganize the table.

Table	Extents	Bytes M	NEXT M	Empty M	Row space M	Blocks M	Pct Full
TST03	65	1,241	20	14	118	1,241	.10
LIKE	3	148	49	24	76	148	.52
VBRK	2	124	4	0	69	124	.56
STXL	35	1,775	40	7	1,021	1,775	.57
VBAK	5	234	49	0	136	234	.58
KOCLU	27	1,889	49	27	1,144	1,889	.61
VBUP	2	866	49	0	570	866	.66
VBUK	2	147	28	0	103	147	.70
VBAP	46	4,314	50	0	3,034	4,314	.70
NASTY	3	137	10	2	97	137	.71
VBPA	5	582	32	0	426	582	.73
LIME	7	2,350	49	0	1,735	2,350	.74
VBRP	45	2,675	49	0	2,029	2,675	.76
WFPRC	30	123	10	7	95	123	.77
VLPMA	16	575	25	23	444	575	.77
EXCDOC	18	432	20	13	337	432	.78
VRPMA	24	700	20	7	549	700	.78
VBEP	4	2,134	49	49	1,698	2,134	.80

Now that we understand the general nature of I/O activity in an Oracle database,
let's look at some global solutions for placing Oracle datafiles onto our disk devices.

Mapping Oracle Disk Architectures

Today's disk devices are normally delivered as complete I/O subsystems, complete with their own memory cache, channels, disk adapters and SCSI adapters. Understanding the architecture requires mapping the number of ports, the size of the disk cache, the number of disk adapters, and the mapping of I/O channels between the disks and the disk cache. Figure 8-7 shows a sample of a disk architecture map for a disk array.

Developing this type of disk map is very important to load balancing within Oracle because there are many possible bottlenecks within the disk array subsystem that can cause slowdowns. In addition to monitoring for disk waits, we also need to monitor for SCSI contention, channel contention and contention between the disk adapters. Fortunately, many of the major disk vendors (EMC, IBM) provide their own proprietary disk utilities (e.g., NaviStar, Open Symmetrics Manager) to perform these disk monitor functions.

The Multiple RAM Buffer Issue

We are also seeing disk arrays being delivered with a separate RAM cache for the disk arrays, as shown in Figure 8-8. These RAM caches can be many gigabytes in size and contain special software tools for performing asynchronous writes and minimizing disk I/O.

The Oracle DBA needs to consider the RAM cache on the disk array, because it changes the basic nature of disk I/O. When Oracle cannot find a data block in one

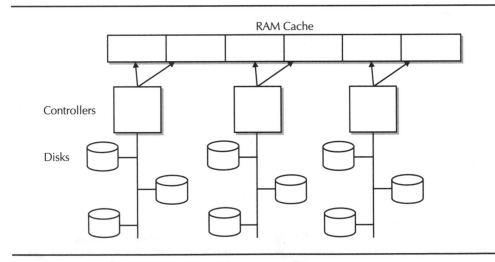

FIGURE 8-7.   *A sample architecture of a disk array*

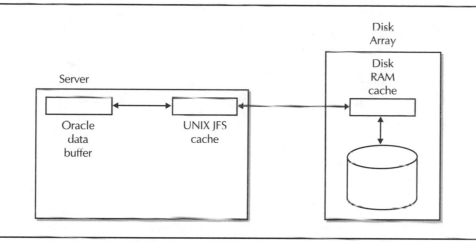

FIGURE 8-8. *Multiple RAM caches with an Oracle database*

of the data buffers in the SGA, Oracle will issue a physical read request to the disk array. This physical read request is received by the disk array, and the disk RAM cache is checked for the desired block. If the desired block is in the RAM cache, the disk array will return the block to Oracle without making a physical disk I/O. The fact that Oracle physical requests may not match actual read requests is a very important point, because it can lead to misleading statistics. For example, the stats$filestatxs table shows the number of reads and writes to files. If you are using a disk array such as EMC, these I/O statistics will not correspond to the actual disk reads and writes. The only conclusive way to check "real" disk I/O is to compare the physical I/O as measured on the disk array with Oracle's read and write statistics. In many cases, the disks are performing less than half the I/O reported by Oracle, and this discrepancy is due to the caching of data blocks on the disk array RAM memory.

Next, let's look at file striping and see how it can be used to load balance the I/O subsystem.

File Striping with Oracle

File striping is the process of splitting a tablespace into small datafiles and placing these datafiles across many disks. With the introduction of RAID (redundant arrays of inexpensive disks), we also have the option of block-interleaf striping (RAID 1), which places each data block in the tablespace on a separate disk.

Other methods of Oracle file striping involve taking a large tablespace and splitting it into many Oracle datafiles. These files may then be spread across many disks to reduce I/O bottlenecks, as shown in Figure 8-9.

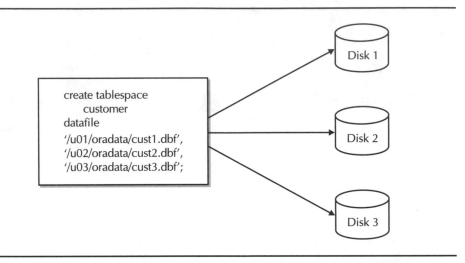

FIGURE 8-9. *Striping a tablespace across multiple disks*

However, manual file striping has become obsolete because of the large size of disks. In 1990, a 20GB database would probably have been composed of 20 physical disks, each within 1GB of storage. With many disks in a database, the Oracle DBA could improve throughput by manually striping the busiest tablespaces across many disks.

Commercial disks are getting larger every year, and it is very difficult to find small disk devices that contain less than 36GB of storage. Just ten years ago, the IBM 3380 disk was considered huge at 1GB of storage. Today, the smallest disks available are 18GB. The larger disks mean that there are fewer disk spindles, and fewer opportunities for manual file striping. Since it is often not possible to isolate Oracle tablespaces on separate disks without wasting a huge amount of disk space, the Oracle administrator must balance active with inactive tablespaces across their disks.

NOTE
There is a new feature in Oracle8i called "single table clusters." By using a cluster, the keys are grouped in the same physical block—reducing I/O and speeding data retrieval by key.

Using RAID with Oracle
As you may know, there are more than six different types (called "levels") of RAID architectures, and each has its own relative advantages and disadvantages. For the

purposes of an Oracle database, many of the RAID schemes do not posses the high performance required for an Oracle database, and are omitted from this discussion. Please note that RAID 5 is not considered in this discussion since the processing overhead for updates makes it too slow for most Oracle applications. Here are the most commonly used RAID architectures for Oracle databases:

- **RAID 0** RAID 0 is commonly referred to as block-level striping. This is an excellent method for performing load balancing of the Oracle database on the disk devices, but it does nothing for high availability since none of the data is duplicated. Unlike manual datafile striping, where the Oracle professional divides an Oracle tablespace into small datafiles, with RAID 0, the Oracle datafile is automatically striped one block at a time across all of the disk devices. In this fashion, every datafile has pieces residing on each disk, and the disk I/O load will become very well balanced.

- **RAID 1** RAID 1 is commonly called disk mirroring. Since the disks are replicated, RAID 1 may involve double or triple mirroring. The RAID 1 architecture is designed such that a disk failure will cause the I/O subsystem to switch to one of the replicated disks with no service interruption. RAID 1 is used when high availability is critical, and with triple mirroring, the mean time to failure (MTTF) for an Oracle database is measured in decades. (Note that disk controller errors may cause RAID 1 failures, although the disks remain healthy.)

- **RAID 0+1** Raid 0+1 is the combination of block-level striping and disk mirroring. The advent of RAID 0+1 has made Oracle-level striping obsolete since RAID 0+1 stripes at the block level, dealing out the table blocks, one block per disk, across each disk device. RAID 0+1 is also a far better striping alternative since it distributes the load evenly across all of the disk devices, and the load will rise and fall evenly across all of the disks. This relieves the Oracle administrator of the burden of manually striping Oracle tables across disks and provides a far greater level of granularity than Oracle striping, because adjacent data blocks within the same table are on different disks.

Note that the use of RAID does not guarantee against catastrophic disk failure. Oracle specifically recommends that all production databases be run in archivelog mode regardless of the RAID architecture, and that periodic Oracle backups should be performed. Remember that there are many components to I/O subsystems—including controllers, channels, disk adapters, SCSI adapters—and a failure of any of these components could cause unrecoverable disk failures of your database. RAID should only be used as an additional level of insurance, and not as a complete recovery method.

Using Oracle with Raw Devices

Because of the high amount of I/O that many Oracle systems experience, many Oracle DBAs consider the use of "raw" devices. A raw device is defined as a disk that bypasses the I/O overhead created by the Journal File System (JFS) in UNIX. The reduction in overhead can improve throughput, but only in cases where I/O is already the bottleneck for the Oracle database. Furthermore, raw devices require a tremendous amount of manual work for both the Oracle administrator and the systems administrator. Oracle recommends that raw devices should only be considered when the Oracle database is I/O bound. However, for these types of Oracle databases, raw devices can dramatically improve overall performance. If the database is not I/O bound, switching to raw devices will have no impact on performance.

In many UNIX environments such as AIX, raw devices are called virtual storage devices (VSDs). These VSDs are created from disk physical partitions (PPs), such that a single VSD can contain pieces from several physical disks. It is the job of the system administrator to create a pool of VSDs for the Oracle administrator. The Oracle administrator can then take these VSDs and combine them into Oracle datafiles. This creates a situation where an Oracle datafile may be made from several VSDs. This many-to-many relationship between Oracle datafiles and VSDs makes Oracle administration more challenging.

In summary, raw devices for Oracle databases can provide improved I/O throughput only for databases that are already I/O bound.

However, this performance gain comes at the expense of increased administrative overhead for the Oracle administrator. We also know that raw devices will only improve the performance of Oracle databases whose Oracle subsystem is clearly I/O bound. For systems that are not I/O bound, moving to raw devices will not result in any performance gains.

The UNIX iostat utility is great for showing those physical disks that have bottlenecks. Since we know the tablespace and table for each hot datafile, we can intelligently move the hot datafiles to a less active disk. Let's begin by exploring the nature of disk load balancing for Oracle.

Load Balancing Disks with Oracle Databases

With terabyte-sized and Web-enabled Oracle8 databases becoming more commonplace, the task of disk load balancing has never been more critical. These huge databases are too massive to be cached in an Oracle data buffer, yet these databases often serve thousands of users who expect instant response times. The most important thing that the DBA can do to minimize disk I/O is to balance the load on the disks.

By placing datafiles strategically on the physical disks, you can minimize the likelihood of any one disk becoming stalled while handling simultaneous I/O requests. This section provides a strategy for collecting I/O information into Oracle tables and generating reports to deliver maximum guidance in the load-balancing process for multiple physical disk systems. The purpose of collecting I/O statistics is to provide data for load balancing. Load balancing involves moving datafiles on the physical disks such that no single disk becomes stalled waiting for simultaneous I/O requests. The best way to start a file placement strategy is to create a transparent disk architecture whereby the DBA can correlate the datafile name to a specific Oracle table or index. Let's explore how we create this type of architecture.

Configuring Oracle Tablespaces and Datafiles

Since different application processes have different I/O patterns, hot disks may appear on different disks at different times during each day. The goal of disk load balancing is to eliminate disk I/O bottlenecks, but it is important to remember that these bottlenecks are transient in nature. Since Oracle transactions happen very quickly, a disk may experience an I/O bottleneck for a very short period, and this short-duration bottleneck may repeat itself thousands of times each day. However, many Oracle administrators make the mistake of summarizing I/O by the hour, and the disk will appear not to have bottlenecks since the I/O spikes will have disappeared in the hourly average, as shown in Figure 8-10.

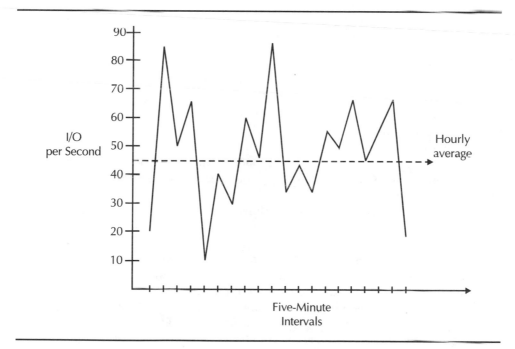

FIGURE 8-10. *Short I/O spikes can be lost with long measurement periods*

To get the most accurate results, you should collect I/O statistics at frequent intervals—preferably no more than ten minutes between samples—over a representative time period, such as a week. Because individual application processes have different I/O patterns, bottlenecks may appear on different disks at various times during each day. And because Oracle transactions happen very quickly, a disk may experience an I/O bottleneck for a very short period—but a short-duration bottleneck may nonetheless repeat itself thousands of times each day. If you make the mistake of summarizing I/O by the hour, as many DBAs do, you won't see these bottlenecks because the I/O spikes will not be evident in the hourly average.

The point is simple: in order to accurately identify and correct disk I/O bottlenecks, you must measure in minor duration, preferably no more than 10 minutes between samples. We will discuss this technique in a following section where we will show how to extend STATSPACK to capture disk iostat information.

The goal of load balancing is to distribute the files across disks so as to achieve a single static optimal I/O throughput. Moving Oracle datafiles to other disks is not a trivial operation, and the datafile must be taken offline before the file can be moved to another disk. However, the good news is that once the I/O subsystem is balanced, the files will not need to be moved unless new processes change the I/O pattern for the disks.

The goal is to find the optimal file placement where overall load balance is achieved for all of the many variations of disk access. Load balancing is essentially the identification of hot disks, and the movement of datafiles to less-used cool disks. As such, disk load balancing is an iterative process since it is possible that relocating a datafile may relieve contention for one process, only to cause I/O contention for an unrelated process. Also, for databases placed on a small number of disks, it is possible that I/O contention cannot be avoided. Consider a 30GB database spread across disks with 20 competing processes for data. On average, ten processes would be queued waiting for I/O from each of the two disks. Clearly, these types of systems will always experience I/O contention.

Within Oracle in any UNIX environment, we have a hierarchical relationship between entities. Each physical disk has many UNIX mount points, each mount point has many Oracle datafiles, and each datafile may have many Oracle tables, as shown in Figure 8-11.

After using data collected by iostat to identify a hot disk, you would use data collected by the Oracle utilities to identify which mount point and file contain the table causing the excessive I/O activity.

Identifying the hot disk is only the beginning of the quest. We must then see what mount point on the disk is causing the problem, which datafile on the mount point, and finally, what Oracle table is causing the excessive I/O. Only with this approach can the Oracle administrator fully understand how to perform disk load balancing. With that in mind, let's look at the first method for collecting Oracle I/O statistics. We will then move on to look at collecting UNIX I/O statistics.

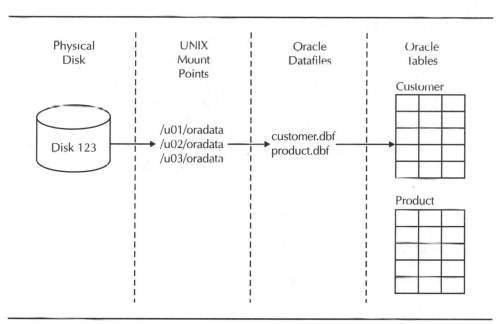

FIGURE 0-11.   *The hierarchy of Oracle file structures on UNIX*

Building the Oracle File-to-Disk Architecture

If you are not using a block-level block striping mechanism such as RAID 0+1, it is a good idea to map each physical disk spindle directly to a UNIX mount point. For example, here is a sample mapping for a set of triple-mirrored disks:

Mount Point	Main Disk	Mirror 1	Mirror 2
/u01	hdisk31	hdisk41	hdisk51
/u02	hdisk32	hdisk42	hdisk52
/u03	hdisk33	hdisk43	hdisk53
/u04	hdisk34	hdisk44	hdisk54
/u05	hdisk35	hdisk45	hdisk55

By mapping the UNIX mount points directly to physical disks, it becomes easy to know the disk location of a hot Oracle datafile. For example, if our STATSPACK hot file report (in the statspack_alert.sql script) indicates that /u03/oradata/prod/books.dbf is consuming an inordinate amount of I/O, we immediately know that /u03 is getting hit, and that /u03 maps directly to disk hdisk33 and its mirrored disks.

Please note that this mapping technology becomes more complex because of the large size of disk spindles. The trend has been toward creating very large disks, and it is not uncommon to find disks that range from 36GB to 72GB. In these cases, many small Oracle databases will reside on a single physical disk, and load balancing becomes impractical. However, this large-disk issue does not imply that the DBA should abandon disk monitoring simply because all of the files reside on a single disk. Remember, high file I/O can be corrected with the judicious use of the Oracle data buffers. For example, a hot table can be moved into the KEEP pool, thereby caching the data blocks and relieving the hot-disk issue.

It is interesting to note that some products such as EMC have developed methods to internally detect hot files and transparently move them to cooler disks. However, this approach has a problem. Blindly moving a hot datafile to a cooler disk is analogous to pressing into an overstuffed pillow: one area goes in, but another area bulges.

It is never simple in the real world. In the real world, the Oracle DBA may find a specific range of data blocks within a datafile that is getting high I/O, and they will segregate these blocks onto a separate datafile. This relates to the point we made earlier in this chapter that the Oracle DBA must always segregate hot tables and indexes onto separate tablespaces.

If you are not using RAID 0+1 or RAID 5, it is simple to write a dictionary query that will display the mapping of tablespaces-to-files and files-to-UNIX mount points. Note that the data selected from the dba_data_files view relies on using the Oracle Optimal Flexible Architecture (OFA). If we use the OFA, the first four characters of the filename represents the UNIX mount point for the file. We can also adjust the substring function in the following query to extract the filename without the full disk path to the file.

Reporting on the Oracle Disk Architecture

If your shop follows the OFA standard, you can write a dictionary query that will report on the disk-to-file mapping for your database. This script assumes that you use OFA names for your datafiles (e.g., */u02/oradata/xxx.dbf*), and that your UNIX mount points map to easily identifiable physical disks. The script here queries the dba_data_files view and reports the mapping.

rpt_disk_mapping.sql

```
set pages 999;
set lines 80;

column mount_point heading 'MP';
```

```
break on mount_point skip 2;

select
    substr(file_name,1,4) mount_point,
    substr(file_name,21,20) file_name,
    tablespace_name
from
    dba_data_files
group by
    substr(file_name,1,4),
    substr(file_name,21,20) ,
    tablespace_name
;
```

Here is the output from this script. Please note that there is a one-to-one correspondence between Oracle tablespaces, physical datafiles, and UNIX mount points.

```
MP      FILE_NAME               TABLESPACE_NAME
----    -------------------     ------------------------------
/u02    annod01.dbf             ANNOD
        arsd.dbf                ARSD
        bookd01.dbf             BOOKD
        groupd01.dbf            GROUPD
        pagestatsd01.dbf        PAGESTATSD
        rdruserd01.dbf          RDRUSERD
        subscrd01.dbf           SUBSCRD
        system01.dbf            SYSTEM
        userstatsd01.dbf        USERSTATSD

/u03    annox01.dbf             ANNOX
        bookx01.dbf             BOOKX
        groupx01.dbf            GROUPX
        pagestatsx01.dbf        PAGESTATSX
        perfstat.dbf            PERFSTAT
        rbs01.dbf               RBS
        rdruserx01.dbf          RDRUSERX
        subscrx01.dbf           SUBSCRX
        temp01.dbf              TEMP
        tools01.dbf             TOOLS
        userstatsx01.dbf        USERSTATSX
```

Now that we know the mapping of our disks to files, we are ready to look at some STATSPACK reports that will display all Oracle datafiles that exceed a threshold value.

STATSPACK Reports for Oracle Datafiles

To perform I/O load balancing, we need to get information about the amount of I/O for an Oracle datafile, relative to the total I/O from the database. Remember, a hot file is not necessarily causing a disk bottleneck. The goal of the following STATSPACK technique is to alert the Oracle DBA to those datafiles that are taking a disproportionate amount of I/O relative to other files in the database.

The script we use for this purpose is called *rpt_hot_files.sql*, and this script is also incorporated into our generalized DBA alert script, *statspack_alert.sql*.

The *rpt_hot_files.sql* script is listed next. Let's take a look at how this script works. The idea is to compare the overall I/O between snapshots (hourly in this case) to the total I/O for the database, as shown in Figure 8-12.

To get the data we need, we rely on two STATSPACK tables:

■ **stats$sysstat** The stats$sysstat table contains two important metrics. These are used to compute the total read I/O and write I/O for the entire database:

■ Total physical reads (*statistic#*=40)

■ Total physical writes (*statistic#*=44)

■ **stats$filestatxs** The stats$filestatxs table contains detailed read I/O and write I/O, totaled by datafile name.

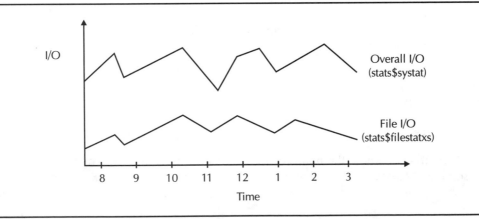

FIGURE 8-12. *Elapsed time I/O comparison*

We then compare the system-wide total for read and write I/O with the individual I/O for each Oracle datafile. This allows us to quickly generate an alert report to tell us which files are having the most I/O activity. If we were judicious in placing important tables and indexes into separate tablespaces and datafiles, this report will tell us exactly which database objects are the most active.

Note that you can adjust the thresholds for the *rpt_hot_files.sql* script. You can set the threshold to 25 percent, 50 percent, or 75 percent, reporting on any files that exceed this threshold percentage of total read and write I/O.

This is a very important script and appears in the generic *statspack_alert.sql* script. It is critical that the DBA become aware whenever an Oracle datafile is consuming a disproportionate amount of disk I/O. The following script is somewhat complex, but it is worth your time to carefully examine it to understand the query. Let's examine the main steps of this SQL statement:

1. We select the individual I/O from stats$filestatxs and compare the value for each file to the total I/O as reported in stats$systat.

2. The WHERE clause determines when a file will be reported. You have the option of adjusting the reporting threshold by commenting out one of the three choices—25 percent, 50 percent, or 75 percent—of the total I/O.

rpt_hot_files.sql

```
set pages 9999;
set feedback off;
set verify off;

column mydate heading 'Yr. Mo Dy  Hr.' format a16
column file_name format a35
column reads  format 99,999,999
column pct_of_tot  format 999


--prompt
--prompt
--prompt  ************************************************************
--prompt  This will identify any single file with a read I/O
--prompt  more than 25% of the total read I/O of the database.
--prompt
--prompt  The "hot" file should be examined, and the hot table/index
--prompt  should be identified using STATSPACK.
--prompt
--prompt  - The busy file should be placed on a disk device with
--prompt    "less busy" files to minimize read delay and channel
--prompt    contention.
```

```
--prompt
--prompt  - If small file has a hot small table, place the table
--prompt     in the KEEP pool
--prompt
--prompt  - If the file has a large-table full-table scan, place
--prompt     the table in the RECYCLE pool and turn on parallel query
--prompt     for the table.
--prompt ************************************************************
--prompt
--prompt


select
   to_char(snap_time,'yyyy-mm-dd HH24')   mydate,
   new.filename                           file_name,
   new.phyrds-old.phyrds                  reads,
   ((new.phyrds-old.phyrds)/
   (
   select
      (newreads.value-oldreads.value) reads
   from
      perfstat.stats$sysstat oldreads,
      perfstat.stats$sysstat newreads,
      perfstat.stats$snapshot   sn1
   where
      sn.snap_id = sn1.snap_id
   and
      newreads.snap_id = sn.snap_id
   and
      oldreads.snap_id = sn.snap_id-1
   and
     oldreads.statistic# = 40
   and
     newreads.statistic# = 40
   and
     (newreads.value-oldreads.value) > 0
   ))*100 pct_of_tot
from
   perfstat.stats$filestatxs old,
   perfstat.stats$filestatxs new,
   perfstat.stats$snapshot   sn
where
   snap_time > sysdate-&1
and
   new.snap_id = sn.snap_id
```

```
and
   old.snap_id = sn.snap_id-1
and
   new.filename = old.filename
and
   -- ***********************************************************
   -- Low I/O values are misleading, so we filter for high I/O
   -- ***********************************************************
   new.phyrds-old.phyrds > 100
and
-- ***********************************************************
-- The following will allow you to choose a threshold
-- ***********************************************************
  (new.phyrds-old.phyrds)*4>   -- This is 25% of total
-- (new.phyrds-old.phyrds)*2> -- This is 50% of total
-- (new.phyrds-old.phyrds)*1.25> -- This is 75% of total
-- ***********************************************************
-- This subquery computes the sum of all I/O during the snapshot period
-- ***********************************************************
(
select
   (newreads.value-oldreads.value) reads
from
   perfstat.stats$sysstat oldreads,
   perfstat.stats$sysstat newreads,
   perfstat.stats$snapshot   sn1
where
   sn.snap_id = sn1.snap_id
and
   newreads.snap_id = sn.snap_id
and
   oldreads.snap_id = sn.snap_id-1
and
  oldreads.statistic# = 40
and
  newreads.statistic# = 40
and
   (newreads.value-oldreads.value) > 0
)
;


--prompt
--prompt
--prompt ***********************************************************
--prompt  This will identify any single file who's write I/O
--prompt  is more than 25% of the total write I/O of the database.
```

```
--prompt
--prompt  The "hot" file should be examined, and the hot table/index
--prompt  should be identified using STATSPACK.
--prompt
--prompt  - The busy file should be placed on a disk device with
--prompt    "less busy" files to minimize write delay and channel
--prompt    contention.
--prompt
--prompt  - If small file has a hot small table, place the table
--prompt    in the KEEP pool
--prompt
--prompt  ************************************************************
--prompt
```

```
select
   to_char(snap_time,'yyyy-mm-dd HH24')  mydate,
   new.filename                          file_name,
   new.phywrts-old.phywrts               writes,
   ((new.phywrts-old.phywrts)/
   (
   select
      (newwrites.value-oldwrites.value) writes
   from
      perfstat.stats$sysstat    oldwrites,
      perfstat.stats$sysstat    newwrites,
      perfstat.stats$snapshot   sn1
   where
      sn.snap_id = sn1.snap_id
   and
      newwrites.snap_id = sn.snap_id
   and
      oldwrites.snap_id = sn.snap_id-1
   and
      oldwrites.statistic# = 44
   and
      newwrites.statistic# = 44
   and
      (newwrites.value-oldwrites.value) > 0
   ))*100 pct_of_tot
from
   perfstat.stats$filestatxs old,
   perfstat.stats$filestatxs new,
   perfstat.stats$snapshot    sn
```

```
where
   snap_time > sysdate-&1
and
   new.snap_id = sn.snap_id
and
   old.snap_id = sn.snap_id-1
and
   new.filename = old.filename
and
   -- **********************************************************
   -- Low I/O values are misleading, so we only take high values
   -- **********************************************************
   new.phywrts-old.phywrts > 100
and
-- **********************************************************
-- Here you can choose a threshold value
-- **********************************************************
 (new.phyrds-old.phywrts)*4>   -- This is 25% of total
-- (new.phyrds-old.phywrts)*2> -- This is 50% of total
-- (new.phyrds-old.phywrts)*1.25> -- This is 75% of total
-- **********************************************************
-- This subquery computes the sum of all I/O during the snapshot period
-- **********************************************************
(
select
   (newwrites.value-oldwrites.value) writes
from
   perfstat.stats$sysstat    oldwrites,
   perfstat.stats$sysstat    newwrites,
   perfstat.stats$snapshot   sn1
where
   sn.snap_id = sn1.snap_id
and
   newwrites.snap_id = sn.snap_id
and
   oldwrites.snap_id = sn.snap_id-1
and
  oldwrites.statistic# = 44
and
  newwrites.statistic# = 44
and
  (newwrites.value-oldwrites.value) > 0
)
;
```

It is highly recommended that the DBA run this STATSPACK report daily so the DBA can constantly monitor for hot datafiles. Here is a sample of the output from this script. Note how it identifies hot files on an hourly basis.

```
************************************************************
This will identify any single file with a read I/O
more than 50% of the total read I/O of the database.
************************************************************


Yr. Mo Dy  Hr. FILE_NAME                               READS PCT_OF_TOT
---------------  ------------------------------------  ----------- ----------
2000-12-14 14    /u02/oradata/prodb1/bookd01.dbf            354         62
2000-12-14 15    /u02/oradata/prodb1/bookd01.dbf            123         63
2000-12-14 16    /u02/oradata/prodb1/bookd01.dbf            132         66
2000-12-14 20    /u02/oradata/prodb1/bookd01.dbf            124         65
2000-12-15 15    /u02/oradata/prodb1/bookd01.dbf            126         72
2001-01-05 09    /u02/oradata/prodb1/system01.dbf           180         63
2001-01-06 14    /u03/oradata/prodb1/perfstat.dbf           752        100
2001-01-06 15    /u02/oradata/prodb1/bookd01.dbf            968         69


************************************************************
This will identify any single file with a write I/O
more than 50% of the total write I/O of the database.
************************************************************


Yr. Mo Dy  Hr. FILE_NAME                              WRITES PCT_OF_TOT
---------------  ------------------------------------  ----------- ----------
2000-12-18 21    /u02/oradata/prodb1/bookd01.dbf           2654         58
2000-12-29 15    /u02/oradata/prodb1/bookd01.dbf           1095         49
```

Now that we have examined how to identify hot files, let's take a look at other useful STATSPACK reports that can tell us about disk activity.

Detailed Disk and File I/O with STATSPACK

Statistics that are captured in the stats$filestatxs table will show details of read and write activity at the file level. However, STATSPACK does not show I/O at the mount point or disk level, and it is up to the Oracle administrator to know the mapping of files to mount points and mount points to disks. On the other hand, statistics that are captured at the UNIX level will show read and write I/O only at the physical disk level. Again, it is up to the Oracle administrator to know all of the mount points and datafiles that reside on each physical disk. If we segregate tables and indexes into separate tablespaces, we know the objects that reside in each file, and we can tell which tables and indexes are experiencing the high I/O.

NOTE
For users of disk array products such as EMC and Net App, you may need third-party products to view I/O statistics. These products include Precise*SQL, or DBView from EMC.

Rather than running the off-the-shelf utilities that generate a printed report for a single time period, you can modify the utilities to collect the I/O data over 5-minute intervals and store the results in Oracle database tables for easy access and report generation:

■ **File statistics** The stats$filestatxs table contains the I/O data collected by STATSPACK. The I/O data includes the actual number of physical reads and writes, the number of block reads and writes, and the time required to perform each operation.

■ **Disk statistics** The next section will explore extending STATSPACK to capture external disk I/O with the UNIX iostat utility and place the data in a STATSPACK extension table called stats$iostat. The stats$iostat table also includes read and write times corresponding to specific dates, but at the disk level. It collects information from the iostat utility, using the script *get_iostat.ksh*.

To provide a cross-reference between the filestat and iostat tables, we added the vol_grp (volume/group) table, which links mount points to physical disks. You need to populate this table manually, based on how your disks are partitioned into mount points. The design of the vol_grp, filestat, and iostat tables lets you aggregate, or average, I/O data over time and summarize it by disk, mount point, tablespace, or datafile.

A STATSPACK Report on Specific I/O Activity

If the DBA is prudent in segregating Oracle objects into distinct tablespaces and datafiles, STATSPACK can be used to create extremely useful reports that show individual I/O or selected datafiles or groups of related datafiles.

The following script accepts a filename "mask" that can be used to report on selected groups of related datafiles. For example, if we have named our customer-related datafiles *customer.dbf*, *custhistory.dbf*, and *custorders.dbf*, the following script can be run to report on all datafile names that contain the string "cust". In the example here, we execute the script with the filename mask to see the I/O history for these datafiles.

rpt_file_io.sql

```
set pages 9999;

column snapdate format a16
column filename format a40
column mydate heading 'Yr.  Mo Dy  Hr.' format a16

select
   to_char(snap_time,'yyyy-mm-dd') mydate,
--    old.filename,
   sum(new.phyrds-old.phyrds)   phy_rds,
   sum(new.phywrts-old.phywrts) phy_wrts
from
   perfstat.stats$filestatxs old,
   perfstat.stats$filestatxs new,
   perfstat.stats$snapshot    sn
where
   new.snap_id = sn.snap_id
and
   old.filename = new.filename
and
   old.snap_id = sn.snap_id-1
and
   (new.phyrds-old.phyrds) > 0
and
   old.filename like '%&1%'
group by
   to_char(snap_time,'yyyy-mm-dd'),
   old.filename
;
```

Here is the output from this script, showing total read and write I/O per day for our cust datafiles:

```
2000-12-12                 833        2770
2000-12-13                   6           9
2000-12-14                   2          80
```

2000-12-15	2	26
2000-12-16	2	4
2000-12-17	2	3
2000-12-18	7	226
2000-12-19	87	556
2000-12-20	141	640
2000-12-21	26	452
2000-12-22	45	368
2000-12-23	10	115
2000-12-24	3	14
2000-12-25	5	54
2000-12-26	169	509
2000-12-27	14	101
2000-12-28	25	316
2000-12-29	13	132
2000-12-30	7	158
2000-12-31	2	129
2001-01-01	4	264
2001-01-02	57	756
2001-01-03	56	317
2001-01-04	1110	123
2001-01-05	1075	386
2001-01-06	20	293
2001-01-07	1	8
2001-01-08	955	1774
2001-01-09	247	1145
2001-01-10	538	1724
2001-01-11	387	1169
2001-01-12	1017	1964
2001-01-13	115	397
2001-01-14	89	443
2001-01-15	22	125
2001-01-16	1267	1667
2001-01-17	646	2082
2001-01-18	588	2359
2001-01-19	46	296

Once gathered, this data can be graphed (see Figure 8-13) to see the detailed activity of the tables and indexes within these datafiles.

This ability of graphing STATSPACK output will be discussed in detail in Chapter 15. Often, the graphical representation of the data is more useful, because the unique I/O signature of the data becomes obvious.

Next, let's examine some STATSPACK tools that can be used to identify potential disk bottlenecks.

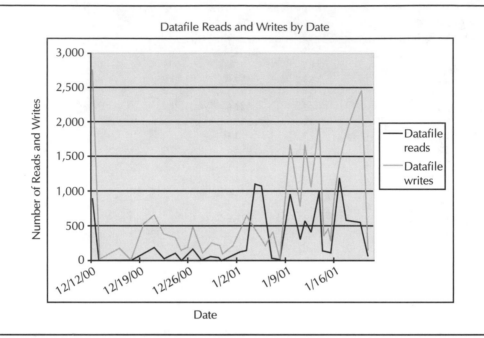

FIGURE 8-13. *File I/O for a selected subset of Oracle datafiles*

A STATSPACK Script to Identify Hot Datafiles

The first step in balancing the load on disks is to find out where they're out of balance by identifying possible bottlenecks. Start by identifying hot disks—those with a disproportionate amount of activity. For example, if one disk in a ten-disk system were experiencing 50 percent of the I/O, measured as the number of reads, writes, or both, you would consider the disk to be hot.

Detecting I/O-Related Slowdowns in AIX

If you are using the IBM AIX operating system, it is easy to detect when a database server may be experiencing I/O slowdowns. An I/O bound database server is usually evidenced by a high value in the wa (wait) column of the UNIX vmstat utility. For example, in the output here we see that 45 percent of the CPU time is being used waiting for database I/O:

```
Prompt> vmstat 5 1

kthr      memory            page                faults        cpu
----- ----------- ------------------------ ------------ ----------
 r  b    avm    fre  re  pi  po  fr   sr  cy  in   sy  cs us sy id wa
 0  0 217485    386   0   0   0   4   14   0 202  300 210 14 19 22 45
```

The Approach to Locating Hot Disks

For other operating environments, we are concerned whenever we see a backlog of I/O tasks waiting to access data on a single disk. For other operating systems, the iostat utility can be used to detect I/O issues.

Once you've identified the hot disks, look closely to find out which files and tables on the disks experience most of the activity, so that you can move them to less-active disks as needed. The actual process of identifying hot files and disks involves running data collection utilities, such as STATSPACK and the UNIX iostat utility, and then using the collected I/O data to pinpoint the sources of excessive I/O measurements.

Here are the cardinal rules for disk I/O:

- There is a difference between a busy disk and a disk that is waiting for I/O to complete. In the next section we will explore the UNIX iostat utility and show how you can identify busy disks.

- If you are using RAID such as RAID 0+1, the Oracle data blocks will be spread randomly across all of the disks, and load will rise and fall in a uniform fashion.

- Senior Oracle DBAs often prefer not to implement RAID striping so that they have more control over the disk I/O subsystem.

- Many disk arrays such as EMC provide sophisticated disk monitoring tools such as Open Symmetrics Manager and Navistar. These tools report on more than simple disk waits, and highlight contention for disks, channels, and disk adapters.

Now that we understand the basic principles behind locating hot disks, let's see how STATSPACK can be extended to capture disk I/O information.

Extending STATSPACK for Disk I/O Data

Our data collection approach relies on I/O information from Oracle and from the physical disks. We will start by using existing STATSPACK tables, but we will also extend STATSPACK to add the disk I/O information. We will use the UNIX iostat utility to capture detailed disk I/O because almost every dialect of UNIX has the iostat utility. However, there is a dialect issue. Just as vmstat has different dialects, iostat is slightly different in each version of UNIX, and the Oracle DBA will need to customize a data collection mechanism according to his or her requirements. Even within the same dialect, there are arguments that can be passed to the iostat utility that change the output display.

The basic iostat utility

The UNIX iostat command syntax looks like this:

```
iostat <seconds between samples> <number of samples>
```

For example, to request five samples, spaced at 10 seconds apart, we would issue the command as follows:

```
iostat -t 10 5
```

Unlike the vmstat utility when all of the data is displayed on one line, the iostat output will have many lines per snapshot, one for each physical disk. Let's begin by taking a short tour of the different dialects of the **iostat** command. We will begin by showing differences between iostat for Solaris and HP/UX, and then show a method for extending STATSPACK to capture STATSPACK data for AIX servers.

iostat on AIX

```
root> iostat 1 1

tty:      tin         tout        cpu:   % user   % sys    % idle    % iowait
          0.0          73                1.0      44.0     56.0       0.0            0.0

Disks:      % tm_act      Kbps     tps    Kb_read    Kb_wrtn
hdisk0        17.0        44.0    11.0       44          0
hdisk1        33.0       100.0    25.0      100          0
hdisk2        15.0        60.0    14.0       56          4
hdisk3        16.0        76.0    19.0       76          0
hdisk4         0.0         0.0     0.0        0          0
hdisk5         0.0         0.0     0.0        0          0
```

Here we see each of the disks displayed on one line. For each disk we see:

- The percentage *tm_act*
- The Kbytes per second of data transfer
- The number of disk transactions per second
- The number of Kbytes read and written during the snapshot period

iostat on HP/UX

```
>iostat 1 5

   device    bps     sps    msps
```

```
c1t6d0       0     0.0     1.0
c2t6d0       0     0.0     1.0
c11t11d0     0     0.0     1.0
c7t11d0      0     0.0     1.0
c11t10d0     0     0.0     1.0
c7t10d0      0     0.0     1.0
c5t10d0      0     0.0     1.0
c10t10d0     0     0.0     1.0
c11t9d0      0     0.0     1.0
c7t9d0       0     0.0     1.0
c5t9d0       0     0.0     1.0
c10t9d0      0     0.0     1.0
c11t8d0      0     0.0     1.0
c7t8d0       0     0.0     1.0
c5t8d0       0     0.0     1.0
c10t8d0      0     0.0     1.0
c5t11d0      0     0.0     1.0
c10t11d0     0     0.0     1.0
c5t12d0      0     0.0     1.0
c7t12d0      0     0.0     1.0
c10t12d0     0     0.0     1.0
c11t12d0     0     0.0     1.0
```

In the HPUX output we see the following columns:

- Device name

- Kilobytes transferred per second

- Number of seeks per second

- Milliseconds per average seek

iostat on Solaris

```
>iostat 1 5
   tty          sd0            sd1            sd6            sd35           cpu
tin tout kps tps serv  kps tps serv  kps tps serv  kps tps serv  us sy wt id
  0    6  53   6   10    0   0    0    0   0    0    0   0    0    0  0  2 97
  0  234   0   0    0    0   0    0    0   0    0    0   0    0    1  0  0 99
  0   80  24   3   10    0   0    0    0   0    0    0   0    0    0  2  2 97
  0   80 120  15    8    0   0    0    0   0    0    0   0    0    0  0  6 94
  0   80   0   0    0    0   0    0    0   0    0    0   0    0    0  0  0 100
```

Unlike the iostat output for HPUX, here we see each disk presented horizontally across the output. We see disks sd0, sd1, sd6, and sd35.

The -x option of the HP/UX iostat utility changes the output from vertical to horizontal. For each disk, we report the reads per second, writes per second, and percentage disk utilization.

```
>iostat -x 1 3
                  extended device statistics
device     r/s    w/s    kr/s    kw/s wait actv   svc_t  %w  %b
sd0        0.0    6.5    1.2     51.6  0.0  0.1    9.6    0   4
sd1        0.0    0.0    0.0      0.0  0.0  0.0    0.0    0   0
sd6        0.0    0.0    0.0      0.0  0.0  0.0    0.0    0   0
sd35       0.0    0.0    0.0      0.0  0.0  0.0    0.0    0   0
nfs1       0.0    0.0    0.0      0.0  0.0  0.0    0.0    0   0
                  extended device statistics
device     r/s    w/s    kr/s    kw/s wait actv   svc_t  %w  %b
sd0        0.0   16.9    0.0    135.3  0.0  0.2    12.3   0   9
sd1        0.0    0.0    0.0      0.0  0.0  0.0    0.0    0   0
sd6        0.0    0.0    0.0      0.0  0.0  0.0    0.0    0   0
sd35       0.0    0.0    0.0      0.0  0.0  0.0    0.0    0   0
nfs1       0.0    0.0    0.0      0.0  0.0  0.0    0.0    0   0
                  extended device statistics
device     r/s    w/s    kr/s    kw/s wait actv   svc_t  %w  %b
sd0        0.0    0.0    0.0      0.0  0.0  0.0    0.0    0   0
sd1        0.0    0.0    0.0      0.0  0.0  0.0    0.0    0   0
sd6        0.0    0.0    0.0      0.0  0.0  0.0    0.0    0   0
sd35       0.0    0.0    0.0      0.0  0.0  0.0    0.0    0   0
nfs1       0.0    0.0    0.0      0.0  0.0  0.0    0.0    0   0
```

Now that we see the differences between the dialects of iostat, let's see how this information can be captured into STATSPACK extension tables.

Defining the STATSPACK table

Because the iostat utility is different on every server, we need to create separate versions of a shell script to capture the disk information. Regardless of the differences in display format, a single Oracle table can be defined to hold the iostat information. Here is the syntax for this table:

```
drop table perfstat.stats$iostat;

create table
perfstat.stats$iostat
(
snap_time           date,
elapsed_seconds     number(4),
hdisk               varchar2(8),
kb_read             number(9,0),
kb_write            number(9,0)
)
tablespace perfstat
storage (initial 20m next 1m )
;
```

```
create index
perfstat.stats$iostat_date_idx
on
perfstat.stats$iostat
(snap_time)
tablespace perfstat
storage (initial 5m next 1m)
;

create index
perfstat.stats$iostat_hdisk_idx
on
perfstat.stats$iostat
(hdisk)
tablespace perfstat
storage (initial 5m next 1m)
;
```

Capturing the iostat Information

The *get_iostat.ksh* script is a UNIX shell script that collects disk-level I/O
information at five-minute intervals. It runs the iostat utility and captures the output
into the iostat table, using the data from the vol_grp table to create the sum_iostat
table as well. Once you've run this script, you have the data required to identify
your system's hot disks and mount points.

get_iostat_solaris.ksh

```
#!/bin/ksh

while true
do
   iostat -x  300 1|\
     sed 1,2d|\
     awk '{ printf("%s %s %s\n", $1, $4, $5) }' |\
   while read HDISK VMSTAT_IO_R VMSTAT_IO_W
   do

     if [ $VMSTAT_IO_R -gt 0 ] and [ $VMSTAT_IO_W -gt 0 ]
     then
        sqlplus -s perfstat/perfstat <<!
        insert into
           perfstat.stats\$iostat
        values
           (SYSDATE, 5, '$HDISK', $VMSTAT_IO_R,$VMSTAT_IO_W);
```

```
        exit
!
    fi
  done
  sleep 300

done
```

Note that this script does not store iostat rows where the values for reads and writes are zero. This is because the stats$iostat table will grow very rapidly, and it is only useful to keep nonzero information. To keep the iostat utility running, you can add a script to your crontab file:

```
#!/bin/ksh

# First, we must set the environment . . . .
ORACLE_SID=prodz1
ORACLE_HOME=`cat /var/opt/oracle/oratab|grep $ORACLE_SID|cut -f2 -d':'`
PATH=$ORACLE_HOME/bin:$PATH
MON=`echo ~oracle/iostat`

#---------------------------------------
# If it is not running, then start it . . .
#---------------------------------------
check_stat=`ps -ef|grep get_iostat|wc -l`;
oracle_num=`expr $check_stat`
if [ $oracle_num -ne 2 ]
 then nohup $MON/get_iostat_solaris.ksh > /dev/null 2>&1 &
fi
```

Once the scripts are created, an entry can be placed into the crontab file to ensure that the iostat monitor is always running. Here is a sample of this crontab file:

```
#*****************************************************************
# This is the daily iostat collector & report for the DBAs and SAs
#*****************************************************************
00 * * * * /home/oracle/iostat/run_iostat_solaris.ksh > \
/home/oracle/iostat/r.lst
```

Generally, you should synchronize the STATSPACK snapshots and *get_iostat.ksh*, so that the file-level and disk-level data are collected during the same time periods. You can run both scripts as often as you like, and you can collect data over long periods of time without adverse effects on database performance. STATSPACK collects file I/O information very quickly from the Oracle database's system global area (SGA) memory. (The actual memory structures that contain the file I/O data are called v$filestat and file$.) The disk I/O data collection is also very fast, usually taking less than one second.

One drawback of this approach is that the data collection tables will eventually become very large. However, you can manage table size by deleting low-I/O datafile entries. For example, you could delete inactive-flle entries with the following SQL:

```
delete from perfstat.stats$iostat
where phys_read < 10 and phys_write < 10;
```

Bear in mind that deleting these entries will skew long-term averages, since the averages will be based only on higher-activity entries.

Although the information collected in stats$iostat and stats$filestatxs is somewhat redundant, the two sets of disk data complement each other. When the iostat results identify a hot mount point, you can turn to the stats$filestatxs results to look at the activity for each datafile residing on the mount point. The stats$filestatxs results also provide more-in-depth information, including the overall time required to perform the reads and writes. From elapsed-time information, you can quickly identify the files that are waiting on disk I/O and see the actual number of physical reads and writes.

Now that we see how to extend iostat for disk information, let's look at some other useful STATSPACK reports that can provide insight into our I/O subsystem.

Generating iostat Reports

Having a wealth of I/O data will be very useful in the process of disk load balancing, but this data is also useful for spotting trends. An application's disk access patterns can vary greatly according to daily or weekly processing needs, so the optimal file placement may not always be obvious. (For example, hdisk32 might be very busy during evening batch processing but largely idle during daytime processing.) And it's possible that relocating a datafile may relieve I/O contention for one process only to cause contention for an unrelated process. Many experienced DBAs say that disk load balancing can be like pressing your fist into an overstuffed pillow: one area goes down, but another area bulges.

In practice, disk load balancing takes several iterations of moving files to find the most workable overall file arrangement. Generally, however, the process of load balancing is well worth the time. Once you have achieved a fairly balanced load, you won't need to move the files unless new processes change the I/O pattern for the disks.

Nonetheless, isolating bottlenecks can be time-consuming and elusive. With the scripts and tables detailed in this section, you can quickly set up a procedure to provide the maximum information you can use for balancing your I/O load and minimizing disk I/O, which is key to keeping response times low. Strategies such as load balancing can go a long way toward improving the speed of your applications and keeping users happy across your network.

Using the I/O information from the stats$iostat table, you can generate trend and alert reports. Both types of reports are easy to generate using SQL, and the combination of the reports will help you identify current bottlenecks as well as spot potential future ones:

■ **High disk I/O**   For each five-minute interval, this report displays the name of any Oracle database file with an I/O value—defined in this case by number of reads—that is more than 50 percent of the total I/O during that interval.

■ **High file I/O**   The alert reports, on the other hand, are intended to identify current bottleneck possibilities—that is, specific datafiles experiencing a disproportionate amount of I/O (for example, those experiencing 20-percent more activity than the average for the mount point).

Often, companies use automated procedures to generate the alert reports and e-mail them to the DBA staff so that they can move these files to less-active mount points as soon as possible.

The following script will generate a sum of all of the I/O, summed by day, hour, or every five minutes.

rpt_disk.sql

```
column hdisk            format a10;
column mydate           format a15;
column sum_kb_read      format 999,999;
column sum_kb_write     format 999,999;

set pages 999;

break on hdisk skip 1;

select
   hdisk,
--   to_char(snap_time,'yyyy-mm-dd HH24:mi:ss') mydate,
--   to_char(snap_time,'yyyy-mm-dd HH24') mydate,
   to_char(snap_time,'day') mydate,
   sum(kb_read)  sum_kb_read,
   sum(kb_write) sum_kb_write
from
   stats$iostat
group by
```

```
    hdisk
    ,to_char(snap_time,'day')
--   ,to_char(snap_time,'yyyy-mm-dd HH24:mi:ss')
--   ,to_char(snap_time,'yyyy-mm-dd HH24')
;
```

Here is the daily summary of disk activity from this script. Note that we see a clear picture of disk I/O activity by physical disk, and we see the changes by the day of the week:

HDISK	MYDATE	SUM_KB_READ	SUM_KB_WRITE
atf0	tuesday	33	1,749
	wednesday	150	7,950
atf2	tuesday	0	4
atf289	tuesday	33	330
	wednesday	150	1,500
atf291	tuesday	0	0
atf293	tuesday	32	1,696
	wednesday	150	7,950
atf4	tuesday	0	0
atf6	tuesday	1	10
atf8	tuesday	0	0
sd0	tuesday	96	160
	wednesday	450	750

Note that this script allows the display of iostat information using several different data formats:

```
to_char(snap_time,'day')
to_char(snap_time,'yyyy-mm-dd HH24:mi:ss')
to_char(snap_time,'yyyy-mm-dd HH24')
```

To change the aggregation of the display information, simply substitute the date format. For example, to see the I/O aggregated by the hour of the day, we substitute the 'day' format string with the 'HH24' format string. Here is the same report aggregating by hour of the day:

HDISK	MYDATE	SUM_KB_READ	SUM_KB_WRITE
atf0	2000-12-26 21	9	477
	2000-12-26 22	12	636
	2000-12-26 23	112	14636
	2000-12-27 07	382	3636
	2000-12-27 08	433	641
atf2	2000-12-26 21	0	4
atf289	2000-12-26 21	9	90
	2000-12-26 22	12	120
	2000-12-26 23	132	5655
atf291	2000-12-26 21	0	0
atf293	2000-12-26 21	8	424
	2000-12-26 22	12	636
	2000-12-26 23	412	1646
	2000-12-27 00	574	4745
	2000-12-27 01	363	3736
	2000-12-27 02	332	432
atf4	2000-12-26 21	23	23
atf6	2000-12-26 21	1	10
atf8	2000-12-26 21	0	9
sd0	2000-12-26 21	24	40
	2000-12-26 22	36	60

Now that we see how we can collect iostat information from a STATSPACK extension table, let's examine how the Oracle DBA uses these reports to detect patterns in disk I/O.

Viewing I/O Signatures with STATSPACK

You will find that your database will develop distinctive I/O signatures. The I/O signature for an OLTP database will be very different than that of a data warehouse, and you can use these I/O signatures to determine regular times when the disk I/O subsystem is overloaded. When we aggregate disk information by day of the week and hour of the day, we can see some very interesting patterns.

NOTE
When developing I/O signatures for your database, it is very important to begin at the global level and drill down for successive detail. For example, after running the global reports, you will find spikes in your database I/O during specific times. Your next step should be to isolate these I/O spikes to specific Oracle database files by closer inspection of the STATSPACK data, and running the rpt_io_pct.sql script to report on specific datafiles.

Let's begin by taking a look at a STATSPACK script to average disk read and write activity by the day of the week.

rpt_avg_io_dy.sql

```
set pages 9999;

column reads  format 999,999,999
column writes format 999,999,999

select
   to_char(snap_time,'day'),
   avg(newreads.value-oldreads.value) reads,
   avg(newwrites.value-oldwrites.value) writes
from
   perfstat.stats$sysstat oldreads,
   perfstat.stats$sysstat newreads,
   perfstat.stats$sysstat oldwrites,
   perfstat.stats$sysstat newwrites,
   perfstat.stats$snapshot    sn
where
   newreads.snap_id = sn.snap_id
and
   newwrites.snap_id = sn.snap_id
and
   oldreads.snap_id = sn.snap_id-1
and
   oldwrites.snap_id = sn.snap_id-1
and
   oldreads.statistic# = 40
and
   newreads.statistic# = 40
and
   oldwrites.statistic# = 41
and
   newwrites.statistic# = 41
having
```

```
    avg(newreads.value-oldreads.value) > 0
and
    avg(newwrites.value-oldwrites.value) > 0
group by
    to_char(snap_time,'day')
;
```

The output from the script will take a running average by the day of the week and display the output as follows:

```
TO_CHAR(S          READS          WRITES
---------    -------------    ------------
friday                  72           2,093
monday                 221           8,896
saturday               211           5,869
sunday                 160           5,056
thursday               338           7,232
tuesday                603          11,765
wednesday              316           7,781
```

This output can then be pasted into an Excel spreadsheet, resequenced, and displayed using the Excel Chart Wizard. In Figure 8-14, we see the I/O signature for an Oracle

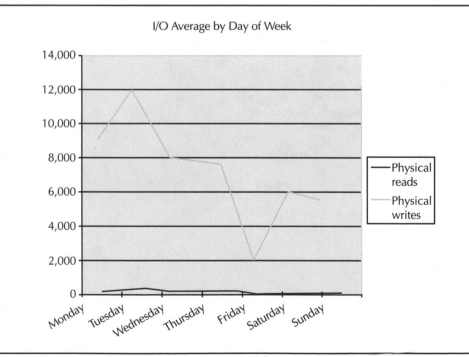

FIGURE 8-14. *Average I/O signature by day of the week*

database. Note that this signature clearly shows peak write activity on Mondays, Tuesdays, and Wednesdays. From this signature, the Oracle DBA knows that this database is loaded during the first part of each week.

Now, let's see how easy it is to change this report to aggregate the data by the hour of the day. The script here is identical to the aggregate averages by day of the week except that the date format string has been changed from 'day' to 'HH24'.

rpt_avg_io_hr.sql

```
set pages 9999;

column reads  format 999,999,999
column writes format 999,999,999

select
   to_char(snap_time,'HH24'),
   avg(newreads.value-oldreads.value) reads,
   avg(newwrites.value-oldwrites.value) writes
from
   perfstat.stats$sysstat oldreads,
   perfstat.stats$sysstat newreads,
   perfstat.stats$sysstat oldwrites,
   perfstat.stats$sysstat newwrites,
   perfstat.stats$snapshot    sn
where
   newreads.snap_id = sn.snap_id
and
   newwrites.snap_id = sn.snap_id
and
   oldreads.snap_id = sn.snap_id-1
and
   oldwrites.snap_id = sn.snap_id-1
and
  oldreads.statistic# = 40
and
  newreads.statistic# = 40
and
  oldwrites.statistic# = 41
and
  newwrites.statistic# = 41
having
   avg(newreads.value-oldreads.value) > 0
and
   avg(newwrites.value-oldwrites.value) > 0
group by
   to_char(snap_time,'HH24')
;
```

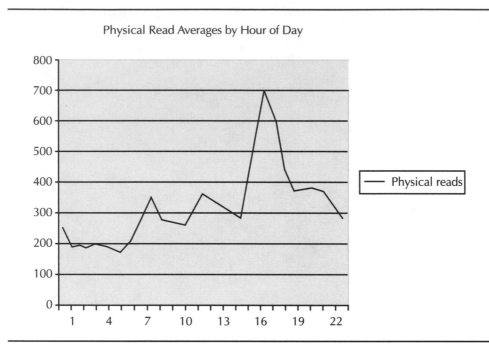

Physical Read Averages by Hour of Day

FIGURE 8-15. *Oracle physical read activity averages by hour of the day*

Now, when we execute this script we see the read and write averages displayed by the hour of the day. Again, we can paste this output into a spreadsheet and create a graphical representation, thereby getting a visual picture of the I/O signature.

TO	READS	WRITES
00	250	6,103
02	180	4,701
03	174	4,580
04	195	5,832
05	191	5,109
06	171	4,669
07	221	4,727
08	354	5,353
09	264	9,531
10	258	7,994
11	249	7,397
12	364	8,499
13	341	7,902
14	326	8,288

15	305	10,891
16	279	9,019
17	692	17,291
18	592	10,444
19	448	9,911
20	385	8,247
21	395	11,405
22	366	9,182
23	271	7,308

The graph in Figure 8-15 (on the facing page) is a graphical representation of the I/O signature of physical reads by hour of the day. Here we see a clear daily trend where the read activity increases throughout the afternoon and a high peak of read activity every day at 6:00 P.M. This information can be extremely valuable to the Oracle DBA. In this example, the DBA could encourage the end-user community to direct their processing to periods before 5:00 P.M.

We can also plot the physical write activity in a graph, as shown in Figure 8-16 In this case, we see a gradual pattern of increasing writes to the database, peaking in the late afternoon. This pattern would be confirmed by an increase in the number of archived redo logs generated later in the day.

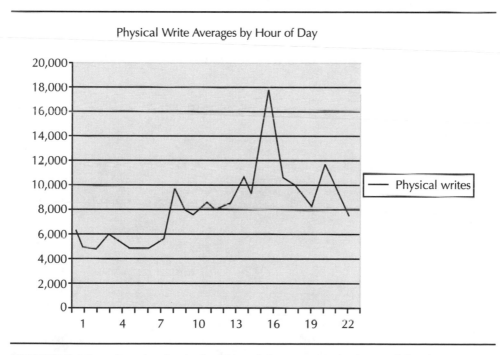

FIGURE 8-16.   *Oracle physical write activity averages by hour of the day*

Conclusion

We have covered an immense amount of material in this chapter, and we should now see the importance of disk load balancing and how to use STATSPACK to monitor the behavior of the disk I/O subsystem. Remember, disk I/O is the single largest component of Oracle performance.

We will now move on to another important topic, the tuning of the Oracle instance. As we noted at the beginning of this chapter, there are many Oracle parameters that directly affect the I/O behavior of the database.

PART
III

Tuning
the Oracle Database
with STATSPACK

CHAPTER
9

Tuning
the Oracle Database
Instance

t this point we have covered all of the external factors that influence Oracle performance and we are ready to look inside Oracle. This next step in Oracle tuning is to inspect the Oracle database instance and examine all of the parameters, configurations, and settings that influence performance. During each phase of instance tuning we will show how STATSPACK information can be used to detect instance performance problems. This chapter will cover the following areas:

- **Overview of the Oracle instance** This will look at the overall architecture of an Oracle instance and show the interrelationships between the components.

- **Tuning the Oracle data buffers** This will include a discussion of the data buffers, and tuning for I/O reduction using the data buffer hit ratio.

- **Overview of tuning the shared pool** This section will explore the shared pool and library cache and show some great STATSPACK scripts for monitoring and tuning shared pool behavior.

- **Pinning objects in the shared pool** This section will describe a technique for ensuring that all packages remain within the RAM memory of the shared_pool.

- **Tuning the library cache** This section will explain the uses of the library cache and show techniques for ensuring that the library cache is functioning properly.

- **Tuning Oracle sorting** This section will show how to monitor sorting for the instance and ensure optimal allocation of sort memory.

- **Tuning rollback segments** This will show techniques for monitoring the rollback segments and identify undesirable conditions.

Once we have completed the tuning of the database instance we are then ready to drill down into more levels of detail. Chapter 10 will examine the settings for tables and indexes and show how they affect Oracle performance, and we will see some useful STATSPACK scripts for monitoring object behavior. We will then move on to look at how STATSPACK can be used to tune the SQL that is run against the database.

Let's begin our discussion of Oracle instance tuning by reviewing the basic structures within a database instance.

An Overview
of the Oracle Database Instance

Before we explore Oracle instance tuning, we must first get a clear idea about the nature of an Oracle instance. At a very general level, an Oracle instance consists of two components: the System Global Area (SGA) and the Oracle background processes, as shown in Figure 9-1.

Within these structures, we find that we can control both the SGA and the background processes by adjusting Oracle parameters. Let's begin with a high-level look at the Oracle SGA.

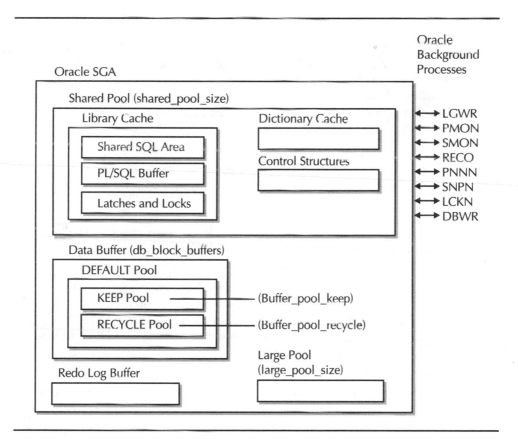

FIGURE 9-1. *An Oracle instance*

The Oracle SGA

When Oracle is started, the Oracle executable issues the **malloc( )** command to create a region of RAM memory. The SGA is commonly called the Oracle region, because it is a region of RAM memory on the database server RAM heap.

The Oracle DBA controls the size of the SGA, and proper SGA management can have a huge impact on performance. However, we must remember that the SGA is a static memory region, and the needs of the Oracle database are constantly changing. Until Oracle9i, the SGA was dynamic and could not be altered. Once Oracle9i becomes commonplace, the dynamic adjustment of the SGA will be possible, and the SGA will reconfigure itself based on the needs of the database. However, changing the SGA requires constant monitoring, and it is sometimes a good approach to develop a general setting for the SGA parameters based on the historical needs of the application.

With STATSPACK, we can observe the historical needs of any application that is running in the SGA, and we can develop a set of global parameters. Using historical STATSPACK information to tune the SGA region works out well because of Oracle's high level of sophistication. Tuning Oracle's memory involves a number of *init.ora* parameters. While there are hundreds of initialization parameters, there are a handful that are very important for Oracle tuning:

- *buffer_pool_keep*   This data buffer pool is used to store small tables that perform full table scans.

- *buffer_pool_recycle*   This pool is reserved for table blocks from very large tables that perform full table scans.

- *db_block_buffers*   This parameter determines the number of database block buffers in the Oracle SGA and represents the single most important parameter to Oracle memory.

- *db_block_size*   The size of the database blocks can make a huge improvement in performance. While the default value is 2,048 bytes, data warehouses and applications that have large tables with full table scans will see a tremendous improvement in performance by increasing *db_block_size* to a larger value. As a general rule, the larger the block size, the less physical I/O, and the faster the overall performance.

- *db_file_multiblock_read_count*   This parameter is used for multiblock reads when performing full table scans or large range scans.

- *large_pool_size*   This is a special area of the shared pool that is reserved for SGA usage when using the multithreaded server.

- *log_buffer*   This parameter determines the amount of memory to allocate for Oracle's redo log buffers. If there is a high amount of update activity, the *log_buffer* should be allocated more space.

- *shared_pool_size*   This parameter defines the pool that is shared by all users in the system, including SQL areas and data dictionary caching. As we will learn later in this chapter, a large *shared_pool_size* is not always better than a smaller shared pool. If your application contains nonreusable SQL, you may get better performance with a smaller shared pool.

- *sort_area_size*   This parameter determines the memory region that is allocated for in-memory sorting. When the stats$sysstat value sorts (disk) becomes excessive, you may want to allocate additional memory.

To see the size of your SGA, you can issue the **show sga** command from SVRMGRL, like this. The output of the **show sga** command appears here:

```
SVRMGR> show sga
Total System Global Area                405323864 bytes
Fixed Size                                  49240 bytes
Variable Size                           354066432 bytes
Database Buffers                         49152000 bytes
Redo Buffers                              2056192 bytes
```

Now let's take a quick look at the important regions within the SGA. We will return to these areas later in this chapter and see how to use STATSPACK to tune each memory area.

The Data Buffer Caches

Starting in Oracle8, the Oracle SGA has three areas of RAM for caching incoming data blocks from disk. They are the DEFAULT pool, the KEEP pool and the RECYCLE pool, as shown in Figure 9-2.

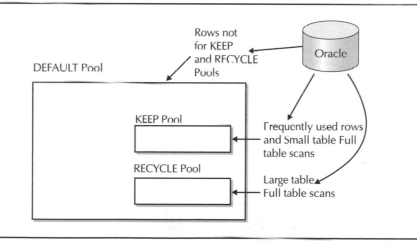

FIGURE 9-2.   *The Oracle data buffer pools*

The buffer caches are in-memory areas of the SGA where incoming Oracle data blocks are kept. On standard UNIX databases, the data is read from disk into the UNIX Journal File System (JFS) buffer where it is then transferred into the Oracle buffer. The size of the data buffers can have a huge impact on Oracle system performance. The larger the buffer cache, the greater the likelihood that data from a prior transaction will reside in the buffer, thereby avoiding expensive physical disk I/O.

The Log Buffer

As you may know, Oracle creates redo logs for all update transactions. These redo logs contain the after image of all row changes and are used to roll forward in cases where Oracle experiences a disk failure. Oracle keeps these redo logs in three separate areas, as shown in Figure 9-3.

As we see in Figure 9-3, the after images are first written to an area of RAM called the log buffer. The images are then transferred to Oracle online redo log files. Finally, the online redo log files are written to the archived redo log file system where they can be used to recover the database.

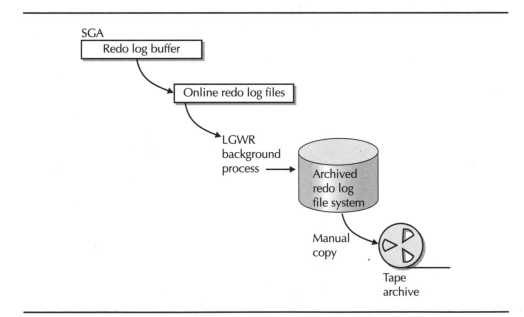

FIGURE 9-3. *The Oracle redo log areas*

The Oracle Shared Pool

After the data buffer caches, the shared pool is the most important area of the SGA. The SGA contains a number of subareas, each with a specific purpose, as shown in Figure 9-4. One of the confounding problems with Oracle is that all of these subareas are controlled with a single parameter called *shared_pool_size*.

It is impossible to dedicate separate regions of memory for the components within the shared pool. The shared pool is normally the second largest memory component within the SGA, depending upon the size of the *db_block_size* parameter. The shared pool holds RAM memory regions for the following purposes:

■ **Library cache**   The library cache stores the execution plan information for SQL that is currently being executed. This area also holds stored procedures and trigger code.

■ **Dictionary cache**   The dictionary cache stores environmental information, including referential integrity, table definitions, indexing information, and other metadata stored within Oracle's internal tables.

■ **Session information**   Stores session information for systems that are using SQL*Net version 2 with Oracle's multithreaded server.

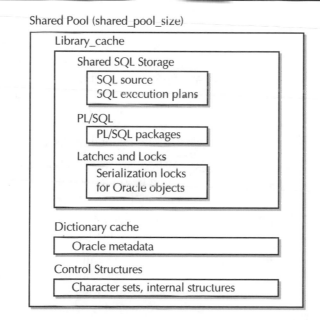

FIGURE 9-4.   *The Oracle shared pool*

Oracle Background Processes

In addition to the SGA region in RAM memory, an Oracle instance also consists of numerous background processes. It is important to remember that an Oracle database is really a very large program running on the server. When the Oracle program needs to perform a specific task, it will spawn a factotum (slave) task to service the task. Table 9-1 provides a listing of the Oracle background processes.

Process	Process Name	Description
Advanced queuing	Aq_tn*xx*	These are the Oracle8 advanced queuing processes that are used to thread processes through the Oracle8 instance.
Archive Monitor	ARCHMON	This is a process on UNIX that monitors the archive process and writes the redo logs to the archives.
Archiver Process	ARCH	This process is only active if archive logging is in effect. This process writes the redo log data files that are filled into the archive log data files.
Callout queues	EXTPROC	There will be one callout queue for each session performing callouts. It was hoped that Oracle8 would multithread these processes, but this feature remains "in the works" for multithreaded environments. As of Oracle8.0.2 beta, callout queues were not working with environments where a multithreaded server was enabled.
Checkpoint processes	CKP*xx*	These are the checkpoint processes that can be started to optimize the checkpoint operation for Oracle logging.
Database Writer	DBWR	This process handles data transfer from the buffers in the SGA to the database files.
Dispatchers	D*nnn*	This process allows multiple processes to share a finite number of Oracle servers. It queues and routes process requests to the next available server.

TABLE 9-1.   *The Oracle Background Processes*

Process	Process Name	Description
Distributed Recoverer	RECO	This is an Oracle process that resolves failures involving distributed transactions.
Listener (SQL*Net v1)	ORASRV	If you are running SQL*Net version 1, this process will be running to service TWO_TASK requests. This parameter was obsoleted in Oracle8.
Listener (Net8)	TNSLSNR	If you are running TCP/IP, this process, known as the TNS listener process, will be running.
Lock Processes	LCKn	This process is used for interinstance locking in an Oracle Parallel Server environment.
Log Writer	LGWR	This process transfers data from the redo log buffers to the redo log database files.
Parallel Query	Pnnn	These background processes are started when Oracle performs a full table scan on a table that is defined as PARALLEL. There will be one background process for each Parallel Query slave, as defined by *DBA_TABLES.DEGREE*.
Process Monitor	PMON	This process recovers user processes that have failed and cleans up the cache. This process also recovers the resources from a failed process.
Servers	Snnn	This process makes all the required calls to the database to resolve user requests. It returns results to the Dnnn process that calls it.
Snapshot queues	Snpxx	These are snapshot process queues.
System Monitor	SMON	This process performs instance recovery on instance startup and is responsible for cleaning up temporary segments. In a parallel environment, this process recovers failed nodes.

TABLE 9-1. *The Oracle Background Processes* (continued)

Most of the Oracle background processes are fully automated and cannot be adjusted. However, there are several *init.ora* parameters that control the background processes.

Important *init.ora* Parameters for Background Processes

It is important to understand that the settings for *init.ora* parameters directly affect the behavior of the Oracle background processes. Here is a list of some of the most important *init.ora* parameters that affect background process behavior.

- *parallel_max_servers*   This is the maximum number of Parallel Query background processes to use when performing a Parallel Query.

- *parallel_min_servers*   This is the minimum number of Parallel Query processes (Pnnn) to be dedicated to a Parallel Query.

- *db_file_multiblock_read_count*   This parameter controls the asynchronous read-ahead feature for Oracle for fast full scans on indexes. In a fast full scan, Oracle reads an entire B-tree index, normally to avoid a sort in the TEMP tablespace.

Now that we have a general understanding of the components that comprise an Oracle instance, let's look deeper into the Oracle data buffer cache. The data buffer cache is one of the most important areas of Oracle instance tuning since it has a direct impact on the amount of disk I/O.

Blocksize and Oracle Disk I/O

I/O is the single most important slowdown in an Oracle database, and the more data we can get in a single I/O, the better the overall performance of Oracle. The cost of reading a 2K block is not significantly higher than the cost of reading an 8K block, and the *db_block_size init.ora* parameter defines the block size for the whole database. However, experiments have shown that almost every Oracle database will run faster with large block sizes and even OLTP databases will run faster with the largest supported block size.

Most neophytes to Oracle will create small block sizes because they see that their average row length is very small, and it seems wasteful to read tiny rows into a huge data block. The problem with this reasoning relates to Oracle's use of indexes. Even in online transaction processing systems where small rows are retrieved, we must remember that Oracle indexes are almost always accessed. The real benefit to large block sizes relates to the Oracle indexes, and not to the row length. As a general rule, the minimum acceptable *db_block_size* is 8K. Oracle data warehouses and systems that perform many full table scans will often benefit from 16K block sizes.

NOTE
When changing a block size from 4K to 8K, the DBA must remember that the size of the SGA will increase because each block will be twice as large. The maximum block size depends on the platform, so you should always consult the operating system specific documentation to find the highest allowed block size for your platform.

When increasing the block size, it is necessary to export the entire database and then redefine the database with the larger block value. This export-import is a time-consuming operation, but it can often result in huge improvements in speed.

The db_file_multiblock_read_count and Oracle

Oracle has an *init.ora* parameter that controls the rate for which blocks are read when long contiguous data blocks are requested. The *db_block_size* parameters can have a dramatic impact on system performance. In addition, there is an important relationship between *db_block_size* and the *db_file_multiblock_read_count* parameter. At the physical level in UNIX, Oracle always reads in a minimum of 64K blocks.

Therefore, the values of *db_file_multiblock_read_count* and *db_block_size* should be set such that their product is 64K. For example:

| 8K blocks | *db_block_size* = 8,192 | *db_file_multiblock_read_count* = 8 |
| 16K blocks | *db_block_size* = 16,384 | *db_file_multiblock_read_count* = 4 |

Again, the *db_file_multiblock_read_count* is most beneficial for systems that perform frequent full table scans, such as data warehouses.

Tuning the Oracle Data Buffers

The purpose of the Oracle data buffers is to reduce disk I/O. As you know, disk I/O is the single largest component to performance, and all tools that reduce I/O are of great interest to someone who is tuning Oracle. Oracle has an insatiable hunger for data buffers, and the addition of buffers will always improve performance by reducing physical disk I/O. We will begin by examining the nature of the data buffers and then explore how the DBA can use STATSPACK to monitor and tune the data buffers for the maximum performance.

Introduction of Data Block Caching

When a SQL statement requests a row, Oracle will first check the internal memory structures to see if the data is already in a data buffer. By caching data blocks in RAM, Oracle avoids doing unnecessary I/O. With the advent of very large SGAs in some 64-bit releases of Oracle, small databases can be entirely cached, and the DBA defines one data buffer for each database block. However, for very large databases, the RAM data buffers cannot hold all of the database blocks and Oracle has a scheme for keeping frequently used blocks in RAM.

When there is not enough room in the data buffer for the whole database, Oracle utilizes a least-recently-used algorithm to determine which database pages are to be flushed from memory. Oracle keeps an in-memory control structure for each block in the data buffer, and moves a data block to the front of the list every time the block is requested. Data blocks that are not frequently referenced will age-out to the end of the data buffer, where they will eventually be erased to make room for a new data block, as shown in Figure 9-5.

Later in this chapter we will see how to use the stats$buffer_pool_statistics table to see the behavior of each of the data buffer pools.

Starting in Oracle8, Oracle provides three separate pools of RAM to hold incoming Oracle data blocks:

- **KEEP pool**   This pool is used to hold tables that are frequently referenced by the application. This normally includes small tables that have frequent full tables scans and reference tables for the application. The KEEP pool is the next evolution of the Oracle7 **table cache** command.

- **RECYCLE pool**   This data pool is reserved for large-table full table scans. Because Oracle data blocks from full table scans are unlikely to be reread, the RECYCLE pool is used so that the incoming data blocks do not "flush out" data blocks from more frequently used tables and indexes.

- **DEFAULT pool**   The DEFAULT pool is used for all table and index access that is not appropriate for the KEEP pool or the RECYCLE pool.

In addition, we must remember that each of these pools are segregated into "hot" and "cool" areas. Please note that Oracle has also dramatically changed the way that data blocks are handled within each of these buffers. In Oracle7, incoming data blocks were always added to the most recently used end of the data buffer. Starting in Oracle8i, incoming data blocks use a midpoint insertion technique. We will go into this in greater detail later in this chapter.

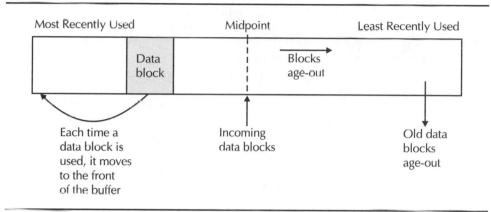

FIGURE 9-5. *Aging data blocks from the RAM block buffer*

To see your current buffer parameters, you can use the server manager utility (svrmgrl) and issue the **show parameters buffer** command.

```
SVRMGR> show parameters buffer
NAME                             TYPE     VALUE
-------- ------------------------ ------- -----------------------------
buffer_pool_keep                 string   500
buffer_pool_recycle              string
db_block_buffers                 integer  6000
log_archive_buffer_size          integer  64
log_archive_buffers              integer  4
log_buffer                       integer  2048000
sort_write_buffer_size           integer  32768
sort_write_buffers               integer  2
use_indirect_data_buffers        boolean  FALSE
```

Here we see the KEEP pool (*buffer_pool_keep*), the RECYCLE pool (*buffer_pool_recycle*) and the DEFAULT pool (*db_block_buffers*).

Full Data Caching

Starting with Oracle8i, it is possible to create a database that is fully cached in the data buffers. Prior to the introduction of the 64-bit versions of Oracle, the maximum size of an Oracle SGA was 1.7 gigabytes. With 64-bit addressing, there is no practical limitation on the size of an Oracle SGA, and the DBA can create database instances with enough data buffers to cache the whole database.

To appreciate the benefit of full data caching, we must remember the time difference between retrieving a data block in RAM vs. fetching a data block from disk. Access time on disks is expressed in milliseconds (thousandths of a second) while RAM speed is expressed in nanoseconds (billionths of a second). In sum, RAM access is faster by two orders of magnitude, and RAM can be thought of as 14,000 times faster than disk.

When fully caching an Oracle database, we must carefully plan for the caching. The multiple data buffer pools are no longer needed when caching the entire database, and most DBAs cache all of the data blocks in the DEFAULT data pool.

Today, any database with less than 20 gigabytes is commonly fully cached, while larger databases still require partial data buffer caches. To calculate the number of data blocks, the DBA simply issues the following command:

```
select
    sum(blocks)
from
    dba_data_files;
```

As the database expands, the DBA must be mindful to increase the *db_block_buffers*, but this approach ensures that all read activity is fully cached. At database startup time, the DBA will invoke a script to load the buffers, generally by issuing a **select count(*) from xxx;** for all of the tables in the database.

This ensures that all data blocks are cached for reads, but write activity will still require disk I/O. With RAM memory getting less expensive every year, Oracle DBAs will continue to make smaller databases fully cached.

The Data Buffer Hit Ratio

The goal of the Oracle data buffers is to keep as many frequently used Oracle blocks in memory as possible. The data buffer hit ratio (DBHR) measures the rate at which a requested data block is found in the buffer pool. As the data buffer hit ratio approaches 100 percent, more data blocks are found in memory, resulting in less disk I/O and better performance. Conversely, if your data buffer hit ratio falls below 90 percent, more data blocks are not found in memory and Oracle must perform a disk I/O to fetch them into the data buffer. Here is the formula for computing the data buffer hit ratio in Oracle8:

```
Cache Hit Ratio = 1 - (Physical Reads - Physical Reads Directs) /
    (session logical reads)
```

In sum, the data buffer hit ratio is the ratio of logical reads to physical reads. There are three *init.ora* parameters that affect the size of the data buffers:

init.ora Parameter	Description
db_block_buffers	Number of blocks in the DEFAULT pool
buffer_pool_keep	Number of blocks in the KEEP pool
buffer_pool_recycle	Number of blocks in the RECYCLE pool

Oracle recommends that the buffer hit ratio stay above 90 percent and the DBA controls the data buffer hit ratio by adding blocks to the *init.ora* parameters.

Many beginning DBAs make the mistake of computing the data buffer hit ratio from the v$ views within Oracle. The v$buffer_pool_statistics view contain the accumulated values for data buffer pool usage, but computing the data buffer hit ratio from the v$ tables will only provide an average since the database was started.

In practice, the more frequently we measure the data buffer hit ratio, the more variation we see. For example, we may see STATSPACK report an hourly data buffer hit ratio of 92 percent, but when we sample the DBHR in five-minute intervals, we will see wide variations in the DBHR, as shown in Figure 9-6.

To see how this variation occurs, let's take a simple example. Imagine a database that is started and ten tasks immediately read ten totally separate blocks. In this case, the data buffer hit ratio would be zero because a requested block always resulted in a physical disk I/O. As a general rule, data warehouses will tend to have lower buffer hit ratios because of their large-table full table scans, while OLTP database will have a higher buffer hit ratio because commonly used indexes are cached in the data buffer.

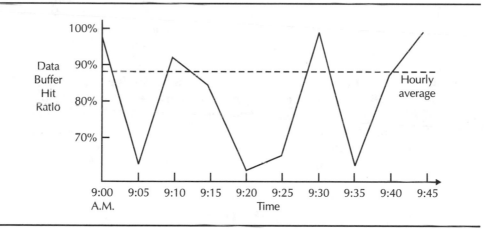

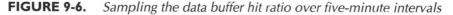

FIGURE 9-6. *Sampling the data buffer hit ratio over five-minute intervals*

To summarize, our goal as the Oracle DBA is to allocate as much RAM as possible to the data buffers without causing the database server to page-in RAM. Whenever the hourly data buffer hit ratio falls below 90 percent, we should add buffers to the block buffers.

NOTE
There is often a RAM problem with very large databases that are running the 32-bit versions of Oracle8i. In these systems, the Oracle software can only reference low memory below the 1.7-gigabyte line. Hence, the only way to create an SGA large enough to keep the DBHR above 90 percent is to install the 64-bit version of Oracle8i.

Now that we understand the basic concepts behind the data buffers, let's go deeper into the internals of the data buffers and see how STATSPACK data can tell us valuable tuning information.

Data Buffer Pool Internals

As we noted, starting with Oracle 8.0, the Oracle data buffer cache was partitioned into multiple disjoint pools named DEFAULT, RECYCLE, and KEEP. In Oracle 8.0, there were issues with the efficiency of the new data pools because they always placed incoming blocks into the most recently used end of each data buffer. Oracle8i contains enhancements to the buffer aging and replacement algorithms in the form of midpoint least recently used insertion and the promotion of most recently used data blocks, and this change has resulted in far better caching of data blocks. Let's take a close look and see why this is true.

New Oracle8i *init.ora* Parameters for Data Buffer Control

Starting in Oracle8i, the buffer cache internal algorithms were dramatically improved and Oracle introduced several new *init.ora* parameters to control aging within the data buffers (Table 9-2). These are all hidden parameters and can be viewed in the stats$parameter table. Of course, Oracle recommends that the DBA should never change a hidden parameter, but advanced Oracle tuning experts often tweak hidden parameters for better performance.

Internal Operations Within the Data Buffer Pools

Prior to Oracle8i, when a data block is fetched into the data buffer from disk, it is automatically placed at the head of the most recently used list. However, this has

Parameter	Default Value	Description
_db_percent_hot_default	50	Percent of DEFAULT buffer pool considered hot
_db_percent_hot_keep	0	Percent of KEEP buffer pool considered hot
_db_percent_hot_recycle	0	Percent of RECYCLE buffer pool considered hot
_db_aging_cool_count	1	Touch count set when buffer cooled
_db_aging_freeze_cr	FALSE	Make CR buffers always be too cold to keep in cache
_db_aging_hot_criteria	2	Touch count that sends a buffer to head of replacement list
_db_aging_stay_count	0	Touch count set when buffer moved to head of replacement list
_db_aging_touch_time	3	Touch count that sends a buffer to head of replacement list

TABLE 9-2.   *Hidden Oracle8 Parameters to Control Buffer Behavior*

changed in Oracle8i. In Oracle8i, a new data buffer is placed in the middle of the block chain, as shown in Figure 9-7.

After loading the data block, Oracle keeps track of the touch count of the data block. If the data block later experiences several touches, it is then moved to the head of the most recently used chain. By inserting new blocks into the middle of the buffer and adjusting the link based on access activity, each data buffer is now partitioned into two sections, a "hot" section that represents the most recently used half of the data buffer, and a "cold" section that represents the least recently used half of the buffer.

This is a huge advancement to the Oracle8i buffers. Essentially, the midpoint insertion scheme creates two pool areas with the DEFAULT, RECYCLE, and KEEP pools. This means that we have a hot and a cold area within each buffer pool, as shown in Figure 9-8, and only those data blocks that are repeatedly requested will move into the hot areas of each pool. This makes each of the data buffers more efficient at caching frequently used data blocks.

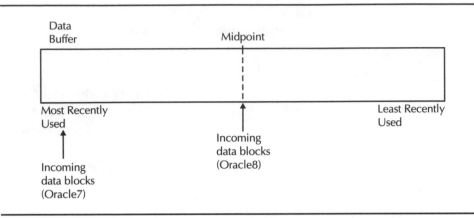

FIGURE 9-7. *Oracle8i placing a new data block in the middle of the chain*

The size of the hot regions is configured by the following *init.ora* parameters:

- *_db_percent_hot_default*
- *_db_percent_hot_keep*
- *_db_percent_hot_recycle*

This new midpoint insertion technique ensures that the most frequently accessed data blocks remain at the head of the most recently used chain because new blocks

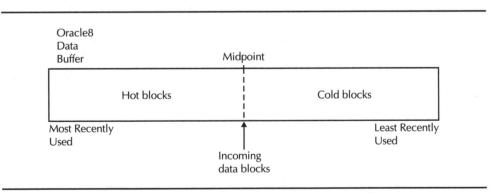

FIGURE 9-8. *The segmentation of each buffer pool in Oracle8i*

only move to the head of the chain if they are repeatedly requested. In sum, Oracle8i data buffer pool management is more efficient than earlier releases.

Finding Hot Blocks Inside the Oracle Data Buffers

Oracle8i maintains an internal X$BH view that shows the relative performance of the data buffer pools. Within the X$BH view we see the following columns:

- **tim**   The tim column is related to the new _DB_AGING_TOUCH_TIME init.ora parameter and governs the amount of time between touches.

- **tch**   the tch column represents the number of times a buffer has been touched by user accesses. This is the touch count that apparently relates directly to the promotion of buffers from the cold region to the hot based on having been touched _DB_AGING_HOT_CRITERIA times.

Since the tch column tracks the number of touches for a specific data block, we can write a dictionary query to display the hot blocks within the buffer:

```
SELECT
     obj       object,
     dbarfil   file#,
     dbablk    block#,
     tch       touches
   FROM
         x$bh
   WHERE
     tch > 10
   ORDER BY
     tch desc;
```

This advanced query technique is especially useful for tracking objects in the DEFAULT pool. Remember, our goal as DBA is to locate hot data blocks and move them from the DEFAULT pool and into the KEEP pool where we allocate enough data blocks to fully cache the table or index.

Before we get into the specifics of tuning the KEEP and RECYCLE pools, let's take a look at how we can measure the historical data buffer hot ratio using STATSPACK. Remember, until Oracle9i, the DBA does not have the luxury of dynamically adding data buffer blocks to the SGA. Hence, a proactive approach to tuning the data buffer is best, and the goal of the DBA is to ensure that the overall I/O patterns are tuned by the configuration of the DEFAULT, KEEP, and RECYCLE pools.

Monitoring Data Buffer Pool Usage with **STATSPACK**

The STATSPACK table for tracking buffer pool utilization is called stats$buffer_pool_statistics. This table contains the following useful columns:

- **name** This is the name of the data buffer (DEFAULT, KEEP, or RECYCLE).

- **free_buffer_wait** This is a count of the number of waits on free buffers.

- **buffer_busy_wait** This is the number of times a requested block was in the data buffer but was unavailable because of a conflict. We will discuss buffer busy waits in detail in Chapter 10.

- **db_block_gets** This is the number of database block gets, which are either logical or physical.

- **consistent_gets** This is the number of logical reads.

- **physical_reads** This is the number of disk block fetch requests issued by Oracle. (Remember, this is not always a "real" read because of disk array caching.)

- **physical_writes** This is the number of physical disk write requests from Oracle. If you have a disk array, the actual writes are performed asynchronously.

The information from these STATSPACK columns can be used to measure several important metrics, the foremost of which is the data buffer hit ratio.

The Data Buffer Hit Ratio and **STATSPACK**

There are two ways to compute the data buffer hit ratio from STATSPACK. In Oracle8i and beyond, the stats$buffer_pool_statistics table contains the required metrics. For Oracle 8.0, the stats$sesstat table should be used to compute the data buffer hit ratio.

NOTE
There is a difference between stats$buffer_pool_statistics in Oracle 8.0 and Oracle8i. If you back-ported STATSPACK into Oracle 8.0, the stats$buffer_pool_statistics view does not give an accurate reading for the data buffer hit ratios for the DEFAULT, KEEP, and RECYCLE pools. Instead, there is only one pool defined as FAKE VIEW.

rpt_bhr.sql   This uses the stats$sysstat table and should be used for Oracle 8.0:

```
set pages 9999;

column logical_reads  format 999,999,999
column phys_reads     format 999,999,999
column phys_writes    format 999,999,999
column "BUFFER HIT RATIO" format 999

select
   to_char(snap_time,'yyyy-mm-dd HH24'),
--   a.value + b.value  "logical_reads",
--   c.value            "phys_reads",
--   d.value            "phys_writes",
   round(100 *
(((a.value-e.value)+(b.value-f.value))-(c.value-g.value)) /
(a.value-e.value)+(b.value-f.v
value)))
          "BUFFER HIT RATIO"
from
   perfstat.stats$sysstat a,
   perfstat.stats$sysstat b,
   perfstat.stats$sysstat c,
   perfstat.stats$sysstat d,
   perfstat.stats$sysstat e,
   perfstat.stats$sysstat f,
   perfstat.stats$sysstat g,
   perfstat.stats$snapshot    sn
where
   a.snap_id = sn.snap_id
and
   b.snap_id = sn.snap_id
and
   c.snap_id = sn.snap_id
and
   d.snap_id = sn.snap_id
and
   e.snap_id = sn.snap_id-1
and
   f.snap_id = sn.snap_id-1
and
   g.snap_id = sn.snap_id-1
and
   a.statistic# = 39
and
   c.statistic# = 39
and
```

```
    b.statistic# = 38
and
    f.statistic# = 38
and
    c.statistic# = 40
and
    g.statistic# = 40
and
    d.statistic# = 41
;
```

rpt_bhr_all.sql   This method is usable for Oracle 8.1 and beyond:

```
column bhr format 9.99
column mydate heading 'yr.   mo dy Hr.'

select
    to_char(snap_time,'yyyy-mm-dd HH24')        mydate,
    new.name                                    buffer_pool_name,
    (((new.consistent_gets-old.consistent_gets)+
    (new.db_block_gets-old.db_block_gets))-
    (new.physical_reads-old.physical_reads))
    /
    ((new.consistent_gets-old.consistent_gets)+
    (new.db_block_gets-old.db_block_gets))     bhr
from
    perfstat.stats$buffer_pool_statistics old,
    perfstat.stats$buffer_pool_statistics new,
    perfstat.stats$snapshot                 sn
where
    (((new.consistent_gets-old.consistent_gets)+
    (new.db_block_gets-old.db_block_gets))-
    (new.physical_reads-old.physical_reads))
    /
    ((new.consistent_gets-old.consistent_gets)+
    (new.db_block_gets-old.db_block_gets)) < .90
and
    new.name = old.name
and
    new.snap_id = sn.snap_id
and
    old.snap_id = sn.snap_id-1
;
```

Here is a sample of the output from this script:

SQL> @rpt_bhr_all

```
yr.   mo dy Hr BUFFER_POOL_NAME        BHR
------------- -------------------- -----
2000-12-12 15 DEFAULT                .92
2000-12-12 15 KEEP                   .99
2000-12-12 15 RECYCLE                .75
2000-12-12 16 DEFAULT                .94
2000-12-12 16 KEEP                   .99
2000-12-12 16 RECYCLE                .65
```

As we can see, this script provides the data buffer hit ratio for each hour for each of the three data buffer pools. Note that we should always see a 99–100-percent DBHR for the KEEP pool. If not, we should add data blocks to this pool, because the size of the KEEP pool should be the sum of the number of data blocks of all objects that are assigned to the KEEP pool.

Next, let's investigate methods for using STATSPACK to identify candidates for the KEEP and RECYCLE pools.

Overview of the New Data Pools

One of the great features of Oracle is the ability to segregate tables based on their characteristics. As you may know, the new data buffer pools are defined in the *init.ora* file, and the syntax looks like this:

```
DB_BLOCK_SIZE=16384
DB_BLOCK_BUFFERS=5000
BUFFER_POOL_KEEP=(1400, 3)
BUFFER_POOL_RECYCLE=(900, 3)
```

After each specification, the first argument is the number of buffer blocks and the second number is the number of LRU latches. Now that we see how the pools are defined, let's revisit the syntax for assigning objects to these pools.

As you know, small tables that experience frequent full table scans should be cached in the data buffers. In Oracle7, this was done with the **cache** command, and in Oracle8 this is done by altering the table to specify the KEEP pool.

In Oracle7, we stated:

```
alter table xxx cache;
```

In Oracle8 we state:

```
alter table CUSTOMER storage (buffer_pool KEEP);
```

Oracle7 did not have an equivalent for the RECYCLE pool because Oracle7 reserved a section at the end of the data buffer for full table scans. As shown in Figure 9-9, by reserving blocks at the least recently used end of the data buffer, Oracle ensured that a full table scan against a huge table would not page-out blocks from more frequently referenced tables and indexes.

In Oracle8 and beyond, the RECYCLE pool is used to receive blocks from large-table full table scans. By isolating the RECYCLE pool, full table scans will never impact the performance of I/O against more frequently referenced tables and indexes. Now that we see the basics, let's explore a technique for identifying tables and indexes for the KEEP and RECYCLE pools.

Locating Tables and Indexes for the KEEP Pool

The Oracle documentation states "A good candidate for a segment to put into the KEEP pool is a segment that is smaller than 10% of the size of the DEFAULT buffer pool and has incurred at least 1% of the total I/Os in the system." In other words, small, highly accessed tables are good candidates for caching.

So, how do we identify small-table full table scans? The best method is to explain all of the SQL that is currently in your library cache and then generate a report showing all of the full table scans in your database at that time. We will introduce a very important script called *access.sql* that will produce these reports in Chapter 15, but for now, let's just assume that we have already explained all of the SQL in our library cache.

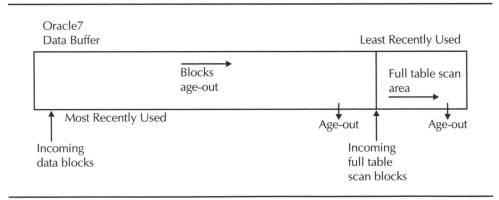

FIGURE 9-9. *The Oracle7 method for handling large-table full table scans*

The access_report Script

This script interrogates the execution plans from the output of access.sql and produces a report of the frequency of full table scans. The details for running this script is explained in Chapter 11.

access_report.sql

```
-- *********************************************************
-- Report section
-- *********************************************************

set echo off;
set feedback on

set pages 999;
column nbr_FTS   format 999,999
column num_rows format 999,999,999
column blocks    format 999,999
column owner     format a14;
column name      format a24;
column ch        format a1;
column K         format a1;

spool access.lst;

set heading off;
set feedback off;
ttitle 'Total SQL found in library cache'
select count(distinct statement_id) from plan_table;

ttitle 'Total SQL that could not be explained'
select count(distinct statement_id) from plan_table where remarks is
not null;

set heading on;
set feedback on;
ttitle 'full table scans and counts|  |Note that "?" indicates in the
table is cached.'
select
   p.owner,
   p.name,
   t.num_rows,
   ltrim(t.cache) ch,
   decode(t.buffer_pool,'KEEP','K','DEFAULT',' ') K,
   s.blocks blocks,
   sum(s.executions) nbr_FTS
```

```
from
  dba_tables t,
  dba_segments s,
  sqltemp s,
  (select distinct
    statement_id stid,
    object_owner owner,
    object_name name
  from
    plan_table
  where
    operation = 'TABLE ACCESS'
    and
    options = 'FULL') p
where
  s.addr||':'||TO_CHAR(s.hashval) = p.stid
  and
  t.owner = s.owner
  and
  t.table_name = s.segment_name
  and
  t.table_name = p.name
  and
  t.owner = p.owner
having
  sum(s.executions) > 9
group by
  p.owner, p.name, t.num_rows, t.cache, t.buffer_pool, s.blocks
order by
  sum(s.executions) desc;
```

The first section of the *access_report.sql* script interrogates the plan table and produces a report showing all full table scans and their frequency. We also have two columns showing if a table is marked as cached (Oracle7) or assigned to the KEEP pool (Oracle8).

This report shows the following columns:

- **OWNER**   The owner of the table.

- **NAME**   This is the table name.

- **NUM_ROWS**   The number of rows in the table as of the last *compute statistics*.

- **C** (Oracle7 only)   This is an Oracle7 column and will display Y if the table is cached, and N if it is not cached.

- **K** (Oracle8 only)   This will display a "K" if the table exists in the KEEP pool.

- **BLOCKS**   This is the number of blocks in the table as defined by the *dba_segments* view.

- **NBR_FTS**   This is the number of full table scans against this table from the data currently in the library cache.

This should give us all of the information we need to identify tables for the KEEP pool. Any small tables (for example, less than 50 blocks) that have a high number of full table scans will benefit from being added to the KEEP pool. In the following report, we see output from an Oracle Applications database, and we see full table scans on both large and small tables.

```
Mon Jan 22                                                              page    1
                    Total SQL found in library cache

                    4600

Mon Jan 22                                                              page    1
                    Total SQL that could not be explained

                    786

Mon Jan 22                                                              page    1
                         full table scans and counts

OWNER        NAME                        NUM_ROWS C K    BLOCKS   NBR_FTS
----------   -------------------------   -------- - -  --------  -------
APPLSYS      FND_CONC_RELEASE_DISJS           39 N K        2    98,864
APPLSYS      FND_CONC_RELEASE_PERIODS         39 N K        2    98,864
APPLSYS      FND_CONC_RELEASE_STATES           1 N K        2    98,864
SYS          DUAL                                N K        2    63,466
APPLSYS      FND_CONC_PP_ACTIONS           7,021 N       1,262    52,036
APPLSYS      FND_CONC_REL_CONJ_MEMBER          0 N K       22    50,174
APPLSYS      FND_CONC_REL_DISJ_MEMBER         39 N K        2    50,174
APPLSYS      FND_FILE_TEMP                     0 N         22    48,611
APPLSYS      FND_RUN_REQUESTS                 99 N         32    48,606
INV          MTL_PARAMETERS                    6 N K        6    21,478
APPLSYS      FND_PRODUCT_GROUPS                1 N          2    12,555
APPLSYS      FND_CONCURRENT_QUEUES_TL         13 N K       10    12,257
AP           AP_SYSTEM_PARAMETERS_ALL          1 N K        6     4,521
APPLSYS      FND_CONCURRENT_QUEUES            13 N K       10     4,078
```

From examining this report, we identify the following files for addition to the KEEP pool. We select those tables with less than 50 blocks that are not already in the KEEP pool (the "K" column).

CAUTION
*Remember that identifying tables for the KEEP pool
is an iterative process. These reports only show you
the SQL that happens to reside in your library cache
at the time you ran the report.*

OWNER	NAME	NUM_ROWS	C	K	BLOCKS	NBR_FTS
PPLSYS	FND_FILE_TEMP	10	N		22	48,611
APPLSYS	FND_RUN_REQUESTS	99	N		32	48,606
APPLSYS	FND_PRODUCT_GROUPS	1	N		2	12,555

Remember, our goal is for the data buffer hit ratio for the KEEP pool to always be 100 percent. Every time we add a table to the KEEP pool, we must also add the number of blocks in the table to the KEEP pool parameter in our *init.ora* file.

Once you have explained all of the SQL in your library cache, you will have a plan table with all of the execution plans and a sqltemp table with all of the SQL source code (see Chapter 11 for details on explaining all of your SQL). Once these tables are populated, you can run a script to generate the KEEP syntax for you. Let's take a look at this script:

access_keep_syntax.sql

```
select
    'alter table '||p.owner||'.'||p.name||' storage (buffer_pool keep);'
from
    dba_tables t,
    dba_segments s,
    sqltemp s,
    (select distinct
        statement_id stid,
        object_owner owner,
        object_name name
    from
        plan_table
    where
        operation = 'TABLE ACCESS'
        and
        options = 'FULL') p
where
    s.addr||':'||TO_CHAR(s.hashval) = p.stid
    and
    t.table_name = s.segment_name
    and
    t.table_name = p.name
```

```
    and
    t.owner = p.owner
    and
    t.buffer_pool <> 'KEEP'
having
    s.blocks < 50
group by
    p.owner, p.name, t.num_rows, s.blocks
order by
    sum(s.executions) desc;
```

To make it easy, we can simply run this script and let Oracle generate the KEEP syntax on our behalf:

```
SQL> @access_keep_syntax

alter table APPLSYS.FND_FILE_TEMP storage (buffer_pool keep);
alter table APPLSYS.FND_RUN_REQUESTS storage (buffer_pool keep);
alter table APPLSYS.FND_PRODUCT_GROUPS storage (buffer_pool keep);
```

The final step is to increase the *buffer_pool_keep init.ora* parameter by the total number of blocks in our tables. The prior value is 1400, and we see that these three tables add 56 blocks to the prior value. Hence we change our *init.ora* parameter as follows:

```
BUFFER_POOL_KEEP=(1456, 3)
```

We are now ready to bounce the database and then execute the output from the access_keep_syntax script.

STATSPACK Tables and KEEP Pool Data
If you want to get extremely sophisticated, you can try to explain the SQL statements that are stored in the stats$sql_summary table. If you are taking the default level-5 STATSPACK snapshots, the stats$sql_summary table will contain the top SQl statements that were in your library cache at the time of each hourly snapshot.

You can simply modify the *access.sql* script from Chapter 11 to use the stats$sql_summary table instead of the v$sqltext.

Advanced KEEP Pool Candidate Identification
In addition to small-table full table scan tables, the KEEP buffer pool may be a good place to keep data blocks from segments that are used frequently and occupy a significant amount of blocks in the data buffer. These are commonly blocks within small reference tables that are accessed via an index and do not appear in our full table scan report.

There is only one window into the internals of the Oracle database buffers: the x$bh internal view. The x$bh internal view contains a great deal of detailed information about the internal operations within the data buffer pools. From the x$bh table, we can count the number of objects in a specific type and the number of "touches" for that object type. It is even possible to use this view to create a picture of all data blocks that are in the buffer.

The following query uses the x$bh view to identify those objects whose blocks average more than five touches and occupy more than twenty blocks in the cache. This will identify tables and indexes that are frequently referenced, and therefore become candidates for inclusion in the KEEP pool.

hot_buffers.sql

```
--     hot_buffers.sql
--     Written by Donald K. Burleson
--        1/22/2001
-- ********************************
-- You MUST connect as SYS
connect sys/manager;
set lines 80;
set pages 999;


column avg_touches format 999
column myname heading 'Name' format a30
column mytype heading 'Type' format a10
column buffers format 999,999

SELECT
   object_type  mytype,
   object_name    myname,
   blocks,
   COUNT(1) buffers,
   AVG(tch) avg_touches
FROM
   sys.x$bh    a,
   dba_objects b,
   dba_segments s
WHERE
   a.obj = b.object_id
and
   b.object_name = s.segment_name
and
   b.owner not in ('SYS','SYSTEM')
GROUP BY
   object_name,
```

```
    object_type,
    blocks,
    obj
HAVING
    AVG(tch) > 5
AND
    COUNT(1) > 20;
```

NOTE
*The hot_buffers.sql script will not run on releases
lower than Oracle8i because the tch column is a
new addition in Oracle 8.1.6.*

Next is the output from this script. The *hot_buffers.sql* script identifies those
objects that are active within the data buffers, both as a function of the number
of data blocks and the number of touches.

Type	Name	BLOCKS	BUFFERS	AVG_TOUCHES
TABLE	PAGE	104	107	44
TABLE	SUBSCRIPTION	192	22	52
INDEX	SEQ_KEY_IDX	40	34	47
TABLE	SEC_SESSIONS	80	172	70
TABLE	SEC_BROWSER_PROPERTIES	80	81	58
TABLE	EC_USER_SESSIONS	96	97	77
INDEX	SYS_C008245	32	29	270

Once you identify hot objects using this script, you are faced with the decision
of segregating the objects into the KEEP pool. As a general rule, you should have
enough available RAM storage for the entire table or index. For example, if you
wanted to add the page table to the KEEP pool, you would need to add 104 blocks
to the *buffer_pool_keep init.ora* parameter.

Because of the transient nature of the data buffers, the results from this script
will be different every time you execute the script. Consequently, some DBAs will
schedule this script to execute every minute whenever they need to see exactly
what is happening inside the data buffers.

Now that we have covered the internals of the KEEP pool, let's turn our attention
to the identification of candidates for the RECYCLE pool.

Tuning the RECYCLE Pool

The RECYCLE pool was created in Oracle8 to provide a reusable data buffer for
transient data blocks. A transient data block is a data block that is being read as a

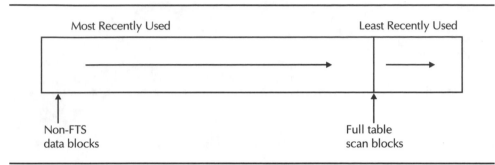

FIGURE 9-10. *The Oracle7 version of the RECYCLE pool*

part of a large-table full table scan and is not likely to be requested again by Oracle in the near future.

In Oracle7, a RECYCLE pool is implemented in the data buffer by reserving blocks at the end of the most recently used chain. These blocks at the end of the buffer were loaded from data blocks from full table scans while all other incoming data blocks went to the head of the data buffer (see Figure 9-10).

Now that we see how the KEEP pool is used, let's discuss the RECYCLE pool and see how it is used for buffering within the SGA.

Identifying Candidates for the RECYCLE Pool

The goal of placing objects into the RECYCLE pool is to segregate large tables that perform frequent full table scans. To see the large-table full table scans, we must return to our full table scan report from *access.sql*:

```
Mon Jan 22                                                          page 1
                          full table scans and counts

    OWNER       NAME                        NUM_ROWS C K    BLOCKS  NBR_FTS
    ----------  --------------------------  -------- - -  --------  --------
    APPLSYS     FND_CONC_RELEASE_DISJS            39 N K         2    98,864
    APPLSYS     FND_CONC_RELEASE_PERIODS         39 N K         2    98,864
    APPLSYS     FND_CONC_RELEASE_STATES           1 N K         2    98,864
    SYS         DUAL                                N K         2    63,466
    APPLSYS     FND_CONC_PP_ACTIONS           7,021 N        1,262    52,036
    APPLSYS     FND_CONC_REL_CONJ_MEMBER          0 N K        22    50,174
```

From this listing, we see one table that is clearly a candidate for the RECYCLE pool. The fnd_conc_pp_actions table contains 1,262 blocks and has had 52,036 full table scans. This is a clear candidate for inclusion into the RECYCLE pool.

CAUTION
*Before blindly assigning a table to the RECYCLE
pool, the prudent DBA should always verify that
the large-table full table scan is legitimate. In many
cases, a poorly tuned query may be performing a
full table scan against the table even though the
query returns far less than 40 percent of the table
rows. As a general rule, large-table full table scans
are only legitimate in systems such as data warehouses where frequent SUM or AVG queries are
required to touch the majority of the table rows.*

Once we have noticed possible candidates for the RECYCLE pool, we can run
a script that will read the plan table generated from *access.sql*. This query will look
for large tables (greater than 1,000 blocks) that are not already assigned to the
RECYCLE pool.

access_recycle_syntax.sql

```
-- ***************************************************
-- Report section
-- ***************************************************

set echo off;
set feedback on

set pages 999;
column nbr_FTS   format 999,999
column num_rows  format 999,999,999
column blocks    format 999,999
column owner     format a14;
column name      format a25;

set heading off;
set feedback off;
select
   'alter table '||p.owner||'.'||p.name||' storage (buffer_pool recycle);'
from
   dba_tables t,
   dba_segments s,
   sqltemp s,
  (select distinct
     statement_id stid,
     object_owner owner,
     object_name name
   from
```

```
        plan_table
    where
        operation = 'TABLE ACCESS'
        and
        options = 'FULL') p
where
    s.addr||':'||TO_CHAR(s.hashval) = p.stid
    and
    t.table_name = s.segment_name
    and
    t.table_name = p.name
    and
    t.owner = p.owner
    and
    t.buffer_pool <> 'RECYCLE'
having
    s.blocks > 1000
group by
    p.owner, p.name, t.num_rows, s.blocks
order by
    sum(s.executions) desc;
```

Here is an example of the output from this script:

```
SQL> @access_recycle_syntax

alter table APPLSYS.FND_CONC_PP_ACTIONS storage (buffer_pool recycle);
```

Remember, before adding any table to the RECYCLE pool, the DBA should extract the SQL source and verify that the query is retrieving more than 40 percent of the rows in the table.

Now that we have covered a technique for finding large-table full table scans from the library cache, let's look at another approach for finding RECYCLE pool candidates that uses the x$bh view.

Advanced RECYCLE Pool Tuning
The following query uses x$bh.tch to identify objects in the buffer cache with single-touch buffer counts totaling more than 5 percent of the total cache. These segments are potentially good candidates for placement in the RECYCLE buffer pool as they are occupying significant cache space with blocks that have not yet been reused.

hot_recycle_blocks.sql

```
set lines 80;
set pages 999;
```

```
column avg_touches format 999
column myname heading 'Name' format a30
column mytype heading 'Type' format a10
column buffers format 999,999

SELECT
    object_type    mytype,
    object_name       myname,
    blocks,
    COUNT(1) buffers,
    100*(COUNT(1)/totsize) pct_cache
FROM
    sys.x$bh     a,
    dba_objects b,
    dba_segments s,
    (select value totsize from v$parameter
         where name = 'db_block_buffers')
WHERE
    a.obj = b.object_id
and
    tch=1   -- This line only works in 8.1.6 and above
and
    b.object_name = s.segment_name
and
    b.owner not in ('SYS','SYSTEM')
GROUP BY
    object_type,
    object_name,
    blocks,
    totsize
HAVING
    100*(COUNT(1)/totsize) > 5
;
```

NOTE
*You must remove the reference to the touch (tch)
column if you are using a release of Oracle prior to
8.1.6. This report is useful in releases prior to 8.1.6,
but you will not be able to tell how many times the
objects have been touched after entry into the pool.*

Here is a sample report from the output of this script. Note that these indexes and
tables comprise more than 5 percent of the space in the data buffer and the data

blocks have only been touched once. This is characteristic of large-table full table scans.

```
Type       Name                                 BLOCKS  BUFFERS PCT_CACHE
---------  ----------------------------------  --------  ------- ---------
INDEX      WIP_REQUIREMENT_OPERATIONS_U1           1042      334      5.57
TABLE      MTL_DEMAND_INTERFACE                     847      818     13.63
TABLE      MTL_SYSTEM_ITEMS                        4227      493      8.22
```

Again, when making a decision to add one of the objects to the RECYCLE pool, you need to consider the number of blocks in the table and the frequency that the table or index appears in the output from this script.

Remember, locating candidates for the RECYCLE pool is an iterative process. Because of the dynamic nature of the data buffer caches, the DBA may want to run this script every minute for several hours to get the full picture of data block activity within the data buffer.

Now that we have covered the monitoring and tuning of the data buffer pools, let's take a look at scripts that can be used to plot the average data buffer hit ratio over specific periods of time.

Trend Reports of the Data Buffer Hit Ratio with STATSPACK

Now that we see how to assign tables and indexes into the proper data buffer, we are ready to examine STATSPACK reports that will show trends in the behavior of the data buffer pools. We can generate average DBHR values along two dimensions:

- Average DBHR by day of the week
- Average DBHR by hour of the day

Each of these reports can provide invaluable information in spotting usage trends within the Oracle database. Remember, activity within the data buffers happens very fast, and sometime a long-tern analysis will provide valuable clues into the processing characteristics of your database. On almost every Oracle database, patterns emerge as the result of regular processing schedules, and these patterns are commonly known as "signatures." In the following examples we will plot the average DBHR for an Oracle8i database running Oracle MRP applications.

Plotting the Data Buffer Hit Ratio by Hour of the Day

Using STATSPACK, you can easily compute the average data buffer hit ratio by the hour of the day. The following script will average the DBHR and present the hourly averages. Let's take a close look at the next script so we can understand how it functions. Note that the script references the stats$buffer_pool_statistics table, which is where we find the values used to compute the DBHR. The problem is that each STATSPACK snapshot gives the values at a specific point in time, while the DBHR is an elapsed-time measure. To convert the snapshots to elapsed-time measures, we join the stats$buffer_pool_statistics table against itself, comparing each snapshot with the snapshot immediately preceding it. Since my STATSPACK collection interval is hourly, the following script computes each hourly DBHR. From the individual DBHR readings, we average the value by selecting the snap_time column with a mask of HH24. This results in an hourly average value for DBHR.

rpt_bhr8i_hr.sql

```
set pages 999;

column bhr format 9.99
column mydate heading 'yr.   mo dy Hr.'

select
   to_char(snap_time,'HH24')        mydate,
   avg(
   (((new.consistent_gets-old.consistent_gets)+
   (new.db_block_gets-old.db_block_gets))-
   (new.physical_reads old.physical_reads))
   /
   ((new.consistent_gets-old.consistent_gets)+
   (new.db_block_gets-old.db_block_gets))
   ) bhr
from
   perfstat.stats$buffer_pool_statistics old,
   perfstat.stats$buffer_pool_statistics new,
   perfstat.stats$snapshot              sn
where
   new.name in ('DEFAULT','FAKE VIEW')
and
   new.name = old.name
and
   new.snap_id = sn.snap_id
and
   old.snap_id = sn.snap_id-1
and
   new.consistent_gets > 0
and
   old.consistent_gets > 0
having
   avg(
   (((new.consistent_gets-old.consistent_gets)+
   (new.db_block_gets-old.db_block_gets))-
```

```
    (new.physical_reads-old.physical_reads))
    /
    ((new.consistent_gets-old.consistent_gets)+
    (new.db_block_gets-old.db_block_gets))
    ) < 1
group by
    to_char(snap_time,'HH24')
;
```

NOTE
*The only problem with this script is that the v$
accumulators will be reset when the instance is
stopped and restarted. When starting a database
and taking a STATSPACK value with a prior value
before the database was stopped, STATSPACK will
invariable return an arbitrary large number. To get
around this problem, we added the* having *clause to
the script to omit any values that are greater than 1.*

Here is the output from the script. Note that we get the average DBHR for each
day. While this report is somewhat interesting, the signature of the database becomes
more evident after we plot the data in an Excel spreadsheet.

yr	BHR
00	.94
01	.96
02	.91
03	.82
04	.80
05	.90
06	.94
07	.93
08	.96
09	.95
10	.84
12	.91
13	.96
14	.95
17	.97
18	.97
19	.95
20	.95
21	.99
22	.93
23	.94

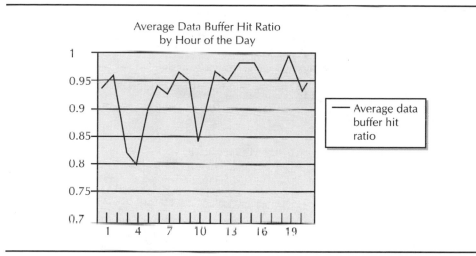

FIGURE 9-11.   *Average data buffer hit ratio by hour of day*

Figure 9-11 shows a plot of the data. Over time, the signature will become more evident, but this database displays some interesting trends.

From this chart we can clearly see that the DBHR dropped below the recommended value of 90 percent at 3:00 A.M., 4:00 A.M., and 10:00 A.M. each day. In this database, it turns out that the end users were submitting huge batch reports between 3:00 A.M. until 5:00 A.M. The problem here is that the DBHR is dropping low at 10:00 A.M., a prime-time online period. The next step would be to review the SQL statements collected in stats$sql_summary for the 9:00 A.M. and 10:10 A.M. periods and see if we can find any rows with a large value for *rows_processed*. This task should then be rescheduled to execute during off-peak processing periods.

Plotting the Data Buffer Hit Ratio by Day of the Week

We can perform a similar analysis for the average DBHR by day of the week. By simply changing the *snap_time* format mask from "HH24" to "day," the averages for each day of the week can be displayed. Here is the script that collected the averages:

rpt_bhr8i_dy.sql

```
set pages 999;

column bhr format 9.99
column mydate heading 'yr.  mo dy Hr.'

select
```

```
    to_char(snap_time,'day')         mydate,
    avg(
    (((new.consistent_gets-old.consistent_gets)+
    (new.db_block_gets-old.db_block_gets))-
    (new.physical_reads-old.physical_reads))
    /
    ((new.consistent_gets-old.consistent_gets)+
    (new.db_block_gets-old.db_block_gets))
    ) bhr
from
    perfstat.stats$buffer_pool_statistics old,
    perfstat.stats$buffer_pool_statistics new,
    perfstat.stats$snapshot                sn
where
    new.name in ('DEFAULT','FAKE VIEW')
and
    new.name = old.name
and
    new.snap_id = sn.snap_id
and
    old.snap_id = sn.snap_id-1
and
    new.consistent_gets > 0
and
    old.consistent_gets > 0
having
    avg(
    (((new.consistent_gets-old.consistent_gets)+
    (new.db_block_gets-old.db_block_gets))-
    (new.physical_reads-old.physical_reads))
    /
    ((new.consistent_gets-old.consistent_gets)+
    (new.db_block_gets-old.db_block_gets))
    ) < 1
group by
    to_char(snap_time,'day')
;
```

Here is the output from the script. Note that the days are presented in alphabetical order, so you must manually resequence the output after pasting it into the spreadsheet for graphing.

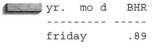
```
yr.  mo d   BHR
--------- -----
friday      .89
```

```
monday      .98
saturday    .92
sunday      .91
thursday    .96
tuesday     .93
wednesday   .91
```

Once the rows are resequenced into day order, it is easy to plot the graph, as shown in Figure 9-12.

This report is especially useful for developing a daily signature. In the case of this database, we see that the DBHR drops on Wednesdays and Fridays. To fully understand this, we would need to use STATSPACK to review the differences between these days and the other days of the week.

Now that we are experts in the data buffer hit ratio, and how to plot and interpret the values, we are ready to move on to other areas of instance tuning. The next section will explore the Oracle database writer and show how STATSPACK can be used to ensure that it is working at optimal levels.

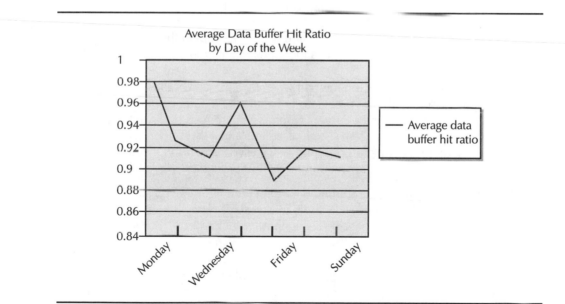

FIGURE 9-12. *The average data buffer hit ratio by day of the week*

Tuning the Database Writer Processes

We may remember that earlier in this chapter we stated that the database writer (DBWR) background processes are responsible for writing dirty data blocks into disk.

For highly active databases, the database writer is a very important Oracle function since the DBWR processes govern the rate at which changed blocks are written to disk. Let's begin with a brief overview of the functions of the DBWR and see how it writes data blocks to disk.

When Oracle detects that a data block in the buffer cache has been changed, the data block is marked as "dirty." Once marked as dirty, the block is queued for a database writer process, which writes the block back to the disk. The DBWR background processes have two responsibilities:

- Scanning the buffer cache, looking for dirty buffers to write

- Writing the dirty buffers to the disk

It is very important to note that every operating system has implemented disk I/O very differently. Hence, the internal process of writing data blocks is specific to the operating system.

Tuning the database writer processes is very important. Within the Oracle data buffer, read-only data blocks can age-out of the buffer but dirty blocks must be retained in the data buffer until the database writer has copied the block to disk.

Oracle offers two *init.ora* parameters for implementing multiple database writers:

- **dbwr_io_slaves**   This is a method whereby a master database writer process spawns additional slave processes to handle the database writes. This option is also used on database servers where asynchronous I/O is not supported. Some UNIX server systems (such as Solaris and AIX) support asynchronous I/O. If your platform does *not* support the asynchronous I/O, you can simulate the asynchronous I/O by defining I/O slave processes.

- **db_writer_processes**   Starting with Oracle 8.0.5, Oracle8 supports true multiple DBWR processes, with no master/slave relationships. This parameter requires that the database server support asynchronous I/O.

Remember, you should only implement multiple database writers when you have a clear indication of writing backlogs. Implementing *db_io_slaves* or *db_writer_processes* comes at a cost in server resources. The multiple writer processes and I/O slaves are intended for large databases with high I/O throughput, and you should only implement multiple database writers if your system requires the additional I/O throughput.

In addition, there are several other *init.ora* parameters that affect the behavior of the DBWR processes:

- **db_block_lru_latches**   This is the number of LRU latches for database blocks. You cannot set *db_writer_process* to a value that is greater than *db_block_lru_latches*.

- **log_checkpoint_interval**   This controls the number of checkpoints issued by the DBWR process. Frequent checkpoints make recovery time faster, but it may also cause excessive DBWR activity during high-volume update tasks. The minimum value for *log_checkpoint_interval* should be set to a value larger than the largest redo log file.

- **log_checkpoint_timeout**   This should be set to zero.

NOTE
Multiple db_writer_process *and* multiple dbwr_io_slaves *are mutually exclusive. If both are set, the* dbwr_io_slaves *parameter will take precedence.*

Now that we understand how the DBWR processes work, let's see where we can go to find information about their performance.

Monitoring the Database Writers with STATSPACK
We can begin our journey by looking at the stats$sysstat table. There are numerous statistics that STATSPACK keeps in this table that provide information about the DBWR behavior.

```
sql> select distinct name from stats$sysstat where name like 'DBWR%'
NAME
------------------------------------------------------------
DBWR Flush object call found no dirty buffers
DBWR Flush object cross instance calls
DDWR buffers scanned
DBWR checkpoint buffers written
DBWR checkpoint write requests
DBWR checkpoints
DBWR cross instance writes
DBWR free buffers found
DBWR incr. ckpt. write requests
DBWR lru scans
DBWR make free requests
DBWR revisited being-written buffer
DBWR skip hot writes
```

```
DBWR summed scan depth
DBWR timeouts
DBWR transaction table writes
DBWR undo block writes
```

Most of these values are of no interest, but a few of them are quite useful. Let's look at the functions of some of the useful values:

- **DBWR checkpoints**   This is the number of checkpoint messages that were sent to the DBWR from Oracle. During checkpoint processing, the log writer hands over to the DBWR a list of modified blocks that are to be written to disk.

- **DBWR buffers scanned**   This is the number of buffers looked at when scanning for dirty buffers to write to the database. This count includes all inspected buffers, including both dirty and clean buffers.

- **Summed dirty queue length**   This is the sum of the queue length after every write request has completed.

- **Write requests**   This is the total number of write requests that were made by Oracle to the database writers.

The main task is determining if the default configuration for the database writers is sufficient for your database. The *summed dirty queue length* and *write requests* are the two metrics in STATSPACK that are useful for measuring the efficiency of the DBWR background processes.

By dividing the summed dirty queue length by the number of write requests, you can get the average length of the queue following the completion of the write.

The following STATSPACK query will measure the dirty queue length for the time period between each snapshot. Any value above 100 indicates a shortage of DBWR processes.

rpt_dbwr_alert.sql

```
-- Written by Donald K. Burleson   1/25/01

set pages 999;

column c1 heading "Write request length" format 9,999.99
column c2 heading "Write Requests"       format 999,999
column c3 heading "DBWR checkpoints"     format 999,999
column mydate heading 'Yr.  Mo Dy  Hr.'  format a16

select distinct
   to_char(snap_time,'yyyy-mm-dd HH24') mydate,
```

```
      a.value/b.value            c1,
      b.value                    c2,
      c.value                    c3
from
      stats$sysstat     a,
      stats$sysstat     b,
      stats$sysstat     c,
      stats$snapshot   sn
where
      sn.snap_id = a.snap_id
and
      sn.snap_id = b.snap_id
and
      sn.snap_id = c.snap_id
and
      a.name = 'summed dirty queue length'
and
      b.name = 'write requests'
and
      c.name = 'DBWR checkpoints'
and
      a.value > 0
and
      b.value > 0
and
      a.value/b.value > 3
;
```

Here is the output from this report. Here we see that the average queue length is quite small, ranging from 2 to 5. According to Oracle, you should only become concerned if the average queue length after writes is more than 50 blocks.

Yr. Mo Dy Hr.	Write request length	Write Requests	DBWR checkpoints
2000-12-25 01	4.71	20,103	44,016
2000-12-25 02	4.62	20,520	44,260
2000-12-25 03	4.51	21,023	45,235
2000-12-25 04	4.31	22,002	47,198
2000-12-25 05	4.13	22,948	49,134
2000-12-25 06	3.96	23,902	51,055
2000-12-25 07	3.81	24,867	52,991
2000-12-25 08	3.67	25,808	54,913
2000-12-25 09	3.54	26,731	56,797
2000-12-25 10	3.42	27,667	58,673
2000-12-25 11	3.31	28,618	60,622
2000-12-25 12	3.20	29,580	62,544
2000-12-25 13	3.10	30,524	64,489
2000-12-25 14	3.01	31,492	66,418

```
2001-01-01 01                    4.70        13,492        31,992
2001-01-01 02                    4.37        14,481        34,007
2001-01-01 03                    4.09        15,486        36,032
```

We can easily extend the STATSPACK report to report on the average values, aggregated by hour of the day and day of the week. This will help the DBA identify trends in database write activity. Next is an example of the STATSPACK script that averages the queue length values by hour of the day:

rpt_dbwr_hr.sql

```
set pages 999;

column c1 heading "Write request length" format 9,999.99
column c2 heading "Write Requests"        format 999,999
column c3 heading "DBWR checkpoints"      format 999,999

select distinct
   to_char(snap_time,'HH24') mydate,
   avg(a.value/b.value)                      c1
from
   stats$sysstat  a,
   stats$sysstat  b,
   stats$snapshot sn
where
   sn.snap_id = a.snap_id
and
   sn.snap_id = b.snap_id
and
   a.name = 'summed dirty queue length'
and
   b.name = 'write requests'
and
   a.value > 0
and
   b.value > 0
group by
   to_char(snap_time,'HH24')
;
```

Here is the output from this script. We can now easily take this output and plot a graphical representation on the data from an Excel spreadsheet (see Figure 9-13).

```
Yr.  Mo Dy  Hr.  Write request length
---------------  --------------------
00                            1.11
01                            2.60
```

02	2.51
03	2.43
04	1.99
05	1.91
06	1.84
07	1.55
08	.96
09	.98
10	.80
11	.75
12	.76
13	.74
14	.74
15	.71
16	.61
17	.99
18	.97
19	.93
20	.86
21	.89
22	.86
23	.95

Here we see that the DBWR is busiest in the early morning hours between midnight and 8:00 A.M. This is because this database does its batch updates during this processing window.

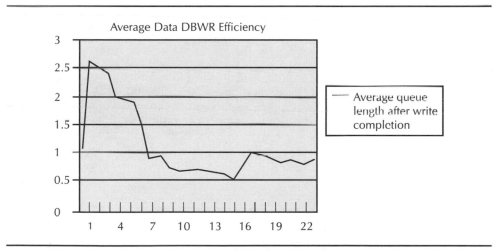

FIGURE 9-13.   *Average queue length after write completion by hour of day*

We can slightly alter this script and aggregate the average queue length, summarized by the day of the week. Here, we take the averages and group them by day.

rpt_dbwr_dy.sql

```
Set pages 999;


column c1 heading "Write request length" format 9,999.99
column c2 heading "Write Requests"        format 999,999
column c3 heading "DBWR checkpoints"      format 999,999

select distinct
   to_char(snap_time,'day') mydate,
   avg(a.value/b.value)                     c1
from
   stats$sysstat  a,
   stats$sysstat  b,
   stats$snapshot sn
where
   sn.snap_id = a.snap_id
and
   sn.snap_id = b.snap_id
and
   a.name = 'summed dirty queue length'
and
   b.name = 'write requests'
and
   a.value > 0
and
   b.value > 0
group by
   to_char(snap_time,'day')
;
```

Here is the output. Again, it is simple to create a graph from this output.

```
Yr.  Mo Dy  Hr.  Write request length
---------------  --------------------
friday                            .18
monday                           2.31
saturday                          .02
sunday                           1.96
thursday                         1.53
tuesday                           .43
wednesday                         .10
```

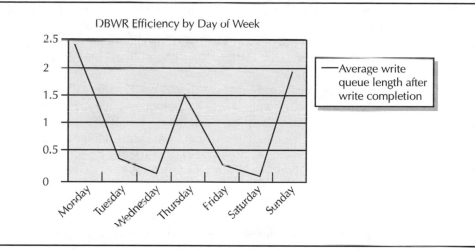

FIGURE 9-14. *Average queue length after write completion by day of week*

Figure 9-14 shows the graph. Here, we see that the overall efficiency of the database writer is fine, but the peak write times are on Monday, Wednesday, and Sunday.

In summary, the database writer processes will work fine for most all Oracle databases without modification. However, when you detect that the summed dirty queue length is too high, you can look at increasing the number of database writer processes.

Now that we understand DBWR, let's look into another important area, the detection and correction of buffer busy waits.

Tuning the Shared Pool

The shared pool component of the Oracle SGA is primarily used to store shared SQL cursors, SQL source and execution plans, stored procedures, and session information, and to function as a RAM cache for the data dictionary and library. The following section will look at the relevant parameters that govern the shared pool and show how STATSPACK can be used to monitor and help tune the shared pool region of RAM.

The size of the shared pool is controlled with the *shared_pool_size init.ora* parameter. This parameter is most often adjusted in response to poor statistics for library cache hits or high SQL reparsing within the library cache, but the shared pool is unlike any other Oracle structure.

There are numerous times when making the shared pool smaller will dramatically improve performance. In fact, many Oracle instances with nonreusable SQL are configured with *shared_pool_size*. Optimally, this setting should be large enough to retain all the reusable library cache objects plus enough to accommodate the maximum total of concurrent nonsharable object sizes.

On the surface, it is counterintuitive that the shared pool performance will get worse as the size increases. In all other areas of Oracle memory, more RAM memory will always result in better performance. The explanation is that memory buffers usually assists performance by eliminating physical disk access. However, in the case of the shared pool and literal SQL, an inverted CPU-memory trade-off develops where more memory actually results in larger data structures to manage with more management overhead due to the nonsharing of library cache objects. This overhead is CPU intensive, so with enough SQL pressure the system becomes CPU bound and performance suffers drastically.

A landmark experiment titled "Piranhas in the Pool" by John Beresniewicz (*Oracle Internals,* 2000) clearly demonstrated this phenomenon, and offered an explanation for this behavior. This paper noted that the failure of SQL statements to utilize bind variables directly contributed to poor performance within the shared pool. Conversely, the use of bind variables (resulting in identical SQL) creates many fewer library cache objects and rapid hashing to the matching object. The library cache latch is thus released more quickly, reducing the latching impact of the library cache latch.

cursor_sharing and the Shared Pool

Starting in Oracle8i (8.1.6), Oracle introduced an exciting new *init.ora* parameter called *cursor_sharing*. *cursor_sharing* is designed to help manage the kinds of problems inherent with nonsharable SQL. The *cursor_sharing* parameter has the following values:

- **FORCE**   Library cache object matching based on exact SQL (or PL/SQL) text match as in pre-8.1.6 Oracle.

- **EXACT**   Oracle automatically substitutes bind variables to replace literals in SQL statements before library cache object matching takes place, causing increased sharing of literal SQL.

When *cursor_sharing* is set to FORCE, Oracle adds an extra parsing process that identifies statements that would be equivalent if they did not contain literal values in the SQL. For systems with dynamic SQL with embedded literal values, the *cursor_sharing* parameter will greatly improve performance.

For example, suppose the following statement was stored in the shared pool:

```
select * from customer where last_name = 'Burleson' and first_name = 'Don';
```

With *cursor_sharing* = FORCE, the following statement will be recognized as identical to the first:

```
select * from customer where last_name = 'Ault' and first_name = 'Mike';
```

The *cursor_sharing* facility will translate the first statement into a host variable equivalent and use its execution plan to execute the second statement:

```
select * from customer where last_name = :var1 and first_name = :var2;
```

The effects of this parameter on systems with lots of literal SQL is astounding. Beresniewicz confirmed that using *cursor_sharing* results in performance advantages similar to those obtained using bind variables. His results confirmed the following performance gains:

- Reduced library cache impact

- Negligible shared pool activity

- Reduced CPU demands

Thus, it is clear that *cursor_sharing* can be used to significantly enhance the performance of high-volume literal SQL and is a great boon to the DBA saddled with such applications.

John Beresniewicz reached the following conclusions:

- The library cache and shared pool memory manager are integral components of the Oracle server designed to create efficiencies and thereby improve performance through the caching and reuse of CPU-intensive steps during SQL processing.

- Applications characterized by high volumes of literal (nonsharable) SQL can compromise these efficiencies, induce additional overhead, and degrade performance.

- Experimental results confirm that this is the case and support the explanation that contention for the shared pool and library cache latches plays a major role in this problem.

- The new *cursor_sharing* initialization parameter introduced in Oracle 8.1.6 addresses and corrects the performance impact of literal SQL by converting it to bind variable format before library cache object matching is undertaken. Results show that this new feature does indeed correct for the performance penalty of literal SQL and promises to be a "silver bullet" for DBAs burdened with pathologically nonsharable SQL.

Now that we see the benefits of *cursor_sharing* on *shared_pool* performance, let's look at some STATSPACK scripts that monitor the performance of the shared pool and the library cache.

Instance Event Waits and STATSPACK

There are several tables within STATSPACK that can be used to give us insight into contention problems within the Oracle instance.

The stats$system_event table contains detailed statistics about system events and the time that they have to wait for service. Unfortunately, the stats$system_event table contains internal events such as *ipc messages* that are not relevant to tuning. Fortunately, the DBA can filter through the events in the stats$system_event table and only report on these events that are interesting to the DBA. These events include:

- Latch-free waits

- Enqueue waits

- Buffer busy waits

- Log writer waits for redo copy latches

- SQL*Net communications events

We are interested in finding times when these events experience an excessive amount of waits and time waiting. The following STATSPACK script will identify those events where time waited is greater than 100 or total waits for the event exceed 100:

rpt_event.sql

```
set pages 999;
set lines 80;

column mydate heading 'Yr.  Mo Dy Hr'       format a13;
column event                                format a30;
column waits                                format 999,999;
column secs_waited                          format 999,999,999;
column avg_wait_secs                        format 99,999;

break on to_char(snap_time,'yyyy-mm-dd') skip 1;

select
   to_char(snap_time,'yyyy-mm-dd HH24')             mydate,
   e.event,
```

```
    e.total_waits - nvl(b.total_waits,0)              waits,
    ((e.time_waited - nvl(b.time_waited,0))/100)  /
    nvl((e.total_waits - nvl(b.total_waits,0)),0)  avg_wait_secs
from
    stats$system_event b,
    stats$system_event e,
    stats$snapshot       sn
where
    e.snap_id = sn.snap_id
and
    b.snap_id = e.snap_id-1
and
    b.event = e.event
and
   (
    e.event like 'SQL*Net%'
    or
    e.event in (
       'latch free',
       'enqueue',
       'LGWR wait for redo copy',
       'buffer busy waits'
      )
   )
and
    e.total_waits - b.total_waits  > 100
and
    e.time_waited - b.time_waited > 100
;
```

Here is the output from this script. As you can see, someone was running a large task on January 22 that stressed several areas within the shared pool and communications subsystem.

```
Yr.  Mo Dy Hr EVENT                                  WAITS AVG_WAIT_SECS
------------ ---------------------------------- -------- -------------
2001-01-22 20 SQL*Net message from client        119,432             1
2001-01-22 20 SQL*Net more data from client          592             0
2001-01-22 20 buffer busy waits                      605             0
2001-01-22 20 enqueue                                826             0
2001-01-22 20 latch free                         128,343             0
2001-01-22 21 SQL*Net message from client         30,249             3
2001-01-22 21 SQL*Net more data from client          253             0
2001-01-22 21 enqueue                                740             0
2001-01-22 21 latch free                          77,247             0
```

In most cases, the resolution to these problems is to add additional blocks to the *shared_pool*, but we can always go back to the stats$sql_summary table to see what

SQL precipitated the problems. Next, let's look at how STATSPACK can be used to monitor background events within the instance.

Monitoring Background Events with STATSPACK

The stats_bg_event summary table provides a wealth of information regarding important background events. To see the list of events, we query the stats_bg_event summary table.

```
  1* select distinct event from STATS$BG_EVENT_SUMMARY
SQL> /

EVENT
------------------------------
buffer busy waits
checkpoint range buffer not saved
control file parallel write
control file sequential read
db file parallel write
db file scattered read
db file sequential read
direct path read
direct path write
enqueue
file identify
file open
free buffer waits
latch free
library cache pin
log file parallel write
log file sequential read
log file single write
log file switch completion
log file sync
pmon timer
process startup
rdbms ipc message
rdbms ipc reply
smon timer
write complete waits
```

The next step is to run a STATSPACK query that will report on those events that exceed our predefined threshold. Note that we remove the *timer* and *message* events since these are seldom of interest when tuning a database.

rpt_bg_event_waits.sql

```
set pages 999;
set lines 80;
```

```
column mydate heading 'Yr.  Mo Dy Hr'      format a13;
column event                               format a30;
column total_waits    heading 'tot waits' format 999,999;
column time_waited    heading 'time wait' format 999,999;
column total_timeouts heading 'timeouts'  format 9,999;

break on to_char(snap_time,'yyyy-mm-dd') skip 1;

select
   to_char(snap_time,'yyyy-mm-dd HH24')            mydate,
   e.event,
   e.total_waits - nvl(b.total_waits,0)            total_waits,
   e.time_waited - nvl(b.time_waited,0)            time_waited,
   e.total_timeouts - nvl(b.total_timeouts,0)      total_timeouts
from
   stats$bg_event_summary      b,
   stats$bg_event_summary      e,
   stats$snapshot       sn
where
   e.event not like '%timer'
and
   e.event not like '%message%'
and
   e.snap_id = sn.snap_id
and
   b.snap_id = e.snap_id-1
and
   b.event = e.event
and
   e.total_timeouts > 50
and
(
   e.total_waits - b.total_waits  > 50
   or
   e.time_waited - b.time_waited > 50
)
;
```

Here is the output. Here we see the time, the event name, the total waits for the event, the time waited, and the total timeouts for the event:

```
Yr.  Mo Dy Hr EVENT                      tot waits time wait timeouts
------------- -------------------------- --------- --------- --------
2000-12-28 12 buffer busy waits                 52         0       45
2001-01-01 00 buffer busy waits                 62         0       60
2001-01-01 01 buffer busy waits                 53         0       49
2001-01-04 01 buffer busy waits                 52         0       46
2001-01-07 18 rdbms ipc reply                   85         0       54
```

```
2001-01-08 17 latch free                 95        0       95
2001-01-17 23 buffer busy waits          82        0       76
2001-01-17 23 latch free                 79        0       78
2001-01-21 23 latch free                 51        0       51
2001-01-22 13 latch free                 55        0       55
2001-01-22 14 latch free                 52        0       52
2001-01-22 20 latch free                 60      104       60
```

This report can provide vital clues for areas of contention within our database. This script is incorporated into the generic *statspack_alert.sql* script, so the DBA is always aware of out-of-bounds conditions inside the database.

Next, let's examine the most important areas of the shared pool, the library cache.

Tuning the Library Cache

The library cache is arguably the most important area of the SGA. The shared SQL areas and the PL/SQL areas reside in the library cache, and this is the true center of activity within Oracle.

The activity of SQL within the library cache is critical to the performance of Oracle. We already discussed the use of *cursor_sharing* to make SQL reusable, but there are some other types of SQL that are always reparsed.

One of the biggest problems with Oracle SQL prior to Oracle8i was that execution plans for SQL could not be stored. In Oracle8i, we have the ability to use the *outline* procedure to store the execution plan for an SQL statement, but Oracle still has problems recognizing "similar" SQL statements. For example, Oracle library cache will examine the following SQL statements and conclude that they are not identical:

```
SELECT * FROM customer;
Select * From Customer;
```

While capitalizing a single letter, adding an extra space between verbs, or using a different variable name might seem trivial, the Oracle software is not sufficiently intelligent to recognize that the statements are identical. Consequently, Oracle will reparse and execute the second SQL statement, even though it is functionally identical to the first SQL statement.

The best way to prevent SQL reloads is to encapsulate all SQL into stored procedures, and place these stored procedures into packages. This removes all SQL from application programs and moves them into Oracle's data dictionary. This method also has the nice side effect of making all calls to the Oracle database look like a logical function. For example, instead of having a complex SQL statement inside a program, you would have a single call to a stored procedure.

There are other ways to make storage reusable within the library cache. The *cursor_space_for_time init.ora* parameter can be used to speed executions within the library cache. Setting *cursor_space_for_time* to FALSE tells Oracle that a shared SQL area can be deallocated from the library cache to make room for a new SQL statement. Setting *cursor_space_for_time* to TRUE means that all shared SQL areas are pinned in the cache until all application cursors are closed. When set to TRUE, Oracle will not bother to check the library cache on subsequent execution calls because it has already pinned the SQL in the cache. This technique can improve the performance for some queries, but *cursor_space_for_time* should not be set to TRUE if there are cache misses on execution calls. Cache misses indicate that the *shared_pool_size* is already too small, and forcing the pinning of shared SQL areas will only aggravate the problem.

Another way to improve performance on the library cache is to use the *init.ora* *session_cached_cursors* parameter. As you probably know, Oracle checks the library cache for parsed SQL statements, but *session_cached_cursors* can be used to cache the cursors for a query. This is especially useful for tasks that repeatedly issue parse calls for the same SQL statement—for instance, where a SQL statement is repeatedly executed with a different variable value. An example would be the following SQL request that performs the same query 50 times, once for each state:

```
select
    sum(dollars_sold)
from
    sales_table
where
    region = :var1;
```

Now that we have reviewed techniques for efficiently using library cache storage, let's look at a STATSPACK report that will show us what is happening inside Oracle. There are several metrics that address the inner workings of the library cache.

Monitoring the Library Cache Miss Ratio

The library cache miss ratio tells the DBA whether or not to add space to the shared pool, and it represents the ratio of the sum of library cache reloads to the sum of pins. In general, if the library cache ratio is over 1, you should consider adding to the *shared_pool_size*. Library cache misses occur during the parsing and preparation of the execution plans for SQL statements. The compilation of a SQL statement consists of two phases: the parse phase and the execute phase. When the time comes to parse a SQL statement, Oracle first checks to see if the parsed representation of the statement already exists in the library cache. If not, Oracle will allocate a shared SQL area within the library cache and then parse the SQL statement. At execution time, Oracle checks to see if a parsed representation of the SQL statement already exists in the library cache. If not, Oracle will reparse and execute the statement.

The following STATSPACK script will compute the library cache miss ratio. Note that the script sums all of the values for the individual components within the library cache and provides an instance-wide view of the health of the library cache.

rpt_lib_miss.sql

```
set lines 80;
set pages 999;

column mydate heading 'Yr.  Mo Dy  Hr.' format a16
column c1 heading "execs"       format 9,999,999
column c2 heading "Cache Misses|While Executing"    format 9,999,999
column c3 heading "Library Cache|Miss Ratio"      format 999.99999

break on mydate skip 2;

select
    to_char(snap_time,'yyyy-mm-dd HH24')   mydate,
    sum(new.pins-old.pins)                 c1,
    sum(new.reloads-old.reloads)           c2,
    sum(new.reloads-old.reloads)/
    sum(new.pins-old.pins)                 library_cache_miss_ratio
from
    stats$librarycache old,
    stats$librarycache new,
    stats$snapshot     sn
where
    new.snap_id = sn.snap_id
and
    old.snap_id = new.snap_id-1
and
    old.namespace = new.namespace
group by
    to_char(snap_time,'yyyy-mm-dd HH24')
;
```

Here is the output. The preceding report can easily be customized to alert the DBA during times when there are excessive executions or library cache misses.

| | | Cache Misses | |
Yr. Mo Dy Hr.	execs	While Executing	LIBRARY_CACHE_MISS_RATIO
2000-12-20 10	10,338	3	.00029
2000-12-20 11	182,477	134	.00073
2000-12-20 12	190,707	202	.00106
2000-12-20 13	2,803	11	.00392

Once this report identifies a time period where there may be a problem, STATSPACK provides the ability to run detailed reports to show the behavior of the objects within the library cache.

Monitoring Objects Within the Library Cache with STATSPACK

Within the library cache, hit ratios can be determined for all dictionary objects that are loaded into the RAM buffer. These objects include tables/procedures, triggers, indexes, package bodies, and clusters. None of these objects should be experiencing problems within the library cache. If any of the hit ratios fall below 75 percent, you can increase the size of the shared pool by adding to the *shared_pool_size init.ora* parameter.

The STATSPACK table stats$librarycache is the table that keeps information about library cache activity. The table has three relevant columns: namespace, pins, and reloads. The first is the namespace, which indicates whether the measurement is for the SQL area, a table or procedure, a package body, or a trigger. The second value in this table is pins, which counts the number of times an item in the library cache is executed. The reloads column counts the number of times the parsed representation did not exist in the library cache, forcing Oracle to allocate the private SQL areas in order to parse and execute the statement.

Let's look at the STATSPACK scripts that we can use to monitor these objects inside the library cache.

STATSPACK Reports for the Library Cache

The following script reports on the details within the objects inside the library cache. While it is often useful to see the specifics for each object, we must remember that the only objects that can be pinned into storage are PL/SQL packages. We will be covering the pinning of packages into the SGA later in this chapter.

rpt_lib.sql

```
set lines 80;
set pages 999;

column mydate heading 'Yr.  Mo Dy  Hr.' format a16
column reloads       format 999,999,999
column hit_ratio     format 999.99
column pin_hit_ratio format 999.99

break on mydate skip 2;

select
```

```
   to_char(snap_time,'yyyy-mm-dd HH24')  mydate,
   new.namespace,
   (new.gethits-old.gethits)/(new.gets-old.gets) hit_ratio,
   (new.pinhits-old.pinhits)/(new.pins-old.pins) pin_hit_ratio,
   new.reloads
from
   stats$librarycache old,
   stats$librarycache new,
   stats$snapshot      sn
where
   new.snap_id = sn.snap_id
and
   old.snap_id = new.snap_id-1
and
   old.namespace = new.namespace
and
   new.gets-old.gets > 0
and
   new.pins-old.pins > 0
;
```

Here is the output. One nice feature of this STATSPACK report is that it shows the activity within the library cache between each snapshot period.

Yr. Mo Dy Hr.	NAMESPACE	HIT_RATIO	PIN_HIT_RATIO	RELOADS
2000-12-20 10	BODY	1.00	1.00	5
	PIPE	1.00	1.00	0
	SQL AREA	.99	.96	2,957
	TABLE/PROCEDURE	1.00	.91	212
	TRIGGER	1.00	1.00	0
	BODY	1.00	1.00	5
	INDEX	1.00	1.00	0
2000-12-20 11	BODY	.99	.99	5
	CLUSTER	1.00	1.00	1
	INDEX	1.00	1.00	0
	PIPE	1.00	1.00	0
	SQL AREA	.98	.99	2,999
	TABLE/PROCEDURE	.99	1.00	221
	TRIGGER	1.00	1.00	0

From this report, the DBA can track the loading of each type of object, and see the balance of the different object types inside the library cache.

Now let's look at the how to pin PL/SQL packages into the library cache.

Pinning Packages in the SGA

It has long been known that placing SQL inside stored procedures has numerous advantages over external SQL. By placing all SQL in packages, system consistency is easy to maintain, all SQL resides inside the data dictionary, and, best of all, the packages can be pinned into the library cache.

As more shops begin encapsulating their SQL into stored procedures, more application code will move away from external programs and into the database engine. Application vendors are delivering their PL/SQL in packages, and more developers are encapsulating their SQL into stored procedures. This has a benefit of having a complete application stored inside the data dictionary.

When a request is made to Oracle to parse an SQL statement or PL/SQL block, Oracle will first check the internal memory structures to see if the parsed object is already in the library cache buffer. In this fashion, Oracle avoids doing unnecessary reparsing of SQL statements. In an ideal world, it would be wonderful if we could allocate memory to hold all SQL, thereby ensuring that Oracle would never reparse a statement.

Library cache objects are paged out based on a least recently used (LRU) algorithm. Once loaded into the RAM memory of the shared pool, stored procedures will execute very quickly, and even though the stored procedure will move to the head of the list each time it is reexecuted, there is still the potential that the stored procedure could age-out of the library cache and need to be reloaded.

To prevent reparsing of SQL inside packages, you can mark packages as nonswappable, telling the database that after their initial load they must always remain in memory. This is called "pinning" or "memory fencing." Oracle provides the procedure dbms_shared_pool.keep for pinning a package. You can unpin packages by using dbms_shared_pool.unkeep.

NOTE
Packages can only be pinned after the instance is started, and they must be repinned each time the database is started. Most DBAs write a script to pin their packages immediately after startup time.

The choice of whether to pin a procedure in memory is a function of the size of the object and the frequency with which it is used. Very large procedures that are called frequently might benefit from pinning, but you might never notice any difference in that case because the frequent calls to the procedure will have kept it loaded into memory anyway.

In an ideal world, the *init.ora shared_pool* parameter would be large enough to accept every package, stored procedure, and trigger your applications might invoke.

Reality, however, dictates that the shared pool cannot grow indefinitely, and you need to make wise choices regarding which objects you pin.

Some Oracle DBAs actively work to encapsulate SQL into stored procedures and the stored procedures into packages. In this fashion, many DBAs identify high-impact procedures and group them into a single package, which is pinned in the library cache.

Because of their frequent usage, Oracle recommends that the standard, dbms_standard, dbms_utility, dbms_describe, and dbms_output packages always be pinned in the shared pool. The following snippet demonstrates how a stored procedure called sys.standard can be pinned:

```
Svrmgrl> connect internal;

@/$ORACLE_HOME/rdbms/admin/dbmspool.sql

EXECUTE dbms_shared_pool.keep('sys.standard');
```

A standard procedure can be written to pin all of the recommended Oracle packages into the shared pool. Here is a sample of such a script:

pin.sql

```
EXECUTE dbms_shared_pool.keep('DBMS_ALERT');
EXECUTE dbms_shared_pool.keep('DBMS_DDL');
EXECUTE dbms_shared_pool.keep('DBMS_DESCRIBE');
EXECUTE dbms_shared_pool.keep('DBMS_LOCK');
EXECUTE dbms_shared_pool.keep('DBMS_OUTPUT');
EXECUTE dbms_shared_pool.keep('DBMS_PIPE');
EXECUTE dbms_shared_pool.keep('DBMS_SESSION');
EXECUTE dbms_shared_pool.keep('DBMS_SHARED_POOL');
EXECUTE dbms_shared_pool.keep('DBMS_STANDARD');
EXECUTE dbms_shared_pool.keep('DBMS_UTILITY');
EXECUTE dbms_shared_pool.keep('STANDARD');
```

Oracle Corporation recommends that you always pin the same packages in the shared pool. For Oracle applications, there is a list of several hundred packages, and the DBA must ensure that these get pinned each time the database starts.

Automated Repinning of Packages

UNIX users might want to add a script to their database startup procedure to ensure that the packages are repinned after each database startup, thereby guaranteeing that all packages are repinned with each bounce of the box. A pinning script might look like this:

```
root> more pin_packs.ksh
ORACLE_SID=prodedi
export ORACLE_SID
su oracle -c "/usr/oracle/bin/svrmgrl /<<!
connect internal;
@pin.sql
exit;
!"
```

Now let's take a look at how we monitor packages inside the library cache and identify candidates for pinning.

Monitoring Packages for Pinning

The following script shows how to look at all packages in the SGA. The output from this listing should show those packages that are frequently used by your application.

memory.sql

memory.sql - Display used SGA memory for triggers, packages, & procedures

```
SET PAGESIZE 60;

COLUMN EXECUTIONS FORMAT 999,999,999;
COLUMN Mem_used   FORMAT 999,999,999;

SELECT SUBSTR(owner,1,10) Owner,
       SUBSTR(type,1,12)  Type,
       SUBSTR(name,1,20)  Name,
       executions,
       sharable_mem       Mem_used,
       SUBSTR(kept||' ',1,4)   "Kept?"
 FROM v$db_object_cache
 WHERE TYPE IN ('TRIGGER','PROCEDURE','PACKAGE BODY','PACKAGE')
 ORDER BY EXECUTIONS DESC;
```

The next output shows the output of *memory.sql*. Here we see that the packages are ordered by the number of executions (in descending order). In this example, we see that *dbms_alert* is a frequently referenced package and should be added to the pinning script.

```
SQL> @memory

OWNER   TYPE      NAME          EXECUTIONS   MEM_USED   KEPT
----    ------    ------        ----------   --------   -----
SYS     PACKAGE   STANDARD         867,600    151,963    YES
```

SYS	PACKAGE BODY	STANDARD	867,275	30,739	YES
SYS	PACKAGE	DBMS_ALERT	502,126	3,637	NO
SYS	PACKAGE BODY	DBMS_ALERT	433,607	20,389	NO
SYS	PACKAGE	DBMS_LOCK	432,137	3,140	YES
SYS	PACKAGE BODY	DBMS_LOCK	432,137	10,780	YES
SYS	PACKAGE	DBMS_PIPE	397,466	3,412	NO
SYS	PACKAGE BODY	DBMS_PIPE	397,466	5,292	NO
HRIS	PACKAGE	S333_PACK	285,700	3,776	NO

Now that we know how to monitor the library cache, lets look at another important component of the shared pool, the data dictionary cache.

Tuning the Dictionary Cache

The data dictionary cache is used to hold rows from the internal Oracle metadata tables, including SQL stored in packages. Let's take a look at how packages interact with the dictionary cache.

When a PL/SQL package is invoked, Oracle first checks the dictionary cache to see if the package is already in memory. Of course, a package will not be in memory the first time it is requested, and Oracle will register a dictionary cache miss. Consequently, it is virtually impossible to have an instance with no dictionary cache misses, because each item must be loaded once.

The data dictionary data is maintained in a separate RAM buffer called the dictionary cache, which is stored in the shared SQL area. The data dictionary cache is accessed for each SQL statement at parse time and again at runtime when the SQL gathers dynamic storage for execution.

The data dictionary cache statistics originate in the x$kqrst structure, where it participates in the v$rowcache view. This data is transferred from v$rowcache into stats$rowcache_summary when a snapshot is requested.

The stats$rowcache_summary table is used to measure dictionary cache activity. Two columns are of interest: gets, and getmisses. The gets column provides the total number of requests for objects of that type. The getmisses column counts the number of times Oracle had to perform a disk I/O to retrieve a row from its dictionary tables.

The data dictionary cache hit ratio is used to measure the ratio of dictionary hits to misses. Bear in mind, however, that this ratio is only good for measuring the average hit ratio for the life of the instance.

The following STATSPACK report displays the summaries for the data dictionary cache for all times when the data dictionary hit ratio has dropped below 95 percent:

rpt_dict_alert.sql

```
set lines 80;
set pages 999;

column mydate heading 'Yr.  Mo Dy  Hr.'              format a16
column c1      heading "Data|Dictionary|Gets"        format 999,999,999
column c2      heading "Data|Dictionary|Cache|Misses" format 999,999,999
column c3      heading "Data|Dictionary|Hit|Ratio"   format 999,999

select
   to_char(snap_time,'yyyy-mm-dd HH24')   mydate,
   sum(new.gets-old.gets)                 c1,
   sum(new.getmisses-old.getmisses)       c2,
   trunc((1-(sum(new.getmisses-old.getmisses)/sum(new.gets-old.gets)))*100) c3
from
   stats$rowcache_summary new,
   stats$rowcache_summary old,
   stats$snapshot sn
where
   new.snap_id = sn.snap_id
and
   old.snap_id = new.snap_id-1
having
   trunc((1-(sum(new.getmisses-old.getmisses)/sum(new.gets-old.gets)))*100) < 95
group by
   to_char(snap_time,'yyyy-mm-dd HH24')
;
```

Here is the listing from this script. We can quickly identify times when the data dictionary experienced a poor hit ratio.

```
SQL> @rpt_dict_alert.sql
```

	Data Dictionary Gets	Data Dictionary Cache Misses	Data Dictionary Hit Ratio
Yr. Mo Dy Hr.			
2000-12-22 02	268,149	34,377	87
2000-12-22 08	976,143	52,311	94
2000-12-23 02	219,912	33,789	84
2000-12-24 06	571,179	54,327	90
2000-12-26 02	277,263	33,915	87
2000-12-27 02	275,961	33,957	87
2000-12-29 02	271,761	34,818	87
2000-12-30 02	407,001	34,587	91
2000-12-31 06	818,496	55,104	93
2000-12-31 11	621,138	38,136	93

```
2001-01-02 02        290,472        35,700         87
2001-01-02 08        661,248        36,918         94
2001-01-02 13        366,282        43,953         88
2001-01-03 02        304,101        36,057         88
2001-01-05 02        302,253        36,519         87
```

We can easily extend this report to see if there is a pattern in the data dictionary gets and misses. The script here computes the average by the hour of the day:

rpt_dict_hr.sql

```
set lines 80;
set pages 999;

column mydate heading 'Yr.  Mo Dy  Hr.'              format a16
column c1     heading "Data|Dictionary|Gets"         format 999,999,999
column c2     heading "Data|Dictionary|Cache|Misses" format 999,999,999
column c3     heading "Data|Dictionary|Hit|Ratio"    format 999,999

select
   to_char(snap_time,'HH24')  mydate,
--   sum(new.gets-old.gets)                c1,
--   sum(new.getmisses-old.getmisses)      c2,
   trunc((1-(sum(new.getmisses-old.getmisses)/sum(new.gets-old.gets)))*100) c3
from
   stats$rowcache_summary new,
   stats$rowcache_summary old,
   stats$snapshot sn
where
   new.snap_id = sn.snap_id
and
   old.snap_id = new.snap_id-1
group by
   to_char(snap_time,'HH24')
;
```

Here is the output from the script. Let's plot the numbers and see if there is a pattern.

```
                          Data
                      Dictionary
                             Hit
Yr.  Mo Dy  Hr.            Ratio
---------------- ----------
00                           99
01                           99
02                           94
03                          100
04                           96
```

05	98
06	98
07	98
08	98
09	98
10	99
11	99
12	99
13	99
14	99
15	99
16	99
17	99
18	99
19	99
20	99
21	98
22	99
23	99

Figure 9-15 shows the graph.

Here we see that the overall data dictionary hit ratio is acceptable, but there is a consistent drop in the data dictionary hit ratio at 2:00 A.M. each morning. Now that we have examined the system-wide dictionary averages, we are ready to drill down and look at the individual types of data dictionary objects.

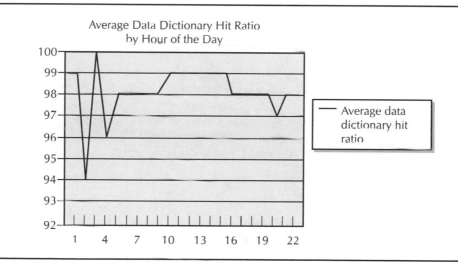

FIGURE 9-15.   *Average data dictionary hit ratio by hour of the day*

The STATSPACK script here displays the details for each parameter type within the data dictionary cache:

rpt_dict_detail.sql

Yr. Mo Dy Hr.	PARAMETER	Data Dictionary Gets	Dictionary Cache Misses	Data Dictionary Usage	Data Object Hit Ratio
2000-12-20 11	dc_objects	1,342	38	22	97
	dc_segments	4,085	10	2	100
	dc_user_grants	414	1	49	100
	dc_object_ids	2,268	39	11	98
	dc_objects	1,335	66	63	95
	dc_segments	2,275	49	61	98
2000-12-20 12	dc_constraints	72	24	8	67
	dc_histogram_defs	229	66	60	71
	dc_object_ids	6,315	94	85	99
	dc_objects	4,048	156	151	96
	dc_segments	6,002	114	105	98
	dc_sequence_grants	97	6	101	94
	dc_synonyms	1,474	49	22	97
2000-12-20 13	dc_object_ids	12,465	86	84	99
	dc_objects	7,234	130	130	98
	dc_segments	13,070	112	113	99
	dc_synonyms	2,718	38	40	99
	dc_users	3,043	1	1	100

While this standard report is useful for showing the activity of the objects, what the DBA really needs is a script to send an alert whenever a frequently used dictionary object type is experiencing a poor hit ratio. The STATSPACK script here will identify all data dictionary object types where the data dictionary hit ratio is less than 80 percent for an object type that had more than 300 gets:

rpt_dict_detail_alert.sql

```
set lines 80;
set pages 999;

column mydate heading 'Yr.  Mo Dy  Hr.'          format a16
column parameter                                 format a20
column c1     heading "Data|Dictionary|Gets"     format 99,999,999
```

```
column c2      heading "Data|Dictionary|Cache|Misses" format 99,999,999
column c3      heading "Data|Dictionary|Usage"        format 999
column c4      heading "Object|Hit|Ratio"             format 999

select
   to_char(snap_time,'yyyy-mm-dd HH24')  mydate,
   new.parameter                         parameter,
   (new.gets-old.gets)                   c1,
   (new.getmisses-old.getmisses)         c2,
   (new.total_usage-old.total_usage)     c3,
  round((1 - (new.getmisses-old.getmisses) /
  (new.gets-old.gets))*100,1)            c4
from
   stats$rowcache_summary new,
   stats$rowcache_summary old,
   stats$snapshot          sn
where
  round((1 - (new.getmisses-old.getmisses) /
  (new.gets-old.gets))*100,1) < 70
and
   (new.total_usage-old.total_usage) > 300
and
   new.snap_id = sn.snap_id
and
   old.snap_id = new.snap_id-1
and
   old.parameter = new.parameter
and
   new.gets-old.gets > 0
;
```

Here is the output. We can clearly see the time when our Oracle database experienced a high reload rate and the type of object. In the next report, we see a low data dictionary cache miss ratio with the *dc_free_extents* object. This may be due to a large load job that was requesting frequent new file extents.

			Data Dictionary Gets	Data Dictionary Cache Misses	Data Dictionary Usage	Object Hit Ratio
Yr. Mo Dy Hr.	PARAMETER					
2001-01-02 20	dc_histogram_defs	4,398	3,595	8,362	18
2001-01-11 22	dc_free_extents	934	316	319	66
2001-01-13 02	dc_free_extents	621	310	305	50
2001-01-19 02	dc_free_extents	626	312	310	50
2001-01-19 07	dc_histogram_defs	1,196	371	367	69
2001-01-19 12	dc_used_extents	453	351	321	23

```
2001-01-20 02      dc_free_extents     317          314          316          1
2001-01-23 02      dc_free_extents     627          313          322          50
2001-01-24 02      dc_free_extents     322          318          314          1
```

Now that we have completed our survey of Oracle's data dictionary cache, let's expand our scope and take a look at how to identify and tune Oracle sorting with the SGA.

Tuning Oracle Sorting

As a small but very important component of SQL syntax, sorting is a frequently overlooked aspect of Oracle tuning. In general, an Oracle database will automatically perform sorting operations on row data as requested by a **create index** or an SQL ORDER BY or GROUP BY statement. In general, Oracle sorting occurs under the following circumstances:

- SQL using the ORDER BY clause

- SQL using the GROUP BY clause

- When an index is created

- When a MERGE SORT is invoked by the SQL optimizer because inadequate indexes exist for a table join

At the time a session is established with Oracle, a private sort area is allocated in RAM memory for use by the session for sorting. If the connection is via a dedicated connection a Program Global Area (PGA) is allocated according to the *sort_area_size init.ora* parameter. For connections via the multithreaded server, sort space is allocated in the *large_pool*. Unfortunately, the amount of memory used in sorting must be the same for all sessions, and it is not possible to add additional sort areas for tasks that require large sort operations. Therefore, the designer must strike a balance between allocating enough sort area to avoid disk sorts for the large sorting tasks, keeping in mind that the extra sort area will be allocated and not used by tasks that do not require intensive sorting. Of course, sorts that cannot fit into the *sort_area_size* will be paged out into the TEMP tablespaces for a disk sort. Disk sorts are about 14,000 times slower than memory sorts.

As we noted, the size of the private sort area is determined by the *sort_area_size init.ora* parameter. The size for each individual sort is specified by the *sort_area_ retained_size init.ora* parameter. Whenever a sort cannot be completed within the assigned space, a disk sort is invoked using the temporary tablespace for the Oracle instance.

Disk sorts are expensive for several reasons. First, they are extremely slow when compared to an in-memory sort. Also, a disk sort consumes resources in the temporary tablespace. Oracle must also allocate buffer pool blocks to hold the blocks in the temporary tablespace. In-memory sorts are always preferable to disk sorts, and disk sorts will surely slow down an individual task as well as impact concurrent tasks on the Oracle instance. Also, excessive disk sorting will cause a high value for free buffer waits, paging other tasks' data blocks out of the buffer.

The following STATSPACK query uses the stats$sysstat table. From this table we can get an accurate picture of memory and disk sorts.

rpt_sorts_alert.sql

```
set pages 9999;

column mydate heading 'Yr.  Mo Dy  Hr.' format a16
column sorts_memory  format 999,999,999
column sorts_disk    format 999,999,999
column ratio         format .99999

select
   to_char(snap_time,'yyyy-mm-dd HH24') mydate,
   newmem.value-oldmem.value sorts_memory,
   newdsk.value-olddsk.value sorts_disk,
   ((newdsk.value-olddsk.value)/(newmem.value-oldmem.value)) ratio
from
   perfstat.stats$sysstat oldmem,
   perfstat.stats$sysstat newmem,
   perfstat.stats$sysstat newdsk,
   perfstat.stats$sysstat olddsk,
   perfstat.stats$snapshot   sn
where
   newdsk.snap_id = sn.snap_id
and
   olddsk.snap_id = sn.snap_id 1
and
   newmem.snap_id = sn.snap_id
and
   oldmem.snap_id = sn.snap_id-1
and
   oldmem.name = 'sorts (memory)'
and
   newmem.name = 'sorts (memory)'
and
   olddsk.name = 'sorts (disk)'
```

```
and
   newdsk.name = 'sorts (disk)'
and
   newmem.value-oldmem.value > 0
   and
   newdsk.value-olddsk.value > 100
;
```

Here is the output from the script. Here, we can clearly see the number of memory sorts and disk sorts, and the ratio of disk to memory sorts.

```
Yr.  Mo Dy  Hr.   SORTS_MEMORY   SORTS_DISK   RATIO
----------------  ------------   ----------   -------
2000-12-20 12           13,166          166   .01261
2000-12-20 16           25,694          223   .00868
2000-12-21 10           99,183          215   .00217
2000-12-21 15           13,662          130   .00952
2000-12-21 16           17,004          192   .01129
2000-12-22 10           18,900          141   .00746
2000-12-22 11           19,487          131   .00672
2000-12-26 12           12,502          147   .01176
2000-12-27 13           20,338          118   .00580
2000-12-27 18           11,032          119   .01079
2000-12-28 16           16,514          205   .01241
2000-12-29 10           17,327          242   .01397
2000-12-29 16           50,874          167   .00328
2001-01-02 08           15,574          108   .00693
2001-01-02 10           39,052          136   .00348
2001-01-03 11           13,193          153   .01160
2001-01-03 13           19,901          104   .00523
2001-01-03 15           19,929          130   .00652
```

This report can be changed to send an alert when the number of disk sorts exceeds a predefined threshold and we can also modify it to plot average sorts by hour of the day and day of the week. The script here computes average sorts, ordered by hour of the day:

rpt_avg_sorts_hr.sql

```
set pages 9999;

column sorts_memory   format 999,999,999
column sorts_disk     format 999,999,999
column ratio          format .99999
```

```
select
   to_char(snap_time,'HH24'),
   avg(newmem.value-oldmem.value) sorts_memory,
   avg(newdsk.value-olddsk.value) sorts_disk
from
   perfstat.stats$sysstat oldmem,
   perfstat.stats$sysstat newmem,
   perfstat.stats$sysstat newdsk,
   perfstat.stats$sysstat olddsk,
   perfstat.stats$snapshot    sn
where
   newdsk.snap_id = sn.snap_id
and
   olddsk.snap_id = sn.snap_id-1
and
   newmem.snap_id = sn.snap_id
and
   oldmem.snap_id = sn.snap_id-1
and
   oldmem.name = 'sorts (memory)'
and
   newmem.name = 'sorts (memory)'
and
   olddsk.name = 'sorts (disk)'
and
   newdsk.name = 'sorts (disk)'
and
   newmem.value-oldmem.value > 0
group by
   to_char(snap_time,'HH24')
;
```

Here is the output from the script. We can now take this data and create a graph in a spreadsheet.

```
TO SORTS_MEMORY   SORTS_DISK
-- ------------   ------------
00       18,855           11
01       19,546           15
02       10,128            5
03        6,503            8
04       10,410            4
05        8,920            5
06        8,302            7
```

07	9,124	27
08	13,492	71
09	19,449	55
10	19,812	106
11	17,332	78
12	20,566	76
13	17,130	46
14	19,071	61
15	19,494	68
16	20,701	79
17	19,478	44
18	23,364	29
19	13,626	20
20	11,937	17
21	8,467	7
22	8,432	10
23	11,587	10

Here is the plot from the output (Figure 9-16). Here we see a typical increase in sort activity during the online period of the day. Sorts rise about 8:00 A.M. and then go down after 6:00 P.M.

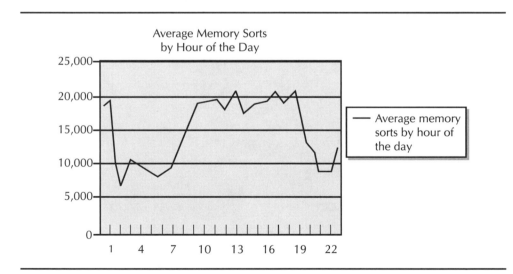

FIGURE 9-16. *Average memory sorts by hour of the day*

Now, let's run the script to compute the averages by the day of the week.

rpt_avg_sorts_dy.sql

```
set pages 9999;

column sorts_memory  format 999,999,999
column sorts_disk    format 999,999,999
column ratio         format .99999

select
   to_char(snap_time,'day')         DAY,
   avg(newmem.value-oldmem.value) sorts_memory,
   avg(newdsk.value-olddsk.value) sorts_disk
from
   perfstat.stats$sysstat oldmem,
   perfstat.stats$sysstat newmem,
   perfstat.stats$sysstat newdsk,
   perfstat.stats$sysstat olddsk,
   perfstat.stats$snapshot    sn
where
   newdsk.snap_id = sn.snap_id
and
   olddsk.snap_id = sn.snap_id-1
and
   newmem.snap_id = sn.snap_id
and
   oldmem.snap_id = sn.snap_id-1
and
   oldmem.name = 'sorts (memory)'
and
   newmem.name = 'sorts (memory)'
and
   olddsk.name = 'sorts (disk)'
and
   newdsk.name = 'sorts (disk)'
and
   newmem.value-oldmem.value > 0
group by
   to_char(snap_time,'day')
;
```

Again, we will take the result set and plot it in a chart. This time, let's plot the disk sorts.

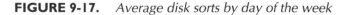

```
DAY         SORTS_MEMORY   SORTS_DISK
---------   ------------   ------------
friday            12,545            54
monday            14,352            29
saturday          12,430             2
sunday            13,807             4
thursday          17,042            47
tuesday           15,172            78
wednesday         14,650            43
```

Figure 9-17 shows the graph. In this database, the activity pattern on Tuesday shows a large number of disk sorts, with another smaller spike on Thursdays. For this database, the DBA may want to pay careful attention to the TEMP tablespaces on these days, and perhaps issue a **alter tablespace TEMP coalesce;** to create continuous extents in the TEMP tablespace.

At the risk of being redundant, we need to reemphasize that the single most important factor in the performance of any Oracle database is the minimization of disk I/O. Hence, the tuning of the Oracle sorting remains one of the most important considerations in the tuning of any Oracle database.

Now, let's turn our attention to the Oracle rollback segments and see how we can use STATSPACK to monitor the rollback segments and tune them for optimal performance.

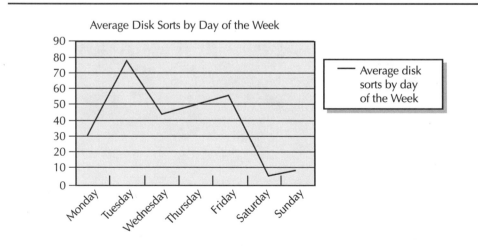

FIGURE 9-17. *Average disk sorts by day of the week*

Tuning the Rollback Segments

Oracle uses rollback segments to maintain the "before" images for rows. Whenever a task terminates with an **abort** or a **rollback**, Oracle goes to the rollback segments and reapplies the previous images for the rows.

Inside the database instance, there needs to be enough rollback segments to accommodate all concurrent update tasks. In addition, the rollback segments must be large enough to hold all of the "before" images between the start and the end (commit or rollback) checkpoints.

There is a relationship between the rollback segments and system latches. A transaction writing rollback data has to first access the transaction table stored in the rollback segment header and acquire a slot in that table. This requires momentary latching of the table to serialize concurrent update to it. If the database is update intensive and has a small number of rollback segments, user transactions will wait on the latch to access the transaction table.

As a general rule, rollback segments should be the same size and created with a large number of small extents. For large transactions, special rollback segments can be created and the task directed to the rollback segment with the **set transaction use rollback segment xxx** command.

The STATSPACK tables provide a table called stats$rollstat that keeps statistics on the behavior of each rollback segment. The important metrics include the number of wraps for each rollback segment and any waits that may happen within a rollback segment.

The script here displays the rollback segment information:

rpt_rbs.sql

```
set pages 9999;

column buffer_busy_wait format 999,999,999
column mydate heading 'Yr.   Mo Dy  Hr.' format a16
column c0 heading "Name"    format 99
column c1 heading "sz now"   format 9,999
column c2 heading "extends" format 9,999
column c3 heading "# trans." format 9,999
column c4 heading "wraps" format 9,999
column c5 heading "High WM" format 999;
column c7 heading "Shrinks" format 999;
column c6 heading "status"
column c8 heading "Waits" format 9,999;

select
    to_char(snap_time,'yyyy-mm-dd HH24')    mydate,
    new.usn                                 c0,
    (new.rssize-old.rssize)/1048576         c1,
```

```
   (new.hwmsize-old.hwmsize)/1048576      c5,
   new.extends-old.extends                c2,
   new.waits-old.waits                    c8,
   new.xacts-old.xacts                    c3,
   new.wraps-old.wraps                    c4,
   new.shrinks-old.shrinks                c7
from
   perfstat.stats$rollstat old,
   perfstat.stats$rollstat new,
   perfstat.stats$snapshot    sn
where
   (new.rssize-old.rssize) > 0
and
   new.xacts-old.xacts > 0
and
   new.snap_id = sn.snap_id
and
   old.snap_id = sn.snap_id-1
and
   new.usn = old.usn
;
```

Here is the output from the STATSPACK script. Here we see the size of each rollback segment, the high-water mark, the number of extends, the number of waits, the number of transactions within the rollback segment, the number of rollback segment wraps, and the number of shrinks within the rollback segments.

Yr. Mo Dy	Hr.	Name	sz now	High WM	extends	Waits	# trans.	wraps	Sh
2001-01-01 01	3	6	6	6	1	1	63	0
2001-01-07 17	1	2	2	2	0	1	73	0
2001-01-10 23	2	6	6	6	1	1	79	0
2001-01-10 23	3	5	5	5	3	1	155	0

Conclusion

This chapter has been dedicated to demonstrating all of the uses for STATSPACK tables when tuning the database instance. Of course, there were many hundreds of additional instance parameters that we did not discuss, but we have covered the most important instance tuning parameters and techniques.

Now that we have a general understanding of the tuning for the instance, we are ready to drill deeper and look into the tuning of specific objects within Oracle. The next chapter will look into the internals of Oracle tables and indexes and show how to tune them for optimal performance. We will also show how to extend STATSPACK to capture tables and index statistics.

CHAPTER
10

Tuning Oracle
Tables and Indexes

able and index tuning can often make a huge impact on the performance of the Oracle database, especially highly volatile databases that are constantly changing their data. This chapter is divided into several important sections:

- Basic Oracle storage parameters and how they affect performance

- Correcting and preventing chained rows

- Reorganizing tables and resequencing Oracle rows for high performance

- Correcting and rebuilding indexes

- Extending STATSPACK to keep object statistics

- Monitoring objects with STATSPACK

Each of these sections contains very important information about the proper methods for tuning Oracle objects. The most important concept in this chapter is that most object-related performance problems can be corrected. Let's begin with a discussion of the basic storage parameters for Oracle objects.

Basic Oracle Storage Parameters and How They Affect Performance

Let's begin this chapter by introducing the relationship between object storage parameters and performance. Poor object performance within Oracle is experienced in several areas:

- **Slow inserts**   Insert operations run slowly and have excessive I/O. This happens when blocks on the freelist only have room for a few rows before Oracle is forced to grab another free block.

- **Slow selects**   Select statements have excessive I/O because of chained rows. This occurs when rows "chain" and fragment onto several data blocks, causing additional I/O to fetch the blocks.

- **Slow updates**   Update statements run very slowly with double the amount of I/O. This happens when **update** operations expand a VARCHAR or BLOB column and Oracle is forced to chain the row contents onto additional data blocks.

- **Slow deletes**   Large **delete** statements can run slowly and cause segment header contention. This happens when rows are deleted and Oracle must relink the data block onto the freelist for the table.

As we see, the storage parameters for Oracle tables and indexes can have an important effect on the performance of the database. Let's begin our discussion of object tuning by reviewing the common storage parameters that affect Oracle performance.

The pctfree Storage Parameter

The purpose of *pctfree* is to tell Oracle when to remove a block from the object's freelist. Since the Oracle default is *pctfree*=10, blocks remain on the freelist while they are less than 90 percent full. As shown in Figure 10-1, once an insert makes the block grow beyond 90 percent full, it is removed from the freelist, leaving 10 percent of the block for row expansion. Furthermore, the data block will remain off the freelist *even after the space drops below 90 percent.* Only after subsequent **delete** operations cause the space to fall below the *pctused* threshold of 40 percent will Oracle put the block back onto the freelist.

The pctused Storage Parameter

The *pctused* parameter tells Oracle when to add a previously full block onto the freelist. As rows are deleted from a table, the database blocks become eligible to accept new rows. This happens when the amount of space in a database block falls below *pctused*, and a freelist relink operation is triggered, as shown in Figure 10-2.

For example, with *pctused*=60, all database blocks that have less than 60 percent will be on the freelist, as well as other blocks that dropped below *pctused* and have not yet grown to *pctfree*. Once a block deletes a row and becomes less than 60-percent full, the block goes back on the freelist. When rows are deleted, data blocks become available when a block's free space drops below the value of

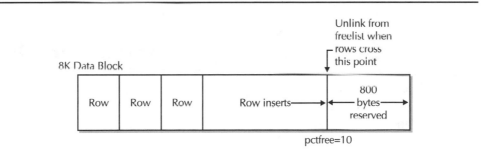

FIGURE 10-1.   *The **pctfree** threshold*

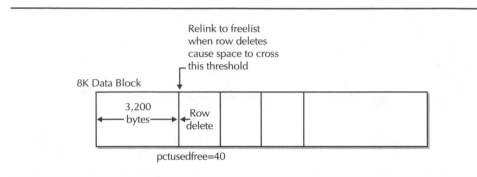

FIGURE 10-2. *The* **pctused** *threshold*

pctused for the table, and Oracle relinks the data block onto the freelist chain. As the table has rows inserted into it, it will grow until the space on the block exceeds the threshold *pctfree*, at which time the block is unlinked from the freelist.

The freelists Storage Parameter

The *freelists* parameter tells Oracle how many segment header blocks to create for a table or index. Multiple freelists are used to prevent segment header contention when several tasks compete to **insert**, **update**, or **delete** from the table. The *freelists* parameter should be set to the maximum number of concurrent update operation.

Prior to Oracle8i, you must reorganize the table to change the *freelists* storage parameter. In Oracle8i, you can dynamically add freelists to any table or index with the **alter table** command. In Oracle8i, adding a freelist reserves a new block in the table to hold the control structures.

The freelist groups Storage Parameter for OPS

The *freelist groups* parameter is used in Oracle Parallel Server (Real Application Clusters). When multiple instances access a table, separate freelist groups are allocated in the segment header. The *freelist groups* parameter should be set the number of instances that access the table. For details on segment internals with multiple freelist groups, see Chapter 13.

NOTE
The variables are called pctfree *and* pctused *in the*
create table *and* ***alter table*** *syntax, but they are
called PCT_FREE and PCT_USED in the dba_tables
view in the Oracle dictionary. The programmer
responsible for this mix-up was promoted to senior
vice president in recognition of his contribution to
the complexity of the Oracle software.*

Summary of Storage Parameter Rules

The following rules govern the settings for the storage parameters *freelists, freelist
groups, pctfree,* and *pctused.* As you know, the value of *pctused* and *pctfree* can
easily be changed at any time with the **alter table** command, and the observant
DBA should be able to develop a methodology for deciding the optimal settings
for these parameters. For now, accept these rules, and we will be discussing them
in detail later in this chapter.

There is a direct trade-off between effective space utilization and high performance,
and the table storage parameters control this trade-off:

- **For efficient space reuse**   A high value for *pctused* will effectively reuse
  space on data blocks, but at the expense of additional I/O. A high *pctused*
  means that relatively full blocks are placed on the freelist. Hence, these
  blocks will be able to accept only a few rows before becoming full again,
  leading to more I/O.

- **For high performance**   A low value for *pctused* means that Oracle will
  not place a data block onto the freelist until it is nearly empty. The block
  will be able to accept many rows until it becomes full, thereby reducing
  I/O at insert time. Remember that it is always faster for Oracle to extend
  into new blocks than to reuse existing blocks. It takes fewer resources for
  Oracle to extend a table than to manage freelists.

While we will go into the justification for these rules later in this chapter, let's
review the general guidelines for setting of object storage parameters:

- Always set *pctused* to allow enough room to accept a new row. We never
  want to have free blocks that does not have enough room to accept a row.
  If we do, this will cause a slowdown since Oracle will attempt to read five
  "dead" free blocks before extending the table to get an empty block.

- The presence of chained rows in a table means that *pctfree* is too low or that *db_block_size* is too small. In most cases within Oracle, RAW and LONG RAW columns make huge rows that exceed the maximum block size for Oracle, making chained rows unavoidable.

- If a table has simultaneous **insert** SQL processes, it needs to have simultaneous **delete** processes. Running a single purge job will place all of the free blocks on only one freelist, and none of the other freelists will contain any free blocks from the purge.

- The *freelist* parameter should be set to the high-water mark of updates to a table. For example, if the customer table has up to 20 end users performing **insert** operations at any time, the customer table should have *freelists*=20.

- The *freelist groups* parameter should be set the number of Oracle Parallel Server instances that access the table.

Freelist Management and Oracle Objects

One of the benefits of having Oracle is that it manages all of the free space within each tablespace. Oracle handles table and index space management for us and insulates humans from the inner workings of the Oracle tables and indexes. However, experienced Oracle tuning professionals need to understand how Oracle manages table extents and free data blocks.

Knowing the internal Oracle table management strategies will help you become successful in managing high-volume performance within Oracle. To be proficient at object tuning, you need to understand the behavior of freelists and freelist groups, and their relationship to the values of the *pctfree* and *pctused* parameters. This knowledge is especially imperative for enterprise resource planning (ERP) applications where poor table performance is often directly related to improper table settings.

The most common mistake for the beginner is assuming that the default Oracle parameters are optimal for all objects. Unless disk consumption is not a concern, you must consider the average row length and database block size when setting *pctfree* and *pctused* for a table such that empty blocks are efficiently placed back onto the freelists. When these settings are wrong, Oracle may populate freelists with "dead" blocks that do not have enough room to store a row, causing significant processing delays.

This dead block problem occurs when the setting for *pctused* allows a block to relink onto the freelist when it does not have enough free space to accept a new row. We will explain the relationship between average row length and freelist behavior later in this chapter.

Freelists are critical to the effective reuse of space within the Oracle tablespaces and are directly related to the *pctfree* and *pctused* storage parameters. When the database is directed to make blocks available as soon as possible (with a high setting of *pctused*), the reuse of free space is maximized. However, there is a direct trade-off between high performance and efficient reuse of table blocks. When tuning Oracle tables and indexes, you need to consciously decide if you desire high performance or efficient space reuse, and set the table parameters accordingly. Let's take a close look at how these freelists affect the performance of Oracle.

Whenever a request is made to insert a row into a table, Oracle goes to a freelist to find a block with enough space to accept a row. As you may know, the freelist chain is kept in the first block of the table or index, and this block is known as the *segment header*. The sole purpose of the *pctfree* and *pctused* table allocation parameters is to control the movement of blocks to and from the freelists. While the freelist link and unlink operations are simple Oracle functions, the settings for freelist link (*pctused*) and unlink (*pctfree*) operations can have a dramatic impact on the performance of Oracle.

The default settings for all Oracle objects is *pctused*=40 and *pctfree*=10. As you may know from DBA basics, the *pctfree* parameter governs freelist unlinks. Setting *pctfree*=10 means that every block reserves 10 percent of the space for row expansion. The *pctused* parameter governs freelist relinks. Setting *pctused*=40 means that a block must become less than 40-percent full before being relinked on the table freelist.

Let's take a closer look at how freelist management works, and how it affects the performance of Oracle. Many neophytes misunderstand what happens when a block is readded to the freelist. Once a block is relinked onto the freelist after a delete, it will remain on the freelist *even when the space exceeds 60 percent.* Only reaching *pctfree* will take the database block off of the freelist.

Linking and Unlinking from the Freelists

As we now know, the *pctfree* and *pctused* table parameters are used to govern the movement of database blocks to and from the table freelists. In general, there is a direct trade-off between performance and efficient table utilization because efficient block reuse requires some overhead when linking and unlinking blocks with the freelist. As you may know, linking and unlinking a block requires two writes: one to the segment header for the freelist head node, and the other to the new block to make it participate in the freelist chain. The following general rules apply to freelists:

- **insert** An **insert** may trigger the *pctfree* threshold, causing a freelist unlink. Since **insert** operations always use the free block at the head of the freelist chain, there will be minimal overhead when unlinking this block.

- **update** An **update** that expands row length is affected by *pctfree*, but it will not cause a freelist unlink since the target block would not be at the head of the freelist chain.

- **delete** A **delete** of rows may trigger the *pctused* threshold and cause a freelist link.

You also need to understand how new free blocks are added to the freelist chain. At table extension time, the high-water mark for the table is increased, and new blocks are moved onto the master freelist, where they are, in turn, moved to process freelists. For tables that do not contain multiple freelists, the transfer is done five blocks at a time. For tables with multiple freelists, the transfer is done in sizes (5*(number of freelists + 1)). For example, in a table with 20 freelists, 105 blocks will be moved onto the master freelist each time that a table increases its high-water mark.

To see how this works, let's review the mechanisms associated with freelist links and unlinks. For the purposes of the following examples, let's use Figure 10-3.

The segment header contains a space to hold a pointer to the first free block in the table. Inside Oracle, a pointer to a block is called a data block address, or DBA for short. The first block on the freelist chain also has a space in the block header to contain the DBA for the next free block, and so on.

Let's explore what happens internally during row operations.

Freelist Unlinks with insert Operations

As new rows are inserted, the block may be removed from the freelist if the free space becomes less than the bytes specified by *pctfree*. Since the block being inserted is always at the head of the freelist chain, only two blocks will be affected.

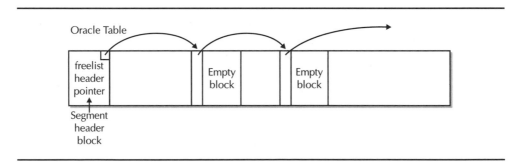

FIGURE 10-3. *A sample freelist chain*

In our example, let's assume that the **insert** has caused block 20 to be removed from the freelist chain:

1. Oracle detects that free space is less than *pctfree* for block 20 and invokes the unlink operation. Since block 20 is the first block on the freelist chain, Oracle reads the data block address (DBA) inside the block header and sees that the next free block is block 60.

2. Oracle next adjusts the freelist header node and moves the DBA for block 60 to the head of the freelist in the segment header. Block 20 no longer participates in the freelist chain, and the first entry in the freelist is now block 60, as shown in Figure 10-4.

Freelist Relinks with update Statements

As updates to existing rows cause the row to expand, the block may be unlinked from the freelist if the free space in the block becomes less than *pctfree*. Of course, this will only happen if the row contains VARCHAR, RAW, or LONG RAW column datatypes, since these are the only datatypes that could expand upon **update**.

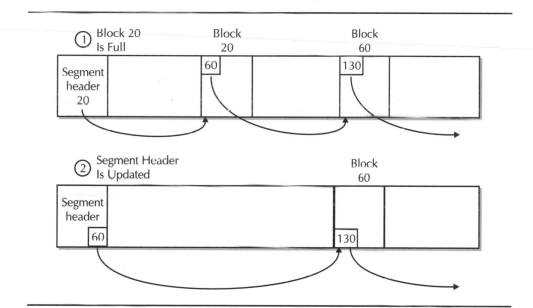

FIGURE 10-4.   *A freelist unlink operation*

Because the updated block is not at the head of the freelist chain, the prior block's freelist pointer cannot be adjusted to omit the block. Note that the dead block remains on the freelist even though it does not have room to accept a row.

The dead block remaining on the list will cause additional Oracle overhead, especially if there is a large number of "unavailable" blocks on the freelist. At runtime, Oracle will incur additional I/Os when reading these freelists, and will try the freelist as many as five times attempting to find a block with enough room to store the new row. After five attempts, Oracle will raise the high-water mark for the table.

Reducing Freelist Relinks

Either of these techniques will cause the freelists to be populated largely from new extents. Of course, this approach requires lots of extra disk space, and the table must be reorganized periodically to reclaim the wasted storage. Freelists relinks can be reduced in two ways:

- Freelists relinks can be "turned down" by setting *pctused* to 1. Setting *pctused* to a low value means that data blocks are not relinked onto the freelist chain unless they are completely empty.

- Use the APPEND hint when adding rows. By using APPEND with inserts, you tell Oracle to bypass the freelists and raise the high-water mark for the table to grab a fresh, unused data block.

TIP
*Remember the cardinal rule of object tuning. There is a direct trade-off between efficient space reuse and fast performance of **insert** statements. If high performance is more important than space reuse, you can use an Oracle8 SQL hint that will bypass freelist checking. By placing **/*+ append */** immediately after the INSERT keyword, Oracle will be directed to increase the high-water mark for the table and place the row into a fresh empty block.*

Now that we understand how freelists operate within each Oracle table and index, we are ready to dig deeper and look at the internals of table management.

Table Internals and Freelists

Inside a segment header (the first block in the table), a freelist is a one-way linked list, with NEXT pointers indicating the data block addresses (DBAs) of the next free block. In addition, when a block is added to the freelist, a flag in the header of the free block is set to indicate that it is on the freelist chain; another bucket in the block header will contain the DBA of the next free block in the segment.

The header node on the freelist chain (in the segment header) contains the DBA of the first block in the freelist and the DBA of the last block in the chain. The last data block in the freelist will have a zero value, indicating that it is the last free block in the freelist chain, as shown in Figure 10-5.

As a table grows, Oracle raises the high-water mark for the table, five blocks at a time, and places these new blocks onto the master freelist in the segment header block. Oracle places the new block at the front of the linked list, changing the pointers for the head and the newly freed block. Figure 10-6 shows what happens when the freelist runs out of blocks. Oracle raises the high-water mark for the table from block 130 to block 135, and then adds links for blocks 130–134 onto the freelist chain. This first-in, first-out linking method allows for very fast unlinking and relinking of data blocks from the freelist.

Now that we see how free blocks are added to the freelist chain, let's examine the details about how Oracle determines when to add blocks to the freelist. To understand the operation of Oracle in a high-update environment, you need to

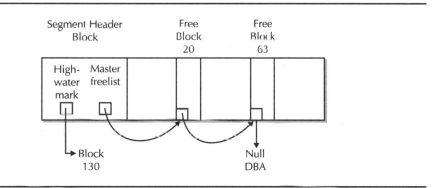

FIGURE 10-5. *The basic composition of a freelist chain*

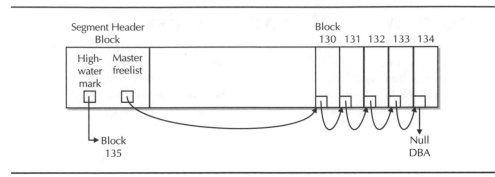

FIGURE 10-6. *Adding a new block to the freelists chain*

understand how Oracle gets free blocks to accept new rows. When a task requests a free block to insert a row, the following steps occur within Oracle:

1. Oracle first looks for the task's own transaction freelist, looking for free blocks.

2. Oracle next looks into the process freelist group for a free block.

3. Oracle then attempts to move blocks from the master freelist to the process freelist. This operation is called a freelist merge and is normally done in chunks of five blocks. Note that Oracle will not look in other process freelists.

4. Oracle then tries to get blocks from other tasks' transaction freelists that have committed their rows. Oracle scans the transaction freelists, moving the committed blocks onto the master freelist.

5. Oracle next bumps up the high-water mark for the table by bumping the high-water mark. This may involve allocating a new table extent.

However, we must note that there are exceptions to this process. When using RAW and LONG RAW columns in a row insert, Oracle will not attempt to insert the row below the high-water mark for the table and will immediately bump the high-water mark to get new blocks. This is also true when *pctused*=1 and when the APPEND hint is used inside an **insert** statement.

Long Data Columns and Freelist Behavior

One of the most confounding problems with some Oracle tables is the use of large columns. The main problem with RAW and LONG RAW, BLOB and CLOB datatypes is that they often exceed the block size, and whenever a column is larger than the database block size, the column will fragment onto an adjacent data block.

This causes Oracle to incur two I/Os instead of one I/O every time the row is accessed. This block-chaining problem is especially prevalent in tables where column lengths grow to thousands of bytes. Of course, it is a good idea to use the maximum supported *db_block_size* for your version of Oracle (usually 8,192 bytes) in an effort to minimize this chaining.

In order to avoid fragmentation of a row, Oracle will always insert table rows containing a RAW or a LONG RAW column onto a completely empty block. Therefore, on insert, Oracle will not attempt to insert below the high-water mark (using freelists) and will always bump the high-water mark, pulling the free blocks from the master freelist. Since Oracle pulls free blocks by raising the high-water mark, it means that Oracle will not reuse blocks once they have been placed on the freelist chain. Actually, free blocks below the high-water mark (i.e., blocks on the freelists) may be used for inserting LONG columns, but only if the block is completely empty. If the block is partially used but still below the *pctused* mark, it will not be used to insert the LONG data.

Remember, multiple freelists can waste a significant amount of disk space. Tables with dozens of freelists may exhibit the "sparse table" phenomenon as the table grows and each freelist contains free blocks that are not known to the other freelists. If these tables consume too much space, the Oracle administrator faces a tough decision. To maximize space reuse, you would want the table to be placed onto a freelist as soon as it is capable of receiving more than two new rows. Therefore, a fairly high value for *pctused* is desired. On the other hand, this would result in slower runtime performance since Oracle will only be able to insert a few rows before having to perform an I/O to get another block.

Long Columns and Freelist Usage

There are cases where large row lengths and an improper setting of *pctfree* can cause performance degradation during SQL **insert** operations. The problem occurs when a block becomes too full to accept another row while the block remains on the freelist. As rows are inserted, Oracle must fetch these blocks from the freelist, only to find that there is not enough room for a row. Fortunately, Oracle will not continue fetching freelist blocks forever. After retrieving five too-small blocks from the freelist, Oracle assumes that there will be no blocks on the freelist that have enough space for the row, and Oracle will grab an empty block from the master freelist, as shown in Figure 10-7.

This problem usually occurs when the row length for the table exceeds the space reserved on the block. For example, with 4K blocks and *pctfree*=10, the reserved space will equal 410 bytes (not counting block header space). Therefore, we may see this problem for any rows that are more than 410 bytes in length.

Now that we understand the internal freelist linking mechanism, let's see how to monitor Oracle to identify when Oracle is waiting because of freelist contention.

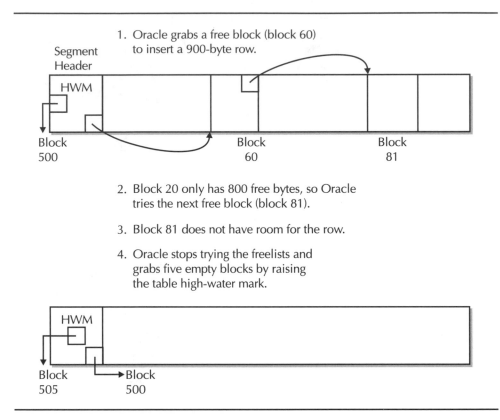

1. Oracle grabs a free block (block 60) to insert a 900-byte row.

2. Block 20 only has 800 free bytes, so Oracle tries the next free block (block 81).

3. Block 81 does not have room for the row.

4. Oracle stops trying the freelists and grabs five empty blocks by raising the table high-water mark.

FIGURE 10-7. *Oracle eventually abandons the freelist and raises the high-water mark*

Setting *pctfree* and *pctused* Based on Average Row Length

It is very important that the DBA understand how the row length affects setting the values for *pctfree* and *pctused*. You want to set *pctfree* such that room is left on each block for row expansion, and you want to set *pctused* so that newly linked blocks have enough room to accept rows.

Here we see the trade-off between effective space usage and performance. If you set *pctused* to a high value—say, 80—a block will quickly become available to accept new rows, but it will not have room for a lot of rows before it becomes logically full again. Remember the rule for *pctused*. The lower the value for *pctused*, the more space will be available on each data block, and subsequent **insert** operations will run faster. The downside is that a block must be nearly empty before it becomes eligible to accept new rows.

The script shown here will generate the table alteration syntax. Please note that this script only provides general guidelines, and you will want to leave the default *pctused*=40 unless your system is low on disk space, or unless the average row length is very large.

pctused.sql

```
rem pctused.sql
set heading off;
set pages 9999;
set feedback off;

spool pctused.lst;
column db_block_size new_value blksz noprint
select value db_block_size from v$parameter where name='db_block_size';

define spare_rows = 2;

select
    ' alter table '||owner||'.'||table_name||
    ' pctused '||least(round(100-
                ((&spare_rows*avg_row_len)/(&blksz/10))),95)||
    ' '||
    ' pctfree '||greatest(round((&spare_rows*avg_row_len)/(&blksz/10)),5)||
    ';'
from
    dba_tables
where
avg_row_len > 1
and
avg_row_len < .5*&blksz
and
table_name not in
 (select table_name from dba_tab_columns b
   where
 data_type in ('RAW','LONG RAW','BLOB','CLOB','NCLOB')
 )
order by
    owner,
    table_name
;

spool off;
```

Now that we understand the table storage parameters and their effect on performance, let's talk about buffer busy waits and see how they relate to object parameters.

Buffer Busy Waits and Freelist Contention

When multiple tasks want to **insert** or **update** rows in a table, there may be contention in the segment header for the table. This contention can manifest itself as a buffer busy wait or a freelist wait. Let's look at some queries that can be run to identify these contention conditions. We are now ready to understand how they occur at the table and index level.

Oracle keeps a v$ view called v$waitstat and the stats$waitstat table for monitoring wait events. The following query shows how many times Oracle has waited for a freelist to become available. As you can see, it does not tell you which freelists are experiencing the contention problems:

```
SELECT CLASS, COUNT
FROM V$WAITSTAT
WHERE CLASS = 'free list';

    CLASS                        COUNT
    --------------               -----------
    free list                       383
```

The main problem with the v$waitstat view and the stats$waitstat table is that they only keep the wait statistics for the whole database, and do not distinguish waits by table or index name. Here, you can see that Oracle had to wait 383 times for a table freelist to become available. This could represent a wait of 383 times on the same table or perhaps a single wait for 83 separate tables. While 383 seems to be a large number, remember that Oracle can perform hundreds of I/Os each second, so 383 could be quite insignificant to the overall system. In any case, if you suspect that you know which table's freelist is having the contention, the table can be exported, dropped, and redefined to have more freelists. While an extra freelist consumes more of Oracle's memory, additional freelists can help throughput on tables that have lots of **insert** statements. Generally, you should define extra freelists only on those tables that will have many concurrent **update** operations.

Using STATSPACK to Find Wait Contention

Now let's look at how STATSPACK can identify these wait conditions. The stats$waitstat table contains a historical listing of all wait events. The stats$waitstat contain the following classes:

```
SQL> select distinct class from stats$waitstat

CLASS
```

```
------------------
bitmap block
bitmap index block
data block
extent map
free list
save undo block
save undo header
segment header
sort block
system undo block
system undo header
undo block
undo header
unused
```

rpt_waitstat.sql

```
set pages 999;
set lines 80;

column mydate         heading 'Yr. Mo Dy Hr'       format a13;
column class                                        format a20;
column wait_count                                   format 999,999;
column time                                         format 999,999,999;
column avg_wait_secs                                format 99,999;

break on to_char(snap_time,'yyyy-mm-dd') skip 1;

select
   to_char(snap_time,'yyyy-mm-dd HH24')             mydate,
   e.class,
   e.wait_count - nvl(b.wait_count,0)               wait_count,
   e.time - nvl(b.time,0)                           time
from
   stats$waitstat       b,
   stats$waitstat       e,
   stats$snapshot       sn
where
   e.snap_id = sn.snap_id
and
   b.snap_id = e.snap_id-1
and
   b.class = e.class
and
(
   e.wait_count - b.wait_count  > 1
```

```
    or
    e.time - b.time > 1
)
;
```

Here is a sample report from this query. Here we see a list of all wait events and the object of the wait. This information can sometimes provide insight into a contention problem within Oracle.

Yr. Mo Dy Hr CLASS	WAIT_COUNT	TIME
2000-12-20 11 data block	2	0
2000-12-20 12 data block	21	0
2000-12-20 12 undo header	5	0
2000-12-20 13 data block	407	0
2000-12-20 13 segment header	3	0
2000-12-20 13 undo block	270	0
2000-12-20 13 undo header	61	0
2000-12-20 16 data block	55	0
2000-12-20 16 undo block	8	0
2000-12-20 16 undo header	5	0
2000-12-20 17 data block	252	0
2000-12-20 18 data block	311	0
2000-12-20 18 undo block	173	0
2000-12-21 00 data block	2,268	0
2000-12-21 00 undo block	744	0
2000-12-21 00 undo header	132	0
2000-12-21 01 data block	2,761	0
2000-12-21 01 undo block	1,078	0
2000-12-21 01 undo header	419	0
2000-12-21 05 data block	7	0
2000-12-21 09 data block	17	0
2000-12-21 09 undo block	8	0
2000-12-21 10 data block	30	0
2000-12-21 10 undo block	29	0
2000-12-21 10 undo header	4	0
2000-12-21 11 data block	139	0
2000-12-21 11 undo header	2	0
2000-12-21 12 data block	17	0
2000-12-21 13 data block	11	0
2000-12-21 14 data block	42	0
2000-12-21 14 undo header	2	0
2000-12-21 15 data block	10	0
2000-12-21 15 undo block	5	0
2000-12-21 16 data block	23	0
2000-12-21 17 data block	17	0
2000-12-21 17 undo block	2	0
2000-12-21 18 data block	122	0

```
2000-12-21 18 undo block              117           0
2000-12-21 18 undo header             19            0
2000-12-21 21 data block              15            0
2000-12-21 22 data block              3             0
2000-12-22 02 data block              59            0
2000-12-22 08 data block              19            0
2000-12-22 09 data block              72            0
2000-12-22 09 undo block              2             0
2000-12-22 10 data block              57            0
2000-12-22 10 undo block              7             0
2000-12-22 10 undo header             3             0
2000-12-22 11 data block              423           0
2000-12-22 11 undo block              10            0
2000-12-22 16 data block              2             0
2000-12-22 17 data block              319           0
2000-12-22 17 undo block              149           0
2000-12-22 17 undo header             44            0
2000-12-22 18 data block              3             0
2000-12-22 18 undo header             2             0
2000-12-22 19 data block              16            0
2000-12-22 20 data block              5,526         0
2000-12-22 20 segment header          30            0
2000-12-22 20 undo block              46            0
```

Note that the segment header and data block waits are often related to competing
update tasks that have to wait on a single freelist in the segment header.

While this STATSPACK report is useful for summarizing wait conditions within
Oracle, it does not tell us the names of the objects that experienced the wait conditions.
The following section will show you how to drill down and find the offending data
block for buffer busy waits.

Finding Buffer Busy Waits with STATSPACK

We are discussing buffer busy waits now because buffer busy waits are usually
associated with segment header contention that can be remedied by adding additional
freelists for the table or index. However, buffer busy waits are measured at the instance
level and it is to our benefit to look at the instance-wide reports on buffer busy waits.

Before proceeding, let's remember that a buffer busy wait occurs when a database
block is found in the data buffer but it is unavailable because another Oracle task
is using the data block. Here is a sample STATSPACK report to display buffer busy
waits for each of the three data buffers.

rpt_bbw.sql

```
set pages 9999;
```

```
column buffer_busy_wait format 999,999,999
column mydate heading 'yr. mo dy Hr.'

select
   to_char(snap_time,'yyyy-mm-dd HH24')        mydate,
   new.name,
   new.buffer_busy_wait-old.buffer_busy_wait buffer_busy_wait
from
   perfstat.stats$buffer_pool_statistics old,
   perfstat.stats$buffer_pool_statistics new,
   perfstat.stats$snapshot                 sn
where
   new.name = old.name
and
   new.snap_id = sn.snap_id
and
   old.snap_id = sn.snap_id-1
and
   new.buffer_busy_wait-old.buffer_busy_wait > 1
group by
   to_char(snap_time,'yyyy-mm-dd HH24'),
   new.name,
   new.buffer_busy_wait-old.buffer_busy_wait
;
```

Here is a sample of the report from this script. Note that it provides instance-wide buffer busy waits and does not tell us the data blocks where the wait occurred. We will see advanced techniques for find the blocks in the next section.

```
yr. mo dy Hr NAME                   BUFFER_BUSY_WAIT
------------ -------------------- ----------------
2000-09-21 15 DEFAULT                             3
2000-10-02 15 DEFAULT                            11
2000-12-11 18 DEFAULT                            20
```

We can enhance this report to show times when the number of buffer busy waits is causing a performance problem. This script alerts when there are more than 400 buffer busy waits between snapshot intervals.

rpt_bbw_alert.sql

```
set pages 9999;

column buffer_busy_wait format 999,999,999
column mydate heading 'Yr. Mo Dy  Hr.' format a16

select
   to_char(snap_time,'yyyy-mm-dd HH24')            mydate,
```

```
      avg(new.buffer_busy_wait-old.buffer_busy_wait) buffer_busy_wait
from
   perfstat.stats$buffer_pool_statistics old,
   perfstat.stats$buffer_pool_statistics new,
   perfstat.stats$snapshot    sn
where
   new.snap_id = sn.snap_id
and
   old.snap_id = sn.snap_id-1
and
   new.buffer_busy_wait-old.buffer_busy_wait > 4000
group by
   to_char(snap_time,'yyyy-mm-dd HH24')
;
```

We can run this script and learn those time periods when buffer busy waits were excessive. This can provide the DBA with valuable clues about the tables and processes that were involved in creating the block wait conditions.

```
SQL> @rpt_bbw_alert.sql

Yr. Mo Dy  Hr. BUFFER_BUSY_WAIT
---------------- ------------------
2001-01-04 01              4,570
2001-01-04 06              4,576
2001-01-04 07              4,582
2001-01-04 11              4,669
2001-01-04 12              4,687
2001-01-04 13              4,692
2001-01-04 14              4,762
2001-01-04 20              4,867
2001-01-04 21              4,875
2001-01-04 23              4,883
2001-01-05 00              4,885
2001-01-07 20              5,462
2001-01-07 21              5,471
2001-01-07 22              5,476
2001-01-07 23              5,482
2001-01-08 00              5,482
2001-01-08 01              5,482
2001-01-08 02              5,484
2001-01-08 03              5,504
2001-01-08 04              5,505
2001-01-08 10              5,365
2001-01-08 11              5,396
2001-01-08 12              5,505
2001-01-08 13              5,943
2001-01-08 14              6,155
2001-01-08 15              6,226
2001-01-08 16              6,767
```

```
2001-01-08 17              14,396
2001-01-08 18              13,958
2001-01-08 19              13,972
2001-01-08 20              13,977
2001-01-08 21              13,979
2001-01-08 22              13,981
2001-01-08 23              13,982
2001-01-09 00              13,986
2001-01-10 23               4,517
2001-01-11 00               5,033
2001-01-16 21               9,048
2001-01-16 22               9,051
2001-01-16 23               9,051
```

We can also gain insight into the patterns behind buffer busy waits by averaging them by the hour of the day. The following STATSPACK script can be used to develop a buffer busy wait "signature."

rpt_avg_bbw_hr.sql

```
set pages 9999;

column buffer_busy_wait format 999,999,999
column mydate heading 'Yr. Mo Dy  Hr.' format a16

select
   to_char(snap_time,'HH24')            mydate,
   avg(new.buffer_busy_wait-old.buffer_busy_wait) buffer_busy_wait
from
   perfstat.stats$buffer_pool_statistics old,
   perfstat.stats$buffer_pool_statistics new,
   perfstat.stats$snapshot    sn
where
   new.snap_id = sn.snap_id
and
   old.snap_id = sn.snap_id-1
having
   avg(new.buffer_busy_wait-old.buffer_busy_wait) > 0
group by
   to_char(snap_time,'HH24')
;
```

Here is the output from this script that we can paste into a spreadsheet for charting. We clearly see the average buffer busy waits for each hour of the day.

```
Yr. Mo Dy  Hr. BUFFER_BUSY_WAIT
---------------- ----------------
00                            155
02                             19
```

03	0
06	5
07	4
08	8
09	28
10	66
11	28
13	31
14	45
15	169
16	61
17	364
18	48
19	34
20	88
22	17
23	186

The chart in Figure 10-8 shows the plot of buffer busy waits during a typical day. Here we see a clear spike in waits at 3:00 P.M. and again at 5:00 P.M. The next step would be to go to the stats$sql_summary table and try to locate the SQL and the underlying tables for these waits.

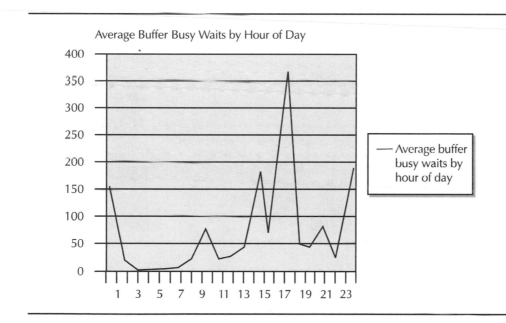

FIGURE 10-8.   *Average buffer busy waits by hour of the day*

Now that we understand the general nature of buffer busy waits, let's move on and see how we can find the exact object that caused the buffer busy wait.

Finding the Offending Block for a Buffer Busy Wait

As we discussed, Oracle does not keep an accumulator to track individual buffer busy waits. To see them, you must create a script to detect them and then schedule the task to run frequently on your database server.

get_busy.ksh

```ksh
#!/bin/ksh

# First, we must set the environment . . . .
ORACLE_SID=proderp
export ORACLE_SID
ORACLE_HOME=`cat /var/opt/oracle/oratab|grep \^$ORACLE_SID:|cut -f2 -d':'`
export ORACLE_HOME
PATH=$ORACLE_HOME/bin:$PATH
export PATH

SERVER_NAME=`uname -a|awk '{print $2}'`
typeset -u SERVER_NAME
export SERVER_NAME

# sample every 10 seconds
SAMPLE_TIME=10

while true
do

    #**************************************************************
    # Test to see if Oracle is accepting connections
    #**************************************************************
    $ORACLE_HOME/bin/sqlplus -s /<<! > /tmp/check_$ORACLE_SID.ora
    select * from v\$database;
    exit
!

    #**************************************************************
    # If not, exit immediately . . .
    #**************************************************************
    check_stat=`cat /tmp/check_$ORACLE_SID.ora|grep -i error|wc -l`;
    oracle_num=`expr $check_stat`
    if [ $oracle_num -gt 0 ]
      then
```

```
  exit 0
fi

rm -f /export/home/oracle/statspack/busy.lst

$ORACLE_HOME/bin/sqlplus -s perfstat/perfstat<<!> /tmp/busy.lst

set feedback off;
select
   sysdate,
   event,
   substr(tablespace_name,1,14),
   p2
from
   v\$session_wait a,
   dba_data_files  b
where
   a.p1 = b.file_id
;
!

var=`cat /tmp/busy.lst|wc -l`

echo $var
if [[ $var -gt 1 ]];
 then
  echo
********************************************************************"
  echo "There are waits"
  cat /tmp/busy.lst|mailx -s "Prod block wait found"\
  don@remote-dba.net \
  Larry_Ellison@oracle.com
  echo
********************************************************************"
 exit
fi

sleep $SAMPLE_TIME
done
```

As we can see from this script, it probes the database for buffer busy waits every 10 seconds. When a buffer busy wait is found, it mails the date, tablespace name, and block number to the DBA. Here is an example of a block alert e-mail:

```
SYSDATE     SUBSTR(TABLESP P2
---------  -------------- ----------
28-DEC-00 APPLSYSD          25654
```

Here we see that we have a block wait condition at block 25654 in the applsysd tablespace. To see the contents of this data block we have several command options:

```
SQL> alter system dump datafile 1 block 25654;
System altered.
```

or:

```
SQL > alter system dump datafile
SQL > '/u03/oradata/PROD/applsysd01.dbf' block 25654;
System altered.
```

or:

```
SQL> ALTER SESSION SET EVENTS 'IMMEDIATE TRACE NAME BLOCKDUMP LEVEL 25654';
System altered.
```

This will then generate a trace file that contains the detailed information about the contents of the data block. In most cases, this will be the first block in the table (the segment header). Let's go to the udump directory and inspect the trace file.

```
oracle*PROD-/u01/app/oracle/admin/PROD/udump
>ls -alt|head
total 5544
-rw-r--r--   1 oracle      dba            69816 Dec 28 14:16 ora_4443.trc
```

Next, we look at the contents of the trace file using the UNIX **more** command.

```
root> more ora_4443.trc

Dump file /u01/app/oracle/admin/PROD/udump/ora_4443.trc
Oracle8 Enterprise Edition Release 8.0.5.1.0 - Production
 .
 .
 .

Block header dump: rdba: 0x00406436
 Object id on Block? Y
 seg/obj: 0x63  csc: 0x00.d3aa2  itc: 9  flg: -  typ: 2 - INDEX
```

Here we see that the object on this block is an index and the object ID is hex 63. We convert the hex 63 and see that our object ID is number 99.

We can then run a query against dba_objects and see the name of the index.

```
SQL> select object_name, object_type
  2  from dba_objects
  3  where object_id=99;
```

```
OBJECT_NAME
---------------------------    ---------------------------------------------------
OBJECT TYPE
---------------
VUST_IDX
INDEX


SQL> select table_name from dba_indexes
  2  where index_name = 'CUST_IDX';

TABLE_NAME
-------------------------------
CUSTOMER
```

So, here we see that our wait event was on the root index node for the *cust_idx* index. This index has only a single freelist and it appears that the contention was caused by multiple tasks competing for an **insert** on the customer table.

Now that we see how to monitor buffer busy waits, let's move on to see how to reorganize Oracle tables for faster performance.

Reorganizing Oracle Tables

There are a number of reasons why the DBA should monitor and periodically reorganize tables. Foremost, the internal structure of Oracle tables is constantly changing because of **update** activities. Since most applications are oriented toward heavy online transaction processing, the internal structures of tables typically become less optimal over time. Reorganization substantially improves table performance.

The specific reasons for reorganizing a table are presented here in their order of importance:

■ **Chained rows can be coalesced** Any rows that chained as a result of row expansion will be coalesced. This does not include any table that contains RAW or LONG RAW columns, since these columns may often chain across blocks, especially with small Oracle block sizes.

■ **Table rows can be physically resequenced in primary index order** By resequencing the table rows to be in the same physical order as the primary index, you can greatly improve the speed of an application. The data can quickly be accessed by queries that use the primary-key index with far less I/O since the adjacent rows reside on contiguous blocks. This is a very important Oracle tuning technique that can reduce system I/O by more than 50 percent for some queries.

■ **Free space within the data blocks can be coalesced**   This is because tables with two freelist groups and 20 freelists, for example, maintain a total of 42 separate freelists, each with its own set of free blocks. Thus, these tables frequently extend even though there is a lot of unused space in the table. A coalesce operation will help any operations that require full table scans of the tables.

■ **Sparse tables with freelist imbalances can be reset**   Table reorganization nullifies all of the freelists within each freelist and freelist group (for OPS tables). A reorganization also lowers the high-water mark for the table to the last allocated block. A table with unbalanced freelists is evidenced by a table that continues to take new extents even though it appears to have a lot of free space within its existing extents. While many Oracle administrators associate multiple freelists with Oracle Parallel Server (using multiple freelist groups), most Oracle databases have tables with simultaneous inserts and updates. Note that while reorganization is a temporary solution to this problem, the permanent solution is to parallelize the table purges, with a separate purge process for each freelist that is defined for the table.

NOTE
Tables with a high number of extents are not on this list. It is an urban legend that tables with hundreds of extents need to be reorganized, and this myth has been perpetuated because high extents are often accompanied with high chained rows. In practice, studies by DBA gurus such a Mike Ault have shown that tables with a high number of extents will often perform faster than tables with a single extent. This is because the rows are more widely distributed along the tablespace.

Now that we have examined the causes of table reorganizations, let's examine some of the methods that are used to reorganize tables. There are several methods available to the Oracle DBA to use for reorganizing tables. These include:

■ The **create table as select** (CTAS) SQL statement

■ Oracle's export/import utilities

■ Oracle's SQL*Loader utility

This table summarizes the benefits of each of these methods.

Method	Benefits	Limitations
create table as select (CTAS) using *order by* or *index* hint	Very fast reorganization, resequencing of the physical rows to reduce I/O	Disk required for duplicate tablespaces
Export/import	Imports tables with referential integrity constraints in the proper order	Very slow, no row clustering possible, difficult for tablespaces
Unload, sort flat file, SQL*Loader	Allow unloaded file to be sorted prior to reload	Somewhat slow, relies on flat files

CAUTION
There are several dangerous third-party products that claim to perform tablespace-level reorganizations and many of these tools are fraught with bugs and are unreliable. The experienced DBA will rely on standard Oracle utilities.

Isolating Large Tables into Separate Tablespaces
In any large database, the DBA should isolate large tables into their own tablespaces to better manage the growth of the table and to make reorganizations easier. The goal is to quickly move the table into a new tablespace with a minimum of service interruption. Let's begin by reviewing the Oracle utilities, their benefits, and their limitations. If you carefully identify and segregate Oracle tables into dedicated tablespaces, the remaining objects will not require reorganization.

We have repeatedly stressed that it is very important to segregate highly volatile tables into separate tablespaces. There are several compelling reasons for segregating your large tables into separate tablespaces. The most important benefit from segregation is improved manageability of the table. If a large, active table resides in its own separate tablespace, you can control the I/O by moving the tablespace to different disks. The other reason for table segregation is improved space usage.

Having too many tables residing in a single tablespace can make reorganization risky. It is far better to isolate the active tables and selectively reorganize the remaining tables as required. As we explained in the previous section, you'll most often reorganize tables that have unbalanced multiple freelists, poor clustering factor of the table to the primary-key index, or chained rows.

Using CTAS to Reorganize a Table

Basically, the **create table as select** (CTAS) statement copies the selected portion of the table into a new table. If you select the entire table with an *order by* clause or an *index* hint, it will copy the rows in the same order as the primary index. In addition to resequencing the rows of the new table, the CTAS statement coalesces free space and chained rows and resets freelists, thereby providing additional performance benefits. You can also alter table parameters, such as initial extents and the number of freelists, as you create the new table. The steps in a CTAS reorganization include:

1. Define a separate tablespace to hold the reorganized table.

2. Disable all referential integrity constraints.

3. Copy the table with CTAS.

4. Reenable all referential integrity constraints.

5. Rebuild all indexes on the new table.

The main benefit of CTAS over the other methods is speed. It is far faster to use CTAS to copy the table into a new tablespace (and then re-create all RI and indexes) than it is to use the export/import method. Using CTAS also has the added benefit of allowing the rows to be resequenced into the same order as the primary index, thereby greatly reducing I/O. Within CTAS, there are two general reorganization methods.

Two Alternatives for Using CTAS

It is always recommended that you resequence the table rows when performing a table reorganization with CTAS because of the huge I/O benefits. You can use the CTAS statement in one of two ways. Each of these achieves the same result, but they do it in very different ways:

- Use CTAS in conjunction with the *order by* clause.

- Use CTAS in conjunction with a "hint" that identifies the index to use.

The approach you choose depends on the size of the table involved, the overall processing power of your environment, and how quickly you must complete the reorganization.

The details of each CTAS approach are discussed more fully next, but in either case, when you create the new table, you can speed the process by using the Oracle *nologging* option (this was called *unrecoverable* in Oracle7). This skips the added overhead of writing to the redo log file. Of course, you cannot use the redo logs to roll forward through a *nologging* operation, and most DBAs take a full backup prior to using CTAS with *nologging*. Let's examine the two methods and see their respective differences.

Using CTAS with the *order by* Clause

When using CTAS with the *order by* clause, you are directing Oracle to perform the following operations, as shown in Figure 10-9.

As we can see, the full table scan can be used with Parallel Query to speed the execution, but we still have a large disk sort following the collection of the rows. Because of the size of most tables, this sort will be done in the TEMP tablespace.

Here is an example of the SQL syntax to perform a CTAS with *order by*:

```
create table new_customer
   tablespace customer_flip
      storage (initial        500m
               next            50m
               maxextents     unlimited)
   parallel (degree 11)
   as select * from customer
   order by customer_number;
```

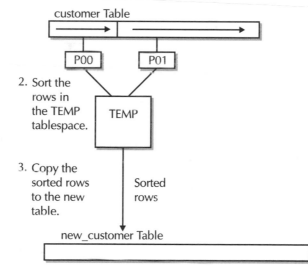

1. Perform a full table scan.

customer Table

P00   P01

2. Sort the rows in the TEMP tablespace.

TEMP

3. Copy the sorted rows to the new table.

Sorted rows

new_customer Table

FIGURE 10-9. *Using CTAS with* order by

Using CTAS with *order by* can be very slow without the *parallel* clause. A parallel full table scan reads the original table quickly (in nonindex order).

As we know from Oracle Parallel Query, the CTAS operation will cause Oracle to spawn to multiple background processes to service the full table scan. This often makes the *order by* approach faster than using the index-hint approach to CTAS. The choice to use *parallel* depends on the database server. If your hardware has multiple CPUs and many (perhaps hundreds of) processes, using *parallel* is likely to be significantly faster. However, if your hardware configuration has a relatively modest number of processes (such as the four specified in the example), the index-hint approach is likely to be faster.

Using CTAS with an Index Hint

The CTAS with an index hint executes quite differently than CTAS with *order by*. When using an index hint, the CTAS begins by retrieving the table rows from the original table using the existing index. Since the rows are initially retrieved in the proper order, there is no need to sort the result set, and the data is used immediately to create the new table, as shown in Figure 10-10.

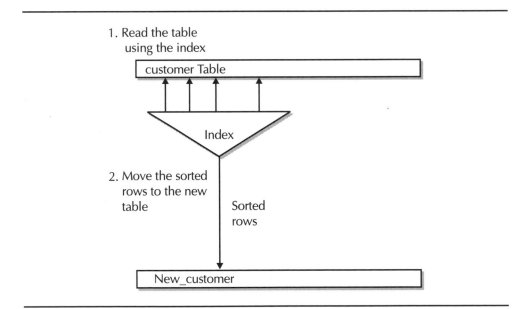

FIGURE 10-10. *Using CTAS with an index hint*

The syntax for CTAS with an index hint appears here:

```
create table new_customer
    tablespace customer_flip
        storage   (initial                 500m
                    next                    50m
                    maxextents              unlimited)
    as select /*+ index(customer customer_primary_key_idx) */   *
    from customer;
```

When this statement executes, the database traverses the existing primary-key index to access the rows for the new table, bypassing the sorting operation. Most Oracle DBAs choose this method over the *order by* approach because the runtime performance of traversing an index is generally faster than using the PARALLEL clause and then sorting the entire result set.

Now that we see how CTAS works for table reorganizations, let's explore a method for reorganizing many tables with CTAS by submitting parallel reorganization tasks.

Reorganizing Multiple Tables with CTAS

Many Oracle DBAs who use the CTAS method segregate the important tables into their own tablespace and define duplicate tablespaces for the table. For example, a customer table might reside in tablespace cust1 until reorganization, when it would move to cust2. Later, during the next reorganization, it would move back to the cust1 tablespace.

When you are reorganizing from one tablespace to another, you should always keep the backup copy of the table and a back-out procedure. The original table can remain online in cases of data inconsistency, and you will never need to perform a full restore if the table becomes corrupt. The only real cost of this duplicate tablespace method is the disk space required to duplicate major reorganized tablespaces.

The following code shows the SQL syntax needed to reorganize a table by copying it from one tablespace to another and changing the table-storage parameters as needed. In addition to the CTAS statement (in this example using the index-hint approach), we see the setup preceding the statement and the renaming and index-creation steps that follow it.

This SQL script creates a new customer table in a new tablespace (cust2) using the CTAS statement with an index hint. Because the new table's rows are physically sequenced in the same order as the primary index, data retrieval for contiguous elements will occur faster and with less I/O. The next time the table is reorganized, it can be copied back to the original tablespace (cust1).

```
connect owner/passwd;
set timing on;
```

```
create table new_customer
tablespace CUST2
    storage (initial         900m
             next            50m
             maxextents      unlimited
             )
unrecoverable
as
select /*+ index(customer customer_key_idx)   */
* from owner.customer;

rename customer to old_customer;
rename new_customer to customer;

create index customer___0 . . . . . ;
```

Now that we see how a single script works, let's expand on this and see how to submit multiple CTAS reorganizations.

Multiplexing Table Reorganization with CTAS

If you have several tables to reorganize, you can save time by running the jobs simultaneously. When you process the table reorganizations in parallel, the total time required to reorganize all the tables is no more than the time required for the largest table. For example, if you need to reorganize 100 gigabytes of table data in a single weekend, the parallel approach is the only way to go.

Below is a Korn shell script you can use to execute the reorganization. The script uses the UNIX **nohup** command to submit simultaneous CTAS reorganizations at the same time.

master_reorg.ksh

```
#!/bin/ksh
# Written by Donald Keith Burleson
# usage: nohup don_reorg.ksh > don_reorg.lst 2>&1 &


# Ensure that running user is oracle . . . . .
oracle_user=`whoami|grep oracle|grep -v grep|wc -l`;
oracle_num=`expr $oracle_user`
if [ $oracle_num -lt 1 ]
 then echo "Current user is not oracle. Please su to oracle and retry."
 exit
fi
```

```
# Ensure that Oracle is running . . . . .
oracle_up=`ps -ef|grep pmon|grep -v grep|wc -l`;
oracle_num=`expr $oracle_up`
if [ $oracle_num -lt 1 ]
  then echo "ORACLE instance is NOT up. Please start Oracle and retry."
  exit
fi


#************************************************************
# Submit parallel CTAS reorganizations of important tables
#************************************************************
nohup reorg.ksh CUSTOMER  >customer.lst   2>&1 &
nohup reorg.ksh ORDER     >order.lst      2>&1 &
nohup reorg.ksh ITEM      >item.lst       2>&1 &
nohup reorg.ksh LINE_ITEM >line_item.lst  2>&1 &
nohup reorg.ksh PRODUCT   >product.lst    2>&1 &
```

We will revisit the CTAS method for table reorganizations when we discuss row resequencing later in this chapter. Next, let's look at row chaining and see how the DBA can reduce I/O by ensuring that all rows reside on a single data block.

Identifying Oracle Tables with Chained Rows

The DBA should always monitor and fix row chaining whenever feasible. However, chained rows will always exist in cases where row length exceeds the database block size. The identification of these tables that do have chained rows is important because of their use of RAW and LONG RAW data columns.

The excessive I/O caused by chained rows can degrade an entire database. To illustrate this problem, consider the following example. An application initially loads data rows that have many VARCHAR columns into 8K blocks. Because the VARCHAR columns are unpopulated, they only consume 80 bytes, and we can fit 90 80-byte rows onto our 8K block size, reserving 10 percent of the block for growth by setting *pctfree*=10, as shown in Figure 10-11.

Several weeks after the initial load of these rows, an **update** job is run that expands the VARCHAR columns from 4 bytes each to 900 bytes each. At update time, Oracle checks to see if there is room for the row to expand on the data block. Since the *pctfree*=10 only reserved 800 bytes, Oracle must chain the row. Oracle retrieves the next data block, only to find that it also does not have room to accept the expanded row. This process continues until Oracle abandons using the freelists,

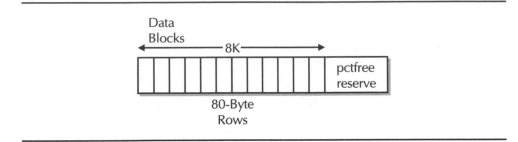

FIGURE 10-11. *Small unexpanded rows in a data block*

and raises the high-water mark for the table and places the expanded row onto a fresh 8K block. In Figure 10-12, we can see that this causes a huge amount of I/O, both at update time and for subsequent retrieval operations. In practice, Oracle is intelligent enough to see that subsequent blocks will not have room for the expanded rows. After a few tries to chain onto subsequent blocks, Oracle gives up and raises the high-water mark to get a fresh block for the chained row.

So, what could we have done to fix this huge mess? Because we know that each expanded row consumes 900 bytes, we can adjust *pctfree* to only allow nine rows on each data block instead of the original 90 rows per block. This way, when the rows expand, there will be room on the data block without any rows chaining. Basically, we want Oracle to unlink the data block from the freelist after nine 80-byte rows (720 bytes) are added to the block, and about 7,500 bytes of free space remain. In Figure 10-13, setting *pctfree*=92 will make the block unlink from the freelist when it is more than 8 percent full.

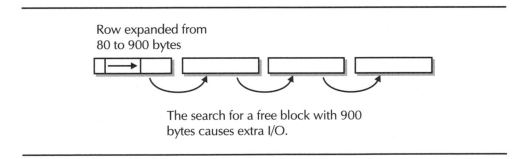

FIGURE 10-12. *Excessive row chaining with Oracle rows*

FIGURE 10-13.   *Storing rows with room for expansion*

NOTE
Please remember that when you do these calculations, a rough approximation is best. You cannot be exact because Oracle reserves space on each block for the block header and footer.

While this may look like space is being wasted on the block, what we are really doing is making room for the later updates. Now, when the subsequent rows are expanded, there is enough room for each row to expand on the original block, as shown Figure 10-14.

Remember, chained rows are bad because they cause excessive I/O, and there are only two causes for chained rows:

■   *pctfree* is set too low to accommodate row expansion.

■   The row length exceeds the database block size.

Identifying Chained Rows

The following script can be run to quickly identify tables in your database that contain chained rows. Note that the use of this script is predicated on the use of

Data Blocks

| 900 | 900 | 900 | | | | | | | 900 | 900 | 900 | | | | |

Rows expand from 80 bytes to 900
bytes without row chaining.

FIGURE 10-14.   *A data block after row expansion*

Oracle's **analyze** command to populate the chain_cnt and num_rows columns
of the dba_tables data dictionary view. Also note that this script does not include
tables that contain RAW or LONG column datatypes, since such columns cause
long rows that commonly span database blocks. Later in this chapter we will
examine STATSPACK scripts that can be used to track chained rows over time.

chained_rows.sql

```
spool chain.lst;
set pages 9999;

column c1 heading "Owner"    format a9;
column c2 heading "Table"    format a12;
column c3 heading "PCTFREE" format 99;
column c4 heading "PCTUSED" format 99;
column c5 heading "avg row" format 99,999;
column c6 heading "Rows"     format 999,999,999;
column c7 heading "Chains"  format 999,999,999;
column c8 heading "Pct"      format .99;

set heading off;
select 'Tables with chained rows and no RAW columns.' from dual;
set heading on;

select
   owner                c1,
   table_name           c2,
   pct_free             c3,
   pct_used             c4,
   avg_row_len          c5,
   num_rows             c6,
   chain_cnt            c7,
   chain_cnt/num_rows c8
from dba_tables
where
owner not in ('SYS','SYSTEM')
and
table_name not in
 (select table_name from dba_tab_columns
   where
 data_type in ('RAW','LONG RAW')
 )
and
chain_cnt > 0
order by chain_cnt desc
;
```

A properly tuned database should not have any row chaining, because the DBA has set *pctfree* high enough to accommodate row expansion. Hence, the report shown here may be used as a database integrity check. Any excessive chained rows should be immediately investigated.

Owner	Table	PCTFREE	PCTUSED	avg row	Rows	Chains	Pct
SAPR3	ZG_TAB	10	40	80	5,003	1,487	.30
SAPR3	ZMM	10	40	422	18,309	509	.03
SAPR3	Z_Z_TBLS	10	40	43	458	53	.12
SAPR3	USR03	10	40	101	327	46	.14
SAPR3	Z_BURL	10	40	116	1,802	25	.01
SAPR3	ZGO_CITY	10	40	56	1,133	10	.01

We can also extend the report to show tables that have long rows. Because of the large row length of some tables with RAW or BLOB columns, you will see chained rows because the row length will exceed the *db_block_size*, forcing the huge rows to chain onto many blocks.

chained_rows.sql

```
set heading off;
select 'Tables with chained rows that contain RAW columns.' from dual;
set heading on;

select
   owner             c1,
   table_name        c2,
   pct_free          c3,
   pct_used          c4,
   avg_row_len       c5,
   num_rows          c6,
   chain_cnt         c7,
   chain_cnt/num_rows c8
from dba_tables
where
owner not in ('SYS','SYSTEM')
and
table_name in
 (select table_name from dba_tab_columns
   where
 data_type in ('RAW','LONG RAW')
 )
and
chain_cnt > 0
order by chain_cnt desc
;
```

Next is an example of the output from this report. Note that many tables have an average row length greater than 4K. If your database supports a large block size, you can remove these chained rows by rebuilding the database with an 8K or 16K block size.

```
Owner       Table     PCTFREE PCTUSED avg row        Rows        Chains   Pct
---------   --------- ------- ------- -------  ------------  ------------  ----
SAPR3       KOCLU          40      60   8,981       597,125       472,724   .79
SAPR3       CDCLSP         40      60     809       712,810       328,989   .46
SAPR3       VBFCL          40      60   5,398       340,917       285,930   .84
SAPR3       EDIDOM         40      60   6,211       158,426       114,859   .73
SAPR3       D01XX          10      40   5,129        76,635        43,791   .57
SAPR3       TSTIJP         40      60   6,559        44,596        22,298   .50
SAPR3       T51GHKU        40      60   1,055        24,393        21,344   .88
SAPR3       D020L          10      40   1,629        84,968         6,294   .07
SAPR3       EUDB           40      60   3,068        13,910         6,028   .43
SAPR3       D010L          10      40  13,454         4,747         4,747   1
```

Again, we must remember that chained rows cause excessive I/O because multiple blocks must be read to access the data. When chained rows are found, the chains can be repaired by reorganizing the tables and resetting *pctfree* to a lower value. Now that we understand how to identify row chaining, let's look at techniques for identifying sparse tables.

Identifying Tables with Long Rows

With the introduction of the RAW and LONG RAW datatypes, many ORACLE tables have table row lengths that exceed the block size. Of course, these long rows will always chain onto several data blocks, and there is nothing that the DBA can do about this chaining except to redefine the whole database with larger block sizes. However, RAW and LONG RAW datatypes can often be redefined in Oracle8 as BLOB, CLOB, or NCLOB datatypes. When using these datatypes, Oracle will automatically move the LOB into offline storage when the column length becomes excessive, thereby preventing chained rows.

However, the DBA still needs to know which tables in their database contain these large rows. The listing here shows an extract from an Oracle database showing all tables where the average row length is greater than one-fourth of the block size:

```
column db_block_size new_value blksz noprint

select value db_block_size from v$parameter where name = 'db_block_size';

select
   table_name,
```

```
   tablespace_name,
   avg_row_len
from
   dba_tables
where
avg_row_len > &blksz/4
order by
   avg_row_len desc
;
```

Here is a sample listing. Here we see all of the tables that have long row lengths.

TABLE_NAME	TABLESPACE_NAME	AVG_ROW_LEN
D010L	PSAPLOADD	15,775
TST03	PDONPROTD	10,041
D010Y	PDONLOADD	7,913
SFDG	PDONDOCUD	7,819
D010Q	PDONLOADD	3,732
SNAP	PDONBTABD	3,250
MONI	PDONSTABD	2,851
MCSI	PDONSTABD	2,781
EUDD	PDONSTABD	2,684
RFDT	PDONBTABD	2,673
DSYO2	PDONCLUD	2,656
SFHOA	PDONSTABD	2,393
DSYO1	PDONCLUD	2,072
SOC3	PDONBTABD	2,018

For example, consider the Oracle table that has an average of 1,700 bytes per row, stored on a 4K block size. For the sake of a simple example, let's say that 4K = 4,000, even though we know that it is really 4,096 bytes. After two rows are added to the block, 3,400 bytes are consumed, and 600 bytes remain in the block. If *pctfree*=10, the block must reach 3,600 bytes to be removed from the freelist, and the block will remain on the freelist even though it cannot hold another entire row. The third row will not chain, and Oracle will grab another free block from the freelist. This is illustrated in Figure 10-15.

Now that we see how to monitor the chaining for our tables, let's revisit the sparse table concept and see how to detect sparse tables.

Identifying Sparse Tables

Sparse tables generally occur when a table is defined with multiple freelists, the table has heavy **insert** and **delete** activity, and the deletes are not parallelized. For example, a table with 20 freelists that has 20 concurrent **insert** processes is purged by a single process, causing all of the free blocks to go to only one of the 20 freelists.

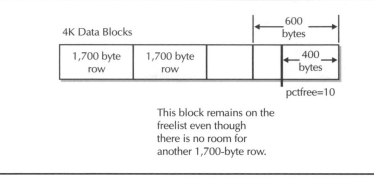

FIGURE 10-15. *A data block on the freelist without room to accept a row*

This causes the table to extend, even though it may be largely empty. Extension occurs because each freelist is unaware of the contents of other freelists.

A sparse table can usually be detected by selecting tables whose actual size (number of rows times average row length) is greater than the size of the next extent for the table. Of course, we must set the number of freelists to the number of simultaneous **insert** or **update** operations, so we cannot reduce the number of freelists without introducing segment header contention.

To see tables with excessive free space, we calculate the average row length (*avg_row_len*) in the data dictionary view and the number of rows (*num_rows*) with a weekly table **analyze** (i.e., **analyze table xxx estimate statistics**). The query here selects tables that contain multiple freelists with more than one extent where there is excessive free space:

sparse.sql

```
column c1   heading "Tablespace";
column c2   heading "Owner";
column c3   heading "Table";
column c4   heading "Bytes M" format 9,999;
column c5   heading "Extents" format 999;
column c7   heading "Empty M" format 9,999;
column c6   heading "Blocks M" format 9,999;
column c8   heading "NEXT M" format 999;
column c9   heading "Row space M" format 9,999;
column c10  heading "Pct Full" format .99;
column db_block_size new_value blksz noprint
select value db_block_size from v$parameter where name = 'db_block_size';
```

```
select
        substr(dt.table_name,1,10) c3,
        ds.extents c5,
        ds.bytes/1048576 c4,
        dt.next_extent/1048576 c8,
        (dt.empty_blocks*4096)/1048576 c7,
        (avg_row_len*num_rows)/1048576 c9,
        (ds.blocks*&blksize)/1048576 c6,
        (avg_row_len*num_rows)/(ds.blocks*&blksize) c10
from    sys.dba_segments ds,
        sys.dba_tables dt
where   ds.tablespace_name = dt.tablespace_name
and     ds.owner = dt.owner
and     ds.segment_name = dt.table_name
and dt.freelists > 1
and ds.extents > 1
and dt.owner not in ('SYS','SYSTEM')
and (avg_row_len*num_rows)/1048576 > 50
and ds.bytes/1048576 > 20
order by c10;
```

Next is an example of the output from this script. When we multiply the number of rows in the table by the average row length, we approximate the actual consumed size of the data within the table. We then compare this value with the actual number of allocated bytes in the table. The idea is that a sparse table will have far more allocated space than consumed space.

Table	Extents	Bytes M	NEXT M	Empty M	Row space M	Blocks M	Pct Full
TST99	65	1,241	20	14	118	1,241	.10
LIKP	3	148	49	24	76	148	.52
VBRK	2	124	4	0	69	124	.56
STXL	35	1,775	40	7	1,021	1,775	.57
VBAK	5	234	49	0	136	234	.58
KOCLU	27	1,889	49	27	1,144	1,889	.61
VBUP	2	866	49	0	570	866	.66
VBUK	2	147	28	0	103	147	.70
VBAP	46	4,314	50	0	3,034	4,314	.70
NAST	3	137	10	2	97	137	.71
VBPA	5	582	32	0	426	582	.73
LIPS	7	2,350	49	0	1,735	2,350	.74
VBRP	45	2,675	49	0	2,029	2,675	.76
WFPRC	30	123	10	7	95	123	.77
VLPMA	16	575	25	23	444	575	.77
EDIDOC	18	432	20	13	337	432	.78
VRPMA	24	700	20	7	549	700	.78
VBEP	4	2,134	49	49	1,698	2,134	.80

As we stated earlier, sparse tables are caused by an imbalance in multiple freelists, and are evidenced by tables that are continuing to extend although they are not very full. In the preceding example, we might take a closer look at the KOCLU, VBRP and TST99 tables because they have a high number of extents while they are largely empty.

Next, let's take a look at a very important concept in object tuning. As we have repeatedly noted, anything that can be done to reduce I/O will improve performance, and resequencing table rows can result in dramatic reductions in expensive disk I/O.

Resequencing Oracle Table Rows for High Performance

Experienced Oracle DBAs know that I/O is the single greatest component of response time and regularly work to reduce I/O. Disk I/O is expensive because when Oracle retrieves a block from a data file on disk, the reading process must wait for the physical I/O operation to complete. Disk operations are 14,000 times slower than a row's access in the data buffers. Consequently, anything you can do to minimize I/O—or reduce bottlenecks caused by contention for files on disk—can greatly improve the performance of any Oracle database.

If response times are lagging in your high-transaction system, reducing disk I/O is the best way to bring about quick improvement. And when you access tables in a transaction system exclusively through range scans in primary-key indexes, reorganizing the tables with the CTAS method should be one of the first strategies you use to reduce I/O. By physically sequencing the rows in the same order as the primary-key index, this method can considerably speed up data retrieval.

Like disk load balancing, row resequencing is easy, inexpensive, and relatively quick. With both techniques in your DBA bag of tricks, you'll be well equipped to shorten response times—often dramatically—in high-I/O systems.

In high-volume online transaction processing (OLTP) environments in which data is accessed via a primary index, resequencing table rows so that contiguous blocks follow the same order as their primary index can actually reduce physical I/O and improve response time during index-driven table queries. This technique is useful only when the application selects multiple rows, when using index range scans, or if the application issues multiple requests for consecutive keys. Databases with random primary-key unique accesses won't benefit from row resequencing.

Let's explore how this works. Consider a SQL query that retrieves 100 rows using an index:

```
select
    salary
from
    employee
where
    last_name like 'B%';
```

This query will traverse the last_name_index, selecting each row to obtain the rows. As Figure 10-16 shows, this query will have at least 100 physical disk reads because the employee rows reside on different data blocks.

Now let's examine the same query where the rows are resequenced into the same order as the last_name_index. In Figure 10-17, we see that the query can read all 100 employees with only three disk I/Os (one for the index, and two for the data blocks), resulting in a saving of over 97 block reads.

The degree to which resequencing improves performance depends on how far out of sequence the rows are when you begin and how many rows you will be accessing in sequence. You can find out how well a table's rows match the index's sequence key by looking at the dba_indexes and dba_tables views in the data dictionary.

In the dba_indexes view, we look at the clustering_factor column. If the clustering factor—an integer roughly matches the number of blocks in the table, your table is in sequence with the index order. However, if the clustering factor is close to the number of rows in the table, it indicates that the rows in the table are out of sequence with the index.

The benefits of row resequencing cannot be underestimated. In large active tables with a large number of index scans, row resequencing can triple the performance of queries.

Finding Queries with Index Range Scans

Using the *access.sql* script to explain all of the SQL in your library cache, it is very easy to identify tables that have a high amount of index range scans. See Chapter 11

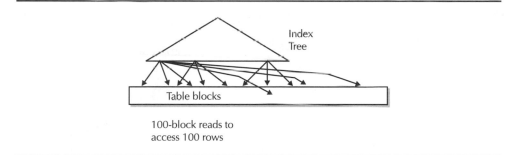

FIGURE 10-16. *An index query on unsequenced rows*

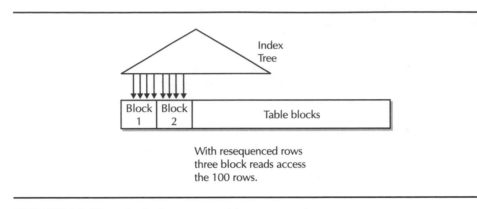

With resequenced rows
three block reads access
the 100 rows.

FIGURE 10-17. *An index query with sequenced rows*

for details on using the *access.sql* technique. Let's examine one of the reports from this script:

```
Tue Nov 07                                                      page
1
                      Index range scans and counts

OWNER      TABLE_NAME          INDEX_NAME            TBL_BLOCKS    NBR_SCANS
---------  ------------------  --------------------  ------------  ------------
READER     ANNO_HIGHLIGHT      HL_ISBN_SEQ_USER_IDX           8        16,738
READER     ANNO_STICKY         ST_ISBN_SEQ_USER_IDX           8        15,900
READER     ANNO_DOG_EAR        DE_ISBN_SEQ_ID_IDX             8         1,191
READER     PAGE                ISBN_VIS_FUNC_IDX             24           813
READER     TOC_ENTRY           ISBN_TOC_SEQ_IDX               8           645
```

In this report we see that all accesses are ranked according to the number of index range scans, and we can quickly identify the tables and indexes that we will use for resequencing.

Next, let's look at index resequencing and see how it improves index performance.

Index Rebuilding Techniques

As we know from DBA 101 class, the goal of an index is to speed the process of finding data. An index file contains a data value for a specific field in a table and a pointer that identifies the record that contains a value for that field. In other words, an index on the last_name field for a table would contain a list of last names and pointers to specific records—just as an index to a book lists topics and page numbers to enable readers to access information quickly. When processing a request, the database optimizer will choose some or all of the available indexes to efficiently locate the requested rows.

Figure 10-18 illustrates some of the concepts of a B-tree index. The upper blocks contain index data that points to lower-level index blocks. The lowest-level blocks contain every indexed data value and a corresponding rowid used for locating the actual row of data.

Normally, these indexes attempt to manage themselves internally to ensure fast access to the data rows. However, excessive activity within a table can cause Oracle indexes to dynamically reconfigure themselves. This reconfiguration involves three activities:

- **Index splitting**   This is when the addition of new table rows cause new index nodes to be created at existing levels (see Figure 10-19).

- **Index spawning**   At some point, the Oracle indexes will reach the maximum capacity for the level and the Oracle index will spawn, creating a deeper level structure (see Figure 10-20).

- **Index node deletion**   As you may know, Oracle index nodes are not physically deleted when table rows are deleted, nor are the entries removed from the index. Rather, Oracle "logically" deletes the index entry and leaves "dead" nodes in the index tree.

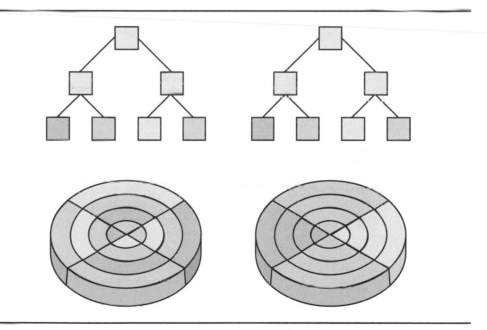

FIGURE 10-18.   *A typical Oracle B-tree index*

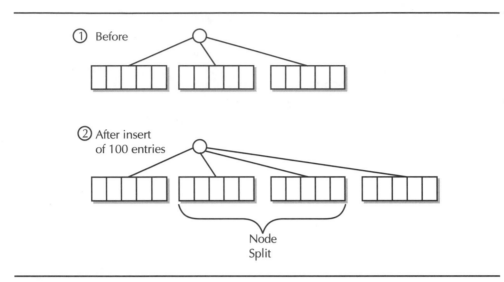

FIGURE 10-19. *Index splitting*

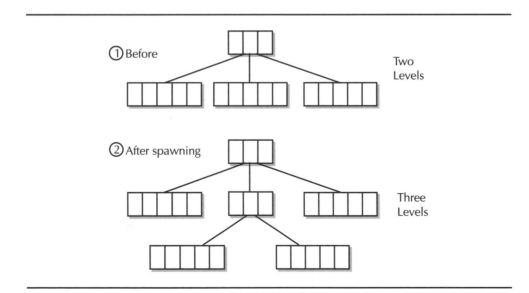

FIGURE 10-20. *Oracle index spawning*

Indexes require rebuilding when deleted leaf nodes appear or when the index has spawned into too many levels of depth. While it is tempting to write a script that rebuilds every index in the schema, bear in mind that Oracle contains many thousands of indexes, and a complete rebuild can be very time consuming. Hence, we need to develop a method to identify those indexes that will get improved performance with a rebuild. Let's look at a method for accomplishing this task.

One vexing issue with Oracle indexes is that the information for an index rebuild must be gathered from two sources:

- The Oracle *analyze index compute statistics* command:

  ```
  ANALYZE INDEX index_name COMPUTE STATISTICS
  ```

- The Oracle *analyze index validate structure* command:

  ```
  ANALYZE INDEX index_name VALIDATE STRUCTURE
  ```

Once we gather information from these sources, we can generate a report with everything we need to know about the index internal structure:

Index acccos	# rep keys	dist. keys	# deleted leaf rows	Height	blk gets per
CUST_IDX	1	423,209	58,282	4	6
EDU_IDX_12	433	36,272	7,231	3	2
CUST_IDX	12	1,262,393	726,361	4	6

From this report, we see several important statistics:

- **The number of deleted leaf nodes** The term "deleted leaf node" refers to the number of index nodes that have been logically deleted as a result of row **delete** operations. Remember that Oracle leaves "dead" index nodes in the index when rows are deleted. This is done to speed up SQL deletes, since Oracle does not have to rebalance the index tree when rows are deleted.

- **Index height** The height of the index refers to the number of levels that are spawned by the index as a result in row inserts. When a large number of rows are added to a table, Oracle may spawn additional levels of an index to accommodate the new rows. Hence, an Oracle index may have four levels, but only in those areas of the index tree where the massive inserts have occurred. Oracle indexes can support many millions of entries in three levels, and any Oracle index that has four or more levels would benefit from rebuilding.

■ **Gets per index access** The number of "gets" per access refers to the amount of logical I/O that is required to fetch a row with the index. As you may know, a logical get is not necessarily a physical I/O since much of the index may reside in the Oracle buffer cache. However, any Oracle index with a number greater than 10 would probably benefit from an index rebuild.

After you analyze the report, you may want to consider rebuilding any index where the height is more than three levels, since three levels will support millions of index entries. Note that Oracle indexes will "spawn" to a fourth level only in areas of the index where a massive **insert** has occurred, such that 99 percent of the index has three levels but the index is reported as having four levels.

The script to make the report is complex because both the **validate structure** and **compute statistics** commands must be executed. The following code snippets are used to generate the report.

id1.sql

```
set pages 9999;
set heading off;
set feedback off;
set echo off;
spool id4.sql;
select '@id2.sql' from dual;
select 'analyze index '||owner||'.'||index_name||' validate structure;',
'@id3.sql;'
from dba_indexes
where
owner not in ('SYS','SYSTEM');
spool off;
set heading on;
set feedback on;
set echo on;
@id4.sql
@id5.sql
```

id2.sql

```
create table temp_stats as
select
name ,
most_repeated_key ,
distinct_keys ,
del_lf_rows ,
height ,
blks_gets_per_access
from index_stats;
```

id3.sql

```
insert into temp_stats
(select
name ,
most_repeated_key ,
distinct_keys ,
del_lf_rows ,
height ,
blks_gets_per_access
from index_stats
);
```

ind_fix.sql

```
Rem ind_fix.sql - Shows the details for index stats

set pagesize 60;
set linesize 100;
set echo off;
set feedback off;
set heading off;

column c1 format a18;
column c2 format 9,999,999;
column c3 format 9,999,999;
column c4 format 999,999;
column c5 format 99,999;
column c6 format 9,999;

spool idx_report.lst;

prompt
prompt
prompt '                       # rep      dist.    # deleted              blk s
prompt Index                  keys      keys     leaf rows   Height     per s
prompt -------------------- ------    ------   ---------  ------    -----

select distinct
  name                  c1,
  most_repeated_key     c2,
  distinct_keys         c3,
  del_lf_Rows           c4,
  height                c5,
  blks_gets_per_access  c6
from temp_stats
where
  height > 3
  or
  del_lf_rows > 10
order by name;
```

```
spool off;

spool id6.sql;

select 'alter index '||owner||'.'||name||' rebuild tablespace
'||tablespace_name||';'
from temp_stats, dba_indexes
where
  temp_stats.name = dba_indexes.index_name
  and
  (height > 3
  or
  del_lf_rows > 10);

select 'analyze index '||owner||'.'||name||' compute statistics;'
from temp_stats, dba_indexes
where
  temp_stats.name = dba_indexes.index_name
  and
  (height > 3
  or
  del_lf_rows > 10);

spool off;
```

id6.sql

```
select 'alter index '||owner||'.'||name||' rebuild tablespace
'||tablespace_name
||';'
from temp_stats, dba_indexes
where
temp_stats.name = dba_indexes.index_name
and
(height > 3
or
del_lf_rows > 10);
select 'analyze index '||owner||'.'||name||' compute statistics;'
from temp_stats, dba_indexes
where
temp_stats.name = dba_indexes.index_name
and
(height > 3
or
del_lf_rows > 10);
spool off;
```

When to Rebuild Indexes

As you may know, you can easily rebuild an Oracle index with the
following command:

```
ALTER INDEX index_name REBUILD TABLESPACE tablespace_name;
```

We might want to rebuild an index if the block gets per access is greater than 5,
since excessive block gets indicate a fragmented B-tree structure. Another rebuild
condition would be cases where deleted leaf nodes comprise more than 20 percent
of the index nodes. Another reason to rebuild is when any index shows a depth
of 4 or greater.

Automating Index Rebuilds

Now that we have identified the candidates for an index rebuild, we can run the
following script during Oracle system downtime to rebuild all of the indexes.

Index rebuilding with the **alter index rebuild** is a very safe command. If anything
goes wrong, Oracle aborts the operation and leaves the existing index in place. Many
DBAs regularly schedule index rebuilds during off-hours with no fear that a problem
might occur. Here is a handy script for generating the **alter index rebuild** syntax:

```
Set heading off;
Set pages 9999;
Spool run_rebuild.sql;

select 'alter index ||owner||'.'||index_name||' rebuild tablespace
'||tablespace_name||';'
from dba_indexes
;

spool off;
@run_rebuild
```

NOTE
*It is interesting to note that Oracle indexing has
changed dramatically between Oracle7 and
Oracle8. While the functions of the indexes
remain the same, the sizes of the indexes have
been reduced by almost 50 percent.*

As we stated, the **alter index** *index_name* **rebuild** command is a very safe way
to rebuild indexes. Here is the syntax of the command:

```
alter index index_name
rebuild
tablespace tablespace_name
storage (initial new_initial next new_next freelists new_freelist_number )
```

Unlike the old-fashioned method of dropping and re-creating the index, the **rebuild** command does not require a full table scan of the table and the subsequent sorting of the keys and rowids. Rather, the **rebuild** command will perform the following steps:

- Walk the existing index to get the index keys.

- Populate temporary segments with the new tree structure.

- Once the operation has completed successfully, drop the old tree, and rename the temporary segments to the new index.

As you can see from the steps, you can rebuild indexes without worrying that you will accidentally lose the index. If the index cannot be rebuilt for any reason, Oracle will abort the operation and leave the existing index intact. Only after the entire index has been rebuilt does Oracle transfer the index to the new B-tree.

Most Oracle administrators run this script and then select the index that they would like to rebuild. Note that the TABLESPACE clause should always be used with the **alter index rebuild** command to ensure that the index is rebuilt in the same tablespace as the existing index. Be aware that you must have enough room in that tablespace to hold all of the temporary segments required for the index rebuild, so most Oracle DBAs will double-size index tablespaces with enough space for two full index trees.

Also note that if you use the PARALLEL option to increase speed when rebuilding indexes, each parallel process will require enough space for the indexes' initial extent size. Hence, if you rebuild indexes with PARALLEL DEGREE 4, you must have four times the space in the target tablespace.

Next. Let's take a look at the most important topic of this chapter—how to extend STATSPACK to capture table and index statistics.

Monitoring Oracle Tables and Indexes with STATSPACK

While the STATSPACK utility does a very good job of monitoring the Oracle databases as a whole, it falls far short on collection of data about the individual tables and indexes within the database. The Oracle DBA is always interested in seeing what is going on within tables and indexes so that he or she can get an idea of the growth of the tables, and keep track of the behavior of each individual object within the database.

Fortunately, it is quite simple to extend the STATSPACK utility to accommodate table information; however, the approach is quite different than the standard STATSPACK snapshots. Whereas the standard STATSPACK snapshots will sample the v$ control structures within the Oracle instance to collect values, a STATSPACK extension for tables and indexes must periodically sample the dba_tables and dba_indexes views from the data dictionary.

When extending STATSPACK to capture statistics for tables and indexes, it is very important to remember that the data dictionary statistics are only current up to the last **analyze** for the table or index. Hence, it is very important that the Oracle DBA issue the **analyze table** and **analyze index** commands immediately prior to running the STATSPACK extension snapshots for tables and indexes.

Unlike the Oracle system statistics that are usually captured by STATSPACK on an hourly basis, the information for tables and indexes can be captured on a weekly basis.

Allocating the STATSPACK Extension Tables

The following script will allocate two tables called stats$tab_stats and stats$idx_stats to hold our weekly snapshots of the table and index metadata. Please note the use of indexes within these tables to avoid full table scans during subsequent report queries.

create_object_tables.sql

```
connect perfstat/perfstat;

drop table perfstat.stats$tab_stats;

create table porfstat.stats$tab_stats
(
    snap_time          date,
    server_name        varchar2(20),
    db_name            varchar2(9),
    tablespace_name    varchar2(40),
    owner              varchar2(40),
    table_name         varchar2(40),
    num_rows           number,
    avg_row_len        number,
    next_extent        number,
    extents            number,
    bytes              number
)
tablespace perfstat
storage (initial 1m next 1m maxextents unlimited)
;

drop table perfstat.stats$idx_stats;

create table perfstat.stats$idx_stats
(
    snap_time          date,
    server_name        varchar2(20),
    db_name            varchar2(9),
    tablespace_name    varchar2(40),
```

```
   owner              varchar2(40),
   index_name         varchar2(40),
   clustering_factor  number,
   leaf_blocks        number,
   blevel             number,
   next_extent        number,
   extents            number,
   bytes              number
)
tablespace perfstat
storage (initial 1m next 1m maxextents unlimited)
;


drop index
   perfstat.tab_stat_date_idx;

create index
   perfstat.tab_stat_date_idx
on
   perfstat.stats$tab_stats
( snap_time )
tablespace perfstat
storage (initial 1m next 1m maxextents unlimited)
;


drop index
   perfstat.idx_stat_date_idx;
create index
   perfstat.idx_stat_date_idx
on
   perfstat.stats$idx_stats
( snap_time )
tablespace perfstat
storage (initial 1m next 1m maxextents unlimited)
;
```

It is important to note that these STATSPACK extension tables contain the name of the database server. In a distributed environment, you can collect STATSPACK table and index information from a variety of servers and transfer the data into a centralized repository.

Collecting the STATSPACK Snapshot for Tables and Indexes

The next step is to populate our STATSPACK extension tables with table and index data from the Oracle data dictionary. In order to get accurate statistics, we must begin by analyzing all of our tables and indexes. Next, we extract the data from the data dictionary and populate the stats$tab_stats and stats$index_stats tables.

The following Korn shell script can be executed once each week to analyze the table and indexes and collect the table and index data. Note that we must set the *oratab* file location and pass the proper ORACLE SID when executing this script.

get_object_stats.ksh

```ksh
#!/bin/ksh


# Validate the Oracle database name with
# lookup in /var/opt/oracle/oratab
TEMP=`cat /var/opt/oracle/oratab|grep \^$1:|\
cut -f1 -d':'|wc -l`
tmp=`expr TEMP`      # Convert string to number
if [ $tmp -ne 1 ]
then
    echo "Your input $1 is not a valid ORACLE_SID."
    exit 99
fi

# First, we must set the environment . . . .
ORACLE_SID=$1
export ORACLE_SID
ORACLE_HOME=`cat /var/opt/oracle/oratab|grep $ORACLE_SID:|cut -f2 -d':'`
export ORACLE_HOME
PATH=$ORACLE_HOME/bin:$PATH
export PATH
MON=`echo ~oracle/obj_stat`
export MON

# Get the server name
host=`uname -a|awk '{ print $2 }'`

$ORACLE_HOME/bin/sqlplus -s perfstat/perfstat<<!

set heading off;
set feedback off;
set echo off;
set pages 999;
set lines 120;

--****************************************************************
-- First, let's get the latest statistics for each table
--****************************************************************
spool $MON/run_analyze.sql
select 'analyze table '||owner||'.'||table_name||' estimate statistics
sample 500 rows;'
from
   dba_tables
```

```
where
   owner not in ('SYS','SYSTEM','PERFSTAT');
--   *****************************
--  Analyze all indexes for statistics
--   *****************************
select 'analyze index '||owner||'.'||table_name||' compute statistics;'
from
   dba_indexes
where
   owner not in ('SYS','SYSTEM','PERFSTAT');
spool off;

set echo on;
set feedback on;

@$MON/run_analyze

connect perfstat/perfstat;

--*******************************************************************
-- Now we grab the table statistics
--*******************************************************************
insert into perfstat.stats\$tab_stats
(
  select
     SYSDATE,
     lower('${host}'),
     lower('${ORACLE_SID}'),
     t.tablespace_name,
     t.owner,
     t.table_name,
     t.num_rows,
     t.avg_row_len,
     s.next_extent,
     s.extents,
     s.bytes
from
   dba_tables   t,
   dba_segments s
where
   segment_name = table_name
   and
   s.tablespace_name = t.tablespace_name
   and
   s.owner = t.owner
   and
   t.owner not in ('SYS','SYSTEM')
--   and
--   num_rows > 1000
);
```

```
--*******************************************************************
-- Now we grab the index statistics
--*******************************************************************
insert into perfstat.stats\$idx_stats
(
   select
      SYSDATE,
      lower('${host}'),
      lower('${ORACLE_SID}'),
      i.tablespace_name,
      i.owner,
      i.index_name,
      i.clustering_factor,
      i.leaf_blocks,
      i.blevel,
      s.next_extent,
      s.extents,
      s.bytes
   from dba_indexes   i,
        dba_segments  s,
        dba_tables    t
   where
      i.table_name = t.table_name
   and
      segment_name = index_name
   and
      s.tablespace_name = i.tablespace_name
   and
      s.owner = i.owner
   and
      i.owner not in ('SYS','SYSTEM')
--    and
--       t.num_rows > 1000
);

exit

!
```

CAUTION
Be sure that you have the correct setting for your
optimizer_mode *before analyzing table and indexes.*
If you have optimizer_mode=choose *and you do not*
have table statistics, analyzing the tables will cause
your SQL to switch from rule-based to cost-based
optimization.

Note that this script also has commented out code to restrict the population of rows to tables that contain more than 1,000 rows. This is because the DBA may only be interested in collecting statistics on the most active tables within their database.

Reports on Tables and Indexes

The following reports are designed to show the DBA changes within the status of individual objects and the overall space usage for the database as a whole. For example, STATSPACK reports can be run against the stats$tab_stats and stats$idx_stats tables to show the total number of bytes allocated within individual tablespaces within the database.

Let's start with the simple STATSPACK report and then move on to the more advanced reporting. One of the advantages of doing weekly snapshots of table and index statistics is that we are able to write easy comparisons between snapshots. The following report is designed to find the most recent snapshot data, go back one snapshot period, and produce a report showing the growth of all significant tables within the Oracle database.

Take a close look at the following report. In the report, you can see how we select the most recent snapshot data from the STATSPACK tables and then use a technique with a temporary table in order to find the immediately previous snapshot. This is an important technique to remember when you start writing your own customized STATSPACK reports and you want to compare the two most recent snapshots within your database.

rpt_bytes.sql

```
--*********************************************************

-- First we need to get the second-highest date in tab_stats
--*********************************************************
set lines 80;
set pages 999;
set feedback off;
set verify off;
set echo off;

drop table d1;

create table d1 as
select distinct
   to_char(snap_time,'YYYY-MM-DD') mydate
from
   stats$tab_stats
```

```
where
   to_char(snap_time,'YYYY-MM-DD') <
     (select max(to_char(snap_time,'YYYY-MM-DD')) from stats$tab_stats)
;


--************************************************************
-- The second highest date is select max(mydate) from d1;
  *************************************************************

set heading off;

prompt Object growth - Comparing last two snapshots
prompt
prompt This report shows the growth of key tables
prompt for the past week.


select 'Old date = '||max(mydate) from d1;
select 'New date = '||max(to_char(snap_time,'YYYY-MM-DD')) from stats$tab_stats;

break on report ;
compute sum of old_bytes on old.table_name;

set heading on;

column old_bytes format 999,999,999
column new_bytes format 999,999,999
column change    format 999,999,999

select
   new.table name,
   old.bytes               old_bytes,
   new.bytes               new_bytes,
   new.bytes - old.bytes     change
from
   stats$tab_stats old,
   stats$tab_stats new
where
   old.table_name = new.table_name
and
   new.bytes > old.bytes
and
   new.bytes - old.bytes > 10000
and
   to_char(new.snap_time, 'YYYY-MM-DD') =
         (select max(to_char(snap_time,'YYYY-MM-DD')) from stats$tab_stats)
and
```

```
     to_char(old.snap_time, 'YYYY-MM-DD') =
           (select max(mydate) from d1)
and
   new.table_name not like 'STATS$%'
order by
   new.bytes-old.bytes desc
;
--*********************************************************
-- First we need to get the second-highest date in idx_stats
--*********************************************************
set lines 80;
set pages 999;
set feedback off;
set verify off;
set echo off;

drop table d1;

create table d1 as
select distinct
   to_char(snap_time,'YYYY-MM-DD') mydate
from
   stats$idx_stats
where
   to_char(snap_time,'YYYY-MM-DD') <
     (select max(to_char(snap_time,'YYYY-MM-DD')) from stats$idx_stats)
;


--*********************************************************
-- The second highest date is select max(mydate) from d1;
--*********************************************************

set heading off;

prompt Object growth - Comparing last two snapshots
prompt
prompt This report shows the growth of key indexes
prompt for the past week.


select 'Old date = '||max(mydate) from d1;
select 'New date = '||max(to_char(snap_time,'YYYY-MM-DD')) from
tats$idx_stats;

break on report ;
compute sum of old_bytes on old.table_name;

set heading on;

column old_bytes format 999,999,999
```

```
column new_bytes format 999,999,999
column change     format 999,999,999

select
   new.index_name,
   old.bytes            old_bytes,
   new.bytes            new_bytes,
   new.bytes - old.bytes    change
from
   stats$idx_stats old,
   stats$idx_stats new
where
   old.index_name = new.index_name
and
   new.bytes > old.bytes
and
   new.bytes - old.bytes > 10000
and
   to_char(new.snap_time, 'YYYY-MM-DD') =
        (select max(to_char(snap_time,'YYYY-MM-DD')) from stats$idx_stats)
and
   to_char(old.snap_time, 'YYYY-MM-DD') =
         (select max(mydate) from d1)
and
   new.index_name not like 'STATS$%'
order by
   new.bytes-old.bytes desc
;
```

Now that we have seen the script, let's take a look at some of the useful information that this report provides. Most DBAs run this report weekly so they can get an object summary report in their mailbox every Monday morning to show them the growth of individual tables and indexes within the Oracle database. These kinds of reports are also interesting to MIS management, especially the parts of the report that show the overall growth of the database. Let's go through each piece of the output from this report individually so we can see exactly what kind of useful information is being gathered inside the STATSPACK extension tables.

The first report shown next gives a summary of table and index growth over the past seven days (or the period between collections). The report starts by displaying information about the most recent snapshot data, and the previous state for which the snapshot was compared. From this we see the table name, the number of bytes in the prior snapshot, and the number of bytes in the new snapshot. We also see the total change in size for the tables during the elapsed time between snapshots. This report provides the DBA with useful information about the rate of growth of key tables within their database, and also provides capacity planning information that is useful for managers who might need to order additional disk or other hardware resources in time to accommodate the growth of the object within the database.

rpt_bytes.sql

Object growth - Comparing last two snapshots

This report shows the growth of key tables
for the past week.

Old date = 2001-01-15

New date = 2001-01-22

TABLE_NAME	OLD_BYTES	NEW_BYTES	CHANGE
MTL_TRANSACTION_ACCOUNTS	40,484,864	43,679,744	3,194,880
GL_JE_LINES	18,653,184	21,315,584	2,662,400
MTL_MATERIAL_TRANSACTIONS	35,692,544	38,354,944	2,662,400
WIP_REQUIREMENT_OPERATIONS	23,445,504	26,107,904	2,662,400
GL_BALANCES	4,808,704	6,406,144	1,597,440
WF_ITEM_ATTRIBUTE_VALUES	18,653,184	20,250,624	1,597,440
PLAN_TABLE	122,880	1,597,440	1,474,560
SQLTEMP	122,880	1,597,440	1,474,560
GL_IMPORT_REFERENCES	6,938,624	8,003,584	1,064,960
MTL_DEMAND_INTERFACE	5,873,664	6,938,624	1,064,960
MTL_CST_ACTUAL_COST_DETAILS	15,458,304	16,523,264	1,064,960
GL_INTERFACE	1,613,824	2,678,784	1,064,960
WF_ITEM_ACTIVITY_STATUSES	6,938,624	8,003,584	1,064,960
SO_EXCEPTIONS	868,352	1,622,016	753,664
AP_INVOICE_DISTRIBUTIONS_ALL	5,341,184	5,873,664	532,480
SO_LINES_ALL	2,146,304	2,678,784	532,480
WF_NOTIFICATION_ATTRIBUTES	4,276,224	4,808,704	532,480
WIP_TRANSACTION_ACCOUNTS	18,653,184	19,185,664	532,480
RA_CUSTOMER_TRX_ALL	548,864	1,081,344	532,480
MTL_DEMAND	2,146,304	2,678,784	532,480
AP_EXPENSE_REPORT_HEADERS_ALL	303,104	589,824	286,720
MRP_RELIEF_INTERFACE	303,104	589,824	286,720
GL_CONS_FLEXFIELD_MAP	16,384	303,104	286,720
RA_REMIT_TOS_ALL	16,384	180,224	163,840
SO_PICKING_LINE_DETAILS	442,368	573,440	131,072
PO_LINES_ALL	3,031,040	3,080,192	9,152
SO_FREIGHT_CHARGES	49,152	81,920	32,768
SO_PICKING_BATCHES_ALL	409,600	442,368	32,768

Object growth - Comparing last two snapshots

This report shows the growth of key indexes
for the past week.

Old date = 2001-01-15
New date = 2001-01-22

INDEX_NAME	OLD_BYTES	NEW_BYTES	CHANGE
WF_ITEM_ATTRIBUTE_VALUES_PK	30,900,224	33,562,624	2,662,400
MTL_CST_ACTUAL_COST_DETAILS_N1	4,276,224	6,406,144	2,129,920
MTL_TRANSACTION_ACCOUNTS_N6	14,393,344	15,990,784	1,597,440
MTL_TRANSACTION_ACCOUNTS_N2	12,263,424	13,328,384	1,064,960

WIP_OPERATION_RESOURCES_N1	2,146,304	3,211,264	1,064,960
WIP_REQUIREMENT_OPERATIONS_U1	7,471,104	8,536,064	1,064,960
MTL_TRANSACTION_ACCOUNTS_N3	9,068,544	10,133,504	1,064,960
WF_ITEM_ACTIVITY_STATUSES_N1	4,276,224	5,341,184	1,064,960
MTL_TRANSACTION_ACCOUNTS_N5	11,730,944	12,795,904	1,064,960
GL_BALANCES_N2	1,736,704	2,596,864	860,160
GL_BALANCES_N3	1,818,624	2,473,984	655,360
GL_BALANCES_N1	2,146,304	2,678,704	532,480
GL_JE_LINES_N1	3,743,744	4,276,224	532,480
MTL_MATERIAL_TRANSACTIONS_N1	6,938,624	7,471,104	532,480
MTL_MATERIAL_TRANSACTIONS_N15	8,003,584	8,536,064	532,480
MTL_MATERIAL_TRANSACTIONS_N3	8,003,584	8,536,064	532,480
MTL_MATERIAL_TRANSACTIONS_N7	4,808,704	5,341,184	532,480
MTL_MATERIAL_TRANSACTIONS_N5	5,873,664	6,406,144	532,480
WIP_REQUIREMENT_OPERATIONS_N2	5,873,664	6,406,144	532,480
WIP_REQUIREMENT_OPERATIONS_N1	8,003,584	8,536,064	532,480
WIP_OPERATION_RESOURCES_U1	1,613,824	2,146,304	532,480
WIP_OPERATION_RESOURCES_N2	1,613,824	2,146,304	532,480
WF_NOTIFICATIONS_ATTR_PK	6,938,624	7,471,104	532,480
MTL_TRANSACTION_ACCOUNTS_N1	6,938,624	7,471,104	532,480
MTL_MATERIAL_TRANSACTIONS_U2	7,471,104	8,003,584	532,480
MTL_MATERIAL_TRANSACTIONS_N9	8,003,584	8,536,064	532,480
WIP_REQUIREMENT_OPERATIONS_N3	6,938,624	7,471,104	532,480
MTL_MATERIAL_TRANSACTIONS_N8	6,938,624	7,471,104	532,480
MTL_MATERIAL_TRANSACTIONS_N2	6,406,144	6,938,624	532,480
MTL_MATERIAL_TRANSACTIONS_N12	3,211,264	3,743,744	532,480
MTL_CST_ACTUAL_COST_DETAILS_U1	7,471,104	8,003,584	532,480
MRP_WIP_COMPONENTS_N1	1,613,824	2,146,304	532,480
MRP_FORECAST_UPDATES_N1	548,864	1,081,344	532,480
GL_IMPORT_REFERENCES_N3	3,211,264	3,743,744	532,480
GL_IMPORT_REFERENCES_N1	1,818,624	2,146,304	327,680
AP_HOLDS_N1	16,384	303,104	286,720
AP_INVOICE_PAYMENTS_N4	589,824	876,544	286,720
GL_JE_LINES_U1	2,310,144	2,596,864	286,720
PO_REQUISITION_HEADERS_N1	16,384	303,104	286,720
PO_REQUISITION_HEADERS_U1	16,384	303,104	286,720
WIP_OPERATIONS_N2	1,163,264	1,449,984	286,720
RCV_TRANSACTIONS_N6	221,184	425,984	204,800
SO_EXCEPTIONS_N1	237,568	434,176	196,608
MRP_RELIEF_INTERFACE_N1	180,224	344,064	163,840
MTL_DEMAND_INTERFACE_N4	507,904	671,744	163,840
MTL_DEMAND_INTERFACE_N6	507,904	671,744	163,840
MTL_DEMAND_INTERFACE_N9	507,904	671,744	163,840
WIP_DISCRETE_JOBS_N7	344,064	507,904	163,840
WIP_DISCRETE_JOBS_N1	180,224	344,064	163,840
MTL_DEMAND_INTERFACE_N8	671,744	835,584	163,840
MTL_DEMAND_INTERFACE_N5	507,904	671,744	163,840
MTL_DEMAND_INTERFACE_N2	835,584	999,424	163,840
SO_EXCEPTIONS_U1	114,688	196,608	81,920
FND_CONCURRENT_REQUESTS_N4	3,735,552	3,768,320	32,768
FND_CONCURRENT_REQUESTS_N5	475,136	507,904	32,768
FND_CONC_RELEASE_CLASSES_U1	606,208	638,976	32,768
MTL_SUPPLY_DEMAND_TEMP_N1	999,424	1,015,808	16,384

Note that this report is sequenced so that the tables with the most growth appear at the top of the report.

The next report is a very useful summary report on database table and index activity. Just like the previous report, this report starts by displaying the most recent snapshot date and the preceding snapshot date. This is done so that the reader of the report knows the duration between reports. Note that this report summarizes all of the information for all tables and indexes within the database. We see as part of the display the database name, followed by counts of the numbers of tables and indexes within the database. Next, we see counts of the total number of bytes within tables and the total number of bytes within indexes for the database.

The second section of this report is the most interesting of all. Here we see the total number of bytes in the prior snapshot as compared to the total number of bytes in the most recent snapshot. The difference between these two values is computed and displayed in bytes.

This type of capacity planning report is covered more thoroughly in Chapter 14, but for now let's just note that we can easily get the total amount of growth of table and index bites between any two snapshot periods that we desire.

The object statistics report script is displayed next. Pay careful attention to the use of temporary tables within the script. We will learn in Chapter 11 that the use of these temporary tables can be used to greatly speed the performance of the query.

What makes this report challenging is that we are comparing summaries between two distinct ranges of rows within the stats$tab_stats table as shown in Figure 10-21.

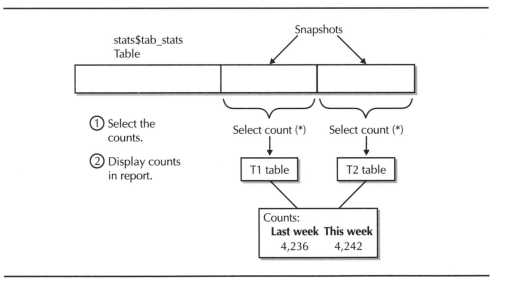

FIGURE 10-21. *Comparing summaries of two ranges with the stats$tab_stats table*

Whereas this query could be performed by joining the stats$tab_stats table against itself, the use of the temporary tables for computing summary information dramatically speeds the execution of the query.

For example, note the following *t1* temporary table. This temporary table is used to store the counts for all tables for the first snapshot period. Once four temporary tables are created with the counts for tables and indexes for the two periods, it is a very quick query to consolidate these counts into a single display.

In fact, without the temporary tables, this query will run for more than four minutes. With the use of the temporary tables, the response time for running this report is almost instantaneous.

rpt_object_stats.sql

```
connect perfstat/perfstat;

set lines 80;
set pages 999;
set feedback off;
set verify off;
set echo off;

--**********************************************************
-- This report compares the max(snap_time) to the second-highest date
--**********************************************************


--**********************************************************
-- First we need to get the second-highest date in tab_stats
--**********************************************************
drop table d1;

create table d1 as
select distinct
   to_char(snap_time,'YYYY-MM-DD') mydate
from
   stats$tab_stats
where
   to_char(snap_time,'YYYY-MM-DD') <
     (select max(to_char(snap_time,'YYYY-MM-DD')) from stats$tab_stats)
;

--**********************************************************
-- The second highest date is select max(mydate) from d1;
--**********************************************************

set heading off;

prompt '*********************************************'
select '  Most recent date '||
         max(to_char(snap_time,'YYYY-MM-DD'))
```

```
from stats$tab_stats;
select '  Older date '||
        max(mydate)
from d1;
prompt '*********************************************'

set heading on;

drop table t1;
drop table t2;
drop table t3;
drop table t4;


create table t1 as
select db_name, count(*) tab_count, snap_time from stats$tab_stats
where    to_char(snap_time, 'YYYY-MM-DD') =
           (select max(to_char(snap_time,'YYYY-MM-DD')) from
tats$tab_stats)
group by db_name, snap_time;

create table t2 as
select db_name, count(*) idx_count, snap_time from stats$idx_stats
where    to_char(snap_time, 'YYYY-MM-DD') =
           (select max(to_char(snap_time,'YYYY-MM-DD')) from
tats$idx_stats)
group by db_name, snap_time;

create table t3 as
select db_name, sum(bytes) tab_bytes, snap_time from stats$tab_stats
where    to_char(snap_time, 'YYYY-MM-DD') =
           (select max(to_char(snap_time,'YYYY-MM-DD')) from
tats$tab_stats)
group by db_name, snap_time;

create table t4 as
select db_name, sum(bytes) idx_bytes, snap_time from stats$idx_stats
where    to_char(snap_time, 'YYYY-MM-DD') =
           (select max(to_char(snap_time,'YYYY-MM-DD')) from
tats$idx_stats)
group by db_name, snap_time;

--*********************************************************
-- This report displays the most recent counts & size totals
--*********************************************************

column tab_bytes format 999,999,999,999
column idx_bytes format 999,999,999,999
column tab_count format 99,999
column idx_count format 99,999
```

```
clear computes;
compute sum label "Total" of tab_count on report;
compute sum label "Total" of idx_count on report;
compute sum label "Total" of tab_bytes on report;
compute sum label "Total" of idx_bytes on report;

break on report;

ttitle 'Most recent database object counts and sizes'

select
   a.db_name,
   tab_count,
   idx_count,
   tab_bytes,
   idx_bytes
from
   perfstat.t1 a,
   perfstat.t2 b,
   perfstat.t3 c,
   perfstat.t4 d
where
   a.db_name = b.db_name
and
   a.db_name = c.db_name
and
   a.db_name = d.db_name
;



-- ***********************************************************
-- These temp tables will compare size growth since last snap
-- ***********************************************************
drop table t1;
drop table t2;
drop table t3;
drop table t4;

create table t1 as
select db_name, sum(bytes) new_tab_bytes, snap_time from stats$tab_stats
where    to_char(snap_time, 'YYYY-MM-DD') =
            (select max(to_char(snap_time,'YYYY-MM-DD')) from
tats$tab_stats)
group by db_name, snap_time;

create table t2 as
select db_name, sum(bytes) new_idx_bytes, snap_time from stats$idx_stats
where    to_char(snap_time, 'YYYY-MM-DD') =
            (select max(to_char(snap_time,'YYYY-MM-DD')) from
tats$idx_stats)
```

```
group by db_name, snap_time;

create table t3 as
select db_name, sum(bytes) old_tab_bytes, snap_time from stats$tab_stats
where    to_char(snap_time, 'YYYY-MM-DD') =
            (select max(mydate) from d1)
group by db_name, snap_time;

create table t4 as .
select db_name, sum(bytes) old_idx_bytes, snap_time from stats$idx_stats
where    to_char(snap_time, 'YYYY-MM-DD') =
            (select max(mydate) from d1)
group by db_name, snap_time;


--**********************************************************
-- This is the size comparison report
--**********************************************************
column old_bytes format 999,999,999,999
column new_bytes format 999,999,999,999
column change    format 999,999,999,999

compute sum label "Total" of old_bytes on report;
compute sum label "Total" of new_bytes on report;
compute sum label "Total" of change    on report;

break on report;
ttitle 'Database size change|comparing the most recent snapshot dates';


select
   a.db_name,
   old_tab_bytes+old_idx_bytes old_bytes,
   new_tab_bytes+new_idx_bytes new_bytes,
   (new_tab_bytes+new_idx_bytes)-(old_tab_bytes+old_idx_bytes) change
from
   perfstat.t1 a,
   perfstat.t2 b,
   perfstat.t3 c,
   perfstat.t4 d
where
   a.db_name = b.db_name
and
   a.db_name = c.db_name
and
   a.db_name = d.db_name
;
```

```
--***********************************************************
-- This is the standard chained row report
--
-- This is for columns without long columns
-- because long columns often chain onto adjacent data blocks
--***********************************************************

column c1 heading "Owner"    format a9;
column c2 heading "Table"    format a12;
column c3 heading "PCTFREE"  format 99;
column c4 heading "PCTUSED"  format 99;
column c5 heading "avg row"  format 99,999;
column c6 heading "Rows"     format 999,999,999;
column c7 heading "Chains"   format 999,999,999;
column c8 heading "Pct"      format .99;

set heading off;
select 'Tables with > 10% chained rows and no LONG columns.' from dual;
set heading on;

select
    owner             c1,
    table_name        c2,
    pct_free          c3,
    pct_used          c4,
    avg_row_len       c5,
    num_rows          c6,
    chain_cnt         c7,
    chain_cnt/num_rows c8
from
    dba_tables
where
    owner not in ('SYS','SYSTEM','PERFSTAT')
and
    chain_cnt/num_rows > .1
and
table_name not in
 (select table_name from dba_tab_columns
    where
 data_type in ('RAW','LONG RAW')
)
and
chain_cnt > 0
order by chain_cnt desc
;

--***********************************************************
-- This chained row report is for tables that have long
-- columns. The only fix for this chaining is increasing
-- the db_block_size
--***********************************************************
```

```
set heading off;
select 'Tables with > 10% chained rows that contain LONG columns.' from
ual;
set heading on;

select7
    owner               c1,
    table_name          c2,
    pct_free            c3,
    pct_used            c4,
    avg_row_len         c5,
    num_rows            c6,
    chain_cnt           c7,
    chain_cnt/num_rows  c8
from
    dba_tables
where
    owner not in ('SYS','SYSTEM','PERFSTAT')
and
    chain_cnt/num_rows > .1
and
table_name in
 (select table_name from dba_tab_columns
    where
 data_type in ('RAW','LONG RAW')
)
and
chain_cnt > 0
order by chain_cnt desc
;
```

Next is the output from the object statistics report. Note we first display the most recent snapshot date with the one immediately preceding it. This is so the reader clearly understands the elapsed time between the snapshots. We immediately get an overall count of the number of tables and indexes that were in the database between the two snapshot periods. We also see the total number of bytes for tables and the total number of bytes for indexes as of the most recent snapshot date.

The next section of the report shows the change in the overall database size. This is the section of the report that the DBA will e-mail to his or her vice presidents and CIO, and other people who are interested in tracking the overall growth of the database.

Some readers may note that this report shows only the sum of dba_tables.bytes, and does not show the whole size of the database. This has always been a confounding issue for DBAs, where the actual bytes consumed by the tables is less than half the total size of their database. This is due to the fact that the object overhead (*pctfree* reserved spaces, indexes, unused spaces in extents and tablespaces) are not reflected in the table sizes. At the highest level, the size of the database will be the sum of all of the data blocks for all of the Oracle data files.

```
'**************************************************!

   Most recent date 2001-01-22

   Older date        2001-01-15

'**************************************************!

Mon Jan 22                                                        page    1
                    Most recent database object counts and sizes

DB_NAME   TAB_COUNT IDX_COUNT    TAB_BYTES        IDX_BYTES
--------- --------- --------- -------------- ----------------
prod          2,861     6,063 1,659,969,536    1,349,140,480
          --------- --------- -------------- ----------------
Total         2,861     6,063 1,659,969,536    1,349,140,480

Mon Jan 22                                                        page    1
                            Database size change
                   comparing the most recent snapshot dates

DB_NAME      OLD_BYTES         NEW_BYTES           CHANGE
--------- -------------- --------------- ----------------
prod       2,873,147,392   3,009,110,016      135,962,624
          -------------- --------------- ----------------
Total      2,873,147,392   3,009,110,016      135,962,624
```

This report clearly shows that the bytes consumed for tables and indexes has grown by 136 megabytes during the past week.

The next section of this report is very interesting to the DBA, and most DBAs automatically e-mail themselves this report on Monday morning so that they can review the number of chained rows that currently exist within their database tables. This report shows the owner, the table name, and the settings for *pctfree* and *pctused*, followed by the average row length, the number of rows, the number of chain rows, and percent of total rows that are chained.

This report is indispensable to the DBA. As you recall from earlier in this chapter, the DBA must be able to track and remedy chained rows by doing periodic reorganizations and adjusting the setting for *pctfree*.

Also note that this chained row report is divided into two sections. The first section reports on tables with chained rows that have no long columns inside them. The second section of the report lists all tables with chained rows for datatypes that do contain RAW, or LONG RAW datatypes. This distinction between short rows and long rows is made because the DBA is unable to correct row chaining in cases where the long columns make the table rows longer than the block size for the individual database. Hence, the DBA is most interested in the first part of this report because he or she can reorganize these tables to remove the chains.

Tables with > 10% chained rows and no LONG columns.

Mon Jan 22   page   1

Owner	Table	PCTFREE	PCTUSED	avg row	Rows	Chains	Pct
OE	SO_OBJECTS	10	70	1,858	87	64	.74
INV	MTL_ABC_COMP	10	70	73	367	44	.12
APPL	FND_PERFORMA	10	40	27,152	20	20	1.00

Mon Jan 22   page   1

Tables with > 10% chained rows that contain LONG columns.

Owner	Table	PCTFREE	PCTUSED	avg row	Rows	Chains	Pct
EULC	DIS_DOCS	10	40	9,873	9	9	100

The next section of this report is used to track only the tables that have extended since the last snapshot period (usually the past week). As we stressed earlier in this chapter, one of the important jobs of the DBA in terms of tuning tables is to have appropriate settings for the NEXT extend size for individual tables and indexes. Given that the DBA has set appropriate sizes to manage the growth of objects within the database, this report is especially useful because it shows only those tables and indexes that have taken extents during the past week. The old adage goes "the squeaky wheel gets the grease," and this report helps the DBA identify the most active tables within the database in terms of **insert** activity. You should also note that this report displays the ORACLE_SID. This is because these STATSPACK extension tables can be populated from many remote databases using Net8 database links to a central STATSPACK repository.

Mon Jan 22   page   1
                          Table extents report
                 Where extents > 200 or table extent changed
                      comparing most recent snapshots

DB	OWNER	TAB_NAME	OLD_EXT	NEW_EXT
prod	GL	GL_CONS_FLEXFIELD_MAP	1	2
	AR	RA_REMIT_TOS_ALL	1	2
	AP	AP_EXPENSE_REPORT_HEADERS_ALL	2	3
	MRP	MRP_RELIEF_INTERFACE	2	3
	OE	SO_FREIGHT_CHARGES	2	3
	GL	GL_INTERFACE	4	6
	INV	MTL_DEMAND	5	6
	APPLSYS	WF_NOTIFICATION_ATTRIBUTES	9	10
	GL	GL_BALANCES	10	13
	OE	SO_PICKING_BATCHES_ALL	13	14
	GL	GL_IMPORT_REFERENCES	14	16
	OE	SO_PICKING_LINE_DETAILS	14	18
	WIP	WIP_TRANSACTION_ACCOUNTS	36	37

GL	GL_JE_LINES	36	41
WIP	WIP_REQUIREMENT_OPERATIONS	45	50
INV	MTL_MATERIAL_TRANSACTIONS	68	73
INV	MTL_TRANSACTION_ACCOUNTS	77	83
PO	PO_LINES_ALL	366	372

Mon Jan 22   page   1

Index extents report
Where extents > 200 or index extent changed
Comparing last two snapshots

DB	OWNER	IDX_NAME	OLD_EXT	NEW_EXT
prod	AP	AP_HOLDS_N1	1	2
	PO	PO_REQUISITION_HEADERS_N1	1	2
	PO	PO_REQUISITION_HEADERS_U1	1	2
	MRP	MRP_FORECAST_UPDATES_N1	2	3
	PO	RCV_TRANSACTIONS_N6	2	3
	AP	AP_INVOICE_PAYMENTS_N4	3	4
	WIP	WIP_DISCRETE_JOBS_N7	3	4
	WIP	WIP_OPERATION_RESOURCES_N1	3	4
	MRP	MRP_WIP_COMPONENTS_N1	4	5
	INV	MTL_DEMAND_INTERFACE_N4	4	5
	INV	MTL_DEMAND_INTERFACE_N9	4	5
	OE	SO_PICKING_HEADERS_N3	4	5
	WIP	WIP_OPERATION_RESOURCES_U1	4	5
	GL	GL_BALANCES_N1	5	6
	INV	MTL_DEMAND_INTERFACE_N8	5	6
	APPLSYS	WF_ITEM_ACTIVITY_STATUSES_N1	5	6
	WIP	WIP_OPERATIONS_N2	5	6
	OE	SO_PICKING_HEADERS_N6	6	7
	GL	GL_BALANCES_N2	7	10
	INV	MTL_MATERIAL_TRANSACTIONS_N5	12	13
	WIP	WIP_REQUIREMENT_OPERATIONS_N2	12	13
	GL	GL_IMPORT_REFERENCES_N1	12	14
	INV	MTL_MATERIAL_TRANSACTIONS_N2	13	14
	INV	MTL_MATERIAL_TRANSACTIONS_N1	11	15
	APPLSYS	WF_NOTIFICATIONS_ATTR_PK	14	15
	WIP	WIP_REQUIREMENT_OPERATIONS_N3	14	15
	APPLSYS	FND_CONCURRENT_REQUESTS_N5	15	16
	GL	GL_BALANCES_N3	12	16
	INV	MTL_CST_ACTUAL_COST_DETAILS_U1	15	16
	INV	MTL_MATERIAL_TRANSACTIONS_N9	16	17
	WIP	WIP_REQUIREMENT_OPERATIONS_N1	16	17
	INV	MTL_TRANSACTION_ACCOUNTS_N3	18	20
	OE	SO_EXCEPTIONS_U1	13	23
	INV	MTL_TRANSACTION_ACCOUNTS_N2	24	26
	OE	SO_EXCEPTIONS_N1	28	52
	INV	MTL_SUPPLY_DEMAND_TEMP_N1	59	60
	APPLSYS	WF_ITEM_ATTRIBUTE_VALUES_PK	59	64
	EUL_MWC	EUL_EXP_EXP1_UK	207	207
	APPLSYS	FND_CONCURRENT_REQUESTS_N2	214	214

In addition to change reports, you can also submit reports that show the current state of your tables. Here is a detail report of table metrics from the stats$tab_stats table, and reports on the data from your most recent snapshot.

rpt_tab.sql

```
column c1  heading "TABLE NAME"       format a15;
column c2  heading "EXTS"             format 999;
column c3  heading "FL"               format 99;
column c4  heading "# OF ROWS"        format 99,999,999;
column c5  heading "#_rows*row_len"   format 9,999,999,999;
column c6  heading "SPACE ALLOCATED"  format 9,999,999,999;
column c7  heading "PCT USED"         format 999;
column db_block_size new_value blksz noprint

select value db_block_size from v$parameter where name = 'db_block_size';

set pages 999;
set lines 80;

spool tab_rpt.lst

select
        table_name         c1,
        b.extents          c2,
        b.freelists        c3,
        num_rows           c4,
        num_rows*avg_row_len  c5,
        blocks*&blksz        c6,
        ((num_rows*avg_row_len)/(blocks*&blksz))*100 c7
from
   perfstat.stats$tab_stats a,
   dba_segments b
where
 b.segment_name = a.table_name
and
   to_char(snap_time,'yyyy-mm-dd') =
      (select max(to_char(snap_time,'yyyy-mm-dd')) from
perfstat.stats$tab_stats)
and
   avg_row_len > 500
order by c5 desc
;

spool off;
```

This is a very interesting report for the Oracle DBA. In this report, from our STATSPACK extension tables, we see the table name, the number of extents, the number of freelists, and the number of rows in the table, followed by additional information on the size of the table. This information includes a metric on the number of rows times the row length, which should be roughly equal to the amount of space the table is consuming.

Next, we see the space allocated to the table, and the percent of the table that is used, which tells us roughly how much of the row space is consumed within the existing extents.

As we discussed earlier in this chapter, this type of report is very useful for identifying sparse tables when a table has multiple freelists. As you may recall, a sparse table is the table that is defined with multiple freelists, and because of a failure to parallelize the purge processes, the multiple freelists are unevenly balanced with free blocks. This causes the table to extend even though the data dictionary shows that the table has a tremendous amount of free space.

```
SQL> @rpt_tab
```

TABLE NAME	EXTS	FL	# OF ROWS	#_rows*row_len	SPACE ALLOCATED	PCT USED
PAGE_IMAGE	138	1	18,067	19,114,886	18,087,936	106
EC_CUSTOMER	3	1	367	219,099	393,216	56
MONOR_BOOKS	1	1	20	13,200	131,072	10
BOOK	1	1	19	12,711	131,072	10
EC_EMAIL_TEMP	1	1	6	3,780	131,072	3
EC_TEMPLATES	1	1	1	837	131,072	1

This report will show sparse tables as those tables that exhibit an increase in extents while at the same time appear to be largely empty

Distributing the Table Reports via E-Mail

Now that we see the value of these reports, we can look at how we can easily automate the e-mail distribution of the statistics reports. As we noted, the summary of size and growth statistics are of interest to top MIS management, and we can automate the distribution by sending them e-mail each week showing the total change in database sizes. Here is the report generation script:

run_object_report.ksh

```ksh
#!/bin/ksh

# Validate the Oracle database name with
# lookup in /var/opt/oracle/oratab
TEMP=`cat /var/opt/oracle/oratab|grep \^$1:|\
cut -f1 -d':'|wc -l`
tmp=`expr TEMP`      # Convert string to number
if [ $tmp -ne 1 ]
then
    echo "Your input $1 is not a valid ORACLE_SID."
    exit 99
fi
```

```
# Here we must set the environment . . . .
ORACLE_SID=$1
export ORACLE_SID
ORACLE_HOME=`cat /var/opt/oracle/oratab|grep $ORACLE_SID:|cut -f2 -d':'`
export ORACLE_HOME
PATH=$ORACLE_HOME/bin:$PATH
export PATH
MON=`echo /export/home/oracle/obj_stat`
export MON


sqlplus perfstat/perfstat<<!
spool ${MON}/stats_rpt.lst
@${MON}/rpt_object_stats
spool off;
exit;
!

#************************************
# Mail the Object Statistics Reports
#************************************
cat $MON/stats_rpt.lst|mailx -s "Weekly Statistics Summary" \
   donald@remote-dba.net \
   jim@us.oracle.com \
   larry@oracle.com
```

Note that you will need to make several changes to customize this report for your environment:

1. The preceding listing uses the Solaris location of the oratab file in /var/opt/oracle. If you are using AIX or HP/UX, you will want to change this to the /etc directory.

2. Make sure you change the e-mail addresses to match the distribution list at your organization.

3. Set the $MON UNIX variable to the location of your object statistics scripts.

Here is an example of the UNIX crontab file that you would use to execute this report generation script:

```
#************************************************************
# These are the statspack extension reports for tables & indexes
#************************************************************
30 07 1 * * /home/obj_stat/get_object_stats.ksh PRODEDI > /dev/null
```

Note from the crontab listing that you must pass your ORACLE_SID as an argument to this script. The crontab entry says to run the report at 7:30 A.M. each Monday, and passes the ORACLE_SID name of PRODEDI to the script.

Conclusion

So far in this book on Oracle tuning with STATSPACK, we have covered the tuning of the external environment, the tuning of the Oracle instance, and now we have covered the tuning of individual Oracle objects within the database. We are now ready to embark on the most challenging part of Oracle tuning: the tuning of the Oracle SQL within the database.

Remember, the chapters in this book are presented in the order that the DBA normally uses when tuning the Oracle database. It is only after the tuning of the individual tables and indexes that the Oracle DBA is ready to tackle the tuning of individual SQL statements within the system. It is also important to remember that the tuning of SQL statements must come after the tuning of the instance and the objects, for several very good reasons. It is only when the instance is well tuned, and Oracle objects can be counted on to behave in a consistent manner, that the Oracle tuning will result in dramatic performance improvements.

The next chapter is going to be one of the longest and most extensive chapters within this text. The tuning of Oracle SQL is an often-overlooked area of Oracle tuning for several major reasons. The primary reason is the sheer complexity of the Oracle SQL. It's not uncommon for a highly active Oracle database to have hundreds, if not thousands, of SQL statements moving through the library cache any given amount of time. In many cases, the Oracle DBA does not know where to start in terms of tuning the Oracle SQL. The second major area is the difficulty in locating the source code for SQL statements. Because Oracle allows client/server environments to communicate remotely, the only evidence that the Oracle DBA will have of SQL statements is what happens to be sitting in the library cache any given moment in time.

The next chapter is very exciting because in addition to being the most tedious and time-consuming, it is also one of the areas of Oracle tuning that will have the most positive impact on database performance. It is not uncommon to take an Oracle SQL statement that runs many hours, and with proper tuning take it down to a query that runs in less than a minute. With that in mind, let's move on and take a look at the tuning of Oracle SQL using the STATSPACK utility.

CHAPTER
11

Tuning Oracle SQL

nce the environment, instance, and objects have been tuned, the Oracle administrator can then focus on what is probably one of the most important single aspects of Oracle tuning: tuning the individual SQL statements that access the database.

This chapter will be presented in two sections. The first section will describe the goals and techniques of SQL tuning and the second section will describe how to use STATSPACK to locate and tune SQL statements. This chapter is intended to be a high-level overview of the major tuning objectives of SQL tuning and the uses of STATSPACK in SQL tuning. For more details about tuning Oracle SQL, see the Oracle Press book *Oracle High-Performance SQL Tuning* (October, 2001), by Don Burleson.

We will review later in this chapter identical queries that can be written a variety of ways with dramatically different execution times while providing identical results. Hence, it is very important when dealing with end-user SQL queries that the end users have some knowledge of the underlying nature of Oracle SQL, and understand how SQL can be used in the most efficient manner.

It is very tempting in this chapter to go into all of the thousands of details that the experienced Oracle professional uses when tuning SQL. However, it is more important for the purpose of this book to show the basic nature of SQL tuning, and how STATSPACK can assist the Oracle DBA in tuning the database engine. Hence, we will focus on Oracle SQL tuning at a very high level, and take a look only at those techniques that will provide large and immediate returns in terms of overall database performance.

Remember, the tuning of SQL can make a huge and immediate impact on performance. Untuned SQL statements can cause millions of extra disk I/Os, and this will slow down even the most robust Oracle database.

Goals of SQL Tuning

Oracle SQL tuning is a phenomenally complex subject, and entire books have been devoted to the nuances of Oracle SQL tuning. However, there are some general guidelines that every Oracle DBA follows in order to improve the performance of their systems. The goals of SQL tuning are simple:

■ **Remove unnecessary large-table full table scans** Unnecessary full table scans cause a huge amount of unnecessary I/O, and can drag down an entire database. The tuning expert first evaluates the SQL based on the number of rows returned by the query. If the query returns less than 40 percent of the table rows in an ordered table, or 7 percent of the rows in an unordered table), the query can be tuned to use an index in lieu of the full table scan. The most common tuning for unnecessary full table scans is adding indexes. Standard B-tree indexes can be added to tables, and bitmapped and function-based indexes can also eliminate full table scans. The decision about removing a full table scan should be based on a careful examination of the I/O costs of the index scan vs. the costs of the full table scan, factoring in the multiblock reads and possible parallel execution. In some cases an unnecessary full table scan can be forced to use an index by adding an index hint to the SQL statement.

■ **Cache small-table full table scans**   In cases where a full table scan is the fastest access method, the tuning professional should ensure that a dedicated data buffer is available for the rows. In Oracle7 you can issue **alter table xxx cache**. In Oracle8 and beyond, the small table can be cached by forcing it into the KEEP pool.

■ **Verify optimal index usage**   This is especially important for improving the speed of queries. Oracle sometimes has a choice of indexes, and the tuning professional must examine each index and ensure that Oracle is using the proper index. This also includes the use of bitmapped and function-based indexes.

■ **Verify optimal JOIN techniques**   Some queries will perform faster with NESTED LOOP joins, others with HASH joins.

These goals may seem deceptively simple, but these tasks comprise 90 percent of SQL tuning, and they don't require a thorough understanding of the internals of Oracle SQL. Let's begin with an overview of the Oracle SQL optimizers.

The Problem of Declarative SQL Syntax

With SQL being a declarative language, there are many options to use when writing an SQL query, and each option may have dramatically different performance. This is a big issue and the Oracle DBA must be constantly on the lookout for malformed and convoluted SQL statements.

Let's illustrate this concept with a simple example. Let's assume that we have a student database for a university and we need to know the names of all students who received an A for any class last semester.

This query can be written in three ways, each providing identical results:

A Standard JOIN

```
SELECT
    *
FROM
    STUDENT,
    REGISTRATION
WHERE
    STUDENT.student_id = REGISTRATION.student_id
AND
    REGISTRATION.grade = 'A';
```

A Nested Query

```
SELECT
    *
FROM
    STUDENT
WHERE
    student_id =
    (SELECT student_id
        FROM REGISTRATION
        WHERE
        grade = 'A'
    );
```

A Correlated Subquery

```
SELECT
    *
FROM
    STUDENT
WHERE
    0 <
    (SELECT count(*)
        FROM REGISTRATION
        WHERE
        grade = 'A'
        AND
        student_id = STUDENT.student_id
    );
```

Each of these queries will return identical results, but with radically different execution plans and different performance. Most experienced DBAs know that the standard JOIN will outperform the other queries, but developers and end users often write convoluted queries to answer a simple question. We will see the shortcomings

of convoluted SQL later in this chapter, but now let's take a quick tour of the
Oracle SQL optimizers.

The Oracle SQL Optimizers

One of the first things the Oracle DBA looks at is the default optimizer mode for their
database. There are two classes of optimizer modes: the rule-based optimizer (RBO)
and the cost-based optimizer (CBO). The Oracle *init.ora* parameters offer four values
for the *optimizer_mode* parameter.

optimizer_mode = RULE

The first, and oldest optimizer mode is RULE. Under the rule-based optimizer, Oracle
uses heuristics from the data dictionary in order to determine the most effective way
to service an Oracle query and translate the declarative SQL command into an actual
navigation plan to extract the data. In many pre-Oracle8i systems, rule-based optimization is faster than cost-based. In fact, Oracle Applications used rule-based
optimization until release 11i.

optimizer_mode = FIRST_ROWS

This is a cost-based optimizer mode that will return rows as soon as possible, even
if the overall query runs longer or consumes more resources. The FIRST_ROWS
optimizer mode usually involves choosing a full index scan over a parallel full table
scan. Because the FIRST_ROWS mode favors index scans over full table scans, the
FIRST_ROWS mode is most appropriate for inline systems where an end user wants
to see some results as quickly as possible.

optimizer_mode = ALL_ROWS

This is a cost-based optimizer mode that ensures that the overall query time is
minimized, even if it takes longer to receive the first row. This usually involves
choosing a parallel full table scan over a full index scan. Because the ALL_ROWS
mode favors full table scans, the ALL_ROWS mode is best suited for batch-oriented
queries where intermediate rows are not required for viewing.

To illustrate the difference between ALL_ROWS and FIRST_ROWS with an
oversimplistic example, consider the following query:

```
select
    last_name
from
    customer
order by
    last_name;
```

This query can be serviced in two ways:

- Perform a full table scan in parallel and sort the rows in the TEMP tablespace. For the sake of illustration, let's assume that this execution plan produces the fastest overall execution time and minimal use of resources, as shown in Figure 11-1.

- Retrieve the rows in *last_name* order by using a *last_name_index*. This technique results in more physical reads, but begins to return sorted rows almost immediately, as shown in Figure 11-2.

optimizer_mode = CHOOSE

Oracle's default optimizer mode is called CHOOSE. In the CHOOSE optimizer mode, Oracle will execute the rule-based optimizer if there are no statistics present for the table, or execute the cost-based optimizer if statistics are present. The danger with using the CHOOSE optimizer mode is in cases where one Oracle table in a complex query has statistics and the other tables do not have statistics. When only some tables contain statistics, Oracle will use the cost-based optimization and estimate statistics (by sampling 5,000 rows) for the other tables in the query at runtime. This can cause significant slowdown in the performance of the individual query. Be careful when using the CHOOSE option. When you give Oracle the ability to choose the optimizer mode, Oracle will favor the cost-based approach if *any* of the tables in the query have statistics. (Statistics are created with the **analyze table** command.) For example, if a three-table JOIN is specified in CHOOSE mode and statistics exist for one of the three tables, Oracle will decide to use the cost-based optimizer. When this happens, the Oracle CBO will inspect the num_rows

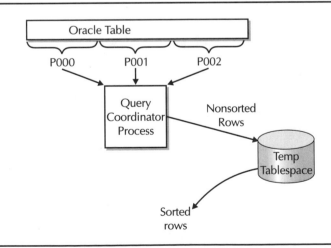

FIGURE 11-1. *Perform a full table scan and a sort (ALL_ROWS)*

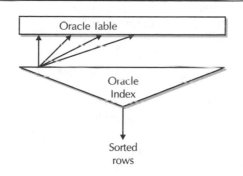

FIGURE 11-2. *Perform an index retrieval (FIRST_ROWS)*

column of the dba_tables view. If num_rows is null, Oracle still estimates statistics based on a 5,000-row sample. If the num_rows column is zero, Oracle will not perform a runtime table analysis. In short, if Oracle analyzes the table at runtime, this action will dramatically slow down the query.

Also, if a cost-based query is issued (i.e., with a hint) and there are no statistics of any tables or indexes, the CBO will choose a driving table—just like the RBO. However, the driving table for the CBO is the first table in the FROM clause, the exact opposite of the RBO.

Disadvantages of Optimizer Modes

Now, let's talk about each of these default modes and observe their relative advantages and disadvantages.

There are major shortcomings in both major optimization modes. The existence of hints indicates that the Oracle optimizers do not always make the most effective execution decision.

CAUTION
The use of any SQL hint except the RULE hint forces the cost-based optimizer to be invoked. Hence, make sure you have analyzed your tables and indexes prior to using any hints.

■ **Rule-based shortcomings**   Often chooses the wrong index to retrieve rows

■ **Cost-based shortcomings**   Often performs unnecessary full tables scans, especially when more than three tables are being joined

The tuning of rule-based SQL is quite different from tuning cost-based SQL. With the rule-based optimizer, the indexing of tables and order of clauses within the SQL statement control the access path in rule-based optimization. The cost-based optimizer automatically determines the most efficient execution path, and the programmer is given hints that can be added to the query to alter the access path.

Remember, the foremost tenet of Oracle SQL tuning is avoiding an unnecessary large-table full table scan. One of the hallmarks of an inefficient SQL statement is the failure of the SQL statement to use all of the indexes that are present within the Oracle database in order to speed up the query.

Of course, there are times when a full table scan is appropriate for a query, such as when you are doing aggregate operations such as a sum or an average, and the majority of the rows (greater than 40 percent for row-sequenced tables and greater than 7 percent for unsequenced tables) within the Oracle table must be read to get the query results. The task of the SQL tuning expert is to evaluate each full table scan and see if the performance can be improved by adding an index.

Most Oracle SQL queries will only be retrieving a small subset of the rows within the table and full table scans are only appropriate when more than 40 percent of the table rows are required. The Oracle optimizers are programmed to check for indexes, and to use indexes whenever possible to avoid excessive I/O. However, if the formulation of a query is inefficient, the cost-based optimizer becomes confused about the best access path to the data, and the cost-based optimizer will sometimes choose to do a full table scan against the table. Again, the general rule is for the Oracle database administrator to interrogate the SQL, and always look for full table scans.

Determining the Threshold for a Full Table Scan

When making the decision to change a full table scan to an index range scan, the primary concern is the speed of the query. In some cases, the full table scan may have more physical disk I/Os, but the full table scan will be faster because of a high degree of parallelism.

In other cases, you need to consider the number of rows retrieved as a function of the clustering of the rows in the table. For example, if your table is clustered or you have manually resequenced the rows in primary-key order, a great many adjacent rows can be read in a single I/O and an index range scan will be faster than a full table scan for up to 40 percent of the table rows. On the other hand, if your table is totally unordered, a request for 10 percent of the table rows may cause the majority of the table data blocks to be read. Of course, you also need to consider the degree of parallelism on the table and the setting for the *db_file_multi_block_read_count init.ora* parameter. Hence, the general guideline for replacing an index range scan is:

- **For row-sequenced tables**   Queries that retrieve less than 40 percent of the table rows should use an index range scan. Conversely, queries that read more than 40 percent of the rows should use a full table scan.

- **For unordered tables**   Queries that retrieve less than 7 percent of the table should use an index range scan. Conversely, queries that read more than 7 percent of the table rows will probably be faster with a full table scan.

Your mileage may vary, so it is always a good idea to test the execution speed in SQL*Plus by issuing the **set timing on** command.

Tuning with Rule-Based Optimization

The rule-based optimizer is the oldest and most stable of the optimizers. The rule-based optimizer is very simple and uses information in the data dictionary to make decisions about using an index. Also, unlike the cost-based optimizer, the order of tables in the FROM clause and the order of Booleans in the WHERE clause affect the execution plan for the query.

Changing the Rule-Based Driving Table

In Oracle's rule-based optimizer, the ordering of the table names in the FROM clause determines the driving table. The driving table is important because it is retrieved first, and the rows from the second table are then merged into the result set from the first table. Therefore, it is essential that the second table return the least amount of rows based on the WHERE clause.

NOTE
The driving table is not always the table with the least amount of rows. The Boolean conditions in the WHERE clause must be evaluated, and the driving table should be the table that returns the smallest number of rows.

With the rule-based optimizer, the table names are read from right to left. Hence, the last table in the FROM clause should be the table that returns the smallest number of rows. For setting the driving table for the rule-based optimizer, consider the following query where the order table has 100,000 rows and the customer table has 50,000 rows.

```
SELECT
    customer_name,
    customer_phone
FROM
    Customer,
    Order
```

```
WHERE
    customer_region = 'WEST'
and
    order_status = 'BACKORDER';
```

In this query, we see that the last table in the FROM clause is the order table, and order will be the driving table. This might make sense since we know that this table has half the rows of the customer table. However, we must first evaluate the WHERE clause to see what table returns the smallest number of rows.

Let's assume that there are 10,000 customers in the WEST region and 30,000 backordered status columns. Given this information, we know that the customer table should be last in the FROM clause because it returns fewer rows.

When the Rule-Based Optimizer Fails to Use the Correct Index

The rule-based optimizer's greatest shortcoming is its failure to use the best index. There are cases where the rule-based optimizer fails to choose the best index to service a query because it is not aware of the number of distinct values in an index. This is especially a problem when values within an index are highly skewed.

For example, let's assume in this example that there are 100,000 retired employees, 20,000 employees in the personnel department, and 500 who are both retired and belong to the personnel department. Let's also assume that we have a nonunique index on both the status and the department columns of our employee table.

We would expect that the most efficient way to service this query would be to scan the most selective index—in this case the department index, scanning the 20,000 retired employees to get the 500 in the personnel department. It would be far less efficient to scan the status index, reading through 100,000 retired employees to find those who work in the personnel department.

```
SELECT
    COUNT(*)
FROM
    employee
WHERE
    department = 'PERSONNEL'
AND
    status = 'RETIRED';
```

With the rule-based optimizer, we see the following execution plan:

```
SELECT STATEMENT
    SORT AGGREGATE
        SELECT BY ROWID EMPLOYEE
            NON-UNIQUE INDEX NON-SELECTIVE RANGE SCAN status_ix(status)
```

Even reversing the order of the items in the WHERE clause does not change the fact that the rule-based optimizer is choosing to scan through all 100,000 retired employees looking for the 500 that belong to the personnel department. With a cost-based optimizer, we see that the selectivity of the indexes is known and that the most efficient index is used to service the request:

```
SELECT STATEMENT
     SORT AGGREGATE
         SELECT BY ROWID EMPLOYEE
             NON-UNIQUE INDEX NON-SELECTIVE RANGE SCAN dept_ix(department)
```

In sum, we need to pay careful attention to the indexes that are chosen by the rule-based optimizer, and either disable the indexes that we do not want used in the query or force the use of the index that we want. To review, indexes can be explicitly specified with the INDEX hint, or unwanted indexes can be disabled by mixing datatypes on the index (i.e., WHERE *numeric_column_value* = 123ll' '), or by specifying a FULL hint in the query.

Tuning with Cost-Based Optimization (CBO)

The cost-based optimizer uses "statistics" that are collected from the table using the **analyze table** and **analyze index** commands. Oracle uses these metrics about the tables in order to intelligently determine the most efficient way of servicing the SQL query. It is important to recognize that in many cases the cost-based optimizer may not always make the proper decision in terms of the speed of the query, and Oracle has provided numerous hints to allow the DBA and developer to tune the execution plan. The cost-based optimizer is constantly being improved, but there are still many cases where the rule-based optimizer will result in faster Oracle queries. One of the first things a seasoned Oracle DBA does when tuning an SQL statement is to add a RULE hint, or use the **alter session set optimizer goal = rule** statement in order to change the default optimizer mode from cost-based to rule-based optimization.

Here is a list of common hints that are used to change the execution plan in the cost-based optimizer:

- **ALL_ROWS**   This is the cost-based approach designed to provide the best overall throughput and minimum resource consumption.

- **AND_EQUAL(*table_name index_name1*)**   Causes merge scans of two to five single-column indexes.

- **CLUSTER(*table_name*)**   Requests a cluster scan of the *table_name*.

- **FIRST_ROWS**   This is the cost-based approach designed to provide the best response time.

- **FULL**   Requests the bypassing of indexes, doing a full table scan.

- **HASH(*table_name*)**   Causes a hash scan of *table_name*.

- **HASH_AJ**   This hint is placed in a NOT IN subquery to perform a hash anti-JOIN.

- **INDEX(*table_name index_name*)**   Requests the use of the specified index against the table. If no index is specified, Oracle will choose the best index.

- **INDEX_ASC(*table_name index_name*)**   Requests to use the ascending index on a range scan operation.

- **INDEX_COMBINE(*table_name index_name*)**   Requests that the specified bitmapped index be used.

- **INDEX_DESC(*table_name index_name*)**   Requests to use the descending index on a range scan operation.

- **MERGE_AJ**   This hint is placed in a NOT IN subquery to perform an anti-JOIN.

- **NO_EXPAND**   Requests the query not to perform OR expansion (i.e., OR concatenation).

- **NO_MERGE**   This hint is used in a view to prevent it from being merged into a parent query.

- **NOCACHE**   This hint causes the table CACHE option to be bypassed.

- **NOPARALLEL**   This hint turns off the Parallel Query option.

- **ORDERED**   Requests that the tables should be joined in the order that they are specified (left to right). For example, if you know that a state table has only 50 rows, you may want to use this hint to make state the driving table.

- **PARALLEL(*table_name degree*)**   For full table scans, this hint requests that the *table_name* query be executed in parallel mode with *degree* processes servicing the table access.

- **PUSH_SUBQ**   This hint causes all subqueries in the query block to be executed at the earliest possible time.

- **ROWID**   Requests a rowid scan of the specified table.

- **RULE**   Indicates that the rule-based optimizer should be invoked (sometimes due to the absence of table statistics).

- **STAR**   This hint forces the use of a star query plan, provided that there are at least three tables in the query and a concatenated index exists on the fact table.

- **USE_CONCAT**   Requests that a UNION ALL be used for all OR conditions.

- **USE_HASH(*table_name1 table_name2*)**   Requests a hash JOIN against the specified tables.

- **USE_MERGE**   Requests a sort merge operation.

- **USE_NL(*table_name*)**   Requests a nested loop operation with the specified table as the driving table.

It is beyond the scope of this chapter to go into all of these hints, so for now just consider hints to be the tools you use to tune cost-based execution plans.

Invoking the Cost-Based Optimizer

Before retrieving any rows, the cost-based optimizer must create an *execution plan* that tells Oracle the order in which to access the desired table and indexes. The cost-based optimizer works by weighing the relative costs for different access paths to the data, and choosing the path with the smallest relative cost. Once the statistics have been collected, there are three ways to invoke the cost-based optimizer:

- **Setting the *init.ora* parameter *optimizer_mode***   all_rows, first_rows or choose

- **ALTER SESSION SET *optimizer_goal***   all_rows or first_rows

- **Cost-based hints**   /*+ all_rows */ or --+ all_rows

These costs for a query are determined with the aid of table and index statistics that are computed with the **analyze table** and **analyze index** commands in Oracle.

```
ANALYZE TABLE xxx ESTIMATE STATISTICS SAMPLE 500 rows;
ANALYZE INDEX xxx COMPUTE STATISTICS;
```

Note that there are documented problems when sampling less than a 25–30-percent sample of the rows in a table. This is due to the way Oracle calculates row counts. Contrary to early documentation, row counts are done using an average row size vs.

total occupied blocks and not a full count. In tables of several million rows, the row counts can be off by as much as 15 percent if a sample of less than 25 percent was used for the analysis.

Gathering Statistics for the CBO

It is important that the statistics be refreshed periodically, especially when the distribution of data changes frequently. As such, the following SQL may be used to run the **analyze** statements for all of the tables and indexes. It is not always a good idea to use Oracle's dbms_utility.analyze_schema or the dbms_ddl.analyze_object packages to perform this task, since a failure on one of the statements can affect the results of subsequent statements. The following script will generate the proper SQL syntax.

analyze.ksh

```
#!/bin/ksh

# First, we must set the environment . . . .
ORACLE_SID=prodb2
export ORACLE_SID
ORACLE_HOME=`cat /var/opt/oracle/oratab|grep ^$ORACLE_SID:|cut -f2 -d':'`
export ORACLE_HOME
PATH=$ORACLE_HOME/bin:$PATH
export PATH

$ORACLE_HOME/bin/sqlplus /<<!

set pages 999
set heading off
set echo off
set feedback off

connect internal;

spool /export/home/oracle/analyze.sql;

select
'analyze table ' ||owner||'.'||table_name||' estimate statistics sample 50
rows;'
from dba_tables
where owner not in ('SYS','SYSTEM','PERFSTAT')'DONALD';

select
'analyze index '||owner||'.'||index_name||' compute statistics;'
from dba_indexes
where owner not in ('SYS','SYSTEM','PERFSTAT');

spool off;
```

```
set echo on
set feedback on

@/export/home/oracle/analyze

exit
!
```

Most shops schedule a script like this to run weekly, or whenever there have been significant changes to the table data. However, it is not necessary to reanalyze tables and indexes that remain relatively constant. For example, a database where the tables have a constant number of rows and indexes where the distribution of values remain constant will not benefit from frequent analysis.

Determining the Default *optimizer_mode*

As we have noted, there are some shortcomings in the cost-based and rule-based optimization, and the DBA must make a decision about the appropriate *optimizer_mode* default for the database. Every database is different, both in the types of queries and the structures of the data. However, there are some general rules that can be applied:

- Pre-Oracle8*i* queries that join three or more large tables will generally benefit from the rule-based optimizer or the first_rows hint.

- Queries that access bitmapped or function-based indexes will benefit from the cost-based optimizer.

- Queries that use star query hints need the cost-based optimizer.

- Databases at Oracle8i and beyond will benefit from the cost-based optimizer.

The choice also depends on the version of Oracle. Oracle recommends that all Oracle7 databases use rule-based optimization, and by Oracle8i, the cost-based optimizer has improved to the point where it can be considered for a default.

Given that any Oracle environment would benefit from both optimizers, there are several choices. The DBA could make the cost-based optimizer the default and use rule hints when required, or they could make rule-based the default and use cost hints and statistics when desired.

Many DBAs conduct a study where they bounce the *init.ora optimizer_mode* and then run the application for a day in each mode and collect statistics. From these overall comparisons, shown in Figure 11-3, the proper default *optimizer_mode* becomes readily apparent.

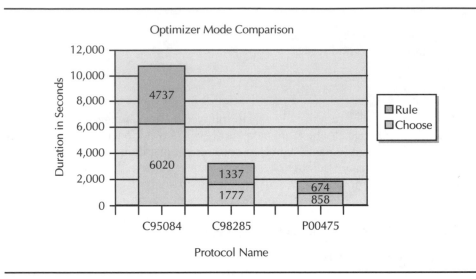

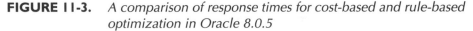

FIGURE 11-3. *A comparison of response times for cost-based and rule-based optimization in Oracle 8.0.5*

In the preceding example, the overall database performance was faster using first_rows, and that was set as the default. After setting the default, individual SQL statements were tuned using the rule hint.

Now let's review some miscellaneous SQL tuning techniques.

Miscellaneous Tuning Techniques

Before we go into detail on the process of tuning, let's look at several important ways to tune individual SQL statements. These topics include:

- Tuning with hints
- Tuning subqueries
- The problem of literal SQL statements
- Tuning with temporary tables
- General rules for writing efficient SQL

Tuning with CBO SQL Hints

There are several hints that can be directly embedded into Oracle SQL. These hints serve the purpose of changing the optimizer path to the data. Remember, hints override all settings for *optimizer_mode* and *optimizer_goal*. While there is not room in this book to go into all of the hints, here are the ones most commonly used when tuning SQL:

- **/*+ rule */**   This hint is normally used when a table experiences a full table scan, even though an index appears on the table. Often, the RBO will use indexes that the CBO will ignore.

- **/*+ full, table=xxx parallel=nn */**   This hint forces a full table scan with Parallel Query. This is commonly used when the query is performing a large aggregation such as SUM or AVG across the whole table.

- **/*+ table=xxx index=xxx */**   This hint forces the use of a specific index. This is commonly used when the RBO chooses a nonselective index to service a query.

- **/*+ first_rows */**   This hint is commonly used with a CBO default to see if the execution plan will improve with cost-based optimization.

- **/*+ use_hash */**   This hint is commonly used with a CBO default to see if the execution plan will improve with a hash join technique.

CAUTION
The cost-based optimizer will not alert you if you have a syntax error in your hint. This is because hints are coded inside comments and comments will be ignored if they contain invalid hint syntax. It is not uncommon to see a DBA add a hint and then not understand why the execution plan has not changed. Hence, be very careful to ensure that you have specified the hint correctly.

Tuning SQL Subqueries

Whenever possible, the use of a subquery within Oracle should be avoided. In most cases, the subquery can be replaced with a standard JOIN operation and thereby avoid the overhead that is associated with subqueries. However, there are circumstances where the use of an Oracle subquery is unavoidable, and this section describes the rules for determining the best way to specify a subquery.

As you may know, Oracle SQL only allows one table to be specified in the FROM clause of a SQL **update** or **delete** statement. As a consequence, the only way to specify values from another table is to place the reference to the other table into a subquery. There is a question about the most efficient way to specify the subquery to update or delete from a table when the operation depends on the values of rows inside other tables. For example, the only way to update table1 based upon corresponding rows in table2 would be to write a subquery to specify the table2 condition.

```
UPDATE
    table1
  set attribute = 'y'
WHERE
  key IN
  (SELECT key from table2);
```

One of the shortcomings of the SQL language is that there are numerous ways to write most SQL statements, and each will return identical results but may have radically different access paths and execution times. Also, while the Oracle SQL optimizer will often detect complex queries and decompose them into equivalent JOIN operations—taking the subquery and converting it into a nested loop JOIN—we cannot always count on the optimal access path to service the query.

In cases where we must use subqueries, there are several options that we need to consider. We have the choice of using a correlated or a noncorrelated subquery, and we also have the choice of using either the IN clause or the EXISTS clause as the comparison condition for the subquery. Hence, there are four possible forms for the subquery:

```
UPDATE TABLE1 . . SET . WHERE key IN (non-correlated sub-query);
UPDATE TABLE1 . . SET . WHERE key IN (correlated sub-query);
UPDATE TABLE1 . . SET . WHERE EXISTS (non-correlated sub-query);
UPDATE TABLE1 . . SET . WHERE EXISTS (correlated sub-query);
```

The Problem of Literal SQL Statements

Many applications are written such that they send SQL statements into the library cache using literal values in the SQL. This is a huge performance issue for Oracle. As you remember from Chapter 9, the purpose of the library cache is to store SQL commands so that they can be reused without reparsing and redeveloping an execution plan every time they are requested.

Next is an actual example from a third-party application that uses Oracle for the database. As you can see, the SQL is identical except for the literal values that exist for *page_unique_id*. This is an excellent example of the nonreusable SQL problem.

```
SELECT a.publisher_name FROM   book a, page b WHERE  b.page_unique_id =
TO_NUMBER('9177') AND b.book_unique_id = a.book_unique_id

SELECT a.publisher_name FROM   book a, page b WHERE  b.page_unique_id =
TO_NUMBER('9182') AND b.book_unique_id = a.book_unique_id
```

```
SELECT a.publisher_name FROM    book a, page b WHERE  b.page_unique_id =
TO_NUMBER('9184') AND b.book_unique_id = a.book_unique id

SELECT a.publisher_name FROM    book a, page b WHERE  b.page_unique_id =
TO_NUMBER('9185') AND b.book_unique_id = a.book_unique_id

SELECT a.publisher_name FROM    book a, page b WHERE  b.page_unique_id =
TO_NUMBER('9194') AND b.book_unique_id = a.book_unique_id

SELECT a.publisher_name FROM    book a, page b WHERE  b.page_unique_id =
TO_NUMBER('9207') AND b.book_unique_id = a.book_unique_id
```

As you can see, each of these statements is identical except for the literal values for *page_unique_id*. When these statements flood the library cache, they consume unnecessary space because they can never be reused. For some systems, the burden on the library cache greatly degrades the performance of the entire system and the DBA must issue periodic **alter system flush shared pool** commands to clean out the non-reusable SQL statements. If we could parameterize this SQL, we would only need a single SQL statement in the library cache:

```
SELECT a.publisher_name FROM    book a,
 page b WHERE  b.page_unique_id = TO_NUMBER(:var1)
 AND b.book_unique_id = a.book_unique_id
```

This would greatly improve the efficiency within the library cache and ensure that all SQL can be reused by subsequent queries. In Oracle8i and beyond, you can use the *cursor_sharing* option to force literal SQL to be reused, and we will cover this later in this chapter.

Now let's look at a query we can use to find these offensive SQL statements.

Whenever possible, it is a good idea to keep all the database SQL inside stored procedures with variables, and place these stored procedures into packages for pinning in the shared pool. By keeping all of the SQL in packages, the DBA will always be able to locate the SQL for tuning purposes. This approach also has the side benefit of ensuring that all SQL statements are identical.

Identifying Nonreusable SQL
We can attempt to locate literal SQL in the v$sql view by grouping and counting SQL statements that are identical up to a certain point based on the observation that most literal SQL becomes textually distinct toward the end of the statement (e.g., in the WHERE clause).

The following query displays the percentage of SQL executed that did not incur an expensive hard parse. Literal SQL will always be fully parsed, so a low percentage may indicate a literal SQL or other SQL sharing problem.

noparse_ratio.sql

```
column noparse_ratio format 999;

SELECT
    100 * (1 - A.hard_parses/B.executions)    noparse_ratio
FROM
    (select
        value hard_parses
    from
        v$sysstat
    where
        name = 'parse count (hard)' ) A,
     (select value executions
      from
          v$sysstat
      where
          name = 'execute count' )        B;
```

Here is the output from this script. Next we see that the SQL parse-to-execute ratio is well over 90 percent, indicating that the majority of the SQL in the library cache can be reused.

```
NOPARSE_RATIO
-------------
           93
```

The following query returns SQL statements having more than ten statements that textually match on the leading substring. This script is a great way to locate nonreusable SQL statements in your database.

find_literal_sql.sql

```
SELECT
    S.sql_text
FROM
    v$sql   S,
    (select
        substr(sql_text,1,&&size) sqltext,
        count(*)
    from
        v$sql
    group by
        substr(sql_text,1,&&size)
    having
        count(*) > 10
          ) D
WHERE
    substr(S.sql_text,1,&&size) =  D.sqltext;
```

Here is an actual excerpt from this script. Note that the output clearly shows the
nonreusable SQL statements.

```
select      ud.*,     u.first_names as referring_user_first_names,     u.last_name
as referring_user_last_name     from users_demographics ud, users u     where
ud.user_id = 362     and ud.referred_by = u.user_id(+)

select      ud.*,     u.first_names as referring_user_first_names,     u.last_name
as referring_user_last_name     from users_demographics ud, users u     where
ud.user_id = 353     and ud.referred_by = u.user_id(+)

select      ud.*,     u.first_names as referring_user_first_names,     u.last_name
as referring_user_last_name     from users_demographics ud, users u     where
ud.user_id = 355     and ud.referred_by = u.user_id(+)

select      ud.*,     u.first_names as referring_user_first_names,     u.last_name
as referring_user_last_name     from users_demographics ud, users u     where
ud.user_id = 361     and ud.referred_by = u.user_id(+)
```

So, now that we have located literal SQL statements, what can we do? If we are
using vendor-supplied code, it is often impossible to get the vendor to make the
SQL queries reusable. Oracle has addressed this problem with the *cursor_sharing*
init.ora parameter in Oracle8i.

Using cursor_sharing in Oracle8i

cursor_sharing is a new initialization parameter in Oracle8i (8.1.6) that is designed
to help manage the clutter problems with nonsharable SQL. *cursor_sharing* can take
the following values:

- **FORCE**   The FORCE option forces statements that may differ in some
  literals, but are otherwise identical, to share a cursor, unless the literals
  affect the meaning of the statement. This is achieved by replacing literals
  with system-generated bind variables and causes increased sharing of
  literal SQL.

- **EXACT (the default value)**   This causes only identical SQL statements to
  share a cursor. This is the standard pre-Oracle8i method.

When *cursor_sharing* is set to FORCE, Oracle adds an extra layer of parsing that
identifies statements as equivalent if they differ only in the values of literals, hashing
them to identical library cache objects. We will see that under the right circumstances
this setting can help solve the performance problems of literal SQL.

CAUTION
Oracle technical support states that cursor_sharing should be set to FORCE only when the risk of suboptimal plans is outweighed by the improvements in cursor sharing. Forcing cursor sharing among similar (but not identical) statements can have unexpected results in some DSS applications and in applications using stored outlines.

Setting *cursor_sharing*=FORCE may be worth considering if your system has these characteristics:

- Are there a large number of statements in the shared pool that differ only in the values of their literals?

- Is the response time low due to a very high number of library cache misses (i.e., hard parses and library cache latch contention)?

In cases where the DBA has added *cursor_sharing*=FORCE, this directive has indeed made the SQL reusable, dramatically reducing the strain on the shared pool. The downside is Oracle's warnings that some SQL can get suboptimal execution plans.

Tuning SQL with Temporary Tables

The prudent use of temporary tables can dramatically improve Oracle performance. Consider the following example: We want to identify all users who exist within Oracle but have not been granted a role. We could formulate the following query:

```
SELECT
    username
FROM
    dba_users
WHERE
    username NOT IN
        (SELECT GRANTEE FROM dba_role_privs);
```

This query runs in 18 seconds. Now, we rewrite the same query to utilize temporary tables:

```
CREATE TABLE temp1 AS
    SELECT DISTINCT USERNAME FROM dba_users;

CREATE TABLE temp2 AS
    SELECT DISTINCT GRANTEE FROM dba_role_privs;
```

```
SELECT USERNAME FROM temp1
WHERE USERNAME NOT in
(SELECT GRANTEE FROM temp2);
```

This query runs in less than three seconds.

Tuning SQL by Adding Indexes

One of the most common techniques for removing an unwanted full table scan is to add a new index to a table. This can often remove an unwanted full table scan or force the query to use a more selective index to service the query. Of course, we must be cautious when adding indexes because a new index may change the execution plan for other SQL statements. It is always a good idea to make all SQL tuning changes by using optimizer plan stability or by adding hints to the SQL.

When tuning by adding indexes, there are two special cases of indexes that are especially useful:

- **Function-based indexes** Whenever a SQL query must use a function (i.e., **WHERE upper(*last_name*)**), a function-based index can remove a full table scan.

- **Bitmapped indexes** It was a common misconception that bitmapped indexes were only appropriate for columns with a very small number of distinct values—say, less than 50. Current research in Oracle8i has shown that bitmapped indexes can substantially improve the speed of queries using columns with up to 1,000 distinct values, because retrieval from a bitmapped index is done in RAM and is almost always faster than using a traditional B-tree index. Most experienced DBAs will look for columns with less than 1,000 distinct values, build a bitmapped index on this column, and then see if the query is faster.

Next let's look at general guidelines for writing efficient SQL.

General Rules for Writing Efficient SQL

There are some general rules available for writing efficient SQL in Oracle regardless of the optimizer that is chosen. These rules may seem simplistic, but they can greatly improve the performance of SQL:

- Never do a calculation or add a built-in function (BIF) to an indexed column. This causes an unnecessary full table scan. In cases where you must use a BIF, the use of function-based indexes can remove the full table scan.

  ```
  WHERE
     Upper(last_name) = 'JONES'
  ```

```
And
    Salary*3 > 100000;
```

■ Avoid the use of NOT IN or HAVING in the WHERE clause. Instead, use the NOT EXISTS clause.

```
WHERE
customer_name NOT IN (select customer_name from customer);
```

■ Never specify numeric values in character form, and character values in numeric form. This invalidates the index and causes full table scans.

```
WHERE
emp_number = '565'
```

■ Avoid specifying NULL in an indexed column.

```
WHERE
last_name is NULL;
```

■ Avoid using the LIKE parameter if = will suffice. Using any Oracle function will invalidate the index, causing a full table scan. In the following example, an index could be created on substr(license_plate,1,3) and an = could be used.

```
WHERE
license_plate LIKE '4YE%';
```

■ Avoid using subqueries when a JOIN will do the job.

```
WHERE
    Student_name IN (select student_name from reg where grade = 'A')
```

■ Always determine the number of row accesses required to service your query. Consider whether the table rows are ordered or unordered, the setting for *db_file_multiblock_read_count*, and the degree of parallelism on the table. In general, if your query will return more than 40 percent of the rows in a row-ordered table, use a full table scan rather than an index scan. If a query returns more than 7 percent of the rows in an unordered table, a full table scan may be faster.

Next, let's move on and look at the overall process of tuning SQL statements.

The SQL Tuning Process

The process of tuning Oracle SQL is both iterative and time consuming. We begin by locating offensive SQL statements either by "fishing" them from the library cache or extracting them from the stats$sql_summary table.

Next, we explain the SQL, tune each statement, and make the changes permanent.

NOTE
If you tune your SQL by adding an index, you can go backwards in time and reexplain historical SQL in the stats$sql_summary table. This technique will verify that the new indexes have improved historical SQL.

There are several steps that are repeated until all major SQL is tuned:

1. Locate offensive and high-impact SQL statements.

2. Extract the offensive SQL syntax.

3. Explain the SQL to get the execution plan.

4. Tune the SQL with indexes and/or hints.

5. Make the tuning permanent with stored outlines or by changing the SQL source.

Step 1: Identify High-Impact SQL in the Library Cache

We begin our investigation into Oracle SQL tuning by viewing the SQL that currently resides inside our library cache. Many people ask where they should start when tuning Oracle SQL. Tuning Oracle SQL is like a fishing expedition; you must first "fish" in the Oracle library cache to extract SQL statements, and rank the statements by their amount of activity.

Oracle makes it quite easy to locate frequently executed SQL statements. The SQL statements in the v$sqlarea view are rank ordered by several values:

- **rows_processed**   Queries that process a large number of rows will have high I/O, and may also have an impact on the TEMP tablespace.

- **buffer_gets**   High buffer gets may indicate a resource-intensive query.

- **disk_reads**   High disk reads indicates a query that is causing excessive I/O.

- **sorts**   Sorts can be a huge slowdown, especially if the sorts are being done on disk in the TEMP tablespace.

- **executions**   The more frequently executed SQL statements should be tuned first, since they will have the greatest impact on overall performance.

You can get lists of SQL statements from the v$sqlarea view or stats$sql_summary table in descending order of any of these variables.

The executions column of the v$sqlarea view and the stats$sql_summary table can be used to locate the most frequently used SQL. When fishing for SQL, you can use a tool to display the SQL in the library cache. The next section will cover two ways to extract high-impact SQL:

- Extract SQL from stats$sql_summary with a STATSPACK SQL top-10 report

- Extract and analyze SQL from the library cache using *access.sql*.

Please note that either of these techniques can be used with either the historical STATSPACK sql_summary table or with the v$sqlarea view. The columns are identical.

STATSPACK SQL Top-10 Report
Here is an easy-to-use Korn shell script that can be run against the STATSPACK tables to identify high-use SQL statements.

rpt_sql.ksh

```
#!/bin/ksh

# First, we must set the environment . . . .
ORACLE_SID=readtest
export ORACLE_SID
ORACLE_HOME=`cat /var/opt/oracle/oratab|grep ^$ORACLE_SID:|cut -f2 -d':'`
export ORACLE_HOME
PATH=$ORACLE_HOME/bin:$PATH
export PATH

echo "How many days back to search?"
read days_back

echo executions
echo loads
echo parse_calls
echo disk_reads
echo buffer_gets
echo rows_processed
```

```
echo sorts
echo
echo "Enter sort key:"
read sortkey

$ORACLE_HOME/bin/sqlplus perfstat/perfstat@!


set array 1;
set lines 80;
set wrap on;
set pages 999;
set echo off;
set feedback off;

column mydate        format a8
column exec          format 9,999,999
column loads         format 999,999
column parse         format 999,999
column reads         format 9,999,999
column gets          format 9,999,999
column rows_proc     format 9,999,999
column inval         format 9,999
column sorts         format 999,999

drop table temp1;
create table temp1 as
   select min(snap_id) min_snap
   from stats\$snapshot where snap_time > sysdate-$days_back;

drop table temp2;

create table temp2 as
select
   to_char(snap_time,'dd Mon HH24:mi:ss') mydate,
   executions                          exec,
   loads                               loads,
   parse_calls                         parse,
   disk_reads                          reads,
   buffer_gets                         gets,
   rows_processed                      rows_proc,
   sorts                               sorts,
   sql_text
from
   perfstat.stats\$sql_summary sql,
   perfstat.stats\$snapshot      sn
where
   sql.snap_id >
   (select min_snap from temp1)
and
```

```
    sql.snap_id = sn.snap_id
order by $sortkey desc
;
spool off;

select * from temp2 where rownum < 11;

exit
!
```

Here is the listing from running this valuable script. Note that the DBA is prompted as to how many days back to search, and the sort key for extracting the SQL.

rpt_sql.ksh

```
How many days back to search?
7
executions
loads
parse_calls
disk_reads
buffer_gets
rows_processed
sorts

Enter sort key:
disk_reads

SQL*Plus: Release 8.1.6.0.0 - Production on Thu Dec 14 09:14:46 2000

(c) Copyright 1999 Oracle Corporation. All rights reserved.


Connected to:
Oracle8i Enterprise Edition Release 8.1.6.1.0 - 64bit Production
With the Partitioning option
JServer Release 8.1.6.1.0 - 64bit Production

MYDATE      EXEC    LOADS   PARSE     READS     GETS ROWS_PROC      SORTS
--------  --------- ------- -------- --------- ---------- --------- -----SQL_TEXT
-------------------------------------------------------------------------
11 Dec 1    866      1      866     246,877 2,795,211      865      4:00:09
DECLARE job BINARY_INTEGER := :job; next_date DATE := :mydate;  broken BOOLEAN :
= FALSE; BEGIN statspack.snap; :mydate := next_date; IF broken THEN :b := 1;
  ELSE :b := 0; END IF; END;

11 Dec 1    863      1      863     245,768 2,784,834      862      1:00:29
DECLARE job BINARY_INTEGER := :job; next_date DATE := :mydate;  broken BOOLEAN :
= FALSE; BEGIN statspack.snap; :mydate := next_date; IF broken THEN :b := 1; ELS
E :b := 0; END IF; END;
```

```
11 Dec 1        866        1      866    245,325    597,647    129,993       866 4:00:09
INSERT INTO STATS$SQL_SUMMARY ( SNAP_ID,DBID,INSTANCE_NUMBER,SQL_TEXT,SHARABLE_M
EM,SORTS,MODULE,LOADED_VERSIONS,EXECUTIONS,LOADS,INVALIDATIONS,PARSE_CALLS,DISK_
READS,BUFFER_GETS,ROWS_PROCESSED,ADDRESS,HASH_VALUE,VERSION_COUNT )   SELECT MIN(
:b1),MIN(:b2),MIN(:b3),MIN(SQL_TEXT),SUM(SHARABLE_MEM),SUM(SORTS),MIN(MODULE),SU
M(LOADED_VERSIONS),SUM(EXECUTIONS),SUM(LOADS),SUM(INVALIDATIONS),SUM(PARSE_CALLS
),SUM(DISK_READS),SUM(BUFFER_GETS),SUM(ROWS_PROCESSED),ADDRESS,HASH_VALUE,COUNT(
1)   FROM V$SQL  GROUP BY ADDRESS,HASH_VALUE  HAVING (SUM(BUFFER_GETS) > :b4  OR
SUM(DISK_READS) > :b5  OR SUM(PARSE_CALLS) > :b6  OR SUM(EXECUTIONS) > :b7 )

11 Dec 0        861        1      861    245,029  2,778,052       860       0 9:00:24
DECLARE job BINARY_INTEGER := :job; next_date DATE := :mydate;  broken BOOLEAN :
= FALSE; BEGIN statspack.snap; :mydate := next_date; IF broken THEN :b := 1; ELSE
E :b := 0; END IF; END;

11 Dec 1        864        1      864    244,587    595,861    129,605       864 2:00:02
INSERT INTO STATS$SQL_SUMMARY ( SNAP_ID,DBID,INSTANCE_NUMBER,SQL_TEXT,SHARABLE_M

EM,SORTS,MODULE,LOADED_VERSIONS,EXECUTIONS,LOADS,INVALIDATIONS,PARSE_CALLS,DISK_
READS,BUFFER_GETS,ROWS_PROCESSED,ADDRESS,HASH_VALUE,VERSION_COUNT )   SELECT MIN(
:b1),MIN(:b2),MIN(:b3),MIN(SQL_TEXT),SUM(SHARABLE_MEM),SUM(SORTS),MIN(MODULE),SU
M(LOADED_VERSIONS),SUM(EXECUTIONS),SUM(LOADS),SUM(INVALIDATIONS),SUM(PARSE_CALLS
),SUM(DISK_READS),SUM(BUFFER_GETS),SUM(ROWS_PROCESSED),ADDRESS,HASH_VALUE,COUNT(
1)   FROM V$SQL  GROUP BY ADDRESS,HASH_VALUE  HAVING (SUM(BUFFER_GETS) > :b4  OR
SUM(DISK_READS) > :b5  OR SUM(PARSE_CALLS) > :b6  OR SUM(EXECUTIONS) > :b7 )
```

It is interesting to note in this output that we see the STATSPACK **insert** statement for the stats$sql_summary table. Next, let's look at a technique that is probably the most valuable script in this book.

Reporting on SQL from the Library Cache

This section explores a technique that runs the Oracle8i **explain plan** statement on all SQL statements in the library cache, analyzes all the execution plans, and provides reports on all table and index access methods.

At first glance, it may be hard to fully appreciate the value of this technique and the information produced by the reports. But if your database has a large library cache, you can get some great insights into the internal behavior of the tables and indexes. The information also offers some great clues about what database objects you need to adjust. The reports are invaluable for the following database activities:

- **Identifying high-use tables and indexes**   See what tables the database accesses the most frequently.

- **Identifying tables for caching**   You can quickly find small, frequently accessed tables for placement in the KEEP pool (Oracle8) or for use with the CACHE option (Oracle7). You can enhance the technique to automatically cache tables when they meet certain criteria for the number of blocks and the number of accesses. (I automatically cache all tables with fewer than 200 blocks when a table has experienced more than 100 full table scans.)

■ **Identifying tables for row resequencing** You can locate large tables that have frequent index range scans in order to resequence the rows, to reduce I/O.

■ **Dropping unused indexes** You can reclaim space occupied by unused indexes. Studies have found that an Oracle database never uses more than a quarter of all indexes available or doesn't use them in the way for which they were intended.

■ **Stopping full table scans by adding new indexes** Quickly find the full table scans that you can speed up by adding a new index to a table.

The script is too long to reproduce in this book, but the source code for the scripts in this book can be found at www.oracle.com/oramag/oracle/00-nov/index.html?o60dba.html

Here are the steps to execute this script:

1. Download the *access.sql* and *access_report.sql* scripts.

2. Issue the following statements for the schema owner of your tables:

```
grant select on v_$sqltext to schema_owner;
grant select on v_$sqlarea to schema_owner;
grant select on v_$session to schema_owner;
grant select on v_$mystat to schema_owner;
```

3. Go into SQL*Plus, connect as the schema owner, and run *access.sql*.

You must be signed on as the schema owner in order to explain SQL statements with unqualified table names. Also, remember that you will get statistics only for the SQL statements that currently reside in your library cache. For very active databases, you may want to run this report script several times—it takes less than ten minutes for most Oracle databases.

Using the access.sql Script with STATSPACK The *access.sql* script can be easily modified to use the stats$sql_summary tables to extract and explain historical SQL statements. All you need to do is change the reference to v$sqlarea to stats_sql_summary, and add the following to the WHERE clause:

```
FROM
    stats$sql_summary s,
    stats$snapshot sn
WHERE
    s.snapshot_id = sn.snapshot_id
AND
    sn,snapshot_id = (select max(snapshot_id) from stats$snapshot;
```

Of course, you can modify the *access.sql* script to extract, explain, and report on any SQL in the stats$sql_summary table. Remember, though, that the SQL stored in the stats$sql_summary table is filtered by the thresholds stored in the stats$statspack_parameter table:

- **executions_th**   This is the number of executions of the SQL statement (default is 100).

- **disk_reads_th**   This is the number of disk reads performed by the SQL statement (default is 1,000).

- **parse_calls_th**   This is the number of parse calls performed by the SQL statement (default is 1,000).

- **buffer_gets_th**   This is the number of buffer gets performed by the SQL statement (default is 10,000).

Remember, a SQL statement will be included in the stats$sql_summary table if any *one* of the thresholds is exceeded.

Now, let's get back to *access.sql* and look at the valuable reports.

The access.sql Reports   As we noted, the *access.sql* script grabs all of the SQL in the library cache and stores it in a table called sqltemp. From this table, all of the SQL is explained in a single plan table. This plan table then queries to produce the following report.

You should then see a report similar to the one listed next. Let's begin by looking at the output this technique provides, and then we'll examine the method for producing the reports. For the purpose of illustration, let's break up the report into several sections. The first section shows the total number of SQL statements in the library cache, and the total number that could not be explained. Some statements cannot be explained because they do not indicate the owner of the table. If your value for statements that cannot be explained is high, you are probably not connected as the proper schema owner when running the script.

Report from access.sql

```
PL/SQL procedure successfully completed.


Mon Jan 29                                                      page    1
                    Total SQL found in library cache

    23907

Mon Jan 29                                                      page    1
                 Total SQL that could not be explained

     1065
```

The Full Table Scan Report   This is the most valuable report of all. Next we see all of the SQL statements that performed full table scans, and the number of times that a full table scan was performed. Also note the C and K columns. The C column indicates if an Oracle7 table is cached, and the K column indicates whether the Oracle8 table is assigned to the KEEP pool. As we recall, small tables with full table scans should be placed in the KEEP pool.

```
Mon Jan 29                                                          page     1
full table scans and counts
               Note that "C" indicates in the table is cached.

OWNER           NAME                          NUM_ROWS C K   BLOCKS  NBR_FTS
--------------  ----------------------------  -------- - - --------  --------
SYS             DUAL                                   N            2   97,237
SYSTEM          SQLPLUS_PRODUCT_PROFILE                N K          2   16,178
DONALD          PAGE                         3,450,209 N      932,120    9,999
DONALD          RWU_PAGE                           434 N            8    7,355
DONALD          PAGE_IMAGE                      18,067 N        1,104    5,368
DONALD          SUBSCRIPTION                       476 N K        192    2,087
DONALD          PRINT_PAGE_RANGE                    10 N K         32      874
ARSD            JANET_BOOKS                         20 N            8       64
PERFSTAT        STATS$TAB_STATS                        N           65       10
```

In this report we see several huge tables that are performing full table scans. For tables that have less than 200 blocks and are doing legitimate full table scans, we will want to place these in the KEEP pool. The larger table full table scans should also be investigated, and the legitimate large-table full table scans should be parallelized with the **alter table parallel degree nn** command.

An Oracle database invokes a large-table full table scan when it cannot service a query through indexes. If you can identify large tables that experience excessive full table scans, you can take appropriate action to add indexes. This is especially important when you migrate from Oracle7 to Oracle8, because Oracle8 offers indexes that have built-in functions. Another cause of a full table scan is when the cost-based optimizer decides that a full table scan will be faster than an index range scan. This occurs most commonly with small tables, which are ideal for caching in Oracle7 or placing in the KEEP pool in Oracle8. This full table scan report is critical for two types of SQL tuning:

- For a small-table full table scan, cache the table by using the **alter table xxx cache** command, (where xxx = table name) which will put the table rows at the most recently used end of the data buffer, thereby reducing disk I/O for the table. (Note that in Oracle8 you should place cached tables in the KEEP pool.)

- For a large-table full table scan, you can investigate the SQL statements to see if the use of indexes would eliminate the full table scan. Again, the original source for all the SQL statements is in the SQLTEMP table. We will talk about the process of finding and explaining the individual SQL statements in the next section.

Next, we see the index usage reports. These index reports are critical for the following areas of Oracle tuning:

■ **Index usage** Ensuring that the application is actually using a new index. DBAs can now obtain empirical evidence that an index is actually being used after it has been created.

■ **Row resequencing** Finding out which tables might benefit from row resequencing. Tables that have a large amount of index range scan activity will benefit from having the rows resequenced into the same order as the index. Resequencing can result in a tenfold performance improvement, depending on the row length. For details on row resequencing techniques, see Chapter 10.

Next, let's look at the index range scan report.

The Index Range Scan Report Here we see the report for index range scans. The most common method of index access in Oracle is the index range scan. An index range scan is used when the SQL statement contains a restrictive clause that requires a sequential range of values that are indexes for the table.

```
Mon Jan 29                                                        page    1
                          Index range scans and counts

OWNER      TABLE_NAME           INDEX_NAME            TBL_BLOCKS    NBR_SCANS
---------  -------------------- -------------------   -----------  ----------
DONALD     ANNO_HIGHLIGHT       HL_PAGE_USER_IN_IDX           16       7,975
DONALD     ANNO_STICKY          ST_PAGE_USER_IN_IDX            8       7,296
DONALD     PAGE                 ISBN_SEQ_IDX                 120       3,859
DONALD     TOC_ENTRY            ISBN_TOC_SEQ_IDX              40       2,830
DONALD     PRINT_HISTORY        PH_KEY_IDX                    32       1,836
DONALD     SUBSCRIPTION         SUBSC_ISBN_USER_IDX          192         210
ARSD       JANET_BOOK_RANGES    ROV_BK_RNG_BOOK_ID_            8         170
PERFSTAT   STATS$SYSSTAT        STATS$SYSSTAT_PK             845          32
12 rows selected.
```

The Index Unique Scan Report Here is a report that lists index unique scans, which occur when the Oracle database engine uses an index to retrieve a specific row from a table. The Oracle database commonly uses these types of "probe" accesses when it performs a JOIN and probes another table for the JOIN key from the driving table. This report is also useful for finding out those indexes that are used to identify distinct table rows as opposed to indexes that are used to fetch a range of rows.

Mon Jan 29   page   1
                              Index unique scans and counts

OWNER	TABLE_NAME	INDEX_NAME	NBR_SCANS
DONALD	BOOK	BOOK_ISBN	44,606
DONALD	PAGE	ISBN_SEQ_IDX	39,973
DONALD	BOOK	BOOK_UNIQUE_ID	6,450
DONALD	ANNO_DOG_EAR	DE_PAGE_USER_IDX	5,339
DONALD	TOC_ENTRY	ISBN_TOC_SEQ_IDX	5,186
DONALD	PRINT_PERMISSIONS	PP_KEY_IDX	1,836
DONALD	RDRUSER	USER_UNIQUE_ID_IDX	1,065
DONALD	CURRENT_LOGONS	USER_LOGONS_UNIQUE_I	637
ARSD	JANET_BOOKS	BOOKS_BOOK_ID_PK	54
DONALD	ERROR_MESSAGE	ERROR_MSG_IDX	48

The Full Index Scan Report   The next report shows all index full scans. As we recall, the Oracle optimizer will sometimes perform an index full scan in lieu of a large sort in the TEMP tablespace. You will commonly see full index scans in SQL that have the ORDER BY clause.

Mon Jan 29   page   1
                              Index full scans and counts

OWNER	TABLE_NAME	INDEX_NAME	NBR_SCANS
DONALD	BOOK	BOOK_ISBN	2,295
DONALD	PAGE	ISBN_SEQ_IDX	744

Although index full scans are usually faster than disk sorts, you can use one of several *init.ora* parameters to make index full scans even faster. These are the *V77_plans_enabled* parameters, renamed *fast_full_scan_enabled* in Oracle8. You can use a fast full scan as an alternative to a full table scan when an index contains all the columns needed for a query. A fast index full scan is faster than a regular index full scan because it uses multiblock I/O as defined by the *db_file_multiblock_read_count* parameter. It can also accept a parallel hint in order to invoke a Parallel Query, just like a full table scan. The Oracle database engine commonly uses index full scans to avoid sorting. Say you have a customer table with an index on the cust_nbr column. The database could service the SQL command **select * from customer order by cust_nbr;** in two ways:

- It could perform a full table scan and then sort the result set. The full table scan could be performed very quickly with *db_file_muiltiblock_read_count init.ora* parameter set, or the table access could be parallelized by using a parallel hint. However, the result set must then be sorted in the TEMP tablespace.

- It could obtain the rows in customer number order by reading the rows via the index, thus avoiding a sort.

Limitations of the access.sql Reports   The technique for generating these reports is not as flawless as it may appear. Because the "raw" SQL statements must be explained in order to obtain the execution plans, you may not know the owner of the tables. One problem with native SQL is that the table names are not always qualified with the table owner. To ensure that all the SQL statements are completely explained, many DBAs sign on to Oracle and run the reports as the schema owner.

A future enhancement would be to issue the following undocumented command immediately before each SQL statement is explained so that any Oracle database user could run the reports:

```
ALTER SESSION SET current_schema = 'tableowner';
```

This would change the schema owner immediately before explaining the SQL statement.

Now that we have covered the SQL reporting, let's move on to look at how the individual SQL statements are extracted and explained.

Step 2: Extract and Explain the SQL Statement

As each SQL statement is identified, it will be "explained" to determine its existing execution plan and then tuned to see if the execution plan can be improved.

Explaining a SQL Statement

To see the output of an explain plan, you must first create a plan table in your schema. Oracle provides the syntax to create a plan table in $ORACLE_HOME/rdbms/admin/utlxplan.sql. The listing here executes *utlxplan.sql* to create a plan table and then creates a public synonym for the plan_table:

```
sql> @$ORACLE_HOME/rdbms/admin/utlxplan
Table created.

sql> create public synonym plan_table for sys.plan_table;
Synonym created.
```

Once the plan table is created, you are ready to populate the plan table with the execution plan for SQL statements.

We start by lifting a SQL statement from the stats$sql_summary table. We will show you the details for extracting the SQL in the next section. Here is the statement that we suspect is not optimized because it takes more than 11 minutes to execute. It is not important that we understand the purpose of this SQL, only that we note the basic structure of the statement.

```
SELECT
B.ISBN,B.BOOK_TITLE,B.EDITION_NBR,B.AUTHOR_NAME,B.THUMBNAIL_TYPE,
B.GLOSSARY_NBR,B.TABLE_CONTENTS_NBR,B.INDEX_NBR,B.PUBLIC_DOMAIN_FLAG,
B.NBR_OF_REVIEWS,B.TOTAL_REVIEW_RATING,S.START_VISUAL_PAGE_NBR,
S.END_VISUAL_PAGE_NBR,S.START_PAGE_SEQ_NBR,S.END_PAGE_SEQ_NBR,
```

```
TO_CHAR(S.START_DATE,'DD-MON-YYYY HH24:MI:SS'),
TO_CHAR(S.END_DATE,'DD-MON-YYYYHH24:MI:SS'),
S.LAST_VIEWED_PAGE_SEQ_NBR,P.VISUAL_PAGE_NBR,
TO_CHAR(S.TIME_LAST_VIEWED,'DD-MON-YYYYHH24:MI:SS'),
S.PROFESSOR_USER_UNIQUE_ID,S.RETURNED_FLAG,
S.TRIAL_SUBSC_FLAG
FROM
    BOOK B,
    SUBSCRIPTION S,
    PAGE P
WHERE
(S.USER_UNIQUE_ID = :b1  AND S.ISBN = B.ISBN  AND S.BOOK_UNIQUE_ID =
P.BOOK_UNIQUE_ID  AND S.LAST_VIEWED_PAGE_SEQ_NBR = P.PAGE_SEQ_NBR )
ORDER BY B.BOOK_TITLE;
```

It is always a good idea to get a visual "pattern" for the SQL statement before you get the execution plan. This statement can be used to extrapolate the following:

```
select
    -----
from
    book,
    subscription,
    page
where
    user = :var
and
    subscription.isbn = book.isbn
and
    subscription.book_id - page.book_id
and
    subscription last_page_nbr_viewed = page page_nbr
```

Here we see a simple three-way table JOIN where the result set is limited for a single user. Now that we understand the basic structure of the query, we can get the execution plan for this SQL statement by inserting the SQL into the following snippet:

```
delete from plan_table where statement_id = 'test1';

explain plan set statement_id = 'test1'
for
SELECT B.ISBN,B.BOOK_TITLE,B.EDITION_NBR,B.AUTHOR_NAME,B.THUMBNAIL_TYPE,
B.GLOSSARY_NBR,B.TABLE_CONTENTS_NBR,B.INDEX_NBR,B.PUBLIC_DOMAIN_FLAG,
B.NBR_OF_REVIEWS,B.TOTAL_REVIEW_RATING,S.START_VISUAL_PAGE_NBR,
S.END_VISUAL_PAGE_NBR,S.START_PAGE_SEQ_NBR,S.END_PAGE_SEQ_NBR,
TO_CHAR(S.START_DATE,'DD-MON-YYYY HH24:MI:SS'),
TO_CHAR(S.END_DATE,'DD-MON-YYYYHH24:MI:SS'),
S.LAST_VIEWED_PAGE_SEQ_NBR,P.VISUAL_PAGE_NBR,
TO_CHAR(S.TIME_LAST_VIEWED,'DD-MON-YYYYH24:MI:SS'),
S.PROFESSOR_USER_UNIQUE_ID,S.RETURNED_FLAG,S.TRIAL_SUBSC_FLAG
```

```
FROM
    BOOK B,
    SUBSCRIPTION S,
    PAGE P
WHERE
(S.USER_UNIQUE_ID = :b1   AND S.ISBN = B.ISBN   AND S.BOOK_UNIQUE_ID =
P.BOOK_UNIQUE_ID   AND S.LAST_VIEWED_PAGE_SEQ_NBR = P.PAGE_SEQ_NBR )
ORDER BY B.BOOK_TITLE;
```

When you execute this code, you instruct Oracle to display the execution plan inside the plan table. To display the data inside the plan table, you can use the following script.

plan.sql

```
SET PAGES 9999;
SELECT  lpad(' ',2*(level-1))||operation operation,
        options,
        object_name,
        position
FROM plan_table
START WITH id=0
AND
statement_id = 'test1'
CONNECT BY prior id = parent_id
AND
statement_id = 'test1';
```

Here is the output from *plan.sql*. This display is known as the execution plan for the SQL statement. It describes in detail all of the access steps that are used to retrieve the requested rows.

OPTIONS	OBJECT_NAME	POSITION
SELECT STATEMENT		
SORT		
ORDER BY		1
NESTED LOOPS		
		1
NESTED LOOPS		
		1
TABLE ACCESS		
FULL	PAGE	1
TABLE ACCESS		
BY INDEX ROWID	SUBSCRIPTION	2

```
            INDEX
RANGE SCAN                    SUBSC_ISBN_USER_IDX              1

        TABLE ACCESS
BY INDEX ROWID                BOOK                            2

            INDEX
UNIQUE SCAN                   BOOK_ISBN                       1
```

9 rows selected.

In this listing we see the TABLE ACCESS FULL PAGE. This is the dreaded full table scan that causes excessive overhead for Oracle. The next question is whether this query needs all of the rows in the page table. Let's look at the WHERE clause for the query:

```
WHERE
    S.USER_UNIQUE_ID = :b1
AND
    S.ISBN = B.ISBN
AND
    S.BOOK_UNIQUE_ID = P.BOOK_UNIQUE_ID
AND
    S.LAST_VIEWED_PAGE_SEQ_NBR = P.PAGE_SEQ_NBR
```

Here we see that the only WHERE condition that applies to the page table is:

```
    S.LAST_VIEWED_PAGE_SEQ_NBR = P.PAGE_SEQ_NBR
```

It then follows that Oracle should be able to retrieve the page rows by using an index on the page_seq_nbr column of the page table and there is no need to perform a time-consuming full table scan.

This statement was extracted from a database where *optimizer_mode*=RULE, so the first thing we can try is to analyze all of the tables and indexes in the query and reexplain the query with a FIRST_ROWS hint:

```
Analyze table page estimate statistics sample 5000 rows.
Analyze table book estimate statistics sample 5000 rows.
Analyze table subscription estimate statistics sample 5000 rows.
Analyze index isbn_seq_idx compute statistics;
Analyze index subsc_pub_name_idx compute statistics;
```

Here is the original explain with the FIRST_ROWS hint:

```
delete from plan_table where statement_id = 'test1';

explain plan set statement_id = 'test1'
for
SELECT /*+ first_rows */
```

```
B.ISBN,B.BOOK_TITLE,B.EDITION_NBR,B.AUTHOR_NAME,B.THUMBNAIL_TYPE,
B.GLOSSARY_NBR,B.TABLE_CONTENTS_NBR,B.INDEX_NBR,B.PUBLIC_DOMAIN_FLAG,
B.NBR_OF_REVIEWS,B.TOTAL_REVIEW_RATING,S.START_VISUAL_PAGE_NBR,
S.END_VISUAL_PAGE_NBR,S.START_PAGE_SEQ_NBR,S.END_PAGE_SEQ_NBR,
TO_CHAR(S.START_DATE,'DD-MON-YYYY HH24:MI:SS'),TO_CHAR(S.END_DATE,
'DD-MON-YYYY HH24:MI:SS'),S.LAST_VIEWED_PAGE_SEQ_NBR,P.VISUAL_PAGE_NBR,
TO_CHAR(S.TIME_LAST_VIEWED,'DD-MON-YYYY HH24:MI:SS'),
S.PROFESSOR_USER_UNIQUE_ID,S.RETURNED_FLAG,
S.TRIAL_SUBSC_FLAG   FROM BOOK B,SUBSCRIPTION S,
PAGE P  WHERE (S.USER_UNIQUE_ID = :b1  AND S.ISBN = B.ISBN  AND
S.BOOK_UNIQUE_ID = P.BOOK_UNIQUE_ID  AND S.LAST_VIEWED_PAGE_SEQ_NBR =
P.PAGE_SEQ_NBR )ORDER BY B.BOOK_TITLE;

@plan
```

Now, when we run *plan.sql*, we see a totally different execution plan without any full table scans:

```
OPERATION
------------------------------------------------------------------------
OPTIONS                 OBJECT_NAME                    POSITION
------------------------ ----- ------------------------------ ----------
SELECT STATEMENT
                                                               27

  SORT
ORDER BY                                                       1

    NESTED LOOPS
                                                               1

      NESTED LOOPS
                                                               1

        TABLE ACCESS
BY INDEX ROWID          SUBSCRIPTION                           1

          BITMAP CONVERSION
TO ROWIDS                                                      1

          BITMAP INDEX
FULL SCAN               SUBSC_PUB_NAME_IDX                     1

        TABLE ACCESS
BY INDEX ROWID          BOOK                                   2

          INDEX
UNIQUE SCAN             BOOK_ISBN                              1

      TABLE ACCESS
BY INDEX ROWID          PAGE                                   2

        INDEX
UNIQUE SCAN             ISBN_SEQ_IDX                           1


11 rows selected.
```

When we reexecute the SQL in SQL*Plus with **set timing on**, the whole query executes in 18 seconds, for a savings of more than 10 minutes! This is just a simple example of the dramatic improvements you can make by tuning your SQL statements.

NOTE
There is a host of third-party tools in the market that show the execution plan for SQL statements. The most common way of determining the execution plan for an SQL statement is by using Oracle's explain plan utility. By using explain plan, the Oracle DBA can ask Oracle to parse the statement, and display the execution class path without actually executing the SQL statement.

Now that we have covered the extraction and explaining of the SQL statement, let's go into more detail on the process of tuning each SQL statement.

Step 3: Tune the SQL Statement

For those SQL statements that possess a nonoptimal execution plan, the SQL will be tuned by one of the following methods:

- Adding SQL hints to modify the execution plan.

- Adding B-tree indexes to remove full table scans.

- Adding bitmapped indexes to all low-cardinality columns that are mentioned in the WHERE clause of the query.

- Rewriting the SQL in PL/SQL. For certain queries, this can result in more than a 20x performance improvement. The SQL would be replaced with a call to a PL/SQL package that contained a stored procedure to perform the query.

By far the most common approach is to add indexes and hints to the query. While we can instantly see the execution plan change as we add indexes and change hints, it is not always immediately evident which execution plan will result in the best performance.

Hence, the DBA will normally take the three most promising execution plans and actually execute the statement in SQL*Plus, noting the total elapsed time for the query by using the SQL*Plus **set timing on** command.

The details of all of the SQL hints are way beyond the scope of this book, but you can get details on all of the hints in the forthcoming Oracle Press book *Oracle High-Performance SQL Tuning* (October, 2001), by Don Burleson.

An Actual Case-Study in SQL Tuning

The first activity of most SQL tuning sessions is to identify and remove unnecessary full table scans. This SQL tuning activity can make a huge difference in SQL performance, since unnecessary full table scans can take 20 times longer than using an index to service the query. Again, here are the basic steps in locating and fixing full table scans:

1. Run the full table scan report to locate SQL statements that produce full table scans.

2. Then query the v$sqltext view to locate the individual SQL statements.

3. Explain the statement to see the execution plan.

4. Add indexes or hints to remove the full table scan.

5. Change the SQL source or store the outline to make the change permanent.

Let's quickly step through these activities and see how easy it is to improve the performance of SQL statements.

Get the Full Table Scan Report

First, we run the *access.sql* script to extract and explain all of the SQL in the library cache. Here is a sample from an actual report:

```
Mon Jan 29                                                      page    1
                        full table scans and counts
                Note that "C" indicates in the table is cached.

OWNER           NAME                       NUM_ROWS C  K    BLOCKS  NBR_FTS
-------------   ------------------------   -------- -- -  --------  -------
SYS             DUAL                                N            2   97,237
SYSTEM          SQLPLUS_PRODUCT_PROFILE             N  K         2   16,178
DONALD          PAGE                      3,450,209 N        932,120    9,999
DONALD          RWU_PAGE                        434 N            8    7,355
DONALD          PAGE_IMAGE                   18,067 N        1,104    5,368
DONALD          SUBSCRIPTION                    476 N  K       192    2,087
DONALD          PRINT_PAGE_RANGE                 10 N  K        32      874
ARSD            JANET_BOOKS                      20 N            8       64
PERFSTAT        STATS$TAB_STATS                     N           65       10
```

Here we see a clear problem with large-table full table scans against the page_image table. The page_image table has 18,067 rows and consumes 1,104 blocks. The report shows 5,368 full table scans against this table. Next, we can run a quick query to display the SQL source from v$sqlarea for the page_image table, looking for a SQL statement that has been executed about 5,000 times:

```
set lines 2000;

select
   sql_text,
   disk_reads,
   executions,
   parse_calls
from
   v$sqlarea
where
   lower(sql_text) like '%page_image%'
and
   executions > 100
order by
   disk_reads desc
;
```

In the result from this query, we will look for SQL statements whose values for executions (5,201) approximate the value in the full table scan report (5,368). From the output, we clearly see the offensive SQL statement:

```
SELECT IMAGE_BLOB   FROM PAGE_IMAGE   WHERE (BOOK_UNIQUE_ID = :b1
  AND PAGE_SEQ_NBR = :b2   AND IMAGE_KEY = :b3 )
  833         5201            148
```

Now that we have the SQL, we can quickly explain it and verify the full table scan:

```
delete from plan_table where statement_id = 'test1';

explain plan set statement_id = 'test1'
for
SELECT IMAGE_BLOB   FROM PAGE_IMAGE   WHERE (BOOK_UNIQUE_ID = :b1
  AND PAGE_SEQ_NBR = :b2   AND IMAGE_KEY = :b3 )
;
```

Here we run the execution plan showing our full table scan:

```
OPERATION
---------------------------------------------------------------------------
OPTIONS                         OBJECT_NAME                     POSITION
---------------------------------------------------------------------------
SELECT STATEMENT
                                                                   168

   TABLE ACCESS
FULL                            PAGE_IMAGE                          1
```

Since this is a very simple query against a single table, we can look directly at the WHERE clause to see the problem. The only condition in the WHERE clause references **upper**(*book_unique_id*), and the Oracle optimizer has not detected a usable index on this column. Since we are in Oracle8, we can create a function-based index using the **upper** function:

```
create unique index book_seq_image_idx
  on page_image
    (book_unique_id,
     page_seq_nbr,
     image_key)
  tablespace bookx
  pctfree 10
  storage (initial 128k next 128k maxextents 2147483645 pctincrease 0);
```

Now we rerun the execution plan and see the full table scan is replaced by an index scan:

```
OPERATION
---------------------------------------------------------------------------
OPTIONS                         OBJECT_NAME                     POSITION
---------------------------------------------------------------------------
SELECT STATEMENT                .

   TABLE ACCESS
BY INDEX ROWID                  PAGE IMAGE                          1

     INDEX
UNIQUE SCAN                     BOOK_SEQ_IMAGE_IDX                  1
```

Problem solved! The query went from an original execution time of 3 minutes to less than 10 seconds.

Now that we see the iterative process of locating and tuning SQL statements, let's look at how third-party GUI tools can speed up the process. This can be very important when the DBA must tune hundreds of SQL statements.

Advanced SQL Execution Plan Analysis

Oracle Corporate Technical Support provides a great supplement to the standard explain plan utility in the form of a SQL*Plus script called *coe_xplain.sql*. This script enhances the SQL analysis by providing additional details about the database and all tables and indexes in the query.

You can download this script from the Oracle Web site at the following URL:

http://coe.us.oracle.com/~csierra/CoE_Scripts/coe_xplain.sql

The purpose of this script is to supplement the standard explain plan output with additional information about the status of the tables and indexes in your database. Let's take a look at how this script is used:

1. First, you download the latest version of the script from Oracle's Web site.

2. Next, you transfer the script to your server.

3. To add your SQL statement, go to section III and paste the SQL statement into the script, making sure that the SQL ends with a semicolon.

4. Finally, you enter SQL*Plus as the schema owner and execute *coe_xplain*.

This script begins by asking you what details you would like in addition to the standard explain plan. Following the data collection, this script generates two files:

- ***coe_statement.lst*** This is a display of the SQL you inserted into section III of the script.

- ***coe_explain.lst*** This file contains the detailed execution plan for the SQL and lots of other useful information.

Let's take a look at the output from this script. When executed, this script prompts the user about the amount of additional detail they need. When analyzing an SQL statement, it is a good idea to request all of the ancillary information.

```
>sqlplus system/manager

SQL*Plus: Release 9.0.3.0.0 - Production on Wed Feb 7 06:38:22 2001
(c) Copyright 2001 Oracle Corporation.  All rights reserved.
Connected to:
Oracle9i Enterprise Edition Release 8.1.6.1.0 - 64bit Production
With the Partitioning option
JServer Release 9.0.3.0.0 - 64bit Production
```

```
SQL> @coe xplain
Unless otherwise instructed by Support, hit <Enter> for each parameter
1. Include count(*) of Tables in SQL Statement? <n/y> y
2. Include Table and Index Storage Parameters? <n/y/d> y
3. Include all Table Columns? <n/y> y
4. Include all Column Histograms? <n/y> y
5. Include relevant INIT.ORA DB parameters? <n/y> y
```

Now that the script has gathered our requirements, it displays the SQL statement and the execution plan for the SQL:

Generating...

```
explain plan set statement_id = 'COE_XPLAIN' into COE_PLAN_TABLE_&&initials for
/*=================================================================
   Generate Explain Plan for SQL statement below (ending with a semicolon ';')
   ================================================================= */
SELECT /*+ first_rows */
B.ISBN,B.BOOK_TITLE,B.EDITION_NBR,B.AUTHOR_NAME,B.THUMBNAIL_TYPE,
B.GLOSSARY_NBR,B.TABLE_CONTENTS_NBR,B.INDEX_NBR,B.PUBLIC_DOMAIN_FLAG,
B.NBR_OF_REVIEWS,B.TOTAL_REVIEW_RATING,S.START_VISUAL_PAGE_NBR,
S.END_VISUAL_PAGE_NBR,S.START_PAGE_SEQ_NBR,S.END_PAGE_SEQ_NBR,
TO_CHAR(S.START_DATE,'DD-MON-YYYY H24:MI:SS'),TO_CHAR(S.END_DATE,
'DD-MON-YYYY HH24:MI:SS'), S.LAST_VIEWED_PAGE_SEQ_NBR, P.VISUAL_PAGE_NBR,
TO_CHAR(S.TIME_LAST_VIEWED,'DD-MON-YYYY HH24:MI:SS'),
S.PROFESSOR_USER_UNIQUE_ID, S.RETURNED_FLAG,S.TRIAL_SUBSC_FLAG
FROM BOOK B, SUBSCRIPTION S, PAGE P  WHERE (S.USER_UNIQUE_ID = :b1
AND S.ISBN = B.ISBN  AND S.BOOK_UNIQUE_ID = P.BOOK_UNIQUE_ID
AND S.LAST_VIEWED_PAGE_SEQ_NBR = P.PAGE_SEQ_NBR )ORDER BY B.BOOK_TITLE;

Explained.


/*========================================================================= */
SET echo off;


Ope  Exec
Typ Order Explain Plan (coe_xplain.sql 8.1/11.5 20010115)
--- ----- --------------------------------------------------------------------
     ----------------------------------------------------------------------------
ROW   11 SELECT STATEMENT Opt_Mode:HINT: FIRST_ROWS Total_Cost:28 (CBO has been used)
SET   10 SORT (ORDER BY) (Cost=28 Card=4 Bytes=500)
ROW    9 . NESTED LOOPS (Cost=24 Card=4 Bytes=588)
ROW    6 .. NESTED LOOPS (Cost=20 Card=4 Bytes=552)
ROW    3 ... TABLE ACCESS (BY INDEX ROWID) OF 'DONALD.SUBSCRIPTION'
  (Cost=15 Card=4 Bytes=196)
ROW    2 .... BITMAP CONVERSION (TO ROWIDS)
ROW    1 ....| BITMAP INDEX ***(FULL SCAN)*** OF
DONALD.SUBSC_PUB_NAME_IDX'
ROW    5 ... TABLE ACCESS (BY INDEX ROWID) OF 'DONALD.BOOK' (Cost=1 Card=22
Bytes=1958)
ROW    4 .... INDEX (UNIQUE SCAN) OF 'DONALD.BOOK_ISBN' (UNIQUE) (Card=22)
ROW    8 .. TABLE ACCESS (BY INDEX ROWID) OF 'DONALD.PAGE'
(Cost=1 Card=13352 Bytes=120168)
ROW    7 ... INDEX (UNIQUE SCAN) OF 'DONALD.ISBN_SEQ_IDX' (UNIQUE) (Card=13352)

Note: Card=Computed or Default Object Cardinality
```

Next, the report will be created and spooled to *coe_statement.lst* and *coe_explain.lst*. The *coe_statement.lst* shows the input SQL statement, but the valuable information is in *coe_explain.lst*. From this listing, we get far more detail than just the execution plan for the SQL. This report contains all of the information for any Oracle object that participates in the query.

First, we see additional information about the internal structure of Oracle tables and indexes:

■ **Section I: Table information**   This section of the report shows all details for the table involved in the query, including the number of rows in the table, the parallel degree, a note if the table is partitioned, the chain count, and the number of freelists for the table.

  ■ **Section I.a: Table statistics**   Next we see details on each table from the data dictionary, including the high-water mark, used blocks, empty blocks, and free space per allocated block. This information can be quite useful for detecting tables where the high-water mark is far above the table's row space.

  ■ **Section I.b: Table storage parameters**   This section displays the PCTFREE, PCTUSED, and extent sizes for each table in the query.

■ **Section II: Index parameters**   This includes everything you would want to know about the index, including the index type, index status parallelism, partitioning, and freelists.

  ■ **Section II.a: Index statistics**   In this section, the report provides details on the cardinality of the index and the number of distinct keys.

  ■ **Section II.b: Index storage parameters**   This section shows all of the indexes and the index column detail.

■ **Section III: Table columns**   The next section displays all of the available information about each table column that participates in the query.

  ■ **Section III.a: Index column statistics**   This section examines all of the available statistics for each column in the query. This includes the column size, cardinality, number of distinct values, and the index selectivity.

  ■ **Section III.b: Table column statistics**   This section of the report shows the individual characteristics of each column that is referenced in the SQL query. It shows all of the CBO statistics that have been collected about each column.

- **Section IV: Histograms**   The histograms section is useful in cases where you may have a table column with a highly skewed distribution of values. As you may know, it is not a good idea to analyze column histograms unless you identify columns where the distribution of values is not uniform.

- **Section V: Oracle initialization parameters**   This section dumps the *init.ora* parameters from the v$parameter view. This completes the overall package, so the analyst will have access to every possible factor that Influences the execution plan for the SQL statement.

This output listing should provide everything that is needed to properly tune the SQL statement, and most professional DBAs make frequent use of this script.

Table Histograms

As you may recall, the following command is used to analyze table columns. The *size* parameter tells Oracle how many distinct buckets to use for the column histograms.

```
analyze table
    CUSTOMER
compute statistics for columns
    CUSTOMER_REGION
size 10;
```

Once analyzed, you can issue SQL commands to see the distribution of values within the table column:

```
column table_name format a20;
column column_name format a25;

select
    table_name,
    column_name,
    endpoint_number,
    endpoint_value
from
    dba_histograms
where
    table_name = 'SUBSCRIPTION'
order by
    column_name
;
```

You can then see the distribution of values by querying the dba_tab_histograms table. The *endpoint_value* shows the column value and the *endpoint_number* shows the cumulative number of rows.

SQL> @disp_hist

TABLE_NAME	COLUMN_NAME	ENDPOINT_NUMBER	ENDPOINT_VALUE
SUBSCRIPTION	BOOK_NAME	0	3.3952E+35
SUBSCRIPTION	BOOK_NAME	1	4.5399E+35
SUBSCRIPTION	BOOK_UNIQUE_ID	0	1
SUBSCRIPTION	BOOK_UNIQUE_ID	1	55
SUBSCRIPTION	COUPON_DISCOUNT_AMOUNT	0	0
SUBSCRIPTION	COUPON_DISCOUNT_AMOUNT	1	0
SUBSCRIPTION	DATE_TIME_SUBSCRIBED	0	2451877.59
SUBSCRIPTION	DATE_TIME_SUBSCRIBED	1	2451952.01

This histogram information should tell you when a data column is skewed, that is, whenever an index column contains an uneven distribution of values, you may want to consider analyzing the column to tell the CBO about the skew.

Making Permanent Changes to Tuned SQL

Tuning the SQL statement is only half of the battle. Once tuned, the DBA must be able to make the tuning change permanent. For some changes, such as adding a new index, the change to the optimizer behavior is automatic. Other changes such as adding hints to SQL require more work to become permanent. There are two approaches to doing this:

- Store an outline for the SQL (Oracle8i).

- Locate the SQL source code and add the hint.

If we have a database where all of the SQL is encapsulated into packages, it is very easy for the DBA to extract the package and change the SQL. If the SQL arrives into Oracle from an external location such as a Pro*C program or a client/server call, we have the time-consuming task of locating the program that sent the SQL statement.

Using Stored Outlines for SQL

If we are using Oracle8i, we have another great option. Oracle8i provides a new package called *outline* that allows the DBA to store a ready-to-run execution plan for any SQL statement. This utility is called *optimizer plan stability* and has several features:

- Parsing and execution time is reduced because Oracle will quickly grab and execute the stored outline for the SQL.

- Tuning of SQL statements can easily be made permanent without locating the source code.

- SQL from third-party products (e.g., SAP, PeopleSoft) can be tuned without touching the SQL source code.

Plan stability allows you to maintain the same execution plans for the same SQL statements, regardless of changes to the database such as reanalyzing tables, adding or deleting data, modifying a table's columns, constraints, or indexes, changing the system configuration, or even upgrading to a new version of the optimizer.

To use optimizer plan stability you must run the *dbmsol.sql* script from $ORACLE_HOME/rdbms/admin. When executed, a new Oracle user called OUTLN is created (with DBA privileges) and a package called outln_pkg is installed to provide procedures used for managing stored outlines.

Oracle provides the **create outline** statement to create a stored outline. The stored outline contains a set of attributes that the optimizer uses to create an execution plan. Stored outlines can also be created automatically by setting the *init.ora* parameter *create_stored_outlines*=TRUE.

For more details on using stored outlines, see your Oracle8i documentation.

Conclusion

This chapter is designed to give you a high-level understanding of how SQL statements are located and tuned. You should remember that SQL tuning is a very complex subject, and this chapter only provides a brief overview.

Next, let's take a look at the Oracle parallel facilities and see how you can tune your database to get improved performance with Oracle Parallel Query.

CHAPTER
12

Tuning with Oracle Parallel Features

here are two main areas of Oracle parallelism: Oracle Parallel Query and Oracle Parallel DML. This chapter will examine each of these features and show how STATSPACK data can be used to assist in the optimal use of parallel features. In the next chapter we will investigate another area of parallelism, Oracle Parallel Server (OPS). In Oracle9i, OPS has been completely revamped and is now called Real Application Clusters (RAC).

One of the most exciting, yet most overlooked, features of Oracle databases is the ability to dedicate multiple query processes to service an Oracle query. The Oracle database has implemented Parallel Query features that allow a query to effectively use both symmetric multiprocessors (SMP) and massively parallel processors (MPP). Using these features, it is possible to read a 1GB table with subsecond response time. Let's begin with a review of these architectures.

NOTE
Oracle Parallel Query only works with databases that perform full table scans. A well-tuned online transaction database will seldom perform full table scans and will not benefit from Oracle Parallel Query.

As we stated, Oracle Parallel Query will only work with queries that perform a full table scan. It is very important that the DBA understand that indexes are the enemy of Parallel Query. To use Parallel Query, you must force the SQL to perform a full table scan. Hence, it follows that Oracle Parallel Query will only improve queries that must read the majority of rows in the table.

Oracle Parallel Query achieves improved speed because multiple processes can be directed to read a table. Parallel Query works best on servers that have multiple CPUs because multiple CPUs allow for simultaneous queries. To find the command to see how many CPUs you have on your database server, see Chapter 6.

Starting with Oracle release 7.2 and above, you can partition a SQL query into subqueries and dedicate separate processors to each one. Here's how it works. Instead of having a single query server to manage the I/O against the table, Parallel Query allows the Oracle query server to dedicate many processes to simultaneously access the whole table (see Figure 12-1).

So what is the optimal amount of Parallel Query slave processes? Let's take a look at the techniques for determining the optimal degree of parallelism.

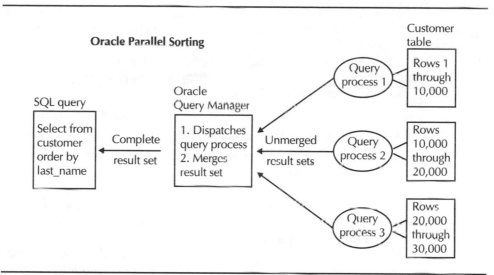

FIGURE 12-1.   *An Oracle Parallel Query with full table scan*

Using Oracle Parallel Query

There are several *init.ora* parameters that are set when using Oracle Parallel Query.
Many of these are default values and are set by Oracle when your database is created.
Oracle Parallel Query can be turned on in several ways. You can turn it on permanently
for a table or you can isolate the Parallel Query to a single table.

Permanent Parallelism

```
Alter table customer parallel degree 35;
```

Single Query Parallelism

```
select /*+ FULL(emp) PARALLEL(emp, 35) */
        emp_name
     from
       emp;
```

Note the use of the double hints in the preceding query. Most Oracle DBAs always use the FULL hint with the PARALLEL hint because they are both required to use Oracle Parallel Query.

Most Oracle DBAs identify those tables that perform full table scans and then alter those tables to specify the degree of parallelism. This way, all full table scans against the tables will invoke Oracle Parallel Query.

Parallel Query init.ora Parameters

There are several important *init.ora* parameters that have a direct impact on the behavior of Oracle Parallel Query:

- *sort_area_size*   The higher the value, the more memory is available for individual sorts on each parallel process. Note that the *sort_area_size* parameter allocates memory for every query on the system that invokes a sort. For example, if a single query needs more memory, and you increase the *sort_area_size*, *all* Oracle tasks will allocate the new amount of sort area, regardless of whether they will use all of the space. It is also possible to dynamically change the *sort_area_size* for a specific session with the **alter session** command. This technique can be used when a specific transaction requires a larger sort area than the default for the database.

- *parallel_min_servers*   This value specifies the minimum number of query servers that will be active on the instance. There are system resources involved in starting a query server, and having the query server started and waiting for requests will accelerate processing. Note that if the actual number of required servers is less than the values of *parallel_min_servers*, the idle query servers will be consuming unnecessary overhead, and the value should be decreased.

- *parallel_max_servers*   This value specifies the maximum number of query servers allowed on the instance. This parameter will prevent Oracle from starting so many query servers that the instance cannot service all of them properly.

- *optimizer_percent_parallel*   This parameter defines the amount of parallelism that the optimizer uses in its cost functions. The default of 0 means that the optimizer chooses the best serial plan. A value of 100 means that the optimizer uses each object's degree of parallelism in computing the cost of a full table scan operation.

NOTE
Cost based optimization will always be used for any query that references an object with a nonzero degree of parallelism. Hence, you should be careful when setting parallelism if your default is optimizer_mode=RULE.

Setting the Optimal Degree of Parallelism

Determining the optimal degree of parallelism for Oracle tasks is not easy. Because of the highly volatile nature of most SMP systems, there is no general rule that will apply to all situations. As you may know, the degree of parallelism is the number of operating system processes that are created by Oracle to service the query.

Oracle states that the optimal degree of parallelism for a query is based on several factors. These factors are presented in their order of importance:

- The number of CPUs on the server.

- The number of physical disks that the tables resides on.

- For parallelizing by partition, the number of partitions that will be accessed, based upon partition pruning (if appropriate).

- For Parallel DML operations with global index maintenance, the minimum number of transaction freelists among all the global indexes to be updated. The minimum number of transaction freelists for a partitioned global index is the minimum number across all index partitions. This is a requirement in order to prevent self-deadlock.

For example, if your system has 20 CPUs and you issue a Parallel Query on a table that is stored on 15 disk drives, the default degree of parallelism for your query is 15 query servers.

There has been a great deal of debate about what number of parallel processes results in the fastest response time. As a general rule, the optimal degree of parallelism can be safely set to *n-1* where *n* is the number of processors in your SMP or MPP cluster.

In practice, the best method is a trial-and-error approach. When tuning a specific query, the DBA can set the query to force a full table scan and then experiment with different degrees of parallelism until the fastest response time is achieved.

Finding the Number of CPUs on Your Database Server

Sometimes the Oracle DBA does not know the number of CPUs on the database server. The following UNIX commands can be issued to report on the number of CPUs on the database server.

Windows NT   If you are using MS Windows NT, you can find the number of CPUs by entering the Control Panel and choosing the System icon.

Linux   To see the number of CPUs on a Linux server, you can **cat** the /proc/cpuinfo file. In the following example, we see that our Linux server has four CPUs:

```
>cat /proc/cpuinfo|grep processor|wc -l
       4
```

Solaris   In Sun Solaris, the **prsinfo** command can be used to count the number of CPUs on the processor.

```
>psrinfo -v|grep "Status of processor"|wc -l
       24
```

IBM-AIX   The following example is taken from an AIX server, and shows that the server has four CPUs:

```
>lsdev -C|grep Process|wc -l

     36
```

HP/UX   In HP UNIX, you can use the glance or top utilities to display the number of CPUs.

> **NOTE**
> *Parallel hints will often speed up index creation even on uniprocessor machines. This is not because there is more processing power available, but because there is less I/O wait contention with multiple processes. On the other end of the spectrum, we generally see diminishing elapsed time when the degree of parallelism exceeds the number of processors in the cluster.*

There are several formulas for computing the optimal parallelism. Oracle provides a formula for computing the optimal parallelism based on the number of CPUs and the number of disks that the file is striped onto. Assume that D is the number of devices that P is striped across (either SQL*Loader striping or OS striping). Assume that C is the number of CPUs available:

```
P = ceil(D/max(floor(D/C), 1))
```

Simply put, the degree of parallelism for a table should generally be the number of devices on which the table is loaded, scaled down so that it isn't too much greater than the number of CPUs. For example, with ten devices and eight CPUs, a good choice for the degree of parallelism is ten. With only four CPUs, a better choice of parallelism might be five.

However, this complex rule is not always suitable for the real world. A better rule for setting the degree of parallelism is to simply use the number of CPUs:

```
P=(number of CPUs)-1
```

As a general rule, you can set the degree of parallelism to the number of CPUs on your server, minus one. This is because one processor will be required to handle the Parallel Query coordinator.

Setting Automatic Parallelism

Oracle Parallel Query allows you to control the number of Parallel Query slave processes that service a table. Oracle Parallel Query processes can be seen on the server because background processes will start when the query is serviced. These factotum processes are generally numbered from P000 through Pnnn. For example, if our server is on AIX, we can create a script to gather the optimal degree of parallelism and pass this argument to the SQL.

parallel_query.ksh

```
#!/bin/ksh
# Get the number of CPUs
num_cpu=`lsdev -C|grep mem|wc -l`
optimal_parallelism=`expr $num_cpu`-1

sqlplus system/manager<<!
select /*+ FULL(employee_table) PARALLEL(employee_table, $optimal_parallelism)*/
employee_name
from
employee_table;
exit
!
```

Resource Contention and Oracle Parallel Query

There are several sources of contention in Oracle Parallel Query. As we already mentioned, Oracle Parallel Query works best on servers that have multiple CPUs, but we can often see disk contention when the whole table resides on the same physical disk. In short, the use of Oracle Parallel Query can precipitate several external bottlenecks. These include:

- **Overloaded processors** This is normally evidenced when the vmstat run queue values exceed the number of CPUs on the server.

- **Disk enqueues** When multiple processes compete for data blocks on the same disk, I/O related slowdowns may occur. This is evidenced by high activity from the UNIX iostat utility.

- **Increased RAM usage** The parallel sorting feature may increase the demands on the server RAM. Each parallel process can allocate *sort_area_size* in RAM to manage the sort.

Let's explore things that we can do to prevent contention-related slowdowns when using Oracle Parallel Query. To be most effective, the table should be partitioned onto separate disk devices, such that each process can do I/O against its segment of the table without interfering with the other simultaneous query processes. However, the client/server environment of the 1990s relies on RAID or a logical volume manager (LVM), which scrambles datafiles across disk packs in order to balance the I/O load. Consequently, full utilization of Parallel Query involves "striping" a table across numerous datafiles, each on a separate device. It is also important to note that large contiguous extents can help the query coordinator break up scan operations more efficiently for the query servers. Even if your system uses RAID or a logical volume manager (such as Veritas), there are still some performance gains from using Parallel Query. In addition to using multiple processes to retrieve the table, the Query Manager will also dedicate numerous processes to simultaneously sort the result set (see Figure 12-2).

As we know, a RAM memory overload can cause swapping on the database server. Because of the parallel sorting feature, it is also a good idea to beef up the memory on the processor. We may also see the TEMP tablespace fall short when using Parallel Query and Parallel DML. Here is an example of the error:

```
SQL> alter session enable parallel dml;

Session altered.

SQL> insert /*+ parallel(customer, 6) */ into customer;
2 select /*+ full(c) parallel(c, 6) */
3 from customer c;
```

```
ERROR at line 3:
ORA-12801: error signaled in parallel query server P000
ORA-01652: unable to extend temp segment by 128000 in tablespace CUSTOMER_TS
```

Disk Contention with Oracle Parallel Query   Many DBAs are surprised
to note that Oracle Parallel Query does not always improve the speed of queries
where the whole table resides on a single physical disk.

The data retrieval for a table on a single disk will not be particularly fast, since
all of the parallel retrieval processes may be competing for a channel on the same
disk. But each sort process has its own sort area (as determined by the
sort_area_size init.ora parameter), so the sorting of the result set will progress very
quickly. In addition to full table scans and sorting, the Parallel Query option also
allows for parallel processes for merge JOINs and nested loops.

Using Parallel Query Hints

Invoking the Parallel Query with hints requires several steps. The most important is
that the execution plan for the query specifies a full table scan. If the output of the
execution plan does not indicate a full table scan, the query can be forced to ignore
the index by using the FULL hint.

The number of processors dedicated to service a SQL request is ultimately
determined by Oracle Query Manager, but the programmer can specify the upper

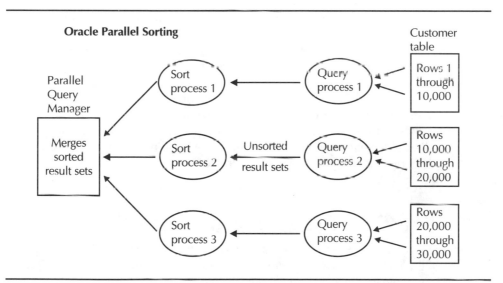

FIGURE 12-2.   *Increase RAM memory demands with Oracle Parallel Query*

limit on the number of simultaneous processes. When using the cost-based optimizer, the PARALLEL hint can be embedded into the SQL to specify the number of processes. For instance:

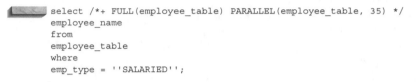

```
select /*+ FULL(employee_table) PARALLEL(employee_table, 35) */
employee_name
from
employee_table
where
emp_type = ''SALARIED'';
```

If you are using an SMP or MPP database server with many CPUs, you can issue a parallel request and leave it up to each Oracle instance to use its default degree of parallelism. For example:

```
select /*+ FULL(employee_table) PARALLEL(employee_table, DEFAULT, DEFAULT) */
employee_name
from
employee_table
where
emp_type = ''SALARIED'';
```

In most cases, it is better for the Oracle DBA to determine the optimal degree of parallelism and then set that degree in the data dictionary with the following command:

```
Alter table employee_table parallel degree 35;
```

This way, the DBA can always be sure of the degree of parallelism for any particular table.

Oracle also provides the *parallel_automatic_tuning init.ora* parameter to assist in setting the best degree of parallelism. When setting *parallel_automatic_tuning*, you only need to specify parallelism for a table, and Oracle will dynamically change the *parallel_adaptive_multi_user* parameter to override the execution plan in favor of maintaining an acceptable overall load on the database. You should also note that setting *parallel_automatic_tuning* will cause extra storage in the large pool because Oracle will allocate message buffers from the large pool instead of the shared pool.

Now let's move on to look at how the Oracle DBA can query the behavior of parallel queries.

Monitoring Oracle Parallel Query

There are several STATSPACK tables and v$ views that can be used to monitor the activity of the Parallel Query background processes. Unfortunately, Parallel Query activity is only measured at the database level, and you cannot find the specific tables that are the target of the Parallel Query. Let's begin by looking at STATSPACK methods for measuring Parallel Query activity.

Monitoring Oracle Parallel Query with STATSPACK

You can query the stats$sysstat table to extract the number of parallelized queries that have been run during each time period between your STATSPACK snapshots.

rpt_parallel.sql

```
set pages 9999;

column nbr_pq format 999,999,999
column mydate heading 'yr.  mo dy Hr.'

select
   to_char(snap_time,'yyyy-mm-dd HH24')        mydate,
   new.value
from
   perfstat.stats$sysstat    old,
   perfstat.stats$sysstat    new,
   perfstat.stats$snapshot   sn
where
   new.name = old.name
and
   new.name = 'queries parallelized'
and
   new.snap_id = sn.snap_id
and
   old.snap_id = sn.snap_id-1
and
   new.value > 1
order by
   to_char(snap_time,'yyyy-mm-dd HH24')
;
```

Here is a sample of the output. This will quickly show the DBA the time periods when full table scans are being invoked.

```
SQL> @rpt_parallel

TO_CHAR(SNAP_ nbr_pq
------------- -------------
2001-03-12 20        3,521
2001-03-12 21        2,082
2001-03-12 22        2,832
2001-03-13 20        5,152
2001-03-13 21        1,835
```

```
2001-03-13 22        2,623
2001-03-14 20        4,274
2001-03-14 21        1,429
2001-03-14 22        2,313
```

In this example we see that there appears to be a period each day between 8:00 P.M. and 10:00 P.M. when tasks are executing parallel queries against tables.

Monitoring Oracle Parallel Query with v$ Views

To see how many Parallel Query servers are busy at any given time, the following query can be issued against the v$pq_sysstat table:

```
select
    statistic,
    value
from
    v$pq_sysstat
where
    statistic = 'Servers Busy';

STATISTIC        VALUE
---------        -----
Servers Busy     30
```

In this case, we see that 30 parallel servers are busy at this moment. Do not be misled by this number. Parallel Query servers are constantly accepting work or returning to idle status, so it is a good idea to issue the query many times over a one-hour period to get an accurate reading of Parallel Query activity. Only then will you receive a realistic measure of how many Parallel Query servers are being used.

This is one other method for observing Parallel Query from inside Oracle. If you are running Oracle on UNIX, you can use the **ps** command to see the Parallel Query background processes in action:

```
ps -ef|grep "ora_p"
```

Parallel Queries and Distributed Objects

Oracle Parallel Query can be simulated when using Net8 to perform remote queries. These types of parallel queries are most useful in distributed databases where a single logical table has been partitioned into smaller tables at each remote node. For example, a customer table that is ordered by customer name may be partitioned into a customer table at each remote database, such that we have a new_york_employee table, a california_employee table, and so on. This vertical table partitioning approach is very common with distributed databases where local autonomy of processing is important.

With the tables partitioned onto different databases at different geographical locations, how can we meet the needs of the corporate headquarters where a complete view is required? How can they query all of these remote tables as a single unit and treat the logical customer table as a single entity? For large queries that may span many logical tables, the isolated tables can then easily be reassembled to use Oracle's Parallel Query facility.

```
create view all_employee as
select * from new_york_employee@manhattan
UNION ALL
select * from california_employee@los_angeles
UNION ALL
select * from japan_employee@tokyo
```

We can now query the all_employee view as if it were a single database table, and Oracle will automatically recognize the *union all* SQL command syntax and fire off simultaneous queries against each of the three base tables. It is important to note that the distributed database manager will direct that each query is processed at the remote location, while the Query Manager waits until each remote node has returned its result set. For example, the following query will assemble the requested data from the three tables in parallel, with each query being separately optimized. The result set from each subquery is then merged by the Query Manager.

```
select
    employee_name
from
    all_employee
where
    salary > 500000;
```

Next, let's look at a method for identifying candidate tables for Oracle Parallel Query.

Finding Candidate Tables for Oracle Parallel Query

The first step in implementing parallelism for your database is to locate those large tables that experience frequent full table scans. Using the *access.sql* script from

Chapter 11, we can begin by observing the full table scan report that was produced by analyzing all of the SQL that was in the library cache:

```
Mon Jan 29                                                         page    1
                       full table scans and counts
              Note that "C" indicates in the table is cached.

OWNER           NAME                    NUM_ROWS C K    BLOCKS  NBR_FTS
-------------   ----------------------  -------- - - --------  --------
SYS             DUAL                             N              2   97,237
EMPDB1          PAGE                   3,450,209 N        932,120    9,999
EMPDB1          RWU_PAGE                     434 N              8    7,355
EMPDB1          PAGE_IMAGE                18,067 N          1,104    5,368
EMPDB1          SUBSCRIPTION                 476 N   K        192    2,087
EMPDB1          PRINT_PAGE_RANGE              10 N   K         32      874
ARSD            JANET_BOOKS                   20 N              8       64
PERFSTAT        STATS$TAB_STATS                N              65       10
```

In this report we see several huge tables that are performing full table scans. For tables that have less than 200 blocks and are doing legitimate full table scans, we will want to place these in the KEEP pool. The larger-table full table scans should also be investigated, and the legitimate large-table full table scans should be parallelized with the **alter table parallel degree nn** command.

CAUTION
The DBA should always investigate large-table full table scans to ensure that they require more than 40 percent of the table rows before implementing Parallel Query on the tables. For details on investigating large-table full table scans, see Chapter 11.

After we have ensured that the tables are legitimate large-table full table scans, we can run a script to generate the parallelization syntax. After running *access_parallel_syntax.sql*, we can extract and execute the syntax. Note that the script here references the sqltemp table that was created by running *access.sql* as the schema owner. From this table, we choose to generate parallelization syntax for all tables that have more than 1,000 blocks and are currently set to **parallel degree 1**.

access_parallel_syntax.sql

```
select
    'alter table '||p.owner||'.'||p.name||' parallel degree 11;'
```

```
from
   dba tables t,
   dba_segments s,
   sqltemp s,
   (select distinct
      statement_id stid,
      object_owner owner,
      object_name name
   from
      plan_table
   where
      operation = 'TABLE ACCESS'
      and
      options = 'FULL') p
where
   s.addr||':'||TO_CHAR(s.hashval) = p.stid
   and
   t.table_name = s.segment_name
   and
   t.table_name = p.name
   and
   t.owner = p.owner
   and
   t.degree = 1
having
   s.blocks > 1000
group by
   p.owner, p.name, t.num_rows, s.blocks
order by
   sum(s.executions) desc;
```

Here is the output from this script. Note that we should manually set the degree of parallelism before running this output in SQL*Plus.

```
SQL> @access_parallel_syntax

alter table EMPDB1.PAGE parallel degree 11;
alter table EMPDB1.PAGE_IMAGE parallel degree 11;
```

Remember, it is not a great problem if the wrong table is marked for Parallel Query. Oracle Parallel Query only works when a full table scan is invoked, so a table that never has full table scans would remain unaffected by Oracle Parallel Query.

Next, let's move on and look at Oracle Parallel DML commands and see how they can help the Oracle DBA improve the speed of database maintenance activities.

Using Parallel DML

Starting with Oracle version 7.2, Oracle introduced parallel **create table as select**, parallel query, parallel index building, and parallel **update**, **insert**, and **delete** functionality. Oracle Parallel DML is used exclusively by the Oracle DBA to improve the speed of database maintenance. As we recall, DML is short for Data Manipulation Language, and DML is normally associated with DBA commands such as **create table**. Here is a list of supported parallel operations.

- Parallel execution of **select** statements
- **create table as select** (CTAS), **alter table**
- **create cluster**, **alter cluster**
- **create index**
- Subqueries in all **update**, **insert**, and **delete** SQL statements

In Oracle8, we see the following additions to parallelism:

- Parallel **insert** (subselect) on partitioned and nonpartitioned tables
- Parallel delete on partitioned tables
- Parallel **update** on partitioned tables
- Parallel **select** using rowid

Turning On Parallel DML

Unlike Oracle Parallel Query, there is no *init.ora* parameter associated with enabling Parallel DML. Parallel DML is only enabled at the session level, and a commit or rollback must be executed prior to enabling a session for Parallel DML.

```
SVRMGRL> ALTER SESSION ENABLE PARALLEL DML;
```

Note that there is no mention of DEGREE in this syntax. When you specify **alter session force parallel DML**, it will use a default level of parallelism unless specified in the hint. Using the default means that the parallelization will be determined by the relevant *init.ora* parameters.

NOTE
Any tables and indexes must have partitions and multiple freelists in order to use Parallel DML. Without multiple freelists, the Parallel DML will "hang" waiting on the segment header, and there will be no improvement in performance.

Parallel DML can be used to speed up **insert**, **update**, and **delete** operations against large database objects. These DML operations are especially useful in a data warehouse environment where tables and indexes tend to be very large. An

update or **delete** statement can be parallelized only on partitioned tables. It is not possible to parallelize these functions on a nonpartitioned table. Once Parallel DML is enabled, an **update** or **delete** statement can be parallelized by setting the table with DEGREE>1 or by using a PARALLEL hint in the statement.

Next, let's look at how Parallel DML can be used by the DBA to speed up table reorganizations.

Parallelizing Oracle Table Reorganizations

You can use parallel **create table as select (PCTAS)** to dramatically reduce the time that it takes to reorganize an Oracle table. For example, in the next listing we create a table with a default PARALLEL option. This directs Oracle to invoke four parallel processes to copy the customer table to new_customer. Also, note the ORDER BY clause, whereby the customer rows are resequenced in the same order as the primary-key index after retrieval of the rows.

```
create table new_customer

tablespace customer_flip
    storage (initial         500m
             next            50m
             maxextents      unlimited
             )
parallel (degree 23)
as
select *
from
    owner.customer
order by
    customer_last_name
;
```

When reorganizing very large tables, parallelization of the full table scan can greatly reduce the overall time required to clean up the table. Next let's look at parallel index rebuilding.

Parallel Index Rebuilding

In Oracle, the **create index** command invokes a full table scan of the target table, so it is appropriate to incorporate parallelism when creating a large index. In the example here, the primary-key index for the customer table is being created with 23 parallel processes, each reading a slice of the table. In this example, we know in advance that the server has 24 CPUs and that the customer table resides in 23 partitions.

```
create index /* parallel 23 */
    customer_key_idx
on owner.customer
```

```
        (""customer_last_name"")
 TABLESPACE
    customer_flip
STORAGE (
    INITIAL 3656K
    NEXT 640K
    MAXEXTENTS UNLIMITED
    FREELISTS 80
    )
;
```

CAUTION
*Whenever parallel sorting is invoked, the DBA
needs to be especially careful about storage within
the TEMP tablespace. As parallel sorts are involved
with operations such as parallel index creation, a
work area will be assigned for each Parallel Query
slave according to the value for the initial extent in
the TEMP tablespace.*

As we discussed in Chapter 10, we can use the **rebuild index** command to
clean up deleted leaf nodes and rebalance a B-tree index. The **alter index rebuild**
command can easily be parallelized, and in this example 23 processes are being
dedicated to rebuilding the index:

```
alter index
    emp_last_name_idx
rebuild
parallel 23
tablespace
    emp_idx
unrecoverable;
```

Also note that the index is being built *unrecoverable*, thereby bypassing the overhead of writing to the redo logs. This is a very common practice in large databases since it is nearly double the speed of a traditional index rebuild. Of course, since the index images are not recorded, you must remember to re-create these indexes following a roll-forward recovery operation.

Conclusion

Now we should have a firm understanding of the role of parallelism within an Oracle database. We are now ready to move on to look at a more sophisticated type of parallelism, whereby many Oracle instances share a single database. This is called Oracle Parallel Server prior to Oracle9i, and it is called Real Application Clusters in Oracle9i and beyond.

CHAPTER
13

Tuning the Oracle
Parallel Server
Environment

his chapter is devoted to tuning issues with Oracle Parallel Server (OPS). This product has been renamed the Real Applications Clusters (RAC) product in Oracle9i, but we will focus on OPS. Tuning the OPS environment is fundamentally the same as tuning any other Oracle database, but with some important exceptions. To understand the differences between tuning a Parallel Server environment and tuning a standard Oracle environment, we need to do a very brief review of the concept surrounding the Oracle Parallel Server product.

Introduction to Oracle Parallel Server Architecture

The central concept behind Oracle Parallel Server is that a single database can have many database instances accessing the database at the same point in time, as shown in Figure 13-1.

The advantage of having many instances share the same database should be obvious to anyone who has ever performed Oracle tuning. Without OPS, each database instance has only one SGA region, and this SGA region services the whole database, with no sharing of the Oracle data buffers, shared pool, and library cache. By isolating these shared pool and data buffer cache components into separate instances, you can get tremendous increases in performance because many independent instances share the same centralized database.

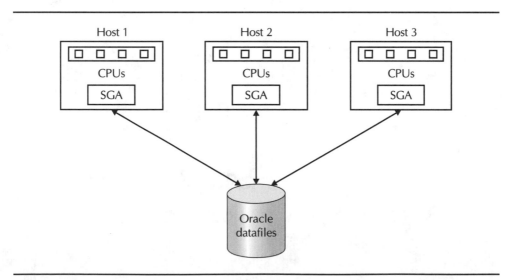

FIGURE 13-1. *An Oracle Parallel Server (OPS) architecture*

Oracle Parallel Server was designed to run on symmetric multiprocessors (SMP) or massively parallel processors (MPP). In an SMP or MPP environment, many central processing units are connected with high-speed links.

With Oracle Parallel Server, several Oracle instances run within different RAM memory, and each independent instance shares access to the same Oracle tables. Within the Oracle Parallel Server, this is called the *shared-nothing parallel server configuration*.

There is a great deal of confusion about the difference between Oracle's Parallel Server and Oracle Parallel Query. While Oracle's Parallel Query can be used with any computer configuration, including stand-alone processors, SMP, or MPP servers, Oracle's Parallel Server can only be used on MPP systems.

The MPP architecture links many processors together, while each server maintains independence. Each MPP server has its own memory and processors, but shares a common disk resource. As such, SMP is sometimes called shared memory multiprocessing and MPP is called shared-nothing multiprocessing.

Oracle Parallel Server only works with MPP, because each node on the MPP box requires its own memory area for the Oracle SGA.

In Parallel Server, careful consideration must be given to the uses of parallelism, because the resulting system could often perform slower than a single-node system. For example, in Parallel Server, the integrated distributed lock manager (IDLM) may force the Oracle database writer to write transactions to the database more frequently than a stand-alone Oracle database.

When planning for Parallel Server tasks, it is important to segregate specific types of tasks to specific nodes, as shown in Figure 13.2. For example, common update routines against customer rows could be segregated onto node 1, while queries against order rows could be segregated onto node 2. Because each Oracle instance has its own complete SGA, a full table scan on one node will not flush any data out of the buffer pool of another node.

Of course, it is not always possible to segregate all data into separate buffer pools, especially with a highly denormalized data warehouse. The Oracle designer will be able to partition the Oracle instances such that similar data queries are launched from the same instance, thereby improving the probability that the data will be waiting in the buffer.

NOTE
It is possible to run Oracle Parallel Query on an Oracle Parallel Server system. In this case, the MPP system would allocate the subqueries evenly across the nodes, and the Concurrency Manager would coordinate the receipt of data from each subquery. Of course, this type of parallel query would run faster than a parallel query on an SMP box because the MPP box has isolated buffer pools. With SMP, the concurrent queries read their data into a common buffer pool.

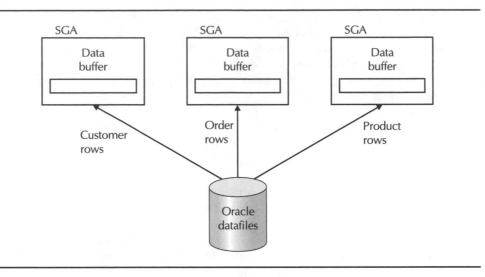

FIGURE 13-2. *Partitioning data on an OPS database*

Unlike an ordinary Oracle database, the disk devices for an OPS environment must be configured such that many separate instances can read from the datafiles that comprise the database. This involves the allocation of *raw* devices. As you may know from your introduction to Oracle tuning, raw devices can be faster in terms of data access because they bypass the Journal File System (JFS) buffer cache in UNIX. However, raw devices are much more difficult to maintain than traditional Oracle files.

Partitioning Data for OPS

The real power of Oracle Parallel Server centers on its ability to allow many instances to share a common database. However, it's important to recognize that Oracle Parallel Server is not good for all systems. In environments where each one of the separate instances may share the same data rows, the excessive overhead in transferring common blocks between instances (called pinging) can negate any performance benefit of OPS.

In short, Oracle Parallel Server is most effective for applications where each instance can have its own control over the majority of the data that is read by that instance. In a sense, each instance is functioning as a separate data buffer cache for different data blocks.

In fact, many organizations that first implemented Oracle Parallel Server and later find out that they have a highly shared data environment will commonly migrate back to a regular Oracle database to reduce the overhead from the IDLM and enjoy even better performance than using OPS.

For example, if we have different classes of end users in our retail organization, we can direct each one of the end users to separate instances, thereby isolating the data to the specific instances. We may have an order entry department that is primarily concerned with the order table in the database. Hence, all of the order records will wind up being cached in the instance to which the end users are directed. Along the same lines, those end users concerned primarily with customer transactions would wind up caching all of the customer data blocks within its own instances data buffers. Again, to continue the example, an area of the organization dealing primarily with products would access the product table in their own separate database instance, thereby providing a level of isolation between the database as a whole and the component tables that are cached within each instance.

It is in these kinds of systems where Oracle can ensure that there is a minimum of pinging that will benefit the most from Oracle Parallel Server environment. However, there are other reasons that people adopt Oracle Parallel Server. Oracle Parallel Server has a very easy method of failover, whereby a failure of one instance (usually a failure in the background processes or the SGA) will not bring the entire system to a standstill. Rather, OPS has facilities that will allow people to be instantly reconnected to one of the remaining live databases and immediately begin caching their data records in the new SGA.

In summary, we see that there are several important distinctions between a standard Oracle database and the Oracle Parallel Server environment:

- All of the instances are sharing a single disk database, and raw partitions must be used on the disk in order to allow the sharing of data between multiple instances.

- Each object within the Oracle Parallel Server environment must be defined with multiple freelist groups. The separate freelist group should be assigned for each and every instance planning on accessing the individual table.

Next, let's look at the core of an OPS system, the Integrated Distributed Lock Manager, or IDLM.

The Integrated Distributed Lock Manager

Many OPS novices are confused by the functions of the Integrated Distributed Lock Manager (IDLM). In Oracle Parallel Server, the limitation of one instance to one database has been lifted, but all of the Oracle instances' SGAs are not running in the same shared memory region. The purpose of the IDLM is to provide locking between instances and to transfer data blocks between multiple data buffers since the data buffers are not shared between the instances.

You can tell if a database is running the IDLM by checking for the LCK process. Just as the RECO process indicates that distributed transactions are enabled, the presence of a LCK background process indicates that the IDLM is active. Traditional distributed systems do not have an IDLM because they are not sharing the same database.

Because you may have many Oracle instances accessing a common database, Oracle has had to come up with a method whereby blocks can be shared between the database instances. In a standard Oracle system, Oracle will always check the data block buffers before doing any I/O against the disk, and in an OPS environment Oracle will first check to see if any of the instances have the desired record within the data buffer.

If OPS discovers that another instance has a data block that is requested by another instance, the Integrated Distributed Lock Manager will ping the other server and transfer the data block memory from one instance to the other, as shown Figure 13-3.

The overhead of the IDLM can often take as many resources as a single database instance, and in databases where there is a high degree of sharing of data blocks between instances, the IDLM pinging can more than outweigh any performance benefit that would be gained by using Oracle Parallel Server.

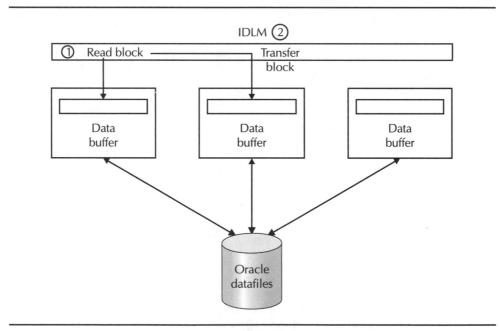

FIGURE 13-3. *Pinging a block within an OPS database*

Before we look at tuning and monitoring OPS, let's take a close look at the proper table storage parameters that are required for OPS.

Configuring the IDLM Within OPS Environment

The configuration of the IDLM and the minimization of pinging are the most important concepts that you need when tuning in OPS database. Just like the Oracle database has initialization parameters, the IDLM also has a configuration file that contains parameters that govern its behavior. This is an example of a configuration file in the OPS system:

$ORACLE_SID.config

```
node_list = "19,23,34,66"
listener_node_list="19,23, 34, 66"
listener_name_list="L_1, L_2, L_3, L_4"
oracle_sid_list="HOME_1, HOME_2, HOME_3, HOME_4"
oracle_home = "/oracle/HOME"

1:oraclesid = "HOME_01"
2:oraclesid = "HOME_02"
3:oraclesid = "HOME_03"
4:oraclesid = "HOME_04"

1:lsnr_name = "L_1"
2:lsnr_name = "L_2"
3:lsnr_name = "L_3"
4:lsnr_name = "L_4"

1:init_ora = "/oracle/HOME/dbs/initHOME_1.ora"
2:init_ora = "/oracle/HOME/dbs/initHOME_2.ora"
3:init_ora = "/oracle/HOME/dbs/initHOME_3.ora"
4:init_ora = "/oracle/HOME/dbs/initHOME_4.ora"

svrmgr_path = "/oracle/HOME/bin/svrmgrl"

# Lock Manager information
lkmgr_env  = "LKPORT-1566; LKMGR_LOG=/oracle/HOME/ops/dlmlog"
lkmgr_args = "-f n -l 237073 -r 236381 -p 800"
```

The top section of the OPS configuration file is quite straightforward, defining the Oracle databases and all the listeners that will be sharing the database. The important information begins at the start of the Lock Manager parameters. As we discussed earlier in this chapter, the IDLM's primary job is to share data buffer blocks between the multiple instances. In order to control the transfer of these data blocks between the separate regions in SGA memory, the IDLM must be able to lock, transfer, and release data blocks in an efficient manner. Again, minimizing pinging is one of the most important jobs of the person tuning the OPS system.

Let's take a look in detail at these Lock Manager parameters. The *lkmgr_args* parameter is the one that has the most impact upon the Oracle database. Here we see several flags:

- **-f (fault-tolerant mode)**   This tells the OPS system whether the database will be run in a fault-tolerant mode. In a fault-tolerant mode, the databases will continue to run even if a single instance crashes, and automatic failover will occur for any client connections that were originally directed to the failed database.

- **-l (number of locks)**   This is the total number of lock buckets to be reserved by the IDLM in order to hold block addresses.

- **-r (number of resources)**   This is the number of resources that will be used by the IDLM.

- **-p (number of processes)**   The number of processes parameter directs the number of processes that can be allocated by the IDLM when performing pinging operations.

In summary, these lock manager arguments determine the overall configuration for the IDLM and, most importantly, the overall performance of the OPS systems.

In addition to the standard initialization files in *init.ora*, there's an ancillary file to the *init.ora* when using Oracle Parallel Server. This ancillary file is called *ocommon.ora*, and this file contains all of the global parameters that are required by the IDLM.

ocommon.ora

```
#### ORACLE OPS PARAMETER

max_commit_propagation_delay = 0

#### ORACLE OPS TUNING PARAMETER
#
# parameter for dba locking:
#
_enable_dba_locking     = true
gc_db_locks             = 0
gc_freelist_groups      = 0
gc_releasable_locks     = 60000
```

```
gc_rollback_locks       = 0
gc_rollback_seqments    = 256
gc_save_rollback_locks  = 0
gc_seqments             = 0
gc_tablespaces          = 0
gc_lck_procs            = 6


#### ORACLE DATABASE ADMINISTRATION PARAMETER
#
remote_login_passwordfile = exclusive
```

Next, let's look at how the standard storage parameters for tables and indexes are altered when we run an OPS database.

Oracle Table Settings for OPS

It is vital to the performance of an OPS database that the DBA properly understand and define the multiple freelist groups that are required by OPS. With Oracle Parallel Server, internal segment header structures become even more complex. Oracle provides an additional OPS table parameter called *freelist_groups*. With multiple freelist groups, extra segment header blocks are defined, one for each freelist group that is defined for the table. For example, assume the following table definition:

```
CREATE TABLE
    CUSTOMER ( . . . )
STORAGE (
  . . .
FREELISTS 5
FREELIST GROUPS 20);
```

Here we see an OPS table defined with 20 freelist groups, meaning that the OPS architecture has 20 instances accessing a single database. Within each freelist group, we see five freelists, indicating that up to five concurrent tasks may be inserting, updating, or deleting rows from this table.

Returning to our example, when the customer table is allocated, Oracle will reserve 20 blocks at the front of the table for space management purposes. Oracle allocates block 1 for the segment header, block 2 for freelist group 1, block 3 for freelist group 2, and so on.

You must define one freelist group for each instance that will be connecting to the database, and enough freelists within each group to support the high-water mark for updates and inserts. However, multiple freelist groups also have a problem relating to the reuse of space within the freelists for the tables and indexes. Because each freelist group is an isolated entity, Oracle is not able to share freelists between the Oracle instances.

Remember, each one of the OPS instances attaches to a separate freelist group, and free blocks are allocated independently of one another within these freelist groups.

Most DBAs begin to run into a problem in the Oracle Parallel Server environment when standard purge routines are executed. In most large OPS environments, it's not uncommon to periodically run purges of transaction information. One of the most common mistakes seen in OPS environments is where the purge routines are run from only one of the instances. When the purge routines are run from only a single instance in an OPS configuration, only that freelist group will receive the empty blocks. The other freelist groups for the table will not get these blocks, and consequently will not be able to access these free blocks to use for later inserts into the database.

This is the same kind of sparse table phenomenon that we discussed in Chapter 10. Again, the remedy for the sparse table phenomenon is to make sure that you parallelize all of your deletes to the same degree for which you have parallelized any **insert** or **update** statements. In other words, if you have three instances doing inserts into the customer table, the customer purge routines should be parallelized so that one-third of the purge runs on each one of the three instances. This will keep the freelists in balance, and will avoid having a largely empty table extending unnecessarily into new free space.

Now, let's take a closer look at the Oracle segment header, as shown in Figure 13-4.

In an Oracle Parallel Server environment with multiple freelist groups, there are three types of freelists in each segment header:

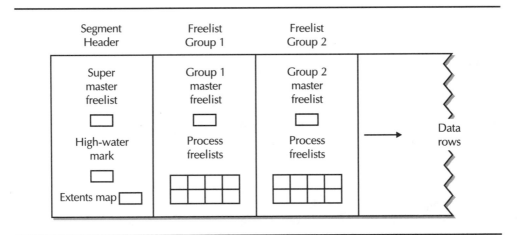

FIGURE 13-4.   *Segment header details for an OPS table with two freelist groups*

- **The master freelist** (aka the common pool)   The master freelist exists for all Oracle segments and resides in the segment header in the first block of the table. With OPS, you have a super master freelist on block 1 of the segment in addition to the master freelists that are dedicated to each freelist group.

- **The process freelist** (aka multiple freelists)   The process freelist is enabled by using the *freelist* parameter in the STORAGE clause when creating the table or index. A process freelist will acquire blocks in two ways. A process freelist can get blocks when a **row delete** occurs, or when a **freelist merge** occurs. A **freelist merge** is a process whereby Oracle moves blocks from the master freelist to the process freelist, usually in chunks of five blocks. If the *freelist_groups* parameter is not used, the process freelist will exist in the segment block header for the table, right next to the master freelist. As you know, multiple process freelists can be defined whenever concurrent updates are expected against the table. Process freelists greatly help reduce contention for freelists in a non-OPS environment, since each **update** process may read its own freelist. The downside is that each freelist exists independently of the other freelists, and blocks that appear on one freelist are not shared with the other freelists.

- **The transaction freelist** (not shown)   The transaction freelist is used by an in-flight program, which performs **delete** or **insert** operations. Unlike the master and process freelists, transaction freelists are allocated in the segment header on an as-needed basis. If there is no room in the segment header for the transaction freelist, the task will wait and incur a "wait on segment header." After the task has ended or committed, the entries are transferred from the transaction freelist to the process freelist in a FIFO manner, with the most recently freed blocks being added to the head of the freelist chain.

While having multiple freelists minimizes contention in regular databases, with OPS a freelist group is used to minimize contention for space within a shared table that is being updated by multiple instances.

As of Oracle OPS release 7.3 and beyond, it is possible to allocate table extents that are "dedicated" to a specific instance. Oracle8 gives you more control over free space if you specifically allocate extents to instances, and it has the side benefit of reducing contention for resources. Consider the following example where we allocate a data file for the exclusive use of instance 10:

```
alter table
    customer
allocate extents
    (size 100m datafile '/oracle/filename' instance 10);
```

Here we see that the customer table has increased by 100MB, and this additional space is exclusively dedicated to instance number ten. Automatic table extension will never dedicate rows to an instance, and the space will go onto the master freelist.

Next, let's get deeper and look at how the OPS environment is tuned.

Tuning the OPS Environment

In a sense, we can think of the shared-nothing configuration as having numerous independent Oracle instances, and we can expect to tune each instance as if it were an independent entity. However, we must always bear in mind that each Oracle instance is competing for the same data block resources. This competition is directly measured by the IDLM.

Oracle Parallel Server only achieves a high degree of parallelism when careful planning has partitioned the tasks onto each instance in such a way that no two instances are constantly competing for data resources. If we find evidence that two Oracle instances are frequently accessing the same data blocks, the first remedy is to move common tasks into the same instance, where they can share the same buffer cache, and eliminate calls to the IDLM.

Indeed, tuning of the Parallel Server is all about IDLM lock contention. Our goal should be to independently tune each Oracle instance and to keep a careful eye on how these instances interact with each other to manage internode locks. As IDLM lock contention is identified, we have numerous options, including repartitioning the application to move tasks to other instances, adding multiple freelists to frequently accessed blocks, or using table replication techniques to alleviate I/O contention.

Here is a very simple monitoring approach to the tuning of an OPS database:

- **Monitor for multiple tasks that modify rows on the same block** When multiple tasks contend for the updating of rows on the same data block, adding freelists or freelist groups may relieve the bottleneck.

- **Monitor the IDLM for lock conversions** If the maximum lock convert rate for your IDLM has been reached, you will need to repartition the application to balance "alike" transactions into common instances.

- **Monitor statistics independently for each Oracle instance** The goal should be to minimize physical I/O by tuning the buffer cache and providing input into an overall load plan. For example, if we discover one instance is heavily loaded when compared to other instances, we can take a look at the partitioning of tasks and rebalance the load by moving tasks onto other instances.

- **Monitor each instance's buffer cache, looking for common data blocks** If the same data blocks show up in multiple buffer caches, move one of the tasks into a common Oracle instance. Remember, the idea of tuning Parallel Server is to segregate common tasks into common instances.

- **Monitor the TEMP tablespace usage within each instance** In OPS, each instance performs its own sorting, but all instances share a common TEMP tablespace. In other words, memory sorts are performed within each instance's *sort_area_size* in RAM, but all disk sorts are performed in the common TEMP tablespace.

It should be apparent that the inherent complexity of parallel processing makes it very difficult to come up with generic tuning techniques. Every parallel system is unique, and the Oracle professional must analyze each system carefully, considering its unique structure and behavior.

As we continue to discuss OPS tuning, let's begin our discussion of tools for monitoring the behavior of the OPS database.

STATSPACK Tables for Monitoring OPS

The STATSPACK utility provides several tables for tracking OPS activity. These tables can be used to provide an instance-wide reporting architecture for Oracle Parallel Server. These are the main STATSPACK tables for OPS. Let's begin by looking at their contents before we look at the reports:

- **stats$sysstat** This table contains numerous global parameters that relate to the behavior of OPS.

- **stats$rowcache_summary** This table shows IDLM activity detail for each instance.

- **stats$sgaxs** This table provides summary information for each instance in the OPS architecture.

The stats$rowcache_summary Table

In addition to information about row cache information within an instance, the stats$rowcache_summary table contains several columns that relate directly to the OPS IDLM:

```
SQL> desc stats$rowcache_summary;
 Name                                      Null?    Type
 ----------------------------------------- -------- ----------------------
 SNAP_ID                                   NOT NULL NUMBER(6)
 DBID                                      NOT NULL NUMBER
 INSTANCE_NUMBER                           NOT NULL NUMBER
 PARAMETER                                 NOT NULL VARCHAR2(32)
 TOTAL_USAGE                                        NUMBER
 USAGE                                              NUMBER
```

```
GETS                                    NUMBER
GETMISSES                               NUMBER
SCANS                                   NUMBER
SCANMISSES                              NUMBER
SCANCOMPLETES                           NUMBER
MODIFICATIONS                           NUMBER
FLUSHES                                 NUMBER
DLM_REQUESTS                            NUMBER
DLM_CONFLICTS                           NUMBER
DLM_RELEASES                            NUMBER
```

This table contains useful information about the internal operations of the DLM. Especially useful is the column dlm_conflicts, which is related to internal bottlenecks within the IDLM.

The stats$sgaxs Table

The stats$sgaxs table contains basic information about each instance in an OPS environment. This is largely a summary table and it does not contain detailed OPS information.

```
SQL> desc stats$sgaxs;
 Name                                     Null?     Type
 ---------------------------------------- -------- ----------------------
 SNAP_ID                                  NOT NULL NUMBER(6)
 DBID                                     NOT NULL NUMBER
 INSTANCE_NUMBER                          NOT NULL NUMBER
 STARTUP_TIME                             NOT NULL DATE
 PARALLEL                                 NOT NULL VARCHAR2(3)
 NAME                                     NOT NULL VARCHAR2(64)
 VERSION                                           VARCHAR2(17)
 VALUE                                             NUMBER
```

The stats$sysstat Table

The stats$sysstat also contains columns that are of interest when tuning OPS. Just like its cousin the v$sysstat table, there are global statistics that relate to the behavior of OPS.

```
SQL> Select distinct name from stats$sysstat where name like 'global%';
global cache blocks corrupt
global cache convert time
global cache convert timeouts
global cache converts
global cache cr block log flush time
global cache cr block log flushes
global cache cr block receive time
global cache cr block send time
```

```
global cache cr block serve time
global cache cr blocks received
global cache cr blocks served
global cache cr requests blocked
global cache cr timeouts
global cache defers
global cache freelist waits
global cache get time
global cache gets
global cache prepare failures
global lock async converts
global lock async gets
global lock convert time
global lock get time
global lock releases
global lock sync converts
global lock sync gets
```

The stats$sysstat STATSPACK table can be used to determine whether lock converts are being performed too often. Excessive lock convert rates usually mean there is contention for a common resource within the database. This resource may be a commonly updated table. For example, inventory management systems often utilize one-of-a kind (OOAK) rows. An OOAK row may be used to keep the order number of the last order, and all application tasks must increment this row when a new order is placed. This type of architecture forces each parallel instance to single-thread all requests for this resource. But how do we identify these types of database resources?

Just as the buffer hit ratio measures contention for data blocks, the lock hit ratio can be used to identify excessive lock conversion by the IDLM. The lock hit ratio should generally be above 90 percent, and if it falls below 90 percent, you should look for sources of data contention. Here is the SQL to determine the lock hit ratio for Oracle Parallel Server:

rpt_idlm.sql

```
column mydate                    heading 'Yr. Mo Dy  Hr.' format a16
column idlm_lock_hit_ratio                         format 999,999,999

select
to_char(snap_time,'yyyy-mm-dd HH24')   mydate,
(a.value - b.value)/(a.value)          idlm_lock_hit_ratio
from
    stats$sysstat     a,
    stats$sysstat     b,
    stats$snapshot    sn
where
    a.name = 'consistent gets'
```

```
and
   b.name = 'global lock converts (async)'
and
   a.snap_id = sn.snap_id
and
   b.snap_id = sn.snap_id
order by
   to_char(snap_time,'yyyy-mm-dd HH24')
;
```

Now that we see the regular STATSPACK tables that capture performance information, let's look at an easy way to extend STATSPACK by including a table to track IDLM behavior.

Extending STATSPACK for OPS Information

Once the IDLM is running, you can run the **lkdump** command to determine the values of IDLM resources and locks, as well as overall IDLM processes. Checking these values is a very critical activity because these values cannot exceed the values defined in your IDLM configuration file. If any one of these values exceeds the value in the configuration file, the IDLM will hang, causing your entire OPS system to lock up.

It is very important to keep track of the high-water mark for these IDLM values. The following script will get the existing initial values for locks, resources, and programs from your *conf* file and compare these values to the maximum values from your Oracle IDLM statistics table. It is a good idea to run this script at least once per day to ensure that the Oracle database does not hang.

Here is the code to create a STATSPACK extension table to hold the IDLM information.

create_idlm_table.sql

```
connect perfstat/perfstat;

drop table perfstat.stats$idlm_stats;

create table perfstat.stats$idlm_stats
(
   snap_time       date,
   pro             number,
   res             number,
   loc             number
)
tablespace perfstat
storage (initial 1m next 1m maxextents unlimited)
;
```

It is always a good idea to keep a running list of these critical IDLM values, and the script here will capture these values and place them into STATSPACK extension tables for later analysis.

get_idlm.ksh

```
# Capture IDLM statistics - 1998 by Donald Keith Burleson
DAY_OF_WEEK=`date +"%A"`
MACHINE_NAME=`hostname`
REPORT_FILE=/oracle/HOME/dba/dlm_monitor.${MACHINE_NAME}.${DAY_OF_WEEK}.log
#
# Set up the file to log the lock to:
#
TIMESTAMP=`date +"%C%y.%m.%d-%H:%M:%S"`
DLM_RESOURCES=`/oracle/HOME/bin/lkdump -a res | head -2 | awk 'getline'`
DLM_LOCKS=`/oracle/HOME/bin/lkdump -a lock | head -2 | awk 'getline' `
DLM_PROCESS=`/oracle/HOME/bin/lkdump -a proc | head -2 | awk 'getline'`
printf "$TIMESTAMP $DLM_RESOURCES $DLM_LOCKS $DLM_PROCESS \n" >>
REPORT_FILE

RES=`echo $DLM_RESOURCES|cut -f2 -d '='`
LOC=`echo $DLM_LOCKS|cut -f2 -d '='`
PRO=`echo $DLM_PROCESS|cut -f2 -d '='`

ORACLE_SID=HOME; export ORACLE_SID;
PATH=$PATH:/oracle/HOME/bin; export PATH;
ORACLE_HOME=/oracle/HOME; export ORACLE_HOME;

/oracle/HOME/bin/sqlplus <<! >> /dev/null

connect perfstat/perfstat;

insert into perfstat.stats$idlm_stats
 values (
   SYSDATE,
   $PRO,
   $RES,
   $LOC );

exit;
!
```

This *get_idlm.ksh* script is normally scheduled to run every five minutes to gather a snapshot of the important IDLM behaviors. Most DBAs place the execution for the script in their UNIX crontab file.

Now that we have defined a table for the IDLM information, we are ready to look at a report from our stats$idlm_stats table. The next script is run against our STATSPACK extension table to report on exceptional conditions within the IDLM.

rpt_idlm_hwm.ksh

```
#! /bin/ksh
# Display high-water mark of IDLM
# Donald K. Burleson
# get the max values . . . .

#grep ^lkmgr_args /oracle/HOME/ops/HOME.conf

MAX_LOC=`grep ^lkmgr_args /oracle/HOME/ops/HOME.conf|cut -f6 -d ' '`
MAX_RES=`grep ^lkmgr_args /oracle/HOME/ops/HOME.conf|cut -f8 -d ' '`
MAX_PRO=`grep ^lkmgr_args /oracle/HOME/ops/HOME.conf|cut -f10 -d ' '|sed -e 's/"//
'`

ORACLE_SID=HOME; export ORACLE_SID;
PATH=$PATH:/oracle/HOME/bin; export PATH;
ORACLE_HOME=/oracle/HOME; export ORACLE_HOME;

unalias rm
rm -f *.tmp

/oracle/HOME/bin/sqlplus <<! > /dev/null

connect perfstat/perfstat;

set newpage 0;
set space 0
set pages 0
set termout off
set feedback off
set echo off
set heading off

spool pro
select max(processes) from perfstat.stats$dlm_stats;
spool res
select max(resources) from perfstat.stats$dlm_stats;
spool loc
select max(locks) from perfstat.stats$dlm_stats;
spool off
exit
!

PRO=`grep '^ ' pro.lst|awk '{print $1}'`
```

```
RES=`grep '^  ' res.lst|awk '{print $1}'`

LOC=`grep '^  ' loc.lst|awk '{print $1}'`

# Now the fun part . . . .

PCT_PRO=`expr $PRO \* 100 \/ $MAX_PRO`
echo "IDLM Process high-water mark is $PRO, or $PCT_PRO percent of max val of
MAX_PRO"

PCT_RES=`expr $RES \* 100 \/ $MAX_RES`
echo "IDLM Resource high-water mark is $RES, or $PCT_RES percent of max val of
MAX_RES"

PCT_LOC=`expr $LOC \* 100 \/ $MAX_LOC`
echo "IDLM Locks high-water mark is $LOC, or $PCT_LOC percent of max val of $MAX_LOC"
```

Again, most DBAs schedule this report to run hourly so they can track changes in
the high-water mark for the IDLM. Next, let's look at the v$ views that can help us
track down OPS locking issues with the IDLM.

Querying the v$ Views for Oracle Parallel Server

Oracle has several v$ views that were created especially for OPS. These views can
be used to tell the DBA the cumulative rate of OPS activity since the instance was
started. Here are the most interesting v$ views for OPS:

- **The v$lock_activity view**   This view is a very good way to determine if
  you have reached the maximum lock convert rate for your IDLM. If the
  maximum lock convert rate has been reached, you will need to repartition
  the application to balance alike transactions into common instances.

- **The v$ping view**   This view tracks the number of IDLM pings that relate
  to this database instance.

The v$ping view is especially useful for showing lock conversions in OPS. Oracle
Parallel Server provides a view called v$ping to show lock conversions. We start
by querying the v$ping view to see if there are any data files experiencing a high
degree on lock conversions, as follows.

ping.sql

```
SELECT
    substr(name,1,10),
    file#,
    class#,
    max(xnc)
FROM
    v$ping
GROUP BY 1, 2, 3
ORDER BY 1, 2, 3;
```

Here is the output from this script. The XNC column is the one that directly relates to lock conversions.

Name	File #	Class #	Max (XNC)
Customer	13	1	556
Customer	13	4	32
Item	6	1	1
Item	3	4	32
Order	16	1	33456

Here, we see that the order table (File 16) may have a problem with excessive lock conversions because of the high value for Max XNC. To further investigate, return to v$ping, and get the sums for File 16, as follows:

```
SELECT
    *
FROM
    v$ping
WHERE
    file#=16
ORDER BY
    block#;
```

Now, we can see additional detail about the contents of File 16, as shown here:

File #	Block #	Stat	XNC	Class #	Name	Kind
16	11	XCUR	5	1	ORDER	Table
16	12	XCUR	33456	1	ORDER	Table
16	13	XCUR	12	1	ORDER	Table

From this output, we can see that block 12 inside File 16 is the source of our contention. The following query against the order table will reveal the contents of the rows in the data block. Remember, data blocks are numbered in hex, so we convert the decimal number 12 to a hexadecimal "C".

```
SELECT
    rowid,
    order_number,
    customer_number
FROM
    ORDER
WHERE
chattorowid(rowid) LIKE '0000000C%';
```

Here we see the results from this query, showing the details for all data rows on this block:

```
ROWID                    ORDER_NUMBER   CUSTOMER_NUMBER
-------------------      ------------   ---------------
0000000C.0000.0008               1212                73
0000000C.0000.0008               1213                73
0000000C.0000.0008               1214                73
```

These results indicate that lock conversion relates to orders placed by customer number 73. Other than a random coincidence, we can assume that there may be freelist contention in the order table as new orders are added to the database. Adding additional freelists will allow more concurrency during SQL **insert** operations, and the value for freelists should be reset to the maximum number of end users who are expected to be inserting an order row at any given time. In Oracle8i, you can issue the following command:

```
alter table
    order
storage
    ( freelists 7 )
;
```

Before Oracle8i, Oracle does not allow the dynamic modification of freelists, because they were physically stored in each data block. So, the only alternative is to drop and re-create the table with more freelists in each block header. Following is the SQL used to drop and re-create the order table:

```
CREATE TABLE
    ORDER_DUMMY
    STORAGE (freelists 10)
AS
SELECT * FROM ORDER;
DROP TABLE ORDER;
RENAME ORDER_DUMMY TO ORDER;
```

Now that we understand the process of using v$ping, let's wrap up and move on to more STATSPACK scripts.

Conclusion

This chapter has been focused on the tuning and monitoring of Oracle Parallel Server. In this chapter we have learned the basic criteria for building an OPS database, and the architectural issues surrounding the use of the IDLM. We are now ready to move on to the final section of this text where we will visit STATSPACK reporting scripts for monitoring virtually every portion of our database.

PART
IV

Database Reporting
with STATSPACK

CHAPTER
14

Monitoring Oracle
with STATSPACK

his chapter is devoted to the various uses of STATSPACK for alerting management to exceptional database conditions. If you have been diligent in creating the STATSPACK extension tables from previous chapters, you should now be able to get reports on virtually every Oracle condition.

We will begin with a review of exception reports that can be used for long-term database performance tuning. Alerts are sometimes called exception reports, and they serve an important role by notifying the DBA to exceptional conditions.

Overview of the Alert Scripts

The scripts presented in the chapter may require customization to meet the requirements of your environment. For example, there are dozens of dialects of UNIX, and dozens of ways to issue UNIX commands. It is recommended that you become familiar with shell programming before attempting to modify any of these scripts.

For example, the command to determine the free space in your database server environment is different in many dialects of UNIX. If you understand shell programming, you can customize the script to handle the differences in dialects. In the following example, we customize the free space command for an Oracle server alert script. Note the use of the $os variable, which is set to the appropriate dialect of UNIX. The script generates the free space commands for IRIX64, AIX, OSF1 and HP/UX.

```
#  This code is because bdf and df -k display free space in different columns
if [ $os = "IRIX64" ]
then
    arch_dir_mp=`${dialect_df} $LOG_ARCHIVE_DEST|grep -v kbytes|awk '{ print $7 }'`
    arch_free_space=`${dialect_df} ${arch_dir_mp}|grep -v kbytes|awk '{ print $3 }'`
fi
if [ $os = "AIX" ]
then
    arch_dir_mp=`${dialect_df} $LOG_ARCHIVE_DEST|grep -v blocks|awk '{ print $7 }'`
    arch_free_space=`${dialect_df} ${arch_dir_mp}|grep -v blocks|awk '{ print $3 }'`
fi
if [ $os = "OSF1" ]
then
    arch_dir_mp=`${dialect_df} $LOG_ARCHIVE_DEST|grep -v blocks|awk '{ print $7 }'`
    arch_free_space=`${dialect_df} ${arch_dir_mp}|grep -v blocks|awk '{ print $3 }'`
fi
if [ $os = "HP-UX" ]
then
    arch_dir_mp=`${dialect_df} $LOG_ARCHIVE_DEST|grep -v kbytes|awk '{ print $6 }'`
    arch_free_space=`${dialect_df} ${arch_dir_mp}|grep -v kbytes|awk '{ print $4 }'`
fi
```

Now, let's explore some of the great information that you can extract from Oracle using these scripts.

Customized Exception Alert Reports for the DBA

There are three categories of reports that are most commonly scheduled by the DBA. Together, these reports give the DBA a complete picture of database activity. Each of these scripts can be located at the Oracle Press Web site at www.oraclepressbooks.com.

This comprehensive set of scripts provides a complete picture of the entire database (see Figure 14-1).

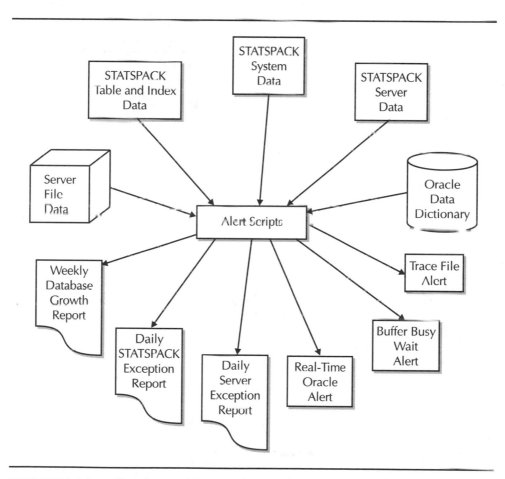

FIGURE 14-1. *The alert architecture for Oracle*

Let's begin by visiting each script and briefly see how it functions.

Daily STATSPACK Alert Report

This STATSPACK alert report is indispensable for any DBA. This script is generally run daily to tell the DBA about any exceptional conditions within their database. There are two script components to this report:

- *statspack_alert.ksh*   This is the Korn shell script to launch and e-mail the report. You can customize this script to send e-mail alerts to anyone within your organization.

- *statspack_alert.sql*   This report uses the standard STATSPACK tables and reports on out-of-bounds conditions. Note that the alert threshold percentages can be adjusted depending on your needs. Most DBAs schedule this report to run every day, and report on the past week. There is a special modified version of this script called *statspack_alert80.sql* for databases that are not on Oracle8i.

To appreciate the value of this report, let's examine the component output from this script.

Hot File Reads Alert

This script reports on files whose reads are greater than (25 percent or 50 percent or 75 percent) of total reads. This code compares the individual I/O for a file from stats$filestatxs with the overall I/O for the period in stats$sysstat. When you find a hot file, you may want to place these files in the KEEP pool or stripe them across multiple disks.

```
*************************************************************
This will identify any single file  with a read I/O
 more than 50% of the total read I/O of the database.

The "hot" file should be examined, and the hot table/index
should be identified using STATSPACK.

- The busy file should be placed on a disk device with
"less busy" files to minimize read delay and channel
contention.

- If small file has a hot small table, place the table
in the KEEP pool

- If the file has a large-table full table scan, place
the table in the RECYCLE pool and turn on parallel query
```

```
for the table.
**************************************************************
```

Yr. Mo Dy Hr.	FILE_NAME	WRITES	PCT OF_TOT
2001-01-05 13	/u04/oradata/temp03.dbf	735,378	38
2001-01-17 16	/u03/oradata/appls.dbf	6,272,242	65
2001-01-23 21	/u04/oradata/temp04.dbf	835,272,262	74

Hot File Writes Alert

This script alerts you to files whose write I/Os are greater than (25 percent or 50 percent or 75 percent) of total writes. This information can help the DBA locate files that are consuming more than a normal proportion of I/O writes. You may want to place these files in the KEEP pool or stripe them across multiple disks.

```
**************************************************************
This will identify any single file with a write I/O
 more than 50% of the total write I/O of the database.

The "hot" file should be examined, and the hot table/index
should be identified using STATSPACK.

- The busy file should be placed on a disk device with
"less busy" files to minimize write delay and channel
contention.

- If small file has a hot small table, place the table
in the KEEP pool

**************************************************************
```

Yr. Mo Dy Hr.	FILE_NAME	WRITES	PCT_OF_TOT
2001-02-05 12	/u02/oradata/bookd01.dbf	1268	38
2001-02-05 13	/u02/oradata/bookd01.dbf	1371	52
2001-02-05 17	/u02/oradata/bookd01.dbf	1489	58
2001-02-05 20	/u02/oradata/bookd01.dbf	807	37
2001-02-05 23	/u02/oradata/bookd01.dbf	840	56

Data Buffer Hit Ratio Alert

This report alerts the DBA to times when the data buffer hit ratio falls below the preset threshold. It is very useful for locating times when decision support type queries are being run, since a large number of large-table full table scans will make the data buffer hit ratio drop. This script also reports on all three data buffers, including the KEEP and RECYCLE pools, and it can be customized to report on individual pools because the KEEP pool should always have enough data blocks to cache all table rows, while the RECYCLE pool should get a very low buffer hit ratio. If the data buffer hit ratio is less than 90 percent, you may want to increase *db_block_buffers*, *buffer_pool_keep*, or *buffer_pool_recycle*. Also note that the Oracle 8.0 version of this alert is available.

```
***********************************************************
When the data buffer hit ratio falls below 90%, you
should consider adding to the db_block_buffer init.ora parameter


***********************************************************
```

yr. mo dy Hr.	Name	bhr
2001-01-27 08	DEFAULT	45
2001-01-27 09	RECYCLE	41
2001-01-27 10	DEFAULT	36
2001-01-27 11	DEFAULT	28
2001-02-02 10	DEFAULT	83
2001-02-02 17	RECYCLE	81
2001-02-03 03	DEFAULT	69
2001-02-03 06	DEFAULT	69
2001-02-03 07	DEFAULT	70

Disk Sorts Alert

If disk sorts are greater than 100/hr, you may want to increase *sort_area_size* or tune SQL to perform index scans. This report is very useful for monitoring the amount of activity against the TEMP tablespace, and it is also useful for ensuring that *sort_area_size* is set to an optimal level. As a general rule, increasing *sort_area_size* will reduce the number of disk sorts, but huge sorts will always need to be performed on disk in the TEMP tablespace.

```
***********************************************************
When there are high disk sorts, you should investigate
increasing sort_area_size, or adding indexes to force index_full scans


***********************************************************
```

TO_CHAR(SNAP_	SORTS_MEMORY	SORTS_DISK	RATIO
2001-01-27 08	6,731	144	.0213935522211
2001-01-27 09	12,532	155	.0123683370571
2001-01-27 10	10,313	147	.0142538543586
2001-01-27 20	6,615	102	.0154195011338
2001-01-28 11	8,574	137	.0159785397714
2001-01-29 04	19,979	111	.0055558336253
2001-01-29 10	13,650	126	.0092307692308
2001-01-29 19	24,293	186	.0076565265714
2001-01-29 21	5,753	102	.0177298800626
2001-01-30 11	17,895	422	.0235820061470
2001-01-31 13	11,821	154	.0130276626343
2001-02-02 14	10,936	129	.0117959034382
2001-02-02 20	13,443	153	.0113813880830
2001-02-02 21	31,355	260	.0082921384149
2001-02-03 05	6,252	135	.0215930902111
2001-02-03 06	6,285	145	.0230708035004
2001-02-03 07	6,313	139	.0220180579756

I/O Wait Alert

This code interrogates the stats$filestatxs.wait_count column to report on any files with an excessive amount of wait activity. If the number of I/O waits appears excessive, the DBA needs to investigate the cause of the waits. High I/O waits on files are commonly associated with buffer busy waits, and may be caused by tables with too few freelists.

```
*************************************************************
When there are high I/O waits, disk bottlenecks may exist
Run iostats to find the hot disk and shuffle files to
remove the contention

*************************************************************
```

SNAPDATE	FILENAME	WAITS
2001-01-28 23	/u03/oradata/PROD/applsysd01.dbf	2169
	/u04/oradata/PROD/applsysx01.dbf	1722
	/u03/oradata/PROD/rbs01.dbf	2016
2001-01-30 16	/u03/oradata/PROD/mrpd01.dbf	1402
2001-01-31 23	/u03/oradata/PROD/applsysd01.dbf	4319
	/u04/oradata/PROD/applsysx01.dbf	3402
	/u03/oradata/PROD/rbs01.dbf	3012

Buffer Busy Wait Alert

Whenever you see buffer busy waits, you have a condition where a data block is in the data buffer but is unavailable. This type of contention is usually for a segment header block of a high-level index node block. Adding freelists for the object often corrects these wait conditions.

```
***********************************************************
Buffer Busy Waits may signal a high update table with too
few freelists. Find the offending table and add more freelists.


***********************************************************
MYDATE          NAME                 BUFFER_BUSY_WAIT
-------------   --------------------  ----------------
2001-01-18 13   DEFAULT                            33
2001-01-28 12   DEFAULT                           120
2001-01-29 03   DEFAULT                            14
2001-02-14 16   DEFAULT                           825
2001-02-21 10   DEFAULT                           332
2001-02-28 09   DEFAULT                            44
```

Redo Log Space Requests Alert

If redo log space requests are greater than 0, you may want to increase the *log_buffer init.ora* parameter. A high number of redo log space requests indicates a high level of **update** activity, and the Oracle log buffer is having trouble keeping up with the volume of redo log images.

```
***********************************************************
High redo log space requests indicate a need to increase
the log_buffer parameter


***********************************************************
TO_CHAR(SNAP_   REDO_LOG_SPACE_REQUESTS
-------------   -----------------------
2001-01-17 23       31
```

Chained Row Alert

When the *table fetch continued row* parameter is greater than 10,000/hr you may have row chaining because of PCTFREE set too low. The *table fetch continued row* can also be triggered by reading data blocks with long columns that exceed the block size. This is common with rows that contain RAW, LONG RAW, NCLOB, CLOB or BLOB datatypes.

```
***********************************************************
Table fetch continued row indicates chained rows, or fetches of
long datatypes (long raw, blob)
```

Investigate increasing db_block_size or reorganizing tables
with chained rows.

```
*******************************************************
```

```
TO_CHAR(SNAP_ TABLE_FETCH_CONTINUED_ROW
------------- ------------------------
2001-01-27 20 29,523
2001-01-27 22 45,338
2001-01-28 00 45,224
2001-01-28 14 44,522
2001-01-29 13 73,350
2001-01-29 14 62,689
2001-01-30 00 41,660
2001-02-01 09 16,308
2001-02-01 14 48,415
2001-02-01 15 56,480
2001-02-01 16 77,914
2001-02-01 17 66,382
2001-02-01 18 59,813
2001-02-01 19 57,564
2001-02-03 04 21,229
```

Shared Pool Contention Alert

Enqueue deadlocks can indicate contention within the shared pool and locking
related problems. Enqueue deadlocks are associated with the deadly embrace
condition where one task is locking resources and another task that is holding
resources requests a lock on the resources of the first task. To prevent these tasks
from waiting forever, Oracle aborts the tasks that requested the lock that caused
the deadly embrace.

```
*******************************************************
```
Enqueue Deadlocks indicate contention within the Oracle
shared pool.

Investigate increasing shared_pool_size

```
*******************************************************
TO_CHAR(SNAP_ ENQUEUE_DEADLOCKS
------------- -----------------
2001-01-28 23                23
2001-02-19 20               341
2001-02-29 01                47
2001-03-04 14               963
2001-03-25 08                55
```

Full Table Scan Alert

Long-table full table scans are only legitimate when the query requires access to more than 40 percent of ordered table rows and more than 7 percent of unordered table rows. Excessive large-table full table scans may indicate poorly tuned SQL that is not using an index.

```
************************************************************
Long-table full table scans can indicate a need to:

- Make the offending tables parallel query
(alter table xxx parallel degree yyy;)
- Place the table in the RECYCLE pool
- Build an index on the table to remove the FTS

To locate the table, run access.sql

See Oracle Magazine September 2000 issue for details

************************************************************


      TO_CHAR(SNAP_        FTS
      -------------    -----------
      2001-01-29 08     17,467
      2001-01-29 09      8,570
      2001-01-29 10      9,008
      2001-01-29 11      8,700
      2001-01-29 12      3,157
      2001-01-29 15      1,599
      2001-01-30 15      2,666
      2001-02-02 09      1,759
      2001-02-02 11      1,423
      2001-02-02 12      1,801
      2001-02-02 15      2,417
      2001-02-02 17      1,024
      2001-02-02 18      1,171
```

Background Wait Alert

This query interrogates the stats$bg_event_summary table to find events with high waits. When background events experience more than 100 time-outs/hr, you may have a locking problem.

```
************************************************************
Excessive waits on background events
************************************************************
```

```
Yr.  Mo Dy Hr EVENT                      tot waits time wait timeouts
------------ ------------------------    -------- --------- --------
2001-01 29 19 latch free                      143         0      142
```

System Waits Alert

This query interrogates the stats$system_event table to locate events where there are excessive waits. If you experience waits on latch free, enqueue, LGWR waits, or buffer busy waits, you need to locate the cause of the contention.

```
******************************************************
Excessive event waits indicate shared pool contention
******************************************************
```

```
Yr.  Mo Dy Hr EVENT                       WAITS AVG_WAIT_SECS
------------ ------------------------   -------- -------------
2001-01-31 11 SQL*Net message from client  95,687          1
2001-01-31 11 SQL*Net more data from client   776          0
2001-01-31 11 enqueue                         997          0
2001-01-31 11 latch free                    2,399          0
2001-01-31 12 SQL*Net message from client  99,974          1
2001-01-31 12 SQL*Net more data from client   992          0
2001-01-31 12 enqueue                       1,071          0
2001-01-31 12 latch free                    2,649          0
```

Library Cache Misses Alert

This query interrogates the stats$librarycache table to look for excessive library cache miss ratios. When the library cache miss ratio is greater than .02, you may want to increase *shared_pool_size*.

```
******************************************************
Excessive library cache miss ratio
******************************************************
                           Cache Misses
MYDATE          execs While Executing LIBRARY_CACHE_MISS_RATIO
------------ ---------- ---------------- ------------------------
2001-01-10 13     2,835            2,122                .02027262
2001-01-24 02     3,381            1,292                .08028927
2001-01-28 15     3,572            2,002                .04111982
2001-01-29 09       121               65                .07073563
```

Database Writer Contention alert

This query looks at the stats$sysstat table for values in *summed dirty queue length*, *write requests*, and *DBWR checkpoints*. When the *write request length* is greater than 3 or you have excessive *DBWR checkpoint waits*, you need to look at tuning the database writer processes.

```
***********************************************************
Excessive length of DBWR processes
***********************************************************
Yr.  Mo Dy Hr  Write request length   Write Requests DBWR checkpoints
------------   --------------------   ------------   ------------
2001-01-31 11                44,201         95,687             12
2001-02-12 14                 2,846          3,028            141
```

Data Dictionary Miss Ratio Alert

This query looks at the stats$rowcache_summary table to compute data dictionary gets, data dictionary cache misses, and the data dictionary hit ratio. This script alerts the DBA to times when requests for data dictionary metadata are high. This problem can sometimes be relieved by increasing the *shared_pool_size init.ora* parameter.

```
***********************************************************
Data Dictionary Miss Ratio below 90% indicates the need
to increase the shared_pool_size
***********************************************************


                            Data      Data
                  Data     Dictionary Dictionary
               Dictionary   Cache      Hit
Yr.  Mo Dy Hr    Gets       Misses     Ratio
------------   --------   ------------ ----------
2001-01-28 05   516,495      55,923         89
2001-01-31 07   753,417      81,438         89
2001-02-03 02   437,913      45,087         89
```

Data Dictionary Object Alert

This report looks into the stats$rowcache_summary table to find individual parameters that experience a low hit ratio. This report can reveal internal contention with the Oracle data dictionary and times of high dictionary metadata requests.

```
***********************************************************
Report when Data Dictionary Hit Ratio for an object
falls below 70%
***********************************************************
```

```
                           Data  Dictionary    Data   Object
                      Dictionary      Cache Dictionary    Hit
Yr.  Mo Dy  Hr.  PARAMETER    Gets   Misses    Usage  Ratio
------- ------ --- ----------- ----------- ----------- ---------- ------
2001-01-28 05    dc_free_extents      954       318      313     67

2001-02-01 03    dc_used_extents      363       338      330      7

2001-02-03 02    dc_free_extents      638       318      314     50
```

Now that we have covered the STATSPACK alert report, let's look at an equally important daily report on the database servers and Web servers.

Daily Server Alert Report

As we noted in Chapter 5, the Oracle DBA is very interested in monitoring conditions on the database servers and Web servers. This script is generally run daily to report on exceptional conditions within any server in the Oracle environment. The data is collected in five-minute intervals and reported with hourly averages. When the DBAs find an out-of-bounds server condition, they can run detailed reports that display the data in five-minute intervals.

run_vmstat.ksh   This is the driver script that submits the vmstat_alert report and e-mails the output to the appropriate staff members.

vmstat_alert.sql   This report provides information on the server conditions that may contribute to poor performance.

The vmstat_alert.sql script gathers the following server information.

■ **Run queue waits**   When the run queue exceeds the number of CPUs, the server is experiencing CPU bottlenecks:

```
Fri Dec 29                                                  page    1
                         run queue > 2
                    May indicate an overloaded CPU

SERVER_NAME      date        hour    runq pg_in pg_ot  usr  sys  idl
---------------- ----------- ------- ---- ----- ----- ---- ---- ----
BAD-01           00/12/22    13        6     0     0   62    7   32
BAD-01           00/12/22    15        3     0     0   82   18    0
BAD-01           00/12/22    17        3     0     0   76   16    8
BAD-01           00/12/27    11        3     0     0   77    5   20
```

■ **RAM swapping**   When page-in operations exist, the maximum RAM capacity of the server has been exceeded:

```
Fri Dec 29                                                  page    1
                         page_in > 1
                    May indicate overloaded memory
```

```
SERVER_NAME       date          hour    runq pg_in pg_ot  usr  sys  idl
----------------  ------------  ------  ---- ----- -----  ---  ---  ---
AD-01             00/12/22      14        0    19     0     1    1   97
AD-01             00/12/26      11        0    32     0     0    0   99
AD-01             00/12/28      17        0     5     0     0    1   99
JANETDB           00/12/22      13        0     3     0     1    3   96
JANETDB           00/12/22      14        0    27     1     6   17   77
JANETDB           00/12/22      15        0     3     0     1    3   96
JANETDB           00/12/22      16        0     7     0     3    9   88
JANETDB           00/12/22      17        0    10     0     4   10   86
JANETDB           00/12/22      18        0     2     1     1    3   96
JANETDB           00/12/23      09        0     2     0     1    3   96
JANETDB           00/12/24      03        0     4     0     1    3   96
JANETDB           00/12/26      10        0     3     0     1    3   96
JANETDB           00/12/26      11        0     2    21     8   17   75
JANETDB           00/12/26      12        0    10    10    13   27   60
JANETDB           00/12/27      09        0    10     0     1    3   96
JANETDB           00/12/27      10        0     5     0     1    3   96
JANETDB           00/12/27      11        0     6     0     1    3   95
JANETDB           00/12/28      03        0     2     0     1    3   96
JANETDB           00/12/28      11        0     2     0     1    3   95
JANETDB           00/12/28      21        0     3     1     2    4   95
```

■ **High CPU**   The DBA is often interested in times when the database CPU utilization is greater than 95 percent.

```
Fri Dec 29                                                       page    1
                           user+system > 70%
                        Indicates an overloaded CPU


SERVER_NAME       date          hour    runq pg_in pg_ot  usr  sys  idl
----------------  ------------  ------  ---- ----- -----  ---  ---  ---
AD-01             00/12/22      08        2     0     0    69    3   28
AD-01             00/12/22      13       12     0     0    89   11    1
AD-01             00/12/22      15        0     0     0    63   29    8
AD-01             00/12/22      17        1     0     0    53   27   20
AD-01             00/12/26      12        1     0     0    77    4   19
AD-01             00/12/27      11        3     0     0    86    6    9
```

Next, let's look at a real-time alert script that can warn the DBA about impending problems in the Oracle environment.

A Real-Time Check for Oracle Problems

The *oracheck.run* script is usually scheduled to run hourly in a production environment to report on any exception condition that may jeopardize the database. This script is quite sophisticated and contains four parameter files that control the level of reporting. The parameter files for this script include:

■ *parm_mount_point_kb_free.ora*   This file contains the threshold for any Oracle mount point. If you are using tablespaces with AUTOEXTEND ON, you must constantly monitor the UNIX mount points to prevent Oracle from hanging on a failure to extend problem.

- ***parm_ts_free.ora*** This file contains the threshold for reporting on full tablespaces.

- ***parm_num_extents.ora*** This file contains the number by which a table or index's extents cannot exceed. For example, placing 600 in this file will cause the DBA to be e-mailed when any object exceeds 600 extents.

- ***parm_alert_log.ora*** This file contains alert log messages that should be reported to the DBA. Next is a common list for this file:

```
>cat parm_alert_log.ora
ORA-00600
ORA-1631
ORA-1650
ORA-1652
ORA-1653
ORA-00447
ORA-00603
ORA-01092
ORA-02050
ORA-1535
```

In addition to the parameter files, we have a Korn shell script that controls the overall execution called *oracheck.run.* This is a Korn shell script that reports on anything that might cause the database to hang up or crash. The idea behind this script is to allow the DBA to repair impending problems before that database crashes. Here are the checks that are performed by this script:

- **Alert log messages** This script e-mails any alert log messages that are found in the alert log. The parameter file *parm_alert_log.ora* contains a list of alert log messages to be reported.

- **Low free space in archived redo log directory** If the archived redo log directory becomes full, our Oracle database will hang up. This alert allows the Oracle DBA to add space before the database hangs.

- **UNIX mount point space alert** The script checks all datafile mount points in Oracle, including the UNIX Oracle home directory. Since most databases now use AUTOEXTEND ON, the DBA must be constantly alert for file systems that may not be able to extend. If the free space in any mount point is less than specified in *parm_mount_point_kb_free.ora*, an e-mail alert will be sent to the DBA.

- **Object cannot extend** This report will alert the Oracle DBA whenever an Oracle table or index does not have room to take another extent. This alert is obsolete if you are using tablespaces with AUTOEXTEND ON, but many DBAs still keep this alert because they want to monitor the growth of the database tables and indexes.

- **Tablespace > nn% free**   This report sends an e-mail alert whenever any tablespaces contain less space than specified by *parm_ts_free.ora*. Again, this alert is obsolete when using AUTOEXTEND ON, but many DBAs still want to see the available space within each tablespace.

- **Object > nnn extents**   This report is very useful for reporting tables and indexes that experience unexpected growth. Whenever a table or index exceeds the number defined in *parm_num_extents.ora*, an e-mail alert will be sent to the DBA.

Here is an actual sample of the e-mail output from this script:

```
NON-EMERGENCY ORACLE ALERT. Mount point /home has less than 250000 K-Bytes free.
```

Next, let's look at a weekly object report that can tell the DBA of the changes to the database in the past week.

Weekly Object Growth Report

This report uses the STATSPACK extension tables for objects to prepare weekly growth reports. For details on collecting these statistics, see Chapter 10.

The *rpt_object_stats.sql* script is a very useful report that approximates the overall growth of the database over the past week. The DBA can quickly compare table and index counts, and see the total growth for table and indexes over the past week. This report is often e-mailed to MIS managers. Let's take a closer look at each section.

Elapsed-Time Section

The first section of the report identifies the snapshots that are used in the comparison. The script identifies the most recent snapshot and compares it to the $n-1$ snapshot.

```
SQL> @/export/home/oracle/obj_stat/rpt_object_stats
Connected.
'**********************************************'

Mon Jan 22                                                        page    1
                            Object growth
                      Comparing last two snapshots


   Most recent date 2001-01-22

Mon Jan 22                                                        page    1
```

```
                          Object growth
                   Comparing last two snapshots

     Older date 2001-01-08

     '*****************************************************!
```

The next section shows the total counts of tables and indexes in the database. This is a very useful report for the DBA to ensure that no new objects have migrated into the production environment. We also see the total bytes for all tables and indexes and the size change over the past week.

This report shows the total growth of tables and indexes for the past week.

```
Mon Jan 22                                              page    1
                Most recent database object counts and sizes

DB_NAME TAB_COUNT IDX_COUNT      TAB_BYTES        IDX_BYTES
-------------- --------- ---------------- ----------------
prodb12       451       674      330,219,520      242,204,672
              -------- --------- ---------------- ----------------
Total         451       674      330,219,520      242,204,672


Mon Jan 22                                              page    1
                     Database size change
                 comparing the most recent snapshot dates

DB_NAME      OLD_BYTES       NEW_BYTES          CHANGE
---------- ----------- ---------------- ----------------
prodb12    467,419,136    572,424,192       105,005,056
           ------------- ---------------- ----------------
Total      467,419,136    572,424,192       105,005,056
```

The next section is primarily for the DBA. It reports on any tables that contain excessive chained rows, where the table has no RAW, LONG RAW, or BLOB type columns. These row chaining problems can generally be resolved by a table reorganization.

```
Mon Jan 22                                              page    1
                 comparing the most recent snapshot dates

Tables with > 10% chained rows and no LONG columns.
Owner      Table        PCTFREE PCTUSED avg row   Rows Chains Pct
--------- ------------ -------- ------- ------- ------- ------- ----
OE        SO_OBJECTS        10      70   1,858      87     64  .74
INV       MTL_ABC_COMP      10      70      73     367     44  .12
APPLSYS   FND_PERFORMA      10      40  27,152      20     19  .99
```

Next we see the chained rows for tables with LONG type column values. These tables cannot be repaired with reorganization because the row length often exceeds the database block size. This is especially true when RAW data columns are stored inline, inside the actual table rows.

Mon Jan 22   page   1
                        comparing the most recent snapshot dates

Tables with > 10% chained rows that contain LONG columns.

Owner	Table	PCTFREE	PCTUSED	avg row	Rows	Chains	Pct
EUL_MWC	DIS_DOCS	10	40	23,912	9	9	100

Next we see a report showing all tables with more than 200 extents, or tables that have extended over the past week. While excessive extents for a table is not a cause for concern, this report will tell the DBA about those critical tables that are growing. This report will help the DBA plan for tablespace growth.

Mon Jan 22   page   1
                              Table extents report
                   Where extents > 200 or table extent changed
                          comparing most recent snapshots

DB	OWNER	TAB_NAME	OLD_EXT	NEW_EXT
prodb1	WOMP	REFERER_LOG	2	1
	WOMP	JANET_SITE_STATISTICS	1	2
	WOMP	EC_CUSTOMER_SERVICE_ACTIONS	1	3
	ORACLE	TOM_ENTRY	2	5
	WOMP	SEC_BROWSER_PROPERTIES	1	8
	WOMP	SEC_SESSIONS	1	10
	WOMP	EC_USER_SESSIONS	1	12
	ORACLE	PAGE_IM3	6	12
	WOMP	EC_PRODUCTS_AUDIT	5	14
	ORACLE	SQLTEMPO	1	17
	ORACLE	PAGE_IMORP	66	125

Mon Jan 22   page   1
                              Index extents report
                   Where extents > 200 or index extent changed
                          Comparing last two snapshots

DB	OWNER	IDX_NAME	OLD_EXT	NEW_EXT
prodb1	ORACLE	ISBN_TOC_SEQ_IDX	1	2
	WOMP	ROV_STAT_PAGE_TYPE_IDX	1	2
	WOMP	SYS_C006210	1	3
	ORACLE	SYS_IL0000005970C00007$$	1	3
	ORACLE	SEQ_KEY_IDX	3	5

Next, let's look at other miscellaneous reports that are helpful for the DBA.

Trace Alert Report

This is a great script for instantly notifying the DBA and developers of the presence of trace files. In a production environment, this script can be used to alert the DBA to production aborts, and it is also useful in development environments, where developers can be e-mailed their trace file dumps when a program aborts. This script is generally executed every five minutes.

The *trace_alert.ksh* script interrogates the Oracle datafile systems to find the locations of all trace and dump files. It then checks these directories and e-mails any trace files to the appropriate staff member. Let's take a close look at the steps in this script.

Set the Environment

The first part of the script ensures that a valid ORACLE_SID is passed to the script:

```
#!/bin/ksh

#*********************************************************
# Exit if no first parameter $1 is passed to script
#*********************************************************
if [ -z "$1" ]
then
    echo "Usage: trace_alert.ksh <ORACLE_SID>"
    exit 99
fi

#*********************************************************
# First, we must set the environment . . . .
#*********************************************************
ORACLE_SID=$1
export ORACLE_SID
ORACLE_HOME=`cat /var/opt/oracle/oratab|grep $ORACLE_SID:|cut -f2 -d':'`
export ORACLE_HOME
ORACLE_BASE=`echo $ORACLE_HOME | sed -e 's:/product/.*::g'`
export ORACLE_BASE
export DBA=$ORACLE_BASE/admin;
export DBA
PATH=$ORACLE_HOME/bin:$PATH
export PATH
MON=`echo ~oracle/mon`
export MON
```

Get Environment Information
Next, we get the name of the database server and the current date:

```
#********************************************************
# Get the server name & date for the e-mail message
#********************************************************
SERVER=`uname -a|awk '{print $2}'`

MYDATE=`date +"%m/%d %H:%M"`


#********************************************************
# Remove the old file list
#********************************************************
rm -f /tmp/trace_list.lst
touch /tmp/trace_list.lst
```

Get the Names of Any Recent Trace or Dump Files
This section issues the UNIX **find** command to locate any Oracle trace or dump files
that were created in the past day:

```
#********************************************************
# list the full-names of all possible dump files . . . .
#********************************************************
find $DBA/$ORACLE_SID/bdump/*.trc    -mtime -1 -print >>  /tmp/trace_list.lst
find $DBA/$ORACLE_SID/udump/*.trc    -mtime -1 -print >> /tmp/trace_list.lst
find $ORACLE_HOME/rdbms/log/*.trc    -mtime -1 -print >> /tmp/trace_list.lst
```

Exit Immediately If No Files Found
This section exits right away if there are no files to e-mail to the DBA and developers:

```
#********************************************************
# Exit if there are not any trace files found
#********************************************************
NUM_TRACE=`cat /tmp/trace_list.lst|wc -l`
oracle_num=`expr $NUM_TRACE`
if [ $oracle_num -lt 1 ]
 then
 exit 0
fi

#echo $NUM_TRACE files found
#cat /tmp/trace_list.lst
```

E-Mail the Trace Files

This section of the code extracts the first 100 lines of each trace and dump file and e-mails them to the DBA and developer staff.

```
#****************************************************
# for each trace file found, send DBA an e-mail message
#   and move the trace file to the /tmp directory
#****************************************************
cat /tmp/trace_list.lst|while read TRACE_FILE
do

    #****************************************************
    #   This gets the short file name at the end of the full path
    #****************************************************
    SHORT_TRACE_FILE_NAME=`echo $TRACE_FILE|awk -F"/" '{ print $NF }'`
    #****************************************************
    #   This gets the file location (bdump, udump, log)
    #****************************************************
    DUMP_LOC=`echo $TRACE_FILE|awk -F"/" '{ print $(NF-1) }'`

    #****************************************************
    # send an e-mail to the administrator
    #****************************************************

    head -100 $TRACE_FILE|\
    mailx -s "$ORACLE_SID Oracle trace file at $MYDATE."\
        don@remote-dba.net\
        terry@oracle.net\
        tzu@oracle.com
```

Move the Trace File

The final step is to move the trace or dump file from its current location to the UNIX /tmp directory. This keeps the dump file locations from getting clogged and ensures that the trace file is periodically deleted. This is because most UNIX administrators remove files from the /tmp directory after they are seven days old.

```
    #****************************************************
    # Move the trace file to the /tmp directory
    # This prevents multiple messages to the developers
    # and allows the script to run every minute
    #****************************************************

    cp $TRACE_FILE /tmp/${DUMP_LOC}_${SHORT_TRACE_FILE_NAME}
    rm -f $TRACE_FILED
```

Next, let's look at a generic alert script that can be used on nondatabase servers to e-mail alerts when a program on a Web server aborts.

Web Server Alert Report

In a production Web environment, it is often useful to alert the staff whenever a program aborts. This script is generally executed every five minutes. The *webserver_alert.ksh* script can be customized to search the dump file location for any Pro*C, C++, or Perl programs. This script requires the following modifications:

- Change the e-mail addresses to match the people who want to be notified of program dumps.

- Change /usr/src/asp/core to the name and location of core files on your Web server.

This is a simple but quite important script. It searches for a core file and instantly e-mails it to alert the staff about a production abort.

webserver_alert.ksh

```ksh
#!/bin/ksh

MYDATE=`date +"%Y%m%d"`

SERVER=`uname -a|awk '{print $2}'`

if [ -f /usr/src/asp/core ]
then

    # Move the file to a dated location . . .
    mv /usr/src/asp/core /tmp/core_$MYDATE

    # send an e-mail to the administrator
    head /tmp/core_$MYDATE|\
    mail -s "EMERGENCY - WebServer $SERVER abort in /tmp/core_$MYDATE"\
        don@remote-dba.net\
        omar@oracle.com\
        carlos@oracle.com
```

Next, let's examine a daemon script that can poll every five minutes for buffer busy waits.

Buffer Busy Waits Alerts

One of the shortcomings of STATSPACK is that it only measures wait at the system-wide level. If you want to track buffer busy waits and sequential read waits with the *block_id* you need to run a real-time script to search for these waits every five minutes. Once you get the block ID, you can dump the block, get the name of the object, and add additional freelists to the object.

The *get_busy.ksh* script will display any buffer busy waits that happen to be occurring when the script is executed and e-mail the information to the Oracle DBA. The DBA can then use the details provided in Chapter 10 to locate the specific block where the buffer busy wait occurred.

This short script performs the following steps:

1. First, the script sets the sample time between checks.

2. It then queries the v$session_wait view, looking for *buffer busy waits* and *db sequential file read waits*.

3. If either of these are found, the script e-mails the waits to the DBA for further investigation.

get_busy.ksh

```
#!/bin/ksh

# First, we must set the environment . . . .
ORACLE_SID=PRODMN1
export ORACLE_SID
ORACLE_HOME=`cat /etc/oratab|grep \^$ORACLE_SID:|cut -f2 -d':'`
export ORACLE_HOME
PATH=$ORACLE_HOME/bin:$PATH
export PATH
MON=`echo ~oracle/mon`
export MON
ORA_ENVFILE=${ORACLE_HOME}/${ORACLE_SID}.env
. $ORA_ENVFILE

SERVER_NAME=`uname -a|awk '{print $2}'`
typeset -u SERVER_NAME
export SERVER_NAME

# sample every 10 seconds
```

```
SAMPLE_TIME=10

while true
do

rm -f /home/oracle/statspack/busy.lst

$ORACLE_HOME/bin/sqlplus -s / <<!>/home/oracle/statspack/busy.lst

set feedback off;
select
 sysdate,
 substr(tablespace_name,1,14),
 p2
 from v\$session_wait a, dba_data_files b
 where
 a.p1 = b.file_id
 and
 event = 'db file sequential read'
 ;

 select
    sysdate,
    substr(tablespace_name,1,14),
  p2
  from v\$session_wait a, dba_data_files b
  where
  a.p1 = b.file_id
  and
  event = 'buffer busy waits'
  ;

!

var=`cat /home/oracle/statspack/busy.lst|wc -l`

echo $var
if [[ $var -gt 1 ]];
 then
   echo
********************************************************************"
   echo "There are waits"
   cat /home/oracle/statspack/busy.lst|mailx -s "Monona block wait found"\
   dburleson@doglog.com \
   dhurley@oracle.com \
   echo
********************************************************************"
 exit
```

```
fi

sleep $SAMPLE_TIME
done
```

Once started, this script is scheduled to check every 10 seconds so that problems can be quickly identified and resolved. Here is an actual report from the e-mail:

```
TO_CHAR(SYSDATE,'Y
------------------
EVENT SUBSTR(TABLESP
---------------------------------------------------------------- ----- --------
P2
----------
000-12-30 00:15:52
buffer busy waits APPLSYSD
       26716
```

A STATSPACK Reactive Report

There are times when the DBA is faced with an imminent performance problem. In cases when the end users are complaining about current poor performance, you can use STATSPACK to quickly see what is going on.

The *quick.ksh* script is great for using STATSPACK to see what is happening right now in your database. Here are the steps in *quick.ksh*:

1. Issue a starting snapshot.

2. Wait for the specified amount of time.

3. Issue an ending snapshot.

4. Run *rpt_last.sql* to compare the beginning and ending values.

Here is the script. Take a minute to see how it produces the report.

quick.ksh

```
#!/bin/ksh

# First, we must set the environment . . . .
ORACLE_SID=$ORACLE_SID
export ORACLE_SID
ORACLE_HOME=`cat /etc/oratab|grep ^$ORACLE_SID:|cut -f2 -d':'`
#ORACLE_HOME=`cat /var/opt/oracle/oratab|grep ^$ORACLE_STD:|cut -f2 -d':'`
```

```
export ORACLE_HOME
PATH=$ORACLE_HOME/bin:$PATH
export PATH

echo "Please enter the number of seconds between snapshots."
read elapsed


$ORACLE_HOME/bin/sqlplus perfstat/perfstat<<!
execute statspack.snap;
exit
!

sleep $elapsed

$ORACLE_HOME/bin/sqlplus perfstat/perfstat<<!
execute statspack.snap;

select
   name,
   snap_id,
   to_char(snap_time,' dd Mon YYYY HH24:mi:ss')
from
   stats\$snapshot,
   v\$database
where
   snap_id > (select max(snap_id)-2 from stats\$snapshot)
;

@rpt_last
```

The *rpr_last.sql* Script

The *rpt_last.sql* script will provide the same information as the statspack_alert report, but it only compares the last two STATSPACK snapshots.

The *rpt_last.sql* script is great for performing stress tests on an Oracle database. You bounce the database, issue a statspack.snap, perform the stress test, run another statspack.snap, and then complete the process with *rpt_last.sql*. This will give you a complete picture of all of the activity within your database during the stress test.

Here is an example of the output from *rpt_last.sql*:

```
>cat rpt_last.lst

TO_CHAR(SNAP_          READS        WRITES
-------------   ------------  ------------
2001-02-01 17      4,881,080           395



*******************************************************************
```

This will identify any single file with a read I/O
 more than 10% of the total read I/O of the database.

The "hot" file should be examined, and the hot table/index
should be identified using STATSPACK.

- The busy file should be placed on a disk device with
"less busy" files to minimize read delay and channel
contention.

- If small file has a hot small table, place the table
in the KEEP pool

- If the file has a large-table full-table scan, place
the table in the RECYCLE pool and turn on parallel query
for the table.
****

MYDATE	FILE_NAME	READS
2001-02-01 17	/u01/oradata/testb1/bookd01.dbf	916,989

1 row selected.

****
This will identity any single file with a write I/O
 more than 10% of the total write I/O of the database.

The "hot" file should be examined, and the hot table/index
should be identified using STATSPACK.

- The busy file should be placed on a disk device with
"less busy" files to minimize write delay and channel
contention.

- If small file has a hot small table, place the table
in the KEEP pool

****
no rows selected
****
When the data buffer hit ratio falls below 90%, you
should consider adding to the db_block_buffer init.ora parameter
****

```
MYDATE             phys_writes BUFFER HIT RATIO
----------------   ------------ ----------------
01 Feb 17:33:47            654               20

Yr.  Mo Dy  Hr.   NAMESPACE        HIT_RATIO PIN_HIT_RATIO     RELOADS
----------------   ----------------  --------- --------------  ------------
2001-02-01 17      SQL AREA              .66           .78           13
                   TABLE/PROCEDURE      1.00           .88           80
                   SQL AREA              .97           .95            8
                   TABLE/PROCEDURE       .74           .30            0
                   BODY                  .00           .00            0
                   CLUSTER              1.00          1.00            0
                   SQL AREA             1.00          1.00            8
                   TABLE/PROCEDURE      1.00          1.00            0
                   BODY                 1.00          1.00            0
                   SQL AREA              .96          1.00           10
                   TABLE/PROCEDURE       .84          1.00            0
                   BODY                  .99           .98            0
                   CLUSTER              1.00          1.00            0
                   SQL AREA              .96          1.00           10
                   TABLE/PROCEDURE       .84          1.00            0
                   BODY                  .99           .99            0
                   CLUSTER              1.00          1.00            0
                   SQL AREA              .97          1.00            8
                   TABLE/PROCEDURE       .85          1.00            0
                   BODY                  .99           .98            0
                   CLUSTER              1.00          1.00            0

21 rows selected.

************************************************************
When there are high disk sorts, you should investigate
increasing sort_area_size, or adding indexes to force index_full scans

************************************************************


Yr.  Mo Dy  Hr.  SORTS_MEMORY  SORTS_DISK         RATIO
----------------  ------------ ------------  ---------------
01 Feb 17:33:47            168            0  .0000000000000

************************************************************
When there is high I/O waits, disk bottlenecks may exist
Run iostats to find the hot disk and shuffle files to
remove the contention
************************************************************
```

```
Yr.  Mo Dy  Hr.  FILENAME                                        WAITS
---------------  ------------------------------------------  ----------
01 Feb 17:33:47  /u01/oradata/testb1/bookd01.dbf                  61342
01 Feb 17:33:47  /u01/oradata/testb1/bookx01.dbf                      9

2 rows selected.
************************************************************
Buffer Bury Waits may signal a high update table with too
few freelists.  Find the offending table and add more freelists.


************************************************************

Yr.  Mo Dy  Hr.  BUFFER_BUSY_WAIT
---------------  --- ------------
01 Feb 17:33:47            61,358


************************************************************
High redo log space requests indicate a need to increase
the log_buffer parameter
************************************************************


no rows selected

************************************************************
Table fetch continued row indicates chained rows, or fetches of
long datatypes (long raw, blob)
Investigate increasing db_block_size or reorganizing tables
with chained rows.
************************************************************


Yr.  Mo Dy  Hr.  TABLE_FETCH_CONTINUED_ROW
---------------  -------------------------
01 Feb 17:33:47                        178


************************************************************
Enqueue Deadlocks indicate contention within the Oracle
shared pool.

Investigate increasing shared_pool_size
************************************************************


Yr.  Mo Dy  Hr.  ENQUEUE_DEADLOCKS
---------------  -----------------
01 Feb 17:33:47                  0

1 row selected.
```

```
*************************************************************
Long-table full table scans can indicate a need to:

- Make the offending tables parallel query
(alter table xxx parallel degree yyy;)
- Place the table in the RECYCLE pool
- Build an index on the table to remove the FTS

To locate the table, run access.sql

See Oracle Magazine September 200 issue for details
*************************************************************


Yr.  Mo Dy  Hr.            FTS
--------------- ------------
01 Feb 17:33:47            0
```

Now that we see the general reports, let's look at how these reports are scheduled in a UNIX environment.

Scheduling and Customizing Oracle Alert Reports

In a UNIX environment, the Oracle DBA can easily control the times when the STATSPACK alert reports are executed. Let's begin by examining a UNIX crontab file that schedules these reports.

A Sample UNIX Crontab to Schedule Oracle Reports and Alerts

The following is a sample of a UNIX crontab file that is used to schedule STATSPACK reports and alert scripts:

```
#*************************************************************
# This is the weekly table and index analyze job for the CBO
#*************************************************************
30 7 1 * * /home/analyze.ksh > /home/analyze.lst
#*************************************************************
# This is the weekly (Monday) object analyze and report for management
#*************************************************************
30 7 * * 1 /home/oracle/obj_stat/get_object_stats.ksh prodb1
00 8 * * 1 /home/obj_stat/run_object_report.ksh prodb1
#*************************************************************
```

```
# This is the daily STATSPACK exception report for the DBAs
#*****************************************************************
30 7 * * * /home/statspack/statspack_alert.ksh prodsid
#*****************************************************************
# This is the daily generic alert report for the DBAs
#*****************************************************************
00 7 * * * /home/mon/oracheck.run prodsid > /home/mon/o.lst
#*****************************************************************
# This is the daily vmstat collector & report for the DBAs and SAs
#*****************************************************************
00 7 * * * /home/vmstat/run_vmstat.ksh > /home/vmstat/r.lst
05 7 * * * /home/vmstat/run_vmstat_alert.ksh prodsid > /home/vmstat/v.lst
09 7 1 * * /home/vmstat/run_vmstat_weekly_alert.ksh prodb1
*****************************************************************
# This is the daily iostat collector & report for the DBAs and SAs
#*****************************************************************
#00 7 * * * /home/iostat/run_iostat_solaris.ksh > /home/iostat/r.lst
#00 7 * * * /home/iostat/run_iostat.ksh prodsid > /home/iostat/v.lst
#*****************************************************************
# This is the every 5 min. trace file alert report for the DBAs
#*****************************************************************
1,3,5,7,9,11,13,15,17,19,21,23,25,27,29,31,33,35,37,39,41,43,45,47,49,51,
53,55,57,59 * * * * /home/mon/trace_alert.ksh prodsid > /dev/null 2>&1
#*****************************************************************
# This code ensures that the daemon to check for buffer busy waits
# is always running.
#*****************************************************************
30 7 * * * /home/mon/run_busy.ksh > /dev/null 2>&1
```

We also need to modify these reports to send the information via e-mail to the appropriate person. The alert reports are designed to spool the output to a known filename, and the DBA just needs to modify the commands that send the e-mail alert to customize the recipients' e-mail addresses.

Let's look at how this works. The following Korn shell code checks the size of the alert report and mails the report to the DBA if alerts were detected by the script:

```
var=`cat /tmp/statspack_alert.lst|wc -l`

if [[ $var -gt 1 ]];
    then
    echo
"*****************************************************************"
    echo "There are alerts"
    cat /tmp/statspack_alert.lst|mailx -s "Statspack Alert" \
    don@oracle.com \
    larry_ellison@us.oracle.com \
```

```
james@us.oracle.com
echo
******************************************************************"
exit
```

Conclusion

This chapter has reviewed a wealth of STATSPACK and shell scripts that can be used to alert the DBA about virtually any Oracle problem. However, most DBAs will take these scripts and customize them according to their individual needs. I encourage you to modify and enhance these reports and alerts, and I welcome sharing STATSPACK code with you. My e-mail address is

don@remote-DBA.net.

Finally, let's wrap up this book by looking at how the STATSPACK data can be used for trend analysis.

CHAPTER
15

Trend Analysis
with STATSPACK

he final chapter in this book is dedicated to the use of STATSPACK information for trend analysis. Because STATSPACK can store data over long time periods, it is easy to extract trend information. This long-term trend data can be plotted and forecasts can be made of future values based on the historical data.

The forecasting techniques can be as simple as a linear regression or as sophisticated as a double-exponential or Gaussian smoothing forecast. The point is that STATSPACK data can be easily graphed to predict future values of database metrics. When creating a forecast, we take existing values from the STATSPACK history and use them to predict a value at a future point in time.

This predictive ability is very useful for any DBA or manager who needs to acquire additional hardware resources such as RAM memory, and a disk of CPU resources.

We will begin this chapter with a discussion on using MS-Excel for plotting STATSPACK data and then move on to look at a wealth of scripts that can be used for trend analysis and forecasting.

Plotting STATSPACK Data Using MS-Excel

Once you have implemented hourly STATSPACK collection, you will develop a great historical database for detailed analysis. In addition to the alerts that we covered in Chapter 14, you can also run STATSPACK reports to provide capacity planning and trend analysis. This can then incorporate linear regression and predictive models so the DBA can predict when to order more disks, RAM memory, and CPU, based on prior consumption rates.

Fortunately, it is not necessary that you purchase an expensive statistical package such as SAS and SPSS. You can use standard Microsoft Excel spreadsheets with chart wizards to make acceptable charts and add forecasts. Let's see how this works.

Plotting STATSPACK Data with a Spreadsheet Chart Wizard

While many third-party products are capable of plotting data for graphical analysis, adequate graphics can be created using Microsoft Excel spreadsheets. The steps for creating the chart are as follows:

1. Run the query in SQL*Plus against the STATSPACK data.

2. Cut and paste the result into the spreadsheet.

3. In MS-Excel, with the data you have just pasted highlighted, choose Data from the drop-down menu and then Text To Columns. This will separate the columns into distinct cells.

4. Press the Chart Wizard button and create a line chart.

5. Choose Chart | Add Trendline to create a forecast line.

To give a simple example, let's take a simple STATSPACK data extract and plot it using the Chart Wizard in MS-Excel. Let's perform an actual analysis and see the steps firsthand. We'll assume that our CIO just contacted us and he or she wants to know the rate of increase in disk read activity for the entire database. The CIO knows that this is not an easy question to answer and gives us two days to assemble and plot the disk read information. Because we know STATSPACK, we know that we can collect and plot this information from the stats$sysstat table in a matter of a few minutes.

Here is a step-by-step description of the process of getting a forecast from STATSPACK data.

Step 1: Customize the STATSPACK Report

We begin by selecting *rpt_io.sql*, which displays hourly physical read and write statistics for the whole database. Because this script reports on each hourly snapshot, we modify the script to compute the average read and writes per day. Note that we have changed the data format string and added the *avg* function to the code.

rpt_io.sql

```
set pages 9999;

column reads   format 999,999,999
column writes  format 999,999,999

select
   to_char(snap_time,'yyyy-mm-dd'),
   avg(newreads.value-oldreads.value) reads,
   avg(newwrites.value-oldwrites.value) writes
from
   perfstat.stats$sysstat oldreads,
   perfstat.stats$sysstat newreads,
   perfstat.stats$sysstat oldwrites,
   perfstat.stats$sysstat newwrites,
   perfstat.stats$snapshot    sn
where
```

```
   newreads.snap_id = sn.snap_id
and
   newwrites.snap_id = sn.snap_id
and
   oldreads.snap_id = sn.snap_id-1
and
   oldwrites.snap_id = sn.snap_id-1
and
  oldreads.statistic# = 40
and
  newreads.statistic# = 40
and
  oldwrites.statistic# = 41
and
  newwrites.statistic# = 41
and
   (newreads.value-oldreads.value) > 0
and
   (newwrites.value-oldwrites.value) > 0
group by
   to_char(snap_time,'yyyy-mm-dd')
;
```

Computing Averages with STATSPACK Scripts

There is often confusion about the proper way to compute average values in STATSPACK queries. For example, the preceding query must subtract the ending snapshot value from the starting snapshot value in order to get the number of reads during the one-hour period between snapshots. When we want to get the average reads per day, we have two options:

```
select
   to_char(snap_time,'yyyy-mm-dd'),
   avg(newreads.value)-avg(oldreads.value),
   avg(newreads.value-oldreads.value)
```

In this snippet we see two methods for computing the average physical reads per day. As it turns out, these variations in computation return identical results:

```
TO_CHAR(SN        READS         READS
---------- ------------ ------------
2000-12-12          193           193
2000-12-13           37            37
2000-12-14           63            63
2000-12-15          100           100
2000-12-16          163           163
2000-12-17          165           165
```

Step 2: Run the Report in SQL*Plus

Now that we have modified the script to compute daily averages, we enter
SQL*Plus and run the report:

```
>sqlplus perfstat/perfstat

SQL*Plus: Release 8.1.6.0.0 - Production on Mon Feb 5 08:21:56 2001

(c) Copyright 1999 Oracle Corporation. All rights reserved.


Connected to:
Oracle8i Enterprise Edition Release 8.1.6.1.0 - 64bit Production
With the Partitioning option
JServer Release 8.1.6.1.0 - 64bit Production

SQL> @rpt_io
```

The report is now displayed on our screen. Now we are ready to highlight and
extract the data to place it in a spreadsheet.

Step 3: Highlight and Copy the Results

The first step is to highlight the data and choose Edit | Copy from the Windows
toolbar (see Figure 15-1).

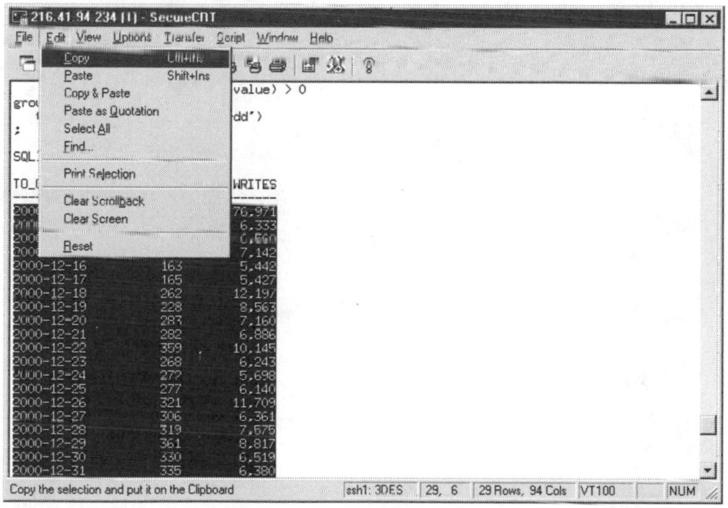

FIGURE 15-1.   *Copying data from SQL*Plus*

Step 4: Open MS-Excel and Paste the Data

In this step, we start Excel, open a spreadsheet, and paste our STATSPACK data into the spreadsheet using Edit | → Paste (or CTRL-V). Note that all of the data still resides in a single column (see Figure 15-2).

Now we need to separate our data into columns in the spreadsheet.

Step 5: Partition the Data into Columns

With our data column highlighted, choose Data from the drop-down menu and then Text to Columns (see Figure 15-3).

We are now guided through a wizard to column delimit the values.

Step 6: Column Delimit the Data

Next, we choose "Fixed width" in the Text to Columns Wizard (see Figure 15-4).

We then accept the defaults for each wizard step and the data will be placed into separate columns.

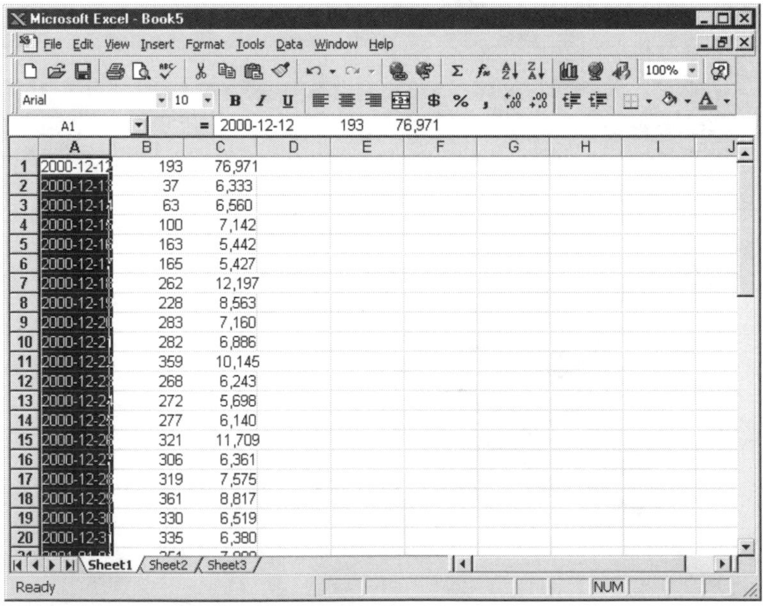

FIGURE 15-2. *Pasting data into a spreadsheet*

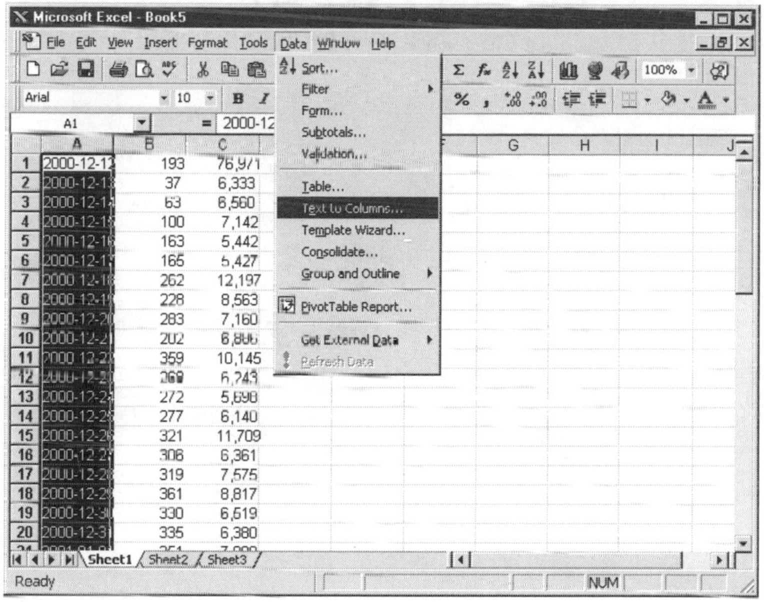

FIGURE 15-3. *Choosing Data | Text to Columns*

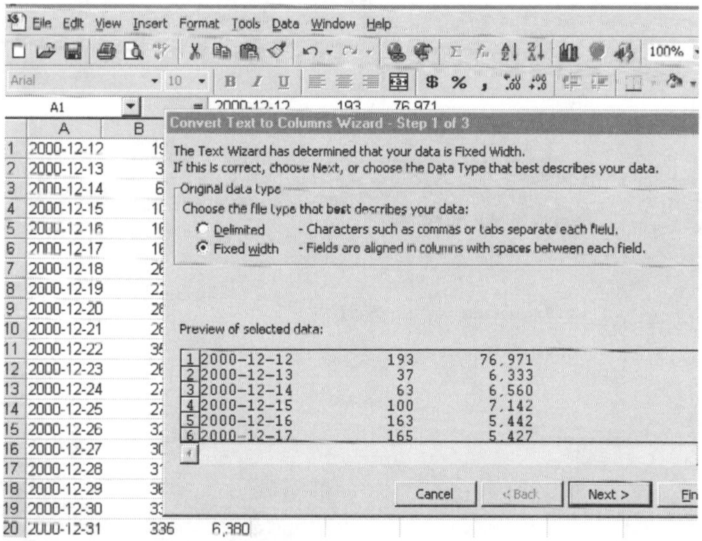

FIGURE 15-4. *Choosing fixed-width column separation*

Step 7: Start the Chart Wizard

In the next step, we highlight the physical reads and press the Chart Wizard button (see Figure 15-5).

Here we see a wizard that will guide us through the process of creating a graph of our STATSPACK data.

Step 8: Choose a Line Chart

Next, we choose a simple line chart (see Figure 15-6).

Step 9: Complete the Chart Wizard and View the Chart

Now we finish the Chart Wizard by accepting the defaults, and we get a basic chart (see Figure 15-7).

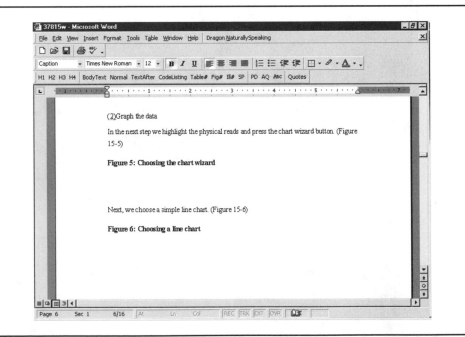

FIGURE 15-5. *Choosing the Chart Wizard*

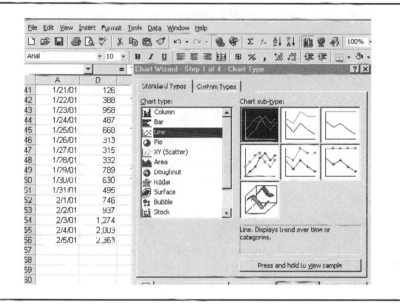

FIGURE 15-6.   *Choosing a line chart*

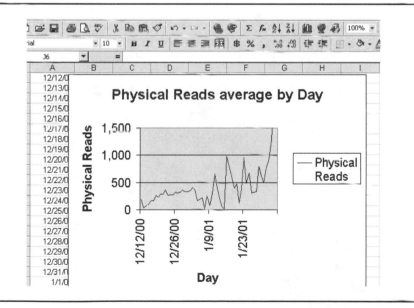

FIGURE 15-7.   *The basic line chart*

Step 10: Add a Trend Line

Finally, we choose Chart | Add Trendline from MS-Excel to add a forecast line.

At this step you are faced with a choice of linear regression techniques, including sum of the least squared, single, double, and triple exponential smoothing methods. In most cases, you will get the most accurate trend line by choosing the default linear trend method. Finally, we display the trend line and the forecast is ready to send to management.

Figure 15-8 shows our completed forecast, ready for management.

Most DBAs will paste the chart in a MS-Word document along with an analysis of the data.

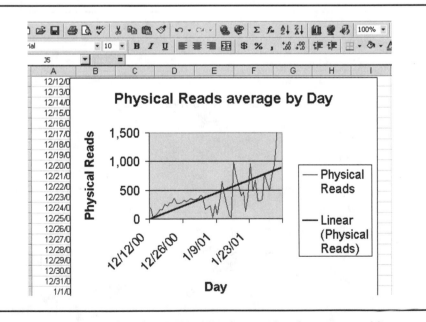

FIGURE 15-8. *A completed STATSPACK chart with a forecast trend line*

Now that we see how to create graphics from our STATSPACK data, let's look at other STATSPACK reports that are useful for forecasting and trend analysis.

STATSPACK Reports for Forecasting

The standard STATSPACK collection mechanism has a host of great information for trend analysis. The scripts I have placed on the companion Web site for this book contain prewritten STATSPACK extract scripts.

There are three types of scripts:

■ **Long-term trend extract scripts**   These simply display the hourly observations for the desired metric.

■ **Averages by hour of the day**   These reports show averages aggregated by the hour of the day. These scripts are in the form *rpt_avg_xxx_hr.sql* and are very useful for identifying regular trends in hourly processing.

■ **Averages by day of the week**   These reports show averages aggregated by day of the week. They are in the form *rpt_avg_xxx_dy.sql* and report on regular trends in daily processing.

Basic STATSPACK Metrics for Trend Analysis

The following STATSPACK data are especially interesting for trend analysis:

■ **Physical reads and physical writes** (*rpt_io.sql, rpt_avg_io_dy.sql, rpt_avg_io_hr.sql*)   These reports are great for showing trends in the physical read and write activity within Oracle. Note that an Oracle physical read is not necessarily an actual disk read because of the RAM caches on most disk arrays.

■ **Data buffer hit ratio** (*rpt_bhr.sql, rpt_avg_bhr_hr.sql, rpt_avg_bhr_dy.sql*)   Plotting the data buffer hit ratio over time can give the DBA great insight into times when the database I/O patterns are changing. Especially useful are the average data buffer hit ratios by hour of the day and day of the week. These will often show theretofore hidden patterns in buffer processing.

■ **I/O waits** (*rpt_io_wait.sql, rpt_avg_io_wait_hr.sql, rpt_avg_io_wait_dy.sql*)   The I/O wait report is useful for showing times when the database was forced to wait for a latch before granting access to an Oracle datafile.

■ **Chained row fetches** (*rpt_chain.sql, rpt_avg_chain_dy.sql, rpt_avg_chain_hr.sql*)   Tracking the fetching of continued rows can help the DBA decide the optimal time to reorganize the database.

- **Full table scans** (*rpt_fts.sql*, *rpt_avg_fts_dy.sql*, *rpt_avg_fts_hr.sql*)
  Tracking full table scans can help the DBA understand those time periods
  when large aggregation or summarization queries are being run. On poorly
  tuned databases, this metric will tell the DBA when to explain the SQL in
  stats$sql_summary for SQL tuning.

- **Cumulative logons** (*rpt_logon.sql*, *rpt_avg_logon_dy.sql*,
  rpt_avg_logon_hr.sql)   This report tracks changes in the cumulative logons
  statistic in stats$sesstat. For lone databases, the hourly and daily average
  reports can show when the end-user community is most active.

- **Sorting activity** (*rpt_sorts.sql*, *rpt_avg_sort_dy.sql*, *rpt_avg_sort_hr.sql*)
  Tracking disk sorts is essential in setting the appropriate value for
  sort_area_size. If the disk sorts are too high, increasing *sort_area_size*
  can greatly improve the performance of sorting tasks.

STATSPACK Extensions for Database Server Trend Analysis

If you implement the STATSPACK extensions for server statistics (see Chapter 5),
you also have scripts to track the following server metrics. The scripts are called
rpt_vmstat.sql, *rpt_vmstat_dy.sql*, and *rpt_vmstat_hr.sql*. These scripts allow you
to choose the metric that you are interested in tracking.

NOTE
*This script requires you to specify the name of the
server. Since the stats$vmstat table collects data
from the database server and the Web servers, you
need to filter the report for the server you are
interested in getting a trend analysis for.*

The database server and Web server reports are especially useful for hardware
trend analysis. These metrics include the following.

- **Run queue trends**   The CPU run queue is a great way to measure the load
  average for the CPU. This data is great for load balancing and forecasting
  when to add more CPUs.

- **Page-in trends**   Any time of nonzero page-in activity indicates a shortage
  of RAM memory. These reports can forecast when the server will exceed
  RAM capacity.

- **CPU trends**   Plotting the average user CPU plus system CPU values can
  tell the DBA the times when the server is overloaded.

Let's start by examining the generic STATSPACK script and see how it is used to track CPU usage. In the next example, we choose to track the average user CPU plus system CPU values.

rpt_vmstat.sql

```
connect perfstat/perfstat;
set pages 9999;

set feedback off;
set verify off;

column my_date heading 'date' format a20
column c2        heading runq     format 999
column c3        heading pg_in    format 999
column c4        heading pg_ot    format 999
column c5        heading usr      format 999
column c6        heading sys      format 999
column c7        heading idl      format 999
column c8        heading wt       format 999


select
 to_char(start_date,'yyyy-mm-dd') my_date,
-- avg(runque_waits)         c2
-- avg(page_in)              c3,
-- avg(page_out)            c4,
avg(user_cpu + system_cpu)           c5,
-- avg(system_cpu)         c6,
-- avg(idle_cpu)           c7,
avg(wait_cpu)          c8
from
   stats$vmstat
where
   server_name = 'prodb1'
group  BY
 to_char(start_date,'yyyy-mm-dd')
order by
 to_char(start_date,'yyyy-mm-dd')
;
```

The following data was generated from running this script:

```
2000-12-20                 6      0
2000-12-21                 6      0
2000-12-22                 4      0
2000-12-23                 6      0
```

2000-12-24	4	0
2000-12-25	7	0
2000-12-26	4	0
2000-12-27	4	0
2000-12-28	5	0
2000-12-29	5	0
2000-12-30	4	0
2000-12-31	4	0
2001-01-01	3	0
2001-01-02	4	0
2001-01-03	24	0
2001-01-04	33	0
2001-01-05	23	0
2001-01-06	14	0
2001-01-07	13	0
2001-01-08	19	0
2001-01-09	22	0
2001-01-10	21	0
2001-01-11	13	0
2001-01-12	13	0
2001-01-13	10	0
2001-01-14	9	0
2001-01-15	21	0
2001-01-16	20	0
2001-01-17	32	0
2001-01-18	25	0
2001-01-19	27	0
2001-01-20	24	0
2001-01-21	24	0
2001-01-22	40	0
2001-01-23	27	0
2001-01-24	25	0
2001-01-25	23	0
2001-01-26	21	0
2001-01-27	18	0
2001-01-28	20	0
2001-01-29	40	0
2001-01-30	29	0
2001-01-31	21	0
2001-02-01	30	0
2001-02-02	33	0
2001-02-03	25	0
2001-02-04	17	0
2001-02-05	27	0

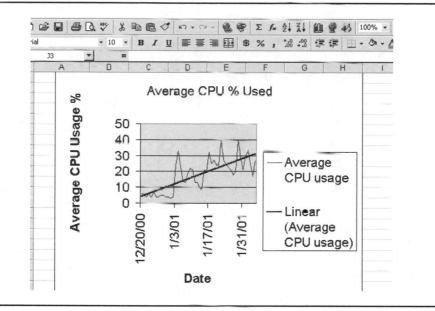

FIGURE 15-9. *A plot of CPU usage over time*

As is, this data is not particularly meaningful, but when plotted, we see a clear trend, as shown in Figure 15-9).

Here we see that the average CPU usage is increasing at a rate of 20 percent per month. At existing rates, the CPU subsystem will reach the maximum capacity in five months. This information can be critical to top IS management who must plan for computer hardware upgrades.

We can quickly modify this script to display page-in values, and we see that this database server is in need of additional RAM. Remember, any nonzero values for RAM page-in indicate that the RAM capacity has been exceeded (see Figure 15-10).

Now, let's look at tracking server trends by hour of the day and day of the week.

Checking Server Trends by Hour

Returning to our basic script, we can easily modify it to capture CPU usage, averaged by hour of the day. Note that all we need to do is to change the date format mask from 'yyyy-mm-dd' to 'HH24'.

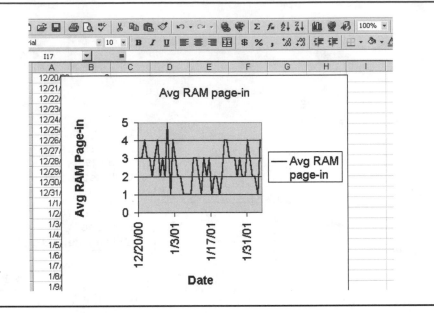

FIGURE 15-10. *A plot of RAM page-in*

rpt_vmstat_hr.sql

```
connect perfstat/perfstat;
set pages 9999;

set feedback off;
set verify off;

column my_date heading 'date' format a20
column c2         heading runq   format 999
column c3         heading pg_in  format 999
column c4         heading pg_ot  format 999
column c5         heading usr    format 999
column c6         heading sys    format 999
column c7         heading idl    format 999
column c8         heading wt     format 999


select
   to_char(start_date,'HH24') my_date,
-- avg(runque_waits)         c2
```

```
--   avg(page_in)            c3
--   avg(page_out)           c4,
avg(user_cpu + system_cpu)            c5
--   avg(system_cpu)          c6,
--   avg(idle_cpu)            c7,
--   avg(wait_cpu)            c8
from
     stats$vmstat
group  BY
   to_char(start_date,'HH24')
order by
   to_char(start_date,'HH24')
;
```

Now, when we run this script, we get the average CPU usage data:

```
date                  usr
-------------------   ----
00                     15
01                     13
02                     13
03                     16
04                     15
05                     14
06                     13
07                     14
08                     17
09                     20
10                     21
11                     21
12                     31
13                     34
14                     37
15                     34
16                     21
17                     21
18                     22
19                     21
20                     19
21                     18
22                     16
23                     15
```

When we plot this data, we clearly see the server gets very busy each day at noon and continues until 3:00 P.M. (see Figure 15-11).

Next, let's modify the script and see trends by day of the week.

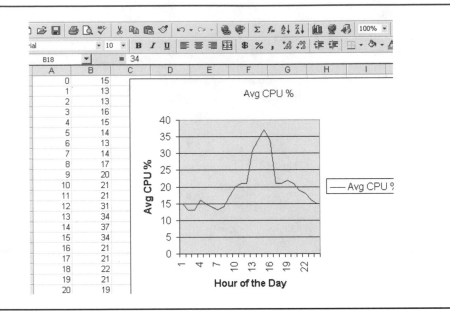

FIGURE 15-11. *A plot of CPU usage by hour of the day*

Plotting Server Statistics by Day of the Week

Next, we change the dat string from 'HH24' to 'day'. This will aggregate the statistics by day of the week. When we run the script, we see the average CPU by day of the week.

```
date                 usr
-------------------- ----
friday                18
monday                53
saturday              14
sunday                14
thursday              20
tuesday               55
wednesday             20
```

When we plot this data, we see that Monday and Tuesday are the busiest processing days of the week (see Figure 15-12).

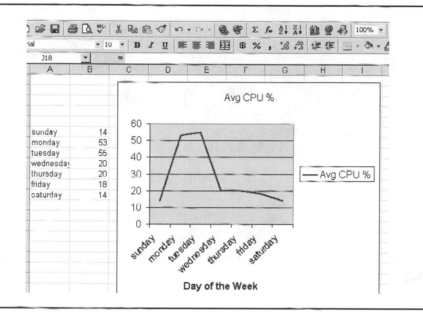

FIGURE 15-12. *A plot of CPU % by day of the week*

Web-Based Plotting of STATSPACK Data

There are several freeware and shareware tools available on the Internet to perform graphical plotting of STATSPACK data. There are dozens of freeware and shareware products on the Internet that can be used to plot STATSPACK data, but we will focus on the most popular tools.

The RRDtool Product

The most popular Web graphing tool is the RRDtool product, which was formerly the graphing and logging component of the MRTG product. It is a GPLed free software product written by the famous Swiss computer scientist Tobi Oetiker.

RRD is the acronym for the round robin database. The RRD system is designed to store and display any form of time-series data such as server, network, and STATSPACK metrics. Extracts can be written to load RRD with STATSPACK data from the Oracle database and the data can then be used to generate trend analysis graphs in GIF format.

The RRDtool product can be downloaded from the following Web site:

http://ee-staff.ethz.ch/~oetiker/webtools/rrdtool/

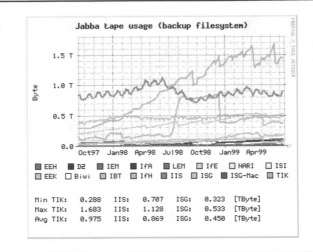

FIGURE 15-13. *An example GIF file created by RRDtool*

RRDtool is very flexible, and is generally used by large Oracle sites to display Oracle, server, and network performance data in Web pages. At the simplest level, RRDtool accepts data sets and creates GIF files that can then be embedded into HTML pages. Figure 15-13 shows an example of a GIF file generated by RRDtool.

Other Web-Based Graphing Tools

There are dozens of interactive Web sites that can be used to generate a plot of STATSPACK data. As a representative sample, let's look at the facility offered at the University of New South Wales in Sidney, Australia. Here is a link to their interactive data plotting Web site:

http://www.phys.unsw.edu.au/3rdyearlab/graphing/graph.html

This Web site accepts data points and creates the appropriate graph based upon your inputs. In the following example, we paste in our STATSPACK data for average CPU usage by hour of the day. As shown in Figure 15-14, we choose a Gaussian fit technique that gives a smooth curve for the average CPU usage.

Next we see the plot for the data (see Figure 15-15). This is presented as a GIF image (General Interchange Format) within the Web page.

To capture this GIF file for inclusion in an HTML page or an MS-Word document, you can simply right-click the image and save it to a local file on your PC (see Figure 15-16).

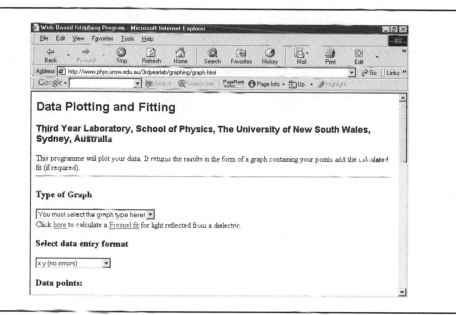

FIGURE 15-14. *An example of an Internet-based plotting utility*

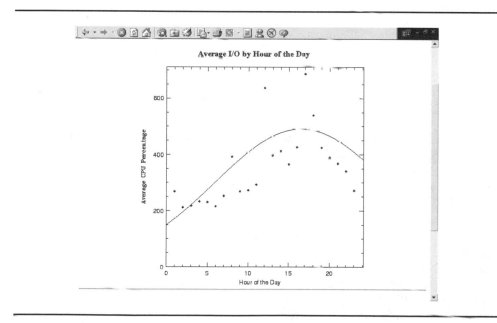

FIGURE 15-15. *A Web-based plot of average CPU percentage*

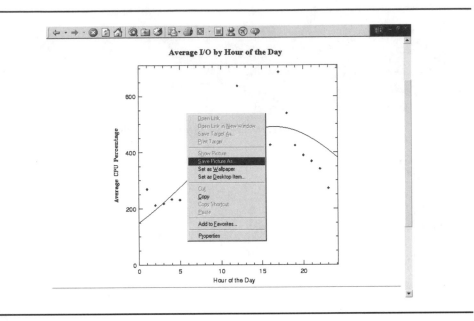

FIGURE 15-16. *Capturing a Web image to a PC file*

To summarize, there are a wealth of graphics tools that can be used to plot STATSPACK data and present it in meaningful formats. Regardless of the method you choose, presenting long-term trends with STATSPACK can provide management with critical strategic planning information.

Conclusion

This chapter has provided a basic starting point for the DBA to extract STATSPACK and plot the data for forecasting purposes. The material in this chapter is intended to give you the general idea of how to present forecasts, but there are far more sophisticated analyses that can be done with the wealth of statistics inside the STATSPACK tables.

As a working DBA who specializes in tuning, I am always excited to hear when a reader has developed a new script or STATSPACK technique. Please feel free to e-mail me if you have any new material to share. My e-mail address is burleson@frontiernet.net.

I wrote this book because there is a huge amount of benefit to using STATSPACK in tuning your database. It is my hope that the material presented in this book has assisted you in your tuning endeavors.

Appendix
of STATSPACK Scripts

he following pages will include an alphabetical listing of all of the scripts that are referenced in this book. The scripts are available online at the Oracle Press Web site at www.oraclepress.com and are reproduced here for your use. These scripts fall into several topical areas.

- **Oracle library cache mining scripts** These are the scripts that can be used to explain all of the SQL in the library cache and produce reports showing the types of table access, as well as the tables and indexes involved in the access.

- **STATSPACK reports** These are listings of all of the STATSPACK scripts.

- **STATSPACK extension scripts** These scripts will be used to extend the standard STATSPACK for disk I/O statistics, UNIX server statistics and Oracle table and index statistics.

Library Cache Mining Scripts

These scripts are a technique that runs the Oracle8i **explain plan** statement on all SQL statements in the library cache, analyzes all the execution plans, and provides reports on all table and index access methods. The reports generated by access_reports.sql are invaluable for the following database activities:

- **Identifying high-use tables and indexes** See what tables the database accesses the most frequently.

- **Identifying tables for caching** You can quickly find small, frequently accessed tables for placement in the KEEP pool (Oracle8) or for use with the CACHE option (Oracle7). You can enhance the technique to automatically cache tables when they meet certain criteria for the number of blocks and the number of accesses. (I automatically cache all tables with fewer than 200 blocks when a table has experienced more than 100 full-table scans.)

- **Identifying tables for row re-sequencing** You can locate large tables that have frequent index range scans in order to re-sequence the rows, to reduce I/O.

- **Dropping unused indexes** You can reclaim space occupied by unused indexes. Studies have found that an Oracle database never uses more than a quarter of all indexes available or doesn't use them in the way for which they were intended.

- **Stopping full table scans by adding new indexes** Quickly find the full table scans that you can speed up by adding a new index to a table.

Here are the steps to execute this script:

1. Download the *access.sql* and *access_report.sql* scripts.

2. Issue the following statements for the schema owner of your tables:

```
grant select on v_$sqltext to schema_owner;
grant select on v_$sqlarea to schema_owner;
grant select on v_$session to schema_owner;
grant select on v_$mystat to schema_owner;
```

3. Go into SQL*Plus, connect as the schema owner, and run *access.sql*.

You must be signed on as the schema owner in order to explain SQL statements with unqualified table names. Also, remember that you will get statistics only for the SQL statements that currently reside in your library cache. For very active databases, you may want to run this report script several times —it takes less than ten minutes for most Oracle databases.

access.sql

```
© 2001 by Donald Keith Burleson - All Rights Reserved
set echo on;
--*********************************************************************
-- Object Access script
--
-- This script is a modification of an Oracle-supplied script.
-- The script creates a stored procedure that executes EXPLAIN
-- PLAN for every SQL statement in the library cache, and runs
-- counting reports against the EXPLAIN PLAN output.
--
-- The following reports are produced:
--
-- 1. Full-table scan counts by table (with num_rows)
-- 2. Table access by ROWID by table
-- 3. Index full scans
-- 4. Index range scans
-- 5. Index unique scans
--
-- Modified from the Oracle script by Donald K. Burleson
-- 3/6/2000  modified to add/use get_sql function by John Beresniewicz
--           NOTE: Oracle8i bug in V$SQLTEXT will cause this not to work there
-- 3/6/2000  modified to work around signed/unsigned problem in hash values
-- 3/6/2000  modified to only call function where LENGTH(SQLTEXT)>1900 chars in length
-- 3/6/2000  modified to try signed AND unsigned hash values
--
-- NOTE: requires direct GRANT SELECT on V_$SQLTEXT
--       requires direct GRANT SELECT on V_$SESSION, V_$MYSTAT
--*********************************************************************
```

```
set serveroutput on size 100000

set echo off;
prompt We first gather all SQL in the library cache and run EXPLAIN PLAN.
prompt This takes awhile, so be patient . . .

--set echo on
--set feedback on

set feedback off
set echo off
-- Drop and recreate PLAN_TABLE for EXPLAIN PLAN
drop table plan_table;
@$ORACLE_HOME/rdbms/admin/utlxplan

Rem Drop and recreate SQLTEMP for taking a snapshot of the SQLAREA
drop table sqltemp;
create table sqltemp
(
  ADDR         VARCHAR2 (16)
 ,HASHVAL      INTEGER
 ,SQL_TEXT     VARCHAR2(2000)
 ,DISK_READS   NUMBER
 ,EXECUTIONS   NUMBER
 ,PARSE_CALLS  NUMBER
 ,PARSE_USER   VARCHAR2(30)
 ,STMT_ID      VARCHAR2(100)
);

--set echo on
set feedback on

CREATE OR REPLACE PROCEDURE do_explain
    (addr IN  VARCHAR2
    ,hash IN INTEGER
    ,sql_text_IN IN VARCHAR2
    ,parse_user_IN IN VARCHAR2
    ,stmt_id_IN IN VARCHAR2 )
AS

    dummy     VARCHAR2(32767);

    dummy1    VARCHAR2(100);

    mycursor INTEGER;
    ret       INTEGER;
    my_sqlerrm VARCHAR2 (85);
    signed_hash NUMBER;
```

```
FUNCTION get_sql(addr_IN IN VARCHAR2, hash_IN IN INTEGER)
RETURN VARCHAR2
IS
   temp_return  VARCHAR2(32767);
   CURSOR sql_pieces_cur
   IS
   SELECT sql_text
     FROM v$sqltext
    WHERE address = HEXTORAW(addr_IN)
      AND hash_value = hash_IN
   ORDER BY piece ASC;
BEGIN
   FOR sql_pieces_rec IN sql_pieces_cur
   LOOP
      temp_return := temp_return||sql_pieces_rec.sql_text;
   END LOOP;

   IF temp_return IS NULL
   THEN
      RAISE_APPLICATION_ERROR(-20000,'SQL Not Found');
   END IF;

   RETURN temp_return;
END get_sql;

FUNCTION current_schema RETURN VARCHAR2
IS
   temp_schema   v$session.schemaname%TYPE;
BEGIN
   SELECT schemaname
     INTO temp_schema
     FROM v$session
    WHERE sid = (SELECT MAX(sid) FROM v$mystat);
   --
   RETURN temp_schema;
EXCEPTION
   WHEN OTHERS THEN RETURN NULL;
END current_schema;

BEGIN
-- adjust signed_hash if hash > 2**31
-- (hash type mismatch between v$sqlarea and v$sqltext)
IF hash > POWER(2,31)
THEN
   signed_hash := hash - POWER(2,32);
ELSE
   signed_hash := hash;
```

```
    END IF;


    dummy1 := 'ALTER SESSION SET CURRENT_SCHEMA ='||parse_user_IN ;


    dummy:='EXPLAIN PLAN SET STATEMENT_ID='''||stmt_id_IN||''' INTO plan_table FOR
;
    IF LENGTH(sql_text_IN) > 1900
    THEN
       BEGIN  -- try to get using hash first, and unsigned hash if not found
          dummy:=dummy||get_sql(addr,hash);

       EXCEPTION
          WHEN OTHERS THEN dummy:=dummy||get_sql(addr,signed_hash);

       END;
    ELSE
       dummy := dummy||sql_text_IN;
    END IF;

    -- JB: optimization = only change schema if different from current
    --IF parse_user_IN != current_schema
    --THEN
    --   dbms_output.put_line(current_schema||' '||parse_user_IN);
    --   mycursor := DBMS_SQL.OPEN_CURSOR;
    --   DBMS_SQL.PARSE(mycursor,dummy1,DBMS_SQL.NATIVE);
    --   ret := DBMS_SQL.EXECUTE(mycursor);
    --   DBMS_SQL.CLOSE_CURSOR(mycursor);
    --END IF;

    mycursor := DBMS_SQL.OPEN_CURSOR;
    DBMS_SQL.PARSE(mycursor,dummy,DBMS_SQL.NATIVE);
    ret := DBMS_SQL.EXECUTE(mycursor);


    DBMS_SQL.CLOSE_CURSOR(mycursor);


    COMMIT;
EXCEPTION -- Insert errors into PLAN_TABLE...
    WHEN OTHERS
    THEN
       my_sqlerrm := SUBSTR(sqlerrm,1,80);
       INSERT INTO plan_table(statement_id,remarks) -- change to plan_table (JB)
       VALUES (stmt_id_IN, my_sqlerrm);
```

```
        -- cleanup cursor id open
        IF DBMS_SQL.IS_OPEN(mycursor)
        THEN
            DBMS_SQL.CLOSE_CURSOR(mycursor);
        END IF;

END;
/

show errors

DECLARE

    CURSOR  c1
    IS
    SELECT
            RAWTOHEX(SA.address)    addr
            ,SA.hash_value          hash
            ,SA.sql_text            sql_text
            ,SA.DISK_READS          diskrds
            ,SA.EXECUTIONS          execs
            ,SA.PARSE_CALLS         parses
            ,DU.username            username
            ,SUBSTR(RAWTOHEX(SA.address)||':'||TO_CHAR(SA.hash_value) , 1,30) stmt_id
      FROM
            v$sqlarea     SA
            ,DBA_USERS    DU
      WHERE
            command_type in (2,3,6,7)
        AND
            SA.parsing_schema_id != 0
        AND SA.parsing_schema_id = DU.user_id;

    CURSOR c2
    IS
    SELECT
            addr
            ,hashval
            ,sql_text
            ,parse_user
            ,stmt_id
      FROM
            sqltemp
      ORDER BY parse_user;

BEGIN
    FOR c1_rec IN c1
```

```
      LOOP
         INSERT INTO
            sqltemp (ADDR
                     ,HASHVAL
                     ,SQL_TEXT
                     ,DISK_READS
                     ,EXECUTIONS
                     ,PARSE_CALLS
                     ,PARSE_USER
                     ,STMT_ID
                     )
            VALUES (c1_rec.addr
                     ,c1_rec.hash
                     ,c1_rec.sql_text
                     ,c1_rec.diskrds
                     ,c1_rec.execs
                     ,c1_rec.parses
                     ,c1_rec.username
                     ,c1_rec.stmt_id
                     );
      END LOOP;
      --
      FOR c2_rec IN c2
      LOOP
         do_explain(c2_rec.addr
                     ,c2_rec.hashval
                     ,c2_rec.sql_text
                     ,c2_rec.parse_user
                     ,c2_rec.stmt_id);
      END LOOP;
   END;
   /

   --show errors

   -- ******************************************************
   -- Report section
   -- ******************************************************

   --@/s001/app/oracle/home/sql/access_report

   --drop procedure do_explain;
   --drop table sqltemp;
   --drop table plan_table;
```

access_keep_syntax.sql

```
-- ***********************************************************
-- Report section
-- ***********************************************************
   © 2001 by Donald Keith Burleson - All Rights Reserved

set echo off;
set feedback on

column nbr_FTS   format 999,999
column num_rows  format 999,999,999
column blocks    format 999,999
column owner     format a14;
column name      format a25;

set heading off;
set feedback off;
select
   'alter table '||p.owner||'.'||p.name||' storage (buffer_pool keep);'
from
   dba_tables t,
   dba_segments s,
   sqltemp s,
  (select distinct
     statement_id stid,
     object_owner owner,
     object_name name
   from
     plan_table
   where
     operation = 'TABLE ACCESS'
     and
     options = 'FULL') p
where
   s.addr||':'||TO_CHAR(s.hashval) = p.stid
   and
   t.table_name = s.segment_name
   and
   t.table_name = p.name
   and
   t.owner = p.owner
   and
   t.buffer_pool <> 'KEEP'
having
   s.blocks < 50
group by
   p.owner, p.name, t.num_rows, s.blocks
```

```
order by
   sum(s.executions) desc;

access_parallel_syntax.sql
-- **********************************************************
-- Report section
-- **********************************************************

set echo off;
set feedback on

-- © 2001 by Donald Keith Burleson - All Rights Reserved
column nbr_FTS   format 999,999
column num_rows format 999,999,999
column blocks    format 999,999
column owner     format a14;
column name      format a25;

set heading off;
set feedback off;
select
   'alter table '||p.owner||'.'||p.name||' parallel degree 11;'
from
   dba_tables t,
   dba_segments s,
   sqltemp s,
  (select distinct
     statement_id stid,
     object_owner owner,
     object_name name
   from
      plan_table
   where
     operation = 'TABLE ACCESS'
     and
     options = 'FULL') p
where
   s.addr||':'||TO_CHAR(s.hashval) = p.stid
   and
   t.table_name = s.segment_name
   and
   t.table_name = p.name
   and
   t.owner = p.owner
   and
   t.degree = 1
having
   s.blocks > 1000
group by
```

```
   p.owner, p.name, t.num_rows, s.blocks
order by
   sum(s.executions) desc;
access_recycle_syntax.sql


--  ******************************************************
--  Report section
--  ******************************************************

set echo off;
set feedback on

--  © 2001 by Donald Keith Burleson - All Rights Reserved
column nbr_FTS   format 999,999
column num_rows format 999,999,999
column blocks    format 999,999
column owner     format a14;
column name      format a25;

set heading off;
set feedback off;
select
   'alter table '||p.owner||'.'||p.name||' storage (buffer_pool recycle);'
from
   dba_tables t,
   dba_segments s,
   sqltemp s,
   (select distinct
      statement_id stid,
      object_owner owner,
      object_name name
   from
      plan_table
   where
      operation = 'TABLE ACCESS'
      and
      options = 'FULL') p
where
   s.addr||':'||TO_CHAR(s.hashval) = p.stid
   and
   t.table_name = s.segment_name
   and
   t.table_name = p.name
   and
   t.owner = p.owner
   and
   t.buffer_pool <> 'RECYCLE'
having
```

```
    s.blocks > 1000
group by
    p.owner, p.name, t.num_rows, s.blocks
order by
    sum(s.executions) desc;
```

access_report.sql

```
-- ********************************************************
-- Report section
-- ********************************************************
-- © 2001 by Donald Keith Burleson - All Rights Reserved

set echo off;
set feedback on

column nbr_FTS   format 999,999
column num_rows  format 999,999,999
column blocks    format 999,999
column owner     format a14;
column name      format a24;
column ch        format a1;
column K         format a1;

--spool access.lst;

set heading off;
set feedback off;
ttitle 'Total SQL found in library cache'
select count(distinct statement_id) from plan_table;

ttitle 'Total SQL that could not be explained'
select count(distinct statement_id) from plan_table where remarks is not null;

set heading on;
set feedback on;
ttitle 'full table scans and counts|  |Note that "?" indicates in the table is cached.'
select
    p.owner,
    p.name,
    t.num_rows,
    ltrim(t.cache) ch,
    decode(t.buffer_pool,'KEEP','K','DEFAULT',' ') K,
    s.blocks blocks,
    sum(s.executions) nbr_FTS
from
    dba_tables t,
```

```
      dba_segments s,
      sqltemp s,
      (select distinct
         statement_id stid,
         object_owner owner,
         object_name name
      from
         plan_table
      where
         operation = 'TABLE ACCESS'
         and
         options = 'FULL') p
where
      s.addr||':'||TO_CHAR(s.hashval) = p.stid
      and
      t.owner = s.owner
      and
      t.table_name = s.segment_name
      and
      t.table_name = p.name
      and
      t.owner = p.owner
having
      sum(s.executions) > 9
group by
      p.owner, p.name, t.num_rows, t.cache, t.buffer_pool, s.blocks
order by
      sum(s.executions) desc;

column nbr_RID   format 999,999,999
column num_rows  format 999,999,999
column owner     format a15;
column name      format a25;

ttitle 'Table access by ROWID and counts'
select
      p.owner,
      p.name,
      t.num_rows,
      sum(s.executions) nbr_RID
from
      dba_tables t,
      sqltemp s,
      (select distinct
         statement_id stid,
         object_owner owner,
         object_name name
      from
```

```
      plan_table
  where
      operation = 'TABLE ACCESS'
      and
      options = 'BY ROWID') p
where
  s.addr||':'||TO_CHAR(s.hashval) = p.stid
  and
  t.table_name = p.name
  and
  t.owner = p.owner
having
  sum(s.executions) > 9
group by
  p.owner, p.name, t.num_rows
order by
  sum(s.executions) desc;


--***************************************************
--   Index Report Section
--***************************************************

column nbr_scans   format 999,999,999
column num_rows    format 999,999,999
column tbl_blocks  format 999,999,999
column owner       format a9;
column table_name  format a20;
column index_name  format a20;

ttitle 'Index full scans and counts'
select
  p.owner,
  d.table_name,
  p.name index_name,
  seg.blocks tbl_blocks,
  sum(s.executions) nbr_scans
from
  dba_segments seg,
  sqltemp s,
  dba_indexes d,
  (select distinct
    statement_id stid,
    object_owner owner,
    object_name name
  from
    plan_table
  where
    operation = 'INDEX'
    and
```

```
       options = 'FULL SCAN') p
where
   d.index_name = p.name
   and
   s.addr||':'||TO_CHAR(s.hashval) = p.stid
   and
   d.table_name = seg.segment_name
   and
   seg.owner = p.owner
having
   sum(s.executions) > 9
group by
   p.owner, d.table_name, p.name, seg.blocks
order by
   sum(s.executions) desc;


ttitle 'Index range scans and counts'
select
   p.owner,
   d.table_name,
   p.name index_name,
   seg.blocks tbl_blocks,
   sum(s.executions) nbr_scans
from
   dba_segments seg,
   sqltemp s,
   dba_indexes d,
   (select distinct
      statement_id stid,
      object_owner owner,
      object_name name
    from
      plan_table
    where
      operation = 'INDEX'
      and
      options = 'RANGE SCAN') p
where
   d.index_name = p.name
   and
   s.addr||':'||TO_CHAR(s.hashval) = p.stid
   and
   d.table_name = seg.segment_name
   and
   seg.owner = p.owner
having
   sum(s.executions) > 9
```

```
group by
   p.owner, d.table_name, p.name, seg.blocks
order by
   sum(s.executions) desc;


ttitle 'Index unique scans and counts'
select
   p.owner,
   d.table_name,
   p.name index_name,
   sum(s.executions) nbr_scans
from
   sqltemp s,
   dba_indexes d,
   (select distinct
      statement_id stid,
      object_owner owner,
      object_name name
    from
       plan_table
    where
       operation = 'INDEX'
       and
       options = 'UNIQUE SCAN') p
where
   d.index_name = p.name
   and
   s.addr||':'||TO_CHAR(s.hashval) = p.stid
having
   sum(s.executions) > 9
group by
   p.owner, d.table_name, p.name
order by
   sum(s.executions) desc;
```

STATSPACK Report Scripts

This is an alphabetical listing of all of the scripts that are referenced in this text.

cleanup_old_stats.ksh

```
#!/bin/ksh
# © 2001 by Donald Keith Burleson - All Rights Reserved

# First, we must set the environment . . . .
ORACLE_SID=readprod
```

```
export ORACLE_SID
ORACLE_HOME=`cat /var/opt/oracle/oratab|grep ^$ORACLE_SID:|cut -f2 -d':'`
export ORACLE_HOME
PATH=$ORACLE_HOME/bin:$PATH
export PATH

$ORACLE_HOME/bin/sqlplus oracle/oracle<<!

select * from v\$database;
set heading off;
set lines 999;

select count(*) from perfstat.stats\$snapshot where snap_time < sysdate - 30;
select count(*) from perfstat.stats\$snapshot where snap_time > sysdate - 30;
delete from perfstat.stats\$snapshot where snap_time < sysdate - 30;
exit
!

count_stats.sql
connect perfstat/perfstat;

set heading off;
-- © 2001 by Donald Keith Burleson - All Rights Reserved

spool run_count.sql;

select
   'select count(*) from perfstat.'||table_name||';'
from
   dba_tables
where
   owner = 'PERFSTAT'
;

spool off

set feedback on;
set echo on;

@run_count
```

create_idlm_table.sql

```
-- © 2001 by Donald Keith Burleson - All Rights Reserved
connect perfstat/perfstat;

drop table perfstat.stats$idlm_stats;
```

```
create table perfstat.stats$idlm_stats
(
   snap_time      date,
   pro            number,
   res            number,
   loc            number
)
tablespace perfstat
storage (initial 1m next 1m maxextents unlimited)
;
```

del_sql_summary.sql

```
-- © 2001 by Donald Keith Burleson - All Rights Reserved
delete from
   perfstat.stats$sql_summary
where
   snap_id in
   (select
      snap_id
   from
      perfstat.stats$snapshot
   where
   snap_time < sysdate -30)
   ;
```

desc.sql

```
-- © 2001 by Donald Keith Burleson - All Rights Reserved
set lines 80;
-- © 2001 by Donald Keith Burleson - All Rights Reserved
set heading off;

spool run_count.sql

select
'desc '||table_name||';'
from dba_tables
where table_name like 'STATS$%';

spool off;

set echo on;
@run_count
```

get_busy.ksh

```ksh
#!/bin/ksh
# © 2001 by Donald Keith Burleson - All Rights Reserved

# First, we must set the environment . . . .
ORACLE_SID=PROD
export ORACLE_SID
ORACLE_HOME=`cat /etc/oratab|grep \^$ORACLE_SID:|cut -f2 -d':'`
export ORACLE_HOME
PATH=$ORACLE_HOME/bin:$PATH
export PATH
MON=`echo ~oracle/mon`
export MON
ORA_ENVFILE=${ORACLE_HOME}/${ORACLE_SID}.env
. $ORA_ENVFILE

SERVER_NAME=`uname -a|awk '{print $2}'`
typeset -u SERVER_NAME
export SERVER_NAME

# sample every 10 seconds
SAMPLE_TIME=10

while true
do

    #*************************************************************
    # Test to see if Oracle is accepting connections
    #*************************************************************
    $ORACLE_HOME/bin/sqlplus s /<<! > /tmp/check_$ORACLE_SID.ora
    select * from v\$database;
    exit
!

    #*************************************************************
    # If not, exit . . .
    #*************************************************************
    check_stat=`cat /tmp/check_$ORACLE_SID.ora|grep -i error|wc -l`;
    oracle_num=`expr $check_stat`
    if [ $oracle_num -eq 0 ]
        then

        rm -f /home/oracle/statspack/busy.lst

        $ORACLE_HOME/bin/sqlplus -s / <<!>/home/oracle/statspack/busy.lst

        set feedback off;
```

```
       select
          to_char(sysdate,'yyy-mm-dd HH24:mi:ss'),
          event,
          substr(tablespace_name,1,14),
          p2
       from
          v\$session_wait a,
          dba_data_files  b
       where
          a.p1 = b.file_id
       and
          event in
          (
            'buffer busy waits',
            'enqueue'
          )
       ;

   !

       var=`cat /home/oracle/statspack/busy.lst|wc -l`

       if [[ $var -gt 1 ]];
        then
          echo "***************************************************************"
          echo "There are waits"
          cat /home/oracle/statspack/busy.lst|\
              mailx -s "Monona block wait found"\
          dburleson@biteme.com
#         dhurley@biteme.com \
          echo "***************************************************************"
        exit
        fi

       sleep $SAMPLE_TIME
    fi
done
```

get_idlm.ksh

```
# Capture IDLM statistics - (c) 1998 by Donald Keith Burleson
DAY_OF_WEEK=`date +"%A"`
MACHINE_NAME=`hostname`
REPORT_FILE=/oracle/HOME/dba_reports/dlm_monitor.${MACHINE_NAME}.${DAY_O
F_WEEK}.log
```

```
#
# Set up the file to log the lock to:
#
TIMESTAMP=`date +"%C%y.%m.%d-%H:%M:%S"`
DLM_RESOURCES=`/oracle/HOME/bin/lkdump -a res | head -2 | awk 'getline'`
DLM_LOCKS=`/oracle/HOME/bin/lkdump -a lock | head -2 | awk 'getline' `
DLM_PROCESS=`/oracle/HOME/bin/lkdump -a proc | head -2 | awk 'getline'`
printf "$TIMESTAMP $DLM_RESOURCES $DLM_LOCKS $DLM_PROCESS \n" >> $REPORT_FILE

RES=`echo $DLM_RESOURCES|cut -f2 -d '='`
LOC=`echo $DLM_LOCKS|cut -f2 -d '='`
PRO=`echo $DLM_PROCESS|cut -f2 -d '='`

ORACLE_SID=HOME; export ORACLE_SID;
PATH=$PATH:/oracle/HOME/bin; export PATH;
ORACLE_HOME=/oracle/HOME; export ORACLE_HOME;

/oracle/HOME/bin/sqlplus <<! >> /dev/null

connect perfstat/perfstat;

insert into perfstat.stats$idlm_stats
 values (
    SYSDATE,
    $PRO,
    $RES,
    $LOC );

exit;
!
```

list_snaps.ksh

```
#!/bin/ksh
# © 2001 by Donald Keith Burleson - All Rights Reserved

# First, we must set the environment . . . .
ORACLE_SID=$ORACLE_SID
export ORACLE_SID
ORACLE_HOME=`cat /etc/oratab|grep ^$ORACLE_SID:|cut -f2 -d':'`
#ORACLE_HOME=`cat /var/opt/oracle/oratab|grep ^$ORACLE_SID:|cut -f2 -d':'`
export ORACLE_HOME
PATH=$ORACLE_HOME/bin:$PATH
export PATH

$ORACLE_HOME/bin/sqlplus perfstat/perfstat<<!
```

```
select
   name,
   snap_id,
   to_char(snap_time,' dd Mon YYYY HH24:mi:ss')
from
   stats\$snapshot,
   v\$database
order by
   snap_id
;
exit
!
```

quick.ksh

```
#!/bin/ksh
# © 2001 by Donald Keith Burleson - All Rights Reserved

# First, we must set the environment . . . .
ORACLE_SID=$ORACLE_SID
export ORACLE_SID
ORACLE_HOME=`cat /etc/oratab|grep ^$ORACLE_SID:|cut -f2 -d':'`
#ORACLE_HOME=`cat /var/opt/oracle/oratab|grep ^$ORACLE_SID:|cut -f2 -d':'`
export ORACLE_HOME
PATH=$ORACLE_HOME/bin:$PATH
export PATH

echo "Please enter the number of seconds between snapshots."
read elapsed

$ORACLE_HOME/bin/sqlplus perfstat/perfstat<<!
execute statspack.snap;
exit
!

sleep $elapsed

$ORACLE_HOME/bin/sqlplus perfstat/perfstat<<!
execute statspack.snap;

select
   name,
   snap_id,
   to_char(snap_time,' dd Mon YYYY HH24:mi:ss')
from
   stats\$snapshot,
   v\$database
```

```
where
   snap_id > (select max(snap_id)-2 from stats\$snapshot)
;

@rpt_last
```

rpt_avg_bbw_dy.sql

```
-- © 2001 by Donald Keith Burleson - All Rights Reserved

column buffer_busy_wait format 999,999,999

select
   to_char(snap_time,'day'),
   avg(new.buffer_busy_wait-old.buffer_busy_wait) buffer_busy_wait
from
   perfstat.stats$buffer_pool_statistics old,
   perfstat.stats$buffer_pool_statistics new,
   perfstat.stats$snapshot    sn
where
   new.snap_id = sn.snap_id
and
   old.snap_id = sn.snap_id-1
group by
   to_char(snap_time,'day')
;
```

rpt_avg_bbw_hr.sql

```
-- © 2001 by Donald Keith Burleson - All Rights Reserved

column buffer_busy_wait format 999,999,999

select
   to_char(snap_time,'HH24'),
   avg(new.buffer_busy_wait-old.buffer_busy_wait) buffer_busy_wait
from
   perfstat.stats$buffer_pool_statistics old,
   perfstat.stats$buffer_pool_statistics new,
   perfstat.stats$snapshot    sn
where
   new.snap_id = sn.snap_id
and
   old.snap_id = sn.snap_id-1
group by
```

```
   to_char(snap_time,'HH24')
;
```

rpt_avg_bhr_dy.sql

```
column logical_reads  format 999,999,999
column phys_reads     format 999,999,999
column phys_writes    format 999,999,999
column "BUFFER HIT RATIO" format 999

select
   to_char(snap_time,'day'),
   avg(round(100 * (((a.value-e.value)+(b.value-f.value))-(c.value-g.value)) /
(a.value-e.value)+(b.value-f.value)))))
        "BUFFER HIT RATIO"
from
   perfstat.stats$sysstat a,
   perfstat.stats$sysstat b,
   perfstat.stats$sysstat c,
   perfstat.stats$sysstat d,
   perfstat.stats$sysstat e,
   perfstat.stats$sysstat f,
   perfstat.stats$sysstat g,
   perfstat.stats$snapshot    sn
where
   a.snap_id = sn.snap_id
and
   b.snap_id = sn.snap_id
and
   c.snap_id = sn.snap_id
and
   d.snap_id = sn.snap_id
and
   e.snap_id = sn.snap_id-1
and
   f.snap_id = sn.snap_id-1
and
   g.snap_id = sn.snap_id-1
and
   a.statistic# = 39
and
   e.statistic# = 39
and
   b.statistic# = 38
```

```
and
   f.statistic# = 38
and
   c.statistic# = 40
and
   g.statistic# = 40
and
   d.statistic# = 41
group by
   to_char(snap_time,'day')
;
```

rpt_avg_bhr_hr.sql

```
-- © 2001 by Donald Keith Burleson - All Rights Reserved

column logical_reads  format 999,999,999
column phys_reads     format 999,999,999
column phys_writes    format 999,999,999
column "BUFFER HIT RATIO" format 999

select
   to_char(snap_time,'HH24'),
   avg(round(100 * (((a.value-e.value)+(b.value-f.value)) (c.value-g.value)) /
(a.value-e.value)+(b.value-f.value))))
        "BUFFER HIT RATIO"
from
   perfstat.stats$sysstat a,
   perfstat.stats$sysstat b,
   perfstat.stats$sysstat c,
   perfstat.stats$sysstat d,
   perfstat.stats$sysstat e,
   perfstat.stats$sysstat f,
   perfstat.stats$sysstat g,
   perfstat.stats$snapshot   sn
where
   a.snap_id = sn.snap_id
and
   b.snap_id = sn.snap_id
and
   c.snap_id = sn.snap_id
and
   d.snap_id = sn.snap_id
and
   e.snap_id = sn.snap_id-1
and
```

```
   f.snap_id = sn.snap_id-1
and
   g.snap_id = sn.snap_id-1
and
   a.statistic# = 39
and
   e.statistic# = 39
and
   b.statistic# = 38
and
   f.statistic# = 38
and
   c.statistic# = 40
and
   g.statistic# = 40
and
   d.statistic# = 41
group by
   to_char(snap_time,'HH24')
;
```

rpt_avg_chain_dy.sql

```
-- © 2001 by Donald Keith Burleson - All Rights Reserved

column table_fetch_continued_row   format 999,999,999

select
   to_char(snap_time,'day'),
   avg(newmem.value-oldmem.value) table_fetch_continued_row
from
   perfstat.stats$sysstat oldmem,
   perfstat.stats$sysstat newmem,
   perfstat.stats$snapshot    sn
where
   newmem.snap_id = sn.snap_id
and
   oldmem.snap_id = sn.snap_id-1
and
   oldmem.name = 'table fetch continued row'
and
   newmem.name = 'table fetch continued row'
and
   newmem.value-oldmem.value > 0
group by
   to_char(snap_time,'day')
;
```

rpt_avg_chain_hr.sql

```
-- © 2001 by Donald Keith Burleson - All Rights Reserved

column table_fetch_continued_row  format 999,999,999

select
   to_char(snap_time,'HH24'),
   avg(newmem.value-oldmem.value) table_fetch_continued_row
from
   perfstat.stats$sysstat oldmem,
   perfstat.stats$sysstat newmem,
   perfstat.stats$snapshot    sn
where
   newmem.snap_id = sn.snap_id
and
   oldmem.snap_id = sn.snap_id-1
and
   oldmem.name = 'table fetch continued row'
and
   newmem.name = 'table fetch continued row'
and
   newmem.value-oldmem.value > 0
group by
   to_char(snap_time,'HH24')
;
```

rpt_avg_fts dy.sql

```
-- © 2001 by Donald Keith Burleson - All Rights Reserved

column long_table_fts     format 999,999,999

select
   to_char(snap_time,'day'),
   avg(a.value) long_table_fts
from
   perfstat.stats$sysstat    a,
   perfstat.stats$snapshot   sn
where
   a.snap_id = sn.snap_id
and
   a.statistic# = 140
group by
   to_char(snap_time,'day')
;
```

rpt_avg_fts_hr.sql

```
-- © 2001 by Donald Keith Burleson - All Rights Reserved

column long_table_fts      format 999,999,999

select
   to_char(snap_time,'HH24'),
   avg(a.value) long_table_fts
from
   perfstat.stats$sysstat      a,
   perfstat.stats$snapshot     sn
where
   a.snap_id = sn.snap_id
and
   a.statistic# = 140
group by
   to_char(snap_time,'HH24')
;
```

rpt_avg_io_dy.sql

```
-- © 2001 by Donald Keith Burleson - All Rights Reserved

column reads   format 999,999,999
column writes format 999,999,999

select
   to_char(snap_time,'day'),
   avg(newreads.value-oldreads.value) reads,
   avg(newwrites.value-oldwrites.value) writes
from
   perfstat.stats$sysstat oldreads,
   perfstat.stats$sysstat newreads,
   perfstat.stats$sysstat oldwrites,
   perfstat.stats$sysstat newwrites,
   perfstat.stats$snapshot    sn
where
   newreads.snap_id = sn.snap_id
and
   newwrites.snap_id = sn.snap_id
and
   oldreads.snap_id = sn.snap_id-1
and
   oldwrites.snap_id = sn.snap_id-1
and
  oldreads.statistic# = 40
```

```
and
   newreads.statistic# = 40
and
   oldwrites.statistic# = 41
and
   newwrites.statistic# = 41
having
     avg(newreads.value-oldreads.value) > 0
and
     avg(newwrites.value-oldwrites.value) > 0
group by
   to_char(snap_time,'day')
;
```

rpt_avg_io_hr.sql

```
-- © 2001 by Donald Keith Burleson - All Rights Reserved

column reads   format 999,999,999
column writes format 999,999,999

select
   to_char(snap_time,'HH24'),
   avg(newreads.value-oldreads.value) reads,
   avg(newwrites.value-oldwrites.value) writes
from
   perfstat.stats$sysstat oldreads,
   perfstat.stats$sysstat newreads,
   perfstat.stats$sysstat oldwrites,
   perfstat.stats$sysstat newwrites,
   perfstat.stats$snapshot   sn
where
   newreads.snap_id = sn.snap_id
and
   newwrites.snap_id - sn.snap_id
and
   oldreads.snap_id = sn.snap_id-1
and
   oldwrites.snap_id = sn.snap_id-1
and
  oldreads.statistic# = 40
and
  newreads.statistic# = 40
and
  oldwrites.statistic# = 41
and
  newwrites.statistic# = 41
```

```
having
    avg(newreads.value-oldreads.value) > 0
and
    avg(newwrites.value-oldwrites.value) > 0
group by
    to_char(snap_time,'HH24')
;
```

rpt_avg_io_wait_dy.sql

```
break on snapdate skip 2

column snapdate format a16
column filename format a40

select
    to_char(snap_time,'day'),
    old.filename,
    avg(new.wait_count-old.wait_count) waits
from
    perfstat.stats$filestatxs old,
    perfstat.stats$filestatxs new,
    perfstat.stats$snapshot    sn
where
    new.snap_id = sn.snap_id
and
    old.filename = new.filename
and
    old.snap_id = sn.snap_id-1
having
    avg(new.wait_count-old.wait_count) > 0
group by
    to_char(snap_time,'day'),
    old.filename
;
```

rpt_avg_io_wait_hr.sql

```
break on snapdate skip 2

column snapdate format a16
column filename format a40
```

```sql
select
   to_char(snap_time,'HH24'),
   old.filename,
   avg(new.wait_count-old.wait_count) waits
from
   perfstat.stats$filestatxs old,
   perfstat.stats$filestatxs new,
   perfstat.stats$snapshot    sn
where
   new.snap_id = sn.snap_id
and
   old.filename = new.filename
and
   old.snap_id = sn.snap_id-1
having
   avg(new.wait_count-old.wait_count) > 0
group by
   to_char(snap_time,'HH24'),
   old.filename
;
```

rpt_avg_logon_dy.sql

```sql
-- © 2001 by Donald Keith Burleson - All Rights Reserved

column current_logons    format 999,999,999

select
   to_char(snap_time,'day'),
   avg(a.value) current_logons
from
   perfstat.stats$sysstat a,
   perfstat.stats$snapshot    sn
where
   a.snap_id = sn.snap_id
and
   a.statistic# = 1
group by
   to_char(snap_time,'day')
;
```

rpt_avg_logon_hr.sql

```sql
-- © 2001 by Donald Keith Burleson - All Rights Reserved
column current_logons    format 999,999,999
```

```
select
   to_char(snap_time,'HH24'),
   avg(a.value) current_logons
from
   perfstat.stats$sysstat a,
   perfstat.stats$snapshot    sn
where
   a.snap_id = sn.snap_id
and
   a.statistic# = 1
group by
   to_char(snap_time,'HH24')
;
```

rpt_avg_sorts_dy.sql

```
-- © 2001 by Donald Keith Burleson - All Rights Reserved
column sorts_memory   format 999,999,999
column sorts_disk     format 999,999,999
column ratio          format .99999

select
   to_char(snap_time,'day'),
   avg(newmem.value-oldmem.value) sorts_memory,
   avg(newdsk.value-olddsk.value) sorts_disk
from
   perfstat.stats$sysstat oldmem,
   perfstat.stats$sysstat newmem,
   perfstat.stats$sysstat newdsk,
   perfstat.stats$sysstat olddsk,
   perfstat.stats$snapshot    sn
where
   newdsk.snap_id = sn.snap_id
and
   olddsk.snap_id = sn.snap_id-1
and
   newmem.snap_id = sn.snap_id
and
   oldmem.snap_id = sn.snap_id-1
and
   oldmem.name = 'sorts (memory)'
and
   newmem.name = 'sorts (memory)'
and
   olddsk.name = 'sorts (disk)'
and
   newdsk.name = 'sorts (disk)'
```

```
and
    newmem.value-oldmem.value > 0
group by
    to_char(snap_time,'day')
;
```

rpt_avg_sorts_hr.sql

```
-- © 2001 by Donald Keith Burleson - All Rights Reserved
column sorts_memory   format 999,999,999
column sorts_disk     format 999,999,999
column ratio          format .99999

select
    to_char(snap_time,'HH24'),
    avg(newmem.value-oldmem.value) sorts_memory,
    avg(newdsk.value-olddsk.value) sorts_disk
from
    perfstat.stats$sysstat oldmem,
    perfstat.stats$sysstat newmem,
    perfstat.stats$sysstat newdsk,
    perfstat.stats$sysstat olddsk,
    perfstat.stats$snapshot   sn
where
    newdsk.snap_id = sn.snap_id
and
    olddsk.snap_id = sn.snap_id-1
and
    newmem.snap_id = sn.snap_id
and
    oldmem.snap_id = sn.snap_id-1
and
    oldmem.name = 'sorts (memory)'
and
    newmem.name = 'sorts (memory)'
and
    olddsk.name = 'sorts (disk)'
and
    newdsk.name = 'sorts (disk)'
and
    newmem.value-oldmem.value > 0
group by
    to_char(snap_time,'HH24')
;
```

rpt_bbw.sql

```
-- © 2001 by Donald Keith Burleson - All Rights Reserved
column buffer_busy_wait format 999,999,999
column mydate heading 'yr.  mo dy Hr.'

select
   to_char(snap_time,'yyyy-mm-dd HH24')         mydate,
   new.name,
   new.buffer_busy_wait-old.buffer_busy_wait buffer_busy_wait
from
   perfstat.stats$buffer_pool_statistics old,
   perfstat.stats$buffer_pool_statistics new,
   perfstat.stats$snapshot                sn
where
   new.name = old.name
and
   new.snap_id = sn.snap_id
and
   old.snap_id = sn.snap_id-1
and
   new.buffer_busy_wait-old.buffer_busy_wait > 1
group by
   to_char(snap_time,'yyyy-mm-dd HH24'),
   new.name,
   new.buffer_busy_wait-old.buffer_busy_wait
;
```

rpt_bg_alert.sql

```
-- © 2001 by Donald Keith Burleson - All Rights Reserved
column mydate heading 'Yr.  Mo Dy Hr'       format a13;
column event                                format a30;
column total_waits    heading 'tot waits' format 999,999;
column time_waited    heading 'time wait' format 999,999;
column total_timeouts heading 'timeouts'  format 9,999;

break on to_char(snap_time,'yyyy-mm-dd') skip 1;

select
   to_char(snap_time,'yyyy-mm-dd HH24')             mydate,
   e.event,
   e.total_waits - nvl(b.total_waits,0)            total_waits,
   e.time_waited - nvl(b.time_waited,0)            time_waited,
   e.total_timeouts - nvl(b.total_timeouts,0)      total_timeouts
from
   stats$bg_event_summary      b,
   stats$bg_event_summary      e,
```

```
   stats$snapshot        sn
where
   e.event not like '%timer'
and
   e.event not like '%message%'
and
   e.snap_id = sn.snap_id
and
   b.snap_id = e.snap_id-1
and
   b.event = e.event
and
   e.total_timeouts > 100
and
(
   e.total_waits - b.total_waits  > 100
   or
   e.time_waited - b.time_waited > 100
)
;
```

rpt_bg_event_waits.sql

```
-- © 2001 by Donald Keith Burleson - All Rights Reserved
set lines 80;

column mydate heading 'Yr.  Mo Dy Hr'      format a13;
column event                               format a30;
column total_waits     heading 'tot waits' format 999,999;
column time_waited     heading 'time wait' format 999,999;
column total_timeouts heading 'timeouts'   format 9,999;

break on to_char(snap_time,'yyyy-mm-dd') skip 1;

select
   to_char(snap_time,'yyyy-mm-dd HH24')           mydate,
   e.event,
   e.total_waits - nvl(b.total_waits,0)           total_waits,
   e.time_waited - nvl(b.time_waited,0)           time_waited,
   e.total_timeouts - nvl(b.total_timeouts,0)     total_timeouts
from
   stats$bg_event_summary       b,
   stats$bg_event_summary       e,
   stats$snapshot       sn
where
   e.event not like '%timer'
and
   e.event not like '%message%'
```

```
and
   e.snap_id = sn.snap_id
and
   b.snap_id = e.snap_id-1
and
   b.event = e.event
and
   e.total_timeouts > 50
and
(
   e.total_waits - b.total_waits  > 50
   or
   e.time_waited - b.time_waited > 50
)
;
```

rpt_bhr.sql

```
-- © 2001 by Donald Keith Burleson - All Rights Reserved

column logical_reads  format 999,999,999
column phys_reads     format 999,999,999
column phys_writes    format 999,999,999
column "BUFFER HIT RATIO" format 999

select
   to_char(snap_time,'yyyy-mm-dd HH24'),
--   a.value + b.value  "logical_reads",
--   c.value            "phys_reads",
--   d.value            "phys_writes",
   round(100 * (((a.value-e.value)+(b.value-f.value))-(c.value-g.value)) /
(a.value-e.value)+(b.value-f.value)))
        "BUFFER HIT RATIO"
from
   perfstat.stats$sysstat a,
   perfstat.stats$sysstat b,
   perfstat.stats$sysstat c,
   perfstat.stats$sysstat d,
   perfstat.stats$sysstat e,
   perfstat.stats$sysstat f,
   perfstat.stats$sysstat g,
   perfstat.stats$snapshot   sn
where
   a.snap_id = sn.snap_id
and
   b.snap_id = sn.snap_id
```

```
and
   c.snap_id = sn.snap_id
and
   d.snap_id = sn.snap_id
and
   e.snap_id = sn.snap_id-1
and
   f.snap_id = sn.snap_id-1
and
   g.snap_id = sn.snap_id-1
and
   a.statistic# = 39
and
   e.statistic# = 39
and
   b.statistic# = 38
and
   f.statistic# = 38
and
   c.statistic# = 40
and
   g.statistic# = 40
and
   d.statistic# = 41
--group by
   --to_char(snap_time,'yyyy-mm-dd HH24')
;
```

rpt_bhr_all.sql

```
-- © 2001 by Donald Keith Burleson - All Rights Reserved

column bhr format 9.99
column mydate heading 'yr.   mo dy Hr.'

select
   to_char(snap_time,'yyyy-mm-dd HH24')        mydate,
   new.name                                    buffer_pool_name,
   (((new.consistent_gets-old.consistent_gets)+
   (new.db_block_gets-old.db_block_gets))-
   (new.physical_reads-old.physical_reads))
   /
   ((new.consistent_gets-old.consistent_gets)+
   (new.db_block_gets-old.db_block_gets))      bhr
from
   perfstat.stats$buffer_pool_statistics old,
   perfstat.stats$buffer_pool_statistics new,
   perfstat.stats$snapshot                     sn
```

```
where
   new.name = old.name
and
   new.snap_id = sn.snap_id
and
   old.snap_id = sn.snap_id-1
;
```

rpt_bhr8i.sql

```
-- © 2001 by Donald Keith Burleson - All Rights Reserved
prompt
prompt
prompt ***********************************************************
prompt  When the data buffer hit ratio falls below 90%, you
prompt  should consider adding to the db_block_buffer init.ora parameter
prompt
prompt ***********************************************************

column bhr format 9.99
column mydate heading 'yr.  mo dy Hr.'

select
   to_char(snap_time,'yyyy-mm-dd HH24')        mydate,
   new.name                                buffer_pool_name,
   (((new.consistent_gets-old.consistent_gets)+
   (new.db_block_gets-old.db_block_gets))-
   (new.physical_reads-old.physical_reads))
   /
   ((new.consistent_gets-old.consistent_gets)+
   (new.db_block_gets-old.db_block_gets))     bhr
from
   perfstat.stats$buffer_pool_statistics old,
   perfstat.stats$buffer_pool_statistics new,
   perfstat.stats$snapshot               sn
where
   new.name in ('DEFAULT','FAKE VIEW')
and
   (((new.consistent_gets-old.consistent_gets)+
   (new.db_block_gets-old.db_block_gets))-
   (new.physical_reads-old.physical_reads))
   /
   ((new.consistent_gets-old.consistent_gets)+
   (new.db_block_gets-old.db_block_gets)) < .90
and
   new.name = old.name
and
```

```
   new.snap_id = sn.snap_id
and
   old.snap_id = sn.snap_id-1
and
   new.consistent gets > 0
and
   old.consistent_gets > 0
;
```

rpt_bhr8i_dy.sql

```
column bhr format 9.99
column mydate heading 'yr.  mo dy Hr.'

select
   to_char(snap_time,'day')        mydate,
   avg(
   (((new.consistent_gets-old.consistent_gets)+
   (new.db_block_gets old.db_block_gets))-
   (new.physical_reads-old.physical_reads))
   /
   ((new.consistent_gets-old.consistent_gets)+
   (new.db_block_gets-old.db_block_gets))
   ) bhr
from
   perfstat.stats$buffer_pool_statistics old,
   perfstat.stats$buffer_pool_statistics new,
   perfstat.stats$snapshot              sn
where
   new.name in ('DEFAULT','FAKE VIEW')
and
   new.name = old.name
and
   new.snap_id = sn.snap_id
and
   old.snap_id = sn.snap_id-1
and
   new.consistent_gets > 0
and
   old.consistent_gets > 0
having
   avg(
   (((new.consistent_gets-old.consistent_gets)+
   (new.db_block_gets-old.db_block_gets))-
   (new.physical_reads-old.physical_reads))
   /
```

```
((new.consistent_gets-old.consistent_gets)+
(new.db_block_gets-old.db_block_gets))
) < 1
group by
to_char(snap_time,'day')
;
```

rpt_bhr8i_hr.sql

```
column bhr format 9.99
column mydate heading 'yr.  mo dy Hr.'

select
   to_char(snap_time,'HH24')        mydate,
   avg(
   (((new.consistent_gets-old.consistent_gets)+
   (new.db_block_gets-old.db_block_gets))-
   (new.physical_reads-old.physical_reads))
   /
   ((new.consistent_gets-old.consistent_gets)+
   (new.db_block_gets-old.db_block_gets))
   ) bhr
from
   perfstat.stats$buffer_pool_statistics old,
   perfstat.stats$buffer_pool_statistics new,
   perfstat.stats$snapshot               sn
where
   new.name in ('DEFAULT','FAKE VIEW')
and
   new.name = old.name
and
   new.snap_id = sn.snap_id
and
   old.snap_id = sn.snap_id-1
and
   new.consistent_gets > 0
and
   old.consistent_gets > 0
having
   avg(
   (((new.consistent_gets-old.consistent_gets)+
   (new.db_block_gets-old.db_block_gets))-
   (new.physical_reads-old.physical_reads))
   /
   ((new.consistent_gets-old.consistent_gets)+
   (new.db_block_gets-old.db_block_gets)) .
```

```
   ) < 1
group by
   to_char(snap_time,'HH24')
;
```

rpt_busy.sql

```
-- © 2001 by Donald Keith Burleson - All Rights Reserved
select
   sysdate,
   substr(tablespace_name,1,14),
   p2
from v$session_wait a, dba_data_files b
where
a.p1 = b.file_id
and
event = 'db file sequential read'
;

select
   sysdate,
   substr(tablespace_name,1,14),
   p2
from v$session_wait a, dba_data_files b
where
a.p1 = b.file_id
and
event = 'buffer busy waits'
;
```

rpt_chain.sql

```
-- © 2001 by Donald Keith Burleson - All Rights Reserved

column table_fetch_continued_row  format 999,999,999

select
   to_char(snap_time,'yyyy-mm-dd HH24'),
   (newmem.value-oldmem.value) table_fetch_continued_row
from
   perfstat.stats$sysstat oldmem,
   perfstat.stats$sysstat newmem,
   perfstat.stats$snapshot    sn
where
   newmem.snap_id = sn.snap_id
and
   oldmem.snap_id = sn.snap_id-1
```

```
and
   oldmem.name = 'table fetch continued row'
and
   newmem.name = 'table fetch continued row'
and
   newmem.value-oldmem.value > 0
;
```

rpt_dbwr.sql

```
-- © 2001 by Donald Keith Burleson - All Rights Reserved
column c1 heading "Write queue length" format 999,999
column c2 heading "DBWR checkpoints" format 999,999
column c3 heading "DBWR Buffers scanned" format 999,999
select
   to_char(snap_time,'yyyy-mm-dd HH24'),
   decode(name, 'summed dirty queue length', value)
   /
   decode(name, 'write requests', value) c1,
   decode(name,'dbwr checkpoints', value) c2,
   decode(name,'dbwr buffers scanned', value) c3
from
   stats$sysstat,
   stats$snapshot
where
   sn.snap_id = s.snap_id
and
   name in ('summed dirty queue length',
                'write requests',
                'dbwr checkpoints',
                'dbwr buffers scanned')
and
   value > 0
;
```

rpt_dbwr_alert.sql

```
-- © 2001 by Donald Keith Burleson - All Rights Reserved
column c1 heading "Write request length" format 9,999.99
column c2 heading "Write Requests"       format 999,999
column c3 heading "DBWR checkpoints"      format 999,999
column mydate heading 'Yr.  Mo Dy  Hr.'  format a16

select distinct
   to_char(snap_time,'yyyy-mm-dd HH24') mydate,
   a.value/b.value                      c1,
   b.value                              c2,
```

```
   c.value                              c3
from
   stats$sysstat   a,
   stats$sysstat   b,
   stats$sysstat   c,
   stats$snapshot sn
where
   sn.snap_id = a.snap_id
and
   sn.snap_id = b.snap_id
and
   sn.snap_id = c.snap_id
and
   a.name = 'summed dirty queue length'
and
   b.name = 'write requests'
and
   c.name = 'DBWR checkpoints'
and
   a.value > 0
and
   b.value > 0
and
   a.value/b.value > 3
;
```

rpt_dbwr_dy.sql

```
-- © 2001 by Donald Keith Burleson   All Rights Reserved
column c1 heading "Write request length" format 9,999.99
column c2 heading "Write Requests"       format 999,999
column c3 heading "DBWR checkpoints"     format 999,999
column mydate heading 'Yr.  Mo Dy  Hr.'  format a16

select distinct
   to_char(snap_time,'day') mydate,
   avg(a.value/b.value)                       c1
--   b.value                              c2,
--   c.value                              c3
from
   stats$sysstat   a,
   stats$sysstat   b,
--   stats$sysstat   c,
   stats$snapshot sn
where
   sn.snap_id = a.snap_id
and
   sn.snap_id = b.snap_id
```

```
--and
--   sn.snap_id = c.snap_id
and
   a.name = 'summed dirty queue length'
and
   b.name = 'write requests'
--and
--   c.name = 'DBWR checkpoints'
and
   a.value > 0
and
   b.value > 0
--and
--   a.value/b.value > 3
group by
   to_char(snap_time,'day')
;
```

rpt_dbwr_hr.sql

```
-- © 2001 by Donald Keith Burleson - All Rights Reserved
column c1 heading "Write request length" format 9,999.99
column c2 heading "Write Requests"       format 999,999
column c3 heading "DBWR checkpoints"     format 999,999

select distinct
   to_char(snap_time,'day') mydate,
   avg(a.value/b.value)                      c1
--   b.value                           c2,
--   c.value                           c3
from
   stats$sysstat  a,
   stats$sysstat  b,
--   stats$sysstat  c,
   stats$snapshot sn
where
   sn.snap_id = a.snap_id
and
   sn.snap_id = b.snap_id
--and
--   sn.snap_id = c.snap_id
and
   a.name = 'summed dirty queue length'
and
   b.name = 'write requests'
--and
--   c.name = 'DBWR checkpoints'
```

```
and
    a.value > 0
and
    b.value > 0
group by
    to_char(snap_time,'day')
;
```

rpt_dict.sql

```
-- © 2001 by Donald Keith Burleson - All Rights Reserved
set lines 80;

column mydate heading 'Yr.  Mo Dy  Hr.'              format a16
column c1       heading "Data|Dictionary|Gets"        format 999,999,999
column c2       heading "Data|Dictionary|Cache|Misses" format 999,999,999
column c3       heading "Data|Dictionary|Hit|Ratio"   format 999,999

break on mydate skip 2;

select
    to_char(snap_time,'yyyy-mm-dd HH24')   mydate,
    sum(new.gets-old.gets)                 c1,
    sum(new.getmisses-old.getmisses)       c2,
    trunc((1-(sum(new.getmisses-old.getmisses)/sum(new.gets-old.gets)))*100) c3
from
    stats$rowcache_summary new,
    stats$rowcache_summary old,
    stats$snapshot sn
where
    new.snap_id = sn.snap_id
and
    old.snap_id = new.snap_id-1
group by
    to_char(snap_time,'yyyy-mm-dd HH24')
;
```

rpt_dict_alert.sql

```
-- © 2001 by Donald Keith Burleson - All Rights Reserved
set lines 80;

column mydate heading 'Yr.  Mo Dy  Hr.'              format a16
```

```
column c1      heading "Data|Dictionary|Gets"           format 999,999,999
column c2      heading "Data|Dictionary|Cache|Misses"  format 999,999,999
column c3      heading "Data|Dictionary|Hit|Ratio"     format 999,999

break on mydate skip 2;

select
   to_char(snap_time,'yyyy-mm-dd HH24')   mydate,
   sum(new.gets-old.gets)                      c1,
   sum(new.getmisses-old.getmisses)         c2,
   trunc((1-(sum(new.getmisses-old.getmisses)/sum(new.gets-old.gets)))*100) c3
from
   stats$rowcache_summary new,
   stats$rowcache_summary old,
   stats$snapshot sn
where
   new.snap_id = sn.snap_id
and
   old.snap_id = new.snap_id-1
having
   trunc((1-(sum(new.getmisses-old.getmisses)/sum(new.gets-old.gets)))*100) < 90
group by
   to_char(snap_time,'yyyy-mm-dd HH24')
;
```

rpt_dict_detail.sql

```
-- © 2001 by Donald Keith Burleson - All Rights Reserved
set lines 80;

column mydate heading 'Yr.  Mo Dy  Hr.'                 format a16
column parameter                                        format a20
column c1      heading "Data|Dictionary|Gets"           format 99,999,999
column c2      heading "Data|Dictionary|Cache|Misses"  format 99,999,999
column c3      heading "Data|Dictionary|Usage"          format 999
column c4      heading "Object|Hit|Ratio"               format 999

break on mydate skip 2;

select
   to_char(snap_time,'yyyy-mm-dd HH24')   mydate,
   new.parameter                           parameter,
   (new.gets-old.gets)                     c1,
   (new.getmisses-old.getmisses)           c2,
```

```
      (new.total_usage-old.total_usage)         c3,
   ROUND((1 - (new.getmisses-old.getmisses) /
   (new.gets-old.gets))*100,1)                   c4
from
   stats$rowcache_summary new,
   stats$rowcache_summary old,
   stats$snapshot           sn
where
   new.snap_id = sn.snap_id
and
   old.snap_id = new.snap_id-1
and
   old.parameter = new.parameter
and
   new.gets-old.gets > 0
and
   (new.total_usage-old.total_usage) > 0
   and rownum < 50
;
```

rpt_dict_dy.sql

```
-- © 2001 by Donald Keith Burleson - All Rights Reserved
set lines 80;

column mydate heading 'Yr.  Mo Dy  Hr.'            format a16
column c1     heading "Data|Dictionary|Gets"       format 999,999,999
column c2     heading "Data|Dictionary|Cache|Misses" format 999,999,999
column c3     heading "Data|Dictionary|Hit|Ratio"  format 999,999

select
   to_char(snap_time,'day')  mydate,
--   sum(new.gets-old.gets)                  c1,
--   sum(new.getmisses-old.getmisses)        c2,
   trunc((1-(sum(new.getmisses-old.getmisses)/sum(new.gets-old.gets)))*100) c3
from
   stats$rowcache_summary new,
   stats$rowcache_summary old,
   stats$snapshot sn
where
   new.snap_id = sn.snap_id
and
   old.snap_id = new.snap_id-1
group by
```

```
    to_char(snap_time,'day')
;
```

rpt_dict_hr.sql

```
-- © 2001 by Donald Keith Burleson - All Rights Reserved
column c1 heading "Write request length" format 9,999.99
column c2 heading "Write Requests"       format 999,999
column c3 heading "DBWR checkpoints"     format 999,999

select distinct
   to_char(snap_time,'day') mydate,
  avg(a.value/b.value)                      c1
--   b.value                                c2,
--   c.value                                c3
from
   stats$sysstat  a,
   stats$sysstat  b,
--   stats$sysstat  c,
   stats$snapshot sn
where
   sn.snap_id = a.snap_id
and
   sn.snap_id = b.snap_id
--and
--   sn.snap_id = c.snap_id
and
   a.name = 'summed dirty queue length'
and
   b.name = 'write requests'
--and
--   c.name = 'DBWR checkpoints'
and
   a.value > 0
and
   b.value > 0
group by
   to_char(snap_time,'day')
;
```

rpt_disk_mapping.sql

```
-- © 2001 by Donald Keith Burleson - All Rights Reserved
set lines 80;
column mount_point heading 'MP';
break on mount_point skip 2;
```

```
select
   substr(file_name,1,4) mount_point,
   substr(file_name,21,20) file_name,
   tablespace_name
from
   dba_data_files
group by
   substr(file_name,1,4),
   substr(file_name,21,20) ,
   tablespace_name
;
```

rpt_enqueue.sql

```
-- © 2001 by Donald Keith Burleson - All Rights Reserved
set lines 80;
column mydate heading 'Yr.  Mo Dy Hr'     format a13;
column name                               format a20;
column gets                               format 999,999;
column waits                              format 999,999,999;
column avg_wait_secs                      format 99,999;

break on to_char(snap_time,'yyyy-mm-dd') skip 1;

select
   to_char(snap_time,'yyyy-mm-dd HH24')            mydate,
   e.name,
   e.gets - nvl(b.gets,0)               gets,
   e.waits - nvl(b.waits,0)                    waits
from
   stats$enqueuestat      b,
   stats$enqueuestat      e,
   stats$snapshot       sn
where
   e.snap_id = sn.snap_id
and
   b.snap_id = e.snap_id-1
and
   b.name = e.name
and
   e.gets - b.gets  > 1
and
   e.waits - b.waits > 1
;
```

rpt_event.sql

```
-- © 2001 by Donald Keith Burleson - All Rights Reserved
set lines 80;

column mydate heading 'Yr.  Mo Dy Hr'     format a13;
column event                              format a30;
column waits                              format 999,999;
column secs_waited                        format 999,999,999;
column avg_wait_secs                      format 99,999;

break on to_char(snap_time,'yyyy-mm-dd') skip 1;

select
   to_char(snap_time,'yyyy-mm-dd HH24')          mydate,
   e.event,
   e.total_waits - nvl(b.total_waits,0)          waits,
   ((e.time_waited - nvl(b.time_waited,0))/100) /
   nvl((e.total_waits - nvl(b.total_waits,0)),0)  avg_wait_secs
from
   stats$system_event b,
   stats$system_event e,
   stats$snapshot      sn
where
   e.snap_id = sn.snap_id
and
   b.snap_id = e.snap_id-1
and
   b.event = e.event
and
  (
   e.event like 'SQL*Net%'
   or
   e.event in (
      'latch free',
      'enqueue',
      'LGWR wait for redo copy',
      'buffer busy waits'
     )
   )
and
   e.total_waits - b.total_waits  > 100
and
   e.time_waited - b.time_waited > 100;
```

rpt_file_io.sql

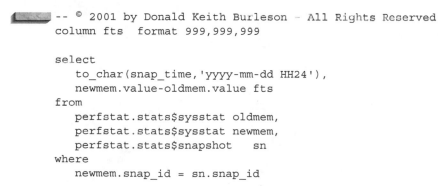

```
-- © 2001 by Donald Keith Burleson - All Rights Reserved
break on snapdate skip 2

column snapdate format a16
column filename format a40
column mydate heading 'Yr.  Mo Dy  Hr.' format a16

select
   to_char(snap_time,'yyyy-mm-dd') mydate,
--   old.filename,
   sum(new.phyrds-old.phyrds)   phy_rds,
   sum(new.phywrts-old.phywrts) phy wrts
from
   perfstat.stats$filestatxs old,
   perfstat.stats$filestatxs new,
   perfstat.stats$snapshot   sn
where
   new.snap_id = sn.snap_id
and
   old.filename = new.filename
and
   old.snap_id = sn.snap_id-1
and
   (new.phyrds-old.phyrds) > 0
and
   old.filename like '%&1%'
group by
   to_char(snap_time,'yyyy-mm-dd'),
   old.filename;
```

rpt_fts.sql

```
-- © 2001 by Donald Keith Burleson - All Rights Reserved
column fts  format 999,999,999

select
   to_char(snap_time,'yyyy-mm-dd HH24'),
   newmem.value-oldmem.value fts
from
   perfstat.stats$sysstat oldmem,
   perfstat.stats$sysstat newmem,
   perfstat.stats$snapshot   sn
where
   newmem.snap_id = sn.snap_id
```

```
and
   oldmem.snap_id = sn.snap_id-1
and
   oldmem.statistic# = 140
and
   newmem.statistic# = 140
and
   newmem.value-oldmem.value > 0;
```

rpt_fts_dy.sql

```
-- © 2001 by Donald Keith Burleson - All Rights Reserved

column fts   format 999,999,999

select
   to_char(snap_time,'day'),
   avg(newmem.value-oldmem.value) fts
from
   perfstat.stats$sysstat oldmem,
   perfstat.stats$sysstat newmem,
   perfstat.stats$snapshot    sn
where
   newmem.snap_id = sn.snap_id
and
   oldmem.snap_id = sn.snap_id-1
and
   oldmem.statistic# = 140
and
   newmem.statistic# = 140
and
   newmem.value-oldmem.value > 0
group by
   to_char(snap_time,'day');
```

rpt_fts_hr.sql

```
-- © 2001 by Donald Keith Burleson - All Rights Reserved
column fts   format 999,999,999

select
   to_char(snap_time,'HH24'),
   avg(newmem.value-oldmem.value) fts
from
   perfstat.stats$sysstat oldmem,
   perfstat.stats$sysstat newmem,
```

```
   perfstat.stats$snapshot   sn
where
   newmem.snap_id = sn.snap_id
and
   oldmem.snap_id = sn.snap_id-1
and
   oldmem.statistic# = 140
and
   newmem.statistic# = 140
and
   newmem.value-oldmem.value > 0
group by
   to_char(snap_time,'HH24');
```

rpt_hot_files.sql

```
-- © 2001 by Donald Keith Burleson - All Rights Reserved
set feedback off;
set verify off;

column mydate      heading 'Yr.  Mo Dy  Hr.' format a16
column file_name   format a25
column reads       format 99,999,999
column pct_of_tot  format 999

prompt
prompt ***********************************************************
prompt  This will identify any single file whose read I/O
prompt  is more than 25% of the total read I/O of the database.
prompt
prompt  The "hot" file should be examined, and the hot table/index
prompt  should be identified using STATSPACK.
prompt
prompt  - The busy file should be placed on a disk device with
prompt    "less busy" files to minimize read delay and channel
prompt    contention.
prompt
prompt  - If small file has a hot small table, place the table
prompt    in the KEEP pool
prompt
prompt  - If the file has a large-table full-table scan, place
prompt    the table in the RECYCLE pool and turn on parallel query
prompt    for the table.
prompt ***********************************************************
prompt

select
```

```
      to_char(snap_time,'yyyy-mm-dd HH24')   mydate,
      new.filename                          file_name,
      new.phyrds-old.phyrds                 reads,
      ((new.phyrds-old.phyrds)/
      (
      select
         (newreads.value-oldreads.value) reads
      from
         perfstat.stats$sysstat oldreads,
         perfstat.stats$sysstat newreads,
         perfstat.stats$snapshot    sn1
      where
         sn.snap_id = sn1.snap_id
      and
         newreads.snap_id = sn.snap_id
      and
         oldreads.snap_id = sn.snap_id-1
      and
        oldreads.statistic# = 40
      and
        newreads.statistic# = 40
      and
        (newreads.value-oldreads.value) > 0
      ))*100 pct_of_tot
from
   perfstat.stats$filestatxs old,
   perfstat.stats$filestatxs new,
   perfstat.stats$snapshot    sn
where
   snap_time > sysdate-&1
and
   new.snap_id = sn.snap_id
and
   old.snap_id = sn.snap_id-1
and
   new.filename = old.filename
and
   -- ***********************************************************
   -- Low I/O values are misleading, so we filter for high I/O
   -- ***********************************************************
   new.phyrds-old.phyrds > 100
and
-- ***********************************************************
-- The following will allow you to choose a threshold
-- ***********************************************************
 (new.phyrds-old.phyrds)*4>  -- This is 25% of total
-- (new.phyrds-old.phyrds)*2> -- This is 50% of total
-- (new.phyrds-old.phyrds)*1.25> -- This is 75% of total
```

```
--   ************************************************************
-- This subquery computes the sum of all I/O during the snapshot period
--   ************************************************************
(
select
    (newreads.value-oldreads.value) reads
from
    perfstat.stats$sysstat oldreads,
    perfstat.stats$sysstat newreads,
    perfstat.stats$snapshot    sn1
where
    sn.snap_id = sn1.snap_id
and
    newreads.snap_id = sn.snap_id
and
    oldreads.snap_id = sn.snap_id-1
and
   oldreads.statistic# = 40
and
   newreads.statistic# = 40
and
   (newreads.value-oldreads.value) > 0
)
;


prompt
prompt ************************************************************
prompt   This will identify any single file whose write I/O
prompt   is more than 25% of the total write I/O of the database.
prompt
prompt   The "hot" file should be examined, and the hot table/index
prompt   should be identified using STATSPACK.
prompt
prompt   - The busy file should be placed on a disk device with
prompt     "less busy" files to minimize write delay and channel
prompt     contention.
prompt
prompt   - If small file has a hot small table, place the table
prompt     in the KEEP pool
prompt
prompt ************************************************************


select
    to_char(snap_time,'yyyy-mm-dd HH24')   mydate,
    new.filename                           file_name,
    new.phywrts-old.phywrts                writes,
   ((new.phywrts-old.phywrts)/
```

```
    (
    select
       (newwrites.value-oldwrites.value) writes
    from
       perfstat.stats$sysstat    oldwrites,
       perfstat.stats$sysstat    newwrites,
       perfstat.stats$snapshot   sn1
    where
       sn.snap_id = sn1.snap_id
    and
       newwrites.snap_id = sn.snap_id
    and
       oldwrites.snap_id = sn.snap_id-1
    and
      oldwrites.statistic# = 44
    and
      newwrites.statistic# = 44
    and
      (newwrites.value-oldwrites.value) > 0
    ))*100 pct_of_tot
from
   perfstat.stats$filestatxs old,
   perfstat.stats$filestatxs new,
   perfstat.stats$snapshot    sn
where
   snap_time > sysdate-&1
and
   new.snap_id = sn.snap_id
and
   old.snap_id = sn.snap_id-1
and
   new.filename = old.filename
and
   -- ***********************************************************
   -- Low I/O values are misleading, so we only take high values
   -- ***********************************************************
   new.phywrts-old.phywrts > 100
and
-- ***********************************************************
-- Here you can choose a threshold value
-- ***********************************************************
 (new.phyrds-old.phywrts)*4>  -- This is 25% of total
-- (new.phyrds-old.phywrts)*2> -- This is 50% of total
-- (new.phyrds-old.phywrts)*1.25> -- This is 75% of total
-- ***********************************************************
-- This subquery computes the sum of all I/O during the snapshot period
-- ***********************************************************
(
```

```
select
    (newwrites.value-oldwrites.value) writes
from
    perfstat.stats$sysstat    oldwrites,
    perfstat.stats$sysstat    newwrites,
    perfstat.stats$snapshot   sn1
where
    sn.snap_id = sn1.snap_id
and
    newwrites.snap_id = sn.snap_id
and
    oldwrites.snap_id = sn.snap_id-1
and
  oldwrites.statistic# = 44
and
  newwrites.statistic# = 44
and
    (newwrites.value-oldwrites.value) > 0
)
;
```

rpt_idlm.ksh

```
#! /bin/ksh
# Display high-water mark of IDLM
# © 1998 Donald K. Burleson
# get the max values . . . .

#grep 'lkmgr_args /oracle/HOME/ops/HOME.conf

MAX_LOC=`grep ^lkmgr_args /oracle/HOME/ops/HOME.conf|cut -f6 -d ' '`
MAX_RES=`grep ^lkmgr_args /oracle/HOME/ops/HOME.conf|cut -f8 -d ' '`
MAX_PRO=`grep ^lkmgr_args /oracle/HOME/ops/HOME.conf|cut -f10 -d ' '|sed -e 's/"//
'`

ORACLE_SID=HOME; export ORACLE_SID;
PATH=$PATH:/oracle/HOME/bin; export PATH;
ORACLE_HOME=/oracle/HOME; export ORACLE_HOME;

unalias rm
rm -f *.tmp

/oracle/HOME/bin/sqlplus <<! > /dev/null

connect perfstat/perfstat;
```

```
set newpage 0;
set space 0
set pages 0
set termout off
set feedback off
set echo off
set heading off

spool pro
select max(processes) from perfstat.stats$dlm_stats;
spool res
select max(resources) from perfstat.stats$dlm_stats;
spool loc
select max(locks) from perfstat.stats$dlm_stats;
spool off
exit
!

PRO=`grep '^ ' pro.lst|awk '{print $1}'`

RES=`grep '^ ' res.lst|awk '{print $1}'`

LOC=`grep '^ ' loc.lst|awk '{print $1}'`

# Now the fun part . . . .

PCT_PRO=`expr $PRO \* 100 \/ $MAX_PRO`
echo "IDLM Process high-water mark is $PRO, or $PCT_PRO percent of max val of
MAX_PRO"

PCT_RES=`expr $RES \* 100 \/ $MAX_RES`
echo "IDLM Resource high-water mark is $RES, or $PCT_RES percent of max val of
MAX_RES"

PCT_LOC=`expr $LOC \* 100 \/ $MAX_LOC`
echo "IDLM Locks high-water mark is $LOC, or $PCT_LOC percent of max val of
MAX_LOC"
```

rpt_idlm.sql

```
column mydate              heading 'Yr.  Mo Dy  Hr.' format a16
column idlm_lock_hit_ratio                           format 999,999,999

select
   to_char(snap_time,'yyyy-mm-dd HH24')  mydate,
   (a.value - b.value)/(a.value) idlm_lock_hit_ratio
from
```

```
    stats$sysstat     a,
    stats$sysstat     b,
    stats$snapshot    sn
where
    a.name = 'consistent gets'
and
    b.name = 'global lock converts (async)'
and
    a.snap_id = sn.snap_id
and
    b.snap_id = sn.snap_id
order by
    to_char(snap_time,'yyyy-mm-dd HH24')
;
```

rpt_idlm_hwm.ksh

```
#! /bin/ksh
# Display high-water mark of IDLM
# © 1998 Donald K. Burleson
# get the max values . . . .

#grep ^lkmgr_args /oracle/HOME/ops/HOME.conf

MAX_LOC=`grep ^lkmgr_args /oracle/HOME/ops/HOME.conf|cut -f6 -d ' '`
MAX_RES=`grep ^lkmgr_args /oracle/HOME/ops/HOME.conf|cut -f8 -d ' '`
MAX_PRO=`grep ^lkmgr_args /oracle/HOME/ops/HOME.conf|cut -f10 -d ' '|sed -e 's/"//
'`

ORACLE_SID=HOME; export ORACLE_SID;
PATH=$PATH:/oracle/HOME/bin; export PATH;
ORACLE_HOME=/oracle/HOME; export ORACLE_HOME;

unalias rm
rm -f *.tmp

/oracle/HOME/bin/sqlplus <<! > /dev/null

connect perfstat/perfstat;

set newpage 0;
set space 0
set pages 0
set termout off
set feedback off
set echo off
```

```
set heading off

spool pro
select max(processes) from perfstat.stats$dlm_stats;
spool res
select max(resources) from perfstat.stats$dlm_stats;
spool loc
select max(locks) from perfstat.stats$dlm_stats;
spool off
exit
!

PRO=`grep '^  ' pro.lst|awk '{print $1}'`

RES=`grep '^  ' res.lst|awk '{print $1}'`

LOC=`grep '^  ' loc.lst|awk '{print $1}'`

# Now the fun part . . . .

PCT_PRO=`expr $PRO \* 100 \/ $MAX_PRO`
echo "IDLM Process high-water mark is $PRO, or $PCT_PRO percent of max val of
MAX_PRO"

PCT_RES=`expr $RES \* 100 \/ $MAX_RES`
echo "IDLM Resource high-water mark is $RES, or $PCT_RES percent of max val of
MAX_RES"

PCT_LOC=`expr $LOC \* 100 \/ $MAX_LOC`
echo "IDLM Locks high-water mark is $LOC, or $PCT_LOC percent of max val of
MAX_LOC"
```

rpt_io.sql

```
column reads  format 999,999,999
column writes format 999,999,999

select
   to_char(snap_time,'yyyy-mm-dd HH24'),
   (newreads.value-oldreads.value) reads,
   (newwrites.value-oldwrites.value) writes
from
   perfstat.stats$sysstat oldreads,
```

```
   perfstat.stats$sysstat newreads,
   perfstat.stats$sysstat oldwrites,
   perfstat.stats$sysstat newwrites,
   perfstat.stats$snapshot    sn
where
   newreads.snap_id = sn.snap_id
and
   newwrites.snap_id = sn.snap_id
and
   oldreads.snap_id = sn.snap_id-1
and
   oldwrites.snap_id = sn.snap_id-1
and
  oldreads.statistic# = 40
and
  newreads.statistic# = 40
and
  oldwrites.statistic# = 41
and
  newwrites.statistic# = 41
and
   (newreads.value-oldreads.value) > 0
and
   (newwrites.value-oldwrites.value) > 0
;
```

rpt_io_pct.sql

```
-- © 2001 by Donald Keith Burleson - All Rights Reserved

column physical_reads   format     999,999,999,999,999
column physical_writes format      999,999,999,999
column pct_reads format 999
column mydate heading 'Yr.  Mo Dy  Hr.' format a16

select
   to_char(snap_time,'yyyy-mm-dd')          mydate,
   sum((newreads.value-oldreads.value))    physical_reads,
   sum((newwrites.value-oldwrites.value)) physical_writes,
   (1-(sum((newwrites.value-oldwrites.value))))/(sum((newreads.value-
ldreads.value))))*100 pct_reads
from
   perfstat.stats$sysstat oldreads,
   perfstat.stats$sysstat newreads,
   perfstat.stats$sysstat oldwrites,
   perfstat.stats$sysstat newwrites,
```

```
   perfstat.stats$snapshot    sn
where
   newreads.snap_id = sn.snap_id
and
   newwrites.snap_id = sn.snap_id
and
   oldreads.snap_id = sn.snap_id-1
and
   oldwrites.snap_id = sn.snap_id-1
and
  oldreads.statistic# = 40
and
  newreads.statistic# = 40
and
  oldwrites.statistic# = 41
and
  newwrites.statistic# = 41
and
   (newreads.value-oldreads.value) > 0
and
   (newwrites.value-oldwrites.value) > 0
group by
   to_char(snap_time,'yyyy-mm-dd')
;
```

rpt_io_wait.sql

```
-- © 2001 by Donald Keith Burleson - All Rights Reserved

break on snapdate skip 2

column snapdate format a16
column filename format a40

select
   to_char(snap_time,'yyyy-mm-dd HH24'),
   old.filename,
   new.wait_count-old.wait_count waits
from
   perfstat.stats$filestatxs old,
   perfstat.stats$filestatxs new,
   perfstat.stats$snapshot    sn
where
   new.snap_id = sn.snap_id
and
   old.filename = new.filename
and
```

```
    old.snap_id = sn.snap_id-1
and
    new.wait_count-old.wait_count > 0
;
```

rpt_last.sql

```
--***********************************************************
--
--   STATSPACK alert report for the DBA
--
--   Created 8/4/2000 by Donald K. Burleson
--   www.dba-oracle.com
--
--   This script is provided free-of-charge by Don Burleson
--   and no portion of this script may be sold to anyone for any reason!
--
--   This script accepts the "number of days back" as an input parameter
--
--   This script can be scheduled to run daily via cron or OEM
--   and e-mail the results to the on-call DBA
--
--***********************************************************

spool rpt_last.lst

-- © 2001 by Donald Keith Burleson - All Rights Reserved
set feedback on;
set verify off;

column reads  format 999,999,999
column writes format 999,999,999

select
    to_char(snap_time,'yyyy-mm-dd HH24'),
    (newreads.value-oldreads.value) reads,
    (newwrites.value-oldwrites.value) writes
from
    perfstat.stats$sysstat oldreads,
    perfstat.stats$sysstat newreads,
    perfstat.stats$sysstat oldwrites,
    perfstat.stats$sysstat newwrites,
    perfstat.stats$snapshot    sn
where
    newreads.snap_id = (select max(sn.snap_id) from stats$snapshot)
and
    newwrites.snap_id = (select max(sn.snap_id) from stats$snapshot)
and
    oldreads.snap_id = sn.snap_id-1
```

```
and
   oldwrites.snap_id = sn.snap_id-1
and
  oldreads.statistic# = 40
and
  newreads.statistic# = 40
and
  oldwrites.statistic# = 41
and
  newwrites.statistic# = 41
;


prompt
prompt
prompt  ************************************************************
prompt  This will identify any single file whose read I/O
prompt  is more than 10% of the total read I/O of the database.
prompt
prompt  The "hot" file should be examined, and the hot table/index
prompt  should be identified using STATSPACK.
prompt
prompt  - The busy file should be placed on a disk device with
prompt    "less busy" files to minimize read delay and channel
prompt    contention.
prompt
prompt  - If small file has a hot small table, place the table
prompt    in the KEEP pool
prompt
prompt  - If the file has a large-table full-table scan, place
prompt    the table in the RECYCLE pool and turn on parallel query
prompt    for the table.
prompt  ************************************************************
prompt
prompt

column mydate format a16
column file_name format a40
column reads   format 999,999,999

select
   to_char(snap_time,'yyyy-mm-dd HH24')   mydate,
   new.filename                           file_name,
   new.phyrds-old.phyrds                  reads
from
   perfstat.stats$filestatxs old,
```

```
   perfstat.stats$filestatxs new,
   perfstat.stats$snapshot    sn
where
   sn.snap_id = (select max(snap_id) from stats$snapshot)
and
   new.snap_id = sn.snap_id
and
   old.snap_id = sn.snap_id-1
and
   new.filename = old.filename
--and
--   new.phyrds-old.phyrds > 10000
and
   (new.phyrds-old.phyrds)*10 >
(
select
   (newreads.value-oldreads.value) reads
from
   perfstat.stats$sysstat oldreads,
   perfstat.stats$sysstat newreads,
   perfstat.stats$snapshot   sn1
where
   sn.snap_id = sn1.snap_id
and
   newreads.snap_id = sn.snap_id
and
   oldreads.snap_id = sn.snap_id-1
and
  oldreads.statistic# = 40
and
  newreads.statistic# = 40
and
  (newreads.value-oldreads.value) > 0
)
;
prompt
prompt ************************************************************
prompt  This will identify any single file whose write I/O
prompt  is more than 10% of the total write I/O of the database.
prompt
prompt  The "hot" file should be examined, and the hot table/index
prompt  should be identified using STATSPACK.
prompt
prompt  - The busy file should be placed on a disk device with
prompt    "less busy" files to minimize write delay and channel
prompt    contention.
prompt
prompt  - If small file has a hot small table, place the table
```

```
prompt     in the KEEP pool
prompt
prompt ************************************************************
prompt

column mydate format a16
column file_name format a40
column writes   format 999,999,999

select
   to_char(snap_time,'yyyy-mm-dd HH24')  mydate,
   new.filename                          file_name,
   new.phywrts-old.phywrts               writes
from
   perfstat.stats$filestatxs old,
   perfstat.stats$filestatxs new,
   perfstat.stats$snapshot    sn
where
   sn.snap_id = (select max(snap_id) from stats$snapshot)
and
   new.snap_id = sn.snap_id
and
   old.snap_id = sn.snap_id-1
and
   new.filename = old.filename
--and
----   new.phywrts-old.phywrts > 10000
and
   (new.phywrts-old.phywrts)*10 >
(
select
   (newwrites.value-oldwrites.value) writes
from
   perfstat.stats$sysstat oldwrites,
   perfstat.stats$sysstat newwrites,
   perfstat.stats$snapshot    sn1
where
   sn.snap_id = sn1.snap_id
and
   newwrites.snap_id = sn.snap_id
and
   oldwrites.snap_id = sn.snap_id-1
and
  oldwrites.statistic# = 40
and
  newwrites.statistic# = 40
and
  (newwrites.value-oldwrites.value) > 0
```

```
)
;

--***********************************************************
-- Alert when data buffer hit ratio is below threshold
--***********************************************************

prompt ***********************************************************
prompt  When the data buffer hit ratio falls below 90%, you
prompt  should consider adding to the db_block_buffer init.ora parameter
prompt
prompt
prompt ***********************************************************
prompt
prompt

column logical_reads  format 999,999,999
column phys_reads     format 999,999,999
column phys_writes    format 999,999,999
column "BUFFER HIT RATIO" format 999

select
   to_char(snap_time,'dd Mon HH24:mi:ss') mydate,
   d.value           "phys_writes",
   round(100 * (((a.value-e.value)+(b.value-f.value))-(c.value-g.value)) /
(a.value-e.value)+(b.value-f.value)))
        "BUFFER HIT RATIO"
from
   perfstat.stats$sysstat a,
   perfstat.stats$sysstat b,
   perfstat.stats$sysstat c,
   perfstat.stats$sysstat d,
   perfstat.stats$sysstat e,
   perfstat.stats$sysstat f,
   perfstat.stats$sysstat g,
   perfstat.stats$snapshot   sn
where
--   (round(100 * (((a.value-e.value)+(b.value-f.value))-(c.value-g.value)) /
(a.value-e.value)+(b.value-f.value)))  ) < 90
--and
   sn.snap_id = (select max(snap_id) from stats$snapshot)
and
   a.snap_id = sn.snap_id
and
   b.snap_id = sn.snap_id
```

```
and
   c.snap_id = sn.snap_id
and
   d.snap_id = sn.snap_id
and
   e.snap_id = sn.snap_id-1
and
   f.snap_id = sn.snap_id-1
and
   g.snap_id = sn.snap_id-1
and
   a.statistic# = 39
and
   e.statistic# = 39
and
   b.statistic# = 38
and
   f.statistic# = 38
and
   c.statistic# = 40
and
   g.statistic# = 40
and
   d.statistic# = 41
;

column mydate heading 'Yr.  Mo Dy  Hr.' format a16
column reloads        format 999,999,999
column hit_ratio      format 999.99
column pin_hit_ratio format 999.99

break on mydate skip 2;

select
   to_char(snap_time,'yyyy-mm-dd HH24')  mydate,
   new.namespace,
   (new.gethits-old.gethits)/(new.gets-old.gets) hit_ratio,
   (new.pinhits-old.pinhits)/(new.pins-old.pins) pin_hit_ratio,
   new.reloads
from
   stats$librarycache old,
   stats$librarycache new,
   stats$snapshot      sn
where
   new.snap_id = sn.snap_id
and
   old.snap_id = new.snap_id-1
```

```
and
    old.namespace = new.namespace
and
    new.gets-old.gets > 0
and
    new.pins-old.pins > 0
;


--************************************************************
-- Alert when total disk sorts are below threshold
--************************************************************
prompt
prompt ************************************************************
prompt  When there are high disk sorts, you should investigate
prompt  increasing sort_area_size, or adding indexes to force index_full scans
prompt
prompt ************************************************************

column sorts_memory  format 999,999,999
column sorts_disk    format 999,999,999
column ratio format .9999999999999

select
    to_char(snap_time,'dd Mon HH24:mi:ss') mydate,
    newmem.value-oldmem.value sorts_memory,
    newdsk.value-olddsk.value sorts_disk,
    (newdsk.value-olddsk.value)/(newmem.value-oldmem.value) ratio
from
    perfstat.stats$sysstat oldmem,
    perfstat.stats$sysstat newmem,
    perfstat.stats$sysstat newdsk,
    perfstat.stats$sysstat olddsk,
    perfstat.stats$snapshot   sn
where
    -- Where there are more than 100 disk sorts per hour
--    newdsk.value-olddsk.value > 100
--and
    sn.snap_id = (select max(snap_id) from stats$snapshot)
and
    newdsk.snap_id = sn.snap_id
and
    olddsk.snap_id = sn.snap_id-1
and
    newmem.snap_id = sn.snap_id
and
    oldmem.snap_id = sn.snap_id-1
and
    oldmem.name = 'sorts (memory)'
```

```
and
   newmem.name = 'sorts (memory)'
and
   olddsk.name = 'sorts (disk)'
and
   newdsk.name = 'sorts (disk)'
and
   newmem.value-oldmem.value > 0
;
--*************************************************************
-- Alert when total I/O wait count is above threshold
--*************************************************************

prompt
prompt  *************************************************************
prompt  When there is high I/O waits, disk bottlenecks may exist
prompt  Run iostats to find the hot disk and shuffle files to
prompt  remove the contention
prompt
prompt  *************************************************************

break on snapdate skip 2

column snapdate format a16
column filename format a40

select
   to_char(snap_time,'dd Mon HH24:mi:ss') mydate,
   old.filename,
   new.wait_count-old.wait_count waits
from
   perfstat.stats$filestatxs old,
   perfstat.stats$filestatxs new,
   perfstat.stats$snapshot    sn
where
   sn.snap_id = (select max(snap_id) from stats$snapshot)
and
   new.wait_count-old.wait_count > 0
and
   new.snap_id = sn.snap_id
and
   old.filename = new.filename
and
   old.snap_id = sn.snap_id-1
;

--*************************************************************
-- Alert when average buffer busy waits exceed threshold
```

```
--************************************************************
prompt ************************************************************
prompt  Buffer Busy Waits may signal a high update table with too
prompt  few freelists.  Find the offending table and add more freelists.
prompt
prompt ************************************************************

column buffer_busy_wait format 999,999,999

select
   to_char(snap_time,'dd Mon HH24:mi:ss') mydate,
   avg(new.buffer_busy_wait-old.buffer_busy_wait) buffer_busy_wait
from
   perfstat.stats$buffer_pool_statistics old,
   perfstat.stats$buffer_pool_statistics new,
   perfstat.stats$snapshot   sn
where
   sn.snap_id = (select max(snap_id) from stats$snapshot)
and
   new.snap_id = sn.snap_id
and
   new.snap_id = sn.snap_id
and
   old.snap_id = sn.snap_id-1
--having
--   avg(new.buffer_busy_wait-old.buffer_busy_wait) > 100
group by
   to_char(snap_time,'dd Mon HH24:mi:ss')
;


--************************************************************
-- Alert when total redo log space requests exceed threshold
--************************************************************
prompt
prompt ************************************************************
prompt  High redo log space requests indicate a need to increase
prompt  the log_buffer parameter
prompt
prompt ************************************************************

column redo_log_space_requests  format 999,999,999

select
   to_char(snap_time,'dd Mon HH24:mi:ss') mydate,
   newmem.value-oldmem.value redo_log_space_requests
from
   perfstat.stats$sysstat oldmem,
```

```
   perfstat.stats$sysstat newmem,
   perfstat.stats$snapshot    sn
where
   sn.snap_id = (select max(snap_id) from stats$snapshot)
--and
--   newmem.value-oldmem.value > 30
and
   newmem.snap_id = sn.snap_id
and
   oldmem.snap_id = sn.snap_id-1
and
   oldmem.name = 'redo log space requests'
and
   newmem.name = 'redo log space requests'
and
   newmem.value-oldmem.value > 0
;


--*********************************************************
-- Alert when table_fetch_continued_row exceeds threshold
--*********************************************************

 prompt
 prompt *********************************************************
 prompt  Table fetch continued row indicates chained rows, or fetches of
 prompt  long datatypes (long raw, blob)
 prompt
 prompt  Investigate increasing db_block_size or reorganizing tables
 prompt  with chained rows.
 prompt
 prompt  See p. 381 "High Performance Oracle8 Tuning" by Don Burleson
 prompt  See p. 102 "Oracle SAP Administration" by Don Burleson
 prompt
 prompt *********************************************************

column table_fetch_continued_row  format 999,999,999

select
   to_char(snap_time,'dd Mon HH24:mi:ss') mydate,
   avg(newmem.value-oldmem.value) table_fetch_continued_row
from
   perfstat.stats$sysstat oldmem,
   perfstat.stats$sysstat newmem,
   perfstat.stats$snapshot    sn
where
   sn.snap_id = (select max(snap_id) from stats$snapshot)
and
   newmem.snap_id = sn.snap_id
```

```
and
   oldmem.snap_id = sn.snap_id-1
and
   oldmem.name = 'table fetch continued row'
and
   newmem.name = 'table fetch continued row'
--and
--    newmem.value-oldmem.value > 0
--having
--    avg(newmem.value-oldmem.value) > 10000
group by
   to_char(snap_time,'dd Mon HH24:mi:ss')
;
prompt
prompt
prompt ************************************************************
prompt  Enqueue Deadlocks indicate contention within the Oracle
prompt  shared pool.
prompt
prompt   Investigate increasing shared_pool_size
prompt
prompt ************************************************************
prompt

column enqueue_deadlocks       format 999,999,999

select
   to_char(snap_time,'dd Mon HH24:mi:ss') mydate,
   a.value enqueue_deadlocks
from
   perfstat.stats$sysstat      a,
   perfstat.stats$snapshot     sn
where
   sn.snap_id = (select max(snap_id) from stats$snapshot)
and
   a.snap_id = sn.snap_id
and
   a.statistic# = 24
--and
--    a.value > 10
;

prompt ************************************************************
prompt   Long-table full table scans can indicate a need to:
prompt
prompt          - Make the offending tables parallel query
prompt            (alter table parallel degree yyy;)
prompt          - Place the table in the RECYCLE pool
```

```
prompt          - Build an index on the table to remove the FTS
prompt
prompt To locate the table, run access.sql
prompt
prompt  See Oracle Magazine September 2000 issue for details
prompt
prompt ************************************************************
prompt

column fts   format 999,999,999

select
   to_char(snap_time,'dd Mon HH24:mi:ss') mydate,
   newmem.value-oldmem.value fts
from
   perfstat.stats$sysstat oldmem,
   perfstat.stats$sysstat newmem,
   perfstat.stats$snapshot   sn
where
  sn.snap_id = (select max(snap_id) from stats$snapshot)
--and
--    newmem.value-oldmem.value > 1000
and
   newmem.snap_id = sn.snap_id
and
   oldmem.snap_id = sn.snap_id-1
and
   oldmem.statistic# = 140
and
   newmem.statistic# = 140
--and
--    newmem.value-oldmem.value > 0
;


spool off;
```

rpt_latch.sql

```
column parent_name    format a33
column where_in_code format a10
column sum_nwfail     format 9,999,999
column sum_sleep      format 9,999,999

column name      format a31              heading 'Latch Name' trunc;
column gets      format 999,999,990      heading 'Get|Requests';
column missed    format 990.9            heading 'Pct|Get|Miss';
column sleeps    format 990.9            heading 'Avg|Sleeps|/Miss';
```

```
column nowai      format 99,999,990      heading 'Nowait|Requests';
column imiss      format 990.9           heading 'Pct|Nowait|Miss';

drop table temp1;
create table temp1 as
select
   to_char(snap_time,'mm-dd-yy')  stats_day,
   min(snap_id)                   min_snap,
   max(snap_id)                   max_snap
from
   stats$snapshot
group by
   to_char(snap_time,'mm-dd-yy')
;

-- Note:  This query requires that the database be up for each entire day
--  If the database is shut-down, and accumulators will be re-set,
--  giving misleading results
select
   stats_day,
   b.name
   , e.gets    - b.gets                                    gets
   , to_number(decode(e.gets, b.gets, null,
     (e.misses - b.misses) * 100/(e.gets - b.gets)))    missed
   , to_number(decode(e.misses, b.misses, null,
     (e.sleeps - b.sleeps)/(e.misses - b.misses)))      sleeps
   , e.immediate_gets - b.immediate_gets                  nowai
   , to_number(decode(e.immediate_gets,
                     b.immediate_gets, null,
                 (e.immediate_misses - b.immediate_misses) * 100 /
                   (e.immediate_gets  - b.immediate_gets)))    imiss
from
   stats$latch          b,
   stats$latch          e,
   temp1
where
   b.snap_id = min_snap
and
   e.snap_id = max_snap
and
   b.name = e.name
and
(
     e.gets-b.gets > 0
or
     to_number(decode(e.gets, b.gets, null,
```

```
     (e.misses - b.misses) * 100/(e.gets - b.gets))) > 0
or
     to_number(decode(e.misses, b.misses, null,
       (e.sleeps - b.sleeps)/(e.misses - b.misses)))      > 0
or
     e.immediate_gets - b.immediate_gets                   > 0
or
     to_number(decode(e.immediate_gets,
                     b.immediate_gets, null,
                   (e.immediate_misses - b.immediate_misses) * 100 /
                   (e.immediate_gets   - b.immediate_gets))) > 0
)
;
```

rpt_latch_misses.sql

```
column parent_name     format a33
column where_in_code   format a10
column avg_nwfail      format 9,999,999
column avg_sleep       format 9,999,999


break on snap_date skip 2;

select
   to_char(snap_time,'mm-dd-yy') snap_date,
   parent_name,
   where_in_code,
   avg(nwfail_count)             avg_nwfail,
   avg(sleep_count)              avg_sleep
from
   stats$latch_misses_summary    lms,
   stats$snapshot                sn
where
   lms.snap_id = sn.snap_id
--and
--  to_char(snap_time,'mm-dd-yy') = to_char(sysdate-9,'mm-dd-yy')
group by
   to_char(snap_time,'mm-dd-yy'),
   parent_name,
   where_in_code
;
```

rpt_lib.sql

```
set lines 80;
-- © 2001 by Donald Keith Burleson - All Rights Reserved

column mydate heading 'Yr.  Mo Dy  Hr.' format a16
column reloads        format 999,999,999
column hit_ratio      format 999.99
column pin_hit_ratio format 999.99

break on mydate skip 2;

select
   to_char(snap_time,'yyyy-mm-dd HH24')  mydate,
   new.namespace,
   (new.gethits-old.gethits)/(new.gets-old.gets) hit_ratio,
   (new.pinhits-old.pinhits)/(new.pins-old.pins) pin_hit_ratio,
   new.reloads
from
   stats$librarycache old,
   stats$librarycache new,
   stats$snapshot      sn
where
   new.snap_id = sn.snap_id
and
   old.snap_id = new.snap_id-1
and
   old.namespace = new.namespace
and
   new.gets-old.gets > 0
and
   new.pins-old.pins > 0
;
```

rpt_lib_miss.sql

```
set lines 80;
-- © 2001 by Donald Keith Burleson - All Rights Reserved

column mydate heading 'Yr.  Mo Dy  Hr.' format a16
column c1 heading "execs"    format 9,999,999
column c2 heading "Cache Misses|While Executing"    format 9,999,999
column c3 heading "Library Cache|Miss Ratio"     format 999.99999

break on mydate skip 2;
```

```
select
   to_char(snap_time,'yyyy-mm-dd HH24')  mydate,
   sum(new.pins-old.pins)                c1,
   sum(new.reloads-old.reloads)          c2,
   sum(new.reloads-old.reloads)/
   sum(new.pins-old.pins)                library_cache_miss_ratio
from
   stats$librarycache old,
   stats$librarycache new,
   stats$snapshot      sn
where
   new.snap_id = sn.snap_id
and
   old.snap_id = new.snap_id-1
and
   old.namespace = new.namespace
group by
   to_char(snap_time,'yyyy-mm-dd HH24')
;
```

rpt_lib_miss_alert.sql

```
set lines 80;
-- © 2001 by Donald Keith Burleson - All Rights Reserved

column mydate heading 'Yr.  Mo Dy  Hr.' format a16
column c1 heading "execs"      format 9,999,999
column c2 heading "Cache Misses|While Executing"   format 9,999,999
column c3 heading "Library Cache|Miss Ratio"      format 999.99999

break on mydate skip 2;

select
   to_char(snap_time,'yyyy-mm-dd HH24')  mydate,
   sum(new.pins-old.pins)                c1,
   sum(new.reloads-old.reloads)          c2,
   sum(new.reloads-old.reloads)/
   sum(new.pins-old.pins)                library_cache_miss_ratio
from
   stats$librarycache old,
   stats$librarycache new,
   stats$snapshot      sn
where
   new.snap_id = sn.snap_id
and
   old.snap_id = new.snap_id-1
and
```

```
   old.namespace = new.namespace
having
   sum(new.reloads-old.reloads)/
   sum(new.pins-old.pins) > .05
group by
   to_char(snap_time,'yyyy-mm-dd HH24')
/
```

rpt_logon.sql

```
-- © 2001 by Donald Keith Burleson - All Rights Reserved

column current_logons      format 999,999,999
column cumulative_logons   format 999,999,999

select
   to_char(snap_time,'yyyy-mm-dd HH24'),
--   a.value cumulative_logons,
   b.value current_logons
from
   perfstat.stats$sysstat a,
   perfstat.stats$sysstat b,
   perfstat.stats$snapshot   sn
where
   a.snap_id = sn.snap_id
and
   b.snap_id = sn.snap_id
and
   a.statistic# = 0
and
   b.statistic# = 1
;
```

rpt parallel.sql

```
-- © 2001 by Donald Keith Burleson - All Rights Reserved

column nbr_pq format 999,999,999
column mydate heading 'yr.  mo dy Hr.'

select
   to_char(snap_time,'yyyy-mm-dd HH24')       mydate,
   new.value
from
   perfstat.stats$sysstat   old,
   perfstat.stats$sysstat   new,
```

```
   perfstat.stats$snapshot   sn
where
   new.name = old.name
and
   new.name = 'queries parallelized'
and
   new.snap_id = sn.snap_id
and
   old.snap_id = sn.snap_id-1
and
   new.value > 1
order by
   to_char(snap_time,'yyyy-mm-dd HH24')
;
```

rpt_rbs.sql

```
-- © 2001 by Donald Keith Burleson - All Rights Reserved

column buffer_busy_wait format 999,999,999
column mydate heading 'Yr.  Mo Dy  Hr.' format a16
column c0 heading "Name"    format 99
column c1 heading "sz now"   format 9,999
column c2 heading "extends" format 9,999
column c3 heading "# trans." format 9,999
column c4 heading "wraps" format 9,999
column c5 heading "High WM" format 999;
column c7 heading "Shrinks" format 999;
column c6 heading "status"
column c8 heading "Waits" format 9,999;

select
   to_char(snap_time,'yyyy-mm-dd HH24')    mydate,
   new.usn                                 c0,
   (new.rssize-old.rssize)/1048576         c1,
   (new.hwmsize-old.hwmsize)/1048576        c5,
   new.extends-old.extends                 c2,
   new.waits-old.waits                     c8,
   new.xacts-old.xacts                     c3,
   new.wraps-old.wraps                     c4,
   new.shrinks-old.shrinks                 c7
from
   perfstat.stats$rollstat old,
   perfstat.stats$rollstat new,
   perfstat.stats$snapshot    sn
where
   (new.rssize-old.rssize) > 0
```

```
and
   new.xacts-old.xacts > 0
and
   new.snap_id = sn.snap_id
and
   old.snap_id = sn.snap_id 1
and
   new.usn = old.usn
;
```

rpt_read_io_file.sql

```
prompt
prompt
prompt  This will identify any single file whose read I/O
prompt  is more than 20% of the total read I/O of the database.
prompt
prompt  The "hot" file should be examined, and the hot table/index
prompt  should be identified using STATSPACK.
prompt
prompt  - The busy file should be placed on a disk device with
prompt    "less busy" files to minimize read delay and channel
prompt    contention.
prompt
prompt  - If small file has a hot small table, place the table
prompt    in the KEEP pool
prompt
prompt  - If the file has a large-table full-table scan, place
prompt    the table in the RECYCLE pool and turn on parallel query
prompt    for the table.
prompt
prompt

column mydate format a16
column file_name format a40
column reads  format 999,999,999

select
   to_char(snap_time,'yyyy-mm-dd HH24')  mydate,
   new.filename                          file_name,
   new.phyrds-old.phyrds                 reads
from
   perfstat.stats$filestatxs old,
   perfstat.stats$filestatxs new,
   perfstat.stats$snapshot   sn
```

```
where
   new.snap_id = sn.snap_id
and
   old.snap_id = sn.snap_id-1
and
   new.filename = old.filename
and
   new.phyrds-old.phyrds > 10000
and
   (new.phyrds-old.phyrds)*20 >
(
select
   (newreads.value-oldreads.value) reads
from
   perfstat.stats$sysstat oldreads,
   perfstat.stats$sysstat newreads,
   perfstat.stats$snapshot    sn1
where
   sn.snap_id = sn1.snap_id
and
   newreads.snap_id = sn.snap_id
and
   oldreads.snap_id = sn.snap_id-1
and
  oldreads.statistic# = 40
and
  newreads.statistic# = 40
and
  (newreads.value-oldreads.value) > 0
)
;
```

rpt_sga_summary.sql

```
column chg_bytes format 999,999,999
column min_bytes format 999,999,999
column max_bytes format 999,999,999
column name        format a25

select
   name,
   min(bytes)              min_bytes,
   max(bytes)              max_bytes,
   max(bytes)-min(bytes)  chg_bytes
from
   stats$sgastat_summary
having
```

```
   min(bytes) < max(bytes)
group by name
;
```

rpt_sorts.sql

```
column sorts_memory  format 999,999,999
column sorts_disk    format 999,999,999
column ratio         format .99999

select
   to_char(snap_time,'yyyy-mm dd HH24'),
   newmem.value-oldmem.value sorts_memory,
   newdsk.value-olddsk.value sorts_disk,
   ((newdsk.value-olddsk.value)/(newmem.value-oldmem.value)) ratio
from
   perfstat.stats$sysstat oldmem,
   perfstat.stats$sysstat newmem,
   perfstat.stats$sysstat newdsk,
   perfstat.stats$sysstat olddsk,
   perfstat.stats$snapshot    sn
where
   newdsk.snap_id = sn.snap_id
and
   olddsk.snap_id = sn.snap_id-1
and
   newmem.snap_id = sn.snap_id
and
   oldmem.snap_id = sn.snap_id-1
and
   oldmem.name = 'sorts (memory)'
and
   newmem.name = 'sorts (memory)'
and
   olddsk.name = 'sorts (disk)'
and
   newdsk.name = 'sorts (disk)'
and
   newmem.value-oldmem.value > 0
;
```

rpt_sorts_dy.sql

```
-- © 2001 by Donald Keith Burleson - All Rights Reserved

column sorts_memory  format 999,999,999
column sorts_disk    format 999,999,999
column ratio format .99999

select
   to_char(snap_time,'day'),
   sum(a.value) sorts_memory,
   sum(b.value) sorts_disk,
   (sum(b.value)/sum(a.value)) ratio
from
   perfstat.stats$sysstat a,
   perfstat.stats$sysstat b,
   perfstat.stats$snapshot   sn
where
   a.snap_id = sn.snap_id
and
   b.snap_id = sn.snap_id
and
   a.name = 'sorts (memory)'
and
   b.name = 'sorts (disk)'
group by
   to_char(snap_time,'day')
;
```

rpt_sql_summary.sql

```
-- © 2001 by Donald Keith Burleson - All Rights Reserved

column sorts_memory  format 999,999,999
column sorts_disk    format 999,999,999
column ratio format .99999

select
   to_char(snap_time,'yyyy-mm-dd HH24'),
   sum(disk_reads) disk_reads,
   sum(buffer_gets) buffer_gets,
   (sum(disk_reads)/sum(buffer_gets)) ratio
from
   perfstat.stats$sql_summary  a,
   perfstat.stats$snapshot   sn
where
```

```
    a.snap_id = sn.snap_id
group by
    to_char(snap_time,'yyyy-mm-dd HH24')
;
```

rpt_top_sql.sql

```
set lines 80;
-- © 2001 by Donald Keith Burleson - All Rights Reserved
set heading off;

select
    to_char(snap_time,'yyyy-mm-dd hh24'),
    substr(sql_text,1,50)
from
    stats$sql_summary a,
    stats$snapshot     sn
where
    a.snap_id = sn.snap_id
and
    to_char(snap_time,'hh24') = 10
or
    to_char(snap_time,'hh24') = 15
order by
    rows_processed desc;
```

rpt_waitstat.sql

```
-- © 2001 by Donald Keith Burleson - All Rights Reserved
set lines 80;

column mydate heading 'Yr.  Mo Dy Hr'      format a13;
column class                               format a20;
column wait_count                          format 999,999;
column time                                format 999,999,999;
column avg_wait_secs                       format 99,999;

break on to_char(snap_time,'yyyy-mm-dd') skip 1;

select
    to_char(snap_time,'yyyy-mm-dd HH24')             mydate,
    e.class,
    e.wait_count - nvl(b.wait_count,0)               wait_count,
    e.time - nvl(b.time,0)                           time
from
    stats$waitstat      b,
```

```
      stats$waitstat       e,
      stats$snapshot       sn
where
   e.snap_id = sn.snap_id
and
   b.snap_id = e.snap_id-1
and
   b.class = e.class
and
(
   e.wait_count - b.wait_count  > 1
   or
   e.time - b.time > 1
)
;
```

run_busy.ksh

```
#!/bin/ksh

# First, we must set the environment . . .
statspack=`echo ~oracle/statspack`
export statspack
ORACLE_SID=PROD
export ORACLE_SID
ORACLE_HOME=`cat /etc/oratab|grep $ORACLE_SID:|cut -f2 -d':'`
export ORACLE_HOME
PATH=$ORACLE_HOME/bin:$PATH
export PATH


#----------------------------------------
# If it is not running, then start it . . .
#----------------------------------------
check_stat=`ps -ef|grep get_busy|grep -v grep|wc -l`;
oracle_num=`expr $check_stat`
if [ $oracle_num -le 0 ]
 then nohup $statspack/get_busy.ksh > /dev/null 2>&1 &
fi
```

statspack_alert.ksh

```
#!/bin/ksh


if [ -z "$1" ]
then
```

```
   echo "Usage: statspack_alert.ksh <ORACLE_SID>"
   exit 99
fi

check=`cat /var/opt/oracle/oratab|grep -i $1|wc -l`
tmp=`expr $check`       # Convert string to number
if [ $tmp -lt 1 ]
then
   echo
   echo "Not a valid ORACLE_SID.  Retry."
   echo
   exit 99
fi

rm -f /tmp/statspack_alert.lst

ORACLE_SID=$1
export ORACLE_SID

ORACLE_HOME=`cat /var/opt/oracle/oratab|grep ^$ORACLE_SID:|cut -f2 -d':'`
export ORACLE_HOME

$ORACLE_HOME/bin/sqlplus /<<!
@/export/home/oracle/statspack/statspack_alert 9
exit
!

var=`cat /tmp/statspack_alert.lst|wc -l`

echo $var
if [[ $var -gt 1 ]];
 then
 echo "********************************************************************"
 echo "There are alerts"
 cat /tmp/statspack_alert.lst|mailx -s "Statspack Alert" don@remote-dba.net
terry.oakes@worldnet.att.net
 echo "********************************************************************"
 exit
fi
```

statspack_alert.sql

```
--***************************************************************
--
--   STATSPACK alert report for the DBA
--
--   Created 8/4/2000 by Donald K. Burleson
--   www.dba-oracle.com
--
--
--   This script accepts the "number of days back" as an input parameter
--
--   This script can be scheduled to run daily via cron or OEM
--   and e-mail the results to the on-call DBA
--
--***************************************************************

-- © 2001 by Donald Keith Burleson - All Rights Reserved
set feedback off;
set verify off;

spool /tmp/statspack_alert.lst

set feedback off;
set verify off;

column mydate heading 'Yr.  Mo Dy  Hr.' format a16
column file_name format a35
column reads   format 99,999,999
column pct_of_tot   format 999


prompt
prompt
prompt ***************************************************************
prompt  This will identify any single file whose read I/O
prompt  is more than 25% of the total read I/O of the database.
prompt
prompt  The "hot" file should be examined, and the hot table/index
prompt  should be identified using STATSPACK.
prompt
prompt - The busy file should be placed on a disk device with
prompt    "less busy" files to minimize read delay and channel
prompt    contention.
prompt
prompt - If small file has a hot small table, place the table
prompt    in the KEEP pool
```

```
prompt
prompt   - If the file has a large-table full-table scan, place
prompt     the table in the RECYCLE pool and turn on parallel query
prompt     for the table.
prompt   ************************************************************

select
   to_char(snap_time,'yyyy-mm-dd HH24')   mydate,
   new.filename                           file_name,
   new.phyrds-old.phyrds                  reads,
   ((new.phyrds-old.phyrds)/
   (
   select
      (newreads.value oldreads.value) reads
   from
      perfstat.stats$sysstat oldreads,
      perfstat.stats$sysstat newreads,
      perfstat.stats$snapshot    sn1
   where
      sn.snap_id = sn1.snap_id
   and
      newreads.snap_id = sn.snap_id
   and
      oldreads.snap_id = sn.snap_id-1
   and
      oldreads.statistic# = 40
   and
      newreads.statistic# = 40
   and
      (newreads.value-oldreads.value) > 0
   ))*100 pct_of_tot
from
   perfstat.stats$filestatxs old,
   perfstat.stats$filestatxs new,
   perfstat.stats$snapshot    sn
where
   snap_time > sysdate-&1
and
   new.snap_id = sn.snap_id
and
   old.snap_id = sn.snap_id-1
and
   new.filename = old.filename
and
   -- ************************************************************
   -- Low I/O values are misleading, so we filter for high I/O
   -- ************************************************************
   new.phyrds-old.phyrds > 100
```

```
and
-- ************************************************************
-- The following will allow you to choose a threshold
-- ************************************************************
  (new.phyrds-old.phyrds)*4>  — This is 25% of total
-- (new.phyrds-old.phyrds)*2>  — This is 50% of total
-- (new.phyrds-old.phyrds)*1.25> — This is 75% of total
-- ************************************************************
-- This subquery computes the sum of all I/O during the snapshot period
-- ************************************************************
(
select
   (newreads.value-oldreads.value) reads
from
   perfstat.stats$sysstat oldreads,
   perfstat.stats$sysstat newreads,
   perfstat.stats$snapshot   sn1
where
   sn.snap_id = sn1.snap_id
and
   newreads.snap_id = sn.snap_id
and
   oldreads.snap_id = sn.snap_id-1
and
  oldreads.statistic# = 40
and
  newreads.statistic# = 40
and
  (newreads.value-oldreads.value) > 0
)
;

prompt
prompt ************************************************************
prompt  This will identify any single file whose write I/O
prompt  is more than 25% of the total write I/O of the database.
prompt
prompt  The "hot" file should be examined, and the hot table/index
prompt  should be identified using STATSPACK.
prompt
prompt  - The busy file should be placed on a disk device with
prompt    "less busy" files to minimize write delay and channel
prompt    contention.
prompt
prompt  - If small file has a hot small table, place the table
prompt    in the KEEP pool
prompt
prompt ************************************************************
```

```
select
   to_char(snap_time,'yyyy-mm-dd HH24')   mydate,
   new.filename                            file_name,
   new.phywrts-old.phywrts                 writes,
   ((new.phywrts-old.phywrts)/
   (
   select
      (newwrites.value-oldwrites.value) writes
   from
      perfstat.stats$sysstat    oldwrites,
      perfstat.stats$sysstat    newwrites,
      perfstat.stats$snapshot   sn1
   where
      sn.snap_id = sn1.snap_id
   and
      newwrites.snap_id = sn.snap_id
   and
      oldwrites.snap_id = sn.snap_id-1
   and
      oldwrites.statistic# = 44
   and
      newwrites.statistic# = 44
   and
      (newwrites.value-oldwrites.value) > 0
   ))*100 pct_of_tot
from
   perfstat.stats$filestatxs old,
   perfstat.stats$filestatxs new,
   perfstat.stats$snapshot    sn
where
   snap_time > sysdate-&1
and
   new.snap_id = sn.snap_id
and
   old.snap_id = sn.snap_id-1
and
   new.filename = old.filename
and
   -- *********************************************************
   -- Low I/O values are misleading, so we only take high values
   -- *********************************************************
   new.phywrts-old.phywrts > 100
and
-- *********************************************************
-- Here you can choose a threshold value
-- *********************************************************
 (new.phyrds-old.phywrts)*4> — This is 25% of total
```

```
-- (new.phyrds-old.phywrts)*2> — This is 50% of total
-- (new.phyrds-old.phywrts)*1.25> — This is 75% of total
-- **********************************************************
-- This subquery computes the sum of all I/O during the snapshot period
-- **********************************************************
(
select
   (newwrites.value-oldwrites.value) writes
from
   perfstat.stats$sysstat     oldwrites,
   perfstat.stats$sysstat     newwrites,
   perfstat.stats$snapshot    sn1
where
   sn.snap_id = sn1.snap_id
and
   newwrites.snap_id = sn.snap_id
and
   oldwrites.snap_id = sn.snap_id-1
and
  oldwrites.statistic# = 44
and
  newwrites.statistic# = 44
and
  (newwrites.value-oldwrites.value) > 0
)
;

--**********************************************************
-- Alert when data buffer hit ratio is below threshold
--**********************************************************

prompt
prompt
prompt **********************************************************
prompt  When the data buffer hit ratio falls below 90%, you
prompt  should consider adding to the db_block_buffer init.ora parameter
prompt
prompt
prompt **********************************************************
prompt
prompt

column bhr format 9.99
column mydate heading 'yr.  mo dy Hr.'

select
   to_char(snap_time,'yyyy-mm-dd HH24')       mydate,
```

```
      new.name                                 buffer_pool_name,
      (((new.consistent_gets-old.consistent_gets)+
      (new.db_block_gets-old.db_block_gets))-
      (new.physical_reads-old.physical_reads))
      /
      ((new.consistent_gets-old.consistent_gets)+
      (new.db_block_gets-old.db_block_gets))     bhr
from
      perfstat.stats$buffer_pool_statistics old,
      perfstat.stats$buffer_pool_statistics new,
      perfstat.stats$snapshot                   sn
where
      snap_time > sysdate &1
and
      (((new.consistent_gets-old.consistent_gets)+
      (new.db_block_gets-old.db_block_gets))-
      (new.physical_reads-old.physical_reads))
      /
      ((new.consistent_gets-old.consistent_gets)+
      (new.db_block_gets-old.db_block_gets)) < .90
and
      new.name = old.name
and
      new.snap_id = sn.snap_id
and
      old.snap_id = sn.snap_id-1
;


-- *********************************************************
-- Alert when total disk sorts are below threshold
-- *********************************************************

prompt
prompt
prompt *********************************************************
prompt  When there are high disk sorts, you should investigate
prompt  increasing sort_area_size, or adding indexes to force index_full scans
prompt
prompt
prompt *********************************************************
prompt
prompt


column sorts_memory  format 999,999,999
column sorts_disk     format 999,999,999
column ratio format .9999999999999
```

```
select
   to_char(snap_time,'yyyy-mm-dd HH24'),
   newmem.value-oldmem.value sorts_memory,
   newdsk.value-olddsk.value sorts_disk,
   (newdsk.value-olddsk.value)/(newmem.value-oldmem.value) ratio
from
   perfstat.stats$sysstat oldmem,
   perfstat.stats$sysstat newmem,
   perfstat.stats$sysstat newdsk,
   perfstat.stats$sysstat olddsk,
   perfstat.stats$snapshot    sn
where
   -- Where there are more than 100 disk sorts per hour
   newdsk.value-olddsk.value > 100
and
   snap_time > sysdate-&1
and
   newdsk.snap_id = sn.snap_id
and
   olddsk.snap_id = sn.snap_id-1
and
   newmem.snap_id = sn.snap_id
and
   oldmem.snap_id = sn.snap_id-1
and
   oldmem.name = 'sorts (memory)'
and
   newmem.name = 'sorts (memory)'
and
   olddsk.name = 'sorts (disk)'
and
   newdsk.name = 'sorts (disk)'
and
   newmem.value-oldmem.value > 0
;


--*************************************************************
-- Alert when total I/O wait count is above threshold
--*************************************************************

prompt
prompt
prompt ************************************************************
prompt  When there is high I/O waits, disk bottlenecks may exist
prompt  Run iostats to find the hot disk and shuffle files to
prompt  remove the contention
```

```
prompt
prompt *******************************************************

break on snapdate skip 2

column snapdate format a16
column filename format a40

select
   to_char(snap_time,'yyyy-mm-dd HH24') snapdate,
   old.filename,
   new.wait_count-old.wait_count waits
from
   perfstat.stats$filestatxs old,
   perfstat.stats$filestatxs new,
   perfstat.stats$snapshot   sn
where
   snap_time > sysdate-&1
and
   new.wait_count-old.wait_count > 800
and
   new.snap_id = sn.snap_id
and
   old.filename = new.filename
and
   old.snap_id = sn.snap_id-1
and
   new.wait_count-old.wait_count > 0
;


--***********************************************************
-- Alert when average buffer busy waits exceed threshold
--***********************************************************

prompt ***********************************************************
prompt  Buffer Busy Waits may signal a high update table with too
prompt  few freelists.  Find the offending table and add more freelists.
prompt
prompt ***********************************************************

column buffer_busy_wait format 999,999,999
column mydate heading 'yr.  mo dy Hr.'

select
   to_char(snap_time,'yyyy-mm-dd HH24')        mydate,
   new.name,
   new.buffer_busy_wait-old.buffer_busy_wait buffer_busy_wait
```

```
from
   perfstat.stats$buffer_pool_statistics old,
   perfstat.stats$buffer_pool_statistics new,
   perfstat.stats$snapshot                sn
where
   snap_time > sysdate-&1
and
   new.name <> 'FAKE VIEW'
and
   new.snap_id = sn.snap_id
and
   old.snap_id = sn.snap_id-1
and
   new.buffer_busy_wait-old.buffer_busy_wait > 1
group by
   to_char(snap_time,'yyyy-mm-dd HH24'),
   new.name,
   new.buffer_busy_wait-old.buffer_busy_wait
;

--************************************************************
-- Alert when total redo log space requests exceed threshold
--************************************************************

prompt ************************************************************
prompt  High redo log space requests indicate a need to increase
prompt  the log_buffer parameter
prompt
prompt ************************************************************

column redo_log_space_requests  format 999,999,999

select
   to_char(snap_time,'yyyy-mm-dd HH24'),
   newmem.value-oldmem.value redo_log_space_requests
from
   perfstat.stats$sysstat oldmem,
   perfstat.stats$sysstat newmem,
   perfstat.stats$snapshot    sn
where
   snap_time > sysdate-&1
and
   newmem.value-oldmem.value > 30
and
   newmem.snap_id = sn.snap_id
and
   oldmem.snap_id = sn.snap_id-1
and
```

```
   oldmem.name = 'redo log space requests'
and
   newmem.name = 'redo log space requests'
and
   newmem.value-oldmem.value > 0
;


--************************************************************
-- Alert when table_fetch_continued_row exceeds threshold
--************************************************************


prompt ********************************************************
prompt  Table fetch continued row indicates chained rows, or fetches of
prompt  long datatypes (long raw, blob)
prompt
prompt  Investigate increasing db_block_size or reorganizing tables
prompt  with chained rows.
prompt
prompt ********************************************************

column table_fetch_continued_row  format 999,999,999

select
   to_char(snap_time,'yyyy-mm-dd HH24'),
   avg(newmem.value-oldmem.value) table_fetch_continued_row
from
   perfstat.stats$sysstat oldmem,
   perfstat.stats$sysstat newmem,
   perfstat.stats$snapshot    sn
where
   snap_time > sysdate-&1
and
   newmem.snap_id = sn.snap_id
and
   oldmem.snap_id = sn.snap_id-1
and
   oldmem.name = 'table fetch continued row'
and
   newmem.name = 'table fetch continued row'
and
   newmem.value-oldmem.value > 0
having
   avg(newmem.value-oldmem.value) > 10000
group by
   to_char(snap_time,'yyyy-mm-dd HH24')
;
prompt
```

```
prompt  ************************************************************
prompt   Enqueue Deadlocks indicate contention within the Oracle
prompt   shared pool.
prompt
prompt   Investigate increasing shared_pool_size
prompt
prompt  ************************************************************

column enqueue_deadlocks      format 999,999,999

select
   to_char(snap_time,'yyyy-mm-dd HH24'),
   a.value enqueue_deadlocks
from
   perfstat.stats$sysstat      a,
   perfstat.stats$snapshot     sn
where
   snap_time > sysdate-&1
and
   a.snap_id = sn.snap_id
and
   a.statistic# = 24
and
   a.value > 10
;

prompt  ************************************************************
prompt   Long-table full table scans can indicate a need to:
prompt
prompt            - Make the offending tables parallel query
prompt              (alter table parallel degree yyy;)
prompt            - Place the table in the RECYCLE pool
prompt            - Build an index on the table to remove the FTS
prompt
prompt To locate the table, run access.sql
prompt
prompt   See Oracle Magazine September 2000 issue for details
prompt
prompt  ************************************************************

column fts  format 999,999,999

select
   to_char(snap_time,'yyyy-mm-dd HH24'),
   newmem.value-oldmem.value fts
from
   perfstat.stats$sysstat oldmem,
   perfstat.stats$sysstat newmem,
```

```
   perfstat.stats$snapshot      sn
where
   snap_time > sysdate-&1
and
   newmem.value-oldmem.value > 1000
and
   newmem.snap_id = sn.snap_id
and
   oldmem.snap_id = sn.snap_id-1
and
   oldmem.statistic# = 140
and
   newmem.statistic# = 140
and
   newmem.value-oldmem.value > 0
;


prompt ***********************************************************
prompt   Excessive waits on background events
prompt ***********************************************************

column mydate heading 'Yr.  Mo Dy Hr'     format a13;
column event                              format a30;
column total_waits    heading 'tot waits' format 999,999;
column time_waited    heading 'time wait' format 999,999;
column total_timeouts heading 'timeouts'  format 9,999;

break on to_char(snap_time,'yyyy-mm-dd') skip 1;

select
   to_char(snap_time,'yyyy-mm-dd HH24')            mydate,
   e.event,
   e.total_waits - nvl(b.total_waits,0)            total_waits,
   e.time_waited - nvl(b.time_waited,0)            time_waited,
   e.total_timeouts - nvl(b.total_timeouts,0)      total_timeouts
from
   stats$bg_event_summary      b,
   stats$bg_event_summary      e,
   stats$snapshot       sn
where
   snap_time > sysdate-&1
and
   e.event not like '%timer'
and
   e.event not like '%message%'
and
   e.snap_id = sn.snap_id
and
```

```
      b.snap_id = e.snap_id-1
and
      b.event = e.event
and
      e.total_timeouts > 100
and
(
      e.total_waits - b.total_waits  > 100
   or
      e.time_waited - b.time_waited > 100
)
;

prompt ************************************************************
prompt  Excessive event waits indicate shared pool contention
prompt ************************************************************

-- © 2001 by Donald Keith Burleson - All Rights Reserved
set lines 80;

column mydate heading 'Yr.  Mo Dy Hr'      format a13;
column event                               format a30;
column waits                               format 999,999;
column secs_waited                         format 999,999,999;
column avg_wait_secs                       format 99,999;

break on to_char(snap_time,'yyyy-mm-dd') skip 1;

select
   to_char(snap_time,'yyyy-mm-dd HH24')            mydate,
   e.event,
   e.total_waits - nvl(b.total_waits,0)            waits,
   ((e.time_waited - nvl(b.time_waited,0))/100) /
   nvl((e.total_waits - nvl(b.total_waits,0)),0)  avg_wait_secs
from
   stats$system_event b,
   stats$system_event e,
   stats$snapshot     sn
where
   snap_time > sysdate-&1
and
   e.snap_id = sn.snap_id
and
   b.snap_id = e.snap_id-1
and
   b.event = e.event
and
   (
```

```
   e.event like 'SQL*Net%'
   or
   e.event in (
      'latch free',
      'enqueue',
      'LGWR wait for redo copy',
      'buffer busy waits'
   )
)
and
   e.total_waits - b.total_waits  > 100
and
   e.time_waited - b.time_waited > 100
;


prompt ********************************************************
prompt  Excessive library cache miss ratio
prompt ********************************************************

column c1 heading "execs"     format 9,999,999
column c2 heading "Cache Misses|While Executing"    format 9,999,999
column c3 heading "Library Cache|Miss Ratio"    format 999.99999


select
   to_char(snap_time,'yyyy-mm-dd HH24')   mydate,
   sum(new.pins-old.pins)                 c1,
   sum(new.reloads-old.reloads)           c2,
   sum(new.reloads-old.reloads)/
   sum(new.pins-old.pins)                 library_cache_miss_ratio
from
   stats$librarycache old,
   stats$librarycache new,
   stats$snapshot      sn
where
   snap_time > sysdate-&1
and
   new.snap_id = sn.snap_id
and
   old.snap_id = new.snap_id-1
and
   old.namespace = new.namespace
having
   sum(new.reloads-old.reloads)/
   sum(new.pins-old.pins) > .05
group by
   to_char(snap_time,'yyyy-mm-dd HH24')
;
```

```
prompt  ***********************************************************
prompt  Excessive length of DBWR processes
prompt  ***********************************************************

column c1 heading "Write request length" format 9,999.99
column c2 heading "Write Requests"       format 999,999
column c3 heading "DBWR checkpoints"      format 999,999

select distinct
   to_char(snap_time,'yyyy-mm-dd HH24') mydate,
   a.value/b.value                   c1,
   b.value                           c2,
   c.value                           c3
from
   stats$sysstat  a,
   stats$sysstat  b,
   stats$sysstat  c,
   stats$snapshot sn
where
   snap_time > sysdate-&1
and
   sn.snap_id = a.snap_id
and
   sn.snap_id = b.snap_id
and
   sn.snap_id = c.snap_id
and
   a.name = 'summed dirty queue length'
and
   b.name = 'write requests'
and
   c.name = 'DBWR checkpoints'
and
   a.value > 0
and
   b.value > 0
and
   a.value/b.value > 3
;

prompt  ***********************************************************
prompt  Data Dictionary Miss Ratio below 90% indicates the need
prompt  to increase the shared_pool_size
prompt  ***********************************************************

column c1     heading "Data|Dictionary|Gets"          format 999,999,999
column c2     heading "Data|Dictionary|Cache|Misses"  format 999,999,999
column c3     heading "Data|Dictionary|Hit|Ratio"     format 999,999
```

```
select
   to_char(snap_time,'yyyy-mm-dd HH24')   mydate,
   sum(new.gets-old.gets)                 c1,
   sum(new.getmisses-old.getmisses)       c2,
   trunc((1-(sum(new.getmisses-old.getmisses)/sum(new.gets-old.gets)))*100) c3
from
   stats$rowcache_summary new,
   stats$rowcache_summary old,
   stats$snapshot sn
where
   snap_time > sysdate-&1
and
   new.snap_id = sn.snap_id
and
   old.snap_id = new.snap_id-1
having
   trunc((1-(sum(new.getmisses-old.getmisses)/sum(new.gets-old.gets)))*100) < 90
group by
   to_char(snap_time,'yyyy-mm-dd HH24')
;


prompt ********************************************************
prompt   Report when Data Dictionary Hit Ratio for an object
prompt      falls below 70%
prompt ********************************************************

set lines 80;
-- © 2001 by Donald Keith Burleson - All Rights Reserved

column mydate    heading 'Yr.  Mo Dy  Hr.'             format a16
column parameter                                       format a20
column c1        heading "Data|Dictionary|Gets"        format 99,999,999
column c2        heading "Data|Dictionary|Cache|Misses" format 99,999,999
column c3        heading "Data|Dictionary|Usage"       format 999
column c4        heading "Object|Hit|Ratio"            format 999

select
   to_char(snap_time,'yyyy-mm-dd HH24')   mydate,
   new.parameter                          parameter,
   (new.gets-old.gets)                    c1,
   (new.getmisses-old.getmisses)          c2,
   (new.total_usage-old.total_usage)      c3,
  round((1 - (new.getmisses-old.getmisses) /
  (new.gets-old.gets))*100,1)             c4
```

```
from
   stats$rowcache_summary new,
   stats$rowcache_summary old,
   stats$snapshot          sn
where
   snap_time > sysdate-&1
and
  round((1 - (new.getmisses-old.getmisses) /
  (new.gets-old.gets))*100,1) < 70
and
   (new.total_usage-old.total_usage) > 300
and
   new.snap_id = sn.snap_id
and
   old.snap_id = new.snap_id-1
and
   old.parameter = new.parameter
and
   new.gets-old.gets > 0
;

spool off;
```

trace_alert.ksh

```
#!/bin/ksh

#*******************************************************
# Exit if no first parameter $1 is passed to script
#*******************************************************
if [ -z "$1" ]
then
   echo "Usage: trace_alert.ksh <ORACLE_SID>"
   exit 99
fi

#*******************************************************
# First, we must set the environment . . . .
#*******************************************************
ORACLE_SID=$1
export ORACLE_SID
ORACLE_HOME=`cat /var/opt/oracle/oratab|grep $ORACLE_SID:|cut -f2 -d':'`
export ORACLE_HOME
ORACLE_BASE=`echo $ORACLE_HOME | sed -e 's:/product/.*::g'`
export ORACLE_BASE
export DBA=$ORACLE_BASE/admin;
```

```
export DBA
PATH=$ORACLE_HOME/bin:$PATH
export PATH
MON=`echo ~oracle/mon`
export MON

#*****************************************************
# Get the server name & date for the e-mail message
#*****************************************************
SERVER=`uname -a|awk '{print $2}'`

MYDATE=`date +"%m/%d %H:%M"`

#*****************************************************
# Remove the old file list
#*****************************************************
rm -f /tmp/trace_list.lst
touch /tmp/trace_list.lst

#*****************************************************
# list the full-names of all possible dump files . . . .
#*****************************************************
find $DBA/$ORACLE_SID/bdump/*.trc   -mtime -1  print >>  /tmp/trace_list.lst
find $DBA/$ORACLE_SID/udump/*.trc   -mtime -1 -print >> /tmp/trace_list.lst
find $ORACLE_HOME/rdbms/log/*.trc   -mtime -1 -print >> /tmp/trace_list.lst

#*****************************************************
# Exit if there are not any trace files found
#*****************************************************
NUM_TRACE=`cat /tmp/trace_list.lst|wc -l`
oracle_num=`expr $NUM_TRACE`
if [ $oracle_num -lt 1 ]
 then
 exit 0
fi
#echo $NUM_TRACE files found
#cat /tmp/trace_list.lst

#*****************************************************
# for each trace file found, send DBA an e-mail message
#  and move the trace file to the /tmp directory
#*****************************************************
cat /tmp/trace_list.lst|while read TRACE_FILE
do
```

```ksh
#***************************************************
#  This gets the short file name at the end of the full path
#***************************************************
SHORT_TRACE_FILE_NAME=`echo $TRACE_FILE|awk -F"/" '{ print $NF }'`
#***************************************************
#  This gets the file location (bdump, udump, log)
#***************************************************
DUMP_LOC=`echo $TRACE_FILE|awk -F"/" '{ print $(NF-1) }'`


#***************************************************
# send an e-mail to the administrator
#***************************************************

head -100 $TRACE_FILE|\
mailx -s "$ORACLE_SID Oracle trace file at $MYDATE."\
    don@remote-dba.net\
    terry@oracle.net\
    tzu@oracle.com
#***************************************************
# Move the trace file to the /tmp directory
# This prevents multiple messages to the developers
# and allows the script to run every minute
#***************************************************

cp $TRACE_FILE /tmp/${DUMP_LOC}_${SHORT_TRACE_FILE_NAME}
rm -f $TRACE_FILED

done
```

webserver_alert.ksh

```ksh
#!/bin/ksh

MYDATE=`date +"%Y%m%d"`

SERVER=`uname -a|awk '{print $2}'`

if [ -f /usr/src/asp/core ]
then

   # Move the file to a dated location . . .
   mv /usr/src/asp/core /tmp/core_$MYDATE

   # send an e-mail to the administrator
   head /tmp/core_$MYDATE|\
   mail -s "EMERGENCY - WebServer $SERVER abort in /tmp/core_$MYDATE"\
      don@remote-dba.net\
```

```
        omar@oracle.com\
        carlos@oracle.com

fi
```

STATSPACK Extension Scripts

vmstat Scripts

create_vmstat_table.sql

```sql
connect perfstat/perfstat;

drop table stats$vmstat;
create table stats$vmstat
(
     start_date              date,
     duration                number,
     server_name             varchar2(20),
     runque_waits            number,
     page_in                 number,
     page_out                number,
     user_cpu                number,
     system_cpu              number,
     idle_cpu                number,
     wait_cpu                number
)
tablespace perfstat
storage (initial 10m
        next       1m
        pctincrease 0)
;
```

get_vmstat_aix.ksh

```ksh
#!/bin/ksh

# First, we must set the environment . . . .
ORACLE_SID=PCT9
export ORACLE_SID
ORACLE_HOME=`cat /etc/oratab|grep \^$ORACLE_SID:|cut -f2 -d':'`
export ORACLE_HOME
PATH=$ORACLE_HOME/bin:$PATH
export PATH
```

```
SERVER_NAME=`uname -a|awk '{print $2}'`
typeset -u SERVER_NAME
export SERVER_NAME

# sample every five minutes (300 seconds) . . . .
SAMPLE_TIME=300

while true
do
   vmstat ${SAMPLE_TIME} 2 > /tmp/msg$$

# This script is intended to run starting at 7:00 AM EST Until midnight EST
cat /tmp/msg$$|sed 1,4d | awk  '{ printf("%s %s %s %s %s %s %s\n", $1, $6, $7,
14, $15, $16, $17) }' | while read RUNQUE PAGE_IN PAGE_OUT USER_CPU SYSTEM_CPU
DLE_CPU WAIT_CPU
   do

      $ORACLE_HOME/bin/sqlplus -s / <<EOF
      insert into perfstat.stats\$vmstat
                         values (
                            sysdate,
                            $SAMPLE_TIME,
                            '$SERVER_NAME',
                            $RUNQUE,
                            $PAGE_IN,
                            $PAGE_OUT,
                            $USER_CPU,
                            $SYSTEM_CPU,
                            $IDLE_CPU,
                            $WAIT_CPU
                               );
      EXIT
EOF
   done
done

rm /tmp/msg$$
```

get_vmstat_linux.ksh

```
#!/bin/ksh

# This is the linux version

# First, we must set the environment . . . .
```

```
#ORACLE_SID=edi1
#export ORACLE_SID
#ORACLE_HOME=`cat /etc/oratab|grep \^$ORACLE_SID:|cut -f2 -d':'`
#export ORACLE_HOME

ORACLE_HOME=/usr/app/oracle/admin/product/8/1/6
export ORACLE_HOME

PATH=$ORACLE_HOME/bin:$PATH
export PATH

SERVER_NAME=`uname -a|awk '{print $2}'`
typeset -u SERVER_NAME
export SERVER_NAME

# sample every five minutes (300 seconds) . . . .
SAMPLE_TIME=300
SAMPLE_TIME=3

while true
do
   vmstat ${SAMPLE_TIME} 2 > /tmp/msg$$


# run vmstat and direct the output into the Oracle table . . .
cat /tmp/msg$$|sed 1,3d | awk '{ printf("%s %s %s %s %s %s\n", $1, $8, $9, $14,
15, $16) }' | while read RUNQUE PAGE_IN PAGE_OUT USER_CPU SYSTEM_CPU IDLE_CPU
   do

      $ORACLE_HOME/bin/sqlplus -s perfstat/perfstat@testb1<<EOF
      insert into perfstat.stats\$vmstat
                      values (
                          sysdate,
                          $SAMPLE_TIME,
                          '$SERVER_NAME',
                          $RUNQUE,
                          $PAGE_IN,
                          $PAGE_OUT,
                          $USER_CPU,
                          $SYSTEM_CPU,
                          $IDLE_CPU,
                          0
                                );
      EXIT
EOF
   done
done

rm /tmp/msg$$
```

get_vmstat_solaris.ksh

```ksh
#!/bin/ksh

# First, we must set the environment . . . .
ORACLE_SID=prodb1
export ORACLE_SID
ORACLE_HOME=`cat /var/opt/oracle/oratab|grep \^$ORACLE_SID:|cut -f2 -d':'`
export ORACLE_HOME
PATH=$ORACLE_HOME/bin:$PATH
export PATH

SERVER_NAME=`uname -a|awk '{print $2}'`
typeset -u SERVER_NAME
export SERVER_NAME

# sample every five minutes (300 seconds) . . . .
SAMPLE_TIME=300

while true
do
   vmstat ${SAMPLE_TIME} 2 > /tmp/msg$$

# Note that Solaris does not have a wait CPU column
cat /tmp/msg$$|sed 1,3d | \
awk  '{ printf("%s %s %s %s %s %s\n", $1, $8, $9, $20, 21, $22) }'\
 | while read RUNQUE PAGE_IN PAGE_OUT USER_CPU SYSTEM_CPU IDLE_CPU
   do

      $ORACLE_HOME/bin/sqlplus -s / <<EOF
      insert into perfstat.stats\$vmstat
                        values (
                           SYSDATE,
                           $SAMPLE_TIME,
                           '$SERVER_NAME',
                           $RUNQUE,
                           $PAGE_IN,
                           $PAGE_OUT,
                           $USER_CPU,
                           $SYSTEM_CPU,
                           $IDLE_CPU,
                           0
                              );
      EXIT
EOF
   done
done

rm /tmp/msg$$
```

get_vmstat_solaris_remote.sql

```ksh
#!/bin/ksh

# First, we must set the environment . . . .
ORACLE_SID=prodb1
export ORACLE_SID
ORACLE_HOME=`cat /var/opt/oracle/oratab|grep \^$ORACLE_SID:|cut -f2 -d':'`
export ORACLE_HOME
PATH=$ORACLE_HOME/bin:$PATH
export PATH

SERVER_NAME=`uname -a|awk '{print $2}'`
typeset -u SERVER_NAME
export SERVER_NAME

# sample every five minutes (300 seconds) . . . .
SAMPLE_TIME=300
SAMPLE_TIME=3

while true
do
   vmstat ${SAMPLE_TIME} 2 > /tmp/msg$$


# Note that Solaris does not have a wait CPU column
cat /tmp/msg$$|sed 1,3d | \
awk '{ printf("%s %s %s %s %s %s\n", $1, $8, $9, $20, 21, $22) }' \
| while read RUNQUE PAGE_IN PAGE_OUT USER_CPU SYSTEM_CPU IDLE_CPU
   do

      $ORACLE_HOME/bin/sqlplus -s perfstat/perfstat@prodb1<<EOF
      insert into perfstat.stats\$vmstat
                      values (
                        SYSDATE,
                        $SAMPLE_TIME,
                        '$SERVER_NAME',
                        $RUNQUE,
                        $PAGE_IN,
                        $PAGE_OUT,
                        $USER_CPU,
                        $SYSTEM_CPU,
                        $IDLE_CPU,
                        0
                            );
      EXIT
EOF
```

```
     done
done

rm /tmp/msg$$
```

rpt_vmstat.sql

```
connect perfstat/perfstat;
-- © 2001 by Donald Keith Burleson - All Rights Reserved

set feedback off;
set verify off;

column my_date heading 'date' format a20
column c2       heading runq   format 999
column c3       heading pg_in  format 999
column c4       heading pg_ot  format 999
column c5       heading usr    format 999
column c6       heading sys    format 999
column c7       heading idl    format 999
column c8       heading wt     format 999


select
 to_char(start_date,'yyyy-mm-dd') my_date,
-- avg(runque_waits)        c2
-- avg(page_in)             c3,
-- avg(page_out)            c4,
avg(user_cpu + system_cpu)           c5,
-- avg(system_cpu)          c6,
-- avg(idle_cpu)            c7,
avg(wait_cpu)            c8
from
   stats$vmstat
group  BY
 to_char(start_date,'yyyy-mm-dd')
order by
 to_char(start_date,'yyyy-mm-dd')
;
```

rpt_vmstat_dy.sql

```
connect perfstat/perfstat;
-- © 2001 by Donald Keith Burleson - All Rights Reserved

set feedback off;
```

```
set verify off;

column my_date heading 'date' format a20
column c2      heading runq   format 999
column c3      heading pg_in  format 999
column c4      heading pg_ot  format 999
column c5      heading usr    format 999
column c6      heading sys    format 999
column c7      heading idl    format 999
column c8      heading wt     format 999


select
 to_char(start_date,'day') my_date,
-- avg(runque_waits)      c2
-- avg(page_in)           c3,
-- avg(page_out)          c4,
avg(user_cpu + system_cpu)          c5,
-- avg(system_cpu)        c6,
-- avg(idle_cpu)          c7,
avg(wait_cpu)             c8
from
   stats$vmstat
group  BY
 to_char(start_date,'day')
order by
 to_char(start_date,'day')
;
```

rpt_vmstat_hr.sql

```
connect perfstat/perfstat;
-- © 2001 by Donald Keith Burleson - All Rights Reserved

set feedback off;
set verify off;

column my_date heading 'date' format a20
column c2      heading runq   format 999
column c3      heading pg_in  format 999
column c4      heading pg_ot  format 999
column c5      heading usr    format 999
column c6      heading sys    format 999
column c7      heading idl    format 999
column c8      heading wt     format 999
```

```sql
select
 to_char(start_date,'day') my_date,
-- avg(runque_waits)         c2
-- avg(page_in)              c3,
-- avg(page_out)             c4,
avg(user_cpu + system_cpu)          c5,
-- avg(system_cpu)           c6,
-- avg(idle_cpu)             c7,
avg(wait_cpu)           c8
from
    stats$vmstat
group  BY
 to_char(start_date,'day')
order by
 to_char(start_date,'day')
;
```

run_vmstat.ksh

```ksh
#!/bin/ksh

# First, we must set the environment . . . .
vmstat=`echo ~oracle/vmstat`
export vmstat
ORACLE_SID=`cat ${vmstat}/mysid`
export ORACLE_SID
ORACLE_HOME=`cat /etc/oratab|grep $ORACLE_SID:|cut -f2 -d':'`
export ORACLE_HOME
PATH=$ORACLE_HOME/bin:$PATH
export PATH


#----------------------------------------
# If it is not running, then start it . . .
#----------------------------------------
check_stat=`ps -ef|grep get_vmstat|grep -v grep|wc -l`;
oracle_num=`expr $check_stat`
if [ $oracle_num -le 0 ]
 then nohup $vmstat/get_vmstat.ksh > /dev/null 2>&1 &
fi

HOUR=`date +"%H"`

#if [ $HOUR -gt 19 ]
#then
   #myvar=`ps|grep get_vmstat|awk '{print $1 }'|wc -l`
   #if [ $myvar -gt 0 ]
   #then kill -9 `ps|grep get_vmstat|awk '{print $1 }'` > /dev/null
```

```
    #fi
#fi
```

run_vmstat_alert.ksh

```ksh
#!/bin/ksh

# First, we must set the environment . . . .
ORACLE_SID=$1
export ORACLE_SID
ORACLE_HOME=`cat /var/opt/oracle/oratab|grep $ORACLE_SID:|cut -f2 -d':'`
export ORACLE_HOME
PATH=$ORACLE_HOME/bin:$PATH
export PATH
vmstat=`echo ~oracle/vmstat`
export vmstat

sqlplus /<<!
spool /tmp/vmstat_$1.lst
@$vmstat/vmstat_alert 7
spool off;
exit;
!

# Mail the report
check_stat=`cat /tmp/vmstat_$1.lst|wc -l`;
oracle_num=`expr $check_stat`
if [ $oracle_num -gt 3 ]
  then
    cat /tmp/vmstat_$1.lst|mailx -s "Oracle vmstat alert" don@remote-dba.net
terry.oakes@worldnet.att.net adamf@oracle.com
fi
```

run_vmstat_linux.ksh

```ksh
#!/bin/ksh

# First, we must set the environment . . . .
vmstat=`echo ~oracle/vmstat`
export vmstat
ORACLE_SID=`cat ${vmstat}/mysid`
export ORACLE_SID

ORACLE_HOME=`cat /etc/oratab|grep $ORACLE_SID:|cut -f2 -d':'`
export ORACLE_HOME
PATH=$ORACLE_HOME/bin:$PATH
```

```
export PATH

#----------------------------------------
# If it is not running, then start it . . .
#----------------------------------------
check_stat=`ps -ef|grep get_vmstat|grep -v grep|wc -l`;
oracle_num=`expr $check_stat`
if [ $oracle_num -le 0 ]
 then nohup $vmstat/get_vmstat_linux.ksh > /dev/null 2>&1 &
fi
```

run_vmstat_rpt.ksh

```
#!/bin/ksh

# First, we must set the environment . . . .
ORACLE_SID=mon1
export ORACLE_SID
ORACLE_HOME=`cat /etc/oratab|grep $ORACLE_SID:|cut -f2 -d':'`
export ORACLE_HOME
PATH=$ORACLE_HOME/bin:$PATH
export PATH
vmstat=`echo ~oracle/vmstat`
export vmstat

echo 'Starting Reports'

for db in `cat ${vmstat}/dbnames|awk '{ print $1 }'`
do
   host=`cat ${vmstat}/dbnames|grep $db|awk '{ print $2 }'`
sqlplus /<<!

select count(*) from perfstat.stats\$vmstat;
exit;
!
done
```

run_vmstat_solaris.ksh

```
#!/bin/ksh

# First, we must set the environment . . . .
vmstat=`echo ~oracle/vmstat`
export vmstat
ORACLE_SID=`cat ${vmstat}/mysid`
```

```
export ORACLE_SID
ORACLE_HOME=`cat /var/opt/oracle/oratab|grep $ORACLE_SID:|cut -f2 -d':'`
export ORACLE_HOME
PATH=$ORACLE_HOME/bin:$PATH
export PATH


#-------------------------------------
# If it is not running, then start it . . .
#-------------------------------------
check_stat=`ps -ef|grep get_vmstat|grep -v grep|wc -l`;
oracle_num=`expr $check_stat`
if [ $oracle_num -le 0 ]
 then nohup $vmstat/get_vmstat_solaris.ksh > /dev/null 2>&1 &
fi

HOUR=`date +"%H"`

#if [ $HOUR -gt 19 ]
#then
    #myvar=`ps|grep get_vmstat|awk '{print $1 }'|wc -l`
    #if [ $myvar -gt 0 ]
    #then kill -9 `ps|grep get_vmstat|awk '{print $1 }'` > /dev/null
    #fi
#fi
```

vmstat.cron.txt

```
00 7 * * * /export/run_vmstat.ksh > /export/home/oracle/vmstat/r.lst
00 7 * * * /export/run_vmstat_alert.ksh prodb1 >
            /export/home/oracle/vmstat/v.lst
```

vmstat_alert.sql

```
set lines 80;
-- © 2001 by Donald Keith Burleson - All Rights Reserved
set feedback off;
set verify off;

column my_date heading 'date       hour' format a20
column c2       heading runq   format 999
column c3       heading pg_in  format 999
column c4       heading pg_ot  format 999
column c5       heading usr    format 999
column c6       heading sys    format 999
column c7       heading idl    format 999
```

```
column c8       heading wt      format 999


ttitle 'run queue > 2|May indicate an overloaded CPU|When run queue exceeds the
number of CPUs| on the server, tasks are waiting for service.';


select
 server_name,
 to_char(start_date,'YY/MM/DD    HH24') my_date,
 avg(runque_waits)       c2,
 avg(page_in)            c3,
 avg(page_out)           c4,
 avg(user_cpu)           c5,
 avg(system_cpu)         c6,
 avg(idle_cpu)           c7
from
perfstat.stats$vmstat
WHERE
runque_waits > 2
and start_date > sysdate-&1
group by
 server_name,
 to_char(start_date,'YY/MM/DD    HH24')
ORDER BY
 server_name,
 to_char(start_date,'YY/MM/DD    HH24')
;

ttitle 'page_in > 1|
May indicate overloaded memory|
Whenever Unix performs a page-n, the RAM memory |
on the server has been exhausted and swap pages are being used.';

select
 server_name,
 to_char(start_date,'YY/MM/DD    HH24') my_date,
 avg(runque_waits)       c2,
 avg(page_in)            c3,
 avg(page_out)           c4,
 avg(user_cpu)           c5,
 avg(system_cpu)         c6,
 avg(idle_cpu)           c7
from
perfstat.stats$vmstat
WHERE
page_in > 1
and start_date > sysdate-&1
```

```
group by
 server_name,
 to_char(start_date,'YY/MM/DD    HH24')
ORDER BY
 server_name,
 to_char(start_date,'YY/MM/DD    HH24')
;

ttitle 'user+system CPU > 70%|
Indicates periods with a fully-loaded CPU subsystem.|
Periods of 100% utilization are only a |
concern when run queue values exceeds the number of CPUs on the server.';


select
 server_name,
 to_char(start_date,'YY/MM/DD    HH24') my_date,
 avg(runque_waits)       c2,
 avg(page_in)            c3,
 avg(page_out)           c4,
 avg(user_cpu)           c5,
 avg(system_cpu)         c6,
 avg(idle_cpu)           c7
from
perfstat.stats$vmstat
WHERE
(user_cpu + system_cpu) > 70
and start_date > sysdate-&1
group by
 server_name,
 to_char(start_date,'YY/MM/DD    HH24')
ORDER BY
 server_name,
 to_char(start_date,'YY/MM/DD    HH24')
;
```

Table and Object Extension Scripts for STATSPACK

create_object_tables.sql

```
connect perfstat/perfstat;

drop table perfstat.stats$tab_stats;
```

```
create table perfstat.stats$tab_stats
(
   snap_time        date,
   server_name      varchar2(20),
   db_name          varchar2(9),
   tablespace_name  varchar2(40),
   owner            varchar2(40),
   table_name       varchar2(40),
   num_rows         number,
   avg_row_len      number,
   next_extent      number,
   extents          number,
   bytes            number
)
tablespace perfstat
storage (initial 1m next 1m maxextents unlimited)
;

drop table perfstat.stats$idx_stats;


create table perfstat.stats$idx_stats
(
   snap_time          date,
   server_name        varchar2(20),
   db_name            varchar2(9),
   tablespace_name    varchar2(40),
   owner              varchar2(40),
   index_name         varchar2(40),
   clustering_factor  number,
   leaf_blocks        number,
   blevel             number,
   next_extent        number,
   extents            number,
   bytes              number
)
tablespace perfstat
storage (initial 1m next 1m maxextents unlimited)
;


drop index
   perfstat.tab_stat_date_idx;

create index
   perfstat.tab_stat_date_idx
on
   perfstat.stats$tab_stats
```

```
( snap_time )
tablespace perfstat
storage (initial 1m next 1m maxextents unlimited)
;


drop index
   perfstat.idx_stat_date_idx;
create index
   perfstat.idx_stat_date_idx
on
   perfstat.stats$idx_stats
( snap_time )
tablespace perfstat
storage (initial 1m next 1m maxextents unlimited)
;
```

get_object_stats.ksh

```
#!/bin/ksh

# Validate the Oracle database name with
# lookup in /var/opt/oracle/oratab
TEMP=`cat /var/opt/oracle/oratab|grep \^$1:|\
cut -f1 -d':'|wc -l`
tmp=`expr TEMP`      # Convert string to number
if [ $tmp -ne 1 ]
then
   echo "Your input $1 is not a valid ORACLE_SID."
   exit 99
fi

# First, we must set the environment . . . .
ORACLE_SID=$1
export ORACLE_SID
ORACLE_HOME=`cat /var/opt/oracle/oratab|grep $ORACLE_SID:|cut -f2 -d':'`
export ORACLE_HOME
PATH=$ORACLE_HOME/bin:$PATH
export PATH
MON=`echo ~oracle/obj_stat`
export MON

# Get the server name
host=`uname -a|awk '{ print $2 }'`

$ORACLE_HOME/bin/sqlplus -s perfstat/perfstat<<!
```

```
set heading off;
set feedback off;
set echo off;
-- © 2001 by Donald Keith Burleson - All Rights Reserved
set lines 120;

--*****************************************************************
-- First, let's get the latest statistics for each table
--*****************************************************************
spool $MON/run_analyze.sql
select 'analyze table '||owner||'.'||table_name||' estimate statistics sample 50
rows;'
from
   dba_tables
where
   owner not in ('SYS','SYSTEM','PERFSTAT');
--   ****************************
--   Analyze all indexes for statistics
--   ****************************
select 'analyze index '||owner||'.'||table_name||' compute statistics;'
from
   dba_indexes
where
   owner not in ('SYS','SYSTEM','PERFSTAT');
spool off;

set echo on;
set feedback on;

@$MON/run_analyze

connect perfstat/perfstat;

--*****************************************************************
-- Now we grab the table statistics
--*****************************************************************
insert into perfstat.stats\$tab_stats
(
  select
     SYSDATE,
     lower('${host}'),
     lower('${ORACLE_SID}'),
     t.tablespace_name,
     t.owner,
     t.table_name,
     t.num_rows,
     t.avg_row_len,
```

```
      s.next_extent,
      s.extents,
      s.bytes
from
   dba_tables    t,
   dba_segments  s
where
   segment_name = table_name
   and
   s.tablespace_name = t.tablespace_name
   and
   s.owner = t.owner
   and
   t.owner not in ('SYS','SYSTEM')
--   and
--   num_rows > 1000
);


--****************************************************************
-- Now we grab the index statistics
--****************************************************************
insert into perfstat.stats\$idx_stats
(
   select
      SYSDATE,
      lower('${host}'),
      lower('${ORACLE_SID}'),
      i.tablespace_name,
      i.owner,
      i.index_name,
      i.clustering_factor,
      i.leaf_blocks,
      i.blevel,
      s.next_extent,
      s.extents,
      s.bytes
   from dba_indexes  i,
        dba_segments  s,
        dba_tables    t
   where
      i.table_name = t.table_name
   and
      segment_name = index_name
   and
      s.tablespace_name = i.tablespace_name
   and
```

```
        s.owner = i.owner
    and
        i.owner not in ('SYS','SYSTEM')
--    and
--        t.num_rows > 1000
);

exit
!
```

rpt_bytes.sql

```
--*********************************************************
-- First we need to get the second-highest date in tab_stats
--*********************************************************
set lines 80;
-- © 2001 by Donald Keith Burleson - All Rights Reserved
set feedback off;
set verify off;
set echo off;

drop table d1;

create table d1 as
select distinct
    to_char(snap_time,'YYYY-MM-DD') mydate
from
    stats$tab_stats
where
    to_char(snap_time,'YYYY-MM-DD') <
      (select max(to_char(snap_time,'YYYY-MM-DD')) from stats$tab_stats)
;

--*********************************************************
-- The second-highest date is select max(mydate) from d1;
--*********************************************************

set heading off;

prompt Object growth - Comparing last two snapshots
prompt
prompt This report shows the growth of key tables
prompt for the past week.


select 'Old date = '||max(mydate) from d1;
select 'New date = '||max(to_char(snap_time,'YYYY-MM-DD')) from stats$tab_stats;
```

```
break on report ;
compute sum of old_bytes on old.table_name;

set heading on;

column old_bytes format 999,999,999
column new_bytes format 999,999,999
column change    format 999,999,999

select
   new.table_name,
   old.bytes            old_bytes,
   new.bytes            new_bytes,
   new.bytes - old.bytes    change
from
   stats$tab_stats old,
   stats$tab_stats new
where
   old.table_name = new.table_name
and
   new.bytes > old.bytes
and
   new.bytes - old.bytes > 10000
and
   to_char(new.snap_time, 'YYYY-MM-DD') =
          (select max(to_char(snap_time,'YYYY-MM-DD')) from stats$tab_stats)
and
   to_char(old.snap_time, 'YYYY-MM-DD') =
          (select max(mydate) from d1)
and
   new.table_name not like 'STATS$%'
order by
   new.bytes-old.bytes desc
;


--********************************************************
-- First we need to get the second-highest date in idx_stats
--********************************************************
set lines 80;
-- © 2001 by Donald Keith Burleson - All Rights Reserved
set feedback off;
set verify off;
set echo off;

drop table d1;
```

```
create table d1 as
select distinct
   to_char(snap_time,'YYYY-MM-DD') mydate
from
   stats$idx_stats
where
   to_char(snap_time,'YYYY-MM-DD') <
     (select max(to_char(snap_time,'YYYY-MM-DD')) from stats$idx_stats)
;

--*********************************************************
-- The second-highest date is select max(mydate) from d1;
--*********************************************************

set heading off;

prompt Object growth - Comparing last two snapshots
prompt
prompt This report shows the growth of key indexes
prompt for the past week.


select 'Old date = '||max(mydate) from d1;
select 'New date = '||max(to_char(snap_time,'YYYY-MM-DD')) from stats$idx_stats;

break on report ;
compute sum of old_bytes on old.table_name;

set heading on;

column old_bytes format 999,999,999
column new_bytes format 999,999,999
column change    format 999,999,999

select
   new.index_name,
   old.bytes              old_bytes,
   new.bytes              new_bytes,
   new.bytes - old.bytes  change
from
   stats$idx_stats old,
   stats$idx_stats new
where
   old.index_name = new.index_name
and
   new.bytes > old.bytes
and
```

```
    new.bytes - old.bytes > 10000
and
    to_char(new.snap_time, 'YYYY-MM-DD') =
            (select max(to_char(snap_time,'YYYY-MM-DD')) from stats$idx_stats)
and
    to_char(old.snap_time, 'YYYY-MM-DD') =
            (select max(mydate) from d1)
and
    new.index_name not like 'STATS$%'
order by
    new.bytes-old.bytes desc
;
```

rpt_obj_stats.sql

```
connect perfstat/perfstat;

set lines 80;
-- © 2001 by Donald Keith Burleson - All Rights Reserved
set feedback off;
set verify off;
set echo off;


--**********************************************************
-- This report compares the max(snap_time) to the second-highest date
--**********************************************************


--**********************************************************
-- First we need to get the second-highest date in tab_stats
--**********************************************************
drop table d1;

create table d1 as
select distinct
    to_char(snap_time,'YYYY-MM-DD') mydate
from
    stats$tab_stats
where
    to_char(snap_time,'YYYY-MM-DD') <
      (select max(to_char(snap_time,'YYYY-MM-DD')) from stats$tab_stats)
;


--**********************************************************
-- The second-highest date is select max(mydate) from d1;
--**********************************************************
```

```
set heading off;

prompt '*********************************************'
select '  Most recent date '||
          max(to_char(snap_time,'YYYY-MM-DD'))
from stats$tab_stats;
select '  Older date '||
          max(mydate)
from d1;
prompt '*********************************************'

set heading on;

drop table t1;
drop table t2;
drop table t3;
drop table t4;


create table t1 as
select db_name, count(*) tab_count, snap_time from stats$tab_stats
where    to_char(snap_time, 'YYYY-MM-DD') =
            (select max(to_char(snap_time,'YYYY-MM-DD')) from stats$tab_stats)
group by db_name, snap_time;

create table t2 as
select db_name, count(*) idx_count, snap_time from stats$idx_stats
where    to_char(snap_time, 'YYYY-MM-DD') =
            (select max(to_char(snap_time,'YYYY-MM-DD')) from stats$idx_stats)
group by db_name, snap_time;

create table t3 as
select db_name, sum(bytes) tab_bytes, snap_time from stats$tab_stats
where    to_char(snap_time, 'YYYY-MM-DD') =
            (select max(to_char(snap_time,'YYYY-MM-DD')) from stats$tab_stats)
group by db_name, snap_time;

create table t4 as
select db_name, sum(bytes) idx_bytes, snap_time from stats$idx_stats
where    to_char(snap_time, 'YYYY-MM-DD') =
            (select max(to_char(snap_time,'YYYY-MM-DD')) from stats$idx_stats)
group by db_name, snap_time;

--*********************************************************
-- This report displays the most recent counts & size totals
--*********************************************************
```

```
column tab_bytes format 999,999,999,999
column idx_bytes format 999,999,999,999
column tab_count format 99,999
column idx_count format 99,999

clear computes;
compute sum label "Total" of tab_count on report;
compute sum label "Total" of idx_count on report;
compute sum label "Total" of tab_bytes on report;
compute sum label "Total" of idx_bytes on report;

break on report;

ttitle 'Most recent database object counts and sizes'

select
   a.db_name,
   tab_count,
   idx_count,
   tab_bytes,
   idx_bytes
from
   perfstat.t1 a,
   perfstat.t2 b,
   perfstat.t3 c,
   perfstat.t4 d
where
   a.db_name = b.db_name
and
   a.db_name = c.db_name
and
   a.db_name = d.db_name
;

--***********************************************************
-- These temp tables will compare size growth since last snap
--***********************************************************
drop table t1;
drop table t2;
drop table t3;
drop table t4;

create table t1 as
select db_name, sum(bytes) new_tab_bytes, snap_time from stats$tab_stats
where    to_char(snap_time, 'YYYY-MM-DD') =
           (select max(to_char(snap_time,'YYYY-MM-DD')) from stats$tab_stats)
group by db_name, snap_time;

create table t2 as
select db_name, sum(bytes) new_idx_bytes, snap_time from stats$idx_stats
where    to_char(snap_time, 'YYYY-MM-DD') =
```

```
                (select max(to_char(snap_time,'YYYY-MM-DD')) from stats$idx_stats)
group by db_name, snap_time;

create table t3 as
select db_name, sum(bytes) old_tab_bytes, snap_time from stats$tab_stats
where    to_char(snap_time, 'YYYY-MM-DD') =
             (select max(mydate) from d1)
group by db_name, snap_time;

create table t4 as
select db_name, sum(bytes) old_idx_bytes, snap_time from stats$idx_stats
where    to_char(snap_time, 'YYYY-MM-DD') =
             (select max(mydate) from d1)
group by db_name, snap_time;

--********************************************************
-- This is the size comparison report
--********************************************************
column old_bytes format 999,999,999,999
column new_bytes format 999,999,999,999
column change    format 999,999,999,999

compute sum label "Total" of old_bytes on report;
compute sum label "Total" of new_bytes on report;
compute sum label "Total" of change    on report;

break on report;
ttitle 'Database size change|comparing the most recent snapshot dates';

select
   a.db_name,
   old_tab_bytes+old_idx_bytes old_bytes,
   new_tab_bytes+new_idx_bytes new_bytes,
   (new_tab_bytes+new_idx_bytes)-(old_tab_bytes+old_idx_bytes) change
from
   perfstat.t1 a,
   perfstat.t2 b,
   perfstat.t3 c,
   perfstat.t4 d
where
```

```
    a.db_name = b.db_name
and
    a.db_name = c.db_name
and
    a.db_name = d.db_name
;


-- ****************************************************************
-- This is the standard chained row report
--
-- This is for columns without long columns
-- because long columns often chain onto adjacent data blocks
-- ****************************************************************

column c1 heading "Owner"    format a9;
column c2 heading "Table"    format a12;
column c3 heading "PCTFREE"  format 99;
column c4 heading "PCTUSED"  format 99;
column c5 heading "avg row"  format 99,999;
column c6 heading "Rows"     format 999,999,999;
column c7 heading "Chains"   format 999,999,999;
column c8 heading "Pct"      format .99;

set heading off;
select 'Tables with > 10% chained rows and no LONG columns.' from dual;
set heading on;

select
    owner              c1,
    table_name         c2,
    pct_free           c3,
    pct_used           c4,
    avg_row_len        c5,
    num_rows           c6,
    chain_cnt          c7,
    chain_cnt/num_rows c8
from
    dba_tables
where
    owner not in ('SYS','SYSTEM','PERFSTAT')
and
    chain_cnt/num_rows > .1
and
table_name not in
 (select table_name from dba_tab_columns
    where
 data_type in ('RAW','LONG RAW','CLOB','BLOB')
 )
```

```
and
chain_cnt > 0
order by chain_cnt desc
;

--*********************************************************
-- This chained row report is for tables that have long
-- columns.  The only fix for this chaining is increasing
-- the db_block_size
--*********************************************************
set heading off;
select 'Tables with > 10% chained rows that contain LONG columns.' from dual;
set heading on;

select
   owner           c1,
   table_name      c2,
   pct_free        c3,
   pct_used        c4,
   avg_row_len     c5,
   num_rows        c6,
   chain_cnt       c7,
   chain_cnt/num_rows c8
from
   dba_tables
where
   owner not in ('SYS','SYSTEM','PERFSTAT')
and
   chain_cnt/num_rows > .1
and
table_name in
 (select table_name from dba_tab_columns
   where
 data_type in ('RAW','LONG RAW','CLOB','BLOB')
 )
and
chain_cnt > 0
order by chain_cnt desc
;

--*********************************************************
-- This report will show all objects that have extended
-- between the snapshot period.
-- The DBA may want to increase the next_extent size
-- for these objects
--*********************************************************
column db format a10
```

```
column owner format a10
column tab_name format a30

break on db;


ttitle 'Table extents report|Where extents > 200 or table extent
    changed|comparing
most recent snapshots'

select /*+ first_rows */
distinct
    a.db_name       db,
    a.owner         owner,
    a.table_name    tab_name,
    b.extents       old_ext,
    a.extents       new_ext
from
    PERFSTAT.stats$tab_stats a,
    PERFSTAT.stats$tab_stats b
where
    a.db_name = b.db_name
and
    a.owner = b.owner
and
    a.table_name = b.table_name
and
(
    b.extents > a.extents
    or
    a.extents > b.extents
    or
    a.extents > 200
)
and
    a.owner not in ('SYS','SYSTEM','PERFSTAT')
and
    a.table_name not in ('PLAN_TABLE')
and
    to_char(a.snap_time, 'YYYY-MM-DD') =
            (select max(to_char(snap_time,'YYYY-MM-DD')) from stats$tab_stats)
and
    to_char(b.snap_time, 'YYYY-MM-DD') =
            (select max(mydate) from d1)
order by
    a.db_name,
```

```
   a.extents
;

column db format a10
column owner format a10
column idx_name format a30

break on db;


ttitle 'Index extents report|Where extents > 200 or index extent changed|Comparing
last two snapshots'

select /*+ first_rows */
distinct
   a.db_name     db,
   a.owner       owner,
   a.index_name  idx_name,
   b.extents     old_ext,
   a.extents     new_ext
from
   PERFSTAT.stats$idx_stats a,
   PERFSTAT.stats$idx_stats b
where
   a.owner not in ('SYS','SYSTEM','PERFSTAT')
and
   a.db_name = b.db_name
and
   a.owner = b.owner
and
   a.index_name = b.index_name
and
(
   b.extents > a.extents
   or
   a.extents > b.extents
   or
   a.extents > 200
)
and
   to_char(a.snap_time, 'YYYY-MM-DD') =
           (select max(to_char(snap_time,'YYYY-MM-DD')) from stats$idx_stats)
and
   to_char(b.snap_time, 'YYYY-MM-DD') =
           (select max(mydate) from d1)
order by
```

```
     a.db_name,
     a.extents
;
```

rpt_tab.sql

```
column c1  heading "TABLE NAME"      format a15;
column c2  heading "EXTS"            format 999;
column c3  heading "FL"              format 99;
column c4  heading "# OF ROWS"       format 99,999,999;
column c5  heading "#_rows*row_len"  format 9,999,999,999;
column c6  heading "SPACE ALLOCATED" format 9,999,999,999;
column c7  heading "PCT USED"        format 999;


-- © 2001 by Donald Keith Burleson - All Rights Reserved
set lines 80;

spool tab_rpt.lst

select
        table_name            c1,
        b.extents             c2,
        b.freelists           c3,
        num_rows              c4,
        num_rows*avg_row_len  c5,
        blocks*16384          c6,
        ((num_rows*avg_row_len)/(blocks*16384))*100 c7
from
   perfstat.stats$tab_stats a,
   dba_segments b
where
 b.segment_name = a.table_name
and
   to_char(snap_time,'yyyy-mm-dd') =
       (select max(to_char(snap_time,'yyyy-mm dd')) from perfstat.stats$tab_stats)
and
   avg_row_len > 500
order by c5 desc
;

spool off;
```

rpt_table_rows.sql

```
--*********************************************************
-- First we need to get the second-highest date in tab_stats
--*********************************************************
set lines 80;
-- © 2001 by Donald Keith Burleson - All Rights Reserved
set feedback off;
set verify off;
set echo off;

drop table d1;

create table d1 as
select distinct
   to_char(snap_time,'YYYY-MM-DD') mydate
from
   stats$tab_stats
where
   to_char(snap_time,'YYYY-MM-DD') <
     (select max(to_char(snap_time,'YYYY-MM-DD')) from stats$tab_stats)
;


--*********************************************************
-- The second-highest date is select max(mydate) from d1;
--*********************************************************

ttitle 'Oracle Object growth|Comparing last two snapshots'

prompt This report shows the growth of key tables within the RovOracle

prompt for the past week.

column old_rows format 9,999,999
column new_rows format 9,999,999

select
   new.table_name,
   old.num_rows                old_rows,
   new.num_rows                new_rows,
   new.num_rows - old.num_rows change
from
   stats$tab_stats old,
   stats$tab_stats new
where
   new.num_rows > old.num_rows
and
```

```
   old.table_name = new.table_name
and
   to_char(new.snap_time, 'YYYY-MM-DD') =
           (select max(to_char(snap_time,'YYYY-MM-DD')) from stats$tab_stats)
and
   to_char(old.snap_time, 'YYYY-MM-DD') =
           (select max(mydate) from d1)
;
```

run_object_report.ksh

```ksh
#!/bin/ksh

# Validate the Oracle database name with
# lookup in /var/opt/oracle/oratab
TEMP=`cat /var/opt/oracle/oratab|grep \^$1:|\
cut -f1 -d':'|wc -l`
tmp=`expr TEMP`       # Convert string to number
if [ $tmp -ne 1 ]
then
   echo "Your input $1 is not a valid ORACLE_SID."
   exit 99
fi


# Here we must set the environment . . . .
ORACLE_SID=$1
export ORACLE_SID
ORACLE_HOME=`cat /var/opt/oracle/oratab|grep $ORACLE_SID;|cut -f2 -d':'`
export ORACLE_HOME
PATH=$ORACLE_HOME/bin:$PATH
export PATH
MON=`echo /export/home/oracle/obj_stat`
export MON


sqlplus perfstat/perfstat<<!
spool ${MON}/stats_rpt.lst
@${MON}/rpt_oracle
@${MON}/rpt_object_stats
spool off;
exit;
!


#***********************************
# Mail the Object Statistics Reports
#***********************************
```

```
cat $MON/stats_rpt.lst|mailx -s "Oracle Weekly Statistics Summary" \
   don@remote-dba.net
# \
#   terry.oakes@worldnet.att.net
```

iostat Reports

create_iostat.sql

```
drop table perfstat.stats$iostat;

create table
perfstat.stats$iostat
(
snap_time          date,
elapsed_seconds    number(4),
hdisk              varchar2(8),
kb_read            number(9,0),
kb_write           number(9,0)
)
tablespace perfstat
storage (initial 20m next 1m )
;

create index
perfstat.stats$iostat_date_idx
on
perfstat.stats$iostat
(snap_time)
tablespace perfstat
storage (initial 5m next 1m)
;

create index
perfstat.stats$iostat_hdisk_idx
on
perfstat.stats$iostat
(hdisk)
tablespace perfstat
storage (initial 5m next 1m)
;
```

get_iostat_aix.ksh

```ksh
#!/bin/ksh

while true
do
    iostat 300 1 | awk  '{ printf("%s ,%s ,%s\n", $1, $5, $6) }' |\
    while read    HDISK VMSTAT_IO_R VMSTAT_IO_W
    do
    if (echo $HDISK|grep -cq hdisk );then

        sqlplus -s / <<EOF
        insert into iostat values
        (SYSDATE, 5, '$HDISK', $VMSTAT_IO_R,$VMSTAT_IO_W);
        EXIT
        EOF
    fi
    done
done
```

get_iostat_solaris.ksh

```ksh
#!/bin/ksh

while true
do
    iostat -x  300 1|\
        sed 1,2d|\
        awk  '{ printf("%s %s %s\n", $1, $4, $5) }' |\
    while read HDISK VMSTAT_IO_R VMSTAT_IO_W
    do

        echo $HDISK
        echo $VMSTAT_IO_R
        echo $VMSTAT_IO_W

        sqlplus -s / <<!
        insert into
            perfstat.stats\$iostat
        values
            (SYSDATE, 300, '$HDISK', $VMSTAT_IO_R,$VMSTAT_IO_W);
        exit
!

    done
    sleep 300

done
```

rpt_disk.sql

```
column hdisk            format a10;
column mydate           format a15;
column sum_kb_read      format 999,999;
column sum_kb_write     format 999,999;

-- © 2001 by Donald Keith Burleson - All Rights Reserved

break on hdisk skip 1;

select
   hdisk,
--    to_char(snap_time,'yyyy-mm-dd HH24:mi:ss') mydate,
--    to_char(snap_time,'yyyy-mm-dd HH24') mydate,
   to_char(snap_time,'day') mydate,
   sum(kb_read)  sum_kb_read,
   sum(kb_write) sum_kb_write
from
   stats$iostat
group by
   hdisk
   ,to_char(snap_time,'day')
--   ,to_char(snap_time,'yyyy-mm-dd HH24:mi:ss')
--   ,to_char(snap_time,'yyyy-mm-dd HH24')
;
```

rpt_hot.sql

```
-- © 2001 by Donald Keith Burleson - All Rights Reserved
set feedback off;
set verify off;

--prompt ***********************************************************
--prompt  This will identify any single disk whose read I/O
--prompt  is more than 25% of the total read I/O of the database.
--prompt
--prompt  The "hot" disk should be examined, and the hot table/index
--prompt  should be identified using STATSPACK.
--prompt
--prompt ***********************************************************
column mydate format a16
column hdisk format a40
column reads  format 999,999,999

select
```

```
   to_char(new.snap_time,'yyyy-mm-dd HH24')   mydate,
   new.hdisk                                  file_name,
   new.kb_read-old.kb_read                    reads
from
   perfstat.stats$iostat old,
   perfstat.stats$iostat new
where
   new.snap_time > sysdate-&1
and
   old.snap_time = new.snap_time-1
and
   new.hdisk = old.hdisk
and
   (new.kb_read-old.kb_read)*10 >
(
select
   (newreads.kb_read-oldreads.kb_read) reads
from
   perfstat.stats$iostat oldreads,
   perfstat.stats$iostat newreads
where
   new.snap_time = newreads.snap_time
and
   newreads.snap_time = new.snap_time
and
   oldreads.snap_time = new.snap_time-1
and
   (newreads.kb_read-oldreads.kb_read) > 0
)
;
--prompt ************************************************************
--prompt  This will identify any single disk whose write I/O
--prompt  is more than 10% of the total write I/O of the database.
--prompt ************************************************************
--prompt
column mydate format a16
column file_name format a40
column writes   format 999,999,999

select
   to_char(new.snap_time,'yyyy-mm-dd HH24')   mydate,
   new.hdisk                                  file_name,
   new.kb_write-old.kb_write                  writes
from
   perfstat.stats$iostat old,
   perfstat.stats$iostat new
where
   new.snap_time > sysdate-&1
```

```sql
and
    old.snap_time = new.snap_time-1
and
    new.hdisk = old.hdisk
and
    (new.kb_write-old.kb_write)*10 >
(
select
    (newwrites.kb_read-oldwrites.kb_read) writes
from
    perfstat.stats$iostat oldwrites,
    perfstat.stats$iostat newwrites
where
    new.snap_time = newwrites.snap_time
and
    newwrites.snap_time = new.snap_time
and
    oldwrites.snap_time = new.snap_time-1
and
    (newwrites.kb_read-oldwrites.kb_read) > 0
);
```

run_iostat_aix.ksh

```ksh
#!/bin/ksh

# First, we must set the environment . . . .
ORACLE_SID=xxxx
ORACLE_HOME=`cat /etc/oratab|grep $ORACLE_SID|cut -f2 -d':'`
PATH=$ORACLE_HOME/bin:$PATH
MON=`echo ~oracle/mon`

#---------------------------------------
# If it is not running, then start it . . .
#---------------------------------------
check_stat=`ps -ef|grep get_iostat_aix|wc -l`;
oracle_num=`expr $check_stat`
if [ $oracle_num -ne 2 ]
 then nohup $MON/get_iostat_aix.ksh > /dev/null 2>&1 &
fi
```

run_iostat_solaris.ksh

```ksh
#!/bin/ksh

# First, we must set the environment . . . .
```

```
ORACLE_SID=prodb1
ORACLE_HOME=`cat /var/opt/oracle/oratab|grep $ORACLE_SID|cut -f2 -d':'`
PATH=$ORACLE_HOME/bin:$PATH
MON=`echo ~oracle/iostat`

#-----------------------------------------
# If it is not running, then start it . . .
#-----------------------------------------
check_stat=`ps -ef|grep get_iostat|grep -v grep|wc -l`;
oracle_num=`expr $check_stat`
if [ $oracle_num -lt 1 ]
 then nohup $MON/get_iostat_solaris.ksh > /dev/null 2>&1 &
fi
```

Index

T

U

V

W

X

INTERNATIONAL CONTACT INFORMATION

AUSTRALIA
McGraw-Hill Book Company Australia Pty. Ltd.
TEL +61-2-9417-9899
FAX +61-2-9417-5687
http://www.mcgraw-hill.com.au
books-it_sydney@mcgraw-hill.com

CANADA
McGraw-Hill Ryerson Ltd.
TEL +905-430-5000
FAX +905-430-5020
http://www.mcgrawhill.ca

GREECE, MIDDLE EAST,
NORTHERN AFRICA
McGraw-Hill Hellas
TEL +30-1-656-0990-3-4
FAX +30-1-654-5525

MEXICO (Also serving Latin America)
McGraw-Hill Interamericana Editores S.A. de C.V.
TEL +525-117-1583
FAX +525-117-1589
http://www.mcgraw-hill.com.mx
fernando_castellanos@mcgraw-hill.com

SINGAPORE (Serving Asia)
McGraw-Hill Book Company
TEL +65-863-1580
FAX +65-862-3354
http://www.mcgraw-hill.com.sg
mghasia@mcgraw-hill.com

SOUTH AFRICA
McGraw-Hill South Africa
TEL +27-11-622-7512
FAX +27-11-622-9045
robyn_swanepoel@mcgraw-hill.com

UNITED KINGDOM & EUROPE
(Excluding Southern Europe)
McGraw-Hill Education Europe
TEL +44-1-628-502500
FAX +44-1-628-770224
http://www.mcgraw-hill.co.uk
computing_neurope@mcgraw-hill.com

ALL OTHER INQUIRIES Contact:
Osborne/McGraw-Hill
TEL +1-510-549-6600
FAX +1 510 883 7600
http://www.osborne.com
omg_international@mcgraw-hill.com

Get Your FREE Subscription to *Oracle Magazine*

Oracle Magazine is essential gear for today's information technology professionals. Stay informed and increase your productivity with every issue of *Oracle Magazine*. Inside each **FREE,** bimonthly issue you'll get:

- Up-to-date information on Oracle Database Server, Oracle Applications, Internet Computing, and tools
- Third-party news and announcements
- Technical articles on Oracle products and operating environments
- Development and administration tips
- Real-world customer stories

Three easy ways to subscribe:

1. Web Visit our Web site at www.oracle.com/oramag/.
You'll find a subscription form there, plus much more!

2. Fax Complete the questionnaire on the back of this card and fax the questionnaire side only to **+1.847.647.9735.**

3. Mail Complete the questionnaire on the back of this card and mail it to P.O. Box 1263, Skokie, IL 60076-8263.

If there are other Oracle users at your location who would like to receive their own subscription to *Oracle Magazine*, please photocopy this form and pass it along.

☐ YES! Please send me a FREE subscription to *Oracle Magazine*.   ☐ NO

To receive a free bimonthly subscription to *Oracle Magazine*, you must fill out the entire card, sign it, and date it (incomplete cards cannot be processed or acknowledged). You can also fax your application to +1.847.647.9735. Or subscribe at our Web site at www.oracle.com/oramag/

SIGNATURE (REQUIRED)	X	DATE	

NAME	TITLE
COMPANY	TELEPHONE
ADDRESS	FAX NUMBER
CITY	STATE	POSTAL CODE/ZIP CODE
COUNTRY	E-MAIL ADDRESS

☐ From time to time, Oracle Publishing allows our partners exclusive access to our e-mail addresses for special promotions and announcements. To be included in this program, please check this box.

You must answer all eight questions below.

1 What is the primary business activity of your firm at this location? *(check only one)*
- ☐ 03 Communications
- ☐ 04 Consulting, Training
- ☐ 06 Data Processing
- ☐ 07 Education
- ☐ 08 Engineering
- ☐ 09 Financial Services
- ☐ 10 Government—Federal, Local, State, Other
- ☐ 11 Government—Military
- ☐ 12 Health Care
- ☐ 13 Manufacturing—Aerospace, Defense
- ☐ 14 Manufacturing—Computer Hardware
- ☐ 15 Manufacturing—Noncomputer Products
- ☐ 17 Research & Development
- ☐ 19 Retailing, Wholesaling, Distribution
- ☐ 20 Software Development
- ☐ 21 Systems Integration, VAR, VAD, OEM
- ☐ 22 Transportation
- ☐ 23 Utilities (Electric, Gas, Sanitation)
- ☐ 98 Other Business and Services _____

2 Which of the following best describes your job function? *(check only one)*
CORPORATE MANAGEMENT/STAFF
- ☐ 01 Executive Management (President, Chair, CEO, CFO, Owner, Partner, Principal)
- ☐ 02 Finance/Administrative Management (VP/Director/ Manager/Controller, Purchasing, Administration)
- ☐ 03 Sales/Marketing Management (VP/Director/Manager)
- ☐ 04 Computer Systems/Operations Management (CIO/VP/Director/ Manager MIS, Operations)

IS/IT STAFF
- ☐ 07 Systems Development/ Programming Management
- ☐ 08 Systems Development/ Programming Staff
- ☐ 09 Consulting
- ☐ 10 DBA/Systems Administrator
- ☐ 11 Education/Training
- ☐ 14 Technical Support Director/ Manager
- ☐ 16 Other Technical Management/Staff
- ☐ 98 Other _____

3 What is your current primary operating platform? *(check all that apply)*
- ☐ 01 DEC UNIX
- ☐ 02 DEC VAX VMS
- ☐ 03 Java
- ☐ 04 HP UNIX
- ☐ 05 IBM AIX
- ☐ 06 IBM UNIX
- ☐ 07 Macintosh
- ☐ 09 MS-DOS
- ☐ 10 MVS
- ☐ 11 NetWare
- ☐ 12 Network Computing
- ☐ 13 OpenVMS
- ☐ 14 SCO UNIX
- ☐ 24 Sequent DYNIX/ptx
- ☐ 15 Sun Solaris/SunOS
- ☐ 16 SVR4
- ☐ 18 UnixWare
- ☐ 20 Windows
- ☐ 21 Windows NT
- ☐ 23 Other UNIX _____
- ☐ 98 Other _____
- 99 ☐ **None of the above**

4 Do you evaluate, specify, recommend, or authorize the purchase of any of the following? *(check all that apply)*
- ☐ 01 Hardware
- ☐ 02 Software
- ☐ 03 Application Development Tools
- ☐ 04 Database Products
- ☐ 05 Internet or Intranet Products
- 99 ☐ **None of the above**

5 In your job, do you use or plan to purchase any of the following products or services? *(check all that apply)*
SOFTWARE
- ☐ 01 Business Graphics
- ☐ 02 CAD/CAE/CAM
- ☐ 03 CASE
- ☐ 05 Communications
- ☐ 06 Database Management
- ☐ 07 File Management
- ☐ 08 Finance
- ☐ 09 Java
- ☐ 10 Materials Resource Planning
- ☐ 11 Multimedia Authoring
- ☐ 12 Networking
- ☐ 13 Office Automation
- ☐ 14 Order Entry/Inventory Control
- ☐ 15 Programming
- ☐ 16 Project Management

- ☐ 17 Scientific and Engineering
- ☐ 18 Spreadsheets
- ☐ 19 Systems Management
- ☐ 20 Workflow
HARDWARE
- ☐ 21 Macintosh
- ☐ 22 Mainframe
- ☐ 23 Massively Parallel Processing
- ☐ 24 Minicomputer
- ☐ 25 PC
- ☐ 26 Network Computer
- ☐ 28 Symmetric Multiprocessing
- ☐ 29 Workstation
PERIPHERALS
- ☐ 30 Bridges/Routers/Hubs/Gateways
- ☐ 31 CD-ROM Drives
- ☐ 32 Disk Drives/Subsystems
- ☐ 33 Modems
- ☐ 34 Tape Drives/Subsystems
- ☐ 35 Video Boards/Multimedia
SERVICES
- ☐ 37 Consulting
- ☐ 38 Education/Training
- ☐ 39 Maintenance
- ☐ 40 Online Database Services
- ☐ 41 Support
- ☐ 36 Technology-Based Training
- ☐ 98 Other _____
- 99 ☐ **None of the above**

6 What Oracle products are in use at your site? *(check all that apply)*
SERVER/SOFTWARE
- ☐ 01 Oracle8
- ☐ 30 Oracle8*i*
- ☐ 31 Oracle8*i* Lite
- ☐ 02 Oracle7
- ☐ 03 Oracle Application Server
- ☐ 04 Oracle Data Mart Suites
- ☐ 05 Oracle Internet Commerce Server
- ☐ 32 Oracle *inter*Media
- ☐ 33 Oracle JServer
- ☐ 07 Oracle Lite
- ☐ 08 Oracle Payment Server
- ☐ 11 Oracle Video Server
TOOLS
- ☐ 13 Oracle Designer
- ☐ 14 Oracle Developer
- ☐ 54 Oracle Discoverer
- ☐ 53 Oracle Express
- ☐ 51 Oracle JDeveloper
- ☐ 52 Oracle Reports
- ☐ 50 Oracle WebDB
- ☐ 55 Oracle Workflow
ORACLE APPLICATIONS
- ☐ 17 Oracle Automotive

- ☐ 35 Oracle Business Intelligence System
- ☐ 19 Oracle Consumer Packaged Goods
- ☐ 39 Oracle E-Commerce
- ☐ 18 Oracle Energy
- ☐ 20 Oracle Financials
- ☐ 28 Oracle Front Office
- ☐ 21 Oracle Human Resources
- ☐ 37 Oracle Internet Procurement
- ☐ 22 Oracle Manufacturing
- ☐ 40 Oracle Process Manufacturing
- ☐ 23 Oracle Projects
- ☐ 34 Oracle Retail
- ☐ 29 Oracle Self-Service Web Applications
- ☐ 38 Oracle Strategic Enterprise Management
- ☐ 25 Oracle Supply Chain Management
- ☐ 36 Oracle Tutor
- ☐ 41 Oracle Travel Management
ORACLE SERVICES
- ☐ 61 Oracle Consulting
- ☐ 62 Oracle Education
- ☐ 60 Oracle Support
- ☐ 98 Other _____
- 99 ☐ **None of the above**

7 What other database products are in use at your site? *(check all that apply)*
- ☐ 01 Access
- ☐ 02 Baan
- ☐ 03 dbase
- ☐ 04 Gupta
- ☐ 05 IBM DB2
- ☐ 06 Informix
- ☐ 07 Ingres
- ☐ 08 Microsoft Access
- ☐ 09 Microsoft SQL Server
- ☐ 10 PeopleSoft
- ☐ 11 Progress
- ☐ 12 SAP
- ☐ 13 Sybase
- ☐ 14 VSAM
- ☐ 98 Other _____
- 99 ☐ **None of the above**

8 During the next 12 months, how much do you anticipate your organization will spend on computer hardware, software, peripherals, and services for your location? *(check only one)*
- ☐ 01 Less than $10,000
- ☐ 02 $10,000 to $49,999
- ☐ 03 $50,000 to $99,999
- ☐ 04 $100,000 to $499,999
- ☐ 05 $500,000 to $999,999
- ☐ 06 $1,000,000 and over

If there are other Oracle users at your location who would like to receive a free subscription to *Oracle Magazine*, please photocopy this form and pass it along, or contact Customer Service at +1.847.647.9630

Form 5

OPRESS

Knowledge is power. To which we say,

crank up the power.

Are you ready for a power surge?

Accelerate your career—become an **Oracle Certified Professional (OCP)**. With Oracle's cutting-edge *Instructor-Led Training*, *Technology-Based Training*, and this *guide*, you can prepare for certification faster than ever. Set your own trajectory by logging your personal training plan with us. Go to **http://education.oracle.com/tpb**, where we'll help you pick a training path, select your courses, and track your progress. We'll even send you an email when your courses are offered in your area. If you don't have access to the Web, call us at 1-800-441-3541 (Outside the U.S. call +1-310-335-2403).

Power learning has never been easier.

ORACLE®
University